Michael Lieb is Professor of English Emeritus
and Research Professor of Humanities
Emeritus at the University of Illinois, Chicago.

Emma Mason is Senior Lecturer in English,
University of Warwick.

Jonathan Roberts is Senior Lecturer in
English, University of Liverpool.

T4-AQL-656

THE OXFORD HANDBOOK OF THE

RECEPTION HISTORY OF THE BIBLE

THE OXFORD HANDBOOK OF THE

RECEPTION HISTORY OF THE BIBLE

Edited by

MICHAEL LIEB

EMMA MASON

and

JONATHAN ROBERTS

Consultant Editor

CHRISTOPHER ROWLAND

OXFORD

UNIVERSITY PRESS

OXFORD
UNIVERSITY PRESS

Great Clarendon Street, Oxford OX2 6DP

Oxford University Press is a department of the University of Oxford.
It furthers the University's objective of excellence in research, scholarship,
and education by publishing worldwide in

Oxford New York

Auckland Cape Town Dar es Salaam Hong Kong Karachi
Kuala Lumpur Madrid Melbourne Mexico City Nairobi
New Delhi Shanghai Taipei Toronto

With offices in

Argentina Austria Brazil Chile Czech Republic France Greece
Guatemala Hungary Italy Japan Poland Portugal Singapore
South Korea Switzerland Thailand Turkey Ukraine Vietnam

Oxford is a registered trade mark of Oxford University Press
in the UK and in certain other countries

Published in the United States
by Oxford University Press Inc., New York

British Library Cataloguing in Publication Data

Data available

Library of Congress Cataloging in Publication Data

Data available

Typeset by SPI Publisher Services, Pondicherry, India
Printed in Great Britain
on acid-free paper by the
MPG Books Group, Bodmin and King's Lynn

ISBN 978–0–19–920454–0

1 3 5 7 9 10 8 6 4 2

CONTENTS

PART II

ACKNOWLEDGEMENTS

The editors would like to thank Lizzie Robottom, Tessa Eaton, Jeff New, Angela Anstey-Holroyd and Lucy Qureshi for assistance with the development and production of this volume. We would also like to warmly thank Sam Fentress for allowing us to use his photograph, 'Jesus the Light of the World', for our cover image; and acknowledge the following institutions for kindly granting us permission rights to reproduce images from their collections: The British Library, London; The Huntingdon Library, California; The Pierpont Morgan Library, New York; São Paulo Museum of Art; Trinity College, Cambridge; and the William Blake Archive (Collection of Robert N. Essick). We would like to dedicate the volume to the memory of Albert C. Labriola, former Professor of English and Distinguished University Professor at Duquesne University.

ALBERT C. LABRIOLA, 1939–2009:
A TRIBUTE

On March 11, 2009, Albert C. Labriola died suddenly and unexpectedly. For those who knew him personally and worked closely with him, the shock of his passing is be especially acute. His contributions as a scholar are widely acknowledged. He assumed editorship of such crucial and demanding projects as the Milton *Variorum Commentary* and the *Songs and Sonets* volume of the Donne *Variorum*. From 1990 until his death, he was editor of *Milton Studies*, the premier annual in the field. During his tenure as editor of *Milton Studies*, he supplemented this annual with such co-edited volumes as *The Miltonic Samson, John Milton: The Writer in His Works, Paradise Regained in Context*, and *Milton and Historicism*. At the same time, he became general editor of the Medieval and Renaissance Literary Studies series published by Duquesne University Press, a series that, with his guidance, has become a major force in the discipline. From 1974 until his passing, he held the office of secretary of the Milton Society of America and editor of its annual bulletin. In this capacity, he helped to oversee and to coordinate the activities of a truly international organization, one that has been a focal point for scholarly exchange for over sixty years. Each of these undertakings involved an ability to devote oneself to the needs and expectations characteristic of that particular calling. Each also required a great deal of time and labor, an understanding of what the job entailed, and the ability to work well with an entire range of individuals. As a result of his efforts, Professor Labriola proved himself indispensable to the scholarly community. Among the many awards he received during his distinguished career was one he valued most—and with characteristic humility felt himself least qualified to receive—that of being named Honored Scholar of the Milton Society of America in 2000. This one sign of recognition represents for the international community of Miltonists the highest goal to which one can aspire.

Professor Labriola's accomplishments extend well beyond his role as editor of commentaries and as coordinator of a press series. The author of over forty notable essays in major periodicals between 1970 and 2009, he produced an imposing body of work that reflects the immense range of his interests. These include not just sixteenth and seventeenth century writers such as Shakespeare, Donne, Crashaw, and Milton, but medieval and modern figures extending from Chaucer, Beckett, and Golding. Crucial to Professor Labriola's scholarly interest was the bearing of

Christian iconography on the literary arts. Here, a series of seminal studies suggest how important iconography was not only to his work on Milton but to his understanding of the Christian world view. Among his essays in this venue, one discovers pivotal articles that focus on the typological and iconic milieu of the Christocentric imagination. One thinks of such studies as "The Aesthetics of Self-Diminution: Christian Iconography in *Paradise Lost*," (1975) and, later in his career, "Iconographic Perspectives on Seventeenth-Century Religious Poetry" (1990) and "The Holy Spirit in Art: The Theological Bearing of Visual Representation" (1996). To these accomplishments must be added his co-authored facsimile editions of two blockbooks, *The Bible of the Poor* (1990) and *The Mirror of Salvation* (2002), both of importance to the dissemination of religious belief through iconography. As scholar, teacher, and colleague, Albert C. Labriola will be sorely missed.

LIST OF ILLUSTRATIONS

LIST OF CONTRIBUTORS

Gordon Allan is a world authority on Joanna Southcott and a member of the Prophecy Project at the University of Oxford.

Atsuhiro Asano is Associate Professor of New Testament Studies at Kwansei Gakuin University.

Zoë Bennett is Director of Postgraduate Studies in Pastoral Theology, Cambridge Theological Federation and Anglia Ruskin University.

Piero Boitani is Professor of Comparative Literature at Sapienza University of Rome.

Brad Braxton Distingushed Visiting Scholar, McCormick Theological Seminary, Chicago, Illinois

John Hedley Brooke is Andreas Idreos Professor Emeritus of Science and Religion, Oxford University, and Honorary Professor of the History of Science, Lancaster University.

John Butt is Gardiner Professor of Music at the University of Glasgow.

Mary Carruthers is Erich Maria Remarque Professor of Literature at New York University.

Jo Carruthers is RCUK Academic Fellow in the Department of Theology and Religious Studies at the University of Bristol.

David J. Clark was Translation Consultant with the United Bible Societies, 1971–2002, and with the Institute for Bible Translation, Moscow, 2002–9.

Peter Clarke is Professor Emeritus Department of Theology and Religious Studies at King's College London and member of the Faculty of Theology, the University of Oxford.

John J. Collins is Holmes Professor of Old Testament Criticism and Interpretation at Yale Divinity School.

Carol Crown is Professor of Art History at the University of Memphis.

Valentine Cunningham is Professor of English Language and Literature at the University of Oxford.

Katharine J. Dell is Lecturer in Divinity at the University of Cambridge and Fellow of St Catharine's College.

Ismo Dunderberg is Professor of New Testament Studies at the University of Helsinki.

Mark Edwards is Tutor in Theology at Christ Church, the University of Oxford.

Michael J. Gilmour is Associate Professor of New Testament and English Literature at Providence College (Manitoba).

Tim Gorringe is St Luke's Professor of Theological Studies at the University of Exeter.

Robin Griffith-Jones is Master of the Temple at the Temple Church, London, and Visiting Lecturer at King's College, London.

David Gunn is A. A. Bradford Professor of Religion at Texas Christian University.

Richard Harries is Gresham Professor of Divinity, and an Honorary Professor of Theology at King's College, London.

Rachel Havrelock is Assistant Professor of English and Jewish Studies at the University of Illinois, Chicago.

Jeremy Holtom is an independent scholar and Teacher of Religious Studies at Dorothy Stringer High School, Brighton.

Jay Emerson Johnson is a member of the core doctoral faculty in theology at the Graduate Theological Union in Berkeley, California.

Paul M. Joyce is University Lecturer in Theology at the University of Oxford.

Judith Kovacs is Associate Professor in the Department of Religious Studies at the University of Virginia.

Albert C. Labriola (1939–2009) was Professor of English and Distinguished University Professor at Duquesne University.

Scott Langston teaches Biblical and Religious Studies at Texas Christian University.

Michael Lieb is Professor of English Emeritus and Research Professor of Humanities Emeritus, University of Illinois at Chicago.

Ann Loades is Professor Emerita of Divinity, University of Durham.

Emma Mason is Senior Lecturer in the Department of English and Comparative Literary Studies, University of Warwick.

Peter Matheson is a fellow of the Department of Theology and Religious Studies, University of Otago.

Kenneth Newport is Professor of Christian Thought at Liverpool Hope University.

Tobias Nicklas is Professor of Exegesis and Hermeneutics of the New Testament at the University of Regensburg.

Paulo Nogueira is Professor of Biblical Literature and of History of Early Christianity at the Universidade Metodista de São Paulo.

George Pattison is Lady Margaret Professor of Divinity at the University of Oxford.

John Riches is Emeritus Professor of Divinity and Biblical Criticism at the University of Glasgow.

Jonathan Roberts is Senior Lecturer in English at the University of Liverpool.

Christopher Rowland is Dean Ireland's Professor of the Exegesis of Holy Scripture at the University of Oxford.

John Sawyer is Emeritus Professor of Old Testament Language and Literature at Newcastle University and Emeritus Professor of Judaism and Biblical Studies at Lancaster University.

Guy Williams is Tutor in Religious Studies and the Philosophy of Religion at Wellington College.

Catrin Williams is Senior Lecturer in New Testament Studies at Bangor University.

Isabel Wollaston is Senior Lecturer in the Department of Theology and Religion at the University of Birmingham.

INTRODUCTION

JONATHAN ROBERTS

THE reception of the Bible comprises every single act or word of interpretation of that book (or books) over the course of three millennia. It includes everything from Jesus reading Isaiah, or Augustine reading Romans, to a Sunday-school nativity play, or the appearance of '2COR4:6' as a stock number on military gunscopes.[1] No one and nothing is excluded. Reception *history*, however, is a different matter. That is usually—although not always—a scholarly enterprise, consisting of selecting and collating shards of that infinite wealth of reception material in accordance with the particular interests of the historian concerned, and giving them a narrative frame. In other words, to get from the plenitude of *reception* to the finitude of *reception history* requires that historians of reception—like any others—envisage parameters: in particular, when reflecting on the history of responses to the Bible, *whose* responses do they deem to be of importance? That is the first, practical, question, and the second, which cannot be disentangled from it, is its theoretical counterpart: how is the choice of material to be justified, and to what end is it being marshalled? These questions are, as it were, the exegetical and hermeneutical faces of reception history, and it is the special character of reception history that they are thought of as interdependent facets of the same whole.

Reception history is grounded in the philosophical hermeneutics of Hans-Georg Gadamer (1900–2002). One of Gadamer's accomplishments as a philosopher was to draw attention to the situated nature of *all* interpretive acts. This situatedness means more than acknowledging that, as an interpreter, I always work from within

[1] http://www.reuters.com/article/idUSTRE60L0SO20100122.

my historical locale; it means acknowledging that my very consciousness exists within that locale. Gadamer famously puts it this way:

History does not belong to us; we belong to it. Long before we understand ourselves through the process of self-examination, we understand ourselves in a self-evident way in the family, society, and state in which we live. The focus of subjectivity is a distorting mirror. The self-awareness of the individual is only a flickering in the closed circuits of historical life. That is why the prejudices of the individual, far more than his judgements, constitute the historical reality of his being. (*Truth and Method*, 276–7)[2]

Gadamer's critique of individual subjectivity has a counterpart in his critique of the dominance of empirical method in intellectual enquiry. The exclusive focus on either subjective experience or empirical knowledge as interpretive paradigms might appear to present an irreconcilable binary, but Gadamer shows these two to be photographic positive and negative images, as it were, developed at the same historical moment. He demonstrates that the Romantic valorization of individual subjective experience is the reverse face of the Enlightenment empiricism whereby subjectivity is disregarded by the individual examining a particular object of study. The model of enquiry that Gadamer advocates is different: as I encounter the past, I must enter a dialogical relationship with it, gradually coming to recognize the alterity of my historical interlocutor, and in the process coming to recognize my own prejudices through that difference (prejudices are not anathema to Gadamer, they characterize historical consciousness itself). The understanding gained thereby is dialogical, and this rapprochement between interpreter and subject is sometimes described by Gadamer as a 'fusion of horizons' (ibid. 305) That metaphor provides a way of thinking about our relationship to the past that is distinct from the one-way (object 7 subject) street of empiricism.

Gadamer is concerned with empiricism as an example of the Enlightenment valorization of 'method', whereby method appears to be a kind of practice that transcends context, that is above history, and that discounts the interpreter. From the Enlightenment, Gadamer argues, the hope grew that a trust and commitment to method alone would provide total understanding of human life. This burgeoning positivism came to be adopted not only in the natural sciences, but in the human sciences as well. The consequent evolution of a false binary of 'reason' and 'tradition' has impoverished human self-understanding ever since. In making this argument, Gadamer is not, of course, disavowing empiricism, but is providing a critique of a historical tradition of interpretation. By showing that consciousness exists as an aspect of historical being, he is able to argue that, from an interpretive perspective, any looking out must, as it were, also mean a looking in. That looking in does not mean a focus on individual subjectivity, but rather implies taking

---

[2] Hans-Georg Gadamer, *Truth and Method*, trans. Joel Weinsheimer and Donald G Marshall, 2nd edn. (London: Continuum, 2004).

account of the historically specific prejudices—the pre-judgements—through which any one of us is granted the ability to think in the first place.

Gadamer argues that understanding comes from open-minded, benevolent dialogue, and when linked to his attempts to recuperate tradition, this leads to him endorsing a way of thinking about the past that can be quite surprising to those schooled in a hermeneutics of suspicion. He depicts tradition as a kind of benevolent inheritance in which the acolyte may trust. The trusting, questioning relationship that can be developed with tradition is a paradigm of his dialogical model of truth. Given Gadamer's attempts to rehabilitate tradition in this way, it is perhaps unsurprising that his work has been so attractive to some theologians. To the relief of those disaffected by poststructuralism, Gadamer appears to provide a philosophically respectable oeuvre that is centrally concerned with the rehabilita-tion of tradition as something that may embody truth. But for those seeking the certitudes of the past this is a double-edged sword, for the reclamation of tradition as a dialogue partner also demands the relinquishment of a foundationalist dream that the meaning of biblical (or indeed any) texts can be settled once and for all. The reason for this necessary relinquishment, of course, is that this hope is itself a hermeneutical sibling of the positivism discussed above.

How, then, have these factors played out in biblical studies? Until recent years reception work on the Bible was principally (though by no means exclusively) a German-language phenomenon.[3] The best-known German-language theologian working in reception history is Ulrich Luz (1938–), and it is in the spirit of reception history to say a little about the context of his work and to quote from the responses of others to that work. Luz is known for his series of commentaries on Matthew's gospel, which pay particular attention to its reception history. Luz's work on Matthew comes out of—and makes sense in the context of—the *Evange-lisch-Katholischer Kommentar* series, which has its own interesting history. The series was born in the post-Second World War situation of the need for rapproche-ment between Protestants and Catholics in the German-speaking world, and is a deliberately ecumenical project which seeks to incorporate the best from the two traditions (the Protestant focus on historical criticism and the Catholic focus on what the church has taught) in a commentary format. The series is, as Ernest Best described it, a 'joint effort by Catholic and Protestant scholars whose native language is German', which 'sets out to bridge the gap between the formal academic

---

[3] This balance has changed in recent years, principally due to the publication of the Blackwell Bible Commentaries series, which is devoted to the reception history of the Bible down the centuries and explores the influence of the Bible on literature, art, music, and film, its role in the evolution of religious beliefs and practices, and its impact on social and political developments. It departs from the dominant paradigm in biblical studies whose major preoccupation is with questions of sources, date, authorship, and above all the original intention, and instead sees all these as part of the history of interpretation and not the foundation upon which other forms of interpretation may be built.

commentary useful to students for passing examinations and writing theses, and the commentary which the minister might use in sermon preparation.'[4] Luz's model of reception history is, then, allied to a particular set of hermeneutical goals, and works within a particular scholarly, ecclesial, didactic, and homiletic tradition.

How, then, has Luz's work been received? In reviewing one of his Matthew commentaries in the *Journal of Biblical Literature*, Donald A. Hagner notes that Luz's reception work 'provides exceptionally rich insight into what might be called the interpretive potential of each passage', and that this has 'revolutionary implications for traditional, historical-critical exegesis in its quest of a single, objective meaning—the intention of the author'. Hagner's review brings out the double-edged character of reception history mentioned earlier. On the positive side (for Hagner), Luz—as a practitioner of reception history—is opening up all sorts of new meanings in the biblical text, further disclosing its immense richness. But on the negative side (for Hagner), he is simultaneously surrendering the quest for a foundational meaning of that text. What concerns Hagner is that Luz puts the 'new meanings' of a text on the same level as the 'original sense', and therefore 'what the author may have intended . . . is regarded as having no special importance'.[5]

Hagner's appeal to the 'original sense' suggests that he is working with a foundationalist hermeneutic which assumes that behind the biblical text's 'supplementary' meanings there must be an empirically verifiable original meaning. Aside from textual meanings not being empirically verifiable in the way that, say, the DNA sequence of a kingfisher may be, the search for an 'original sense' implies that original senses are singular, not plural. But of course it may be the case that 'original meanings' are themselves intrinsically multivalent, and that the hermeneutical genius of painters such as Rembrandt and writers such as Kierkegaard lies in their ability to sense and explore those multifaceted meanings. Reception history also picks up this variety of meanings by showing us different individuals and groups seeing the same texts from different angles. Seen in this way, empirical scholarly research is one more kind of exploration, not one that exists on a separate or superior plane, but one that can exist in dialogue with the others. It is not the purpose of this volume to make the argument against hermeneutical positivism—that discussion can be found in the works of a range of philosophers including Gadamer and Richard Rorty, and it is a premise rather than a conclusion of reception history. Nonetheless, even if we accept the idea of 'tradition' as a sort of contained multivalency, difficult questions still remain. In particular, what this volume must ask—because assumptions about this topic have been central to the

[4] Ernest Best, 'Recent Foreign New Testament Literature', *Expository Times*, 93: 1 (1981), 13–18, at 13.
[5] Donald A. Hagner, 'Review: Matthew 8–20, by Ulrich Luz. Trans. James E. Crouch. Hermeneia. Minneapolis: Fortress, 2001.', *Journal of Biblical Literature*, 121: 4 (Winter 2002), 766–9 at 768.

reception work in biblical studies—is how decisions are reached about 'tradition' itself.

Luz's work demonstrates how the concept of 'tradition' can be a way of putting parameters on the multivalency of the biblical text by setting out what is and is not acceptable to the interpreter. As Hagner points out, it is not the case for Luz that '*any* or *every* interpretation of a text is acceptable' (ibid., p. 767). Luz may not have a foundationalist commitment to the 'original sense' of the text, but in setting out parameters for separating 'valid interpretations from false ones' (ibid.) he has replaced that commitment with a different kind of foundationalism: a belief in what he calls the '"trajectory" of biblical texts' and 'the totality of the Christian faith' (p. 768), and what Hagner describes as 'the essential elements of the history of Jesus and congruence with an expression of love' (p. 767). This all sounds benevolently ecumenical, but the complication is that Luz's parameters are not universals: they are shaped by the very tradition that he then uses them to define. The 'expression of love', for example, is not simply a given, and certainly not something that is restricted to Christianity. There is a great deal of interpretive work packed into those parameters, and to the degree that Luz treats such concepts as givens—as they may be within his own theological/denominational setting—he is operating a kind of contextual foundationalism. This circularity raises concerns for critics such as Mark Elliott who writes, 'I wonder: when it comes down to considering what the theological legacy of Matthew is, should we accept that Matthew had no more to say than moral advice and tips in favour of an ecclesiological identity? This could too easily be the way that Luz has "brokered" Matthew for scholarship and the Church.'[6]

It is impossible to judge these matters from the outside, because the experiential truth of a particular tradition may only be evident to those within it. Perhaps this suggests that if one is sure of one's own tradition, then the reception enterprise works well. But what if one inhabits a multicultural, multi-disciplinary, multi-faith environment—such as a university? In that case, what are the parameters of 'validity' to be? Or to come back to the beginning of this introduction, what material do we decide to interest ourselves in? Given the billions of individual lives shaped for better or worse by the Bible over the millennia, it is a contentious task to compile a work that says 'in the total history of humankind's reading of the Bible, *these* are the voices that matter'. If this was, say, *The Oxford Handbook of the Reception History of Genesis amongst English Non-Conformists, 1770–1800*, then these parameters would already be provided, and the philosophical questions might be muted. But in the present case, the task—in terms of time, place, and religious tradition—is completely open-ended, and this brings the hermeneutical questions that all reception history faces right to the fore.

---

[6] Mark W. Elliott, 'Effective-history and hermeneutics of Ulrich Luz', JSNT, 33:2 (forthcoming).

It should now be apparent how the current volume differs from the kind of work that Luz does, because unlike his work, it is not attempting to found its discussion in a particular model of religious faith. In so far as the editors, the publishing press (OUP), and the majority of contributors share a tradition, it is that of the university. Yet almost the opposite is true of the subjects of discussion. From the outset the editors intended to foreground rather than occlude the hermeneutical questions raised above, and did so by commissioning a highly diverse set of responses to the Bible. The chapters include studies of the Bible not just of individuals and groups from Jewish and Christian backgrounds, but from Islamic, Hindu, Gnostic, and agnostic backgrounds too; the chronological range stretches from biblical times to the present day, and covers locations including Europe, India, Japan, Latin America and the United States. This diversity is also reflected in the contributors, who—despite largely sharing an academic background—are of any or no religious position, and write from many countries around the globe.

As a practice, reception history is undatable, as there is nothing new in collating the responses of different readers to a particular text: a scrapbook of reviews of a work, a collection of letters to an author responding to his or her writing, a gallery collection or museum exhibition—each of these may constitute a reception history. Nonetheless, the accompanying hermeneutical questions raised by the practice of reception history are often not in evidence. In the present case these are of great importance, because, as I suggested above, they put the question of who owns the Bible centre stage. Take one instance: the cover of this book. Other volumes in this series are adorned by details of venerable ancient manuscripts that have a reassuringly scholarly aura about them. We have chosen a photograph of a neon sign in Lampe, Missouri, beaming the message 'Jesus is the light of the world'. Why? The image is a work by the US photographer Sam Fentress, who has spent twenty-five years travelling his home country recording the ways in which the Bible—here a slightly modified John 8:12—has become a part of everyday life. Whether or not he thinks of himself in this way, Fentress is a kind of reception historian, and his work provides a complex, human insight into the place of the Bible in the United States. In engaging with this sort of work, this volume is not, however, ignoring the more traditional academic approach to reception history, but in the spirit of Gadamer is attempting to provide space for a dialogical relationship between what that has meant and what that might mean, between the dominant scholarly lines of interpretation of a range of biblical books, and new scholarly readings of moments of biblical reception, many of which have not been part of that tradition. Our challenge, then, in planning and editing this book has been to provide a structure in which the essential movement—the dialogue between the traditional and the novel—can be made visible. To this end, the volume is in two parts.

The chapters in Part I provide a survey of the outline, form, and content of a number of key biblical books which have been influential in the history of interpretation.

In most cases[7] these chapters provide an overview of scholarly post-Enlightenment readings of the form and content of each book. This tradition provides a helpful panoramic view against which to locate the more specific case studies of Part II, and gives readers some sense of the features of our selected biblical books which have led to particular readings in the history of interpretation. The following books are considered in this first section: Genesis, Judges, Job, Psalms, Isaiah, Ezekiel, Daniel, the Gospel of John, Romans, First Corinthians, Galatians, Revelation. Part II offers a series of in-depth case studies of particular key passages or books with due regard for the specificity of their socio-historical context. There is no attempt to be exhaustive in coverage of either books or contexts. These case studies are deliberately close readings which show the contingent character of the particular interpretations in question, and in some cases the relationship of this character to wider patterns of interpretation. We have aimed to ensure that a range of different historical circumstances and different books and methods of interpretation are covered. Many of the chapters consider the specific appropriation of a particular book at a particular time and place. To take some examples of the variety of what is to come: Jo Carruthers looks at the celebration of Purim at Terezin, a transit camp, and at the incorporation of the figure of Hitler into the celebration of Purim during the Second World War; John Hedley Brooke examines the 1860 debate and intellectual fall-out in Oxford between Wilberforce and Huxley over the relationship of Genesis 1–2 to the new work on evolution; Jay Emerson Johnson scrutinizes the impact on the Anglican communion of the conventional wisdom that 'sodomy' in Genesis 19 concerns a sexual act; Robin Griffith-Jones takes another contemporary starting-point: Dan Brown's *The Da Vinci Code*, and—resisting the temptation to dismiss this as an 'airport novel'—uses it to open out current assumptions about Jesus' marital status that inhibit readers from seeing, for example, the echoes of Adam and Eve in the encounter of Jesus and Mary in the Garden in John 20; Zoë Bennett examines John Ruskin annotating a page of a manuscript medieval Gospel lectionary in the unspoken context of his grief over the death of Rose la Touche. In addition, there are chapters on artists who have—in astonishingly innovative and diverse ways—reimagined the Bible in different media: Dante, Handel, Blake, and Bob Dylan; and theologians who have rethought the same: Luther wrestling with Galatians, Barth with Romans, Augustine and Pelagius likewise, and Kierkegaard with Matthew 6. There are also chapters that provide wider surveys of hermeneutical appropriation, notably Valentine Cunningham's concluding chapter on the sometimes parasitic, sometimes symbiotic relationships of biblical studies, literary studies, and cultural theory.

As this brief overview indicates, we have not tried to establish a consensus view on reception history, but what we hope to reflect is that no individual, school, or group does or can own biblical reception. There is, and can be, no single common

---

[7] There is no set formula here. David Gunn's essay on Judges, for example, forms a crossover piece anticipating elements of Parts II in Part I Study.

denominator between these readings, as their richness and value lies in their multiplicity and diversity. Nonetheless, even though there is not quite a dialogue going on between these pieces, there is often a sense of them coexisting in a world in which they share the same hermeneutical strategies without even knowing it. It is a thought-provoking and disconcerting experience, for example, to read alongside one another Michael Lieb's discussion of Black Nationalism and anti-Semitism in the Nation of Islam; Brad Braxton's discussion of contemporary African American preaching that endorses economic materialism at the cost of forgetting its own history of exploitation; Jay Emerson Johnson's mention of African American readings of the New Testament that critique Paul on slavery, but accept him on sexuality; Peter Clarke's discussion of the Rastafarian apocalyptic vision of a holocaust of all whites; and Ann Loades's discussion of Elizabeth Cady Stanton, whose abolitionist husband would not make a stand on women's rights for fear it would undermine his work on slavery.

In the case of the present volume, the material is hermeneutically stimulating precisely because it will not coalesce. The more history of reception of the Bible one reads, the clearer it becomes that the human importance of the Bible does *not* lie in a single foundational meaning that, by dint of scholarly effort, may finally be revealed. This is not a resignation to postmodernism, but an acknowledgment that both inside and outside the doors of academia all of us live in a changing world in which engagements with the Bible are themselves ever changing. It is a world in which there are always new engagements between readers and the Bible (or 'Bibles', as that text shifts according to manuscript translation and tradition), and those engagements will never stabilize. No amount of taxonomical or theological effort will alter this, as the matter is ontological, not pragmatic: individually and corporately, we change through time; in its singleness and multiplicity the Bible changes too. In describing this relationship between texts and readers, empirical studies can only provide half the story, as reading itself is a process full of mystery: the quiet translocation of the reader into other times and scenes, the silent communion with voices long dead. The act of reading is both as light and present, and as dark and inscrutable, as consciousness itself. There can be no meaning except through the conjunction of readers and texts, and at no point can a clear line be drawn to divide where texts end and readers begin. The reception history of the Bible is the practice of making worldly records of those manifest and mysterious individual and corporate experiences of the biblical text. It is a recognition of the dynamic, living relationship between texts and readers, rather than an attempt to isolate and stabilize textual meanings from the mutability of human life.

PART I

CHAPTER 1

....

GENESIS

....

RACHEL HAVRELOCK

GENESIS holds the undisputed place as the first book of the Bible. No matter the canon, it is the point of beginning. Every subsequent biblical book to some degree relates to Genesis. In some cases, as in the prologue to the Gospel according to John, which returns to the beginning of time and interprets Genesis 1 in light of Proverbs 8, reference is explicit (Boyarin 2004: 95–8). In other cases, as in Deuteronomy's synopsis of Jacob's life (Deut. 26:5–9) or Paul's account of Abraham and his wives (Gal. 4:22–31), writers show their acquaintance with ancestral narratives by retelling them. The cataclysmic end predicted by the prophets and detailed in Revelation collapses the very categories put into place at creation. Genesis is not only the first, but also the foundational text of the Bible.

Many beginnings unfold in Genesis. Chapter 1 provides a cosmic view of the world that comes into being at God's command, whereas chapters 2 and 3 narrow the focus to two humans and the ultimate exigencies of an agrarian economy. The first murder is recorded in chapter 4, along with the origin of cities, metal tools, and music. The flood story in chapters 6 through 10 provides the account of a new beginning marked by a rainbow indicating a renewed, covenantal relationship between God and humanity (9:12–17). Linguistic difference can be said to emerge as a result of building the Tower of Babel (11:1–9). With the introduction of Abram and Sarai a new ethnicity with a particular destiny comes into relief. This ethnicity, often defined in terms of a nation, is built up from one family. Family life is, for the most part, the subject of chapters 12–50 and appears to be the most contentious realm of human life.

What this founding family represents has been the subject of centuries of speculation. As precursor to the Exodus and the legal codes of Leviticus and

Deuteronomy, Genesis purports to describe an earlier phase of Israelite religion. For example, when God reveals the divine name Yahweh to Moses, He claims that it was not known by Abraham, Isaac, and Jacob (Exod. 6:3). Thus a chronology is set up in which the nascent devotion of the ancestors sets the stage for the revelation of a comprehensive religious system. Although readers are warned against viewing Genesis as 'a preliminary stage', many scholars do believe that it casts light on the nature of household religion in ancient Israel (Albertz 1994: 29). Carol Meyers interprets the family stories, in particular the story of the Garden of Eden, as reflecting the social organization and economic realities of an agrarian and pastoral community located in an arid, mountainous region (Meyers 1988: 53–62). Naomi Steinberg, also concerned with questions of social organization, perceives a kinship system based on the patrilineal principle of marrying within a group descended from a common male ancestor (1993: 6–14). Literary scholars perceive the tensions, latent enmities, and plots that drive family life in every era (Alter 1981: 23–46, 155–77; Pardes 1992: 60–78; Sternberg 1985: 285–308).

CHRONOLOGY AND CONTENT

The material in Genesis can be divided in many ways. One such division follows the sequence of the book and brackets sub-units such as the Primordial History (Gen. 1–11), the ancestral tales (Gen. 12–36), and the sustained, almost novella-like account of Joseph in Egypt (Gen. 37–50). With some important exceptions, these sub-units loosely cohere with genre distinctions. The stories in Genesis 1–11, for example, belong to the genre of myth; they are sacred stories that describe how the world and humanity came into being (Dundes 1984: 3). The stories of Abraham and Sarah; Rebecca and Isaac; Jacob, Rachel, and Leah and their families can be appropriately classified as legends, stories about founding figures and the places they establish that purport to unfold in historical time. While the account of Joseph can be considered a legend, it also has a particular literary quality. Although the story of Joseph follows a plot more complex and labyrinthine than those of Abraham and Jacob, Gabriel Josipovici has warned against separating the ups and downs of Joseph's life from the life of Jacob that begins with Jacob's birth in chapter 25 and only ends with his death in chapter 49 (Josipovici 1988: 77).

The stories overlap to an extent that the insistence on such divisions can impede the understanding of how the texts interact within the book as a whole. In fact, repetition is a distinguishing feature of Genesis. The repetition of specific plot sequences has been identified as constituting a type-scene, a recurrent event that allows comparison across texts (Alter 1981: 47–62). For example, Abraham at two junctures (12:10–20; 20) and Isaac (26:1–16) seek refuge at the court of a foreign ruler during a famine and protect themselves with the claim that their wives are their sisters. This parallel construction, the type-scene, creates an interpretive context that can help determine the poetics of specific writers (Hendel 1997), the particularities of character, or the nature of a locale. Through the device of the type-scene, the use of recurrent motifs and the notion of a covenant transmitted from one generation to the next, the stories of Genesis invite comparative and intertextual readings.

Genesis 1–11

In highly structured, symmetrical prose, Genesis 1:1–2:4 portrays God ordering a primordial chaos into distinct realms like water, sky, and land (Cassuto 1978: 11–17). The generative potency of Divine speech, described as the 'logos' model of creation, has been understood as a polemic against the notion that at the beginning of time God battled with chaos in the form of a watery monster, the 'agon' model of creation (Fishbane 2003: 34–6). In this story of creation, the categories of male and female are created simultaneously, both 'in the image' of God (1:27). A woman emerges from the body of a man in the Garden of Eden story (2:4b–3:24). However, a midrash explains that God created an androgyne in Genesis 1:27 and only separated it into male and female bodies in Genesis 2:22 (Genesis Rabbah 8:2–3).

The Garden of Eden, with its trees, rivers, and precious stones, is lost due to the eating of a fruit (3:6), but the text in Genesis says nothing of the devil or the Fall. The talking snake operates as a trickster and sets the stage for the trickster tales to follow. The loss of Eden functions etiologically as an explanation for why women and men must toil for their bread (3:16–19), at the same time that it is the first in a chain of stories in which humanity transgresses a border of some sort resulting in punishment as well as increased knowledge.

While Adam and Eve lose Eden and must ever after farm the land, their son Cain is cursed to wander the earth and is unable to farm the land. The blood that he spills by murdering his brother contaminates both the earth and his person (4:11–12). However, Cain builds a city, enabling the urban arts as the result of knowledge gained through his crime of fratricide (4:17–22).

Genesis 6 begins with a crossing of the border between heaven and earth when the sons of God procreate with the daughters of man. Their hybrid offspring, the Nephilim, are heroes who seem to outlive the 120-year time-limit placed on human life as penalty for this miscegenation. Through a comparison with Atrahasis, the Babylonian flood myth, scholars have suggested that the subsequent flood in Genesis is aimed at silencing the noise of these unions and purifying this divine–human sexual intermixing.

Internal to the flood story is God's desire to wipe the earth clean of rotten human action and intention. The ark that God instructs Noah to build serves as a kind of womb in which the seeds of future life are preserved. After the waters subside and God signals future stability through the rainbow, the survivors revert to their insidious ways. Noah gets drunk; his son, Ham, humiliates him; and a fraternal hierarchy of masters and slaves ensues (9:18–27).

Despite the penalties incurred up to this point, the unchastened people try to infiltrate the realm of the divine one last time. Once again a city is built, but this time with a tower that aims for heaven. God nips this overreaching in the bud by scrambling human language into a variety of tongues. Since different languages necessitate different countries, the primordial history draws to a close with the image of a centre that has become diffuse (11:9).

Genesis 12–36

The ancestral legends in this section of Genesis are organized according to the concept of generations. The main players in the first generation are Abraham and Sarah; in the second Isaac and Rebecca; and in the third Jacob, Rachel, and Leah. Who is a major and who a minor player in each generation is not predetermined so much as worked out over the course of the stories. Abram breaks from all that is familiar and travels with his wife Sarai, and nephew Lot, to Canaan. He builds altars at Canaanite sites in Shechem, the environs of Bethel, and the Negev and escapes to Egypt during a famine before parting from his nephew and watching him walk toward Sodom. Lot is not entirely abandoned to a fate among the Sodomites, since Abram releases him from captivity following a war in which Sodom, Gomorrah, and the other Cities of the Plain are looted (14), and surely has him in mind when he negotiates with God to spare the city of Sodom (18:22–33). With Lot absent and Sarai, Abram's wife, barren, the family, counter to God's promise, seems to be shrinking rather than growing. Sarai engineers a surrogacy, but Hagar, the surrogate, perceives an elevation of her status once she becomes pregnant. With Abram's permission Sarai oppresses Hagar, who runs away into the wilderness where she receives a prophecy concerning a son who is to be called Ishmael.

Everyone's fate changes when God establishes a covenant with Abram and Sarai. As a result, their names become Abraham and Sarah in order to reflect the fact that they will engender nations and kings (17:5–6, 15–16). Despite the fact that Ishmael is circumcised (17:25–6) and promised to be the father of twelve tribal chiefs and one large nation (17:20), he is not a proper recipient of the covenant. Covenantal transformation continues when an angelic visitation enables Sarah to conceive (18), and Lot, spared the blaze visited on Sodom, produces the rival nations of Moab and Ammon through incest (19). Abraham, father of many nations, shows himself ready to sacrifice both his sons when he exiles Ishmael with an inheritance of bread and water (21) and leads Isaac to a sacrificial altar on a mountain-top.

Although God promised Abraham land stretching from the Euphrates to the Mediterranean Sea, he enters into tense negotiations with Ephron the Hittite in order to acquire a burial plot for Sarah (Sternberg 1991: 33). After Sarah's burial at the Cave of Machpelah in Hebron, Abraham dispatches his servant to the very homeland he abandoned in order to find a wife for Isaac. Rebecca identifies herself as the ideal bride when she helps the stranger (24:18–19), extends hospitality (24:25), and voluntarily agrees to leave her home for a distant land (24:58). In this text, Rebecca displays qualities analogous to Abraham's.

Between his near-sacrifice and his blindness, there is not much of a story about Isaac. Perhaps Isaac's poor judgement in favouring Esau leads the editors to truncate his biography. It is Rebecca, acting as patriarch in Isaac's place, who makes the choice of Jacob as Isaac's heir, although she endangers him in the process. Jacob conspires with his mother to gain his father's blessing through subterfuge, then must abandon his home in order to escape Esau's wrath. Jacob's flight from home and his return frame the adult phase of his life. Prior to his departure, Jacob is very much a son of the household caught up in the drama of reversing the priorities bestowed by his twin brother's earlier birth. After his return, his sons appear as the more active characters.

Leaving home with the intangible assets of birthright and blessing, the youthful Jacob sleeps with a stone for a pillow and dreams of a ladder in which angels of God ascend and descend. A dream journey of increasing proximity to God mirrors his physical movements. For example, the dream of seeing the angels is balanced and extended by Jacob's nocturnal wrestling with a divine being prior to his return home (32:4–33). This wrestling with God is the prototypical act that defines Israel. God renames Jacob 'Israel', because he has wrestled with gods and men and has wrested a blessing. On the basis of this paradigmatic encounter, contention can be said to be valued over obedience. The children of Israel are not meant to be passive, even toward God.

Genesis 37–50

Is parental favouritism in line with God's will? This question that disturbs the reader as Ishmael is put out of Abraham's house and Esau is left to beg a blessing from his father yields contradictory answers in the Joseph story. The favouritism shown to Joseph by Jacob—made undeniably evident by his ornamented coat—stirs up a bloodthirsty jealousy among Joseph's brothers. Joseph also inherits an active dream-life from his father, but the dreams that he recounts publicly concern his destiny rather than the movements of angels. In fact, God is not a central figure in the Joseph story. God never speaks to Joseph, and when Joseph speaks of God he seems to be referring to his own powers. In an Egyptian jailhouse, Joseph urges an imprisoned sommelier to reveal his dreams, with the assurance that 'interpretations belong to God, so tell (your dreams to) me' (40:8). Similarly Joseph attributes Pharaoh's dreams and his interpretations to God (41:25–32). Once reunited with his brothers who sold him into slavery, Joseph seems to excuse them of their actions with the conclusion, 'it wasn't you who sent me here, but God' (45:8). Now in a position of power over his brothers, Joseph strips them of the power they once had over him. On the basis of this plot-line, it seems that the favouritism that stoked the fraternal jealously was part of God's plan to save Israel from a famine and eventually bring them home (46:1–4).

Although Joseph's trials and triumphs may be the means of saving Jacob's family, Jacob, it seems, chooses the wrong favourite. Joseph serves as the patron ancestor of the northern kingdom of Israel, which is ultimately defeated by Assyria and lost to posterity (Josipovici 1988: 85). In contrast, the southern kingdom of Judea, descended from Judah, survives a long line of empires and promises deliverance in the form of a Messiah son of David (for the development of this tradition, see Carr 1996: 303–4). In light of this historical trajectory, Joseph's complicity in the appropriative economics of Egypt and Judah's noble protection of his father Jacob and brother Benjamin (43:8–10, 44:18–34) have karmic undertones. The question of why the story of Judah's seduction by his outcast daughter-in-law Tamar (38) interrupts the sale of Joseph (37) and his service in Potiphar's house (39) has been answered in literary terms by Alter through the theme of 'the deceiver deceived' that runs through both stories (Alter 1981: 10). Yet one also notices that it is precisely when Joseph is removed from Israel's household that the messianic line springs up through Tamar's son, Perez (see Ruth 4:18–22 and Matt. 1:1–16).

Joseph does not make it into the list of the forefathers. 'God is always the God of Abraham, Isaac and Jacob; we never hear of the God of Abraham, Isaac, Jacob and Joseph' (Josipovici 1988: 88). The intricate plot and sustained narrative concerning Joseph represents devolution rather than improvement. As much as he is successful in his resilience and resilient in his success, Joseph remains something of a suspect character. God initiates no covenant with him, he easily finds a place in the pharaonic system, and his brothers remain afraid of him (50:15–18). The position of his story at the end of Genesis may be another means of casting aspersion on Joseph's character.

In biblical literature, endings often indicate erosions or the end of an established social institution. For example, the Five Books of Moses (Torah) end with the acknowledgment that no prophet will ever equal Moses. He must then be succeeded by Joshua, a military leader. The Book of Judges concludes with a civil war and the near extinction of the tribe of Benjamin, and so the tribal system gives way to the monarchy in 1 Samuel. Elisha, the last prophet of deeds, gives way to the Book of Isaiah and the prophets of words. Based on these comparisons, the fact that Joseph is never named with the God of Abraham, Isaac, and Jacob can be understood as an indication that the ancestral relationship with God reaches its end with Joseph. The prophetic alternative is subsequently introduced with Moses at the beginning of Exodus. The fact that the ancestral bond with God terminates with Joseph and that the prophet Moses and Aaron the high priest are both from the tribe of Levi suggests that Jacob's love of Joseph does not coincide with God's.

GENRE

Genesis is a book that displays cohesion of form. It is written in prose that represents a divergence from other antique creation accounts such as the Babylonian *Enuma Elish*, the Canaanite *Baal* Epic, and Hesiod's *Theogony*, which are written in epic verse. Poetry does appear in Genesis primarily as the language of curse (3:14a–19; 9:25) and blessing (9:26–7; 14:19–20; 24:60; 27:28–9; 48:15–16; 49:2–27),[1] but it predicts events rather than narrating them in the style of epic. The shift from prose to poetry signals a change in discourse. But the prose, memorably described by Erich Auerbach as 'fraught with background', is poetic in so far as it adheres to a deeply structured chiastic form (Auerbach 1953: 12). The poetry mirrors the chiastic structure on a smaller scale through syntactic parallelism. The poetic nature of the prose and the often prosaic poetics of Genesis evoke a time in which the future is woven into the texture of the past.

Accounting for Genesis as a collection of legends began with Hermann Gunkel at the dawn of the twentieth century (Gunkel 1901). The legends, according to Gunkel, do not record historical events but rather point toward popular, pre-national memories. They are a species of folklore rooted in the life-setting (*Sitz im Leben*) of a tribal system. Although Gunkel's analysis was rooted in an evolutionary scheme that relied too heavily on a dichotomy between legend and history, his instinct about Genesis as folklore has proven correct (see Niditch 1987 and 1993). The more current designation for Genesis is myth, which doesn't mean that it is 'untrue' in contrast to a 'true' category of science, but rather that the book makes foundational claims about the world and how it came into being.

Myths describe the creation of the world as a means of setting out a social charter (Malinowski 1948: 74–88). How things began becomes the justification for how they must be. In Genesis 1:1–2:4, for example, God orders the universe by separating elements such as darkness and light and placing boundaries between them. This is the foundation story for the *Kohanim*, the priestly class of Israel. As God enforced

---

[1] Poetry is also used for an oath (4:23–4), which may indeed operate as a curse, and for pre-natal prophecy (16:11–12; 25:23), likely a fatalistic form of blessing.

separation between the elements of creation, so the priests must uphold distinctions of class, category, and cleanliness. In this view, to efface social boundaries is to invite God to unleash chaos.

Myth is also believed to emerge from ritual or to provide something of a script for ritual. As God rests from his creative labours on the seventh day, so the beneficiaries of creation are instructed to set aside the seventh day as a Sabbath (Lev. 23:3).

Claude Lévi-Strauss has described myth as hinging upon binary opposition that is ultimately mediated by a trickster figure. Several oppositions are at work in the Garden of Eden story: between human and animal, between man and woman, and between God and human. Enter the snake, an animal that interacts with the humans, intervenes between the man and the woman, and speaks of God's anxiety about the humans becoming too God-like. On all counts the snake serves as a trickster who brings about the transformation of everything with which he comes into contact.

Freudian notions about the violent undercurrent of family life find support in Genesis. The potential violence of the father becomes hauntingly apparent as Abraham is prepared to sacrifice his beloved son, Isaac, at God's behest (Gen. 22), and the desire of the son to usurp the father's role comes across when Reuben, Jacob's firstborn, beds his father's concubine (35:22). Myth is further an operative category because identity is articulated in myth and Genesis speaks about the formation of collective identity at every turn.

CANAAN

Each story in Genesis works to produce a portrait of the Promised Land, a portrait not as geographic or topological as it is political and ethnic. The stories map the land by describing the relationships between Israel and its neighbours in terms of familial relationship. In this way, neighbouring nations are characterized as troublesome relatives. The type of mapping that transpires in Genesis attests to the role of myth in sanctioning and sanctifying territory.

Specific tales relate to distinct historical periods and yet work together to produce the space of the land rather than a historical chronology. Figures like Isaac and Ishmael are best understood as founding ancestors whose actions express certain typical features of national character; something like the 'wild-ass' aspect of Ishmael is best understood as Israelite polemic (Gen. 16:12). Such myths come into being at particular moments. For example, the boundary established between Jacob and his Aramean uncle, Laban, in the region of Gilead relates to the rise of Aram in the mid- to late ninth century BCE, and the tense relationship between Isaac and Ishmael references the rise of Ishmaelite tribes in the Negev desert between the eighth and sixth centuries BCE (Hendel 2005: 47). Ancestral wanderings, wars, and reconciliations signify the contacts, conflicts, and treaties of ancient Israel and are best understood as reflecting the time in which the stories came about rather than the events they portray.

The narration of political interaction as ancestral precedent lends an inevitable quality to the relationships, a sense that because things were this way at the beginning so they are ever destined to be. Since Ishmael's 'hand will be against everyone, and everyone's hand against him' (16:12), the Israelites should not trust their Arab neighbours. Despite the fact that this prophecy was likely written during a period of raids or skirmishes with Ishmaelites, it becomes frozen as an ineluctable characteristic of a nation. The specific moments of time embedded in Genesis assume a simultaneous quality. In fact, the cover-up of authorship and date is so thorough that scores of modern archaeologists and philologists have not been able to crack the code. This simultaneity, nowhere better expressed than in the rabbinic dictum, 'There is no early or late in Torah' (Babylonian Talmud, Pesahim 6b), is perceptible on the spatial plane of Genesis. The land mapped through the stories of Genesis exists in concurrent relationship with Babylonia, Moab, Ammon, Ishmael, Aram, Edom, and Egypt, even though these nations rose to power in different periods. In every case, the land of Israel is defined in opposition to these other nations and a coherent national identity emerges through the articulation of borders with them.

Abram breaks from the past by distancing himself from his family and birthplace, which is identified as 'Ur of the Chaldees'. His origins are meant to evoke Babylonia, synonymous with Chaldea in the Neo-Babylonian period, yet also convey associations with the Amorite and Aramean cultures (Hendel 2005: 47–54). The story of Abraham went through several revisions in the name of matching social reality. Abraham's descendants, extending to the Judeans exiled by the Babylonians in 587 BCE, found themselves always negotiating a relationship with a larger, better-armed country in the Syro-Mesopotamian region. The spectre of these military powers may also be perceptible in the gleeful revenge fantasy that is the Tower of Babel (11:1–9) ('Babel' is the Hebrew name for Babylonia).

After migrating from Mesopotamia and orienting himself with Canaan, Abraham heads to Egypt in order to survive a famine. Egypt is a place of treacherous sustenance, where food is acquired at the price of an assault on familial integrity. This episode, amplified in the Book of Exodus, sounds a warning against seeking alliance or sanctuary in Egypt.

Israel's regional relationships are figured in terms of a family tree: those relatives who are not recipients of the covenant are positioned on the other side of the border from Israel. Geographic borders double as markers of distinct identities, but neighbouring countries are also imagined as kin, however estranged. The first and fundamental separation occurs when Abraham and his nephew Lot part ways. Lot migrates to the Jordan river valley and Abraham holds fast in the Canaanite hills (Gen. 13). In the next generation, Isaac inherits the land, or at least the concept of the land, while Ishmael's legacy lies in the desert. Where Abraham and Lot and the descendant nations of Israel and Moab/Ammon are separated by the Jordan river, there is a more porous frontier between Isaac and Ishmael. Ishmael is prophesied, 'to dwell beside all of his brothers' (16:12), and the Ishmaelites were indeed a nomadic people encamped in the desert abutting Beer-sheba, Isaac's hometown.

Even before Jacob and Esau are born, a rivalry between two nations begins. Esau is the older, heartier brother, associated with the hunt and the red mountains of southern Jordan known to us as Petra. His opposite, Jacob, sits in tents evidently scheming how to displace him. Jacob prevails, although the act of overriding his brother costs him some twenty years of his life spent labouring for next to nothing for his uncle and father-in-law Laban. Some measure-for-measure justice is meted out when Laban tricks him into marrying his firstborn daughter, Leah, instead of the younger Rachel. When Jacob returns, he is terrified and necessarily contrite about his brother. Yet Esau is the one who appears to have transcended the competition when he greets his brother with hugs, kisses, and tears (33:4). Jacob's character involves more of the same duplicity; he offers a complex excuse for trailing behind his brother on the way to Edom and then goes in the opposite direction (33:17–18). By the time Jacob settles in Shechem, boundaries have been set between his territory and those of Aram, associated with Laban, and Edom, the terrain of Esau.

The position that the absence of boundaries leads to social dissolution becomes evident in the rape of Dinah, Jacob's daughter (Gen. 34). Dinah is a young girl who seeks peers among the women of Shechem, but ends up being raped by the city's eponymous prince. After the king brokers a marriage-deal with Jacob, Dinah's brothers, Simeon and Levi, murder the groom and his fellows, who had submitted to circumcision as a bride-price. Considering the rape of Dinah in light of other national foundation stories premised on the rape of women, Helena Zlotnick describes it as a means of drawing an otherwise invisible cultural boundary across the bodies of women (Zlotnick 2002: 48). Although Jacob's heirs live alongside the people of Canaan, they are cautioned to avoid marriage and mixing.

GENEALOGY

Genesis is not only a book about brothers and geopolitics, but also one about birth and genealogy. For ancient audiences, the kinship pattern was 'likely the primary component of the tradition' (McCarter 1988: 17). Genealogies serve as interludes between narratives (2:4; 5:1; 6:9; 10:1; 11:10–32; 22:20–4; 25; 36; 37:15), and the drama of birth runs parallel to that of demarcating territory. The genealogies, which take the form of lists of who begot whom, serve the dual purpose of setting the contours of nations and establishing heredity as a principle of continuity. While they begin with a universal scope as in the Table of Nations of Genesis 10, the genealogies narrow by the end of Genesis to include only the descendants of Jacob (46:7–27). With Genesis in mind, Derrida maintains that genealogies are contexts that account for the unique phenomenon of genius by associating it with genetics (Derrida 2006: 27–8). Indeed, adaptability and talent are transmitted among generations along with blessing. However, the persistence of relationships external to the family shows that 'this ethnic group is part of the entire coherence of humanity' (Crüsemann 2002: 66).

Although the migrations of women only exert indirect influence on the map that emerges from the pages of Genesis, they are the key figures in establishing the genealogical line. The centrality of birth to the plot-lines of Genesis is introduced in Genesis 1, when God blesses the first male and female with the command to 'be fruitful and multiply and fill the earth' (1:28), as well as when Eve gives birth after being expelled from Eden and calls her son Cain, 'Because I have created a man with God' (4:1). Thereafter creating life is not easy for the would-be mothers of Israel. When Sarah's surrogacy backfires (16), she forces the issue of women's place in the covenantal system by protesting about her barrenness. It is not enough to bless men with fertility or to cite them alone as the founders of nations. God changes Sarah's name, yet when it comes to the covenant she presents an anomaly. Her husband and son can be circumcised, but she cannot. For this reason, Sarah is unable to formally constitute a covenantal subject. Although never explicitly labelled as such, conception, or the absence of blood, signals Sarah's partnership in God's plan for Israel. It can be said that, by advocating for her motherhood, Sarah initiates a covenantal relationship with God.

In Rebecca's case, the struggle is internal when Jacob and Esau contend with one another in the womb (25:22). Her enquiry into the meaning of the unrest leads to an oracle from God that she will be the mother of two nations. Rachel's infertility is intertwined with the competition with her sister and co-wife Leah. In the name of maintaining her status as beloved wife and securing a place in the clan, Rachel tries pleading with Jacob (30:1), using surrogacy (30:3–8), and finding a medicinal aid (30:14–15). In so far as she contends with her father's power over her, her sister's jealousy, and God's frustration of her plans to found a family, Rachel's struggle parallels Jacob's. The parallel is made explicit in the name that she bestows on Naphtali, the second child that she claims through surrogacy. After the birth, Rachel says, 'Wrestlings of God I have wrestled with my sister and *prevailed*, so she called him Naphtali' (30:8). Rachel's naming of Naphtali echoes God's renaming of Jacob, 'Your name will no longer be Jacob, but Israel, because you have wrestled with God and with men and *prevailed*' (32:29). Rachel and Jacob both prevail in contests waged simultaneously with people and with God.

Even the more fertile Leah undergoes a period in which she cannot conceive, and uses her servant Zilpah as a surrogate (30:9–13). Although she is not the beloved of

Jacob, Leah is redeemed through the chronology of the Bible. As the mother of Levi, the progenitor of priests, and 'the lion cub Judah' (49:9), Leah becomes, like Jacob, the founder of a nation whose descendants supplant those of a sibling. It is the tribe of Judah and not the tribes of Joseph who survive. Through the names that they bestow upon their sons, Rachel and Leah articulate the various characters ascribed to the tribes of Israel. As evident in the story of Joseph, the competition expressed through these names is likewise transmitted.

Although Rebecca has something of a pre-story before she meets Isaac (24:15–61) and Rachel shepherds her father's flocks (29:9), women occupy the narrative stage primarily when the subject is the birth of sons (Fuchs 1999: 128). The emphasis on the transmission of covenant involves anxiety about continuity, and this anxiety in turn redirects the focus of the story from men to women. However, in the framework of Genesis birth and genealogy become issues concerning the perpetuation of male institutions.

The organization of Genesis according to generations has other inclusive effects. In the covenant established with Abraham, Jewish interpreters have read an eternal assurance of divine protection. Many Christian interpreters, in contrast, have emphasized the unique personal relationship with God that can arise through acts that attest to one's faith. In Genesis, human caprice in the forms of preference and rivalry reverberates in the realms of the future and the Divine.

WORKS CITED

ALBERTZ, R. (1994), *History of Israelite Religion in the Old Testament Period.* vol. 1: *From the Beginnings to the End of the Monarchy.* Louisville, Ky.: Westminster/John Knox Press.

ALTER, R. (1981), *The Art of Biblical Narrative.* New York: Basic Books.

AUERBACH, E. (1953), *Mimesis: The Representations of Reality in Western Literature.* Trans. Willard Trask. Princeton: Princeton University Press.

BOYARIN, D. (2004), *Borderlines: The Partition of Judaeo-Christianity.* Philadelphia: University of Pennsylvania Press.

CARR, D. M. (1996), *Reading the Fractures of Genesis: Historical and Literary Approaches.* Louisville, Ky.: Westminster/John Knox Press.

CASSUTO, U. (1978), *A Commentary on the Book of Genesis: Part I, From Adam to Noah.* Trans. Israel Abrahams. Jerusalem: Magnes Press.

CRÜSEMANN, F. (2002), 'Human Solidarity and Ethnic Identity: Israel's Self-Definition in the Genealogical System of Genesis', in Mark G. Brett (ed.), *Ethnicity and the Bible,* 57–77. Boston and Leiden: Brill.

DERRIDA, J. (2006), *Geneses, Genealogies, Genres & Genius: The Secrets of the Archive,* trans. Beverley Bie Brahic. New York: Columbia University Press.

DUNDES, A. (1984), 'Introduction', in *Sacred Narrative: Readings in the Theory of Myth.* Berkeley: University of California Press.

FISHBANE, M. (2003), *Biblical Myth and Rabbinic Mythmaking*. New York: Oxford University Press.

FUCHS, E. (1999), 'The Literary Characterization of Mothers and Sexual Politics in the Hebrew Bible', in Alice Bach (ed.), *Women in the Hebrew Bible: A Reader*. New York: Routledge.

GUNKEL, H. (1901), *The Legends of Genesis*, trans. W. H. Carruth. Chicago: Open Court. Repr., with Introduction by W. F. Albright. New York: Schocken, 1964.

HENDEL, R. (1997), 'The Poetics of Myth in Genesis', in S. Daniel Breslauer (ed.), *The Seductiveness of Jewish Myth: Challenge or Response?*, 157–70. Albany, NY: SUNY Press.

——(2005), *Remembering Abraham: Culture, Memory, and History in the Hebrew Bible*. New York: Oxford University Press.

JOSIPOVICI, G. (1988), *The Book of God: A Response to the Bible*. New Haven: Yale University Press.

MCCARTER, P. K. (1988), 'The Patriarchal Age: Abraham, Isaac and Jacob', in Hershel Shanks (ed.), *Ancient Israel: A Short History from Abraham to the Roman Destruction of the Temple*, 1–30. Washington, DC: Biblical Archaeology Society.

MALINOWSKI, B. (1948), *Magic, Science and Religion, and Other Essays*. Boston: Beacon Press.

MEYERS, C. (1988), *Discovering Eve: Ancient Israelite Women in Context*. New York: Oxford University Press.

NIDITCH, S. (1987), *Underdogs and Tricksters: A Prelude to Biblical Folklore*. New York: Harper & Row.

——(1993), *Folklore and the Hebrew Bible*. Minneapolis: Fortress/Augsburg.

PARDES, I. (1992), *Countertraditions in the Bible: A Feminist Approach*. Cambridge, Mass.: Harvard University Press.

STEINBERG, N. (1993), *Kinship and Marriage in Genesis: A Household Economics Perspective*. Minneapolis: Fortress Press.

STERNBERG, M. (1985), *The Poetics of Biblical Narrative: Ideological Literature and the Drama of Reading*. Bloomington: Indiana University Press.

——(1991), 'Double Cave, Double Talk: The Indirections of Biblical Dialogue', in Jason P. Rosenblatt and Joseph C. Sitterson, Jr. (eds.), *'Not in Heaven': Coherence and Complexity in Biblical Narrative*, 28–57. Bloomington: Indiana University Press.

ZLOTNICK, H. (2002), *Dinah's Daughters: Gender and Judaism from the Hebrew Bible to Antiquity*. Philadelphia: University of Pennsylvania Press.

FURTHER READING

BRENNER, A. (1993) 'Female Social Behaviour: Two Descriptive Patterns Within the "Birth of the Hero" Paradigm', in Athalya Brenner (ed.), *A Feminist Companion to Genesis*. Sheffield: Sheffield Academic Press.

BRETT, M. G. (2000), *Genesis: Procreation and the Politics of Identity*. London and New York: Routledge.

DRIVER, S. R. (1911), *The Book of Genesis*. London: Methuen.

Eskenazi, T. C. and A. Weiss (eds.) (2008), *The Torah: A Women's Commentary*. New York: Union of Reform Judaism Press.

Fishbane, M. (1998), *Biblical Text and Texture: A Literary Reading of Selected Texts*. Oxford: Oneworld.

Fox, E. (1989), 'Can Genesis Be Read as a Book?', *Semeia*, 46: 31–40.

Gunkel, H. (1922), 'Die Komposition der Joseph-Geschichten', *ZDMG* 76, nf 1: 55–71.

Havrelock, R. (2008), 'The Myth of Birthing the Hero: Heroic Barrenness in the Hebrew Bible', *Biblical Interpretation*, 16: 154–78.

Hendel, R. (2008), 'Other Edens', in D. Scholoen (ed.), *Exploring the Longue Durée: Essays in Honor of Lawrence E. Stager*. Winona Lake, Ind.: Eisenbrauns.

Niditch, S. (1985), *Chaos to Cosmos: Studies in Biblical Patterns of Creation*. Chico, Calif.: Scholars Press.

Speiser, E. A. (1964), *Genesis*. The Anchor Bible Commentary. Garden City, NY: Doubleday.

Von Rad, G. (1972), *Genesis: A Commentary*. Philadelphia: Westminster Press.

Westermann, C. (1984–6), *Genesis: A Commentary*. Minneapolis: Augsburg.

CHAPTER 2

··

JOB

··

JOHN F. A. SAWYER

THE Book of Job tells the story of a comfortable, law-abiding citizen suddenly, for no apparent reason, struck down by a series of spectacular disasters. Messengers run in, one after the other, with news that his property has been raided and his animals stolen, lightning has struck his flock and he has lost both sheep and shepherds; all his sons and daughters, with their families, have been killed at a banquet. Then he himself is struck down with an excruciating and hideously disfiguring skin disease, and forced to give up his position as respected elder statesman in his community to live in squalor outside the city gate. A brief prose narrative at the beginning informs us that Job's sufferings, unknown to him, were engineered in heaven as a test of his integrity, but the main part of the book, which is in verse, makes no mention of this, and his attempts to find an explanation, along with those of his 'comforters', come to nothing. In the end Yahweh speaks to him 'out of the whirlwind' (38:1) and restores his fortunes.

Job in the Bible is remembered for his 'righteousness', along with Noah and Daniel (Ezek. 14:14), and for his proverbial patience (James 5:11), and we may assume that from an early period he was the subject of one or more legends which provide the framework for the biblical book. But it is significant that the book is grouped, both in Christian scripture and in the Hebrew Bible, with two great poetical books, Psalms and Proverbs, rather than with any of the prose narratives in the Pentateuch or the 'Former Prophets' (Joshua–Kings).

LITERARY STRUCTURE

The main characters in the book are Job, his three old friends Eliphaz the Temanite, Bildad the Shuhite, and Zophar the Naamathite, who come to comfort him (2:11–13), and the young Elihu who appears later (32:1–6). They are all non-Israelites. The exact location of their places of origin is unknown, but in biblical tradition Uz, where Job comes from, has Edomite connections (Lam. 4:21; cf. Gen. 36:28), as have Eliphaz and Teman (Gen. 36:10–11), while Shuah, where Bildad comes from, is related to Midian (Gen. 25:32), Zophar the Naamathite may be Ammonite (cf. 1 Kgs 14:21, 31), and Elihu the Buzite an Arab (Jer. 25:23). The appearance in the prologue of Sabaeans (Arabia) and Chaldaeans (Babylonia) confirms the foreign setting of the book (Gordis 1965: 66–8).

There is also a remarkable feature of the language they use about God which appears to make the same point. While Yahweh's name appears in the narrative framework of the book, all of them, including Job, with one conspicuous exception which surely proves the rule (12:9), avoid the name of Israel's God, using instead a variety of other names, particularly *eloah*, 'God' (the singular of *elohim*) and *shaddai*, 'the Almighty', which occur far more frequently in Job than in any other book in the Bible (Driver and Gray 1921: pp. xxxv–xxxvi). Job had heard of Yahweh: in fact at the beginning of the story he quotes a Yahwistic saying: 'The Lord (Hebr. *YHWH*) gives, the Lord takes away: Blessed be the name of the Lord', 1:21), but only after his suffering and anguish does he come to know him personally. In his own words, 'I had heard of thee by the hearing of the ear, but now my eye sees thee' (42:5). One effect of this is that, when Yahweh finally addresses Job (38:1; 40:1) and the comforters (42:7), these are moments of revelation, comparable to the conversion of the kings of Syria (2 Kgs 5:15) or Babylon (Dan. 4:34–7), and must be taken into account in the interpretation of the book.

The literary structure of the book confirms this. We may consider Job's colourful lament in chapter 3 as belonging more to the prologue than to his dialogue with the comforters, just as his final confession is part of the epilogue (42). Within this framework the main part of the book (4–41) reveals an impressive symmetrical structure (Sawyer 1979). At the centre-point is a hymn in which wisdom is defined as 'fearing Yahweh and departing from evil' (28:28), exactly the words used to describe Job at the beginning of the book, but with the name Yahweh substituted for God (1:1). The three cycles of speeches by Job and the comforters which come before the hymn (4–27) correspond to the three speeches after it by Job, Elihu, and Yahweh. But while the former fade out, incomplete and inconclusive—Bildad's third speech is only a few verses long (25) and Zophar makes no third speech at all— the latter rise to a climax beginning with Job's humble *apologia pro vita sua* (29–31) and ending with the dazzling, uncompromising poetry of the Yahweh speeches (38–41). The literary independence of chapter 28 is confirmed by the occurrence of the name

Yahweh, and gives it a dramatic function, rather like that of a Greek chorus (Junker 1959: 54) or a 'musical interlude' (Gordis 1965: 278), marking the transition from human failure to divine intervention by the God of Israel.

The intervention of the gods in human affairs is reminiscent of Greek mythology and has obvious parallels also in the Gilgamesh Epic as well as in many biblical narratives. But the dramatic irony, by which the reader knows what is being planned in heaven while the human characters do not, is rare in the Bible. Normally Yahweh reveals his plans to his people in a strikingly personal way, whether to individuals like Abraham or, through his prophets, to the whole people. The scenes in heaven in which Yahweh discusses human events with Satan and the other members of his divine court (Hebr. *bene elohim*, 'sons of God', Job 1:6–12; 2:1–6) have a number of biblical parallels, notably the prophecy of Micaiah ben Imlah (1 Kgs 22:19–23) and the vision of Isaiah (Isa. 6). In both cases a prophet has personally witnessed the scene and recounts it in the first person ('I saw the Lord'). In Job, by contrast, only the reader is informed about the ways of Yahweh.

The Yahwistic literary framework of the book, however, accounts for only five of the forty-two chapters (1–3; 28; 42). The rest is composed of a series of speeches by Job, his comforters, and Yahweh. The first part is in the form of a dialogue (4–27). The appropriateness of this literary form for philosophical discussion is confirmed by its universal popularity, both in the ancient Near East (e.g. the Babylonian 'Dialogue about Human Misery': *ANET* 438–40) and classical literature (Plato, Cicero, Aesop). But Job's 'dialogue' with his comforters is a dialogue only in form. The character of the participants is for the most part irrelevant, with the possible exception of the distinctively pompous and patronizing Eliphaz, and, while there are some cases where one speaker picks up on a comment made by a previous speaker, these are infrequent. For the most part the speeches are independent compositions, loosely placed in the structure of a dialogue. Indeed, Job's speeches, read on their own, have an impressive literary unity (Rosenberg 1977).

The second part of the book consists in effect of three long monologues, leaving little room for actual dialogue. First comes Job's soliloquy, which is in three parts. A touching account of how things were before misfortune struck (29) is contrasted with an agonizing description of his present plight ('my lyre is turned to mourning', 30:31), a social outcast, mocked, despised and humiliated, and in great physical pain (30). In the third part of his speech Job protests his innocence by listing all the social and ethical principles he has lived his life by (31), in a manner reminiscent of the 'Negative Confession' of those facing death in Egyptian funerary texts (*ANET* 34). Next, the angry young Elihu addresses Job by name a number of times (33:1, 31; 37:14) and quotes him once (34:5–6), but again his long speech is a monologue, in which, like Yahweh, he dismisses the three older comforters as failures ('they answer no more: they have not a word to say', 32:15) and expresses his own view at great length (32–7).

Finally, Yahweh's speech 'out of the whirlwind' (38:1; 40:6) does not address Job by name, but is written almost entirely in the second-person singular, contrasting Job's weakness with divine wisdom and omnipotence: 'Where were you when I laid the foundation of the earth?' (38:4). To maintain the dialogue framework, Job makes a brief statement in reply to Yahweh at the midpoint of the speech (40:3–5), but the climax describing the awesome power of Leviathan is written in the third person (41:12–34), almost as though Job is no longer there. In the end, however, personal contact between Israel's God and the four foreign protagonists is established, first by Job's answer (42:1–6), which Yahweh accepts (42:9), and then by Yahweh's direct words to Eliphaz, Bildad, and Zophar (42:7–9).

SOME HISTORICAL-CRITICAL PROBLEMS

Inconsistencies in style and structure, some extremely difficult Hebrew, and the problem of dating such a work have occupied scholars for several centuries and still account for a very large proportion of most commentaries. Could the same author have written both the poetic dialogue and the prose sections at the beginning and end of the book? How is it that Job apparently refers to his sons as still living (19:17), when according to the prologue they had all been killed? The 'patient Job' of the prologue is a very different character from the angry, protesting Job of the main part of the book. Which of the characters could have uttered chapter 28, considered by most, on both stylistic and theological grounds, to be an independent composition? Why is there no mention of Elihu in the literary framework of the book, especially at the end when the other three comforters are named? The relevance of parts or all of the Yahweh speeches has also been questioned, as has the effectiveness of the 'happy ending' which, far from picking up the themes introduced in the prologue, in many ways undermines the whole argument of the book. There seems to be plenty of evidence for the later 'expansion, mutilation or other modification' of an original text (Driver and Gray 1921: p. xxxvii).

As our initial discussion of the literary structure of the book illustrates, recent scholarship has tended to favour a more holistic approach to biblical literature, not least because centuries of readers found it possible to discuss and interpret the Book of Job, like the Pentateuch and the Book of Isaiah, in its present form, and the value of some of their interpretations is being increasingly appreciated. Nevertheless, some of the historical-critical questions are justified and the proposed solutions often interesting, even although there is wide disagreement amongst scholars on most of them. It must also be said that some of the commentators concerned are clearly motivated as much by the subjective desire to reconstruct a shorter and more effective book, as by strictly literary, linguistic, or historical considerations.

First, let us look at one of those passages widely believed to be 'later additions'. The value of the Elihu speeches (32–7) was already questioned by Gregory the Great, while a typical critical judgement from modern times is that of S. R. Driver, who describes them as 'prolix, laboured and sometimes tautologous' (Driver 1913: 429). Elihu has nothing new to add to what has already been said by the others. He is superfluous, and his removal would make very little difference apart from shortening the book. Indeed, if his speeches were not there, the appearance of Yahweh would follow immediately after Job's soliloquy in which he pleads for an answer (31:35; cf. 30:14), and would give the book a tighter, more dramatic structure. Linguistic arguments, which are rather less subjective, include the fact that there is a significant concentration of Aramaisms in Elihu's speeches, and his preferred name for God is El, rather than the *Eloah*, 'God' and *Shaddai*, 'Almighty' of the other speakers. Perhaps most convincing is the absence of any reference to Elihu in the rest of the book.

The question then arises as to why these six chapters were inserted. A number of scholars propose that they were added by the author himself later in life, perhaps simply to add the voice of youth to the debate and therefore in a different style. Or it could have been for structural reasons, so that three speeches in the second half of the book, those of Job, Elihu, and Yahweh, would balance the three cycles of dialogue in the first half (see above). More interesting is the suggestion that the position of the Elihu speeches, entirely separate from those of the three old comforters and next to the Yahweh speeches, deliberately gives prominence to one particular view of suffering, namely, that suffering is not punishment for sin, but a 'source of moral discipline and a spur to ethical perfection' (Gordis 1965: 115). Eliphaz's words 'Happy is the man whom God reproves!' (Job 5:17) are said in the context of traditional wisdom teaching on divine retribution (cf. Prov. 3:11–12) and do not really anticipate Elihu. Elihu's speeches may be a later addition, representing the thoughts of an older, more mature writer, but nonetheless profound and, within the debate, original. One scholar actually describes them as the 'summit and crown of the Book of Job' (Cornill 1907: 428).

Critical discussion of chapter 28 and the Yahweh speeches runs along similar lines. From a literary point of view chapter 28 is universally held to be poetry of the highest quality, but widely regarded as a later addition as it could not have been uttered by any of the characters: if it were spoken by Job, for example, it would anticipate and undermine the Yahweh speeches. Perhaps it was written by the same author as the rest of the book, but added later (Dhorme 1967: p. xcvii). The Yahweh speeches (38–41) are less often rejected as later insertions, not least because it would be hard to envisage a book ending either at chapter 31 or with the Elihu speeches. But the variation in literary quality as between its two parts, divided by Job's feeble intervention (40:3–5), has often been noted, and the speeches about a hippopotamus and a crocodile in chapters 40–1 rejected, while the first part, 'unsurpassed in world literature' according to some (Peake 1905: 43), is retained.

We turn now to consider the date of the book. The biblical reference to Job along with two other folk heroes, Noah and Daniel (Ezek.14), suggests that elements in the book are very ancient. The story of Noah's flood has long been compared to a well-known passage in the Gilgamesh Epic (*ANET* 93–6) and other ancient Mesopotamian texts, while the Ugaritic legend of a righteous king called Dan'el who loses his son Aqhat because of the jealousy of the goddess Anat (*c.*1400 BCE), provides interesting evidence for an aspect of the Daniel legend, not found in the biblical book (Margalit 1989). A number of parallels to the Book of Job have also been quoted from Egyptian and Mesopotamian literature. The Egyptian 'Dialogue between a man and his soul on whether to commit suicide' (*c.*2000 BCE), for example, laments the breakdown of normal social and moral conditions (*ANET* 405–7); and there is a lengthy poem beginning 'I will praise the Lord of Wisdom' (*Ludlul bel nemeqi*), sometimes rather misleadingly called the 'Babylonian Job', which contains a passage in which the reasons for innocent suffering are explored (*ANET* 434–7; Lambert 1967: 27). There are substantial differences, however, between such writings and the Hebrew Job, which has more significant parallels within the Hebrew Bible, particularly in Psalms, Proverbs, Ecclesiastes, and Deutero-Isaiah.

The language of the Book of Job is likewise unable on its own to help us date it. Aramaisms are relatively common (not only in the Elihu speeches), and this is usually taken as pointing to a date in the sixth century BCE at the earliest, or more likely the Second Temple period when the use of Aramaic was increasingly widespread (Hurvitz 1974). The absence of any obvious Persian or Greek influence might perhaps suggest a date early in that period. Jerome mentions Arabic, alongside Hebrew and Aramaic, in the preface to his Latin translation (Weber 1994: 731), and scholars have long noted cases where the meaning of a Hebrew word is known only by reference to an Arabic cognate (Grabbe 1977). One theory proposed to explain the strangeness and difficulty of the language of Job is that it is a translation from an Aramaic or Arabic original, but this seems unlikely, and in any case would only tell us something about the author and perhaps where he lived, but not when. The evidence of the ancient versions, including the Greek, which differs significantly from the Hebrew in places (Pope 1973: 95–6), and the Targum discovered at Qumran, is not sufficient to prove the existence of another ancient textual tradition alongside the Masoretic text.

The period in biblical history when the most original discussions about suffering appear to have taken place is the Babylonian Exile in the sixth century BCE. At least one author during that time of national crisis questioned the teaching that suffering is always punishment for sin, and introduced some new ideas into the debate. The anonymous author of Isaiah 40–55 ('Deutero-Isaiah') begins by suggesting that the disasters that had afflicted Judah were out of proportion to the sins they had committed (Isa. 40:2; cf. 54:7–8), and later argues that in certain cases Yahweh can use innocent suffering for a saving purpose (53). Parallels with the Book of Job are striking, and have led many to conclude that it comes from the same exceptionally creative period or soon after.

THEOLOGICAL AND PHILOSOPHICAL ISSUES

The brief prose prologue must be considered as merely setting the scene for what is a major poetical composition on the problem of suffering in a world created and ruled by Yahweh. But its literary function should not be underestimated. In the first place, it establishes the innocence of Job: 'he is blameless and upright, one who feared God and turned away from evil (1:1) . . . in all this he did not sin or charge God with wrong . . .'(1:22; cf. 2:10). Indeed, he is a legend, like Noah and Daniel, who were saved by their righteousness (Ezek.14:14). Thus the theory that suffering is always punishment for sin is ruled out from the start. There is the additional point that the exceptionally severe forms of suffering that afflict Job and his family are out of all proportion to any possible minor sin he might have inadvertently committed. The detailed narrative of the relentless series of personal catastrophes that befall him, entirely unexpectedly, is intended to make this point absolutely clear, as are the reactions of his wife and his three friends. His wife, described by Augustine as the 'devil's assistant' (*diaboli adiutrix*), tells him to 'curse God and die' (2:9) (Newsom 1998: 139–40.), while his friends 'rend their garments and sprinkle dust upon their heads' as if he were already dead and they had come to mourn, rather than comfort, him (2:12–13).

   The other element in the prologue which is both theologically and ethically significant is the glimpse the reader is given into heaven, where Yahweh is seen to be discussing Job with one of the members of his heavenly court. The role of this character, known as 'the adversary', or perhaps 'prosecutor' (Hebr. *ha-satan*; cf. 1 Kgs 11:14, 23, 25), and not yet identified with Satan (cf. Mark 1:13; Rev. 20:2), appears to be that of devil's advocate, challenging Job's integrity and provoking Yahweh into giving him the authority to test it. The notion that Job's sufferings are the result of decisions taken in heaven is reminiscent of the activities of Zeus and the Fates in Homer (e.g. *Iliad* 19. 86–94), and even comes close to Shakespeare's famous image: 'Like flies to wanton boys, are we to the gods; they kill us for their sport' (*King Lear*, IV. i. 35–6). Job almost comes to this conclusion himself later in the book (10).

   The adversary's challenge, however, is from a moral perspective entirely justified, focusing as it does on the question of whether Job's innocence is motivated by self-interest. First, take away his house, his wealth, and his family and see whether he still 'fears God and turns away from evil'. Then, when Job's integrity is unaffected by losing everything that belongs to him, the adversary, still not satisfied, says: 'Skin for skin! All that a man has he will give for his life . . . touch his bone and his flesh, and he will curse thee to thy face' (2:4). Job was a like a snake that can slough off its outer skin and survive. So the 'satan' afflicted him with an abhorrent skin disease that covered his body 'from the sole of his foot to the crown of his head' (cf. Isa. 1:6). There has been some discussion as to what exactly the skin disease was, but more pertinent is the observation that skin diseases, of whatever kind, are among the commonest symptoms of poverty, and thus the second part of Job's test is that he was forced to join the ranks of the marginalized, outside the city gates, like Lazarus (Luke 16:20; Gutierrez 1987: 6). Yahweh's confidence in 'his servant' Job is vindicated. Job passes both tests and maintains his integrity, each time citing a religious saying, one of them a Yahwistic blessing (1:21), in which he expresses his faith that whatever happens is God's will and we have no reason to complain. The prose narrative ends with a picture of the three friends sitting in silence beside Job, certainly their most effective gesture of comfort.

Chapter 3 is about death. It is a lament by Job in which he reveals the extent of the psychological and spiritual damage caused by the disasters that have befallen him. Although it is written in verse, like most laments (cf. Ps. 22:1–18; Jer. 20:14–18), it is thus a continuation of the prologue, completing the setting of the scene for the ensuing dialogue. First Job curses the day he was born, indeed the night when he was conceived, summoning experts in the dark arts to help him delete that day from the calendar (3:8). Then he asks, if he had to be born why could he not have died at birth? Death would have been preferable, because 'there the wicked cease from troubling . . . the prisoners are at ease together . . . and the slave is free from his master'. There are few passages in the Hebrew Bible that give such a benign description of the underworld (cf. Sir. 41:2–4), and again its purpose is to stress the intensity of Job's suffering. It is not a change in the character of Job between the prologue and the dialogue, as many scholars have argued, but a change in his situation, both physical and psychological. When people long for death 'more than for hidden treasure . . . and are glad when they find the grave' (3:21–2), then the problem of suffering in God's world is at its most acute.

A number of logical solutions are proposed by Job and the three comforters in the next twenty-four chapters. The most frequent is the 'Deuteronomic' view (cf. Deut.28) that suffering is punishment for sin. The fundamental importance of this ethical teaching, namely, that if you behave well you will be rewarded, is stressed throughout the Book of Job, and beautifully expressed in some of the comforters' speeches (e.g. 11:13–20). Indeed, the book has a 'Deuteronomic' ending in which Job is richly rewarded. But in the context of Job's experience, it is irrelevant. The logical deduction that when someone suffers he must have sinned, albeit unwittingly, does not apply to Job, and in the mouths of the comforters sounds painfully cold and self-righteous (e.g. 5:8–16). Similarly inappropriate is the argument that no one is without sin, not even the angels (4:17–21). This almost implies that everybody suffers equally, which is manifestly not the case, as it is the disproportionate nature of Job's suffering that is one of the key issues debated.

Job also offers some theories sparked off by the intensity of his personal experience of suffering, his 'existential passion' (Brueggemann 2003: 294). Nowhere does he question the existence of God, but he makes some terrifying suggestions about God's nature. Perhaps suffering has nothing at all to do with punishment, and therefore God's intervention in human affairs is haphazard and indiscriminate: 'He destroys both the blameless and wicked' (9:22). Or perhaps God is fallible, since it looks as though he does not always punish the right person: 'Are your eyes mere human eyes? Do you see as human beings see?' (10:4 NJB). Has he made a mistake? Or suppose God enjoys watching us suffer: maybe the reason he lavished so much care in creating us in all our complexity and sensitivity was because he wanted to see how we would react to pain, 'like flies to wanton boys' (10:8–17). It is clear from the language and structure of the book that the author rejects all these explanations, as he does any questioning of the belief in the existence of God. If there were no God, Job's moral and theological problems, and those of the comforters, would disappear, but that logical option is not considered

The other theological solution which is missing from the debate is a belief in life after death, where the injustices of this world are set right in the next: 'and those who sleep in the dust shall awake, some to everlasting life and some to shame and everlasting contempt' (Dan.12:2). Certainly Job's celebrated words beginning 'I know that my Redeemer liveth . . .' (19:25 AV) have strong eschatological associations in the Hebrew text as it stands ('at last . . . he will arise . . . I shall see . . . my eyes shall behold . . .'), but these are no doubt due to later developments, like those already evident in Daniel (Sawyer 1973: 232–3), which earned them a famous role in Handel's *Messiah*, and on their own they do not provide sufficient grounds for changing the whole plot of the book.

There is, however, one other explanation offered in the Book of Job as to why the innocent suffer. Suffering is a discipline which even the wise can profit from: 'Happy is the man whom God reproves' (5:17). These are the words of Eliphaz, but it is Elihu who develops the theory most eloquently: 'Behold, God is exalted in his power; who is a teacher like him? (36:22) . . . God does all these things, twice, three times, with a man, to bring his soul back from the Pit that he may see the light of life' (33:29–30). Many believe the Elihu speeches reflect the experience of an older, wiser author and have been added later. However that may be, as they stand they challenge both the other three comforters' rejection of Job's innocence and Job's argument that God is unjust. The idea that suffering can have a beneficial function is developed in a different direction in the Suffering Servant passage in Isaiah 53, and taken to its ultimate conclusion in the Christian doctrine that salvation comes only through the suffering and death of Christ. But in the present context it must be said that, while it is certainly true that the experience of suffering can strengthen and enrich, it often breaks and embitters even the world's wisest and most god-fearing citizens.

It remains to consider the ending of the book. This consists of three separate sections, each raising some intriguing theological questions, and on none of which can it be said that there is scholarly agreement. First, there are the two magnificent speeches of Yahweh, each introduced as being delivered 'out of the whirlwind' (38:1, 40:6) and each intended as a rebuke to Job ('Shall a faultfinder contend with the Almighty?', 40:2). The image of a whirlwind frequently accompanies spectacular descriptions of divine intervention, whether to rescue Israel (Ps. 77:18; Isa. 29:6) or to destroy the wicked (Nahum 1:3), but it was also by a whirlwind that Elijah was taken up to heaven (2 Kgs 2:1, 11). Either way, commentators suggest that its function here is to place the emphasis as much on Job's first terrifying encounter with Israel's God as on what Yahweh actually says (Rowley 1976: 19–20). In his suffering, in his experience of solidarity with the poor, Job was able to enter into a closer relationship with God than was possible before (Gutierrez 1987: 48).

The speeches themselves contain an accumulation of examples illustrating how ignorant, weak, and helpless human beings are when confronted by the wonders of nature, and no explanation of why innocent people like Job suffer (von Rad 1972: 225–6). The first speech (38–9) draws on some of the most beautiful imagery in the Bible to describe, on the one hand, the creation of the earth, the sea, and the sky, and, on the other, the skills and instincts of a variety of animals and birds. The second, in two extended poems, chooses the hippopotamus (Hebr. *behemoth*) and the crocodile (Hebr. *leviathan*) as prime examples from untamed nature, or, as some suggest, two mythical creatures symbolizing cosmic powers which only God can master (4 Ezra 6:49, 51; Job 3:8; Isa. 27:1). The contrast between this view and that of Genesis 1, where humankind is the high point of creation and is given 'dominion over the fish of the sea and over the birds of the air . . .' (Gen.1:28; cf. Ps. 104), is striking (Greenberg 1987: 298), and recalls a cynical allusion made by Job himself to Psalm 8 (7:17–18), as well as some of his other comments on the miserable plight of human beings in this world (10).

Job's response to the Yahweh speeches is in two parts. In the first he is silenced and simply capitulates: 'I have spoken once . . . but I will proceed no further' (40:4–5). But his second, longer response is more complicated (42:2–6). The usual view is that he admits he was wrong to challenge God, often in disrespectful and near-blasphemous language, and 'repents in dust and ashes' (42:6). But it has been suggested that, since the actual content of the debate is not addressed by Yahweh, Job's 'repentance' must be about something else. In Hebrew the word 'repent' is followed by a preposition which much more frequently means 'about, concerning' than 'in', suggesting that Job has accepted he was wrong to lament and mourn ('dust and ashes'). According to this interpretation he does not retract any of his arguments, and the dialogue ends with a defiant Job and a God that fails to convince him (Miles 1995: 429–30).

The 'happy ending', in which Job is restored to a life of prosperity and happiness (42:7–17), has been seen by some as a vindication of the comforters' view that after all there is a causal connection between righteousness and prosperity. This is not borne out by the text, however, as the point is made that what Job has said, including perhaps even his most intemperate outbursts, is praised by God, at the expense of his three friends whose folly has aroused God's wrath. Furthermore, the enormity of what he has been through, for which he is never given an explanation, is not forgotten. On the contrary, all his friends and relations come to offer their sympathy and comfort, although, as a number of scholars have noted, lost children can never be replaced and we may imagine that Job is like Rachel: 'weeping for her children, she refuses to be comforted for her children because they are not' (Jer. 31:15; Fackenheim 1980: 202).

Within the limits of the Book of Job, where from beginning to end the author affirms his belief in the power of God and the integrity of his hero, the conclusion seems to be that, on the one hand, the nature of God is so complex that speculation about it can only lead to oversimplification, frustration, or blasphemy, while on the other, the vicissitudes of human experience are also so complex that the search for patterns of cause and effect is doomed from the start. But suffering, however intense and however incomprehensible, irrational, or undeserved, makes no difference to anyone whose has based his life on belief in God. Job's answer to suffering is the defiant belief in an all-powerful and all-loving God, in spite of the evidence, not because of it.

Works Cited

ANET: Ancient Near Eastern Texts Relating to the Old Testament, ed. J. B. Pritchard. Princeton: Princeton University Press, 1950.

Brueggemann, W. (2003), *An Introduction to the Old Testament: The Canon and Christian Imagination*. Louisville, Ky.: Westminster/John Knox.

Cornill, C. H. (1907), *Introduction to the Canonical Books of the Old Testament*, trans. G. H. Box. New York: Williams & Norgate.

Dhorme, E. (1967), *A Commentary on the Book of Job*. London: Nelson.

Driver, S. R. (1913), *Introduction to the Literature of the Old Testament*. Edinburgh: T. & T. Clark.

——and Gray, G. B. (1921), *The Book of Job, together with a New Translation* (International Critical Commentary). Edinburgh: T. & T. Clark.

Fackenheim, E. (1980), 'New Hearts and the Old Covenant', in L. H. Silberman, J. L. Crenshaw, and S. Sandmel (eds.), *The Divine Helmsman: Studies on God's Control of Human Events*. New York: KTAV Publishing House.

Gordis, R. (1965), *The Book of God and Man: A Study of Job*. Chicago and London: University of Chicago Press.

Grabbe, L. (1977), *Comparative Philology and the Text of Job: A Study in Methodology* (SBL Dissertation Series). Missoula, Mont.: Scholars Press.

GREENBERG, M. (1987), 'Job', in R. Alter and F. Kermode (eds.), *The Literary Guide to the Bible*, 283–304. London: Collins.

GUTIERREZ, G. (1987), *On Job: God-Talk and the Suffering of the Innocent*. Maryknoll, NY: Orbis Books.

HURVITZ, A. (1974), 'The Date of the Prose Prologue of Job Linguistically Reconsidered', *Harvard Theological Review*, 67: 17–34.

JUNKER, H. (1959), 'Das Buch Hiob', in F. Nötscher (ed.), *Echter Bibel*, vol. 4. Würzburg: Echter Verlag.

LAMBERT, W. G. (1967), *Babylonian Wisdom Literature*. Oxford: Clarendon Press.

MARGALIT, B. (1989), *The Ugaritic Poem of AQHT: Text, Translation, Commentary*. Berlin and New York: de Gruyter.

MILES, J. (1995), *God: A Biography*. London and New York: Simon & Schuster.

NEWSOM, C. A. (1998), 'Job', in C. A. Newsom and S. H. Ringe (eds.), *Women's Bible Commentary*. Louisville, Ky.: Westminster/John Knox.

PEAKE, A. S. (1905), *Job* (The Century Bible). Edinburgh: T. C. & E. C. Jack.

POPE, M. E. (1973), *Job* (Anchor Bible). Garden City, NY: Doubleday.

ROSENBERG, D. (1977), *Job Speaks*. New York: Harper & Row.

ROWLEY, H. H. (1976), *Job* (New Century Bible Commentary). London: Marshall, Morgan & Scott.

SAWYER, J. F. A. (1973), 'Hebrew Terms for the Resurrection of the Dead', in *Vetus Testamentum*, 23: 218–34.

——(1979), 'The Authorship and Structure of the Book of Job', *Journal for the Study of the Old Testament Supp.*, 11: 253–7.

VON RAD, G. (1972), *Wisdom in Israel* (orig. *Weisheit in Israel*, Neukirchen-Vluyn, 1970). London: SCM Press.

WEBER, R. (ed.) (1994), *Biblia Sacra iuxta vulgatam versionem*. 4th edn. Stuttgart: Deutsche Bibelgesellschaft.

FURTHER READING

The magisterial commentary of David Clines, (*Job 1–20* (Dallas, Tex.: Word Books, 1989); *Job 21–37* (Nashville, Tenn.: T. Nelson, 2006), *Job 38–42* (Nashville, Tenn.: Nelson, 2010) is by far the most comprehensive and detailed currently available. Also valuable are the commentaries of H. H. Rowley (1976), Norman Habel, in the Old Testament Library Series (Philadelphia: Westminster Press, 1985), and J. L. Crenshaw in the *Oxford Bible Commentary*, ed. J. Barton and J. Muddiman (Oxford: Oxford University Press, 2001). Walter Brueggemann's succinct introduction (2003) is extremely useful, as are the important studies of Job by Robert Gordis (1965), Gustavo Gutierrez (1987), and Edwin Good, *In Turns of Tempest: A Reading of Job, with a Translation* (Stanford: Stanford University Press, 1990).

....

CHAPTER 3

PSALMS

....

KATHARINE J. DELL

OUTLINE

....

Books Within a Book

The Book of Psalms is amongst the Writings in the canon of the Old Testament and has from early times been used as a book of worship and prayer in Jewish and Christian communities. The book has no title as such, but at the end of Psalm 72 'the prayers of David' is a key phrase. Rabbinic tradition, however, has preferred *tehillim*, 'praises', and, interestingly, 'praise' and 'prayer' together describe the contents of the Psalter. The title *tehillim* is thus what one finds in Hebrew Bibles today.[1] 'Psalms' comes from the Greek *Psalmoi*, 'songs of praise'. The Psalter contains 150 psalms, and is itself divided into five books with varying numbers of psalms in each, varying also in length and differing greatly in theological content. Each of the five books contains a doxology—Ps. 41:13; 72:19; 89:52; 106:48; 150—which is evidence of some deliberate arrangement. The shortest psalm is 117 (two verses) and the longest 119 (176 verses). The fact of five books is thought to have followed a Pentateuchal model, the five corresponding to the five books of the 'Torah'—Genesis, Exodus, Leviticus, Deuteronomy, and Numbers. Terrien (2003) believes that exploration of this model and these connections would be a fruitful line of further research. He also thinks that the pattern of early liturgical calendars might have affected this division into five. This arrangement would have occurred primarily when the Psalter was being written down and

---

[1] The Qumran community refers to the 'Book of Praises'.

finalized in late post-exilic times, although there were clearly groupings of psalms that existed at an earlier stage and it may be that the first three books reached a fixed form before the latter two. Increasingly scholars are finding method in the alignment of certain psalms (see below), and so the process may not be as random as once believed.

The headings to the psalms (contained by 116 out of 150 psalms and ranging from one word to a long sentence) may have formed a reason for their collection, in that psalms attributed to certain figures, be they King David or temple singers such as Asaph, who was assigned a singing role by David in 1 Chronicles 16:7, seem to have been put together in groups. For example, most of the psalms in Book 1 have super-scriptions linking them to David (with the exception of Pss. 1–2, 10, 33) and most of the psalms of Asaph are in Book 3, Psalms 73–83 within 73–89. Furthermore, thirteen of the seventy-three 'Davidic' psalms are linked to particular historical events in David's life. Some psalms have a double attribution (e.g. to David and Jeduthun, Pss. 39 and 62). One key arrangement is what is known as the Elohistic Psalter, the use of the divine name Elohim in preference to Yahweh in Psalms 42–83, essentially most of Books 2 and 3. Elsewhere in the Psalter both are used, but Yahweh more predominantly. This indicates that an early Elohistic psalter, a kind of 'mini-psalter, may have existed from pre-exilic times which has been incorporated into the larger work. Another sub-group seems to be psalms that betray a northern interest (e.g. Ps. 80), which were no doubt collected and preserved in the south after the fall of the northern kingdom in 722 BCE. The Psalter was probably finished sometime between the age of the Chronicler and that of Sirach. This has not always been the scholarly view, with pre-critical scholars taking the Davidic attribution at face value and early critical scholarship in the late nineteenth and early twentieth centuries favouring the Macca-bean period of the second century BCE. However, this suggestion does have some mileage. The great interest of the Chronicler in David and in temple worship must have influenced the way the Psalter started to come together (in particular, the addition of the headings). Furthermore, the Chronicler tells us of the appointment of groups of singers to sing particular psalms (1 Chron. 16:7), and adds that these musicians 'composed a canticle' (vv. 8–36, which is in fact an amalgam of fragments from the Psalter). This suggests an important stage along the way to finalization, but not fully so. Sirach says in 47:8 that David 'sang hymns with the whole of his heart'. Verse 10 of his prologue suggests that there were 'other books of our fathers' in existence, and this may include a book of psalms amongst others.

Collections of psalms found at Qumran[2] indicate that Books 1–3 may have had a rather more fixed form from earlier times than the other two. These three books are found at Qumran with the same psalms in the same order—whilst in relation to Books 4–5, there is clearly some fluidity about their contents. Indeed, other psalms were found there that represent psalmic compositions by the community

---

[2] There are fragments of 115 biblical psalms and a scroll (11Q Psa) containing 39 psalms.

itself.[3] A note from Qumran mentions that David composed 3,600 psalms and 446 songs, plus four for the stricken, totalling 4,050. The psalms of Books 1–3 have a predominance of laments and nationalistic psalms, whilst the psalms of Books 4–5 have a more didactic and eschatological emphasis and move towards a crescendo of worship, the final five psalms being framed with 'praise the Lord', which reaches its peak in Psalm 150. This differing emphasis between the books may reveal a changing purpose for the Psalter over time. This process has not ceased with canonization, in that different early translations of the Bible contain extra psalms, notably the Septuagint, which contains one extra psalm (151). How the Psalter gained the shape in which we have it today is of interest, and so there has been considerable focus in recent times on the final form of the text and canonization process (see below).

There appear to be important relationships between psalms at the beginning and ending of the Psalter, that is, Psalms 1 and 2 and 150, and also psalms at the 'seams' of the individual books (Wilson 1985). For example, Psalm 1 is often seen as a wisdom psalm intended to put the Psalter into the context of didactic study (which may have been one of its later contexts), added as a preface to the Psalter. Psalm 2 would then open the 'Davidic' collection, giving it eschatological significance. Such possible interrelationships do not stop there. Wilson's suggestion that royal psalms are found at the seams of Books 1–3 (Wilson 1986), that is, Psalms 21, 72, 89, and 41 (it is disputed whether this psalm is royal), has been criticized for giving too much significance to particular psalms. Furthermore, no reason has been given for the non-royal psalms also found at the seams (e.g. Pss. 42–3 and 71). There are increasing attempts to counter any idea of randomness in the collection. A similar line to this is being taken in Proverbs research—seeing patterns in what appear to be simply 'lists' of two-line sentences (Heim 2001). Vestiges of earlier pairings, such as Psalms 104–6, 111–13, 115–17, and 146–50 (all of which either begin and/or end with 'Hallelujah'), or groupings according to festival contexts, for example the enthronement psalms (Pss. 93, 96–9) that concern God's kingship, are also possible (see below). I wonder, however, if the quest for editorial connections between psalms has become rather subjective in relation to what a particular interpreter finds there. D. M. Howard (1993) expresses this well when he writes that soon 'every pair of adjacent psalms will be shown to have significant . . . links between them'. There is also evidence of later shaping within individual psalms, for example Psalm 89, which is essentially a psalm praising the covenant with David, but which contains a gear-change in verse 38 that indicates a recognition that the covenant has now been broken (presumably with the events of Exile). There is also an interesting field of enquiry into the redactional purpose of the whole, whether it be didactic, legal, or eschatological. Whybray (1996) argues that there is insufficient evidence for the idea that the Psalter was compiled as a book for private spiritual

---

[3] Qumran's own *Hodayot* comprise 25 psalms.

reading (e.g. Anderson 1980). Whilst there are elements of its use in private devotion, this is not enough to orientate the whole book in that direction, nor do scholarly suggestions of alternatively didactic, legal, or eschatological reshapings of the Psalter dictate the overall form of the final text.

A Davidic Psalter?

The figure of David dominates the Psalter in the many attributions of psalms to his name in the headings. The Masoretic texts contains seventy-three such designations, whilst the Septuagint increases this to eighty-five. Many psalms simply say 'Of David'. Others attempt to find a location for a psalm in an event of his life (Pss. 3, 7, 18, 51, 52, 54, 56–7, 59–60, 63, 142). He had a reputation for singing and playing the lute (1 Sam. 18:10; Amos 6:5). The tradition certainly has remembered him as the great psalm-writer, rather as Moses is the great lawgiver and Solomon the ultimate wise king. Whether these titles are, however, mainly honorific is open to debate. Most scholars nowadays would attribute some psalms to David (e.g. Pss. 2, 10, 18), but not many, whilst in contrast Davidic authorship was simply assumed by scholars before the rise of biblical scholarship. The Psalms also contain references that clearly refer to the Davidic line and hence to other Davidic kings (e.g. Ps. 72, 'Of Solomon') or simply indicate a king figure (e.g. Pss. 20–1, 45, 72, 89, 101, 110, 132, 144).[4] Others portray David or a king figure in an eschatological light (e.g. Ps. 2:8–9), which has led Christians in particular to align a future David with Jesus, born of the line of David.

The issue mainly revolves around the psalm headings—were they always attached to the psalm in question or are they an addition from the last stages of the compilation of the book? Are they an attempt at authorization, with hindsight? Or are we to take them in any way at face value? Goulder (1982, 1990, 1996, 1998) argues that psalm headings should be taken more seriously and may well have been attached to the psalm from earliest times. He aligns small collections of psalms alongside narrative material, in particular from the Books of Samuel, which describe the monarchic period. He also argues (1990) for the alignment of smaller portions of the Psalter with liturgical occasions in ancient Israel, for example Psalms 90–106 with the Feast of Tabernacles. Similar questions can be asked of the musical notations—how integral to the psalm are they? Eaton (2005) gives a full account of musical and performance elements in the Psalms. They refer either to a tune to which a particular psalm is to be sung, or to an instrument which accompanies it. They reveal the use of psalms in a worship situation, although the second temple was probably not the first place in which psalms would have been sung (nor indeed are all to be confined to a temple context, many representing the work of individuals outside that setting). Are these notations original to the

---

[4] We also find Ps. 90 attributed to Moses.

psalm, or again are we seeing 'the hymnbook of the second temple' (a phrase long coined by scholars to describe the final ordering of the Psalter)?

FORM

Psalms as Poetry

The Psalms are poetry, and hence concise in their structure. They make use of parallelism in terms of rhythm, length, and meaning. Balance in rhythm is usually expressed under the rubric of metre (the same number of accented syllables in each half of a line of poetry), yet this is not regular in psalmic poetry. Rhythmic balance is more predominant, arising out of the presence of parallelism. The parallelistic line is composed of two parts that relate to each other in various ways—so B is connected to A but has a supporting or expanding role (see Kugel 1981). Many studies have focused on these technical matters (e.g. Fokkelman 2003 on the number of syllables per colon). e.g. Ps. 119). Of particular interest in some psalms, such as Psalms 25, 34, 111, 112, and 145, is the use of the acrostic in which the full Hebrew alphabet is used in sequence. The sequences vary, but in Psalm 119, the prime example of an acrostic in the Psalter, eight lines begin with each of the twenty-two letters in sequence. Furthermore, each line has eight synonyms for the law—with two exceptions in vv. 90 (nine synonyms) and 122 (no synonyms). Other techniques are used in this poetry, such as repetition, deliberate ambiguity, and the use of metaphor. The Psalms are rich in the use of metaphor. God is depicted variously as king, judge, shepherd, rock, portion, light, warrior, father, and farmer. The people are vine, tree, sheep, or quiver. The wicked are as grass, chaff, or dust. This technique gives a richness to the language which makes it vivid and memorable.

Rhetorical criticism, which seeks to uncover the persuasive elements of the text, is linked to form in its emphasis on repetition, chiasms, structure, and figurative language. The structure of a psalm is thus of main concern. Small sections that show signs of the foreshadowing of an idea, or its reiteration, are of interest, as also persuasive elements in psalms, plays on words, direct and indirect speech, changes of speaker, and so on. Whether this is authorial intention or whether such techniques are simply structurally there is open to debate.

Form Criticism

Attempts to classify the Psalms began in the nineteenth century, notably from De Wette (1823), but were taken up more famously and definitively in the early twentieth century by Gunkel (1904, 1926; see also 1998). De Wette found four major categories of psalm—individual laments, national laments, psalms reflecting evil in the world, and theodicy psalms. He later found six main types of psalms—hymns, national psalms, Zion and temple psalms, royal psalms, laments, and reflective psalms. Gunkel found five main types and numerous minor ones. His main types were hymn, communal lament, individual lament, individual thanksgiving, and royal psalm. Alongside hymns he included enthronement psalms and Zion psalms, and alongside individual psalms of lament, psalms of confidence. Amongst his minor types were sayings of blessing and curse, pilgrimage psalms, victory psalms, thanksgiving songs of Israel, and Torah psalms. He used the German term *Gattung*, meaning 'genre' or 'type'. Scholars prior to this had focused on historical-critical aspects, asking about the original date and historical context of each psalm, and there was a nineteenth-century consensus that most psalms had nothing to do with David but, rather, were post-exilic. Thus, Psalm 137, which speaks of the Babylonian Exile (unusually, since most psalms contain very few historical clues), was regarded as one of the earliest psalms. The contrast between older views and those of fifty years later is shown by the irony that while Duhm (1899) thought that Psalm 137 was the earliest psalm in the Psalter, Engnell (1967) believed it to be the latest. In fact scholars such as Duhm had found late contexts in the Maccabean period (second century BCE) for many psalms.

Gunkel not only overturned the nineteenth-century idea that the Psalms were late (although he did believe that many were later forms of early 'types'), but he shifted interest away from a one-off date or event for each psalm and the idea that they were individually penned by an author or poet, to the recurring occasion on which a psalm might have been sung and its communal origin and use. Furthermore, he showed that a literary classification and analysis of the Psalms had much more mileage than the attempt to date pieces of literature that were essentially undateable. Gunkel's emphasis was on form—hence the use of the term 'form criticism'—as he used the form of each type as a mode of classification. A good example is the hymn, of which there are approximately thirty-five in the psalter (e.g. Pss. 46, 135, 146), which begins with a summons to praise—that is, an invitation to song or hymnic introduction (Section A). This is followed by a transitional passage (B) giving the reason(s) for praising God. The main part of the hymn (C) is a historical retrospect on the works of salvation that God has effected in the past which leads to the necessity of praising him in the present. Whilst these three elements are found in all hymns, each is different and contains the parts in different degrees, sometimes with one section much more dominant (usually C) or sometimes with all three repeated twice, as in Psalm 47. One problem, then, with this categorization was that there are very few 'pure' forms of any one genre—many psalms are either slightly variant or hybrids. Another problem with Gunkel's classifications was that some groupings were clearly made more on the grounds of content and possible *Sitz im Leben* ('situation in life') than on the grounds simply of form. Thus it is generally regarded that the term 'genre', which includes element of form, content, and context, is a better one. Although Gunkel helpfully isolated major types of psalm, his categories were enumerated such that his final category has to be 'Other', which includes anything that didn't fit into other patterns! This suggests that he tried to over-classify according to this principle. However, it opened up psalm study in a fruitful way for its time and in a lasting manner, and became a starting point for the conclusions of others as they sought not only to find recurring forms and occasions, but also to reconstruct the wider context of possible festival and worship use in early Israel.

CONTENT

Types of Psalm

It is clear that some categories of psalm range together better on grounds of content than on grounds of form. Within Gunkel's categories the royal psalms are one example, the wisdom/Torah psalms another. Indeed, with the so-called wisdom psalms the content is quite diverse and the classification only based on the character of the biblical wisdom books—Proverbs, Job, and Ecclesiastes. More recently other attempts to classify the content in a more theological way have been attempted (see below).

Festivals

The royal psalms in particular, but also many other psalms, came to be regarded as evidence of the early worshipping life of ancient Israel. Building on a strictly literary analysis were those scholars who sought to find a cultic, festival context for the psalms. This was not to find a strictly historical context, but rather a recurring occasion on which these psalms might have been recited. Such work had the effect of bringing many psalms to life in a fresh and exciting way. Mowinckel (1921–4), Gunkel's pupil, was the pioneer of this method, and argued for an Autumn New Year enthronement festival in ancient Israel at which a number of psalms would have been sung on an annual basis. He found evidence for this reconstruction in the ancient Near Eastern world in the Babylonian Akitu festival. He believed that every year the king would have been ritually dethroned and then enthroned again as evidence of a cyclical view of the king as guarantor of the order that could so easily descend into chaos. The essential psalms that fitted this pattern were Psalms 2, 18, 20, 21, 72, 89, 101, 110, 132, and 144. These ideas were built upon and varied by other scholars. Eaton (1986) found psalms (enthronement psalms) to play an important and central role in this festival. Kraus (1979) posited a royal Zion festival rather than an autumn, new year enthronement one. Weiser (1962) argued that the alignment of other psalms suggested a covenant festival that may have existed alongside an autumnal one.[5] This seemed to be evidenced from Deuteronomy (31:9 ff.) and may well have formed a focus of Israelite thanksgiving for the key saving events of their history. This may, however, have been a seven-yearly festival only, as Deuteronomy indicates. The problem is, however, that there is no solid evidence for such a reconstruction.

The use of the psalms in Jewish festivals today suggests that autumn was a key time for thanksgiving, with the Feast of Tabernacles (Booths) taking place as a major festival, but that is a far cry from the possible *Sitz im Leben* they originally inhabited. Because of the lack of definite proof, scholarly interest has moved away from such festival reconstructions, but it has been an important stage, not least in bringing the psalms alive in possible original recurrent cultic and communal contexts, and in showing that the psalms are not a literary genre that belonged to Israel alone, but rather are part of a much wider ancient Near Eastern enterprise. Of course, many psalms do not fit into a communal context but are individual laments and thanksgivings. Whilst the ingenious idea of 'corporate personality' (Wheeler Robinson 1981) allowed the 'I' to become the 'We' in communal worship, this cannot account for all psalms, many of which may have been private prayers from the beginning (nineteenth-century scholars saw most of the psalms (one-sidedly) in this light). The 'I' may well have had a representative function, alternatively, with king, army chief, or high priest being candidates for the role. Any of these can represent the nation, with the 'enemies' of the lament psalms in particular possibly representing foreigners who threaten the nation (e.g. Eaton 1986, amongst others).

The Wider Ancient Near Eastern World

It is clear that the psalms should be grounded in the wider ancient Near Eastern world, and some Israelite psalms may well have been modelled upon (even borrowed from) other cultures; for example, Psalm 29 has close resemblances to a Canaanite hymn to Baal, god of the storm: features include the sevenfold voice of God, God's appearance in the clouds, and references to the cedars of Lebanon and Syria (from which Baal's temple was built). Psalm 82 may well have come from an originally polytheistic milieu in its description of God in council in authority over other gods. Psalm 104, the psalm to God as creator (most similar to Egyptian

---

[5] It is often forgotten that Mowinckel (1921–4) too gave a place to psalms about the covenant in his Autumn New Year festival, but considered them secondary to the main psalms of that festival.

hymns to Atun), depicts God as creator of the sun and rider of the clouds, and Psalm 68:16 has God dwelling on a mountain, a feature of a number of ancient Near Eastern religious texts. A fruitful line of research has been study of psalms from Ras Shamra (Ugarit)—as in the work of Dahood (1966–70)—and Qumran, and comparison of these texts with the Israelite Psalter. Such discoveries demonstrate that writing psalms was not a distinctively Israelite phenomenon. Given that Israelite religion took over originally Canaanite sanctuaries in various places, such as Bethel and Dan, it is likely that the Israelites also came into contact with Canaanite worship, ritual, and musical practices and psalms (Terrien 2003). They appear also to have made use of Canaanite myth, especially the idea of God overcoming a chaos dragon. Not only Egyptian and Canaanite but also Mesopotamian links have been found. The creation myth of God versus a dragon was also prominent in Babylonian myth. Psalm 19a has God as creator of the sun as well as bridegroom and strong man, which recalls the Babylonian hymn to Shamash. Mesopotamian lament tradition may also have influenced laments in the Psalter. Recent work has asked questions about the link of psalms with popular religion, rather than simply with the official religions of other nations (Gerstenberger 1985).

The Role of the Psalms

The assumption tends to be made that the psalms are intended for worship, and so they are, worship of both a communal and individual nature, with psalms able to be adapted to both situations. But is this as far as their role goes? The suggestion has been made of prophetic links (e.g. Johnson 1979, Bellinger 1984), for example Psalms 75:3–6 and 81:9–11, which would align some psalms closely to prophecy and the prophetic role. This would suggest a role in persuading worshippers to change their ways. Terrien (2003) points out a musical link with the prophet Elijah in 2 Kings 3:14–15—as a minstrel plays, the hand of the Lord comes upon Elijah. He also notes that in the post-exilic temple, the Levites who had a key musical role also prophesied—to music (according to 1 Chron. 25:1). Another suggestion is of an instructional role, which Terrien (2003) sees as watering the psalms down when he writes: 'Such a sapientialization of a hymnal by scribes risked rendering it abstract, and even anemic.' There is, however, considerable evidence of the presence and importance of wisdom psalms,[6] which may have come from circles of sages in the recognition that, amongst the many areas of life represented in the Psalter (law, prophecy, etc.), wisdom has its own place and may have had a role in cultic life. Rather than being simply a redactional tool (which it probably was too), wisdom

---

[6] It is hard to decide how many psalms to classify as wisdom psalms, but on a broad definition the following are possible: Pss. 1, 14, 19, 25, 32, 33, 34, 36, 37, 39, 49, 51, 53, 62, 73, 78, 90, 92, 94, 104, 105, 106, 111, 112, 119, 127, and 128.

psalms are part of the formation of the Psalter in that wisdom was a recognized stream of thought from early times (Dell 2004). Didactic elements are found especially in Psalms 1–2 at the beginning of the Psalter and increasingly in Books 4–5, suggesting an important role in its shaping. Perhaps this material was used in teaching contexts from time to time. There are clear links with the law (e.g. Pss. 1 and 119); a natural partner for the psalms given that keeping legal prescriptions was such a key part of temple life. As with wisdom, law is both an integral and a redactional element in the Psalter. Essentially this role is a religious and pious one, allowing the worshipper to use the psalms in prayer to God, which brings us back to the primary worship context.

THEOLOGY

Theological 'Types'

Increasingly the psalms are evaluated in strictly theological terms, without recourse to literary types or cult-historical contexts. In fact, rather than five or six form-critical 'types' scholars have suggested just two categories—'prayer and praise' (Crenshaw 2001); or 'prayer and petition' (Westermann 1981), or indeed three—disorientation, reorientation, orientation (Brueggemann 1980, 1984). Brueggemann's model is more about the effect that the psalm has on the reader than a comment on classification—it either disorientates readers by forcing them to question accepted norms (mainly the laments), reorients them by offering alternative paths to follow (mainly thanksgiving psalms), or orients them to a particular way of life (mainly hymns). There is an accompanying interest in the rhetoric of the psalms—in the way that the text persuades its worshipper/readers (linking up with stylistic features and with recurrent context and context today). This interest in the theological content of the psalms and in their theological/religious role in many ways bridges the gap between the academic study of psalms and the use made of them in worshipping communities.

Overall Themes

Accompanying the interest in the final coming together of the Psalter, into clusters, groups, books, and a final book, has been an interest in overall themes. The overriding theological theme of Psalms 1–89, for example, has been seen (by Wilson 1985) as the promise of the covenant with David. Whilst this suggestion in no way indicates the diversity of content in those eighty-nine psalms, it is nonetheless a helpful comment in theological terms in the attempt to characterize parts of the whole Psalter and ultimately the whole itself. From Psalm 90 onwards the eternal kingship of God is stressed, as is the importance of right living. Once again a shift occurs in Books 4–5, in a move from king to God (as king) and from covenant to ethics, law, and eschatology. Wilson argues that the movement in the Psalter shows how the covenant with David became bankrupt and the kingship of Yahweh took its place. The purpose of Psalms 2, 72, and 89 is to document the failure of the Davidic covenant, and later psalms in Books 4 and 5 (also the shaping Psalm 1) shift the emphasis to individual relationship with God in the present and the coming reign of God in the future. Interest in the overall shape of the Psalter leads Terrien (2003) to see Psalm 90 as a particularly pivotal psalm. After the conclusion of Book 3 in Psalm 89, Moses intercedes in Psalm 90. A nationalistic spirit gives way to a more universalistic one, and this sapiential meditation leads to a broadening of scope. This is followed by Psalm 91, a prayer on the triumph of the faith. Terrien also sees Psalm 73 as a contender for this pivotal role and decides that both have a claim and form two poles. McCann (1987), on rather different grounds, describes Psalm 73 as demonstrating 'Old Testament theology in miniature' and notes its strategic position between protest and prayer. Whether such 'central' psalms can indeed be found is a matter for discussion. Another model is the observation of the increase in liturgical guilds and cultic events starting in Book 3 and culminating in Psalms 113–18 (for three major festivals) and 120–34 (for pilgrims) in Book 5. Westermann (1962) put emphasis on Psalm 119 as a pivotal point in the Psalter—combined with Psalm 1, it placed obedience to the law as a key concern. Brueggemann's (1991) more theological model is to see the Psalter as 'bounded by obedience and praise', the title of his article. Psalm 1 begins with the call to obedience to God's law, whilst Psalm 150 is an expression of pure, unbounded praise.

   Interest in such themes has inevitably led to questions about the place of the psalms in Old Testament theology as a discipline. The psalms are clearly key in that theology (see H.-J. Kraus 1979). The fact that they contain so many of the diverse genres of Israelite life and thought indicates, in my view, that this book is a watershed of genres. It has been described as a 'little treatise of biblical theology'.[7] Indeed, if we only had the Book of Psalms and not the rest of the Old Testament it would give us a good impression of what is contained in the rest—the history of salvation, God as creator and orderer of the world with his king dominant over the social order, covenant and law, prophecy and wisdom. In that sense the Book of Psalms truly provides a centrepiece for the Old Testament, possibly even a 'centre' theologically, as scholars have been keen to find it. Terrien (2003) even suggests its centrality as regards different interest-groups in ancient Israel when he writes: 'More than any other book of the Hebrew Bible, the Psalter can reconcile priests,

---

[7] This is cited by Terrien (2003: 44), but it is unclear from his corresponding footnote from where the quotation comes.

prophets, sages and musicians' (p. 61). He puts a particular stress on the role of
musicians in not only performing the psalms but also shaping them in a prior oral
tradition. Terrien (1978; 2003) draws out the centrality of the theme of the 'presence
of God' in the Psalter, a concept that reveals a tension between a present and absent
God. He describes psalmists as 'captives of the Presence, even the Presence of the
hidden God' (2003: 46). He writes: 'The motif of Yahweh's presence seems to
constitute, alone, the generative and organic power of such a theology' (ibid.).
This forms an interesting contrast to views that regard the Psalter as essentially
human-centred—for Terrien it is ultimately theocentric. Terrien sees the human/
divine interplay as ever present, with the temple as the meeting-place of divine
transcendence and cultic presence.

Universal, Life-centred Prayers

Increasingly the psalms and the Psalter as a whole are viewed as universal, life-
centred prayers, despite inevitable nationalistic elements that belong to their
specific context in the life of Israel. They celebrate life over death (although
death is not without mention, and Sheol, the place of the dead, is widely featured).
Westermann advocates a 'life-centred' reading, arguing that cultic interpretations
of the psalms fail to convey their nature as universal prayers, representing the two
basic aspects of prayer, notably praise and lament. They have been read and used in
worship very differently in Jewish and Christian communities over the centuries,
and often those differences have been a source of strife. However, in the modern
world, with the coming together of Jewish and Christian scholarship on the psalms
and with the increased appreciation on both sides of differing ways of praying the
psalms, there has been a productive confluence of input (see Gillingham 2007).
Even outside any religious context, there is much in the psalms that simply reflects
human emotions and relationships.

It should not be forgotten, however, as Terrien (2003) emphasizes, that much of
the content of the psalms is about God and the experience of God. Although there
are lesser beings represented in some psalms (e.g. Ps. 82), they are never praised but
are always subservient to God himself. It is only ever to God himself that praise is
given. The threat of chaos (as at creation) is ever present—in the form of suffering,
illness, enemies—but God can provide the necessary relief from such woes. God
overcomes the chaos and establishes his power and order in the world. His name,
'Yahweh', is a personal one, revealed to Israel initially but radiating out to a wider
context. He also has other designations and titles, some known from earlier tribal
circles, others simply epithets of praise. The use of the generic name for God,
El/Elohim, is also found, which has arguably more universal overtones and emphasizes his unique authority. Images of God's face and sheltering wings, as well as
his 'kingship', add to the richness of the portrayal of God. A particularly intense

experience of God is to be had in the temple, and there he makes himself especially known—hence the home of the psalms in the Jerusalem temple (Zion) underlines the intense experience of God that they represent. David/the king is God's representative on earth and hence the channel of much of this devotion. The king and individuals were able to bring to God in their psalmic prayers their most profound emotions of suffering and praise, and simply the process of offering up a lament often led to a change within the psalm towards praise. Psalm 73 is a good example of a troubled soul, musing on the seemingly misplaced rewards for the wicked rather than the righteous, until a turning-point comes in verse 17 when the psalmist goes into the sanctuary and suddenly sees things the right way round. It seems that a profound experience of God in the temple, through the medium of psalmic plea, led to this change.

Reading the Psalms

The beginning of this chapter stated that Psalms is a book, albeit a book of five books. In a post-modern world there is considerable interest in the 'reader' of the book. In this case we might add 'the worshipper', who might be slightly different from 'the reader' in their presuppositions and response. This involves an interaction from many different contexts with what is in the text as it stands, as it is printed in our bibles. It opens up the subjective side of the hermeneutical circle in the awareness that no two readers are alike and that therefore no psalm speaks identically to each person. Of course, groups of people tend to read similarly, traditions within religious faiths have their own prescriptions, and so on. But this is essentially where the history of interpretation begins—with the reader.

WORKS CITED

ANDERSON, G. W. (1980), 'Sicut Cervus': Evidence in the Psalter of Private Devotion in Ancient Israel', *Vetus Testamentum*, 30: 388–97.

BELLINGER, W. H. (1984), *Psalmody and Prophecy.* JSOT Supp. 27. Sheffield: SAP.

BRUEGGEMANN, W. (1980), 'Psalms and the Life of Faith: A Suggested Typology of Function', *JSOT* 17: 3–32.

——(1984), *The Message of the Psalms: A Theological Commentary.* Minneapolis: Augsburg.

——(1991), 'Bounded by Obedience and Praise: The Psalms as Canon', *JSOT* 50: 63–92.

CRENSHAW, J. L. (2001), *The Psalms: An Introduction.* Grand Rapids, Mich.: Eerdmans.

DAHOOD, M. (1966–70), *Psalms.* Anchor Bible. New York: Doubleday.

DE WETTE, W. M. L. (1823), *Commentar über die Psalmen.* Heidelberg: Mohr.

DELL, K. J. (2004), '"I will solve my riddle to the music of the lyre" (Psalm XLIX 4 [5])': 'A Cultic Setting for Wisdom Psalms?' *Vetus Testamentum*, 54/4: 445–58.

DUHM, B. (1899), *Die Psalmen*. Freiburg: J. C. B. Mohr (Paul Siebeck).

EATON, J. (1986), *Kingship and the Psalms*. Sheffield: JSOT Press.

——(2005), *The Psalms: A Historical and Spiritual Commentary with an Introduction and New Translation*. London and New York: Continuum.

ENGNELL, I. (1967), *Studies in Divine Kingship in the Ancient Near East*. Oxford: Blackwell.

FOKKELMAN, J. P. (2003), *Major Poems of the Hebrew Bible at the Interface of Prosody and Structural Analysis*, vols. 1–3. Studia Semitica Neerlandica. The Hague: Van Gorcum.

GERSTENBERGER, E. (1985), 'Singing a New Song', *Word and World*, 5: 409–44.

GILLINGHAM, S. E. (2007), *Psalms Through the Centuries*. Oxford: Blackwell.

GOULDER, M. (1982), *The Psalms of the Sons of Korah*. JSOT Supp. 20. Sheffield: JSOT Press.

——(1990), *The Prayers of David (Psalms 51–72)*. JSOT Supp. 233, Sheffield: SAP.

——(1996), *The Psalms of Asaph and the Pentateuch*. JSOT Supp. 233, Sheffield: SAP.

——(1998), *The Psalms of the Return (Book V, Psalms 107–150)*. JSOT Supp. 258, Sheffield: SAP.

GUNKEL, H. (1904), *Ausgewählte Psalmen*. Göttingen: Vandenhoeck & Ruprecht.

——(1926), *Die Psalmen*. Göttingen: Vandenhoeck & Ruprecht.

——(1998), *An Introduction to the Psalms: The Genres of the Religious Lyric of Israel*. Macon, Ga.: Mercer University Press, 1998 (orig. *Einleitung in die Psalmen*, HAT, Göttingen: Vandenhoeck & Ruprecht, 1928–33, completed by J. Begrich).

HEIM, K. M. (2001), *Like Grapes of Gold Set in Silver: Proverbial Clusters in Proverbs 10:1–22:16*. BZAW 273. Berlin and New York: de Gruyter.

HOWARD JR., D. M. (1993), 'Editorial Activity in the Psalter: A State of the Field Survey', in C. McCann Jr. (ed.), *The Shape and Shaping of the Psalter*, 42–51, 72–82. JSOT Supp. 159. Sheffield: JSOT Press.

JOHNSON, A. R. (1979), *The Cultic Prophet and Israel's Psalmody*. Cardiff: University of Wales Press.

KRAUS, H.-J. (1979), *Theologie der Psalmen*. BKAT 15/3. Neukirchen-Vluyn: Neukirchener Verlag.

KUGEL, J. (1981), *The Idea of Biblical Poetry*. New Haven: Yale University Press.

McCANN, J. C. (1987), 'Psalm 73: A Microcosm of Old Testament Theology', in K. Hoglund (ed.), *The Listening Heart*, 247–57. JSOT Supp. 58. Sheffield: JSOT Press.

MOWINCKEL, S. (1921–4), *The Psalms in Israel's Worship*, 2 vols. Oxford: Blackwell.

TERRIEN, S. (1978), 'The Psalmody of Presence', in *The Elusive Presence: Toward a New Biblical Theology*. New York: Harper & Row.

——(2003), *Psalms*. ECC. Grand Rapids, Mich.: Eerdmans.

WEISER, A. (1962), *The Psalms*. OTL. London: SCM Press.

WESTERMANN, C. (1962), 'Zur Sammlung des Psalters', *Theologia Viatorum*, 8: 278–84.

——(1981), *Praise and Lament in the Psalms*. Atlanta, Ga.: John Knox Press.

WHEELER ROBINSON, H. (1981), *Corporate Personality in Ancient Israel*. Edinburgh: T. & T. Clark.

WHYBRAY, R. N. (1996), *Reading the Psalms as a Book*. JSOT Supp. 222. Sheffield: SAP.

——(1997), 'Psalm 119: Profile of a Psalmist', in M. L. Barré SS (ed.), *Wisdom, You Are My Sister: Studies in Honor of Roland E. Murphy O. Carm. on the Occasion of his 80th Birthday*, 31–43. CBQ Monograph Series 29. Washington, DC: The Catholic Biblical Association of America.

WILSON, G. H. (1985), *The Editing of the Hebrew Psalter*. SBLDS 76. Chico, Calif.: Scholars Press.

——(1986), 'The Use of Royal Psalms at the 'Seams' of the Hebrew Psalter', *JSOT* 35: 85–94.

Further Reading

Brueggemann, W. (1991), *Abiding Astonishment: Psalms, Modernity, and the Making of History*. Louisville, Ky.: Westminster/John Knox Press.

Clements, R. E. (1965), *God and Temple*. Oxford: Blackwell.

Davidson, R. (1998), *The Vitality of Worship: A Commentary on the Book of Psalms*. Grand Rapids, Mich.: Eerdmans; Edinburgh: Handsel.

Day, J. (1992), *Psalms*. Old Testament Guides. Sheffield: Sheffield Academic Press.

Gillingham, S. (1994), *The Poems and Psalms of the Hebrew Bible*. Oxford: Oxford University Press.

Magonet, J. (1994), *A Rabbi Reads the Psalms*. London: SCM Press.

Ringgren H. (1963), *The Faith of the Psalmists*. London: SCM Press.

Spieckermann H. (1989), *Heilsgegenwart: eine Theologie der Psalmen*. FRLANT 148. Göttingen: Vandenhoeck & Ruprecht.

CHAPTER 4

···

ISAIAH

···

JOHN F. A. SAWYER

THE Book of Isaiah is one of the longest in the Bible. Jeremiah and Chronicles are about the same length but have had far less influence on the subsequent history of Judaism and Christianity. In Jewish lectionaries there are twice as many passages from Isaiah as there are from Jeremiah. Isaiah played a major role in the literature and theology of the Qumran community, and in the NT he is far more frequently alluded to or quoted, often by name, than any other prophet (Blenkinsopp 2006: 89–221). While apocryphal legends grew up around Jeremiah, Daniel, Habakkuk, and other 'Writing Prophets', and there is the whole *merkavah* mystical tradition based on Ezekiel 1, there is nothing to compare with the Martyrdom and Ascension of Isaiah, particularly in its elaborate Christian (Ethiopic) version (Knibb 1985: 143–76). It is no exaggeration to say that for 2,000 years there is hardly any aspect of western culture to which the language and imagery of Isaiah has not contributed something significant (Sawyer 1996). Only the Book of Psalms is longer and arguably even more popular and influential (Gillingham 2008). What was it about Isaiah that produced this unique phenomenon? What are the Isaianic themes and images that played so prominent a role in the history of Christianity that he was to become known as the 'fifth evangelist'? In seeking answers to these questions, we shall look first at Jewish and Christian perceptions of Isaiah, and then at some of the results of modern research.

I

According to the rabbis, Isaiah was unique among the prophets and second only to Moses in that he saw God face to face (Isa. 6:1; cf. Deut. 34:10). This is a reference to the account of Isaiah's heavenly vision in chapter 6, which introduces several of the most distinctive features of the book that bears his name. First, the words of the seraphim beginning 'Holy, holy, holy' (6:3) had a prominent role, probably from very ancient times, both in Jewish worship as the *Qedushah* in the *Amidah* or 'Eighteen Benedictions' recited three times daily (Elbogen 1933: 37–41), and in the Christian liturgy as the *Sanctus* in the West and the *Trisagion* in the East (cf. Rev. 4:8) (Spinks 1991). But they also echo throughout the book in the distinctively Isaianic title 'the Holy One of Israel' (twenty-four times) or 'the Holy One of Jacob' (29:13) or simply 'the Holy One (10:17; 40:25; 43:15), together with references to God's 'holy mountain' (seven times, from 11:9 to 66:20); his 'holy city' (48:1; 52:1), only here in the Prophets (cf. Neh.11:1, 18; Dan. 9:24); his 'holy people' (62:12; 63:18); and even his 'Holy Spirit' (63:10, 13), only here and Psalm 51:12. The ethical significance of the name is made clear by the prophet's reaction ('Woe is me . . . for I am a man of unclean lips!', 6:5) and elsewhere spelt out with uncompromising clarity in the context of his attacks on social injustice: 'But the Lord of hosts is exalted in justice, and the Holy God shows himself holy in righteousness' (e.g. 5:16; cf. vv. 19, 24). In this respect as well the rabbis compared Isaiah to Moses, as the prophet who reduced the number of commandments to two: 'keep justice and do righteousness' (56:1; tMakk. 24a).

They also found in Isaiah's vision a corollary to the holiness of God and his demand for justice and righteousness. Of all the prophets Isaiah had the reputation for being the most cruel in his verbal attacks on his own people. According to a well-known ancient Jewish midrash, the reason why one of the seraphim burned his lips with a coal from the altar (Isa. 6:6–7) was to punish him for this (Ginzberg 1975: 612–13). Hosea, Amos, Micah, Jeremiah, and the other prophets utter many bitter prophecies of judgement against their people, but none directs them so explicitly and personally at the citizens of Judah and Jerusalem as does Isaiah (cf. 1:1; 2:1). Sad to say, Isaiah's ferocious polemic against his own people was frequently used by Christian writers and preachers, especially in the early church and the Middle Ages, as scriptural authority for some of their bitterest attacks on the Jews. If one of their own prophets could accuse them of being blind (6:9–10) and stubborn (65:2), behaving like drunkards (29:9), and having blood on their hands (1:15: cf. Matt. 27:25), then so could they. For those who believe the Jewish people have been rejected, a sentence like 'Jerusalem has stumbled and Judah has fallen' (3:8) lends itself all too easily to a supersessionist interpretation (Sawyer 2003a).

He is also known in the rabbinic literature, however, following a tradition already present in Ben Sira (Sir. 48:24), as 'the prophet of consolation' (tBer. 57b). The rabbis contrasted Moses's stern words of warning (e.g. Lev. 26:38) with Isaiah's prophecies of salvation, and the pedestrian language of Ezekiel with the regal elegance of his prophecies of comfort for those in distress (Hag. 14a). Although we do not have evidence for Jewish lectionaries much before the Middle Ages, we can be sure the rabbis had in mind passages from chapters 40–61, which contain the eight 'Consolation' *haftarot* (readings from the Prophets). These are traditionally recited on the eight Sabbaths following the Fast on the Ninth of Ab, in the summer, when the destruction of the temple is commemorated: e.g. 'For the LORD will comfort Zion; he will comfort all her waste places' (51:3; cf. 49:13; 52:9) (Berlin and Brettler 2004: 861, 2116). To these we might add three poignant verses from Isaiah which conclude the 'prayer in the house of mourning', printed at the end of the *Authorized Daily Prayer Book* and beginning: 'As one whom his mother comforts, so I will comfort you' (66:13; cf. 60:20; 25:8) (Singer 1962: 324).

Not only does Isaiah contain these and many other 'comfortable words', but the structure of the book is designed to highlight the theme of comfort after disaster, forgiveness after judgement, hope after despair. This is by no means confined to Isaiah: the Book of Amos is another conspicuous example (9:11–15), and it is characteristic of the Deuteronomistic literature (Joshua–Kings) to structure history in a way that highlights some hopeful sign after disaster (e.g 2 Kgs 25:27–30) (Alt 1991). But nowhere is the point so consistently and elaborately made as in Isaiah. In chapters 1–12 prophecies of judgement are balanced by prophecies of hope (e.g. 2:1–4; 9:1–7; 11:1–9), culminating in a Song of Thanksgiving beginning: 'I will give thanks to thee, O Lord, for . . . thou didst comfort me' (12:1). The prophecies against the world's nations (11–23) are followed by the so-called Isaiah apocalypse (24–7): 'He will swallow up death for ever, and the Lord God will wipe away tears from all faces' (25:8), and the whole book ends with the vision of a new heaven and a new earth (65:17–25; 66:22–3), where 'the wolf and the lamb shall feed together' (65:25).

Most striking, however, is chapter 40, beginning 'Comfort, comfort my people', which introduces a sequence of passages where the theme is developed in new images and new arguments so distinctive as to suggest a change of author ('Deutero-Isaiah') and a different historical context. While in chapter 39 Jerusalem is still standing, albeit under the threat of Babylonian invasion, in chapters 40–55 the city is in ruins (44:26–8) and the people in exile (43:5–6). The opening verses of Deutero-Isaiah introduce two of the most powerful themes in the book. First, the audience—that is to say, all those who had given up all hope and are now to be 'comforted'—is defined in parallel as 'my people' (masculine) and 'Jerusalem' (feminine) (40:1–2). This anticipates much of the rest of the book, which is taken up with memorable poetic accounts of the suffering, rejection, and final redemption of these two 'characters', Israel (or 'Jacob my servant') and Jerusalem (or 'the daughter of Zion') (Sawyer 1989). There are repeated appeals to them individually to 'fear not' (e.g. 40:9; 43:1, 5; 44:8; 54:4) alongside promises ('I will not forget you', 49:15; cf. 44:21) and reassurances ('I love you', 43:4; cf. 54:10), until finally 'he will share the spoil with the strong' (53:12) and 'she will put on her beautiful garments again, Jerusalem the holy city' (52:1).

Second, there is the notion that their suffering had been disproportionate to what they deserved: '(Jerusalem) has received from the Lord's hand double for all her sins' (40:2). This goes beyond divine forgiveness to a new appreciation of the exceptional severity of what had befallen Jerusalem and her citizens, and is developed later in the astonishing image of God as an apologetic husband (54:6–10). He admits that he lost his temper with her, 'in overflowing wrath for a moment' (54:8), and promises never to do it again: 'For the mountains may depart and the hills be removed, but my steadfast love shall not depart from you' (54:9–10). There are obvious parallels with the story of the Suffering Servant in the previous chapter, in that God takes full responsibility ('it was the will of the Lord to bruise him', 53:10), the suffering is not simply punishment for sin (53:9), and, most comforting of all, it is over (49:5; 53:10–12).

Finally, Jewish tradition has always viewed Isaiah as the prophet of Jerusalem par excellence, and, particularly in modern times, found inspiration in Isaianic language about Zion (Sawyer 2003b). Isaiah's focus from beginning to end is the city of Jerusalem. What little biographical material there is in the book locates Isaiah and his prophecies firmly in Jerusalem (cf.1:1; 2:1; 7:3). There are detailed accounts of his role in the story of Jerusalem's miraculous escape from Sennacherib's army (36–7), Hezekiah's recovery from illness (38), and the arrival in Jerusalem of envoys from Babylon (39). But it is the accumulation of epithets and images, many of them unique to, or uniquely developed in, Isaiah that is so striking. The earliest occurrences of the phrases 'holy city' (48:1; 52:1) and 'faithful city' (1:21, 26) are in Isaiah. The only place where Jerusalem is called 'the city of David' outside the historical books is in Isaiah (22:9; cf. Luke 2:4, 11), and the epithets 'city of righteousness' (1:26) and 'Ariel' (29:1, 7) are unique to Isaiah. The word 'Zion' occurs more frequently in Isaiah than in any other book of the Bible, including Psalms, as does the phrase 'Mount Zion'. Not surprisingly, a number of place-names in the modern State of Israel are derived from Isaiah, including Mevasseret Tziyyon ('O thou that tellest good tidings to Zion', 40:9 AV) and Rishon le-Tziyyon ('first to Zion', 41:27 AV).

Again, there are two images of Zion especially prominent in Isaiah. First, the image of the 'holy mountain' or the 'mountain of the Lord' is at the centre of a number of Isaiah's best-known prophecies: 'the mountain of the house of the Lord shall be established as the highest of the mountains' (2:2); 'they shall not hurt or destroy in all my holy mountain' (11:9); 'on this mountain the Lord of hosts will … swallow up death for ever' (25:6–8) (von Rad 1965). Second, there is the personification of the city as a woman, sometimes named as 'the daughter of Zion'.

Her sinful behaviour is compared to that of a harlot (1:21) and her destruction and exile to the plight of an abandoned wife (49:14; 50:1; 54:6) or a mother bereft of her children (54:1); but these are contrasted with images of her defiantly tossing her head in the face of foreign aggressors (37:22), throwing off the chains of slavery (52:2), and, miraculously, becoming once more a loving mother (66:7–14) (Sawyer 1989).

II

In the prologue to his Latin translation, Jerome (c.342-420) explains why Isaiah should be considered more an evangelist than a prophet: 'for he records all the mysteries of Christ and the Church (*universa Christi Ecclesiaeque mysteria*) so clearly that you would think he was describing what had already happened, rather than foretelling the future' (Weber 1994: 1096). He also singles out two themes to which he says Isaiah pays particular attention, the mission to the gentiles and the coming of Christ (*de vocatione gentium et de adventu Christi*), and warns against Jewish falsification of scripture (*de falsitate scripturarum*). Such Christian perceptions of Isaiah go back before Jerome, to Paul, the other four evangelists, the apologists, and the early Church Fathers, and this is how the book was almost universally interpreted by Christians down to the advent of historical criticism. Let us look in turn at Jerome's three points, beginning with the last, Jewish falsification of scripture.

It was Isaiah in Greek that played such a central role in Christian origins and the subsequent history of the Church. The Hebrew original had little impact on the development of Christian tradition, despite the occasional efforts of Jerome and others to apply their knowledge of Hebrew to biblical interpretation. Even though most of the Christian Bible was originally written in Hebrew, there were rarely ever more than a handful of Christian Hebraists before the Renaissance (McKane 1989). Hebrew remained the sacred language of the Jews, however, and the insights of Jewish scholars, infinitely better qualified to handle the Hebrew text, were treated for the most part with contempt by Christians. This helps to explain why traditional Jewish and Christian perceptions of Isaiah are so different, and why the book became such a battleground in the stormy relations between Jews and Christians down the centuries (Sawyer 2003a). Jerome's selection of the mission to the gentiles and the coming of Christ as the two most distinctive features of Isaiah's prophecy nicely illustrates this.

No other prophet emphasizes the worldwide implications of his message more frequently and more eloquently than Isaiah. The 'ends of the earth' are mentioned in Isaiah and Psalms more than in any other book of the Bible, while the distinctively Isaianic term 'coastlands' (RSV; 'islands' AV), in texts like 'Listen to me, O coastlands, and hearken you people from afar!' (49:1; cf. 41:1; 42:4), is rare outside the Book of Isaiah (van Winkle 1985). The notion that one day all the nations of the world will come to Jerusalem is expressed repeatedly in different terms, from 'out of Zion shall go forth the law' (2:3, cf. Mic. 4:2) and 'the wealth of nations shall come to you' (60:1–9; 66:12), to the revolutionary idea that the temple will become 'a house of prayer for all peoples' (56:7; cf. Mark 11:17) (Beuken 1990).

It is therefore no surprise that it is his words and images on the role of the gentiles in God's plan that are most often quoted in the NT. Matthew cites Isaiah 42:1–4 in full (in a Greek translation) because it refers twice to the Servant's mission to the gentiles. The phrase 'a light to the gentiles' (42:6; 49:6), quoted by the aged Simeon (Luke 2:32) and Paul (Acts 13:47; cf. 26:23) is a striking example. Language used in a different context later is quoted in the NT in support of Christ's mission to the gentiles: thus, the passage beginning 'the people that walked in darkness have seen a great light' (9:1 MT) is cited, not because of what follows ('For to us a child is born . . .'), but because it comes immediately after a prophecy believed to be about Christ's ministry in 'Galilee of the nations' (Matt. 4:15–16). Similarly, Paul cites 'the root of Jesse', not in relation to Christ's Davidic ancestry (11:1), but because it 'shall stand as an ensign to the gentiles: him shall the nations seek' (11:10, cf. Rom. 15:12).

Oracles against the foreign nations are a regular part of biblical prophecy (cf. Jer. 46–51; Ezek. 24–32; Amos 1–2), and Isaiah is no exception (13–23). His colourful and influential description of the descent of the king of Babylon into the underworld is well known (14). But even here Isaiah twice introduces a generous element which is rarely present elsewhere. First, his oracle against the Moabites contains not only cries of sympathy for their plight (15:5; 16:11), but also a remarkable appeal for justice and the humane treatment of outcasts and refugees (16:3–5). Scholars have sought to remove the anomaly in various ways: for example, by pointing out that the appeal is rejected in subsequent verses: 'therefore let Moab wail . . .' (vv. 6–7) (Childs 2001: 131–2). The language is hardly typical of Israel's enemies, however, and is better understood as an isolated—but in Isaiah by no means unique—call for justice and peace. The other astonishing exception concerns Egypt and Assyria. Isaiah prophesies that one day these two traditional enemies of Israel will be united and worship together (19:23), and then ends his 'Oracle concerning Egypt' with a blessing: 'Blessed be Egypt my people, and Assyria the work of my hands, and Israel my heritage' (19:25). Scholars argue that this was no doubt influenced by events in the Second Temple period, when prosperous Jewish communities were established in Egypt (cf.19:18) and Mesopotamia (cf. Jer. 29:1–7), but it is nonetheless consistent with the distinctive Isaianic concern for the gentiles (cf. Blenkinsopp 2006: 129–37).

Jerome's other observation on Isaiah was that he was particularly interested (*omnis ei cura*) in the coming of Christ. Prophecies about the coming of a royal saviour who 'will judge the poor with righteousness' (11:4; cf. 9:7; 16:5; 32:1) are not in themselves distinctively Isaianic (cf. Jer. 23:5; Ezek. 34:23–4). The one exception is the Greek version of the 'Immanuel prophecy' in 7:14. The Hebrew original had very little impact on its Jewish readers, and the name Immanuel is never found as a messianic title in Judaism. But the Greek version cited at the beginning of Matthew's Gospel with explicit reference to the Virgin Mary (Matt.1:23) is by far the most often-quoted verse from Isaiah in Christian art and architecture as well as literature, liturgy, and theological discourse, and had the effect of putting Isaiah in the forefront of OT heralds of Christ. If Isaiah could foretell the exact nature of Christ's coming so accurately in this verse, then there must surely be many other examples, and Christian interpreters turned with particular enthusiasm to the Book of Isaiah. Indeed, they found it was possible, with very little exegetical imagination, to find Isaianic references to almost every detail of the Gospel account of the life, ministry, death, and resurrection of Christ, as well as some details not given in the Gospels (Sawyer 1996: 49–50).

But Jerome noticed another feature of the Isaianic tradition which has no parallel in the other prophets. A number of passages describe the coming of a saviour in the past tense, as though it had already happened. On the one hand, there is the celebration of the birth of a royal heir: 'For to us a child is born, to us a son is given' (9:6), while on the other there is a sequence of passages in which the prophet tells the story, all in the past, of an individual appointed by God to 'bring forth justice to the nations' (42:1), who suffered persecution (49:4; 50:6; 53:3, 7, 8–9) and gave his life for his people (53:12). Whatever the explanation of this phenomenon, it is unique and, with the Immanuel prophecy, accounts more than anything else for the special role played by the Book of Isaiah in the history of Christianity.

III

Modern biblical scholars focus on the Hebrew text rather than the ancient versions, and on the original historical context or contexts of the book rather than its role in Judaism and Christianity, the assumption being that the true meaning of the text cannot be established without first determining who wrote it and in what context. One effect of this is to rule out many of the traditional Christian interpretations as scientifically impossible. The Immanuel prophecy, in the original Hebrew, for example, says nothing about a virgin (7:14), and, if the date of the Servant Songs is fixed in the sixth century BCE, then they cannot refer to Jesus. Yet for humanist and other non-Christian scholars Isaiah remains one of the most discussed books in the Bible, while for Christian scholars, although *The Struggle to Understand Isaiah as Christian Scripture* becomes more difficult in the 'post-Reformation period' (Childs 2004: 230–64), Isaiah continues to occupy a central position in their research. The reasons for this must be different. Let us look at three different modern approaches, the historical, the canonical, and the postmodern.

By the middle of the twentieth century the historical-critical analysis of the Book of Isaiah had reached a consensus that, while some passages reflect the eighth century BCE and the reigns of Ahaz and Hezekiah, (7:1; 14:28; 36:1), if not those of Uzziah and Jotham, as the title claims (1:1; cf. 6:1), most of the book comes from much later, particularly the Babylonian Exile in the sixth century. It was no longer possible to speak of a single prophet, be he the 'prophet of consolation' of Jewish tradition or the 'fifth evangelist' of Christian interpreters. Instead, it contains a number of individual voices, each one reflecting, to a greater or lesser extent, its own social and political context. For example, most scholars would attribute some of the most powerful language and imagery, particularly in chapters 1–12, 28–31, and 36–9, to an original eighth-century prophet called Isaiah, who witnessed the Assyrian destruction of all Judah's neighbours and the unexpected survival of Jerusalem in 701 BCE. He was one of the great eighth-century prophets, whose 'ethical monotheism' (5:16) and attacks on cultic institutions (1:10–11) for many scholars, especially Protestants, marked them out as a high point in OT theology, but he towered above them as the founder of an 'Isaianic tradition' with its distinctive focus on Jerusalem and the holiness of God (Bright 1981: 286–7).

There is also broad agreement on the dating of chapters 40–55 ('Second Isaiah' or 'Deutero-Isaiah'), which, unlike most of the rest of the book, show a remarkable unity of style and structure, very different from the earlier chapters, and make specific reference to historical conditions and events in the middle of the sixth century, such as the appearance on the political scene of Cyrus (44:28; 45:1). Very striking is the repeated formula of explicit monotheism ('besides me there is no god', 44:6; cf. 45:5, 6, 14, 18, 21, 22; cf. Deut. 4:35, 39), which may reflect a more exclusive theology facilitated perhaps by the actual destruction of all rival sanctuaries, including Assyrian ones, and the nationalist, centralizing reforms of Josiah (2 Kgs 22–3) in the last decades of the previous century (Beuken 1974). Some radical, even subversive, references to the temple in chapters 56–66 ('Third Isaiah' or 'Trito-Isaiah'), notably 56:7 ('my house shall be called a house of prayer for all peoples') and 66:1–3 ('Heaven is my throne . . . what is the house you would build for me . . . ?'), probably reflect controversy surrounding the role of the Second Temple in the late sixth or early fifth century BCE (Smith 1995: 128–72).

No such consensus exists, however, on the dating of many other parts of the book. It has been suggested, for example, that 'Josianic redactors' had a significant role in shaping some of the earlier chapters, particularly those describing the destruction of the Assyrians and the ideological mythology of Zion, but there remains disagreement on exactly which passages to attribute to them (Barth 1977). References to a flourishing Jewish community in Egypt (19:18–25), together with the possible mention of Aswan (49:12 1QIsaA), may reflect conditions there in fifth-century

BCE Elephantine (Childs 2001: 144–5), while some of the language and imagery of the so-called 'Isaiah Apocalypse' (24–7) may be even later, according to some commentators (Kaiser 1974: 177–9). Literary parallels in the Ugaritic literature confirm the great antiquity of some of it (e.g. 27:1) (Gordon 1966: 1–9), but tell us little about its date and composition. Thus, questions about the date and composition of the Book of Isaiah became extremely complex, involving the fragmenting of the text, not only into three 'Isaiahs' (1–39; 40–55; 56–66), but into numerous short passages, each with its own provenance and prehistory. Attempts to find solutions to such historical puzzles still take up much space in most of the numerous commentaries on Isaiah, and undoubtedly constitute one of the chief reasons for its continuing fascination for scholars.

For many Christian scholars the book is part of the canon, and therefore, in some sense, the 'Word of God', whatever the conclusions of their historical-critical endeavours. Thus, for example, the quest for an original Isaiah led to the discovery of the 'genius' of an eighth-century prophet (Driver 1891: 263) and a 'hero of faith' (Skinner 1896: p. xlii), whose experience of the holiness of God, involving religious awe as well as an ethical imperative, together with faith in the special role of his city Jerusalem and a Davidic 'messiah', speaks directly to the Church today, without the need for elaborate typologies or christological interpretations, or a belief in the miraculous powers of the prophets to foretell the future. Thus, 'when lifted to a more transcendent and ultimate plane some of the motifs of the Zion ideology may be held to be eternally true' (Clements 1980: 88–1). The same goes for parts of 'Deutero-Isaiah', particularly the four 'Servant Songs', interpreted as exilic compositions rather than prophecies of Christ. The notion of vicarious suffering may be found in the story of Moses offering to die for his people (Exod. 32:32) and in the scapegoat ritual on the Day of Atonement (Lev. 16), but nowhere is it described in such detail as it is here in chapter 53 (vv. 4–6; 10–12). The chapter is thus 'linked dogmatically to Jesus Christ in terms of its ontology' (Childs 2001: 422), not because a sixth-century BCE prophet foresaw the coming of such a saviour.

The canonical approach to OT interpretation involves another modification in the historical-critical process. While acknowledging the overwhelming historical probability that its many separate parts were originally composed at different times, in different contexts and by different people, particular attention must be paid to the canonical shape of each book (Tull 2006). Thus, a correct understanding of Isaiah 24–7, for example, whatever the date of its original composition, requires the recognition that its reuse and redevelopment of themes and images from earlier chapters (1–12; 13–23) marks a growth and deepening of thought, entirely missed by a more atomistic historical-critical approach (Sweeney 1988). The words of God to his heavenly court, overheard by the prophet at the beginning of chapter 40 ('Comfort my people') recall Isaiah's heavenly vision in chapter 6, but substitute comfort for judgement (Seitz 1990). Such a holistic approach would also note how the analysis of suffering in chapter 53 picks up and transforms the words of 1:5–6, and how the use of key motifs like 'the Holy One of Israel' and 'Zion', which recur throughout the whole book, can be studied in terms of a literary or theological development.

One other canonical issue concerns the relationship between Isaiah and the NT. Both are in the same canon and few would dispute the fact that the Book of Isaiah played a crucial role in Christian origins (Blenkinsopp 2006: 129–221). Whether or not this goes back to Jesus himself, and his own personal use and interpretation of the book, it is impossible to say (Hooker 1998). Surprisingly, there is only one passage in the NT about vicarious suffering where Isaiah 53 is quoted (1 Pet. 2:24–5) and none in the Gospels, but the Book of Isaiah as a whole is, after Psalms, the most-quoted OT book, and Isaiah is mentioned by name in the NT more often than any other prophet apart from Moses and Elijah (fourteen times in the Gospels; eight times in Paul and Acts). The OT quotations in the NT, however, are never in the original Hebrew, so that how the NT interprets the OT is no more helpful in the quest for the original meaning of the text than is the LXX or the other ancient versions. So long as the goal of OT interpretation is the meaning of the canonical Hebrew text, the NT evidence must remain, like the LXX, an early stage in the book's reception history. In fact, the evidence of the rabbinic literature is in many ways more relevant, semantically, than that of the ancient versions, including NT Greek quotations.

This brings us to the last of our three modern approaches, postmodern interpretations. The term is widely used to denote a reaction against some of the characteristics of historical criticism, particularly the privileging of one meaning, whether a reconstructed original meaning or a canonical meaning authorized by the Church (Aichele 2001: 1–12). Central to all varieties of postmodernism is the role of the reader in the interpretive process, and the notion that meaning is a function of the interaction between reader and text. In this respect postmodernism represents a return to a pre-critical age when, for example, the Church Fathers were well aware that texts have more than one meaning, and believed that the literal meaning may often be less important, for the Church, than a spiritual, moral, or allegorical interpretation. It is a simple fact that millions of Christians can and have read Isaiah 53 as an account of Christ's passion, and this is evidence that that is what the chapter means in certain clearly defined homiletical, liturgical, and devotional contexts. They have also read the book, for hundreds of years, as a single literary work by a single author and made good sense of it.

Clearly a Christian interpretation is not the only meaning the text can have—there are many others, including Jewish interpretations and a variety of reconstructed originals. But if any is to be privileged in a Christian context, then arguably it should be a traditional christological interpretation of the Greek or Latin or English version. The same applies, *mutatis mutandis*, to Jewish interpretations, which are usually based more closely on the Hebrew text (Berlin and Brettler 2004: 780–916). Modern historians, philologists, and archaeologists will continue to focus on ancient meanings in the context of eighth-century Jerusalem or sixth-century Babylon or the Second Temple period, those amongst them who happen to be Christians rejoicing in the many signs of continuity between the Testaments (Childs 2004: 304–9). But their monopoly of the Book of Isaiah has now been broken, and its extraordinary afterlife in the history of Judaism, Christianity, and western culture in general can now be studied with the same degree of scientific rigour and sensitivity as the original Hebrew.

WORKS CITED

AICHELE, G. (2001), *The Control of Biblical Meaning: Canon as Semiotic Mechanism*. Philadelphia: Trinity Press International.

ALT, A. (1991), *The Deuteronomistic History* (orig. *Die deuteronomistische Geschichte*, 1943). Sheffield: Sheffield Academic Press.

BARTH, H. (1977), *Die Jesaja-Worte in der Josiazeit* (WMANT 48). Neukirchen-Vluyn: Neukirchener Verlag.

BERLIN, A. and M. Z. BRETTLER (eds.) (2004), *The Jewish Study Bible*. Oxford: Oxford University Press.

BEUKEN, W. A. M. (1974), 'Isaiah LIV: The Multiple Identity of the Person Addressed', *OTS* 19: 29–70.

——(1990), 'The Main Theme of Trito-Isaiah: "The Servants of YHWH"', *JSOT* 47: 67–87.

BLENKINSOPP, J. (2006), *Opening the Sealed Book: Interpretations of the Book of Isaiah in Late Antiquity*. Grand Rapids and Cambridge: William B. Eerdmans.

BRIGHT, J. (1981), *A History of Israel*, 3rd edn. Philadelphia: Westminster Press.

CHILDS, B. S. (2001), *Isaiah: A Commentary*. Louisville, Ky.: Westminster/John Knox.

——(2004), *The Struggle to Understand Isaiah as Christian Scripture*. Grand Rapids and Cambridge: William B. Eerdmans.

CLEMENTS, R. E. (1980), *Isaiah and the Deliverance of Jerusalem: A Study of the Interpretation of Prophecy in the Old Testament* (JSOTS 13). Sheffield: JSOT Press.

DRIVER, S. R. (1891), *Introduction to the Literature of the Old Testament*. Edinburgh: T. & T. Clark.

ELBOGEN, I. (1933), *Jewish Liturgy: A Comprehensive Liturgy* (orig. *Die judische Gottesdienst in seiner geschichtlichen Entwicklung*, 1913), trans. R. P. Scheidlin). Philadelphia: Jewish Publication Society.

GILLINGHAM, S. (2008), *Psalms Through the Centuries*, vol. 1. Oxford: Blackwell Publishing.

GINZBERG, L. (1975), *The Legends of the Jews*. Philadelphia: Jewish Publication Society.

GORDON, C. H. (1966), 'Leviathan: Symbol of Evil', in A. Altmann (ed.), *Biblical Motifs: Origins and Transformations*. Cambridge, Mass: Harvard University Press.

HOOKER, M. D. (1998), 'Did the Use of Isaiah 53 to Interpret his Mission Begin with Jesus?', in W. H. Bellinger Jr. and W. R. Farmer (eds.), *Jesus and the Suffering Servant: Isaiah and Christian Origins*, 88–103. Harrisburg, Pa.: Trinity Press International.

KAISER, O. (1974), *Isaiah 13–39: A Commentary*. London: SCM Press/Phildelphia: Westminster.

KNIBB, M. (1985), 'Martyrdom and Ascension of Isaiah' in J. H. Charlesworth (ed.), *The Old Testament Pseudepigrapha*, 1. 143–76. London: Darton, Longman & Todd; Garden City, NY: Doubleday.

McKANE, W. (1989), *Selected Christian Hebraists*. Cambridge: Cambridge University Press.

SAWYER, J. F. A. (1989), 'Daughter of Zion and Servant of the Lord in Isaiah: A Comparison', *Journal of Studies of the Old Testament*, 44: 89–107.

——(1996), *The Fifth Gospel: Isaiah in the History of Christianity*. Cambridge: Cambridge University Press.

——(2003a), 'Isaiah and the Jews: Some Reflections on the Church's Use of the Bible', in C. Exum and H. Williamson (eds.), *Reading from Right to Left: Essays in Honour of David Clines*, 390–401. Sheffield: Sheffield Academic Press.

——(2003b), 'Isaiah and Zionism', in P. R. Davies and A. G. Hunter (eds.), *Sense and Sensitivity: Essays on Biblical Prophecy, Ideology and Reception in Tribute to Robert Carroll*, 246–69. Sheffield: Sheffield Academic Press.

SEITZ, C. R. (1990), 'The Divine Council: Temporal Transition and New Prophecy in the Book of Isaiah', *JBL* 109: 229–47.

SINGER, S. (ed.) (1962), *Authorised Daily Prayer Book of the United Hebrew Congregations of the British Commonwealth of Nations*, 2nd rev. edn. London: Eyre & Spottiswood.

SKINNER, J. (1896), *The Book of the Prophet Isaiah*. Cambridge: Cambridge University Press.

SMITH, P. A. (1995), *Rhetoric and Redaction in Trito-Isaiah* (VT Supp. 62). Leiden: E. J. Brill.

SPINKS, B. D. (1991), *The Sanctus in the Eucharistic Prayer*. Cambridge: Cambridge University Press.

SWEENEY, M. A. (1988), 'Textual Citations in Isaiah 24–27: Toward an Understanding of the Redactional Function of Chapters 24–27 in the Book of Isaiah', *JBL* 107: 39–52.

TULL, P. K. (2006), 'One Book, Many Voices: Conceiving of Isaiah's Polyphonic Message', in *As Those Who Are Taught: The Interpretation of Isaiah from the LXX to the SBL*. Atlanta, Ga.: Society of Biblical Literature.

VAN WINKLE, D. W. (1985), 'The Relationship of the Nations to Yahweh and to Israel in Isaiah XL–LV', *VT* 35: 446–58.

VON RAD, G. (1965), 'The City on the Hill' (orig. in *Evangelische Theologie*, 8 (1949), 211–15), trans. in *The Problem of the Hexateuch and Other Essays*, 232–42. Edinburgh and London: Oliver & Boyd.

WEBER, R. (ed.) (1994), *Biblia Sacra iuxta vulgatam versionem*, 4th edn. Stuttgart: Deutsche Bibelgesellschaft.

FURTHER READING

Probably the most useful single-volume commentary on the whole book is that of the late Brevard Childs (2001). Important studies of parts of it include Marvyn Sweeney's *Isaiah 1–39, with an Introduction to Prophetic Literature*, in the Forms of Old Testament Literature series (Grand Rapids, Mich.: Eerdmans, 1996), Hugh Williamson, *The Book Called Isaiah: Deutero-Isaiah's Role in Composition and Redaction* (Oxford: Clarendon Press, 1994), and Elizabeth Achtemeier, *The Community and Message of Isaiah 56–66* (Minneapolis: Augsburg Publishing House 1982). *New Visions of Isaiah*, ed. Roy Melugin and Marvyn Sweeney (Sheffield: Sheffield Academic Press 1996), is an interesting collection of essays by members of the SBL 'Formation of Isaiah' Seminar, and valuable examples of modern reading strategies are Ed Conrad, *Reading Isaiah* (Minneapolis: Fortress Press 1991), Kathryn Pfisterer Darr, *Isaiah's Vision and the Family of God* (Louisville, Ky.: Westminster/John Knox 1994), and Peter D. Quinn-Miscal, *Reading Isaiah: Poetry and Vision* (Louisville, Ky.: Westminster/John Knox, 2001).

CHAPTER 5

....

EZEKIEL

....

PAUL M. JOYCE

FROM esoteric mysticism through to visits from spaceships, there can be few if any books of the Bible that have generated a more diverse and challenging reception history than the Book of Ezekiel. Before embarking on a survey of that remarkable story of a text through time and culture, it is important briefly to get a sense of the nature of this book that has proved so fertile in its afterlife.

OUTLINE, FORM, AND MAJOR THEMES
....

A distinctive feature of the Book of Ezekiel is the extent to which it is arranged in a systematic and thematic fashion. It is in many ways the most orderly of the prophetic books. The major sections of the book are as follows: chapters 1–3, presenting the prophetic call of Ezekiel; chapters 4–24, concerning YHWH's judgement upon Judah and Jerusalem; chapters 25–32, containing oracles against foreign nations; chapter 33, constituting the 'turning point' of the book; chapters 34–7, focusing upon hopes for the restoration of Judah; chapters 38–9, dealing with the episode of Gog of Magog; and chapters 40–8, presenting a detailed vision of the temple.

As to the form of the book, it is presented in the autobiographical first-person voice of the prophet Ezekiel himself. It is largely in prose, but with substantial poetic sections (e.g. chs. 7, 19). Like Ezekiel the man, the book associated with him exemplifies both prophetic and priestly features. Some discern the beginnings of apocalyptic style in Ezekiel. The work features three great visions (in chs. 1, 8–11, and 40–8), and these have played a significant part in the liveliness of its reception history. The book presents a clear progression from judgement to promise, but with numerous elements of symmetry linking the first and second halves of the book. With all of these features, one has to recognize the hands of editors, though they may well have stood in close continuity with Ezekiel, in matters of form as well as of theology. (For a detailed form-critical review, see Hals 1989.)

The major themes of the book are dictated by the traumatic times in which its life began. The ministry of Ezekiel responds to the profound theological questions posed by the Babylonian crisis of the early sixth century BCE. Judah had been stripped of her land, her city, her temple, and of not one but two kings—in sum, it seemed that she had lost her status as the chosen people of YHWH. Ezekiel articulated the theological meaning of this national crisis: the disaster was YHWH's powerful and just act, punishing his own people for their sins. This must be read in the light of catastrophic events that had already come upon Israel; Ezekiel—already deported—offers a key to understanding the disaster that has engulfed the nation.

Ezekiel is distinctive in emphasizing that the present generation is punished for its own sins and not for the sins of previous generations (ch. 18). There has been a long tradition of interpretation that has insisted that Ezekiel wished to stress individual responsibility: in other words, the moral independence of contemporary individuals. However, this must be contested, particularly on the ground that Ezekiel's overriding concern is consistently to explain a disaster that is national and thereby collective. Explicit calls to repentance are infrequent in Ezekiel (14:6; 18:30–2). Wherever a call to repentance is found in Ezekiel it is in a context where it is quite clear that the judgement is unavoidable and indeed already happening; and so repentance cannot offer a means of averting judgement. Rather, the call to repentance serves three functions: to act as a rhetorical device, underlining the responsibility of Israel for the now inevitable (indeed present) disaster; to express a concern that the exiles should conduct their lives in accordance with God's will; and also to anticipate a time when YHWH will grant a new beginning.

After the grim first half of the book, the second features many wonderful passages of restoration (such as the revival of the dry bones in ch. 37 or the life-giving river of ch. 47). In Ezekiel the new future is never earned by righteousness, but is promised for God's own reasons; right behaviour follows only afterwards, as a consequence (as in 36:22–32). In Ezekiel all depends on God's continuity of providential activity: YHWH acts because he is YHWH and must be known to be YHWH. In the use of a range of formulae and motifs in Ezekiel we find evidence of a distinctive emphasis on the absolute centrality of YHWH and his self-manifestation, a radical theocentricity that is of an order difficult to parallel anywhere in the Hebrew Bible. The so-called 'Recognition Formula' or 'Proof-Saying' is the most characteristic expression of this: 'and you [or they] shall know that I am YHWH'

[NRSV: 'The LORD']. Others are the phrase 'in the sight of the nations', various formulae that speak of YHWH acting for the sake of his 'name', and also the theme of divine holiness. It is in such a theological context that we read of the gift of a 'new heart' and a 'new spirit' (36:26–7; cf. 11:19), the primary purpose of which is to preclude the otherwise inevitable danger of YHWH having to punish his people again, with the renewed risk of the profanation of his 'name' that would bring. Israel's response is so important that YHWH himself promises to make it possible.

Finally, the theological geography of the book may be highlighted. Ezekiel opens with the great vision of chapter 1, where the divine throne itself is witnessed in far-off Babylonia. YHWH is with his people in exile, no longer tied to the land of Israel. Chapter 1 here anticipates the departure of YHWH from the temple that will be recounted in chapters 10–11. This affirmation of YHWH's presence with the exiles is one of the distinctive contributions of Ezekiel; it is, however, as though the price of this presence with his dispersed people is that YHWH has abandoned his temple. But in the final section of the book comes the grand return of the deity to his shrine (ch. 43), echoing many ancient Near Eastern models. This is a rich theology, with a finely balanced dialectic between the presence of YHWH with his people wherever they are and his honouring of the particular location of the revelation of his holiness (see further Joyce 2007).

MAIN LINES OF INFLUENCE

The Book of Ezekiel exercised a significant influence on the later writings of the Hebrew Bible. For example, Fishbane has explored the relationship between Ezekiel 44:1–14 and Isaiah 56:1–8 (Fishbane 1985: 138, 142). Ezekiel has influenced the content and more especially the form of Haggai and Zechariah 1–8. Even more striking is the mark Ezekiel has made within Daniel (e.g. Dan 7; 10), Joel (esp. Joel 2–3), and Deutero-Zechariah (e.g. Zech. 14). More generally, the Book of Ezekiel had a pervasive effect on the development of apocalyptic, both within and beyond the canon (Rowland 1982). Some discussion of the social context of apocalyptic has suggested that it arose in marginal circles opposed to central priestly authority (Hanson 1979); however, as a book exhibiting both priestly and apocalyptic features, Ezekiel fits badly within such a polarized model, and indeed discussion of the evidence of Ezekiel (especially chs. 38–9) has played a significant role in the challenging of this so-called Plöger–Hanson hypothesis (Cook 1995).

Ezekiel's name, which is used rarely even in his own book (Ezek. 1:3 and 24:24), is never mentioned elsewhere in the Hebrew Bible, but Ezekiel does feature in the Apocrypha, specifically in Ecclesiasticus (Sirach), which makes explicit reference to the prophet within the context of a survey of great figures in Jewish tradition (Sir. 49:8: 'It was Ezekiel who saw the vision of glory, which God showed him above the chariot of the cherubim'). The following verse can be construed to say that Ezekiel mentioned Job, which would presumably be an allusion to Ezekiel 14:14, 20.

In frequency of citation Ezekiel generally fares less well in post-biblical tradition than either Isaiah or Jeremiah. Nonetheless, 4 Maccabees 18:10–18 (*c.* first century CE) includes Ezekiel among 'the law and the prophets', referring to the words of 37:3, 'Can these bones live?' At much the same time, Philo was writing his *De specialibus legibus*, which features seven quotations from Ezekiel; among these, when paraphrasing the ceremonial commandments, Philo (*Spec.* 1.84) seems closer to Ezekiel 44:17–18 than to Leviticus 16:4. Josephus comments on Ezekiel among other classical prophets in his *Antiquities*; he tantalizingly states that Ezekiel 'left behind two books' (*Ant.* 10.5.1 [79]). Some have interpreted this in the light of the rabbinic notion that the Book of Ezekiel comprised two halves, the second more hopeful than the first (cf. b. B. Bat. 14b). Alternatively, the reference could be to the so-called *Apocryphon of Ezekiel*. Though extant only in fragments and mostly in quotations in Greek from the Christian Fathers, this seems to stand in some relation to the biblical Ezekiel. It may have been a work in its own right or it could have its origin as a midrash on the canonical book; three of the five extant fragments bear some similarity to Ezekiel. While some scholars are sceptical about the five extant fragments necessarily being from one work, Mueller (1994) has influentially argued that they are indeed from a single source, which was Jewish (rather than Christian) and written in Hebrew. He proposes a dating of *c.* first century BCE–first century CE. Repentance and judgement are recurrent themes in the *Apocryphon*, with eschatological overtones. The title is drawn from Epiphanius' introduction to the longest and best-known fragment, which he attributes to Ezekiel's 'own apocryphon' (*Panarion* 64.70). This features a parable about two men, one lame and the other blind, who are punished for robbing a king's garden. Stone, Wright, and Satran (2000) have provided an excellent resource for the study of these and other apocryphal Ezekiel materials.

In passing, it should be explained that the *Exagoge* of 'Ezekiel the Tragedian' (*c.* second century BCE) is a drama that recounts the story of the Exodus from Egypt. It includes a non-biblical scene in which Moses has a vision of God enthroned on Sinai; there is some affinity with the vision of Ezekiel 1, but the name of the author could be merely coincidental (Robertson 1985).

The evidence of the Dead Sea Scrolls suggests that the priestly oriented eschatological prophecy of Ezekiel had a considerable impact at Qumran. Prominent among the Ezekiel material that exercised a particular influence are the opening throne vision and the related material in chapter 10, the condemnation of the nation in chapters 16 and 23, the dry bones of chapter 37, and the final temple vision of chapters 40–8. Brooke has speculated that, given the recurrence of certain passages in the relatively small body of Qumran Ezekiel materials, it may be that there were 'excerpted texts', which gathered these and similar Ezekiel texts for community use (Brooke 1992: 318–21). While there are no extant running *pesharim* devoted to providing interpretations of Ezekiel (in the manner of the Habakkuk Commentary), indirect references abound. Particularly worthy of mention is 4Q Second Ezekiel, otherwise known as 'Pseudo-Ezekiel' (*c.* mid-first century BCE; found in fragments 4Q383–91, most importantly 4Q385). This is an example of so-called 'rewritten Bible', and is an apocryphal work modelled on the Book of Ezekiel (Brady 2005). It is available in a Principal Edition (Dimant 2001). Pseudo-Ezekiel amplifies such material as Ezekiel 1, 10, and 37. There is evidence that the work was known to early Christian writers, specifically the author of the *Letter of Barnabas* and the author of the *Apocalypse of Peter.* Moreover, Pseudo-Ezekiel is striking in the way it draws together material from Ezekiel and Isaiah in a manner similar to some use of scripture in the New Testament, for example, Revelation 4. Bauckham (1996) argues that Pseudo-Ezekiel is in fact the same work as the aforementioned *Apocryphon of Ezekiel* known from fragments in the Christian Fathers, but most scholars doubt such an identification (e.g. Cook 1996: 534).

There are allusions to many Ezekiel motifs within the sectarian literature of Qumran; to a large extent this reflects the apocalyptic nature of that community. For example, according to the Damascus Document the community of the new covenant arose 390 years after the destruction of Jerusalem (CD 1:6–10; cf. Ezek. 4:5). The document also quotes, with some significant minor differences, Ezekiel 9:4 and 44:15 (CD 19:11–12; 3:21–4:2). The start of the War Scroll refers to the 'wilderness of the peoples' (cf. Ezek. 20:35), and the same document features the name 'Gog' (cf. Ezek. 38–9). The pervasive self-designation of the Qumran cove-nanters as 'sons of Zadok' seems dependent on Ezekiel 44. Several non-sectarian compositions, found at Qumran but lacking the specific characteristics distinctive of the Qumran community, such as the Temple Scroll (11QTemple) and the work called *The New Jerusalem*, make use of Ezekiel 40–8 in particular. That these works do not seem to have originated in the community itself serves only to highlight the breadth of the influence of Ezekiel at this time.

The work known as the *Lives of the Prophets* includes a section on Ezekiel, in which a legend about the death of the prophet is recorded: 'He died in the land of the Chaldeans during the captivity . . . The ruler of the people Israel killed him there as he was being reproved by him concerning the worship of idols.' The notion that Ezekiel experienced opposition in Babylonia could perhaps echo the biblical refer-ence to the binding of Ezekiel (Ezek. 3:25: 'As for you, mortal, cords shall be placed on you, and you shall be bound with them, so that you cannot go out among the people'). Hare (1985: 383) suggests that the New Testament Letter to the Hebrews 11:37 ('They were stoned to death, they were sawn in two, they were killed by the sword') may refer respectively to Jeremiah, Isaiah, and Ezekiel. Scholars are divided about the date of the *Lives of the Prophets*; most would place it *c.* first century CE

(Schwemer 1995/1996), but Satran (1995) has argued that it derives from the Byzantine period. (On Ezekiel in extra-biblical traditions, see further Wright 1998.)

Of special importance in the reception history of Ezekiel is the tradition of Merkabah mysticism, an influential if controversial phenomenon within post-biblical Judaism, associated particularly with Johanan ben Zakkai (Gruenwald 1980). Such mysticism focused on the inaugural vision of Ezekiel. The word *merkābâ* ('chariot') is not found in Ezekiel, which speaks rather of a moving 'throne' (*kissē'*), but the word is used in Sirach 49:8. Meditation on Ezekiel 1 sometimes led to the experience of ecstasy, and this became the classic case of a biblical passage being regarded as the bearer of esoteric mysteries about the nature and even the appearance of God himself. The so-called 'Riders of the Chariot' engaged in 'soul ascents' to the palaces of heaven, where they saw God and his holy angels. Allusions to such mysticism are found in a range of rabbinic texts; these include, in the Babylonian Talmud, b. HΩag. 14b, in the Palestinian Talmud, y. HΩag. 77a, in the Tosefta, t. Hag. 2:1, and in the *Mekilta* de R. Simeon ben Yohai, Mishpatim 21:1. At Qumran, *c.* first century BCE, the *Songs of the Sabbath Sacrifice* represent a particularly early example of such mysticism, clearly dependent on Ezekiel (esp. chs. 1, 10, and 40–8) (Newsom 1985). The text is available in a Principal Edition (Eshel 1998). It is striking that Ezekiel is connected to both the Merkabah tradition and, as we noted earlier, incipient apocalyptic. In fact Rowland (1982) sees Merkabah mysticism as related very closely to apocalyptic (interpreted more in terms of cosmology than of eschatology), and indeed presents Ezekiel 1 as the tap-root of the apocalyptic tradition. Some recent work in the history of Jewish mysticism has strengthened the case for seeing Ezekiel as central to the development of the mystical tradition (Elior 2004).

The dangers relating to Merkabah mysticism were a concern in certain circles; this was one of the features associated with Ezekiel that led some in ancient times to regard the book as problematic. Nevertheless, Ezekiel is frequently quoted, with standard formulae for citing scripture (including 'as it is written'), in the Mishnah (e.g. m. Yoma 8:9 cites Ezek. 36:25; m. Mid. 2:5 cites Ezek. 46:21-22). The Ezekiel Targum (Levey 1987) evidences parallels between Ezekiel's reaction to the destruction of the temple in 587 BCE and responses to the destruction of 70 CE. The development of the hope of resurrection within post-exilic Judaism owes something to Ezekiel's expression of the hope of national restoration in the striking vision of the valley of dry bones (Ezek. 37). In Judaism, as in Christianity, there is a strong trend towards literal rather than metaphorical interpretation of the passage (Greenberg 1997: 749–51). The portrayal of this passage in the Dura Europos synagogue wall-paintings in Mesopotamia (*c.* third century CE) is representative of the ongoing role of Ezekiel in Judaism. The Jewish tradition of exegesis of Ezekiel has been rich, numbering among its major medieval contributors Kara, Rashi, Eliezer of Beaugency, and Kimhi, and among those in the modern era David and Jehiel Altschuler and Malbim.

As a biblical prophet, Ezekiel enjoys a place of honour within Islam (Schussman 1998). However, Ezekiel (Arabic *Hizqil*) is, like Isaiah and Jeremiah, never mentioned by name in the Qur'an. Both the dry bones of Ezekiel 37 and the Gog of Magog material of chapters 38–9 are alluded to, but not explicitly linked with *Hizqil*. A few late Islamic sources identify an obscure Qur'anic personality with *Hizqil*: there are two references in the Qur'an (21:85–6 and 38:48) to a figure called *Dhu al-Kifl* ('One endowed with responsibility' or perhaps 'One doubly endowed'). The link is tenuous, but one explanation is that it may rest on a supposed connection with Ezekiel's onerous responsibility as a watchman (Ezek. 3:16–21, 33:1–9). Of related interest is an Islamic shrine to *Hizqil* (equated with *Dhu al-Kifl*) at al-Kifl in Iraq, venerated historically also by Jews.

If we turn to the place of Ezekiel in Christianity, though by no means one of the most frequently cited Old Testament books (and never mentioned by name), Ezekiel has left its mark on the New Testament. The image of the Good Shepherd (John 10) owes much to Ezekiel 34 (Manning 2004). More than once the resurrection language of the New Testament seems to allude to Ezekiel 37 (e.g. Matt. 27:52; Rev. 11:11). The Book of Revelation reflects the symbolism of Ezekiel at numerous points (e.g. the four living creatures in Rev. 4 and Gog and Magog in Rev. 20:7–10; cf. Sänger 2006). Goulder (1980–1) characteristically argued that much of the Book of Revelation is shaped by liturgical reading of Ezekiel. Second Corinthians is indebted to Ezekiel at various places (e.g. 3:3; 6:16–17). The depth of Paul's dependence on Ezekiel is acknowledged by Young and Ford (1987: 74–6). Less widely recognized is the extent to which more generally the emergence of a theology of 'grace' among the exilic prophets provides crucial background to Paul's interpretation of the Christian gospel. Some have read 2 Corinthians 12:2–4 as suggesting a link with Merkabah mysticism; indeed Bowker (1971) argued that Paul's conversion experience on the Damascus road took place in the context of such a vision.

The 'statutes that were not good' of Ezekiel 20:25 have puzzled both Jews and Christians. For the Christians these always referred to the commandments of the Torah itself or their interpretation, whereas for the Jews (sometimes perhaps reacting to Christian interpretations) they never referred to the Torah but only to rabbinic rules or pagan laws (cf. Van der Horst 1992).

Ezekiel plays a recurrent, if unobtrusive, role in both patristic and scholastic literature (Dassmann 1988: 1151–83; Neuss 1911; 1912; Stevenson and Glerup 2008). Some of the great figures in Christian tradition have given close attention to the book. Within the patristic era, Origen and Gregory the Great devoted homilies to it. Origen's massive and influential commentary survives only in fragments, but major commentaries by both Jerome and Theodoret are extant. An interesting case is provided by Jerome's handling of Ezekiel 44:2: 'This gate shall remain shut; it shall not be opened, and no one shall enter by it; for the LORD, the God of Israel, has entered by it; therefore it shall remain shut.' This verse is used as scriptural authority for the doctrine of the virgin birth, a reading facilitated in various ways by Jerome's Latin rendition. The Christian Fathers continued to find inspiration in Ezekiel's inaugural vision (Christman 2005). They generally made much of Ezekiel 37 as a proclamation of the final resurrection of the dead. This features prominently in early church art, but, surprisingly, Ezekiel 37 rapidly disappears in western art, and does not feature, for example, in the great twelfth-century cycle of wall-paintings based on Ezekiel in the Doppelkirche Church at Schwarzrheindorf, near Bonn (Odell 2005). Distinguished among medieval expositors of Ezekiel were the so-called Victorines, especially Hugh (1096–1141) and Andrew (1110–75) of St Victor, Paris. They were noted for their insistence on the literal sense of the Bible, and Andrew in particular drew systematically upon Jewish interpretation (Patton 1998*a*), features which characterized also the work of Nicholas of Lyra (*c*.1270–1349) (Patton 1998*b*).

In later times the prophet's radical theocentricity was much admired by John Calvin (1509–64). His sermons on Ezekiel of 1552–4 offer intriguing material on his exposition of the visions, including those on the restoration of Israel, Gog and Magog, and also the great temple vision. They constitute a striking specimen of literal historical exegesis with a christological perspective. Calvin produced a commentary on chapters 1–20: this consists of revised transcripts of his last lectures, delivered in 1563–4 and first appearing in print in the year after his death. Calvin's account of the inaugural vision becomes a statement of his doctrine of providence, and he finds support in Ezekiel 11:19–20 for his doctrine of total depravity (Calvin 1994: 41, 271). John Donne (1572–1631), poet and dean of St Paul's, London, declared: 'Amongst the four great ones, our prophet Ezekiel is the greatest . . . the extraordinary greatness of Ezekiel, is in his extraordinary depth, and mysteriousness.' The ancient Jewish tradition of mystical speculation on Ezekiel spread to Christian circles, for example, in J. Reuchlin's work of 1517 *De arte cabalistica* (Reuchlin 1993). Another example of contact between Jewish and Christian scholars is found in the influence of rabbinic authorities on the Ezekiel translations of the English and Dutch Authorized Versions (Lloyd Jones 1968–9; Verdegaal 1986).

In the modern period, much valuable work has been done in historical-critical mode better to understand the Book of Ezekiel in its ancient context. But it would be a mistake to imagine that such work does not reflect the era of the reception of Ezekiel from which it derives. There are clear examples of the way the perspectives of such readers have a marked influence on interpretation, and occasionally distort the text. For example, Ezekiel gained favour among some critics on account of his supposed individualism, such ideas surviving well into the twentieth century. Or again, Protestant prejudice about priests has sometimes been found. Kennett closed a chapter on Ezekiel with the words: 'He was the father of Judaism, but of a Judaism in which the Gospel could not germinate . . . Of Ezekiel's teaching the almost inevitable outcome was Caiaphas, while Jeremiah marked out the way which led to Jesus Christ' (Kennett 1928: 58). Ezekiel has occasionally in modern times been compared unfavourably with other prophets, such as Hosea (cf. Robinson 1948); Ezekiel is not generally perceived as a congenial character, with whom readers can readily identify and onto whom they can project their sentiments and their spiritual aspirations. Some modern interpreters have attempted to render Ezekiel's theology more sympathetic, playing down the extent to which Ezekiel's God is merely concerned for his reputation and emphasizing the place of compassion and forgiveness (e.g. Carley 1975: 59), but this has been at the expense of accuracy. Recent times have seen an emergence of critical commentary work that is ready to be bold about its openly theological, indeed confessional, task (e.g. Jenson 2009).

One interesting feature of the quest for the historical Ezekiel in the modern era (reflecting a preoccupation of the times) has been the attempt to diagnose Ezekiel's condition in terms of a psychological illness that might explain his bizarre behaviour (e.g. Broome 1946). More recently, Halperin (1993) revived this approach, offering a thoroughgoing reductionistic Freudian reading. More nuanced psychological readings have been offered since (see Ellens and Rollins 2004). Feminist criticism, reading familiar passages with new eyes, has provided an impetus for a reassessment of the place of women and the feminine in Ezekiel. The sexually explicit, perhaps even pornographic, content has led some critics to consider the book seriously problematic if not downright immoral. Chapters 16 and 23 in particular have both generated a great deal of writing over recent years (e.g. Van Dijk Hemmes 1993; Kamionkowski 2003).

The place of Ezekiel in modern literature is not insignificant. William Blake's indebtedness to the book was considerable, as is seen in *The Marriage of Heaven and Hell*, where, in one of his 'memorable fancies', the prophets Isaiah and Ezekiel dine with the author. The play *Juno and the Paycock* by the Irish writer Sean O'Casey ends with an anguished plea that Ireland's 'hearts o' stone' be replaced with 'hearts o' flesh' (cf. Ezek. 11:19; 36:26); during the ongoing Irish troubles of the later twentieth century the rock band U2 evoked the same Ezekiel theme in *Like a Song...* ('A new heart is what I need...O God, make it bleed'). Blake also produced memorable illustrations of several scenes from Ezekiel; another striking artistic representation is Marc Chagall's *Vision d'Ezéchiel*, in which he portrays the living creatures of chapter 1, giving the human figure breasts.

Perhaps one of the most bizarre legacies of Ezekiel is found in the legend of the last of the British giants, Gog and Magog, whose statues stand in London's Guildhall; these figures appear to derive their names, by an obscure route, from the Gog of Magog who makes war on the people of Israel in chapters 38–9. The influence of the book remains evident in sayings such as 'wheels within wheels' (cf. 1:16) and 'like mother, like daughter' (16:44), and in African-American spirituals, such as 'Dem Bones' (cf. ch. 37).

Ezekiel has long played an important part in millennial speculation, not surprisingly in view of its historical association with apocalyptic material. Such links were strongly evident in the latter part of the twentieth century. As in ancient times so in modern, the opening chapter of Ezekiel has continued to exercise a strangely powerful appeal and influence, and has not infrequently been read in terms of aliens and Unidentified Flying Objects (Lieb 1998). Von Däniken's best-selling book *Chariots of the Gods?* (1969) interpreted the passage in terms of extraterrestrial visitors, and allusions to the same Ezekiel imagery were observed in Steven Spielberg's 1977 film *Close Encounters of the Third Kind*, while Collin Higgins's 1982 film, *The Best Little Whorehouse in Texas*, features a scene in which an appearance of a shooting star in the night sky leads on to a citation of Ezekiel 1 and reference to 'what the Bible says about the spaceships in Ezekiel'.

Ezekiel plays a prominent role of a very different kind in another film, Quentin Tarantino's influential *Pulp Fiction* (1994), of which the oft-repeated refrain is adapted from Ezekiel 25:17: 'I will execute great vengeance on them with wrathful punishments. Then they shall know that I am the LORD, when I lay my vengeance on them.' Though it can hardly be denied that vengeance is a strong feature of the first half of the book, it is sobering to reflect that brutal violence is what the word 'Ezekiel' currently evokes for many. But this is but one landmark in the rich afterlife of the Book of Ezekiel, and it cannot be doubted that this great text will continue to generate new insights and to make a very significant religious and cultural impact over the centuries to come.

WORKS CITED

BAUCKHAM, R. (1996), 'The Parable of the Royal Wedding Feast (Matthew 22:1–14) and the Parable of the Lame Man and the Blind Man (*Apocryphon of Ezekiel*)', *JBL* 115: 471–88.

BOWKER, J. W. (1971), '"Merkavah" Visions and the Visions of Paul'. *JSS* 16: 157–73.

BRADY, M. (2005), 'Biblical Interpretation in the "Pseudo-Ezekiel" Fragments (4Q383–391) from Cave Four', in M. Henze (ed.), *Biblical Interpretation at Qumran: Studies in the Dead Sea Scrolls and Related Literature*, 88–109. Grand Rapids and Cambridge: Eerdmans.

BROOKE, G. J. (1992), 'Ezekiel in Some Qumran and New Testament Texts', in J. Trebolle Barrera and L. Vegas Montaner (eds.), *The Madrid Qumran Congress: Proceedings of the International Congress on the Dead Sea Scrolls, Madrid 18–21 March, 1991*, Studies on the Texts of the Desert of Judah 11/1, pp. 317–37 Leiden: Brill and Madrid: Editorial Complutense.

BROOME, E. C. (1946), 'Ezekiel's Abnormal Personality', *JBL* 65: 277–92.

CALVIN, J. (1994), *Ezekiel I: Chapters 1–12*, Calvin's Old Testament Commentaries: The Rutherford House Translation, rev. edn., vol. 18. Grand Rapids, Mich.: Eerdmans and Carlisle: Paternoster.

CARLEY, K. W. (1975), *Ezekiel among the Prophets*, SBT II:31. London: SCM.

CHRISTMAN, A. R. (2005), 'What Did Ezekiel See?': Christian Exegesis of Ezekiel's Vision of the Chariot from Irenaeus to Gregory the Great, The Bible in Ancient Christianity 4. Leiden and Boston: Brill.

COOK, S. L. (1995), Prophecy and Apocalypticism: The Postexilic Social Setting. Minneapolis: Fortress.

——(1996), Review of Mueller 1994. JBL 115: 532–4.

DASSMANN, E. (1988), 'Hesekiel', in Reallexikon für Antike und Christentum, 14: 1132–91.

DIMANT, D. (2001), 'Pseudo-Ezekiel', Principal Edition, pp. 7–88 and plates i–iii in Qumran Cave 4. XXI, Parabiblical Texts, Part 4: Pseudo-Prophetic Texts, Discoveries in the Judaean Desert, XXX. Oxford: Clarendon Press.

ELIOR, R. (2004), The Three Temples: On the Emergence of Jewish Mysticism. Oxford and Portland: Littman Library of Jewish Civilization.

ELLENS, J. H. and W. G. ROLLINS (eds.) (2004), Psychology and the Bible: A New Way to Read the Scriptures, vol. 2: From Genesis to Apocalyptic Vision (Westport and London: Praeger).

ESHEL, E. (1998), 'Songs of the Sabbath Sacrifice', Principal Edition, pp. 173–401 and plates xvi–xxxi in Qumran Cave 4. VI, Poetical and Liturgical Texts, Part 1, Discoveries in the Judaean Desert, XI. Oxford: Clarendon Press.

FISHBANE, M. (1985), Biblical Interpretation in Ancient Israel. Oxford: Oxford University Press.

GOULDER, M. D. (1980–1), 'The Apocalypse as an Annual Cycle of Prophecies', New Testament Studies, 27: 342–67.

GREENBERG, M. (1997), Ezekiel 21–37. Anchor Bible 22A. New York: Doubleday.

GRUENWALD, I. (1980), Apocalyptic and Merkavah Mysticism, Arbeiten zur Geschichte des antiken Judentums und des Urchristentums 14. Leiden: Brill.

HALPERIN, D. J. (1993), Seeking Ezekiel: Text and Psychology. University Park, Pa.: Pennsylvania State University Press.

HALS, R. M. (1989), Ezekiel, FOTL 19. Grand Rapids, Mich.: Eerdmans.

HANSON, P. D. (1975; revised edn, 1979), The Dawn of Apocalyptic: The Historical and Sociological Roots of Jewish Apocalyptic Eschatology. Philadelphia: Fortress.

HARE, D. R. A. (1985), 'The Lives of the Prophets', in J. H. Charlesworth (ed.), The Old Testament Pseudepigrapha, 2. 379–99. New York: Doubleday.

JENSON, R. W. (2009), Ezekiel, Theological Commentary on the Bible series. Wheaton, Ill.: Brazos and London: SCM.

JOYCE, P. M. (2007), Ezekiel: A Commentary, LHBOTS 482. New York and London: T. & T. Clark/Continuum.

KAMIONKOWSKI, S. T. (2003), Gender Reversal and Cosmic Chaos: A Study on the Book of Ezekiel, JSOT Supp. 368. London: Sheffield Academic Press.

KENNETT, R. H. (1928), Old Testament Essays. Cambridge: Cambridge University Press.

LEVEY, S. H. (1987), The Targum of Ezekiel: Translated, with a Critical Introduction, Apparatus and Notes, The Aramaic Bible 13. Wilmington, Del.: Michael Glazier and Edinburgh: T. & T. Clark.

LIEB, M. (1998), Children of Ezekiel: Aliens, UFOs, the Crisis of Race, and the Advent of End Time. Durham, NC, and London: Duke University Press.

LLOYD JONES, G. (1968–9), 'Jewish Exegesis and the English Bible', ASTI 7: 53–63.

MANNING, G. T., JR. (2004), Echoes of a Prophet: The Use of Ezekiel in the Gospel of John and in Literature of the Second Temple Period, JSNT Supp. 270. London and New York: T. & T. Clark International.

MUELLER, J. R. (1994), *The Five Fragments of the Apocryphon of Ezekiel: A Critical Study*, Journal for the Study of the Pseudepigrapha, Supplement Series 5. Sheffield: Sheffield Academic Press.

NEUSS, W. (1911), *Die Entwicklung der theologischen Auffassung des Buches Ezechiel zur Zeit der Fruhscholastik*. Bonn.

——(1912), *Das Buch Ezechiel in Theologie und Kunst bis zum Ende des XII Jahrhunderts*, Beiträge zur Geschichte des Alten Mönchtums und des Benediktinerordens 1–2. Münster: Aschendorff.

NEWSOM, C. (1985), *Songs of the Sabbath Sacrifice: A Critical Edition*, HSS 27. Atlanta, Ga.: Scholars Press.

ODELL, M. S. (2005), *Ezekiel*, Smyth and Helwys Bible Commentary. Macon, Ga.: Smyth & Helwys.

PATTON, C. L. (1998*a*), 'Hugh and Andrew of St Victor', in D. K. McKim (ed.), *Historical Handbook of Major Biblical Interpreters*, 106–12. Downers Grove and Leicester: Inter-Varsity Press.

——(1998*b*), 'Nicholas of Lyra', in D. K. McKim (ed.), *Historical Handbook of Major Biblical Interpreters*, 116–22. Downers Grove and Leicester: Inter-Varsity Press.

REUCHLIN, J. (1993), *De arte cabalistica: On the Art of the Kabbalah*, trans. with introduction by G. L. Jones. Lincoln, Nebr., and London: University of Nebraska Press.

ROBERTSON, R. G. (1985), 'Ezekiel the Tragedian', in J. H. Charlesworth (ed.), *The Old Testament Pseudepigrapha*, 2. 803–19. New York: Doubleday.

ROBINSON, H. W. (1948), *Two Hebrew Prophets: Studies in Hosea and Ezekiel*. London: Lutterworth.

ROWLAND, C. C. (1982), *The Open Heaven: A Study of Apocalyptic in Judaism and Early Christianity*. London: SPCK.

SÄNGER, D. (ed.) (2006), *Das Ezechielbuch in der Johannesoffenbarung*, Biblisch-theologische Studien 76. Neukirchen-Vluyn: Neukirchener.

SATRAN, D. (1995), *Biblical Prophets in Byzantine Palestine: Reassessing the 'Lives of the Prophets'*, Studia in Veteris Testamenti Pseudepigrapha 11. Leiden: Brill.

SCHUSSMAN, A. (1998), 'The Prophet Ezekiel in Islamic Literature: Jewish Traces and Islamic Adaptations', in M. E. Stone and T. A. Bergren (eds.), *Biblical Figures Outside the Bible*, 316–39. Harrisburg, Pa.: Trinity Press International.

SCHWEMER, A. M. (1995/1996), *Studien zu den frühjüdischen Prophetenlegenden*, 2 vols. Texte und Studien zum Antiken Judentum 49, 50. Tübingen.

STEVENSON, K. and M. GLERUP (eds.) (2008), *Ezekiel, Daniel*, Ancient Christian Commentary on Scripture, Old Testament 13. Downers Grove, Ill.: Inter-Varsity Press.

STONE, M. E., B. G. WRIGHT, and D. SATRAN (eds.) (2000), *The Apocryphal Ezekiel*, Early Judaism and its Literature series 18. Atlanta, Ga.: SBL.

VAN DER HORST, P. W. (1992), '"I gave them laws that were not good": Ezekiel 20:25 in Ancient Judaism and Early Christianity' in J. N. Bremmer and F. García Martínez (eds.), *Sacred History and Sacred Texts in Early Judaism: A Symposium in Honour of A. S. van der Woude*, Contributions to Biblical Exegesis and Theology 5, 94–118. Kampen: Kok Pharos.

VAN DIJK-HEMMES, F. (1993), 'The Metaphorization of Woman in Prophetic Speech: An Analysis of Ezekiel xxiii', *VT* 43: 162–70.

VERDEGAAL, C. M. L. (1986), 'The Jewish Influence on the Ezekiel Translation of the English and Dutch Authorized Versions', in J. Lust (ed.), *Ezekiel and his Book*, BETL 74, 111–19. Leuven: Leuven University Press/Peeters.

VON DÄNIKEN, E. (1969), *Chariots of the Gods? Unsolved Mysteries of the Past*. London: Souvenir.

WRIGHT, B. G. (1998). 'Talking with God and Losing His Head: Extrabiblical Traditions About the Prophet Ezekiel' in M. E. Stone and T. A. Bergren (eds.), *Biblical Figures outside the Bible*, 290–315. Harrisburg, Pa.: Trinity Press International.

YOUNG, F. and D. F. FORD (1987), *Meaning and Truth in 2 Corinthians*, Biblical Foundations in Theology. London: SPCK.

FURTHER READING

BLOCK, D. I. (1997, 1998), *The Book of Ezekiel*, NICOT, 2 vols. Grand Rapids and Cambridge: Eerdmans.

COOK, S. L. and C. PATTON (2004), *Ezekiel's Hierarchical World: Wrestling with a Tiered Reality*, SBL Symposium Series 31. Atlanta, Ga.: Society of Biblical Literature.

MEIN, A. (in preparation), *Ezekiel Through the Centuries*, Blackwell Bible Commentary. Oxford: Blackwell.

ODELL, M. S. and J. T. STRONG (eds.) (2000), *The Book of Ezekiel: Theological and Anthropological Perspectives*, SBL Symposium Series 9. Atlanta, Ga.: Society of Biblical Literature.

ZIMMERLI, W. (1979/1983), *Ezekiel*, Hermeneia, 2 vols. Philadelphia: Fortress.

——(1982), *I am Yahweh*, ed. W. Brueggemann. Atlanta, Ga.: John Knox Press.

CHAPTER 6

....

DANIEL

....

JOHN J. COLLINS

THE Book of Daniel is found among the Writings in the Hebrew Bible, but appears as fourth among the Major Prophets in the Greek Bible. Daniel is traditionally grouped among the Prophets in Christian Bibles. The differing placements point already to different assessments of the genre and character of the book.

Canonical placement is not, however, the only anomaly in the Book of Daniel. The form of the book found in the Hebrew Bible is bilingual: chapters 1:1–2:4a and 8–12 are in Hebrew, but from chapter 2:4b to the end of chapter 6 is in Aramaic. The transition to Aramaic occurs when the Chaldeans address the king in that language; thereafter the narrative simply continues in Aramaic. There is no obvious occasion for the return to Hebrew at the beginning of chapter 8. Moreover, the Greek translation includes additions in chapter 3 (the Prayer of Azariah and the Song of the Three Young Men), and also includes two additional stories, Bel and the Serpent, and Susanna. These additional materials were most probably originally composed in Hebrew or Aramaic, but they are not extant in these languages. The oldest preserved text is the Greek. The additional materials are accepted as part of the book in the Roman Catholic Bible, but they are relegated to the Apocrypha in Protestant Bibles. Moreover, the Old Greek translation of Daniel was replaced in Church usage by the translation of Theodotion. The two Greek translations differ widely, especially in chapters 4 to 6.

THE GENRES

....

Perhaps the most significant anomaly associated with the book, however, is the variation in genre. The first six chapters are stories about Daniel and his compa- nions, who were supposedly taken captive to Babylon by King Nebuchadnezzar at the time of the destruction of Jerusalem. Daniel supposedly lived until the time of King Cyrus of Persia. Bel and the Serpent and Susanna are also stories, with Daniel as the protagonist. Chapters 7–12, in contrast, consist of revelations received by this Daniel, and explained to him by an angel. These revelations concern the time of the end, which was apparently still in the distant future, and have a strongly eschatological orientation. The stories in chapters 1–6, in contrast, are not concerned with eschatology, except in the case of Nebuchadnezzar's dream in chapter 2.

The Stories in Chapters 1–6

The stories in the first part of the book are set at the Babylonian court. Daniel and his companions, we are told, were selected for training in the service of the king. They are thereby placed in a situation with conflicting claims on their loyalty. On the one hand, they are consistently loyal to the king. On the other, their ultimate loyalty is to their God. Accordingly, Daniel's companions refuse to bow down before the statue erected by the king, and Daniel persists in praying to his God even when forbidden to do so. Daniel and his companions refuse the royal food, and adopt a vegetarian diet, presumably in deference to the Jewish food laws, although these are not mentioned explicitly. While he and his companions behave respectfully towards the kings, Daniel denounces Belshazzar for his arrogance and indulgence in very blunt terms in Daniel 5. There is some variation in the attitudes of the pagan kings. Nebuchadnezzar is so impressed with Daniel's ability to tell his dream and interpret it, in chapter 2, that he acknowledges that 'your God is God of gods and Lord of kings', and promotes Daniel and his friends to positions of authority over the affairs of Babylon. His conversion appears to be short-lived, however, as it has to be repeated in chapters 3 and 4. In chapter 4 the king only acknowledges the God of Daniel after he has been reduced to a bestial state for seven years. Belshazzar, who succeeds Nebuchadnezzar in chapter 5, seems unaware of his father's experience. Darius the Mede, who succeeds Belshazzar in chapter 6, is by far the most sympathetic of the gentile rulers. In contrast to the kings, the gentile courtiers are consistently depicted either as rivals or as enemies of Daniel and his friends. The stories in chapters 2 and 4 illustrate Daniel's superiority over the Babylonians in his ability to know and interpret dreams. In chapters 3 and 6 the Babylonian courtiers are openly hostile, and try to plot the downfall of the Judeans. This is also the case in the story of Bel and the Serpent.

The stories in Daniel 1–6 have many legendary, miraculous features. Daniel's companions are preserved unharmed in the middle of a fiery furnace, and Daniel survives in the lions' den. Nebuchadnezzar is transformed for a time into a beast. Belshazzar receives an ominous warning in the form of mysterious writing on a wall. These stories serve to illustrate, in the words of Daniel 4, that 'the Most High is sovereign over the kingdom of mortals'. They provide moral lessons, both as positive examples and as illustrations of hubristic behaviour that should be avoided. They strain credibility at many points, and are often at variance with our knowledge of history from other sources. Belshazzar was never actually king in Babylon, although he was regent in the absence of his father. No such figure as Darius the Mede is known to history. The stories are concerned to inspire a sense of awe, and are not constrained by considerations of realism. The additional stories of Bel and the Serpent and Susanna are much more realistic. In both of these stories Daniel resolves problems by his wit and ingenuity. Bel and the Serpent, however, has a variant form of the story of Daniel in the lions' den, with the added embellishment that the prophet Habakkuk is miraculously transported to Babylon to bring him food.

Dreams and revelations play an important part in some stories, but they are not the main point of the plot. In chapter 2 Daniel recounts and interprets Nebuchad-nezzar's dream, but the theme of the chapter as a whole is the superiority of Daniel to the Chaldean wise men, which is taken to reflect the superiority of his God. The king is so impressed with Daniel's ability to tell his dream and interpret it that he scarcely pays any attention to the content of the dream, which predicts the ultimate demise of Babylonian power. In other cases the story recounts how the dreams were fulfilled, as a way of teaching a moral lesson. In chapter 4 Nebuchadnezzar has a dream, which is then fulfilled, about his transformation into a beast. When he is restored, he acknowledges the supremacy of the Most High God. The mysterious writing on the wall in chapter 5 announces in advance the fate that befalls Belshazzar at the end of the chapter. Again, there is a moral lesson about the fall of the haughty. Only Nebuchadnezzar's dream in chapter 2 concerns matters that extend into the distant future.

Modern scholarship has made various attempts to classify these tales. Most often, they are classified as 'court tales', because of their setting at the royal court, or 'Diaspora tales', because of their exilic setting (Wills 1990). They are clearly related to the story of Joseph in Genesis 37–50 and to the Book of Esther. There are also significant parallels with the tales from Near Eastern courts in Book 1 of Herodotus' history. The stories in Joseph, Esther, and Daniel may also be taken to represent early examples of the Jewish novel or short story (Wills 1995: 40–67), although some scholars would dispute whether there is enough coherence between novelistic Jewish stories to allow us to speak of a genre. Some scholars have taken these stories to inculcate 'a life-style for the Diaspora' (Humphreys 1973). In the case of Daniel, the main point would be to illustrate how Jews could work in the service of a foreign king and still be faithful to their God.

The Visions

Chapters 7–12, in contrast, are accounts of visions and revelations which are given to Daniel and are interpreted for him by an angel. These revelations are almost entirely concerned with matters that are still in the future, from Daniel's perspective. Angels figure prominently in them, and the final revelation in chapters 10–12 concludes with a prophecy of the resurrection of the dead. The kind of visionary material in Daniel 7–12 is closely related to the Apocalypse, or Book of Revelation, in the New Testament, and is usually called 'apocalyptic'.

There is some formal variation in the visions in Daniel 7–12. Chapters 7 and 8 are symbolic visions, which are interpreted for Daniel by an angel. In Chapter 9 the revelation comes by way of an interpretation of a prophecy in the Book of Jeremiah, according to which Jerusalem was to be desolate for seventy years. The chapter contains a lengthy prayer by Daniel. The only vision is the apparition of the angel Gabriel, who provides the interpretation. Chapter 10:1 says that Daniel had a vision, and that a word was revealed to him, but again the only vision described is the apparition of the interpreting angel. At the end of the angel's revelation, Daniel sees two other angels who discuss the length of time 'until the end of these wonders' (12:6).

The Apocalyptic Genre

The recognition that apocalyptic literature is generically different from prophecy only came about in the nineteenth century, when the First Book of Enoch was brought to England from Ethiopia by a Scottish traveller, and translated into English by Richard Laurence (Laurence 1821). First Enoch consists mainly of revelations, which Enoch allegedly received when he was taken up to heaven and shown the heavenly tablets on which the course of history was predicted. The revelations are explained to him by angelic guides. They describe not only the course of history, but also the mysteries of the cosmos, as well as a final judgement, leading to eternal life with the angels for the righteous or to eternal punishment for the wicked. There were evident analogies between these revelations and what we find in Daniel, but also in 4 Ezra (2 Esdras 3–14), which was preserved in Latin in the Apocrypha, and the Greek Sibylline Oracles, which had been rediscovered in the Renaissance (Lücke 1832). In the course of the nineteenth century several other such 'apocalypses' came to light: 2 (Syriac) Baruch, 3 (Greek) Baruch, 2 (Slavonic) Enoch, the Apocalypse of Abraham (preserved in Slavonic), the Testament of Abraham (preserved in Greek). Consequently, it became apparent that such literature constituted a genre, and that Daniel and Enoch were not unique from a literary point of view (Koch 1972: 18–22).

The apocalyptic genre was evidently related to prophecy, and this relationship was clearer in some cases than in others. Some apocalypses (including Daniel) are primarily concerned with the course of history; others (including much of the Enoch literature) are concerned more with otherworldly mysteries (Collins 1979: 21–59; 1998: 1–42). Nonetheless, it was apparent that even the historically oriented apocalypses differed from earlier prophecy in significant ways.

First, the historical predictions in the apocalypses typically concerned events long after the time of the visionary. For example, many of the predictions in Daniel demonstrably relate to the time of the Maccabean revolt in the second century BCE, although Daniel supposedly lived during the Babylonian Exile. The chronological gap was even greater in the case of Enoch, who supposedly lived before the Flood. Consequently, it was inferred that these writings were pseudepigraphical: they were not actually written by Daniel and Enoch, but by people of a much later time.

Second, the revelations were usually couched in mysterious language, which had to be explained to the visionary by an angel. There were precedents for the interpreting angel in the later prophetic books (Ezek. 40–8; Zechariah), but the apocalyptic visions were much more elaborate and baroque than what we find in the earlier prophets (Niditch 1983). Angels figure far more prominently in the apocalypses than in prophetic literature. Daniel is the only book in the Hebrew Bible where angels (Michael, Gabriel) are mentioned by name.

Third, the predictions in the apocalypses cover a much longer time-span than the prophetic books, and often divide history into periods (four kingdoms, ten generations, and so on).

Finally, the apocalypses envision a judgement of the individual dead, with eternal reward and punishment. Although there are a few references to resurrection in the prophetic literature (Ezek. 37; Isa. 26), these are most readily understood as metaphors for the restoration of the Israelite people. The apocalypses are also concerned with the restoration of Israel, but the expectation of individual judge-ment made an enormous difference in the worldview of these books, and was exceptionally important for the emergence of Christianity (Collins 1974).

Moreover, the apocalypses, including Daniel, typically lack oracular speech in the name of the Lord, and seldom engage in direct moral exhortation and denun-ciation in the manner of Amos or Jeremiah. Instead, the apocalypses attain their effect by framing human decisions against a backdrop of angelic and demonic activity and the anticipation of a final judgement.

But while the distinction between prophetic and apocalyptic literature is impor-tant for modern scholarship, it was not drawn explicitly before the nineteenth century. Prior to that time, the main question about the genre of Daniel was whether it belonged with the Prophets, where it is found in the Christian Bible, or rather among the sapiential and instructional literature of the Writings, as in the Hebrew Bible.

Prophecy or Wisdom?

Because of the visionary material in the second half of the book, Christian readers often assume that Daniel self-evidently belongs among the Prophets. On this view, Daniel was placed among the Writings in the Hebrew Bible only because the collection of Prophets was already closed when the book was composed. (Alternatively, it has been suggested that Daniel was initially regarded as a prophet, but that his book was moved to the Writings by the rabbis, who were disillusioned with apocalyptic prophecy after the failure of the revolts against Rome; see Koch 1985). But it is also possible that the placement of the book in the Hebrew Bible reflects a judgement on its genre, which privileges the stories with which the book begins rather than the visions in its later half. Rabbinic tradition focused on these stories as test-cases of moral dilemmas; for example, should Daniel have been so concerned for the welfare of King Nebuchadnezzar, who was not only a pagan but the destroyer of Jerusalem? The stories could be taken to exemplify the importance of pure food (ch. 1), of prayer at the prescribed times (ch. 6) and of the rejection of idolatry, and fidelity to the God of Israel, even under threat of death (chs. 3, 6). Daniel then could be classified appropriately with wisdom books such as Proverbs, which are also primarily instructional literature.

The sapiential aspects of Daniel have come to the fore again in modern scholarship. Gerhard von Rad famously argued that apocalypticism had its roots in wisdom literature rather than in prophecy (von Rad 1965: 2. 330). This thesis has not been widely accepted, because of the obvious differences between Daniel on the one hand, and Proverbs or Qoheleth on the other. But scholars have increasingly recognized that the apocalypses do contain a kind of wisdom. Daniel and his friends are sages, wise men at the Babylonian court. Even the heroes in the time of persecution in Daniel 11 are referred to as *maskilim*, wise men. The interest in geography and the heavenly world in the Enoch literature is also a sapiential interest, as it concerns a kind of knowledge. So while the wisdom of Daniel is very different from that of Proverbs or Qoheleth, it is a kind of wisdom nonetheless.

Yet it is the visionary, prophetic character of the book that has most impressed interpreters through the ages. This has also had an impact on the way the tales in chapters 1–6 have been read. Because the dream of Nebuchadnezzar in Daniel 2 is closely related to the vision in Daniel 7, this has strengthened the impression that the whole book is concerned with predicting the course of history. Even though the three youths in the fiery furnace, and Daniel in the lions' den, do not actually die, their stories have been read as metaphors for resurrection, in light of the prediction in Daniel 12.

MAJOR THEMES

More than any other biblical book, Daniel seems to provide predictions of the course of history, its division into periods, and the time of its end. These aspects of the book have fed eschatological speculation for more than two thousand years.

The Four Kingdoms

The periodization of history is especially evident in chapters 2 and 7. In chapter 2 the content of Nebuchadnezzar's dream is revealed to Daniel. It involved a great statue, in human form. The head was of gold, the chest and arms of silver, the middle and thighs of bronze, the legs of iron, and the feet partly iron and partly clay. This statue was toppled by a stone not cut by human hands. Then the stone grew into a great mountain and filled the whole earth. Daniel interprets this dream in terms of a sequence of kings and kingdoms. Nebuchadnezzar of Babylon is the head of gold. After him will arise another kingdom, inferior to his. Then a third kingdom, of bronze, will rule over the earth. A fourth kingdom will be strong as iron, and will shatter all the others, but it shall be a divided kingdom, as in part the iron will be mixed with clay. The stone that shatters the statue and becomes a mountain represents a kingdom that will be set up by the God of heaven, and that will never be destroyed.

The representation of history as a sequence of metals of declining value is known from a number of ancient sources (Collins 1993: 162–5). The most famous of these is Hesiod's *Works and Days* 109–201. Hesiod describes a sequence of five ages—golden, silver, bronze, one that is not identified with a metal, and iron. The fourth age breaks the pattern of decline and is inserted to accommodate the heroes of Greek legend. Hesiod, who lived about 700 BCE, was evidently adapting an older schema of four ages and four metals.

A closer parallel to Daniel is found in the Persian *Bahman Yasht*, or *Zand-I Vohuman Yasn*, chapter 1. There we read that Ahura Mazda showed 'the wisdom of all-knowledge' to Zoroaster. Through it he saw 'the trunk of a tree, on which there were four branches: one of gold, one of silver, one of steel and one of mixed iron'. These are explained to him as 'the four periods which will come' in the millennium of Zoroaster. The golden period is the reign of Zoroaster. The second and third periods are identified with the reigns of Sassanian kings, and the fourth period is the evil sovereignty of 'the divs with dishevelled hair' (often thought to be an allusion to the Greeks). The motif of mixed iron is especially interesting as a parallel to Daniel. Both the Persian text and the biblical one are concerned with a sequence of kingdoms rather than with the ages of humankind, as in Hesiod. Both see history as a process of decline. The biblical text differs from the others in speaking explicitly of a future kingdom of God, which would reverse the decline of history and restore a golden age. It is possible, however, that some such reversal was also implied both in Hesiod and in the Persian text.

The motif of four kingdoms, followed by a fifth that is everlasting, appears again in Daniel 7. In this case it is Daniel who has the dream, and the imagery is different. He sees four great beasts coming up out of the sea. The first is like a lion, and has eagle's wings. The second is like a bear, and the third like a leopard with wings on its back. The fourth is not compared with a specific animal, but it stamps with its feet, suggesting perhaps an elephant. This fourth beast has iron teeth and ten horns, and then a further horn sprouts up, which proves to be especially obnoxious. The scene then changes to a divine 'Ancient of Days' on his throne, before whom a court assembles. The beasts are judged. The fourth is executed and thrown in the fire, while the others are allowed to live on for a time. Then 'one like a son of man' appears, coming with the clouds of heaven. The Ancient One confers on him the everlasting kingdom.

This dream, or night vision, is explained to Daniel by an angel. The four beasts are four kings that will arise on the earth, but the holy ones of the Most High will receive the kingdom. Daniel asks for further clarification about the fourth beast. This, he is told, represents a kingdom, from which ten kings will arise and another after them. The final king will speak words against the Most High and 'wear out' the holy ones of the Most High. Finally this kingdom will be destroyed and its dominion will be given to the people of the holy ones.

The connotations of this imagery are rather different from that of chapter 2. The beasts rising from the turbulent sea evoke the old Near Eastern myths of creation in which a god does battle with a chaos monster, often associated with the sea (Collins 1993: 286–94). While the second and third kingdoms are passed over rather briefly, it is not apparent that they represent progressive decline, like the metals in chapter 2. All the beasts seem to be in rebellion against God. The iron teeth of the fourth beast, however, recall the iron legs of the statue in Nebuchadnezzar's dream. This fourth kingdom receives considerably more attention in chapter 7 than in chapter 2, and is portrayed as considerably worse than all before it. Nonetheless, most interpreters over the centuries have harmonized the two dreams and regarded them as complementary.

In the context of the Book of Daniel, the four kingdoms are most easily identified as Babylonian, Median, Persian, and Greek, since these are the only kingdoms mentioned explicitly in the book. Much of the book is set in the reigns of Nebuchadnezzar and Belshazzar of Babylon. Chapters 6 and 9 are set in the reign of the fictional Darius the Mede, and chapter 10 in the reign of Cyrus of Persia. The coming of the Greek kingdom is only mentioned, by the angel Gabriel, in chapter 10:20. But the kingdoms are not identified either in chapter 2 or in chapter 4. Consequently, it was possible to offer new identifications in different historical periods. Around the turn of the Common Era, it seemed self-evident that the fourth kingdom was Rome (so Josephus, Ant. 10.276; 4 Ezra 12). In a later era the Muslims, or more specifically the Turks, would be so identified.

For most Christian interpreters, down to modern times, it seemed self-evident that the 'one like a son of man' should be identified as Jesus, or, if one respected the pre-Christian, Jewish context of the book, the messiah. This identification is implied already in the Gospels, which implicitly identify the Son of Man who will come on the clouds of heaven as Jesus (Yarbro Collins 1993). Modern scholarship has cast doubt on the messianic interpretation. There is no clear reference to a messiah elsewhere in Daniel. Opinion has been divided between the view that the 'one like a son of man' is a collective symbol for the Jewish people (e.g. Hartman and DiLella 1978: 218–19) and the view that he should be identified as an angelic figure, most probably Michael, who appears as the 'prince of Israel' in Daniel 10:21 and 12:1 (Collins 1993: 304–10). There is a similar dispute about the holy ones of the Most High. Christian interpreters have traditionally assumed that the reference was to Christian 'saints'. Modern historical critics have often taken them to be the Jewish people, or a segment thereof. Others have pointed out that 'holy ones' in the Bible and in the Dead Sea Scrolls are usually angels, and argued that the reference here is to the heavenly host, although 'the people of the holy ones' must still be the Jewish people (Collins 1993: 313–17). The traditional assumption that human saints were in question still allowed plenty of room for debate as to their precise identification.

Chronological Predictions

Several passages in the Book of Daniel predict the length of time that must elapse before the end of persecution and the coming of the kingdom of God. The most elaborate of these is found in chapter 9. Daniel prays for illumination regarding 'the number of years that, according to the word of the Lord to the prophet Jeremiah, must be fulfilled for the devastation of Jerusalem, namely seventy years' (Dan. 9:2). In response, the angel Gabriel appears to him and explains that the seventy years are really seventy weeks of years, or 490 years. Seven weeks would pass 'from the time that the word went out to restore and rebuild Jerusalem until the time of an anointed prince' (9:25). Then sixty-two weeks would pass uneventfully, but at the end of this period 'an anointed one shall be cut off', and 'the troops of the prince who is to come shall destroy the city and the sanctuary' (9:26). For the last half-week of years before the decreed end, this 'prince who is to come' 'shall make sacrifice and offering cease; and in their place shall be an abomination that desolates'.

Several other predictions in Daniel are related to this final period of half a week of years, or three-and-a-half years, between the desolation of the sanctuary and the 'end'. According to Daniel 7:25, the little horn of the fourth beast would prevail for 'a time, times, and half a time', which is to say, three-and-a-half years. Other passages give the number of days. In Daniel 8 one holy one (angel) asks another: 'For how long is this vision concerning the regular burnt offering, the transgression that makes desolate, and the giving over the sanctuary and host to be trampled?' And he answered him: 'For two thousand three hundred evenings and mornings; then the sanctuary shall be restored to its rightful state.' The 'evenings and mornings' refer to the twice-daily sacrifice in the temple. The number is equivalent to 1,150 days, which is a little less than three-and-a-half years. At the end of Daniel

12, however, we read: 'from the time that the regular burnt offering is taken away and the abomination that desolates is set up, there shall be one thousand two hundred ninety days. Happy are those who persevere and attain the thousand three hundred thirty-five days' (12:11–12). The different numbers are most easily understood as revisions, to extend the period when the earlier dates passed.

The passage in Daniel 8 makes clear that the period in question was the duration of the desecration of the temple. Modern scholars understand this as a reference to the desecration of the Jerusalem temple by Antiochus Epiphanes in the second century BCE, and this reference was sometimes recognized in antiquity, most famously by the pagan philosopher Porphyry (third century CE). But in fact that desecration only lasted three years. It is likely that within the Book of Daniel itself the focus shifted from the restoration of the temple to the end of history, which according to Daniel 12 would be marked by the resurrection of the dead. The numbers of days in Daniel 12:11–12, are followed by instruction to Daniel: 'But you, go your way, and rest; you shall rise for your reward at the end of days.' It would seem, then, that the 'end' in question was no longer the restoration of the temple but the end of history.

Regardless of when we date the Book of Daniel, it is apparent that history did not end in the predicted number of days. Nonetheless, Daniel's prophecy was not discredited. The historian Josephus, writing in the late first century CE, said that Daniel was one of the greatest prophets, 'for he was not only wont to prophesy future things, as did the other prophets, but he also fixed the time at which these would come to pass' (Ant. 10.267). For many centuries, down to modern times, people have tried to infer the length of time remaining until the end of the world from the numbers in the Book of Daniel. The principle of interpretation is obvious: if seventy years could mean seventy weeks of years, why should not 'years' also be taken metaphorically, especially since 'with the Lord one day is as a thousand years, and a thousand years as a day' (2 Pet. 3:8; cf. Ps. 90:4)? Consequently, Daniel's numbers have remained fertile ground for speculation, long after the literal number of years had passed.

An Anointed One Cut Off

One other aspect of Daniel 9 has played a fateful role in the history of interpretation. There are two references to an anointed one. Daniel 9:25 says that 'until there is an anointed ruler will be seven weeks', and 9:26 says that 'after the sixty-two weeks the anointed one will be cut off'. The Greek translation of Theodotion, however, combines the seven weeks and the sixty-two weeks, so that both verses can be taken to refer to the same anointed figure. Traditional Christians then took 9:26 as a prophecy of the death of Christ, which in turn became a fixed point in calculating the time remaining until the end of the world. Modern scholars take 9:25 as a reference to the high priest Joshua, at the time of the restoration in the

Persian period, and 9:26 as a reference to the murder of the high priest Onias III in the second century BCE.

The Abomination of Desolation

Also noteworthy in Daniel 9 is the reference to 'the abomination that makes desolate'. There are similar allusions in chapters 8:13 and 11:31. The installation of this abomination is related to the disruption of the temple cult. The earliest interpretation of this phrase is found in 1 Maccabees 1:54, which says that in 167 BCE, during the persecution under Antiochus Epiphanes, the gentile authorities 'erected a desolating sacrilege upon the altar of burnt offering'. The reference seems to be to a pagan altar superimposed on the great altar of sacrifice in the Jerusalem temple. St Jerome thought the reference was to a statue of Zeus Olympios, set up in the temple, but the older interpretation found in 1 Maccabees is more reliable. In the New Testament the abomination was understood as future, eschatological, and apparently related to the destruction of Jerusalem (Matt. 24:15; Mark 13:14). In later tradition it was sometimes interpreted as the Antichrist (so Hippolytus).

Daniel 11 was also interpreted traditionally in terms of an Antichrist. Approximately half the chapter, beginning in 11:21, deals with the career of an arrogant king, who is identified in modern scholarship as Antiochus Epiphanes, the Syrian king who tried to suppress the Jewish cult in the Maccabean era. This identification was made already in antiquity by the philosopher Porphyry, whose interpretations were often followed by Jerome. On this point, however, Jerome parted company with him. If all the predictions in Daniel 11:21–45 are referred to Antiochus Epiphanes, then it must be admitted that some of them were not fulfilled, since Antiochus did not die as predicted in the land of Israel. Porphyry seized on this point gleefully, to discredit the prophecy. Jerome, and a long line of Christian interpreters after him, argued that this prophecy could not refer to Antiochus, and must refer to a future eschatological figure, the Antichrist.

Martyrdom

Daniel 11 also provided a prototype for martyrdom, since the wise teachers in the time of persecution lay down their lives, and are subsequently vindicated in the resurrection. The stories in Daniel 3 and 6 were read in light of this passage. Even though the three young men and Daniel did not actually die, they too were willing to lay down their lives rather than deviate from their religious observances.

In the history of interpretation, however, the moral example provided by these and other stories was overshadowed by the predictive aspects of the book. It is mainly as a guide to the future that Daniel would have its impact on both Jewish and Christian traditions.

WORKS CITED

COLLINS, J. J. (1974), 'Apocalyptic Eschatology as the Transcendence of Death', *Catholic Biblical Quarterly*, 36:21–43.

——(1993), *Daniel*. Hermeneia; Minneapolis: Fortress.

——(1998), *The Apocalyptic Imagination*. Grand Rapids, Mich.: Eerdmans.

——ed. (1979), *Apocalypse: The Morphology of a Genre*. Semeia 14. Missoula: Society of Biblical Literature.

HARTMAN, L. F. and A. A. DiLELLA (1978), *The Book of Daniel*. Anchor Bible 23. New York: Doubleday.

HUMPHREYS, W. L. (1973), 'A Life-Style for Diaspora: A Study of the Tales of Esther and Daniel', *JBL* 92: 211–23.

KOCH, K. (1972), *The Rediscovery of Apocalyptic*. Naperville, Ill.: Allenson.

——'Is Daniel Also Among the Prophets?' *Interpetation*, 39: 117–30.

LAURENCE, R. (1821), *The Book of Enoch the Prophet*. Oxford: Oxford University Press.

LÜCKE, F. (1832), *Versuch einer vollständigen Einleitung in die Offenbarung Johannis und in die gesamte apokalyptische Literatur*. Bonn: Weber.

NIDITCH, S. (1983), *The Symbolic Vision in Biblical Tradition*. Chico, Calif.: Scholar's Press.

RAD, G. VON (1965), *Theologie des Alten Testaments*. 2 vols. 2nd edn. Munich: Kaiser.

WILLS, L. M. (1990), *The Jew in the Court of the Foreign King: Ancient Jewish Court Legends*. Minneapolis: Fortress.

——(1995), *The Jewish Novel in the Ancient World*. Ithaca, NY: Cornell.

YARBRO COLLINS, A. (1993), 'The Influence of Daniel on the New Testament', in Collins 1993: 90–112.

FURTHER READING

The classic commentary of J. A. Montgomery, *A Critical and Exegetical Commentary on the Book of Daniel*. ICC. Edinburgh: T. & T. Clark, 1927 remains indispensable on textual and philological matters. A concise form-critical commentary and outline of the structure can be found in J. J. Collins, *Daniel with an Introduction to Apocalyptic Literature*. Forms of Old Testament Literature; Grand Rapids, Mich.: Eerdmans, 1984. A full, up-to-date commentary can be found in Collins 1993. Also useful, from a more conservative theological perspective, is J. Goldingay, *Daniel*. Word Biblical Commentary; Dallas: Word, 1988. A very thorough commentary on Daniel 1–4 can be found in K. Koch, *Daniel 1–4*. Biblische Kommentar; Neukirchen: Neukirchener Verlag, 2005. Wills 1990 provides an excellent introduction to the court tales. On the apocalyptic genre, see Collins (ed.), 1979 and Collins 1998.

CHAPTER 7

....

JUDGES

....

DAVID M. GUNN

THE Book of Judges begins with a brief account of the Israelite tribes' settlement in the land after Joshua's death (Judg. 1). Despite their victories they are unable to drive out all the Canaanites and an angel puts them on notice that these remaining inhabitants will test them. The narrator sums up what transpires (2:11–19). The Israelites forsook Yahweh ('the LORD'), the god of their fathers, and followed the gods of the peoples around them. Angered, Yahweh brought enemies to oppress them, but, for their rescue, then raised up 'judges'. Yet despite gaining 'rest', the Israelites persisted in apostasy so that Yahweh again oppressed and, responding to their groans of affliction, delivered them. This summary prefaces a series of stories about individual judges who deliver their people from the divinely instigated oppression of their enemies. Each story has its own preface telling of apostasy, punishment, and repentance, though the formula fragments as the book progresses.

Othniel defeats Cushan-rishathaim, king of Mesopotamia (3:7–1). Ehud, a Benjaminite, deceives and assassinates Eglon, king of Moab (3:12–30). Deborah and Barak gather an army in Ephraim to defeat the iron chariots of Jabin, king of Canaan, whose general, Sisera, is deceived and killed by a woman, Jael (4:1–5:31). Gideon variously tests the LORD's summons to him before his small band throws the Midianites into fatal confusion (6:1–8:35); his son, Abimelech, who is not called a judge, murders his own half-brothers and seizes power as a king before eventually being struck down by a millstone cast by another woman, at Thebez (9:1–57). Jephthah, engaged by the men of Gilead who had previously disowned him, wins a victory over the Ammonites, but at the expense of a vow that demands his daughter's sacrifice (10:1–12:7). The barren wife of Manoah bears a son, Samson, who finds himself in conflict with the Philistines, loves Delilah, who betrays him to his enemies, and brings death to himself and thousands in the Philistine house of the god Dagon (13:1–16:31).

Two remaining stories, without the formulaic preface or a judge/deliverer, have long been viewed as an appendix. Micah, with money stolen from his mother, hires a Levite to be a private priest but loses him to some marauding Danites looking for a priest and a city of their own (18:1–31). Another Levite lets his wife (a secondary wife; KJV translates 'concubine') be ravaged by a gang at Gibeah and sets in train a destructive civil war between Benjamin and the other tribes; the latter rescue Benjamin from extinction by forcing the young women of Shiloh to marry the Benjaminite survivors (19:1–21:25).

For a large part of the book's history, from late antiquity, the predominant way of reading Judges by Christians has been typologically, treating the text as a predictive code. Thus Samson's life and death prefigure Christ's saving deeds and death. While sometimes seeming arbitrary, such interpretation is usually anchored in some textual detail and metaphorical possibility. Philistine Gaza, whose gates Samson removes, represents death. As Samson renders the city open, so Christ defeats death and opens the gates of Limbo. Though almost all the stories have found their typological interpreters, Gideon's miraculous tests and Samson's great feats have enjoyed special favour. But with the advent of printed, vernacular translations of the Bible, coupled with rising rates of literacy in the early modern period, the arcane codes of typology (and allegory) found in Judges by medieval scholars gradually lost ground to literal-historical interpretations more directly accessible to the expanding readership. In the vernacular, laypeople could read and hear the narratives of Judges as tales of ancient events and figures, not unlike the stories of Greece and Rome that were also being rediscovered. Delilah, for example, was always easier to read, literally, through the lens of the popular story of a great man brought down by a temptress than as (typologically—and polemically) the Jewish 'synagogue' conspiring to have Jesus crucified, or (allegorically) representing an aspect of humankind, (feminine) flesh betraying (masculine) rational sense (Gunn 2005: 179). Nonetheless, Judges was for most readers not just a collection of ancient tales but scripture. Governing its interpretation, moreover, was another scriptural text, namely Hebrews 11: 32–4. After instancing at length how, by faith, biblical figures had acted from Genesis to Joshua, Paul (ascribed as the book's author) asks rhetorically: 'And what shall I more say? For the time would be too short for me to tel of Gedeon, of Barak and of Sampson, and of Jephte, also of David, and Samuel, and the Prophets . . .' (Geneva Bible). To Judges, then, as elsewhere in the Bible, readers looked for religious inspiration and moral guidance. The stories taught lessons for life. But Hebrews 11 also complicated things, since many of the judge's stories did not match their readers' expectations as models of faithful living. Deception, for example, was crucial to Ehud's and Jael's successful assassinations (and Jael is praised by Deborah, the judge), linking these figures to Delilah, the betrayer. Jephthah vowed rashly, unnecessarily, and contrary to the Mosaic law, in the view of many readers. Yet they also believed that the apostle Paul singled him out for high praise in Hebrews 11—for some reason! Moral problems such as these occasioned much debate and varying interpretations through the centuries.

The goal of most post-enlightenment historical-critical analysis of Judges has been to shed light on the political and religious history of ancient Israel. Most scholars have reconstructed that history from the evidence of the biblical text itself, treating Judges as a source-book, though some have tried to correlate the book with other ancient historical records and with archaeological excavations. There is broad agreement that the story of piecemeal and incomplete settlement in Judges 1 is a reliable account (in contrast to the unified conquest in Joshua 10–12). Likewise it is commonly argued that the stories of the main section were originally local in scope, that local heroes have been transformed into national deliverers in a composite history of all Israel; by adding a theological preface (2:6–3:6) and the reiterated 'framework' passages (telling of apostasy, punishment, and cry for help) the ancient editor(s) refashioned the stories to show that Israel's history was determined by its religious fidelity or infidelity (reward and punishment). For modern scholars, however, the true history lies behind the text, hidden in the diverse origins of stories or distorted in the conflation of sources by authors and editors over time. Consequently, much energy has been directed towards determining what sources and revisions have led to the present composition; and here there however, literary-critical and feminist scholars have taken a different turn, exploring again the meaning of the stories and book in their extant form and focusing in particular on the prominent role of women and the ubiquity of violence.

The exercise of violence, endemic to Judges, has caused serious misgivings, particularly throughout the modern period. Deist philosopher Voltaire (1694–1778) is scathing about Ehud's assassination and includes him in his *Philosophical Dictionary* (1764) under the entry 'Fanaticism'. He attacks the regicide as being akin to the treacherous slaying of Julius Caesar, also in the name of liberty, and lumps the biblical text in with John Milton's defence of the 'judicial assassination' (Voltaire's phrase) of Charles I. For his part, poet and politician Milton (1608–74) appealed to Ehud's example precisely to justify the regicide (1651: ch. 4).

Perhaps Samson more than any other judge exemplified the problem. Luther, manoeuvring for the favour of the princes, argues that use of force is the prerogative of rulers following their Christian duty, not individuals furthering their own cause, even if the objective is to punish evil. Samson he concedes to be an exception, allowable because he was acting under God's special grace. 'First become like Samson,' he suggests, 'and then you can also do as Samson did' (1523: 104). Again Milton, parliamentary apologist, takes the other view. Despite the opposition of his countrymen, 'who did not balk at slavery', Samson at Lehi (15:9–19), whether prompted by God or not, took it on himself as a deed of piety to slay, by his own hand, a host of his country's tyrannical masters (1651: ch. 4).

A major dimension of violence in Judges concerns the conduct of war. The Bible has for centuries been used to stake out ground in public affairs, in proposing and defending systems of governance, and in debating the justice of war. One text yielding pertinent lessons was the story of war between Benjamin and the other Israelite tribes (Judg. 20–1) following the rape of the Levite's wife (Judg. 19). Reception of this text is the subject of the remainder of this chapter. My starting-point is a sermon in mid-nineteenth-century London, its context a national fast-day proclaimed for the support of British arms against an insurrection in India. A key issue is what should be the appropriate response to perceived violent outrage. Then I move to some earlier addresses, also designed for national fast-days, this time in the context of the American insurrection which became the War of Independence. Here we see views from both sides, the same text speaking differently depending on which side of the Atlantic the fast-day is observed. Many viewed the American rebellion as a civil war, which is how, too, they read the Benjaminite war. In Britain, civil war, as parliament struggled with the monarchy for power, was what above all marked out the seventeenth century. It was a defining time in the history of British governance, and the story of the Benjaminite war has a place in it. Again the question of proportionate response is at issue. Finally, I look to the period just preceding the civil war, to a remarkable appropriation of this story that reads it in a very different vein from most, finding irony where others have found example.

The final story of Judges runs as follows. The Levite had gone to Bethlehem from the hill country of Ephraim to retrieve his wife, who had run off to her father's house. On the way back home an Ephraimite living in Benjaminite Gibea gave them lodging, but men of the city sought to rape the Levite, who put his woman out for them to assault instead. Finding her dead in the morning, he cut her up into twelve pieces. These bits he sent throughout Israel, demanding that the tribes take action, to which they agreed after hearing him in Mizpah. The Benjaminites, however, refused to give up the culprits. Having consulted the oracle, the Israelites twice went into battle unsuccessfully, with great loss of life, but after penitential fasting and sacrifice, at the third attempt they successfully slaughtered all but 600 Benjaminites. Realizing now that they had nearly exterminated one of their own tribes, and having vowed never to give their daughters in marriage to the Benjaminites, the Israelites sought a solution. First they slaughtered the inhabitants of Jabesh-Gilead for not aiding them, but spared 400 young women to give to the surviving Benjaminites. Then they pressured the men of Shiloh to allow their daughters to be seized from a festival by the remaining 200 Benjaminites. So the problem was solved.

In 1857, on 7 October, the Revd John Baillie preached at All Souls', Langham Place, in London on the insurrection against the British in India that became known (to the British) as the Indian Mutiny (Sugirtharajah 2005: 77–81; the sermon was reported in *The Times*, 8 Oct. 1857, p. 7). Baillie's text was Judges 20:12, where the Israelites send messengers to the tribe of Benjamin after the assault, saying: 'What wickedness is this that is done among you?' The minister was responding to months of lurid (and often unsubstantiated) accounts of violence, including rape, visited upon British civilians in northern India by the rebelling sepoys (Indian soldiers in the British army). Among the gruesome news, no doubt etched into the congregation's consciousness, was the infamous Cawnpore (Kanpur) massacre which ended on 15 July with some 200 European women and children being hacked to pieces and thrown into a well (Sugirtharajah 2005: 60–3; English 1994; Mukherjee 1994; Hibbert 1980). Some were dead, others, it was reported, still dying. No one survived. Another sermon in London, a month earlier, on 'India's Ills and England's Sorrows', conveys the prevailing mood. The preacher was the young C. H. Spurgeon (1834–92), who was to become one of the most popular preachers in Britain:

My brethren, our hearts are sick nigh unto death with the terrible news … our race so cruelly butchered in the land of the East. … Alas! alas, for our brethren there! They have died; alas for them! They have been slain by the sword of treachery. … O England! weep for thy daughters with a bitter lamentation; let thine eyes run down with rivers of blood for them. Had they been crushed within the folds of the hideous boa, or had the fangs of the tiger been red with their blood, happy would their fate have been compared with the indignities they have endured! … God's fairest creatures stained; those loved ones, who could not brook the name of lust, given up to the embraces of incarnate devils! Weep, Britain, weep, weep for thy sons and for thy daughters! (Spurgeon 1857a)

Baillie's sermon was occasioned by Queen Victoria's proclamation that on 7 October, throughout England and Ireland, 'a public day of solemn fast, humiliation, and prayer be observed … so both we and our people may humble ourselves before Almighty God in order to obtain pardon of our sins, and in the most devout and solemn manner send up our prayers and our arms for the restoration of tranquillity [in India]' (Sugirtharajah 2005: 64). Certainly the Revd Baillie was devoutly offering up British arms for divine approval and solemnly seeking vengeance: 'the avenging work must be done—the outraged law of society must be vindicated.' Here he was taking a clear stand in a debate that was raging over Britain's response to the rebellion, fuelled by a clemency resolution from the Governor-General of India, Charles Canning, at the end of July (*The Times* mockingly dubbed him 'Clemency' Canning). The preacher finds the biblical text 'exactly parallel' to 'our own case'. It gave biblical warrant for the exercise of vengeance against the evildoers, even if that meant wiping out all the sepoys (a mainstay of the British army) as the Israelites came close to wiping out the Benjaminites. In the event, Baillie's call was answered. Sugirtharajah sums up the aftermath: 'The retribution was swift and barbaric. The violence unleashed was unimaginable' (2005: 79).

While it is not difficult to understand a thirst for vengeance, there is more to the Revd Baillie's response than this. For one thing, there was the question about what the British were doing in India, which Baillie understandably wants to dismiss (now is not the time for questions, he tells his flock), since it might complicate the issue of responsibility for things going so terribly wrong. Not everyone in Britain was convinced that it should rule India, nor that British rule was without serious faults. Spurgeon himself had acknowledged as much: 'It is for us to-day humbly to confess our crime. The government of India has been a cruel government; it has much for which to appear before the bar of God. Its tortures—if the best evidence is to be believed—have been of the most inhuman kind; God forgive the men who have committed such crimes in the British name.' But Spurgeon, too, had raised the question only to dismiss it: 'But those days are past. May God blot out the sin.' The present concern was the 'cold-hearted cruelty' of others. Nonetheless, behind these dismissals of the question of how British rule was administered lies a larger conviction. God had placed England, another clergyman told his YMCA audience a decade earlier, 'in a position to advance or retard the highest interests of our species, such as a nation never occupied before'. It was a fervent hope, then, that in ages to come people of other lands would refer to the English not as invaders, introducing a foreign yoke, 'but as the benefactors who, bringing the light of truth, cast a radiance on the path of their benighted fathers, by which they discovered first of all the way to God, and then to the arts, laws and institutions of civilization; to the interchanges of friendship, and the endearments of home' (Arthur 1846: 75, 79).

Mixed into the outrage Baillie expresses, therefore, is a deep feeling of betrayal, a shocked sense of the ingratitude of the ruled, intolerable behaviour if civilization (for the sake of the greater population of India) was to prevail (for similar sentiments in imperial New Zealand, see Gunn 1998). A violent response, to the point of extermination, was appropriate. Britain's role as civilizer of the pagan world was at stake. Spurgeon also preached on the appointed fast-day, and he was as convinced as Baillie of where God stood: unlike those 'implacable [pagan] deities' delighting in blood, 'our God delights in mercy, and in the deliverance of Britain from its ills'. Unite in prayer, and the day will come when 'the world shall see what Britain's God has done, and how he has heard her cry' (Spurgeon 1857b). But mercy was for the British, not the rebels.

The idea of the fast-day, to set the nation at right with God and prosper arms, was not new when Victoria proclaimed it, though it had not been invoked in some time. But in the eighteenth century the national fast-day found many an occasion. In July 1775, at the outset of the American rebellion which became the War of Independence, a fast-day was appointed by the Continental Congress—a day set aside for prayers seeking forgiveness and blessing (and 'His smiles on American Councils and arms', as John Adams put it). In his sermon to the Great Valley Baptist Church in Pennsylvania, the minister, David Jones (1736–1820), preached that it was legitimate for Christians to have recourse to war, as a last resort, in defence of freedom against 'absolute slavery and despotism' (*Defensive War in a just*

Cause Sinless, 1775). All would not be easy, he warned. Most likely they would meet with some defeats. '[B]ut even if this should be the case; let us not be discouraged; for so it was with Israel in their first battles with Benjamin, but in the third battle the whole tribe of Benjamin is cut off, save six hundred men.' Three years later Jacob Cushing (1730–1809), minister of the church at Waltham, Massachusetts, preached at the site of the opening skirmish, near Lexington in Massachusetts (*Divine Judgments Upon Tyrants*, 1778). Like Jones, he addressed the issue of just war and again appealed to the war against the Benjaminites as scriptural warrant for the colonists' taking up arms against the king. In particular he dwelt passionately on the atrocity that had triggered the conflict. As the subtitle of his printed sermon has it: '*In commemoration of the Murderous War and Rapine, inhumanely perpetrated, by two brigades of British troops, in that town...*'

It was clear to these colonists that the Judges text advocated forceful response to injustice and atrocity, and that it provided scriptural warrant for the rebellion. On the other side of the Atlantic, however, the Revd John Fletcher (1729–85), Methodist vicar of Madeley in Shropshire and a good friend of evangelist John Wesley, was equally clear that the colonists were in the wrong and God was emphatically not on their side (*The Bible and the Sword*, 1776). Fletcher supports his view with 'a similar case, in which God testified his approbation of a fast connected with a fight; yea, with a bloody civil war'. And so he recounts briefly the story of Judges 19–20, before drawing an analogy: 'Certain sons of Belial, belonging to the city of Boston, beset a ship in the night, overpowered the crew, and feloniously destroyed her rich cargo.' He refers, of course, to the famous 'Boston Tea Party' in December 1773 which came to be seen as a contributing cause of the revolution. In response to the British government imposing taxes (including duties on tea) and then allowing the British East India company to undercut the American tea merchants, a group of colonists, calling themselves the sons of liberty, boarded an East India vessel in Boston harbour, seized her cargo, and destroyed it.

Fletcher elaborates a parallel between the sons of Belial who beset the visitors to Gibea and the sons of Belial who beset the ship in the 'inhospitable harbour of Boston'. In both cases, instead of giving up the culprits to justice, the towns resist lawful authority and, just as the Benjaminites rallied around Gibeah, so the other colonists set themselves against the 'sons of Great Britain' on behalf of Boston, and 'by taking up arms against the king to protect felons, made themselves guilty both of felony and high treason'.

What lesson can be drawn from the parallel? God did not forbid the Israelites from bringing their obstinate brethren to reason by force of arms but gave directions for battle. To be sure there were grievous losses at first, 'But alas! the righteousness of a cause, and the divine approbation, do not always ensure success to those who fight in the cause of virtue' (as Jones, from the other side of the struggle, warned). But then the people wept and fasted before the Lord, and consequent upon that action were the Benjamites delivered into their hand. No doubt the colonists, like the surviving Benjaminites, would come to rue the day they threw in their lot with law-breakers. Even a bloody civil war is better than allowing the mobbing sons of Belial 'to commit with impunity all the crimes which their lust, rapaciousness, and ferocity prompt them to'.

By naming the crime of Boston as one of 'lust, rapaciousness, and ferocity', he brings directly to mind the rapist men of Gibeah and seals the link he is making between the biblical outrage and that of the North American colony. Ferocity, then, would seem an appropriate response. Yet, remarkably, Fletcher does not leave it at this. By degrees the sermon retreats from the sharp dichotomies of good and evil and the claim to God's side. At the heart of the evangelical Methodist's piety was a conviction of the boundless grace of God. The fast, he says, should be not only for 'ourselves, and those who fight our battles', but also, with 'hearts full of forgiving love, and Christian sympathy', for 'our American brethren'.

A contemporary of the Revd Fletcher was Mrs Trimmer (ne Sarah Kirby, 1714–1810), author of *Fabulous Histories*, the first book in English to teach children to be kind to animals, but also well known for her six-volume *Sacred History* (1782–6), written to facilitate the study of scripture in schools and families. Mrs Trimmer moved in well-to-do circles, was acquainted with the queen, and believed that Britain was hugely fortunate in being a well-ordered society undergirded by the Church of England's moderation of religion. She preferred not to talk about the war. When she comes to the end of Judges she clearly finds the text a problem. Her disquiet leads her to read it in a very Anglican 'middle way', avoiding any hint of a present-day application: 'In the war between the Benjamites and the other tribes, great losses were sustained on both sides; neither party had any reason to hope for the protection and assistance of GOD, and they were made instruments of punishment to each other.'

In an aside, we might note that American composer William Billings (1746–1800) also adapted a biblical text, Psalm 137, to the Boston incident. His 'Lamentation over Boston' (1778), written while the British occupied the city, knows that God was on the colonists' side: 'By the Rivers of Watertown we sat down and wept, when we remember'd thee, O Boston. | As for our Friends, Lord God of Heaven, preserve them, defend them, deliver and restore them unto us. | For they that held them in bondage requir'd of them to take up arms against their brethren. Forbid it, Lord. | God forbid! Forbid it Lord, God forbid! That those who have sucked Bostonian Breasts should thirst for American Blood!' (Gillingham 2008: 161–2). Billings sees in the incident the prospect of civil war but refrains from taking his poem towards the violent end of his biblical model—'Happy shall he be, that taketh and dasheth thy little ones against the stones' (Ps. 137:9 AV).

The English Civil War (1642–51) was a struggle over religious and political differences between supporters of Charles I and parliament. It led to the temporary removal of the Church of England as the state church, the execution of the king, and the ascendency of, variously, parliament, the Puritans, Presbyterianism, and Oliver Cromwell, lasting until 1660 when Charles II was restored to the throne. Immediately upon the execution of Charles in 1649 a memoir appeared purporting to come from the king himself and portraying him as a royal martyr (*Eikon Basilike*, 1649). Alarmed at the book's rapidly growing popularity, parliament banned it and commissioned poet and politician John Milton (1608–74) to write a rebuttal justifying the beheading of the king. Milton's book (*Eikonoklastes*, 1649) appeared swiftly but did not match its rival's popularity. Ten years later, on the eve of the monarchy's restoration, the public hangman burned the book. Milton was imprisoned and narrowly escaped execution.

In the memoir Charles charged parliament with acting unduly harshly against the Catholic rebellion in Ireland in 1641, so making the rebellion worse, and deserving a curse such as Jacob called down upon his sons Simeon and Levi (Gen. 49:7) when they slaughtered all the men of Shechem in retaliation for the rape of their sister Dinah (Gen. 34) by Hamor the prince of Shechem (1649: ch. 12). Milton responds that the king seems little concerned for those who had lost fathers, brothers, wives, and children through the Irish rebels' cruelty, and that retaliation is not, as the king supposes, 'unevangelical'.

At issue is whether it is right 'for a Nation by just Warr and execution to slay whole Families of them who so barbarously had slaine whole Families before'. Milton's position, then, is similar to that of John Baillie two centuries later. Ferocity is best matched with ferocity. And like Baillie, Milton's biblical warrant is Judges 19–21: 'Did not all Israel doe as much against the Benjamits for one Rape committed by a few, and defended by the whole Tribe?' He is here drawing on established lines of argument by Puritan writers regarding just war and holy war, going back at least to the previous century to Henry Bullinger's influential sermon 'Of War' (1577). Bullinger (1504–75), whose sermons were required reading for Elizabethan clergy, extends standard Augustinian just-war theory to include the duty of the magistrate 'to make war upon men which are incurable, whom the very judgment of the Lord condemneth and biddeth to kill without pity or mercy'. Bullinger cites the Benjaminites as being such, 'rejecting all justice and equity', and like 'at this day those arrogant and seditious rebels which trouble commonweals and kingdoms . . .'.

Milton later returned to this theme and text, assailing Charles as wholly accountable for the bloodshed and destruction of families during the Civil War. He defends both the restraint of the 'magistrates and people' against the king's provocations and their eventual prosecution of the war, appealing again to Judges 19–21 for support: 'All Israel saw that without much shedding of blood she could not avenge the outrage and murder of the Levite's wife; did they think that for this reason they must hold their peace, avoid civil war however fierce, or allow the death of a single poor woman to go unpunished?' (1651: ch. 5).

That the death of 'a single poor woman' should not go unpunished is hard to gainsay. Milton knows how to win a reader's sympathy. Similarly, Baillie and Spurgeon in the nineteenth century sharpen the focus upon raped and murdered mothers, wives, and daughters, so speaking to every father, husband, and son who knew that his manly role was to protect the weaker sex. Yet there are real differences between the writers. The Victorian preachers enjoyed considerable security and advocated harsh measures to be taken in a distant land. Milton lived in a society constantly in or on the brink of turmoil, where what he advocated could well become the cause of his own demise. Harsh measures were for him a matter of survival—his own and his state's.

Milton lived and wrote in dangerous times. But the seventeenth century saw other ways of reading this biblical story. In 1628, early in Charles I's reign, a young English cleric, Robert Gomersall (1602–c.1646), educated at Oxford, wrote a narrative poem on Judges 19–20 called *The Levite's Revenge*, a work laced with irony that expresses deep aversion to the prospect of civil war.

The narrator recounts the aftermath of the rape, parodying the excesses of political speech, as the messenger to Judah—'Carrying the head of the dismembered corse, | With such a voice which sorrow had made hoarse, | (Lest he should rave too highly)'—at length whips up the crowd, who fall into a great passion. 'Such was the people's fury. They're so hot | That they will punish what we credit not, | And be as speedy as severe...' Some elders, however—'...some | who loathed the bloody accents of the drum'—oppose their rage and urge against a rush to judgement. '"Stay", says one, | "And be advised before you be undone".' The speaker poses the crucial issue of proportionate response by conjuring up the realities of war—rape, destruction, neglect, insecurity, and death: 'We yet have cities proudly situate, | We yet have people: be it not in Fate | That your esteem of both should be so cheap | To wish those carcasses and these on heap.' He confronts—and counters—his critics. He is not 'sin's advocate'; he makes no excuse for the wrongdoers of Gibeah. In addition to the woman's death, sodomy was their crime (and a capital crime in seventeenth century England), for that was their intent.

> But whose intent? O pardon me, there be
> Benjamites spotless of that Infamy.
> Shall these be joined in punishment?

These lines powerfully conjure up the question Abraham asks God, in Genesis 18, of the decision to destroy Sodom (were there no women and children, let alone men, in Sodom 'spotless of that Infamy'?), a question which receives no satisfactory answer. Wistfully, in his own voice, the poet finally imagines another way, when 'Kings might put up their swords, | And every quarrel might conclude in words'.

Gomersall also wrote, in Jacobean drama's dark mode, *The tragedie of Lodovick Sforza, duke of Millan* (1628*b*), republished a few years later with *The Levite's Revenge*. In his dedicatory letter he compares his play to a sermon. 'But is not this to preach? . . . If I make the ambitious see that he climbes but to a fall, the usurper to acknowledge, that blood is but a slippery foundation of power, all men in general to confesse that the most glorious is not the most safe place: is not this to cry downe Ambition and Usurpation?' He explains the book's allegorical frontispiece, showing a wolf enthroned while another mauls a sheep: 'It was when Industry did sleepe | The Wolfe was Tutor to the Sheep | And to amaze a plainer man, | The thief was made the guardian' (Foakes 1985: 167–8). The genre harks back to Thomas Kyd's *The Spanish Tragedie* (published 1592), Thomas Middleton's *Revenger's Tragedie* (1607), and John Webster's *The Duchess of Malfi* (1614; published 1623). The plays explore a macabre world of corruption and moral ambiguity, where revenge entails excess and horror piles on horror. Gomersall, therefore, was well versed in the satiric and the cynical. But in both *Lovovick Sforza* and *The Levite's Revenge* he strives to find a moral order in a deeply unsettled world.

Jacobean drama is not the only clue to the cultural context of Gomersall's interpretation. As a young poet and clergyman, he almost certainly delved into the works of another clergyman with a reputation for his verse as well as his distinctive exposition of the history books of the Old Testament, Judges included. Joseph Hall (1574–1656), a moderate Calvinist, was chaplain to James I and tutored Prince Henry, who died young. He later became bishop of Exeter and then Norwich, and in turn an object of parliament's attacks on the bishops (and was imprisoned in the Tower), finally being evicted from his bishopric. A fine pulpit orator, in earlier years his satiric verse was among the first in English (*Vergidemiarum*, 1597–8) and he introduced the satiric 'character' into English prose, for which he earned Milton's scorn years later. His *Contemplations upon the Principall Passages of the Holy History* were published early in the seventeenth century (from 1612 to 1626, with Judges in 1615), and much consulted throughout that century and the next. Hall reads his Bible with a keen eye for narrative detail and drama, shrewdly construing motives and imaginatively supplying his biblical characters with explanatory speech and interior monologue. As a writer of satiric verse, he has a sharp eye for the dissembler or self-deceiver and the ironic possibilities of his biblical texts. And, for his times, he is a sympathetic reader, often willing to accommodate the foibles of the human cast of his biblical histories. Judges provides him ample opportunities (Gunn 2005).

Hall responds more conventionally than Gomersall to the bizarre twists of Judges 19–20. He sets up, however, an ironic tone at the outset as he delves into the characters' motives. Understanding that the woman had 'played the whore' (so KJV) against her husband, Hall as narrator wonders at her father's readiness to receive her home. Why, he asks, did the father not say: 'What? Doest thou thinke to find my house an harbor for thy sinne? Whiles thou wert a wife to thine husband, thou wert a daughter to me; Now thou art neither; . . . I had rather be a just man, than a kind Father; Get thee home therefore to thy husband, crave his forgivenesse upon thy knees, redeeme his love with thy modesty and obedience; when his heart is once open to thee, my doores shall not be shut.' Switching back to his own voice, Hall declares the moral underlying the speech-not-said: 'Indulgence of Parents is the refuge of vanity, the bawd of wickednesse, the bane of children.' But if the father took another path, so too did the injured Levite: 'What husband would not have said, She is gone, let shame and griefe goe with her . . . ?' But this the Levite does not say; instead he goes to bring her back. Hall again epitomizes this alternative motivation: 'Love procures truer servitude than necessity: Mercy becomes well the heart of any man, but most of a Levite. He that had helped to offer so many sacrifices to God for the multitude of every Israelites sins, saw how proportionable it was, that man should not hold one sin unpardonable.'

In short, as Hall begins to contemplate the text he invites his reader to seek alternative perspectives. Gomersall does so radically. A century later another writer with a gift for satire and an eye for human fallibility certainly borrowed inspiration (and more) from Hall. Novelist and clergyman Laurence Sterne (1713–68), famous for *Tristram Shandy* and his innovative narratorial style, was also a popular preacher. Among several expositions of Old Testament narratives in his *Sermons of Mr Yorick* (1766) is 'The Levite and his Concubine', on Judges 19–20. Sterne's sermon opens with storytelling that rapidly becomes a complex dialogue of inter-secting and interjecting voices or perspectives (Prickett 1996: 123–4). To the reader of Hall's *Contemplations*, however, the voices, perspectives, and style are familiar. The preacher has been enjoying the good bishop's reception of the same story (Gunn 2006). In tune with the times, where wit trumped moralizing, Sterne wears his morality more lightly on his sleeve than Hall. His narratorial style is perhaps more flexible and his irony more comic. But both preachers shared a gift for satire and took pleasure in idiosyncrasy. Both saw ambiguities in their biblical story. Yet neither saw what the young Jacobean poet saw—deep darkness at the story's heart.

In Judges 19–20 Gomersall read a text that satirizes prejudice and excess, self-serving and self-defeating piety and politics. His text is a guide, if guide at all, as to what *not* to do. Only in recent years, influenced by literary theory, feminist criticism, deconstruc-tion, and a century of catastrophic wars and attempted exterminations, have readers ventured, like Gomersall, to read this text of rape and war with a jaundiced eye. Most other uses, whether of Milton, Fletcher, or Baillie, read a text that maps civil behaviour. Milton, perhaps because of what he needs politically from this text, reads it in literal-historical fashion as a straightforward account of what happened, and so uses it as a template, a guide for action in a similar situation. This has been the predominant way Protestants have read narrative texts since the Reformation.

Gomersall is unusual in reading for irony. Voltaire—a serious critic of his culture—is unusual in reading to discredit the texts. One of the obvious things in common among our users is that they assume that the Bible carries authority for most of their audience or readership. Jael is a problem not simply because she treacherously kills a man—Lady Macbeth does as much—but because the text appears to bestow divine approval on her and the culture takes for granted the text's divine authority. Milton, Fletcher, and Baillie are intent on matching their take on the text to the contemporary political scene, because they understand that the Bible is a religious and cultural classic that lends weight to their arguments and seals them with divine approval. In other words, in these social contexts biblical authority underwrites the Bible's value as cultural currency.

Because Judges is a narrative book, most interpreters intent on making some application to their own times must abstract from the plot, characters, or dialogue some principle which will bridge the ancient text and the present-day situation, course of action, or moral choice. There is much room for slippage here and interpretations are bound to vary, even when the interpreters keep looking to an expositional tradition for guidance. This process of finding meanings to use also involves crucial choices of other biblical texts, like Hebrews 11, to help control those meanings. And a narrative text, especially told in such sparse style, always offers gaps to filled, such as why Jael killed Sisera or the Levite butchered his concubine or God allowed the slaughter of many Israelites before granting them victory. Usually interpreters find textual pegs (so to speak) upon which to hang their imagination. Although Gomersall apparently invents the elderly nay-sayer's plea for restraint, the speaker's description of the war's outcome—rape, pillage, death, and destroyed cities—could just as well summarize the biblical text's account of what follows in the war with Benjamin. The poet has read that outcome back into the call for peace. But textual clues for filling gaps will also vary according to the eye of the beholder.

Predominantly, of course, as I hope I have indicated in this brief exploration, the social locations and contingent purposes of our interpreters have left a large mark on how they have read, what interpretations they have produced, and to what purposes they have put their productions. If reception history has one particular value useful to me today it is its ability to demonstrate empirically that the meanings of scripture are, as they have been through the centuries, in the hands of its readers. Living and working, as I do, in the southern Bible Belt of the United States, I judge that to be no mean use.

Works Cited

ARTHUR, THE REVD W. (1846), 'The Extent and Moral Statistics of the British Empire'. *Exeter Hall Lectures: 1845–46.* London.

BULLINGER, HENRY [JOHANN HEINRICH] (1578), *Fiftie godlie and learned sermons, diuided into five decades conteyning the chiefe and principall pointes of Christian Religion. Translated out of Latine into English, by H.I. student in diuinitie.* London (1577).

[Charles I] (1649), *Eikon basilike, the pourtraicture of His Sacred Maiestie in his solitudes and sufferings.* London. [Perhaps 'ghosted' by the kings's chaplain, John Gouden.]

CUSHING, JACOB (1778), *Divine Judgments Upon Tyrants: And Compassion To The Oppressed: A Sermon Preached at Lexington, April 20th, 1778*. Boston.

ENGLISH, BARBARA (1994), 'The Kanpur Massacres in India in the Revolt of 1857', *Past and Present*, 142: 169–78.

FLETCHER, JOHN (1776). *The Bible and the Sword: or, The Appointment of the General Fast vindicated: In an Address to the Common People concerning the propriety of repressing obstinate licentiousness with the sword, and of fasting when the sword is drawn for that purpose*. London. In Ellis Sandoz (ed.), *Political Sermons of the American Founding Era: 1730–1805*, 559–78. Indianapolis: Liberty.

FOAKES, R. A. (1985), *Illustrations of the English stage, 1580–1642*. Stanford: Stanford University Press.

GIBBON, JOHN (1661), 'How May We Be So Spiritual, as to Check Sin in the First Rising of It?', in James Nichols (ed.), *Puritan Sermons 1659–1689*, vol. 1, sermon V, pp. 87–111. Wheaton, Ill.: Richard Owen Roberts, 1981.

GILLINGHAM, SUSAN (2008), *Psalms Through the Centuries*, vol. 1. Blackwell Bible Commentaries. Oxford: Blackwell Publishing.

GOMERSALL, ROBERT (1628*a*), *The Levite's Revenge: Containing Poetical Meditations upon the 19. and 20. Chapters of Judges*, in *Poems* (1633). London.

——(1628*b*), *The Tragedie of Lodovick Sforza, duke of Millan*, in *Poems* (1633). London.

GUNN, DAVID M. (1998), 'Colonialism and the Vagaries of Scripture: Te Kooti in Canaan (A Story of Bible and Dispossession in Aotearoa/New Zealand)', in Tod Linafelt and Timothy K. Beal (eds.), *God in the Fray: A Tribute to Walter Brueggemann*. 127–42. Minneapolis: Fortress Press.

——(2003), '"Lawless Riot and Intestine Division": Judges 19–21 and Civil War in England and North America, 1628–1786', in J. Cheryl Exum and H. G. M. Williamson (eds.), *Reading from Right to Left: Essays on the Hebrew Bible in Honour of David J. A. Clines*, 216–28. London and New York: T. & T. Clark.

——(2005), *Judges*. Blackwell Bible Commentaries. Oxford: Blackwell Publishing.

——(2006), 'The "Good Commentator": On Joseph Hall, Laurence Sterne, Biblical Narrative and the Eighteenth-Century Novel', in Wesley Bergen and Armin Siedlecki (eds.), *Voyages in Uncharted Waters: Essays on the Theory and Practice of Biblical Interpretation in Honor of David Jobling*, 96–109. Sheffield: Phoenix.

HALL, JOSEPH (1615), *Contemplations upon the Principall Passages of the Holie History, The Third Volume*, in *The Works of Joseph Hall B. of Exceter*. London, 1634.

HIBBERT, CHRISTOPHER (1980), *The Great Mutiny: India 1857*, chs. 9–10. Harmondsworth: Penguin Books.

JONES, DAVID (1775), *Defensive War in a Just Cause Sinless: A Sermon Preached On the Day of the Continental Fast*. Philadelphia.

LUTHER, MARTIN (1523), *Temporal Authority: to What Extent it Should be Obeyed*, in Walter I. Brandt (ed.), *The Christian in Society*, II [45], 75–129. Philadelphia: Muhlenberg.

MILTON, JOHN (1649), *Eikonoklastes, in Answer To a Book Intitl'd* Eikon Basilike . . . London.

——(1651), *A Defence of the People of England* [*Pro populo anglicano defensio*, 2nd edn.], in *Complete Prose Works of John Milton*, 4. 285–537. New Haven: Yale University Press.

MUKHERJEE, RUDRANGSHU (1994), 'The Kanpur Massacres in India in the Revolt of 1857: Reply', *Past and Present*, 142: 169–78.

PRICKETT, STEPHEN (1996), *Origins of Narrative: The Romantic Appropriation of the Bible*. Cambridge: Cambridge University Press.

SPURGEON, C. H. (1857*a*), 'A Sermon delivered on Sabbath Morning, September 6, 1857 . . . at the Music Hall, Royal Surrey Gardens', in *The New Park Street Pulpit*, no. 150, www. spurgeon.org/sermons/0150.htm.

——(1857*b*), 'Fast-Day Service held at the Crystal Palace, Sydenham, on Wednesday, October 7th, 1857', in *The New Park Street Pulpit*, nos. 154–5, www.spurgeon.org/sermons/0154.htm.

STERNE, LAURENCE (1766/1966), 'The Levite and his Concubine', in *Sermons of Mr Yorick*, III.3 [18], in Melvin New (ed.), *The Sermons of Laurence Sterne*, 4. 167–76. Gainsville, Fla.: University Press of Florida.

SUGIRTHARAJAH, S. R. (2005), 'Salvos from the Victorian Pulpit', in *The Bible and Empire: Postcolonial Explorations*, 60–97. Cambridge: Cambridge University Press.

Voltaire [Arouet, François-Marie] (1764). *Philosophical Dictionary: A–I*, trans. Peter Gay. New York: Basic Books, 1962.

FURTHER READING

The material in this chapter is drawn in part from previous work (Gunn 2003, 2006) where further data and discussion may be found. R. S. Sugirtharajah's book *The Bible and Empire* (2005), which pointed me to Baillie's sermon, offers a much richer account of the Indian rebellion and explores other fascinating uses of the Bible in empire. The volume on Judges in the Blackwell Bible Commentaries series (Gunn 2005) is an extensive survey of the reception history of the whole book. *Judges and Method* (2nd edn. 2007), edited by Gale Yee, looks at new approaches to the Book of Judges, including a reception-history study of Jephthah's daughter in Bible illustration. For late-twentieth-century shifts in understanding Judges 19–21, see Stuart Lasine, 'Guest and Host in Judges 19', *Journal for the Study of the Old Testament*, 30 (1984), 37–59; Phyllis Trible, *Texts of Terror: Literary-Feminist Readings of Biblical Narratives* (1984); Barry Webb, *The Book of Judges: An Integrated Reading* (1987); Mieke Bal, *Death and Dissymmetry: The Politics of Coherence in the Book of Judges* (1988); Lillian Klein, *The Triumph of Irony in the Book of Judges* (1989); Danna Nolan Fewell, 'Judges', in Carol Newsom and Sharon Ringe (eds.), *The Women's Bible Commentary* (1988); and Cheryl Exum, *Fragmented Women: Feminist (Sub)versions of Biblical Narratives* (1993).

CHAPTER 8

THE GOSPEL OF JOHN

CATRIN H. WILLIAMS

IF the significance or impact of a text could be measured by the variety of memorable designations attributed to it by subsequent interpreters, the Gospel of John would, simply on this basis alone, be granted pride of place among the New Testament writings. The distinctiveness of John's style and content, especially when compared to the other three canonical Gospels, has given rise to a number of striking epithets, from the widely quoted 'spiritual Gospel' coined by Clement of Alexandria (c.155–220 CE, cited in Eusebius, *Historia Ecclesiastica* 6.14.7) to its popular description, eighteen centuries later, as 'the maverick Gospel' (Kysar 2007). Its designation as a 'Gospel of surprises' (Lindars 1990: 9), though less well known, is particularly apt, because it captures the fact that, in John's Gospel, things are rarely as they first appear. Although the simplicity of its language may initially give the impression that this is a relatively straightforward text, bubbling under the surface is a profound message clothed in evocative symbols that open up all kinds of interpretative possibilities.

Many of the surprising elements in John's Gospel are, inevitably, also puzzles. In a text that supplies its readers and hearers with several aids to secure comprehension, how can it, at the same time, incorporate so many complex and ambiguous features? No other New Testament text displays such fondness for the repetition of its key themes, as well as for explanatory comments like translations of Hebrew and Aramaic words (e.g. 1:38, 42; 4:25; 9:7) and guiding notes on customs (2:6; 4:9) and characters (e.g. 3:1; 7:5; 19:38). Yet, as literary approaches to John's Gospel have particularly highlighted (Culpepper 1983; Thatcher 2000), its symbolic language and deliberate play on the literal and figurative meanings of words (e.g. 3:3–5; 4:10–11; 8:21–2), though sometimes explained for the benefit of readers/hearers (e.g. 2:21–2; 7:39; 12:33), project the image of Jesus as a 'stranger from heaven' (de Jonge 1977) whose riddles lead, certainly for his dialogue partners within the text, to confusion rather than clarification. And if the Gospel's (sometimes rather basic) interpretative asides presuppose a broad audience from a variety of cultural backgrounds, how can this be reconciled with its sophisticated, often deeply allusive, interaction with the practices, expectations and, not least, the scriptural heritage of first-century Judaism? Perhaps one of the greatest surprises is that the Gospel, for all its theological subtlety and literary sophistication, contains many unexpected breaks or tensions ('aporias'). In what is largely a carefully crafted text, a clear awkwardness can be detected at various points in the narrative. Thus, for example, although Jesus' words, 'Rise, let us be on our way' (14:31), suggest that they signal the ending of his farewell speech to the disciples, the discourse continues for a further three chapters. Similarly, after apparently ending the Gospel with a succinct statement of its purpose (20:30–1), another resurrection narrative is appended in chapter 21.

As far as the awkward tensions are concerned, the most plausible solution is that they are textual indicators that the Gospel was not composed in one sitting, but, over a period of time, underwent different stages of composition and revision, including the addition of new material like chapters 15–17 and 21 (see Ashton 2007: 42–53). The function of John's symbolic language has become the subject of more vigorous debate. Some propose that it represents a 'closed system of metaphors' in a book originally intended for insiders (Meeks 1972: 68–9), while those who view the Gospel's doors as left open for outsiders, at least to those who were already Christian believers, highlight the didactic role of its special language (Phillips 2006: 57–71; cf. Bauckham 2001). Whether the Gospel was initially aimed at those within or also at those outside the Johannine community, there is no doubt that a number of its wordplays, riddles, and use of irony belong to a communicative strategy designed to enable readers/hearers to gain a fuller understanding of John's message. Furthermore, while the many explanations included in the text are intended as tools to assist comprehension, they also reflect the author's awareness of the various levels at which the message could be grasped by a culturally diverse audience. What seems certain, and will underpin much of the discussion in this chapter, is that the roots of John's Gospel belong firmly within the traditions of Judaism, and that one of its primary aims is to offer what it regards as the definitive interpretation of the relationship of Jesus to Jewish beliefs and practices.

This selection of surprises merely scratches the surface of the puzzles posed by John's Gospel, but it does offer some clues as to why this most fascinating, and enigmatic, of biblical texts has engaged the attention of readers and hearers down the centuries and, as a result, has enjoyed such a rich history of interpretation.

THE SHAPE OF JOHN'S NARRATIVE

The text of John's Gospel, in its present form, can be divided into two main parts framed by a prologue (1:1–18) and an epilogue (21:1–25). The first major section depicts the public ministry of Jesus (1:19–12:50) and the second contains Jesus' Farewell Discourse to his disciples and an account of his death and resurrection (13:1–20:31). Although several themes appear in different configurations throughout the text, the structural divisions reveal a close alignment between the order of various episodes and the distribution of key themes and motifs, some of which will be examined in later sections of this chapter.

Mapping out its content and structure also throws into sharp relief the major differences, and also some noteworthy points of contact, between John and the other three canonical (Synoptic) Gospels. Even though John's narrative stands firmly apart from the others in terms of vocabulary, style, and much of its content, the resemblances between their narrative outlines of Jesus' ministry, death, and resurrection cannot be denied. The dominant view during the second half of the twentieth century was that links between John and the Synoptics pointed to their use of a common pool of oral tradition. However, a growing number of scholars now favour some form of dependence by John on the Synoptic Gospels, particularly on Mark, given the striking similarities between the order and content of some Johannine passages and those in Mark that also attest the author's redactional activity (e.g. John 6:1–71 and Mark 6:30–9:1; cf. Mackay 2004). Due to an increasing emphasis on the highly oral/aural environment in which John's Gospel was composed (cf. Dewey 2001), the debate about the precise nature of the 'use' of existing texts is now entering a new phase, because John's familiarity with Mark may not be due to reliance on a written version of the text but through its oral performance(s) and subsequent recollection from memory.

That John significantly parts company from the Synoptic Gospels, and had access to a wealth of other material, becomes evident in his prologue of celebration to the eternal Word who becomes incarnate in the historical figure of Jesus of Nazareth (1:1–18). His origins are set against a cosmic stage, 'in the beginning' (1:1), as preparation for his depiction as the agent of creation (1:3) in whom there is life and light (1:4–5). The themes of conflict and ignorance (1:5, 10) anticipate the division between those who reject the mission of the Word and those who, through belief in him, become children of God (1:11–13). The theme of revelation dominates the final part of the prologue, because Jesus, as the embodiment of the divine Word, both manifests his glory (1:14) and, as Son, makes known the invisible God (1:18). Even if the prologue was added during the later stages of the Gospel's composition, its focus on revelation and division offers a gateway to what, from a literary and theological perspective, will become the central themes of the narrative.

The selection of miraculous works or 'signs' and lengthy discourses and dialogues that make up the Johannine account of Jesus' public ministry (1:19–12:50) all serve to disclose his identity, his relationship with the Father, and the life-giving purposes of his mission. It begins with a second introduction which places Jesus firmly on the historical stage (1:19–51), and, through the testimony of John the Baptist and the responses of the first disciples, presents him as the fulfilment of Jewish expectations. Seeking and finding Jesus are familiar motifs in these initial encounters (cf. 1:38, 39, 41, 45, 46), while quests for Jesus and his work continue to dominate his ministry 'from Cana to Cana' (2:1–4:54; cf. Painter 1991: 129–73). The response to Jesus by initiators of these quests ranges from confusion to varying levels of recognition, but he encounters little open hostility during these early stages of his earthly mission.

A marked change of tone occurs from chapter 5 onwards. Jesus' ministry causes division (7:43; 9:16; 10:19), and he engages in a series of bitter disputes with opponents described as 'the Jews' or Pharisees (5:16–18; 7:14–24; 8:12–59; 10:22–39). These scenes of confrontation depict Jesus as a defendant on trial (Lincoln 2000), whose testimony is rejected by those accusing him of breaking the law (e.g. 5:16; 8:13; 9:16) and of blasphemy (8:59; 10:33). Their attempts to arrest and even kill Jesus fail at this point (cf. 8:59; 10:39), because the time for him to die has not yet arrived. Nevertheless, Jesus' raising of Lazarus (11:1–44) initiates rapid movement towards the hour of his departure (cf. 11:45–53), with the narrative recording numerous episodes which anticipate his death (12:1–26) before reflecting on the unbelief encountered by Jesus during his ministry (12:37–40).

Having withdrawn with 'his own', Jesus prepares his disciples, through instruction and prayer, for the future after his departure to the Father (13:1–17:26). The act of foot-washing (13:3–20) illustrates his commandment that, by following his example (13:12–18; 15:13–14), the disciples are to love one another (13:34–5; cf. 14:15; 15:12). They are reassured that Jesus will not leave them as orphans (14:18); by departing to his Father, he will prepare a place for them (14:2–3) and will come and abide with them (e.g. 14:18–20; 16:16–22) in a relationship characterized by unity and mutual love (cf. 15:1–11, 12–17). Jesus promises the sending of the Spirit, 'the Paraclete', who will guide the disciples to the truth (16:13) and disclose the sin of unbelief (16:8–9). In the prayer that brings the Farewell Discourse to a close, Jesus announces the completion of his mission (17:1–5, 6–8), and, with the aid of the now familiar themes of unity, love and glory, sets out his requests on behalf of present and future believers (17:9–19, 20–6).

While the passion narrative (18:1–19:42) largely follows the order of the Synoptic accounts, many of its distinctive features crystallize in narrative form the Gospel's earlier interpretative expressions of Jesus' death. It fulfils his prediction that he will be lifted up so that whoever believes in him will receive eternal life (3:14; cf. 8:28; 12:32–4), a 'lifting up' that connotes both his physical elevation on the cross and his exaltation. Jesus' death as exaltation, and glorification (12:23; 13:31–2), accounts, to a large degree, for the fact that the passion narrative does not focus on suffering but, with much dramatic irony, on Jesus' kingship (18:33–7; 19:2–5, 14–15, 19–22) and control over events (18:4–8; 19:17, 25–7; cf. 10:17–18). Jesus' final cry on the cross, 'It is completed' (19:30), encapsulates his death as the fulfilment of his mission to reveal the Father and accomplish his work (cf. 4:34; 18:11).

Jesus' death undoubtedly occupies a central place in John's understanding of revelation and salvation, although the resurrection narrative (20:1–29) proves, in many respects, to be the culmination of John's Gospel. Jesus' hour of glorification, whereby he returns to the Father, involves not only his death, but also his resurrection and ascension (cf. 7:39; 12:16). The importance of faith in, and recognition of, the risen Jesus is emphasized in a series of scenes, while his bestowal of the life-giving Spirit (20:22) serves to affirm the truth of his claim that he possesses and mediates life (cf. 5:24–5, 26; 11:25). It therefore comes as no surprise that the themes of life and (in all likelihood the strengthening of already existing) faith feature as integral components of the Gospel's statement of purpose: 'These [signs] are written so that you may believe that Jesus is the Messiah, the Son of God, and that through believing you may have life in his name' (20:31). John's narrative, in its present form, continues with a chapter recounting how the appearance of the risen Jesus in Galilee leads to a miraculous catch of fish (21:1–14) and to a dialogue clarifying the roles of Peter and the Beloved Disciple (21:15–24).

JESUS' MISSION IN THE WORLD: CONTRASTS AND CONFLICT

If the mapping out of John's narrative helps to clarify its shape and content, examining the sequence of events, and the connection between them, reveals that the central element of its plot is Jesus' mission to/in the world. This is evident from the many mission statements and the prominence of 'sending' language in the text, which, as we shall see, is a key component of Johannine christology. How the plot unfolds can be described in several ways (cf. Culpepper 1995; Stibbe 1994: 32–53), but setting out its development according to the three-stage movement of com-mission, complication, and resolution (Lincoln 2000: 17–19, 159–66) ensures that due attention is given to the purpose and outcome of Jesus' mission, and to the conflict encountered by him during his ministry. The 'commission' involves the sending of Jesus into the world to carry out the tasks of revealing God (1:18; 17:6, 26), bringing life (3:16; 10:10) and light (8:12; 12:46), bearing witness to the truth (18:37), and bringing judgement (5:22; 8:16). The theme of conflict ('complication') is concretized in the opposition to Jesus from his human adversaries and from

Satan, while the 'resolution' of the plot is effected by Jesus' death, bringing about
the accomplishment of his work, including the judgement of those who reject him
(cf. 19:11) and the overthrow of 'the ruler of this world' (12:31; 14:30; 16:11).

Integrally related to the plot of John's story is the underpinning of its worldview
by the belief in two essentially different realities, with the result that the account of
Jesus' mission is permeated by a language of contrasts: life and death, light and
darkness, heaven and earth, above and below, truth and lies. Of decisive importance is John's use of the term 'world' (*kosmos*) in spatial-vertical terms to distinguish between the heavenly reality ('above') and the earthly reality ('below'). Jesus
says to 'the Jews': 'You are from below, I am from above; you are of this world, I am
not of this world' (8:23; cf. 18:36). Because the world below, inhabited by human
beings, is under the power of the devil ('the ruler of this world'), it becomes a
symbol of alienation from God. However, John does not embrace an absolute form
of 'spatial' dualism, because God's initiative through Jesus seeks to bridge the gap
between these different spheres of existence (Smith 1995: 81; cf. Barrett 1982: 106–14:
'dualism in motion'). By his descent from heaven (cf. 3:13, 31), Jesus offers revelation and salvation to the world, the object of God's love (3:16–17).

In addition, John employs the term 'world' to express the opposition to Jesus,
which, in horizontal terms, takes place on earth (1:10: 'the world did not know
him'; cf. 7:7; 15:18). It reflects a form of ethical dualism that centres on the
importance of human decision. Those who believe in Jesus are assured life (5:24;
6:35) and light (3:21; 12:36), but those who reject him remain enslaved to a world
dominated by darkness (1:5; 12:46), sin (8:21, 34), and death (8:24). This division is
directly linked to the Johannine theme of judgement (*krisis*). Although 'judgement'
terminology sometimes possesses the negative connotation of condemnation (3:17,
18; 12:47), particularly to express the consequences of rejecting Jesus, it primarily
denotes the process of separation, and relates closely to Jesus as 'the light of the
world' (8:12; 9:5) who exposes believers and unbelievers, depending on whether or
not they see the light (cf. 9:39). Judgement, therefore, is already at work in Jesus'
earthly ministry; in his many confrontations with opponents (e.g. 5:1–47; 8:12–59;
10:22–39) and trials before the Jewish and Roman authorities (18:19–24; 18:28–
19:16), earthly categories are turned on their head because Jesus' accusers in fact
bring judgement upon themselves.

A particularly difficult interpretative issue is the fact that, more often than not,
those who accuse Jesus and vehemently oppose him during his ministry are
described as 'the Jews' (*hoi Ioudaioi*). Whereas the Synoptic Gospels tend to
concentrate more on individual Jewish groups, especially the Pharisees and the
Sadducees, as the chief opponents of Jesus, John's Gospel singles out 'the Jews' as a
hostile force seeking to kill Jesus (cf. 5:18; 8:40; 10:31). In line with its dualistic
outlook, it characterizes them as being 'of this world' (8:23), 'not from God' (8:47),
and, because of their unbelief, accuses them of being children of the devil (8:44).
The profound hermeneutical challenges posed by John's negative depiction of

'the Jews' have long been recognized (most recently by Motyer 2008; Lieu 2008), because, although the Gospel 'may not itself be anti-Semitic, it has given aid and comfort to anti-Semites' (Smith 1995: 169). John's use of the designation *hoi Ioudaioi* is, in fact, complex and varied; characters who are themselves Jewish are at times distinguished from 'the Jews' (e.g. 1:19; 3:25; 9:22), and some 'Jews' are more sympathetic than antagonistic towards Jesus (cf. 10:21; 11:45; 12:9). Consequently, attempts have been made to equate the hostile *hoi Ioudaioi* with the religious authorities or, alternatively, with the inhabitants of Judea. Neither proposal can account for all the evidence (cf. 11:45–6 and 6:41, 52), unless, in the case of the latter proposal, there is some loosening of the geographical focus so that *hoi Ioudaioi* denotes a distinct religious group with adherents both within and outside Judea (cf. Boyarin 2002). The religious nature and intensity of the disputes between Jesus and 'the Jews' are, in fact, widely held to shed light on the historical circumstances from which John's Gospel emerged, belonging to what has been described as its 'two-level drama' depicting both the story of Jesus and the situation of the evangelist and his group (Martyn 1968). Its portrayal of 'the Jews' may, then, have developed in the context of a conflict with a local Jewish community, whose rejection of Jesus as the messiah led to the expulsion of the Johannine Christians from the synagogue (cf. 9:22; 12:42; 16:2). Reconstructing John's social location can help to explain, but does not remove, the text's hostility towards 'the Jews', although it may offer some valuable insights into the strategies used by the Johannine side to define themselves over against a group with whom they shared a common Jewish heritage, but with whom there was profound disagreement about the significance of Jesus in relation to that heritage.

SYMBOLS, SIGNS, AND JESUS' OFFER OF LIFE

If judgement results in the condemnation of those who reject Jesus' revelation, those who believe in him are rewarded with 'eternal life' (*zōē aiōnios*). This phrase stems from the Jewish concept of 'the life of the age to come' (cf. LXX Dan. 12:2), but it is used by John to denote a present eschatological reality. The offer of life, like the process of judgement, has definitively taken place in Jesus, who is 'the resurrection and the life' (11:25; cf. 3:36; 14:6). As Jesus shares God's prerogative of giving life (5:21), those who believe in him have *already* passed from death to life (5:24), even though, in a few passages, the more traditional belief in a future resurrection is also affirmed (cf. 5:28–9; 6:39–40). The emphasis is not upon the long duration of the 'life' that death cannot touch, but upon its particular quality and intrinsic difference from physical/material life. This is the life that Jesus himself, like God, possesses (5:26; 6:57; cf. 1:4), and believers, through new birth (1:12–13; 3:3, 5), can participate in this life by entering into a relationship of intimate communion with the Father and the Son (17:3).

The centrality of the concept of 'life' in John's Gospel is further confirmed by the use of Jesus' words and actions as vehicles to express his life-giving purposes. This, for example, is what binds together the memorable metaphorical 'I am' statements, for the claims made with the aid of images like bread (6:35), light (8:12; 9:5), and vine (15:1, 5) convey various aspects of Jesus' role as the giver of life. As with the offer of 'living water' (4:10), a number of the 'I am' declarations draw on earthly images to symbolize the life 'from above', a function sometimes misunderstood by characters within the text (e.g. 4:10; 6:32–42). In this respect, the seven carefully selected signs recounted in the first half of the narrative (2:1–11; 4:46–54; 5:1–18; 6:1–15; 6:16–21; 9:1–41; 11:1–53) can be categorized as 'symbolic actions' (Koester 2003: 79–140). As miraculous deeds, they operate on the material level and centre on tangible realities (Jesus changes water into wine, heals an official's son, heals a lame man, feeds a crowd with bread, walks on water, gives sight to a blind man, raises Lazarus from the dead), but, as signs, they point beyond themselves to Jesus' true identity and, in particular, to his role as the one who bestows eternal life. Thus, in the first sign, the abundance of wine symbolizes the new life offered by Jesus (cf. 10:10; Isa. 25:6–9; Amos 9:13; Sira 31:27), as does the scripturally evocative depiction of the disciples reaching the other side of the sea upon 'receiving' Jesus (6:21; cf. Williams 2000: 225–8). In the case of the other signs, readers/hearers are directed to Jesus' life-giving significance by subtle 'signifiers' within the narrative (cf. 4:50, 53–4; 9:39; 11:25–6) or through a subsequent discourse (5:19–29; 6:25–65). The connection with Jesus' bestowal of eschatological life is most fully explicated in the seventh, and most significant, of the Johannine signs, because the raising of Lazarus to physical life serves as a symbolic enactment of Jesus' claim to be 'the resurrection and the life' (11:25) and as a concrete manifestation of his earlier promise that 'the hour is coming, *and is now here*, when the dead will hear the voice of the Son of God, and those who hear will live' (5:25; cf. 11:38–44).

JESUS, THE HEAVENLY EMISSARY
AND SON OF GOD

Life, according to John's (original) conclusion, is the consequence of belief in Jesus as 'the Messiah, the Son of God' (20:31). Both of these titles feature prominently in confessions and disputes about Jesus' identity (e.g. 1:41, 49; 7:41–2; 10:24; 11:27; 19:7), but, in this final summary statement, their function as the content of Johannine belief cannot be appreciated in isolation from the christological portrayal that unfolds in kaleidoscopic form within the Gospel. Underpinning this statement is an exalted christology which introduces new dimensions of meaning to the titles 'Messiah' and 'Son of God', and offers a presentation of Jesus that cannot be contained in these two titles. From beginning to end, in narratives and discourses, and in a manner unparalleled in the Synoptic Gospels, the focus of John's Gospel is its intricately woven claims about Jesus' heavenly origin, his relationship with the Father, and his sending as Son to make God known in the world.

Its christological agenda is unequivocally set out in the prologue (1:1–18), whose identification of Jesus with the eternal Word (*logos*) provides readers/hearers with a vantage-point from which to view the ensuing narrative. To state that the Word was 'in the beginning' with God (1:1) amounts to a declaration of timeless existence, one to which Jesus also lays claim during his earthly ministry (cf. 8:58; 17:5). In addition, the first verse seeks to express the relationship between the Word and God ('the Word was with God'), followed by a declaration, 'the Word was God', whose precise meaning continues to be debated due to the subtleties of the Greek text. It neither claims that the Word is 'divine' nor that he is a second god, but it does affirm that the Word is to be identified with God (*theos*) at the same time as maintaining his separate identity ('with God'). It is significant that Jesus is also called *theos* in 1:18 (if one accepts the reading 'the only-begotten, God') and in the confession made by Thomas, 'My Lord and my God' (20:28). Thus, although *theos* is not a title claimed by the earthly Jesus, its attribution to him at these two key points in the Gospel expresses the conviction that he is the definitive revelation of God. As the vehicle of God's disclosure in the world, the Word becomes flesh and reveals his glory (1:14). And since 'no one has ever seen God' (1:18; cf. Exod. 33:20), the revelation mediated by the Son is superior to that received in the past by figures like Moses (1:17), because only the Son is in direct and personal communion with the Father. It is through the Son, in his own person, that humankind receives the authentic revelation of light and life (1:4–5), grace and truth (1:14, 16) and the invisible God (1:18).

'Word' as a christological title disappears after the prologue, but the interest in the nature of the relationship between Jesus and God is sustained in the narrative that follows. Some of Jesus' strongest assertions about his identity are made in confrontation with 'the Jews', whose accusation that he is making himself equal to God (5:18–19; 10:33; cf. 19:7) may reflect issues shaping the conflict between Johannine Christians and synagogue Jews (Meeks 1990). Jesus' opponents interpret his claims (5:17: 'My Father is still working, and I also am working'; 10:30: 'The Father and I are one') as a direct challenge to Jewish monotheism, but he responds that, as God's emissary and obedient Son, they are not incompatible with belief in the one God, since he only does what the Father has commissioned him to do (cf. 5:19; 10:32, 37–8). The repeated stress, in these and other passages, on the 'sending' of Jesus (e.g. 5:23–4, 36–7; 7:29; 10:36; 17:18) indicates that his depiction as God's authorized envoy is to be explained against the background of Jewish notions of agency (Borgen 1968). Based on the principle that the one who is sent (Hebrew: *shaliach*) is endowed with the full authority of the sender (m.Berakot 5:5: 'An agent is like the one who sent him'), the agent is to be treated like the sender, to whom the agent returns after carrying out his mission in total obedience. Jesus, therefore, functions as the unique emissary, because the Father 'has placed all things in his hands' (3:35). His words and works are those of God, including the giving of life and executing judgement (5:21–2, 27). The Son acts in dependence upon the one who sent him (7:28; 8:42; 10:37; 12:49) and commits himself obediently to the will of the Father (4:34; cf. 5:30; 6:38). During his earthly life he speaks and acts in unity with God (10:30), so that to see and know him is to see and know the Father (12:45; 14:7, 9). After completing his mission, Jesus returns to the one who sent him (cf. 7:33; 16:5).

Jewish notions of agency, even when combined with the Father–Son language, do not fully encompass the presentation of Jesus as the emissary of God. John's conviction that Jesus' authority as divine agent is due to his heavenly origins, as well as his unparalleled relationship with the God whom he fully represents, has led to the proposal that other strands within Jewish tradition may also have contributed to the shaping of Johannine christology, including traditions about God's principal angel, his chief agent, who bears God's name (cf. 5:43; 17:6, 11, 26) and glory (cf. 12:41; 17:5, 22, 24), and is entrusted with his authority and power (Ashton 2007: 281–96; cf. Meeks 1990: 317–18). Such traditions would provide a framework whereby, as with the *logos* christology, Jesus can be linked to God in the closest possible terms without infringing on the authority of the one God.

Certain facets of the presentation of Jesus' relationship with God are intended to bolster what is undoubtedly one of its dominant themes, the impossibility of seeing God other than through Jesus: 'Not that anyone has seen the Father except the one who is from God; he has seen the Father' (6:46; cf. 1:18; 14:9). Central to this claim is the intimate and unique nature of Jesus' status as divine Son; he offers unmediated revelation of the invisible God because he is the 'only-begotten Son' (1:14; 3:16, 18) who is 'in the bosom of the Father' (1:18). His heavenly origins explain why he alone can lay claim to have seen God; with the aid of the descent–ascent pattern, Jesus constantly reiterates the claim that he has come from above where he has dwelt with the Father from the beginning, and, as a result, he 'testifies to what he has seen and heard' (3:31–2; cf. 8:38; 17:4–5). Even figures from Israel's ancient past did not see God, but are to be remembered as witnesses to Jesus: Abraham rejoiced because he saw Jesus' day (8:56), Moses wrote about him in the law (1:45; cf. 5:46), and it was a vision of Jesus as the divine glory that led Isaiah to speak about him (12:41).

The significance of Jesus as the definitive revelation of God finds expression in Jesus' proclamation of the words 'I am (he)' (*egō eimi*). He declares to 'the Jews', 'You will die in your sins unless you believe that I am (he)' (8:24; cf. 8:28; 13:19), and they pick up stones to kill him upon hearing him proclaim, 'Before Abraham was,

I am' (8:58). To these may be added the occurrences of *egō eimi* where a predicate is implied (4:26; 18:5, 8; cf. 6:20), although its pronouncement by Jesus as he walks on the sea (6:20) and the dramatic response of the arresting party in the garden (18:6) indicate that it amounts to more than a form of self-identification, but points to Jesus' divine status and authority, particularly in view of John's fondness for polyvalent words and expressions. The key that unlocks the christological signifi-cance of these 'I am' statements is the use of the same phrase in the Greek versions of Isaiah (e.g. Isa. 41:4; 43:10; 46:4) and Deuteronomy 32:39 to express Yahweh's claim to unique sovereignty. Jesus can also utter the divine self-proclamation *egō eimi* because he is the eternal Word incarnate, the heavenly emissary, the Son who speaks in unity with the Father who sent him.

THE SPIRIT AND 'THE REMEMBERING COMMUNITY'

The Johannine Jesus, from the outset of his earthly mission, openly manifests his identity with the aid of exalted christological claims, and yet, during his ministry, even his own disciples fail to grasp fully the significance of his words and deeds. The true import of his teaching often escapes them (cf. 4:31–4; 11:7–16), even within the context of his farewell speech to them (13:36–8; 14:4–5, 8–9; 16:16–18, 25).

The search for the key that unlocks this enigma of 'hidden revelation' must begin with John's explicit linking of the gift of the Spirit to Jesus' glorification (7:38–9). When the risen Jesus breathes the Spirit upon his disciples (20:22), it fulfils his earlier words: 'If I do not go away, the Paraclete will not come to you; but if I go, I will send him to you' (16:7). There is much debate about the origins of the Johannine use of 'Paraclete' (*paraklētos*), the term used consistently for the Spirit in the Farewell Discourse (14:16–17, 26; 15:26; 16:7–11, 12–15), but, on each occasion, a clear description is given of the Paraclete's role in relation to the hostile world (16:8–11) and, in particular, to the disciples. Jesus assures them that, through the abiding presence of the Paraclete—his agent and successor—their relationship with him continues despite his physical absence (14:16–17). The Paraclete will carry on Jesus' work of teaching the disciples, reminding them of all that Jesus said (14:26) and testifying on his behalf (15:26). Continuity, in this respect, does not amount to reproducing the words of the earthly Jesus. The final saying (16:12–15) establishes a clear distinction between what Jesus, due to the disciples' limited capacity, was able to communicate during his ministry (16:12) and the fuller disclosure made available after his glorification: the Spirit of truth will instruct the disciples and guide them into all the truth (16:13). This disclosure will include 'the things to come', but the uniqueness of Jesus' revelation is still maintained, because whatever the Paraclete declares will in fact belong to Jesus (16:13–15).

Not only the post-resurrection period, but also Jesus' earthly ministry is regarded by John as 'a storehouse of revelation waiting to be unpacked by the Spirit of truth' (Hall 1991: 217), as exemplified by the promise that the Paraclete will *remind* the disciples of all that Jesus said to them (14:26; cf. 16:4). That the Spirit's activity involves the elucidation, rather than mere recall, of Jesus' words is strongly suggested by other statements about the disciples' post-glorification memory. After Jesus' veiled declaration about the temple (of his body), it is remarked that, following his resurrection, 'his disciples remembered that he had said this; and they believed the scripture and the word that Jesus had spoken' (2:22). Similarly, in the account of Jesus' entry into Jerusalem it is stated: 'His disciples did not understand these things at first; but when Jesus was glorified, then they remembered that these things had been written of him and had been done to him' (12:16). 'Remembering', in both cases, points to the disciples acquiring greater insight into what had hitherto been obscure or partially hidden. And, despite the lack of explicit reference to the Spirit's involvement, this interpretative recollection is clearly placed within the period after the gift of the Spirit. It appears that, for John, it is the Paraclete-inspired memory promised by Jesus that enables the disciples to comprehend his revelation more fully. Furthermore, in the context of a discourse (John 13:31–16:33) in which the envisaged future resonates with the 'now' of the evangelist and his group, the disciples act as representatives of the Johannine 'remembering community' whose post-Easter perspective moulds its understanding of Jesus' earthly mission.

The relevance of a post-glorification remembering should not, consequently, be restricted to those individual words and events (2:22; 12:16) where the post-resurrection perspective is brought to the surface. Together with other textual indicators (7:39; 14:26; 15:26; 16:13–15; 20:9), these statements indicate, in a more conscious manner than anything encountered in the Synoptic Gospels, that John's Gospel has been significantly shaped by the Spirit-inspired memory of Jesus (Dahl 1976: 28; Hurtado 2007: 203). This is implied by Jesus' promise that the Paraclete will bring to remembrance 'all' that he has said (14:26), and by the (deliberate) framing of Jesus' public ministry with references to the disciples' remembering of his words and deeds (Painter 2007: 242). John, in other words, bears witness to a process of intertwining the post-Easter 'present' and the pre-Easter 'past', and although the narrative displays a distinct awareness of the difference between these two perspectives, the post-Easter remembrance so deeply permeates the story of the pre-Easter Jesus that the one is largely inseparable from the other.

The intermingling of two temporal perspectives is part and parcel of John's literary and theological design, and, for that reason, it yields important insights into how this Gospel 'works'. It not only underscores the necessity of Jesus' glorification and the gift of the Spirit, but also seeks to secure the identity of the earthly Jesus with the glorified Lord. The close intertwining indicates that, for John, Jesus of Nazareth and the risen Lord cannot, and need not, be disconnected from each other; the christological insights revealed through the Spirit simply disclose what, from a Johannine viewpoint, has always been true of Jesus (cf. Hurtado 2007: 206): he is the incarnate Word, God's agent and only Son, who brings revelation into the world. To recognize the correlation of these two perspectives within the text is to make a decisive first step towards unravelling one of John's Gospel's many surprising, and challenging, puzzles.

WORKS CITED

ASHTON, J. (2007), *Understanding the Fourth Gospel*, 2nd edn. Oxford: Clarendon Press.

BARRETT, C. K. (1982), 'Paradox and Dualism', in *Essays on John*, 98–115. London: SPCK.

BAUCKHAM, R. (2001), 'The Audience of the Fourth Gospel', in R. T. Fortna and T. Thatcher (eds.), *Jesus in Johannine Tradition*, 101–11. Louisville, Ky.: Westminster John Knox Press.

BORGEN, P. (1968), 'God's Agent in the Fourth Gospel', in J. Neusner (ed.), *Religions in Antiquity: Essays in Memory of E. R. Goodenough* Leiden: E. J. Brill, 137–48.

BOYARIN, D. (2002), 'The Ioudaioi in John and the Prehistory of "Judaism"', in J. C. Anderson, P. Sellew, and C. Setzer (eds.), *Pauline Conversations in Context: Essays in Honor of Calvin J. Roetzel*, 216–39. Sheffield: Sheffield Academic Press.

CULPEPPER, R. A. (1983), *Anatomy of the Fourth Gospel: A Study in Literary Design*. Philadelphia: Fortress Press.

——(1995), 'The Plot of John's Story of Jesus', *Interpretation*, 49: 347–58.

DAHL, N. A. (1976), 'Anamnesis: Memory and Commemoration in Early Christianity', in *Jesus in the Memory of the Early Church*. Minneapolis: Augsburg Publishing House, 11–29.

DEWEY, J. (2001), 'The Gospel of John in Its Oral-Written Media World', in R. T. Fortna and T. Thatcher (eds.), *Jesus in Johannine Tradition*, 239–52. Louisville, Ky.: Westminster John Knox Press.

HALL, R. G. (1991), *Revealed Histories: Techniques for Ancient Jewish and Christian Historiography*. JSPSS 6; Sheffield: JSOT Press.

HURTADO, L. W. (2007), 'Remembering and Revelation: The Historic and Glorified Jesus in the Gospel of John', in D. P. Capes, A. D. DeConick, H. K. Bond, and T. A. Miller (eds.), *Israel's God and Rebecca's Children: Christology and Community in Early Judaism and Christianity. Essays in Honor of Larry W. Hurtado and Alan F. Segal*, 195–213. Waco, Tex.: Baylor University Press.

JONGE, M. DE (1977), *Jesus: Stranger from Heaven and Son of God*. Missoula: Scholar's Press.

KOESTER, C. R. (2003), *Symbolism in the Fourth Gospel: Meaning, Mystery. Communion*, 2nd edn. Minneapolis: Fortress Press.

KYSAR, R. (2007), *John, the Maverick Gospel*, 3rd edn. Louisville, Ky.: Westminster John Knox Press.

LIEU, J. (2008), 'Anti-Judaism, the Jews, and the Worlds of the Fourth Gospel', in R. Bauckham and C. Mosser (eds.), *The Gospel of John and Christian Theology*, 168–82. Grand Rapids, Mich.: Eerdmans.

LINCOLN, A. T. (2000), *Truth on Trial: The Lawsuit Motif in the Fourth Gospel*. Peabody: Hendrickson.

LINDARS, B. (1990), *John*. New Testament Guides. Sheffield: JSOT Press.

MACKAY, I. D. (2004), *John's Relationship with Mark: An Analysis of John 6 in the Light of Mark 6–8*. WUNT 2:182. Tübingen: Mohr Siebeck.

MARTYN, J. L. (1968), *History and Theology in the Fourth Gospel*, 1st edn. Louisville, Ky.: Westminster John Knox Press (3rd edn. 2003).

MEEKS, W. A. (1972), 'The Man from Heaven in Johannine Sectarianism', *Journal of Biblical Literature*, 91: 44–72.

——(1990), 'Equal to God', in R. T. Fortna and B. R. Gaventa (eds.), *The Conversation Continues: Studies in Paul and John in Honor of J. Louis Martyn*, 309–21. Nashville, Tenn.: Abingdon Press.

MOTYER, S. (2008), 'Bridging the Gap: How Might the Fourth Gospel Help Us Cope With the Legacy of Christianity's Exclusive Claim Over Against Judaism?', in R. Bauckham and C. Mosser (eds.), *The Gospel of John and Christian Theology*, 143–67. Grand Rapids, Mich.: Eerdmans.

PAINTER, J. (1991), *The Quest for the Messiah: The History, Literature and Theology of the Johannine Community*. Edinburgh: T. & T. Clark.

——(2007), 'Memory Holds the Key: The Transformation of Memory in the Interface of History and Theology in John', in P. N. Anderson, F. Just, and T. Thatcher (eds.), *John, Jesus, and History*, Vol. 1: *Critical Appraisals of Critical Views*, 229–45. SBL Symposium Series 44; Atlanta, Ga.: Society of Biblical Literature.

PHILLIPS, P. M. (2006), *The Prologue of the Fourth Gospel: A Sequential Reading*. LNTS 294. London: T & T Clark.

SMITH, D. M. (1995), *The Theology of the Gospel of John*. Cambridge: Cambridge University Press.

STIBBE, M. W. G. (1994), *John's Gospel*. New Testament Readings. London: Routledge.

THATCHER, T. (2000), *The Riddles of Jesus in John: A Study in Tradition and Folklore*. SBL Monograph Series 53. Atlanta, Ga.: Society of Biblical Literature.

WILLIAMS, C. H. (2000), *I am He: The Interpretation of 'Anî Hû' in Jewish and Early Christian Literature*. WUNT 2:113. Tübingen: Mohr Siebeck.

FURTHER READING

ASHTON, J. (1991), *Understanding the Fourth Gospel*, 1st edn. Oxford: Clarendon Press (2nd edn. 2007).

——ed. (1997), *The Interpretation of John*, 2nd edn. Edinburgh: T. & T. Clark.

BIERINGER, R. *et al.*, eds. (2001), *Anti-Judaism and the Fourth Gospel: Papers of the Leuven Colloquium, 2001*. Assen: Royal Van Gorcum.

BULTMANN, R. (1971), *The Gospel of John: A Commentary*. Philadelphia: Westminster.

BROWN, R. E. (1966, 1970), *The Gospel According to John*. 2 vols. Anchor Bible; New York: Doubleday.

118   CATRIN H. WILLIAMS

CULPEPPER, R. A. and C. C. BLACK, eds. (1991), *Exploring the Gospel of John*. Louisville, Ky.: Westminster John Knox Press.

LINCOLN, A. T. (2000), *Truth on Trial: The Lawsuit Motif in the Fourth Gospel*. Peabody: Hendrickson.

SMITH, D. M. (1995), *The Theology of the Gospel of John*. Cambridge: Cambridge University Press.

CHAPTER 9

ROMANS

GUY J. WILLIAMS

THE LETTER, ITS FORM AND CONTENT

Paul's letter to the Romans is an extraordinary text with an extraordinary history. It can make a strong claim to be the most interpreted book in the Bible. Readings of the epistle have played key roles during major developments in Christian thought (Augustine, Luther, Barth, etc.), and beyond these famous episodes there lies a vast quantity of less well-known readings, analyses, and appropriations. In terms of modern scholarly literature, we find a mind-boggling array of research with seemingly endless bibliographies being a common feature of monographs and commentaries. With all of this attention being lavished upon one document, it is reasonable to ask what it is about the text itself which may have caused its distinctive and elevated status. What is the letter to the Romans and what is it about?

Needless to say, the basic genre of the piece is self-evident: we are dealing with a letter from an apostle to a church. However, it might be useful to establish a more precise description of what Romans actually is; what *type* of letter did Paul intend to write? It could be a personal communication, or something more official. It could be meant to disseminate general teachings, or respond to some particular and urgent situation. Naturally, because of the limitations of the evidence, scholars are divided on this matter. The claim that Romans offers an explanation of Paul's basic theological perspectives has led some to offer the suggestion that the text operates as a kind of 'testament letter' or treatise (e.g. Bornkamm 1991). Others, however, have envisaged a much more practical and concrete function for the text, perhaps presenting Paul's credentials to an unfamiliar community, even making this an 'ambassadorial letter' (Jewett 1982). Ultimately, the diversity of the letter seems to frustrate attempts to pin it down to any given genre or format. It contains highly personal touches (16:1ff.), yet gives quite general arguments (1:18ff.). It addresses the practical logistics of Paul's mission (15:22ff.), yet also seemingly speaks to the human condition (7:7ff.). However we wish to describe it, Romans remains a letter of great complexity.

Within the detail of the text, an array of different literary forms and conventions find their place. As one might expect from a letter, Romans begins with a formulaic epistolary opening (1:1–17) and ends with exhortations and personal comments (15:14–16:27). As literary devices, these features are certainly recognizable (e.g. 'Paul, a slave of Christ Jesus . . . to all those beloved of God in Rome', 1:1, 7). However, mixed in with these familiar idioms are literary curiosities. Romans seems to be far too long for a normal letter, and even the prescript stretches on for a decidedly odd seven verses (1:1–7). Scholars have pointed out that this may have been quite perplexing for Paul's first-century readers (Moo 1996: 40). Aspects of the letter at times seem to bend literary rules, making the job of classifying this work all the more difficult.

Another distinctive side to the literary shape and form of Romans lies in Paul's quite extensive quotation and exposition of Scripture. Although he quotes from the OT in other letters, in Romans this seems to be more detailed and more developed. Scripture shapes both what he writes and how he writes. For instance, in 3:1 Paul poses the question 'what advantage has the Jew?' and soon follows up with an answer rooted in the Psalms and the familiar refrain 'as it is written' (*kathōs gegraptai*, 3:4). Then, just six verses later, we find the same refrain again and an extensive quotation covering nine verses (3:10–18). Paul does not handle this material with precision and does not even distinguish between the different parts of the Bible he mixes together. Nevertheless, the texts he employs seem to be driving what he has to say. Scripture is something which Paul argues with and around, giving his letter to the Romans a discursive or investigative feel. At times, it is as though Paul is trying to have a three-way conversation with himself, the Bible, and the addressees of his letter. It is a literary approach which fits with his wider argumentative prose style.

This point leads on to the nature and quality of Paul's Greek. Surely one of the key factors in the history of interpretation has been the interpretable nature of what is written. In this respect, the letter to the Romans is intriguingly, compellingly badly written. It lacks precision, finesse, and even at times basic clarity. Yet, at the very same moment, it carries along a fascinating and quick-witted argument. Possibly more than anything else, it is this duality between the strong rhetorical-theological agenda of the letter and the imperfect Greek which presents it which has sparked so much interest in what Paul has to say. Certainly, he is dealing with important matters, but his expression of these leaves interpreters with their options open. He 'asks questions he does not answer and begins lists he does not finish'

(Muddiman 2006: 90). All of this provides a wealth of possibilities for detailed exegesis. A simple illustration of this is found in the famous and much-interpreted verse 1:17: 'for the righteousness (*dikaiosunē*) of God is revealed from faith to faith (*pistis*), just as it is written, "the righteous one shall live by faith" (or, "the one who is righteous by faith shall live").' Each sub-clause of this crucial sentence can conceivably be read in a number of different ways, providing quite different theological perspectives. What Paul says seems to be pregnant with meaning, but the question is, *which* meaning?

While the nuance of Paul's words may be open to interpretation, the actual content of the Greek text is, on the whole, fairly secure. For the majority of the letter, most significant manuscripts of Romans tend not to yield major variant readings. Throughout history, this has meant that interpreters of Paul have usually been able to accept the words on the page without further ado. However, that is not quite the end of the matter, for modern scholarship has identified some notable variants in the text at the beginning and end of the letter (see Gamble 1977). Some of these have raised questions over the letter's original context (notably, the absence of 'in Rome' from 1:7, 15 in Origen and the manuscript 'G'). Yet, possibly the most serious question for the textual integrity of the letter is that of whether to include 15:1–16:23—a significant chunk which is absent from numerous Latin Vulgate manuscripts. If we remove this part from our bibles, we are left with a fourteen- or fifteen-chapter version of Romans which has quite a different feel from the received text. It could have been that Paul took a letter originally addressed to another city and added the latter part before sending it on to Rome (so Lake 1919: 350 ff.) or, quite the reverse, Paul may have taken his letter originally addressed to Rome and supplemented it with extra greetings before directing it elsewhere (e.g. Ephesus, so Manson 1991). Beyond this, there is also the related and tricky question of where (if anywhere) we should place the final doxology of the letter (16:25–7), since this tends to move around in the manuscript tradition. Nevertheless, despite these intriguing problems in the text, contemporary scholars are still mostly satisfied with the sixteen-chapter form of the letter and its basic contents. When talking about Paul's letter to the Romans, they tend to be confident that the scope of this document is identifiable.

OUTLINE AND MAJOR THEMES

In describing the general outline and thematic content of Romans, it can be easy to lose sight of the diversity of the subject-matter which Paul covers. With the desire to find an over-arching thesis or focus for the letter, there may be a risk of placing slightly too much emphasis upon the apparent logicality of the structure and argument. The issue of Paul's status as a genuine theological thinker (or not) touches upon all of his major letters, though Romans seems to be a major battleground in this respect (e.g. contrast the approaches of Räisänen 1987 and Dunn 1998). Does Paul carefully draw together the strands of a major theological opus, or does he meander through a number of issues of interest and importance? Given the complexity of that problem, it pays to take a balanced view. On the one hand, Romans is not a tightly argued intellectual masterpiece; that would be an exaggeration. Yet, on the other hand, neither is Romans devoid of coherence and rigour. Major points are developed and sustained, and their consequences are thought through. Naturally, then, a reasonably clear structure emerges, despite the odd digression. Although minor variations are given from commentary to commentary, most contemporary Pauline scholars tend to arrive at the same basic divisions within the text.

The first obvious part forms the introduction (1:1–17), including the prescript (1:1–7) and thanksgiving (1:8–15) of the letter. Although this is a curiously long letter opening, it is still clear and recognizable as such. The extra material which Paul has crammed into his lengthy prescript is perhaps indicative of significant themes for the letter as a whole: the gospel of Christ resurrected and the apostleship among the gentiles. Similarly, the inflated thanksgiving touches upon the gospel of God's son and Paul's 'harvest' among the gentiles. It also seems likely that Paul's crucial words about the gospel and faith in 1:16–17 are meant to round off this first section, since they reinforce his sentiments from the thanksgiving, while 1:18 seems to mark a change of tone.

The next major section (1:18–4:25) ties together a number of different strands of thought around the main issues of justification/righteousness and the inclusion of the gentiles on that basis (see Byrne 2007: 26, 62). Paul's initial focus upon the wrath of God and the terrible wickedness of man (1:18ff.) primarily seems to pave the way for the claim that God's judgement is equal upon all, good and evil, regardless of whether one nominally lives under the law or not (2:11). The requirements of the law should be written upon the heart (2:15). Paul's focus upon internal or spiritual obedience raises questions concerning the value of traditional Jewish observance, so he feels obliged to defend the 'advantage' of the Jew (3:1ff.). All the while, he thus faces the difficult balancing act of maintaining that Jews still are no freer from sin than 'Greeks' (i.e. gentiles, 3:9). The ultimate destination of this first major discussion lies in the connection between two key elements in Paul's vocabulary: faith/faithfulness/trust (*pistis*) and justice/righteousness (*dikaiosunē*). This brings the crucial statement that 'a person is justified by faith, apart from the works of the law' (3:28), and the example of Abraham is given to illustrate this point (4:1ff.).

The next major division lies in Paul's discussion of the salvation of believers (5:1–8:39), a hope grounded in the justification which he has just described.

The tendency of most modern commentators to link chapter 5 with chapters 6–8 represents a departure from the great Reformation commentators, who tended to associate it with chapters 1–4. It could be argued that 5:1 indicates an attempt simply to draw out the consequences of the argument in chapters 1–4 ('Therefore, since we are justified...'). However, it is clear that this transitional chapter is taking the argument in a new direction; the focus quickly shifts to Christ's death and the reconciliation it has brought (5:6–11). Paul addresses 'Christian existence' (Morgan 1995: 36), the status of the person who is justified. The life and hope received is then thoroughly contrasted with the rule of sin and death (5:12–6:23), and is given further definition through an intriguing discussion of the connection between the law and sin, written entirely in the first person (7:7–25). All of this leads up to the climactic and optimistic chapter 8, which describes a life free from condemnation and guided by the Spirit. Rhetorically speaking, Paul has led his readers from the depths of sin at the beginning of the letter to the high-point of his gospel: nothing in creation—not even the angels and powers—will be able to separate the believer from the love of God (8:39).

A clear change in focus occurs in chapter 9, with Paul embarking upon a fairly lengthy discussion of the problem of Israel's election (9:1–11:36). Modern scholarship has gradually changed its views on this particular section. It was once the case that chapters 9–11 were regarded as something of an anomaly, without any clear role in the wider theology or rhetoric of the letter. It was even suggested that they once formed a separate document (e.g. Dodd 1932: 148–50), integrated into Romans without a direct link to what preceded and followed. However, more recently the importance of Israel has been seen as an integral part of the letter. Paul, it is now assumed, wrote about the Jewish people because he genuinely cared about them and anticipated their salvation (11:26). Paul injects his own personality into this section ('I myself am an Israelite...', 11:1), presumably to demonstrate that his gospel does not exclude or compromise the value of his own people. If Paul and Abraham can fit with the demands and hopes set out in chapters 1–8, then why cannot the rest of Israel?

The final main discussion of the letter to the Romans is chiefly concerned with various types of ethical behaviour (12:1–15:13). This begins with very general principles in chapter 12 ('be transformed', 'let love be genuine', etc.), but then moves on to the specifics of dealing with the civil authorities (13:1–7). Chapter 14 has more focus and argument, as Paul tackles those who pass judgement on their 'weak' fellows in the church (14:10), chiefly on the grounds that they 'observe the day' and abstain from certain foods (14:5–6). Certainly, he attempts to give very clear advice to the recipients of the letter on this matter, hammering home his point about mutual tolerance with a final rhetorical flourish (15:1–13).

Paul then begins gradually drawing his letter to a close, with a rather extended conclusion and series of greetings (15:14–16:27). He refers back to the boldness of his letter (15:15) and reviews the progress of his mission thus far (15:19-21), broaching his own desire to make a visit to Rome in the near future (15:22–33). Paul then gives a long list of greetings and commendations (16:1–23) which, as we have already noted, has fallen under the suspicion and speculation of a minority of modern scholars, as possibly being an addition to the original text. The final doxology (16:25–7) is perhaps the least secure part of the text, but still makes quite a fitting end to the letter; it re-emphasizes the gospel to the gentiles and the value of obedience.

So, what we find across the sixteen chapters of Romans is a complex and multi-themed letter, addressing a number of different (but mostly related) points. There is a fair dose of morality here, from warnings about wicked conduct (1:18ff.) to advice about eating and abstaining from food (14:1ff.). It is also clear that justice/righteousness (*dikaiosunē*) is a central concern of the letter, however we are meant to interpret it. Finally, Israel and Judaism, which has often been seen as one of the 'minor' issues, has tended to jump out of the text in recent times. With changing perspectives on Paul in current scholarship, it only seems reasonable to place heavy emphasis upon his cultural and religious origins among the Jewish people.

Now, having dealt with the outline and major themes of the letter, it remains for us to take a closer look at some of the key issues of interpretation in Romans. How is it that the text poses a challenge to its readers, and how might it be understood? Although distinguishing between the relative importance of different issues is a very subjective business, we shall attempt to consider these broadly in the order of their significance for the modern reception and interpretation of the letter. This leads us straight to what many have regarded as the epicentre of Pauline and Reformation theology: faith and justification.

FAITH AND JUSTIFICATION

The connection between faith (*pistis*) and justification (*dikaiōsis* and cognates) in Romans is a crucial issue for modern interpreters, both because of its importance within the text itself (*pistis* occurs forty times, *dikaiosunē* thirty-four times) and because of external, historic reasons. Paul's apparent teaching or theology of 'justification by faith' has been a central concern for NT studies ever since the time of Martin Luther, who made it the key to his reforms. Despite many challenges and reassessments of this idea, the view that faith leads to righteousness is still often identified as one of Paul's main theories. However, a number of questions now face the modern scholar: What exactly did Paul teach on this matter? Where did he get his ideas from? And finally, how important is this within the wider scheme of his gospel?

Concerning the content of Paul's teaching, the interpreter's first task is to establish an understanding of his cherished but slightly obscure ideal of moral and religious status: *dikaiosunē*. Scholars have long lamented the impossibility of translating this word with a precise English equivalent. One could opt for 'righteousness', but this might be too individualistic, lacking the connotation of goodness more widely distributed (for example, in English a 'self-righteous' person is one obsessed by their own personal morality). By contrast, one could render *dikaiosunē* with 'justice', but this seems to weigh too heavily on fairness and objective moral decisions, lacking some of the personal and pietistic dimension. Suffice it to say, therefore, that we are dealing with a term with a certain breadth to it; this does not imply an inherently narrow conception of grace or virtue.

Determining the meaning of *dikaiosunē* in Romans actually falls within the scope of detailed exegesis rather than general lexicography. That is to say, given its wide scope of possible reference, it is important to uncover its meaning by its context; instead of just asking: 'What does this mean?' one should rather ask: 'What does this mean *here*?' Needless to say, a full study of this would be a lengthy task beyond the scope of this current chapter, so one should refer to an up-to-date commentary. However, a number of broad observations may still be made.

First, Paul attaches specific value to what he calls 'the *dikaiosunē* of God' (1:17; 3:21, 22, 25, 26; 10:3; cf. 2 Cor. 5:21). Faced by this crucial phrase, the interpreter has two main choices; the genitive ('of God') may be taken as possessive ('the *dikaiosunē* which God has'), or it may be taken as denoting origin ('the *dikaiosunē* which comes from God'). Those who favour the first option tend to see this as an eschatological power: God's goodness and majesty are revealed at the end time (see Muddiman 2006: 96–7). This perhaps gives Paul's whole teaching on 'justification' an eschatological spin; *dikaiosunē* can be attained because it is currently and finally being revealed. Interpreters favouring the second option are more likely to see God's *dikaiosunē* as a forensic quality: it is the state of justice or acquittal which is granted to believers (see Seifrid 1992: 214 ff.). Naturally, this reading tends to place emphasis upon the status of the individual before God. The precise meaning, then, is difficult to establish. We may even wish to see the truth as lying somewhere between these two options; perhaps God both manifests *and* supplies his righteousness on earth.

The next main point we could make is the one which Luther elevated to a position of central importance. The status of being just/righteous (*dikaios*) is not something which a human achieves for him/herself, but rather people 'are justified by [God's] grace as a gift' (3:24). Given the context of this comment, Paul seems to be saying that justification is not granted by observance of the Jewish law but instead depends on faith (*pistis*). This viewpoint, it must be emphasized, probably does not constitute an attempt on Paul's part to condemn Judaism as a false religion (a point which Protestant interpreters have often failed to see). On the contrary, going back to his argument earlier in the letter, Paul seems to be working through the consequences of his key moral assumption: 'there is no one who is righteous' (3:10). Therefore, though the Jewish law is *good* in many respects (3:1ff.; 7:7), it cannot achieve what Paul regards as most important; it cannot *make* a person *dikaios*. This is a flaw inherent in humankind itself, rather than some peculiar wickedness of Judaism.

The moral pessimism of this third chapter in Romans is striking, so it is small wonder that it has plotted the pathways down which later theological writers have run their arguments. The view of God's grace as an unmerited free gift has proved to be something of a theological time-bomb, exploding every so often in the history of the Church. We may witness Augustine arguing against Pelagius that grace 'is not rendered for any merits' (*Nature and Grace*, ch. 4), deliberately picking off the key points from Romans 3:23–4. Later, Luther's teaching on justification is found to be motivated by a close reading of this exact same part of scripture, interpreted also through the lens of Augustine. Paul, then, whether intentionally or not, pioneered points of great theological importance and resonance with his rather terse but rich account of the free gift of grace.

Finally, and immediately after laying down the basics on faith and justification, Paul then moves on to make an application of his arguments, showing the foundational significance of what he has said for his mission among the gentiles. This idea is illustrated through the example of Abraham (4:1ff.). The crux of the argument seems to be that God regarded Abraham as righteous *before* he was physically circumcised (4:10), establishing the principle that righteousness (*dikaiosunē*) is granted by faith (*pistis*), rather than by the works of the law. This allows Paul to re-focus his readers' understanding of the promise made to Abraham: it was not given to his descendants 'through the law' but instead 'through the righteousness of faith' (4:13). Thus, Paul defends his view that justification belongs to *all* those who follow the example of Abraham's faithfulness, inclusive of the gentiles. The scope and intention behind this passage provides a further interesting problem. It could be that Paul is trying to persuade Jewish Christians to shift allegiance away from the wider Jewish community, joining up with gentile Christians (so Watson 1986: 178). Alternatively, it could be argued that Paul is trying to bring Jewish and gentile Christian identities together under the example of a common 'prototype' (so Esler 2003: 184). Whichever is the case, it is at least certain that Paul regards Abraham as *the* role model for his non-Jewish followers; Abraham demonstrates the supreme value of faith.

Having described Paul's arguments concerning faith and justification, we might briefly consider where such ideas could have come from. The origins and development of this teaching have long been a source of debate in modern biblical studies. The 'standard' view of Protestant critical interpreters earlier in the twentieth century was that justification by faith developed as a targeted critique of 'rabbinic' or 'legalistic' Judaism. It was assumed that Paul's fellow Jews regarded the law rather mechanically as a kind of formula for religious success; if someone followed all the rules, God regarded this person as righteous. This account of Paul's teaching on justification may ultimately be traced back to the work of F. C. Baur, who interpreted Pauline Christianity as having arisen through intellectual conflict with Judaism (see Baur 1873–5). However, it would seem that this approach to justification bears little resemblance to the Judaism of the Second Temple period or, indeed, to the faith which Paul alludes to in his letter to Rome. For example, if we read the Thanksgiving Hymns from Qumran (Vermes 1998: 243ff.), we encounter Jews from the same time period as Paul praising God for the mercy he has shown, even though it is *not* well-deserved. Meanwhile, in Romans we find that Paul simply has no intention of portraying himself as an opponent of Judaism, or of portraying the law as a kind of false intellectual system. For Paul, negotiating the limitations of the law is a complex and sensitive matter. The majority of scholarly readings of Romans today start from this basic observation.

However, if the theme of justification in Romans does not constitute an attack on Jewish legalism, one is obliged to offer some alternative explanation for the trajectory of Paul's thinking. Contemporary scholarship offers a number of possibilities, most of which demand a more positive reassessment of Paul's attitude towards Judaism in Romans and his other letters. Perhaps the best-known of these alternative accounts is what may loosely be described as the 'new perspective' on Paul (a term coined in 1982 by Dunn: Dunn 1990). Broadly speaking, this refers to the view that Paul emphasized the link between faith and righteousness as a means of defending gentile Christian practice (i.e. without circumcision, food laws, and so on) and breaking down the barriers between gentile and Jewish Christians. This represents a more social and pragmatic view of what Paul was trying to achieve, without placing all of the emphasis upon individualistic faith. The new perspective has met with fairly widespread approval, for, although it is not without its critics, the ethos of bringing people together does at least have quite a secure footing in the letter to the Romans. As Paul asks, 'Is God the God of Jews only? Is he not also the God of the gentiles? Indeed, he is also the God of the gentiles, for God is one . . .' (3:29–30).

Paul's teaching on faith and justification makes fascinating reading and certainly repays careful study. Yet, it remains extremely difficult to pin down why exactly this one part of Romans has had such a far-reaching impact, much greater than any other part of the letters. It may simply be that what Paul argued was profoundly true or insightful, as many have claimed throughout the ages. However, the continuing echoes of his teaching may also result more generally from the radical social horizon of what he has to say. Paul plays down the importance of traditional moral codes, questions the value of long-standing religious consensus, and dismisses the idea of earning credit by service or good deeds. All of these attitudes have the potential to be redeployed as criticisms of a religious status quo, as indeed was dramatically the case in the Reformation.

A PERSONAL APPEAL

A related concern to the issue of faith/righteousness is sin, and on this point one particular interpretive puzzle in Romans has challenged the ingenuity of NT scholars for centuries. That is, Paul seemingly speaks of himself in the passage

7:7–25 in a highly personal way, ending with a dramatic flourish: 'Wretched man that I am! Who will save me from this body of death?' (7:24). This wretched man is a person who fails to do the deed he wishes, but instead does 'the very thing I hate' (7.15). It is difficult to know the exact capacity in which Paul could be using this language. Is this some dramatization of the past, when he was persecuting the church? This is possible, but the lack of a consistent past tense in this passage would be rather curious in this case. Could it be that Paul continued to regard his life as a constant struggle with sin? This is also possible, although Paul seems to focus on wider lessons concerning sin, rather than just his own personal problems. Then there is another option: might it be that Paul is telling a story about sin, which has plagued the individual ('I') since time immemorial? Christ would then offer a new hope at the end of the narrative (7:25). Again, this may be what is intended, though it is difficult to say. After all, Paul's use of the first person is striking, and it is hard to imagine that this passage is not at least partially self-referential. Finally, there is one further option: could Paul be describing the general Christian life in terms of an ongoing battle with the power of sin? This possibility suffers from the same difficulty as the previous suggestion: surely Paul has himself at least somewhat in view.

In an earlier era of scholarship many biblical commentators opted for the last of these options, which is the Lutheran view. Although Christians are 'justified', they still expect to be bound to sin. As Luther put it, believers are at the same time both just and sinners (*simul iustus et pecattor*). Paul, then, would simply be using himself as an illustration of this fact. This once-popular reading, however, has long since fallen by the wayside. As several scholars have noted, the claim that all Christians are persistently afflicted by sin 'is impossible to coordinate with the details of Rom 5–6' (Jewett 2006: 442); Paul has only just stated that believers effectively have been 'freed from sin' (6:7). So, it is difficult to defend the Lutheran view, although it is not without notable modern supporters (especially Dunn 1988: 1. 411–12).

No single consensus has emerged in the most recent scholarly readings of this passage, and it seems likely that the mystery concerning Paul's precise intentions here will continue to perplex scholars for generations to come. The same options continue to be debated, all having a ring of plausibility but no hard proof. Nevertheless, one particular development may foreshadow progress in the years to come. Rhetorical analysis of this passage has revealed that Paul was following a well-known Greco-Roman technique known as *prosopopoeia*, a 'speech in charac- ter' (so Stowers 1995). This represents the idea that one can make a speech in the first person as a means of enhancing the emotional impact of an argument. Possibly, then, scholarly attention should shift to the argumentative point Paul was trying to make, rather than focusing narrowly on the ambiguous personal background of his language. Hopefully, such analysis may improve our under-standing of the wider context of the letter and may clarify the agenda Paul was trying to set in terms of sin. As I have suggested, this may demand a departure from some of the more established readings of this enigmatic passage.

JEWS AND JUDAISM

As mentioned in describing the outline of the letter, chapters 9–11 have traditionally been regarded as an odd or intrusive feature in Paul's correspondence with Rome. They have a fairly strong and self-contained message, a message which is not obviously a development of the theology of justification which Protestant commentators have tended to regard as the focus of the letter. Indeed, for a long period of time chapters 9–11 were regarded as a special and separate discourse on the predestination of humanity to salvation or damnation—another Protestant preoccupation with its roots in Augustine's reading of scripture.

However, over the last fifty years or so these traditional scholarly readings of Romans 9–11 have been almost entirely abandoned. First, it seems unlikely that Paul would indulge in a major theological diversion which was not relevant to the main thrust of the letter. Secondly, the idea that Paul would write of grace and election in purely abstract terms is implausible, given recent attempts to reconstruct the social context of the letter. Finally, there is a related point, that Paul would probably have quite a concrete concern for the long-term salvation of his Jewish kinsmen; the psychological portrait of Paul as a man who had severed all his links with his Jewish past hardly finds significant support among today's scholars.

Therefore, we may perhaps say that the reading of this passage among scholars is as much a reflection of current relations between Christians and Jews as it is a reflection of changing methods and analyses. This socially engaged reading of Romans 9–11 goes back to Luther himself, who was once convinced that the prophecy of 11.26 had only failed to materialize because of the bad example of the pope (Luther, *That Jesus Was Born a Jew*; see *Jewish Encyclopedia*: Martin Luther). However, as Luther's own brand of Christianity failed to win significantly more Jewish converts than the pope's, his positive reading of the Jews in Romans 9–11 disappeared. So today, with the greater rapprochement between Christian and Jewish scholars, the positive reading abandoned by Luther now seems to be back in vogue.

Given this tangled background, how then are we to approach this passage? A common starting-point among current critical interpreters is to take Paul's positive statements about Israel at face value. For example: 'they are the Israelites; to them belong the adoption, the glory, the covenants, the giving of the law, the worship and the promises' (9:4). These are significant observations and are not to be interpreted away merely as artificial rhetorical devices. We might assume that Paul means what he says; he genuinely cares for his fellow Jews. This then creates quite a difficult problem for scholars. How is it possible to square Paul's positive appraisal of Israel's covenant with his apparently competing claim that God *only* favours those who display faith (*pistis*), regardless of whether they are Jew or gentile? There is a tension which modern scholars face here, arguably of Paul's own creation.

The solution which Paul seems to opt for is given through what recent scholars have dubbed 'the jealousy motif' (as outlined by Bell 1994). That is, Paul regards the relative success of his gentile mission as a possible cause for jealousy amongst the Jewish people, which will ultimately result in their full salvation. By a mysterious and convoluted route, God is ensuring the deliverance of his chosen people by first accepting non-Jewish Christians. So, we arrive at the rather startling conclusion: 'Stubbornness has come upon a part of Israel, until such time as the full number of gentiles has entered in. And thus all Israel will be saved' (11:25–6).

However, the apparent universal application of this statement has puzzled some commentators. *All* Israel? The salvation of every last Jewish person stands in some friction with the most established teaching of the Christian Church. Thus, some have attempted to interpret these words differently from their surface meaning. Perhaps 'all' can be taken to mean 'most, with a few exceptions'. Likewise, perhaps 'Israel' can be taken to mean 'elect believers, gentiles and Jews'. Although such readings sit more easily with common Christian expectations, they do not work well with the Greek text of Paul's letter. The Greek *pas* really does mean 'all' rather than 'most'. By the same token, 'Israel' in this letter is specifically, ethnically Jewish in reference (see especially 11:1 in this respect). It seems most likely, therefore, that Paul really does use the jealousy motif to account for the salvation of all Jews, however difficult this may be to square with more familiar doctrines.

So, the motives behind Paul's subtle and intriguing argument concerning the Jews are twofold. First, he needs chapters 9–11 to address a question which arises from his argument earlier in the letter: if what he says about faith and righteousness is true, then where does that leave Israel? Surely, that must have been a pressing question for all members of the early church. The second part of Paul's motivation lies in the concrete setting of the letter. Reading between the lines, Jewish believers must have been a significant practical issue for the apostle; he emphasizes his own Jewish heritage, appeals to scripture, defends the validity of the promises to Israel, and rules out gentile gloating over unbelieving Jews (11:22 ff.). There is a practical and social dimension to the argument which only quite recently has come to the forefront. The issue of Judaism brought out Paul's pragmatic and creative sides; his solution is novel and attempts to please all interested parties, Jews and gentiles alike. Whether this actually worked for Paul in practice, it is impossible to say.

MORALIZING AND CONDEMNATION

One final issue in the letter to the Romans arises in a part of the text which has come to the forefront in recent Christian ethical debate: the moralizing and condemnation found in the first couple of chapters. On an initial and casual reading, there is much which offends the eye and good taste in Paul's condemnation of sinful humanity in 1:18 ff. First, the transition from 1:17 is hardly smooth: the discussion of God's wrath (*orgē*) seems to come out of the blue and it is not until 3:21 that Paul gets back on track with his discussion of faith and righteousness. Secondly, modern literary fashion tends to regard judgemental stereotyping as low and unsophisticated, though this is precisely what Paul indulges in here. Seemingly, most gentiles are to be regarded as animal-worshiping and violent sexual deviants— a view which does not stand up to real historical scrutiny.

The interest of modern scholarship in this part of the letter is an obvious and natural occurrence. Without a care in the world, Paul barges through issues which represent a moral minefield for modern believers. Apparently, he deals with non-Christian religions (they are foolish and corrupt, 1:20–5), homosexual relationships (they are shameless and unnatural, 1:26–7), and many other crimes of the secular world (malice, murder, slander, etc., 1:28–32). Needless to say, such views tend to be divisive. The biblical scholar is thus given the rather difficult task of trying to establish exactly what Paul might have been trying to communicate with such language and his reasons for placing it here.

To grasp some of the intentions behind this rather lengthy and difficult passage, it is perhaps best to begin with the conclusion which Paul tries to draw out from his criticisms and condemnations. For the most part, scholars have identified 3:9–20 as the end-point for this argument. Paul seeks to establish what we might call 'the universality of sin', as emerges very clearly from his choice of scriptural quotation: 'There is no one who is righteous, not even one.' (3:10; cf. Ps. 14:3). It would thus appear that the ultimate aim of this section is to show that all humans are guilty of some measure of sin, regardless of whether they attempt to observe the Jewish law or not. Indeed, attempting to live a blameless life by the law simply will not work out, because 'through the law there is recognition of sin' (3:20). Despite the slightly long-winded and meandering nature of the two chapters leading up to this, it is precisely this point which Paul must make before setting out on his discussion of faith and righteousness.

Thus, it would seem that Paul is not simply being a grumpy and negative writer in 1:18 ff.; he has a specific point he wants to prove and keeps a rhetorical destination in sight. Through this progressive and bleak picture, he wishes to identify Jews and gentiles *together* (so Esler 2003: 154), failing to live lives which are truly righteous in the sight of God. He is creating the need which 3:21 ff. will supply.

Given that Paul's general intentions may now be somewhat clearer, the content of his harsh remarks may also receive a measure of clarification. The first part of this is targeted directly at gentiles (1:18–32). In view of Paul's background and social mores, it is natural that he should start things off with a Jewish critique of the non-Jewish world. He would have been at home with such material and it underpins the conclusion he reaches in 3:9–20. The Jewish flavour of what Paul says becomes apparent as soon as it is compared with documents from the same era: notably, the Book of Wisdom (15:1 ff.) and the works of Philo of Alexandria (*The Contemplative Life* 3 ff.). Scholarly readings of this material have also shifted in recent years, as an anti-Jewish reading of the opening chapters of Romans has looked less and less tenable (see Gager 2000: 112). Paul actually begins his description of the moral landscape through a simple repetition of common Jewish attitudes, building on familiar and reliable ground.

So, having unpacked the rhetorical context for Paul's attack on gentile life, we can see that his comments are hardly original. Other Jewish writers used exactly the same imagery. It is most likely that Paul's depiction of non-Jewish religion and sexuality is derived from stock imagery from within the Jewish community, rather than genuine experience of these at first hand. What we have, then, is a cartoon image of moral corruption, without any sincere attempt to address the reality on the ground. Modern biblical scholarship is largely aware of this fact, but still feels obliged to treat Paul's comments with a moral seriousness which they probably do not deserve. For example, much ink is spilled over the precise nuance of Paul's contention that homosexual relationships are 'unnatural' (*para phusin*, 1:26), since this issue stirs up so much emotion in modern Christianity (see Scroggs 1983).

Paul's focus clearly shifts in 2:1 ff., in a passage which must have been very difficult for him to write and consequently is difficult for later readers to interpret. Having dealt with the sinfulness of the gentile world, Paul now needs to highlight the failings of the Jewish people too; that is the only possible way in which he can conclude that 'there is no one who is righteous'. In pursuit of that point, his main claims seem to be, first, that Jews are also susceptible to moral corruption (2:17 ff.), and secondly, that physical circumcision is of no use if the law is not followed (2:25 ff.); what matters is what is upon a person's heart. In former times, biblical scholars regarded this as a kind of special critique of Judaism, or a rejection of a false religion (a view going back to Luther 1961: 37 ff.). This interpretation finds few supporters today, as it is reasonably clear that Paul's target is a blanket condemnation of all humanity, without singling out Jews for special criticism.

Closer reading of chapter 2 may actually reveal an apostle who is unwilling to depart from his Jewish roots. Some contemporary scholars have read this passage as an attempt to have it both ways; Paul wishes to deny the moral superiority of Judaism while at the very same time affirming its truth and lasting value. Certainly, he must have had mixed feelings when penning this part of the letter, as is shown by some of the trickier parts of the text. For example, in 2:6–11 Paul gives what appears to be solid Jewish teaching: '[God] will pay back each according to his deeds.' There will be immortality for the good and torment for the wicked. But how can this possibly fit with the claim that *faith* justifies, beyond any works? Some would argue that this passage simply contradicts that teaching on justification (e.g. Räisänen 1987). This implies that Paul had quite a conflicted attitude, remaining supportive of his ancestral faith, even to the point of intellectual compromise. However, other scholars attempt to iron-out the creases in Paul's thought (e.g. Moo 1996: 135ff.). For example, one might claim that Paul's talk of 'the good' is simply shorthand for the Christians who will receive eternal life from faith. The difficulty remains, though, of why Paul should refer to a repayment on the basis of *works* (*erga*, 2:6).

As perhaps may now be appreciated, the moralizing and condemnation of chapters 1–3 reflects quite a complex agenda for Paul. This is not simply a bad-tempered rant. On the contrary, this passage poses two particularly significant and interesting interpretive problems. First, why does Paul engage in such harsh (and arguably unfair) criticism of the gentile world? Secondly, we must ask, what understanding of Judaism does he try to develop at this point? Modern scholarship has much to say on both questions. Despite getting sidetracked at a number of points, Paul stays focused upon his pessimistic conclusion: no one is really righteous. Surveying the whole history of the interpretation of this letter, we can see that this key assumption has persistently resurfaced.

CONCLUSION: CHANGING PERSPECTIVES

As was noted at the beginning of this chapter, Romans is a complex, fascinating, and much-interpreted document. Although traditional assumptions about the text's role in Paul's theological agenda have been challenged and in some cases abandoned, it is fair to say that scholarly interest in this letter has not really waned. The letter to the Romans does not perhaps have the kind of dogmatic pre-eminence which it once had in the minds of many (especially German) critical commentators, but it has found a new importance in a number of scholarly readings. Once, Luther placed this text at the theological heart of Paul's gospel. Now it is a focal point for the kaleidoscope of different readings, methodologies, and historical reconstructions which characterize modern Pauline studies.

Particularly notable in recent years has been the ascendancy of interpretations grounded in rhetoric and social history. On the one hand, recent studies have sought to dissect Paul's language in terms of the argumentative structure *within* the text: how does it convey his ideas, particularly when compared with the techniques used by well-known orators of Greco-Roman society? On the other hand, some would try to describe the social framework *behind* the text: what different parties have a stake in Paul's letter? How would they define their identities? And, how would Paul seek to negotiate such sensitive matters?

Overall, then, the importance of Romans has not diminished; it is more the case that scholarly interest in the letter has grown more diffuse. This is a document which finds new life with changing perspectives. Because of its difficult Greek and pregnant phrases, Paul's letter to the Romans has perhaps achieved a curious and ironic feat: it is at once the least readable and most well-read book of the NT.

Works Cited

BAUR, F. C. (1873–5), *Paul the Apostle of Jesus Christ*, 2 vols. Trans. A. Menzies. London: Theology Translation Fund Library.

BELL, R. H. (1994), *Provoked to Jealousy: The Origin and Purpose of the Jealousy Motif in Romans 9–11*. Tübingen: Mohr/Siebeck.

BORNKAMM, G. (1991), 'The Letter to the Romans as Paul's Last Will and Testament', in Donfried 1991: 16–28.

BYRNE, B. (2007), *Romans*, Sacra Pagina 6. Collegeville: Liturgical Press (paperback edn.).

Citations of Patristic and Reformation sources from the Christian Classics Ethereal Library (www.ccel.org).

DODD, C. H. (1932), *The Epistle of Paul to the Romans*. Moffatt New Testament Commentary. London: Hodder & Stoughton.

DONFRIED, K., ed. (1991), *The Romans Debate*. Peabody: Hendrickson (rev. edn.).

DUNN, J. D. G. (1988), *Romans*, 2 vols. WBC 38a–38b, Waco, Tex.: Word Books.

——(1990), *Jesus, Paul and the Law*. London: SPCK.

——(1998), *The Theology of the Apostle Paul*. Edinburgh: T. & T. Clark.

ENGBERG-PEDERSEN, T., ed. (1995), *Paul in his Hellenistic Context*. Minneapolis: Fortress Press.

ESLER, P. F. (2003), *Conflict and Identity in Romans: The Social Setting of Paul's Letter*. Minneapolis: Fortress Press.

GAGER, J. G. (2000), *Reinventing Paul*. Oxford: Oxford University Press.

GAMBLE, H. Y. (1977), *The Textual History of the Letter to the Romans: A Study in Textual and Literary Criticism*. SD 42. Grand Rapids, Mich.: Eerdmans.

JEWETT, R. (1982), 'Romans as an Ambassadorial Letter', *Interpretation*, 36: 5–20.

——(2006), *Romans: A Commentary*. Hermeneia. Philadelphia: Fortress Press.

Jewish Encyclopedia (published by Funk & Wagnalls, 1906) cited from JewishEncyclopedia. com (www.jewishencyclopedia.com).

LAKE, K. (1919), *The Earlier Epistles of St Paul: Their Motive and Origin*. London: Rivingtons.

LUTHER, M. (1961), *Lectures on Romans*. Trans. W. Pauck. Philadelphia: Westminster Press.

MANSON, T. W. (1991), 'St Paul's Letter to the Romans—and Others', in Donfried 1991: 1–15.

MCCOSKER, P. J., ed. (2006), *What Is It That the Scripture Says? Essays in Biblical Interpretation, Translation and Reception in Honour of Henry Wansbrough OSB*. LNTS 316. Edinburgh: T. & T. Clark.

MOO, D. (1996), *The Epistle to the Romans*. NICNT. Grand Rapids, Mich.: Eerdmans.

MORGAN, R. (1995), *Romans*. NT Guides. Sheffield: Sheffield Academic Press.

MUDDIMAN, J. (2006), 'Making Sense of Romans', in McCosker 2006: 89–101.

RÄISÄNEN, H. (1987), *Paul and the Law*. WUNT 29. Tübingen: Mohr/Siebeck (rev. edn.).

SCROGGS, R. (1983), *New Testament and Homosexuality: Contextual Background for Contemporary Debate*. Philadelphia: Fortress Press.

SEIFRID, M. A. (1992), *Justification by Faith: The Origin and Development of a Central Pauline Theme*. Supp. NovT 68. Leiden: Brill.

STOWERS, S. K. (1995), 'Romans 7.7–25 as a Speech-in-Character', in Engberg-Pedersen 1995: 180–202.

VERMES, G. (1998), *The Complete Dead Sea Scrolls in English*. London: Penguin Books.

WATSON, F. (1986), *Paul, Judaism and the Gentiles: A Sociological Approach*. SNTSMS 56. Cambridge: Cambridge University Press.

FURTHER READING

Recommended commentaries are Byrne 2007; C. E. B. Cranfield, *The Epistle to the Romans*, 2 vols. ICC. Edinburgh: T. & T. Clark, 2004 (orig. 1975–9); Jewett 2006; E. Käsemann, *Commentary on Romans*. London: SCM, 1980. For orientation and general interpretive issues: Donfried 1991; Morgan 1995. For a recent and accessible introductory reading of Romans: N. T. Wright, *Paul for Everyone: Romans*, 2 vols. London: SPCK, 2006–7.

CHAPTER 10

1 CORINTHIANS

JUDITH L. KOVACS

INTRODUCTION

One of the earliest surviving Christian writings, Paul's First Letter to the Corinthians provides a fascinating picture of the life of one early Christian community and the challenges its members faced as they attempted to live out the gospel as a tiny minority in the midst of a pagan world. It also gives a first-hand glimpse of Paul's work as missionary and teacher. Written to a church Paul founded (Acts 18:1–17) and knows especially well, in response to a letter from the Corinthians asking him for guidance (7:1), the letter gives advice on healing factions in the community (chs. 1–4), sexual morality (chs. 5–7), how to relate to the civil and religious institutions of the pagan world (6:1–11; chs. 8–10), and various aspects of Christian worship (chs. 11–14). It also reveals a great deal about Paul's theology, as he brings the central affirmations of the gospel to bear on the everyday realities of Christians' lives. The letter begins with a powerful presentation of the cross of Christ as the paradoxical revelation of God's wisdom and power (1:17–25) and concludes with an extended discussion of the general resurrection of the dead and God's final triumph over evil (15:1–58). It includes the earliest extant version of the words of institution of the Eucharist (11:23–5), a striking image of the church as the 'body of Christ' (12:12–31) and a poetic paean to self-giving love (13:1–13) that was to have much resonance through the centuries.

Approach of this Study

Ever since the mid-third century, when the great exegete Origen devoted a series of sermons to it, countless interpreters have discussed this letter in detail, giving a chapter-by-chapter commentary. It has had considerable influence on the development of Christian theology and ethics (Bray 1999; Kovacs 2005) and has found resonance in liturgy, poetry, and song. The present chapter is an example of how 1 Corinthians is interpreted by a biblical scholar in the twenty-first century, drawing on a tradition of historical-critical study of the Bible that reaches back to the Enlightenment. A secondary aim is to provide a few glimpses into the long and rich reception history of the letter. More than any other Pauline letter, 1 Corinthians is concerned with a large number of particular questions and problems. One challenge it presents to interpreters is that our only source for the particulars of the situation it addresses is what we can infer from Paul's words themselves. For example, he says in 1 Corinthians 9:3: 'This is my defence to those who would examine me', and he warns the Corinthians against overvaluing human teachers and making arrogant boasts (3:5; 4:18). From such verses interpreters have often concluded that Paul had 'opponents' in Corinth, and much attention has been given to trying to reconstruct their teaching (Adams and Horrell 2004: 1–128). While such questions will be mentioned, this chapter will eschew speculative reconstruction of the situation that lies behind the letter and stick as closely as possible to the text itself. Verses from the letter will be cited after the New Revised Standard Version translation.

1 Corinthians 1:1–17: Salutation, Situation, Primary Themes

The salutation in 1:1–3 follows the form of ancient letters, with names of sender and recipient and words of greeting:

Paul, called to be an apostle of Christ Jesus by the will of God, and our brother Sosthenes, To the church of God that is in Corinth, to those who are sanctified in Christ Jesus, called to be saints, together with all those who in every place call on the name of our Lord Jesus Christ, both their Lord and ours: Grace to you and peace from God our Father and the Lord Jesus Christ.

Paul claims a double authority: as an apostle sent by God and founder of the church in Corinth (3:10; 4:15; 9:1; see also Acts 18:1–17). 'Apostle' means 'one who is sent'; Paul believes he was commissioned by Jesus Christ to spread the good news of his death and resurrection and to foster the growth of Christian communities.

He greets the Corinthian Christians as the 'church of God', an expression that at this early date (around the year 54) refers not to an established institution or a building but to a small community that met in private houses. He calls them 'holy ones' (or 'saints') who have been 'sanctified'. These words signal a perspective that will pervade the letter: Paul emphasizes the communal nature of Christian life and regards the fledgling community as a holy space, an outpost of the divine rule in the midst of a world where evil forces are still at work. Later in the letter (3:16–17) he will call the church God's 'temple'—a strong image in a time when the temple in Jerusalem still stood and temples of Greco-Roman gods were everywhere to be seen.

There follows a 'thanksgiving' section (as in Rom. 1:8–15; Phil. 1:3–11; 1 Thess. 1:2–10), which anticipates themes that will be important in what follows:

I give thanks to my God always for you because of the grace of God that has been given you in Christ Jesus, for in every way you have been enriched in him, in speech and knowledge of every kind—just as the testimony of Christ has been strengthened among you—so that you are not lacking in any spiritual gift as you wait for the revealing of our Lord Jesus Christ. He will also strengthen you to the end, so that you may be blameless on the day of our Lord Jesus Christ. God is faithful; by him you were called into the fellowship of his Son, Jesus Christ our Lord. (1:4–9)

Paul begins and ends this letter by celebrating divine grace (1:3–4; 16:23), expressing his keen awareness that salvation is possible only because of God's free gift. Other themes introduced here are: eloquence (cf. 2:1–5; 4:20), knowledge (cf. 1:18–25; 2:1–16; 3:18–20; 8:1–13; 13:2), and spiritual gifts (cf. 12:1–14:38). The references to 'the end' and 'the day of our Lord Jesus Christ' foreshadow the subject of chapter 15: the *eschaton* or 'endtime' when Christ will return. Paul refers to this as Christ's 'revealing'; the Greek word is *apokalypsis*, which is the Greek title of the Revelation of John. Paul's teaching has much in common with this book, including his conviction that the Christ's victory over evil powers will be completed at the *eschaton*.

In 1:10–17 Paul turns to the specific situation that has prompted his letter: it has been reported to him that the community is already divided, with various subgroups championing their leaders, Paul, Apollos, or Cephas (Peter), and some claiming 'I belong to Christ' (1:10–12). It appears that Apollos was particularly influential, since Paul refers to him several times in the letter (3:4–6, 22; 4:6; 16:12; on his activity in Corinth see also Acts 18:24–19:1). In response to this factionalism Paul says he is glad that he baptized only a few in Corinth (1:14–16); this suggests that the factions may have involved special loyalty towards the leader by whom one was baptized. In verse 17 Paul focuses on the gospel—that is, the 'good news' he preaches—providing the topic sentence for the next part of the letter: 'For Christ did not send me to baptize but to proclaim the gospel, and not with eloquent wisdom, so that the cross of Christ might not be emptied of its power.'

1 CORINTHIANS 1:18–4:21: DIVINE WISDOM—PAUL'S RESPONSE TO THE PROBLEM OF DIVISIONS

Paul's gospel centres on two salvific events: the death of Jesus Christ on the cross and his resurrection (15:3–8). In 1:18–2:5 he meets head-on the scandal of the cross: how could God's messiah have suffered such an ignominious death? By human standards this is sheer folly; but in fact—as Paul has come to know only through the grace of God (15:8–11)—the cross is the paradoxical revelation of God's wisdom and power. Wisdom based on anything else, he argues, is false wisdom. This polemic against wisdom that is merely human, together with the polemic in 8:1–13 against those who boast of their knowledge (*gnosis* in Greek, a word also used in 3:21; 4:18; 13:2), has led many interpreters to suppose that Paul had opponents in Corinth who claimed to be wiser than he (Adams and Horrell 2004: 71–9). To reinforce his claim that God reveals himself through apparent foolishness and weakness, Paul points to the humble origins of the Corinthian believers (1:26: 'Not many of you were wise by human standards, not many were powerful, not many were of noble birth'). Christians are to boast only in Christ Jesus, 'who became for us wisdom from God, and righteousness and sanctification and redemption' (1:30). Paul himself, when he brought the gospel to Corinth, was weak and unprepossessing, making no show of eloquence or high-sounding wisdom (2:1–5).

After this vigorous defence of divine 'folly', Paul's argument takes a surprising turn in 2:6–16. He now says: 'Yet among the mature (or 'the perfect') we do speak wisdom, though it is not a wisdom of this age or of the rulers of this age, who are being destroyed' (2:16; NRSV translates 'doomed to perish'). Here Paul interprets the cross from another point of view, as the locus of a conflict between suprahuman spiritual powers: on the one side the Spirit of God who has enabled Paul and the Corinthian believers to recognize God's gifts (2:10–16), and on the other side the 'rulers' (2:6–8), which probably refers to evil spiritual powers along with human leaders. The crucifixion, Paul implies here, is God's paradoxical and surprising triumph over the evil powers. This is understood only by those who are spiritual (*pneumatikoi*) not by the 'unspiritual' or 'soulish' (*psychikoi*, a word difficult to translate).

In 3:1–4 Paul returns to the factions mentioned in 1:10–12. Because of their quarrelling the Corinthian believers are like children; thus he could not teach them the wisdom for the 'mature' (or 'perfect'). While they ought to be 'spiritual' they are still 'fleshly' (*sarkikoi*)—that is, dominated by impulses that are merely human. Paul warns against boasting in leaders such as himself and Apollos, pointing out that they are only servants of God. The Corinthian church is like a field, 'planted' by Paul and 'watered' by Apollos, and a building constructed jointly by Paul and other workers (3:5–15). 'Do you not know', he asks, 'that you are God's temple and that God's Spirit dwells in you?' (3:16; in Greek 'you' is a plural form). The eschatological horizon introduced in 1:7–8 reappears when Paul predicts that God will destroy anyone who destroys his temple (3:17). Even the leaders revered by the different factions will be subject to God's judgement and their work tested 'in the fire'(3:10–15).

Next Paul insists that he and Apollos, as mere servants, will be judged at the *eschaton* when Christ returns; it is not for the Corinthians to pronounce judgement or boast in their leaders (4:1–7). He seeks to deflate their arrogance through irony: 'Already you have been filled!... Quite apart from us you have become kings! Indeed I wish that you had become kings, so that we might be kings with you!' (4:8). The idea that God's elect will be given a special role in the endtime, as rulers or judges, appears in Daniel 7:9, Matthew 19:28, and Revelation 20:4–6; Paul himself says in 6:2–3 that Christians will judge the world and angels. Based on 4:8 and 15:12 (where Paul asks: 'How can some of you say there is no resurrection of the dead?'), some interpreters think that Christians in Corinth did not share Paul's eschatological orientation but maintained an overly 'realized eschatology', that is, a belief that all the blessings of the endtime were already available in the present (Adams and Horrell 2004: 107–18).

In contrast to this glorified view of the situation of Christians in the present, Paul portrays his own weakness: 'God has exhibited us apostles as last of all, as though sentenced to death, because we have become a spectacle to the world, to angels and to mortals.... We have become like the rubbish of the world' (4:9, 12). He admonishes the Corinthians to follow his example, reminding them that he is their 'father' in Christ Jesus and promising to visit them soon, the Lord willing, and to put those who are arrogant to the test (4:14–21).

1 CORINTHIANS 5–7: QUESTIONS OF SEXUAL MORALITY

In chapters 5–7 Paul takes up several specific questions of Christian praxis. In earlier chapters he had emphasized his humble status as 'servant' of God (3:5), but here he presents a different face, making rulings about allowable conduct in an authoritative voice. The dominant theme is sexual morality, as Paul discusses a case of incest (5:1–5), a claim of some Corinthians that they are free to sleep with prostitutes (6:12–20), and questions about marriage and sexual relations (7:1–40). He also touches on how Christians are to function within the dominant society, specifically, whether they should make use of normal law-courts (6:1–11).

Paul delivers a strong rebuke for a specific case of sexual misconduct: a Christian is sleeping with his father's wife (5:1–5). He solemnly declares his judgement: this man must be 'handed over to Satan for the destruction of the flesh, so that his spirit may be saved on the day of the Lord' (5:3–5). The reference to Satan recalls the 'rulers of this age' of 2:6–8 who were unable to thwart the divine plan of salvation. In Paul's apocalyptic view, evil spiritual powers are still active in the world despite their initial defeat in the cross of Christ. The church is a holy community, a divine outpost in a world where evil forces are at work (1:2; see also Gal. 1:4). Handing over to Satan seems to mean excommunicating the offender from the church, thus putting him back into the realm where Satan has power. Paul pronounces this drastic punishment with a view to the offender's ultimate salvation; the 'destruction of his flesh' probably refers to his evil impulses rather than his physical body. Contrary to what some of his interpreters think, Paul does not maintain a dualism of body and spirit (or soul). While 'flesh' sometimes refers to the stuff of the body (e.g. in 7:28; 15:50), Paul also uses the word in contrast to 'spirit' to designate two warring impulses: the 'flesh' prompts rebellion against God and the 'spirit' obedience (Gal. 5:16–25; Rom. 8:2–9). As chapters 6 and 15 will make clear, Paul does not view salvation as the escape of the spirit (or soul) from the body. True to his Jewish heritage, he considers the human being, body and spirit, as a unity, and he looks for the resurrection of the body.

Excursus: Basic Principles of Paul's Ethics

Paul's treatment of this specific case exemplifies three principles that underlie all the specific advice he gives in 1 Corinthians. Although he quotes from 'the law', that is, the Law of Moses contained in the books of Exodus through Deuteronomy (9:8, 9; 14:21, 34), this is not his primary moral criterion. In 15:56 he says that the law is 'the power of sin'; in other letters he contrasts the power of the gospel with this law (Rom. 3:21; 10:4; Gal. 3:13; 2:20). He does not envision a new Christian *system* of law to replace the old law. Instead, he gives advice tailored to specific situations that is unified by his understanding of the Christian calling. Again and again, he reminds the Corinthians that they are called to: (1) live in light of the gospel of Jesus Christ; (2) remember what time it is; (3) act so as to 'build up' the church.

Paul's gospel centres on the crucifixion and resurrection of Jesus Christ. Frequently his advice for specific situations amounts to: 'Remember the gospel! And let your lives be guided by it.' In 5:7–8, for example, he explains the rationale for his pronouncement of excommunication: 'For our paschal lamb, Christ, has been sacrificed. Therefore, let us celebrate the festival, not with the old yeast, the yeast of malice and evil, but with the unleavened bread of sincerity and truth.' (See similar reminders of the cross in 6:20; 7:23; 8:11; 10:16–17; 11:27). Moral action is not a *means* of salvation (see Rom. 3:21–4:7) but a *consequence* of accepting the gospel; it is living out the new life given by divine grace. The other half of Paul's gospel—the proclamation that Jesus Christ has been raised from the dead—figures similarly in his moral exhortations. In response to Christians who claim freedom to sleep with prostitutes (6:13–14), Paul does not cite a law or general moral principle but instead recalls Christ's resurrection: 'The body is meant not for fornication but for the Lord, and the Lord for the body. And God raised the Lord and will also raise us by his power.'

These verses also reflect a second reference point by which Paul judges moral issues: eschatology. From the beginning (1:6–8) to the end of this letter (16:22) Paul portrays himself and his fellow Christians as poised between two advents of Christ (see also 7:26–31; 11:26; ch. 15). He describes believers as those 'on whom the ends of the ages have come' (10:11), and reminds them to live in expectation of the second coming, when Christ will complete his victory over evil and death (15:12–58). So in 5:5 Paul expresses concern that the incestuous man may be saved in the 'day of the Lord', that is, when Jesus returns as eschatological judge (on the future judgement see also 3:13–15; 11:32).

The third general principle that undergirds Paul's moral advice is that the individual should always act in such a way as to benefit his fellow believer and the church as a whole. When he addresses the case of incest his concern reaches beyond the offender to the effect on the community of their tolerating the man's sin: 'And you are arrogant! Should you not rather have mourned, so that he who has done this would have been removed from among you? . . . Do you not know that a little yeast leavens the whole batch of dough?' (5:2, 6). The church in Corinth is a temple, a holy place (3:16) which has been polluted by the sin of the incestuous man. Paul compares it to a 'building' built upon the foundation of Christ (3:10), and speaks frequently of 'building up' (8:1, 10; 10:23; 14:3–4, 17). Every action should 'build up' the church. This means that actions that may be permissible in themselves are to be avoided if they harm another Christian (8:7–13; 14:1–5).

These principles are also evident in chapter 6. Paul criticizes the Corinthians for bringing their disputes into pagan law-courts instead of adjudicating them within the church (6:1–8). Putting this in eschatological perspective, he reminds them that they are destined to judge angels (6:3) and enumerates unrighteous actions that will merit exclusion from the kingdom of God (6:9–11). He then returns to questions of sexual ethics, addressing the claim of some that they are free to do whatever they want, including sleeping with prostitutes (6:12–20). Perhaps these Corinthians have taken Paul's preaching of a law-free gospel in a direction he did not intend. He writes: ' "All things are lawful for me," but not all things are beneficial' (6:12). The phrase 'All things are lawful for me' is the first of several that NRSV encloses in quotation-marks (see also 6:13; 7:1; 8:1, 4, 8), reflecting the translators' judgement that Paul is quoting slogans current among the Corinthians, which he then proceeds to qualify, in this case with: 'But not all things are beneficial.' The verses that follow appeal to the gospel and to eschatology. They also display Paul's high regard for the body: 'The body is not meant for fornication but for the Lord, and the Lord for the body'—a point he reinforces by reminding the Corinthians of the resurrection of Christ and the expected resurrection of believers (6:14). His final argument is an appeal to the cross of Christ: 'You were bought with a price; therefore glorify God in your body' (6:20).

Next Paul turns to questions the Corinthians had posed in a letter: 'Now concerning the matters about which you wrote' (7:1; cf. 8:1; 12:1). In a discussion that was to have enormous influence on the development of Christian sexual ethics, he considers marriage and sexual relations. His advice is mixed, and this has led to very different understandings of the chapter's implications for Christian practice. On the one hand Paul orders married couples to have regular sexual relations (7:3–5), counsels against divorce (7:10–14), says that engaged men and widows who marry 'do well' (7:28, 36, 38–9), and calls both marriage and celibacy 'spiritual gifts' (7:7). On the other hand he expresses a preference that all share his unmarried state (7: 7, 40), portrays marriage as an antidote to excessive passion that might bring a person under Satan's power (7: 2, 5, 9, 36), and says that the engaged person and the widowed do 'better' not to marry (7:27, 38, 40). The reasons Paul gives for preferring celibacy to marriage are that it facilitates single-minded devotion to the Lord (7:32–5) and that the *eschaton* is near. The eschatological perspective is prominent in 7:17–31 (see 7:26, 29, 31), where Paul considers circumcision, slavery, and the use of wealth along with marriage. In all of these matters he counsels the Corinthians to remain in the state in which God called them (7:17, 20, 24), because 'the present form of this world is passing away' (7:31).

1 CORINTHIANS 8–10: CHRISTIANS AND GRECO-ROMAN RELIGION

Chapters 8–10 remind us that the little house-church in Corinth existed in a world in which the temples of Greco-Roman gods were a prominent part of daily life. Paul considers whether Christians may eat meat from animals sacrificed in pagan temples, some of which would end up in butcher shops (10:25), and discusses whether they may attend pagan dinner parties, which might be held in temple complexes (8:10; 10:27). Referring to pagan cult statues as 'idols' that represent demons (10:20), Paul contrasts these 'so-called gods' with the 'one God, the Father, from whom are all things and for whom we exist, and one Lord, Jesus Christ, through whom are all things and through whom we exist' (8:6), a confession that recasts the central Jewish prayer, the Shema (Deut. 6:4), and gives evidence of Paul's high view of Jesus Christ. He then considers those he calls 'the weak' whose faith might be shaken if they see their fellow Christians ('the strong') eating meat that has been offered to idols (8:7–9). Their faith is 'weak' in that they have residual fear of the 'idols'. Paul says there is nothing intrinsically wrong with eating 'idol meat'—Christians are free in such matters (8:8–9). But more important than individual freedom is the principle of 'building up': the 'strong' should not eat 'idol-meat' if this endangers the faith of the 'weak'. If they do so, they have forgotten the meaning of the cross: 'By your knowledge those weak believers—for whom Christ died—are destroyed' (8:11).

In chapter 9 Paul offers his life as an example of self-restraint: he will 'endure anything' rather than cause offence (9:12). Responding to criticisms of his ministry (9:3), he defends his right to receive compensation for his work of evangelism but points out that he has not exercised this right. Verses 19–23 make the more general point that Paul has adapted himself to many different situations: 'I have become all things to all people that I might by all means save some' (9:22).

To strengthen his advice concerning 'idol meat' Paul adduces, in 10:1–11, an exegesis of the stories of the exodus from Egypt (Exod. 1–15) and the wandering of the Israelites in the wilderness (Exod. 16–Num. 21). Comparing the crossing of the sea to baptism and eating of manna in the wilderness to the Eucharist, he concludes: 'These things occurred as *typoi* for us' (10:6). The NRSV translates the word *typoi* with 'examples', thereby underscoring the context in 10:6–14, where Paul argues that the Corinthians, like the ancient Israelites, are in danger of committing idolatry. Early interpreters, however, understood *typoi* to mean 'types' or 'figures', and saw this passage as an important model for how Christians should interpret the Old Testament (Kovacs 2005: 159–65). Later the word 'typology' came to designate a particular type of symbolic exegesis, similar to, but often contrasted with, 'allegory'.

Once again Paul reminds the Corinthians of the eschatological perspective that should inform their action: 'These things . . . were written down to instruct us, on whom the ends of the ages have come' (10:11). Then, in 10:14–22, he turns to the Eucharist to argue that participation in the table of Christ excludes any sharing in the 'table of demons'. To conclude the discussion of 'idol meat' he offers himself as a model for being thankful to God in all things and adapting one's action to what love requires in each different situation (10:27–33). Although the Corinthians are free to eat whatever is sold in the markets and to attend pagan dinner parties, they should follow Paul's example and limit their freedom if doing so will 'build up' their fellow Christians.

1 CORINTHIANS 11–14: CHRISTIAN WORSHIP

In chapters 11–14 Paul turns his attention to the internal life of the Christian community, addressing various problematic aspects of their gatherings for worship: the dress of female prophets (11:1–16), disorder in celebrations of the Eucharist (11:17–34), the exercise of 'spiritual gifts' such as speaking in tongues (chs. 12–14), lack of order in worship (14:26–33), and the participation of women (14:33–6). Paul's main concern in 11:1–16 is to convince women prophets to cover their heads when they prophesy, but subsequent commentary has focused less on this concrete point and more on a justification Paul gives for this directive: 'Christ is the head of every man, and the husband is the head of his wife, and God is the head of Christ' (11:3). Paul offers several other arguments why female prophets should wear head-covering, including the creation of Eve from Adam (11:9) and Genesis 1:26, which he understands to say that only the man was created in the 'image of God', not the woman (11:7)—a curious interpretation, when Genesis says: 'God created man in the image of God; male and female he created them.' Interpreters frequently pass over the fact that Paul does not limit the prophetic activity of women. It is difficult to see how this implicit support squares with his command in 14:33–6 that women should remain silent in gatherings for worship.

Particularly important for Christian theology and practice is 11:23–6, the earliest version we possess of the words of institution of the Eucharist. The traditional words are framed by a description of how the Lord's Supper is celebrated in Corinth (11:17–22) and Paul's own theological interpretation of it (11:27–34). In the latter section he warns of serious consequences for those who partake of the bread and wine in an unworthy manner: 'For all who eat and drink without discerning the body, eat and drink judgement against themselves' (11:29).

Chapters 12 and 14 continue the theme of worship by considering 'spiritual gifts'—that is, special abilities or functions given by the Spirit. Paul mentions a number of 'spiritual gifts', including utterances of wisdom and knowledge, faith, healing, performing miracles, discernment of spirits, and the interpretation of tongues (12:8–10), but he concentrates on the gifts of prophecy and *glossolalia*. Both are forms of inspired speech. Whereas the prophet utters a message from God in an ordinary human language, *glossolalia*, or 'speaking in tongues', involves sounds that are not generally intelligible, which Paul calls 'tongues of angels' (13:1). The house-church in Corinth had no ordained leaders, and worship was a lively affair. 'When you come together,' Paul says, 'each one has a hymn, a lesson, a revelation, a tongue, or an interpretation' (14:26). From his argument it appears that the dramatic gift of speaking in tongues was especially prized. Paul boasts: 'I thank God that I speak in tongues more than all of you' (14:18), but he urges the Corinthians to limit their exercise of this gift in order to 'build up' the church (14:3–5, 12, 26). It is better, he says, to speak five words in a language others can understand than 10,000 words in a 'tongue'.

This central principle of 'building up' is reinforced in two sections that are among the best-loved and most influential of the letter: Paul's depiction of the church as 'the body of Christ' in 12:12–31 and the semi-poetic encomium to love in 13:1–13. Just as a body is made up of diverse but interdependent parts, so the members of Christ's 'body', with their varied gifts and abilities, are dependent on each other; all rise or fall together. In 13:1–3 Paul describes love's superiority to all the spiritual gifts; then he enumerates the many virtues of love: 'Love is patient; love is kind; love is not envious or boastful or arrogant or rude.... It bears all things, believes all things, hopes all things, endures all things' (13:4–7). Once again, he speaks of the eschatological context of Christian life. It is love—not the spiritual gifts so prized in Corinth or human knowledge—that endures to the end (13:8–10). Paul looks forward to the *eschaton*, when his imperfect knowledge will be replaced by something much richer: 'For now we see in a mirror, dimly, but then we will see face to face. Now I know only in part; then I will know fully, even as I have been fully known' (13:12).

1 CORINTHIANS 15–16: THE GOSPEL, THE ESCHATON, AND THE PRESENT SITUATION

Chapter 15 has been a crucial text for Christian theology, especially for discussions of christology and the afterlife, and it has occasioned many debates. It contains a concise summary of Paul's gospel (15:1–11), followed by the most detailed treatment in the New Testament of the *eschaton*. Paul begins with a traditional confession of faith that centres on the cross and resurrecton of Jesus Christ, and includes a list of witnesses to the resurrected Christ (15:3–7) to which he adds his own name: 'Last of all, as to one untimely born, he appeared also to me' (15:8). He sees this appearance to one who had persecuted the church as a supreme example of divine grace (15:9–11).

Paul quotes the traditional creed in order to reiterate and clarify his teaching about the *eschaton*, the final consummation of God's plan for human salvation. He treats this subject at length because he has heard that the Corinthians find it difficult. He writes: 'How can some of you say that there is no resurrection of the dead?' (15:12). He does not explain exactly what these sceptics maintained—whether they claimed there was no life after death, or, whether, as gentiles (see 12:2), they believed the soul was immortal but could make nothing of the Jewish idea of resurrection of the body. The latter seems more probable. Paul argues that it makes no sense to believe in the resurrection of Christ but not the general resurrection of the dead, which was an important feature of Jewish eschatology attested in Daniel 12:2–3, Jewish apocalypses, and many New Testament books (e.g. Luke 14:14; 20:33–6; John 5:29; 11:24; Acts 17:32). Paul insists that resurrection is a two-act drama: Christ's resurrection is the 'firstfruits', after which the resurrection of all believers must follow inevitably (15:12–20). This will take place at the second coming of Christ:

Then comes the end, when [Christ] hands over the kingdom to God the Father, after he has destroyed every ruler and every authority and power . . . the last enemy to be destroyed is death. . . . When all things are subjected to him, then the Son himself will also be subjected to the one who put all things in subjection under him, so that God may be all in all. (15:24–8)

In 2:6–16 Paul had portrayed the cross as a preliminary victory over evil powers; here he describes the conclusion of that victory, with the triumph over death, the 'last enemy'. These verses were much discussed by the church fathers, who found difficult the suggestion that Christ's kingdom would have an end. Another point that occasioned much debate was the statement 'that God may be all in all', which some understood to imply universal salvation. The phrase has also prompted much reflection on God as the source of everything good and the ultimate satisfaction of all human desires (Kovacs 2005: 252–60).

After this forceful articulation of his eschatological hope, Paul anticipates a question someone might ask: 'How are the dead raised? With what kind of body do they come?' (15:35). The resurrection body, he argues, will be a transformed version of the present body. While 'flesh and blood cannot inherit the kingdom of God' (15:50), the body will be raised and transformed into something more glorious, 'a spiritual body' that cannot perish (15:35–54). To explain the continuity and the discontinuity between the present body and the resurrection body Paul uses the image of a seed that is transformed into a plant; he also points out that there are many different kinds of heavenly and earthly bodies (15:35–41). This resurrection and transformation will take place for all at once, when the 'last trumpet' sounds and death is 'swallowed up in victory' (15:51–8).

Chapter 16, which focuses on Paul's situation and his travel plans, reminds us that 1 Corinthians is a real letter, addressed to a specific community, written from and intended for a particular situation. Paul writes from Ephesus, where he has a promising mission field but also 'many adversaries' (16:9). He hopes to visit the Corinthian church soon and to spend some time with them, and he wants their help for his further mission (16:5–7). He discusses the travel plans of his co-workers Timothy and Apollos and thanks the Corinthians for the emissaries they have sent to him (16:10–12, 17–18). His exhortation in 16:15–16 that they subject themselves to Stephanus, Fortunatus, and Achaicus recalls the problem of divisions addressed in chapters 1–4.

As we have seen throughout 1 Corinthians, the mundane and the theological are intricately connected for Paul. So this chapter full of travel plans and personal greetings (16:13–22) echoes theological themes that have been important earlier in the letter. In 16:1–4 Paul's concern for 'building up' the church is extended beyond the little community in Corinth when he asks the Corinthians to participate in a collection he is taking up for the church in Jerusalem, an act that symbolizes the unity of the church. His eschatological perspective peeks through in the admonition to 'keep alert' (16:13) and in the Aramaic phrase 'Marana tha' (16:22), which means 'May our Lord come!' He closes, as he began (1:3), by speaking of God's grace: 'I, Paul, write this greeting with my own hand. Let anyone be accursed who has no love for the Lord. Our Lord, come! The grace of the Lord Jesus be with you. My love be with all of you in Christ Jesus' (16:21–4).

Works Cited

ADAMS, D. and D. G. HORRELL (2004), *Christianity at Corinth: The Quest for the Pauline Church*. Louisville, Ky.: John Knox Press.

BRAY, G. (ed.) (1999), *Ancient Christian Commentary on Scripture: 1–2 Corinthians*. Downers Grove, Ill.: InterVarsity Press.

KOVACS, J. L. (ed.) (2005), *The Church's Bible: 1 Corinthians*. Grand Rapids, Mich.: Eerdmans.

Further Reading

COUSAR, C. (1996), *The Letters of Paul*. Nashville, Tenn.: Abingdon Press.

FEE, GORDON (1987), *The First Epistle to the Corinthians*. Grand Rapids, Mich.: Eerdmans.

FURNISH, V. P. (1999), *The Theology of the First Letter to the Corinthians*. Cambridge: Cambridge University Press.

HAYS, R. (1997), *First Corinthians*. Louisville, Ky.: John Knox Press.

MITCHELL, M. (1991), *Paul and the Rhetoric of Reconciliation: An Investigation of the Language and Composition of 1 Corinthians*. Louisville, Ky.: Westminster/John Knox Press.

MURPHY-O'CONNOR, J. (1990), *St. Paul's Corinth: Texts and Archeology*, 3rd edn. Collegeville, Minn.: Liturgical Press.

THISELTON, A. (2000), *The First Epistle to the Corinthians: A Commentary on the Greek Text*. Grand Rapids, Mich.: Eerdmans.

CHAPTER 11

....

GALATIANS

....

JOHN RICHES

PAUL's short letter to the congregation which he had founded in Galatia, it is not too much to say, has had an extraordinary influence on the subsequent development of religious cultures across the world.

It addressed an issue crucial for the development of the Christian church in the first and second centuries, namely that of its relations with the religious traditions preserved in what Christians would come to call the Old Testament but which Paul and his contemporaries referred to as the 'Writings' or the 'Law and the Prophets'. This in turn had long-term effects on the relations between Christians and Jews, as their (various) communities grew further and further apart. In this respect, Galatians was a major source of theological inspiration for the 'heretic' Marcion, possibly the first Christian theologian to reflect seriously on Paul's thought, who read Paul's gospel as proclaiming a strange new God, sharply contrasted with the harsh God of justice of the Old Testament. Other interpreters would draw back from finding such a sharp division in Paul's letter, while nevertheless seeing it as setting clear lines of division between the church and Jewish observances.

Marcion was not alone in reading Paul as depicting a world under the sway of dark powers from which it needed to be rescued by a quite contrary force (Gal. 1:4). Marginalized groups, Gnostics and Manicheans, who embraced various forms of cosmological dualism, also sought support for their views in Galatians. They would in the end be suppressed, but their influence was widespread. Augustine himself had at one stage been a 'hearer' (adherent) of the Manichees and engaged in vigorous debate with them after his conversion and ordination. The threat—and attraction—of such dualist readings of Galatians are never far away over the first 1,500 years of its interpretation: it is most clearly seen in orthodox rejections of such a reading. Luther, with his remarkable sensitivity to Paul's rhetoric, comes closest to embracing a Marcionite position, as he repeatedly lists the law among those forces which oppress and hold men and women in bondage: death, sin, the devil, and the Law!

But the letter was not only beloved of the more deviant groups who drew inspiration from Christian beliefs and scriptures. It also, with its talk of a new creation which had come to birth with the resurrection of Jesus, played a vital role in shaping the new forms of Christian culture which began to replace the world of antiquity once the church emerged from its position of marginality in the Roman Empire during the fourth century. At the end of that century no fewer than three of the major Fathers of the Church wrote commentaries on Galatians: John Chrysostom, Jerome, and Augustine. These three figures, for whom their Galatians commentaries were doubtless of varying degrees of importance, shaped respectively the development of Eastern Orthodoxy and Western Catholic and Reformation Christianity. The lines of influence are certainly not straightforward, but there can be no doubt that Augustine and Jerome were aware of the differences of interpretation that they were offering (they engaged in a lengthy and heated correspondence over the nature of Peter and Paul's conflict at Antioch). This is an important point which will be developed in what follows: in his letter Paul invites the Galatians to allow themselves to be led by the Spirit into the new creation inaugurated through Christ's death and resurrection. That is an extremely open invitation. It offers a new world to all those who are willing to make a radical break with their past (neither circumcision nor un-circumcision any longer counts), to be crucified with Christ to the world. But what this new world will be like, how it will be structured and organized, are all matters which are left gloriously open. Those who live in this new world will be free from the old powers which previously held them in bondage, but how free? Will they be able to lead a life free of sin? The law was clearly part of the old age which has been superseded by the age of faith, but does this mean that it is no longer binding on Christians? How far, to pose a continually disturbing question, does the advent of this new world mean that God has changed the manner in which he deals with the world and his people, 'the Israel of God', as Paul refers to them?

It is not just those writing at the beginning of the Constantinian era who are inspired by the sense of the radically new in Galatians. Even Aquinas, writing from the relative stability of medieval Christianity, sees Galatians as being a letter essentially about newness, renewal: cast out the old to make room for the new (Lev. 26:10). Christianity needs to be constantly purged from what is old: from what is at best a figure of the new to come, but which also stands for the error, the guilt, and the punishment from which the new world is to be freed by the new teaching of Christ, the new righteousness, the new glory (*Prologus: Super Epistolam ad Galatas Lectura*, 563). Aquinas, seeking to renew Christian theology through his engagement with the Bible and Aristotle, appealed to the radical sense of renewal with which Paul's letter was embued.

However, the point at which Galatians reaches the height of its influence is almost certainly the Reformation, where it provides the main support for Luther's doctrine of justification by faith alone which was to transform the religious and social complexion of Europe. Luther incorporated much of what he had learnt from Galatians in his *Freedom of the Christian*, a popular tract of enormous influence. Here the revolutionary force of Paul's letter is harnessed by Luther as never before or since. Luther describes the letter as his Kaethe von Bora (referring to his wife); it was clearly a deep source of comfort to him in the continuing attacks of anxiety which beset him from time to time as he struggled with a troubled conscience. Yet even though Galatians undoubtedly provided Luther with support and encouragement, it was also the letter which provided one of the key texts for the Roman Catholic counter-challenge to the Reformation at the Council of Trent. The phrase 'faith working through love' (Gal. 5:6) became a slogan for those who argued that faith alone could not bring justification; it needed to be informed by love infused into the soul.

Luther gave lectures on the letter on at least three occasions, and there are numerous editions of these lectures taken down by one of his followers, Reginald of Piperno. The influence of Luther's *Commentary on Galatians* is itself a fascinating story. It was the book that helped Bunyan escape from his religious torments and which he described as the book dearest to him next to the Bible. A reading from its preface converted Charles Wesley; his brother John eventually reacted to it more negatively and found it deeply deficient in its understanding of law.

One could go on. Particular verses or passages of the letter have been of particular interest to particular groups. Paul's account of the conflict between Peter and himself in chapter 2 was at the centre of F. C. Baur's account of the development of early Christian theology. He saw the two leaders as representing two very different versions of the gospel which would eventually be synthesized in 'early Catholicism'. Galatians' doctrine of freedom has inspired liberation and advocacy theologians, and Galatians 3:28, with its proclamation of the oneness in Christ of Jew and gentile, slave and free, male and female, has been a rallying-point in debates about women's ordination and in the civil-rights struggles in North America. Down the ages, Galatians 2:20 ('It is no longer I who live, but Christ who lives in me') has been a key text for Christian mystical theology, and in the last hundred years has also attracted the attention of Zen Buddhists. On one reading of Galatians 5:17 ('The desires of the flesh are against the spirit and the desires of the spirit are against the flesh'), Paul's doctrine of the divided self has been the source of much destructive introspection in western Christianity, and this has provoked a fierce criticism of Lutheran readings of Paul, in an attempt to shift the responsibility for these torments away from Paul. (This is actually somewhat odd, in view of the fact that Luther found in Galatians the antidote to such torments and Bunyan derived the same comfort from Luther's commentary!) Yet the same verse has also been, for John Chrysostom and the eastern churches, an encouragement to a life of asceticism and disciplined obedience which is achievable.

What, then, is it about this book and the communities which received it that gives it such remarkable power to influence the lives of so many? What is it about the nature of Paul's rhetoric and diction (the letter was, for the most part, dictated), about the nature of the letter form, about the particular circumstances of its composition (the occasion of the letter, Paul's purpose in writing), and about Paul's own particular formation and experience that gave it such power? And what was it about the wider cultural and religious dynamics of the time and of the communities which subsequently read and embodied the ideas and images of the letter in their corporate lives that made people in very different situations so responsive to what Paul had written long before?

To put the questions like that is, I hope, to make it clear that there can be no one single answer. All of the factors just listed could have contributed, and probably did contribute, to the influence and effects of the letter. What follows is a brief attempt to look at some of them in the light of Galatians' subsequent reception.

THE LETTER FORM AND PAUL'S RHETORIC AND DICTION

Galatians is a letter, written to be read out aloud to a particular group of hearers, addressing quite specific concerns in the life of their community. As a letter it is, of course, one-sided. We hear only one side of the conversation/argument and have to work out for ourselves who the recipients are, what the issues are, what the tone of voice is, what may have been said, what is a counter-argument to something previously argued by the recipients, or indeed by other parties to the dispute/conversation not here addressed.

All of these difficulties are present with the Galatians letter. We can, it is true, say some things about the situation with a good deal of confidence. Paul had established a congregation which was non-observant as far as the Jewish law was concerned, which had experienced in its early days various, largely unspecified, charismatic happenings (speaking in tongues, healings . . . ?), but which was now beginning to turn to the observance of the law, much encouraged by other travelling Jewish Christian missionaries. It is clear too that this dispute was by no means without a history. Paul recounts how some time earlier he and Peter had had a fierce disagreement over the necessity of observing Jewish food laws. At Antioch (on the coast in Syria), Paul and Peter had eaten with the gentiles (who would not have been observant), but then, when people came from Jerusalem, Peter had withdrawn and returned to his traditional Jewish ways. This was a crucial issue for the early church and would divide it for some centuries, with a Jewish-Christian body separating from the 'Great Church' which would go on to become the church of the Empire. Vital matters of principle are at stake here for the future of this body, as the vehemence of Paul's language indicates (e.g. Gal. 1:1, where he curses any one who challenges his gospel).

Other things are somewhat less clear. We do not know for sure where the congregation/s were located; we are far from sure what the constitution of the congregation was: were they gentile converts, Jewish believers in Christ, a mixture of the two? Certainly there were other outsiders involved who had caused trouble in the congregation and whose influence Paul was trying to counter. It seems reasonably clear that there were voices in the congregation who were urging the members to become law-observant, to follow some or all of the law's prescriptions: food laws, observation of festivals, circumcision, and so on. This Paul opposes as a betrayal of the gospel which he has been preaching, which brought them a new life in the Spirit.

But we would, of course, always like to hear more of the other side's arguments, what grounds they gave for their views, who they appealed to—the apostles in Jerusalem, Abraham, Moses—what social pressures they were under which made them want to take this course, all this and much more. When Paul brings Abraham into the argument, is he picking up remarks that have been made by those opposed to him or is he bringing a new motif into the debate which, he hopes, may clinch it for some or all of his hearers? Is he appealing to Jews or is he hoping that Abraham will also have authority for gentile converts who want to become law-observant? In short, as a letter it is a communication which is peculiarly linked to a particular situation which is not easy for us to reconstruct. Not all the issues at stake are equally clear; it is difficult to reconstruct what is being said by the various parties to the debate, and this in turn makes it to difficult to locate the precise context of Paul's arguments in the letter which we have.

There is another consequence of Paul's use of the letter form in such a charged situation. With the exception of the last few verses, Paul dictated this letter, leaving the actual penning of his message to a professional scribe. The number of corrections that this permits is low, and there is much which is less than clear, sometimes comprehensively ambiguous. At the same time there is a passion and spontaneity about Paul's prose which shows him as no mean orator, albeit one who allows his thought to run its course, taking him into some surprising places. All of this gives ample opportunity for Paul to produce sentences that are less than unambiguously clear. When Paul, for instance, says (and his scribe writes, Gal. 5:17), 'the flesh desires against the spirit and the spirit against the flesh; for these are opposed/contrasted with one another that you may not do the things that you wish', is he talking about the good things that they want to do or the bad—or indeed about anything that they might will? Is Paul saying that they can resist what is wrong; or that they are unable to do the good that they want; or that they can never do what they want (that they do not enjoy the freedom to carry through anything that they purpose to undertake)? It is no exaggeration to say that this verse has been the source of very different kinds of Christian anthropology. In the West it has often been associated with the notion of the divided self, more or less paralysed by the inner conflict between flesh and the spirit, with the result that it is unable to do the good that it desires. For Chrysostom, however, Paul in speaking of the desires of the flesh and the spirit is referring not to warring forces *within* the human self but to different goals which the self can set itself. The Spirit teaches us to distinguish the good from the bad in order that we can resist being carried away by our fleshly desires.

And there is more to be said. The very urgency of the situation means that this is no ordinary communication. As Paul writes, the church faces its first major controversy, which will decide whether it is to be one of the forms of Judaism struggling to control the future of the Jewish community or whether it will sever its links with that body, while at the same time maintaining its links with the theological traditions of the Hebrew scriptures. To put it that way is to reveal something of the ambiguity and difficulty of Paul's task. Paul is overwhelmed by the newness of what he has experienced in his life as a follower of Jesus Christ, by what has been revealed to him: his letter finishes with a great outpouring about the coming new creation which makes all the old distinctions between circumcision and un-circumcision simply irrelevant: how could he tolerate his converts' reverting to a way of life and a mindset which would restore power to such forms of religion? At the same time, he follows Jesus the Messiah and regards the writings of the Hebrew Bible as 'scriptures', revelatory of God's will, purposes, and actions. He wants to assert the continuity of this new way of life ('new creation') with what has gone before in the history of Israel (this new church is the 'Israel of God'), while asserting that this new form of life is one which breaks all ties with what has gone before ('new creation'). It is this deep tension in his position which gives it its dynamic and power and makes it attractive to the innovators, 'heretics', and reformers (with or without a capital 'r'). At the same time, it is also a vital document for those who, like Augustine, Jerome, and Chrysostom, are seeking to construct a new culture, who need the resources of the scriptures, old and new, to create a whole new world to replace the world of antiquity, of classical culture.

PAUL'S CULTURAL IDENTITY

Paul would have been particularly sensitive to the tensions and conflicts between the old and new which we have just been considering. He is, he tells us in his Letter to the Philippians (3:4–6), someone fully educated in the traditions of his people, *who has been shaped by Jewish worship*, the observation of Jewish rituals and food laws as understood by the Pharisees, whose traditions were preserved in Hebrew; he is someone who lives within the world of 'the scriptures', which he would have read or heard in either Hebrew or Greek. At the same time, he is a Greek-speaker familiar with standard classical rhetorical figures and tropes, who was in all likelihood familiar not only with the kinds of debates which Platonizing Jewish writers like Philo of Alexandria conducted in their writings, but also with those of Stoic philosophers. Moreover, Paul was also familiar with movements of thought which had entered Judaism in the previous two centuries or more, probably from the East. This kind of apocalyptic thought spoke of revelations of hidden mysteries to seers and of a dramatic end to the present—evil—world. Paul, that is to say, was something of a hybrid, steeped in Jewish culture but with more than one foot in the diverse cultures of the Greek-speaking Mediterranean world.

And this hybridity will allow him to be read in surprisingly different ways by later theologians. It is instructive to look at the way that what he says about the law is later interpreted. In this letter Paul portrays the law as a temporary measure which comes 430 years after the promise God makes to Abraham and whose time comes to an end with the advent of faith. More strictly, what he says is that 'we' were kept locked up under the law until the revelation of the faith which was to come (Gal. 3:17–23). The law, that is to say, is part of the old age which is passing away, which was an age of bondage to 'weak and beggarly powers'. Christ has redeemed those who were formerly under the law, so that they might receive sonship, and has sent the Spirit of God into their hearts crying 'Abba, father' (Gal. 4:1–11). Until the time of Calvin, almost all Christian interpreters of the letter took this to mean that once Christ, and therefore the age of faith, had come, the law no longer had a function for those who believed. Previously they (or at least those of them who had been Jewish) had been watched over, taught, held under guard by, and enslaved to, the law (Paul's metaphors allow a good deal of freedom of interpretation), but now they are led by, instructed by, the Spirit, so that they are no longer subject to the law—so that, indeed, to go back to observance of the law would be to return to slavery. Chrysostom has Paul despairingly ask the Galatians: how could you so degrade yourselves as to go back to the law? The law was like an elementary teacher teaching the basics of grammar, whereas they were now under a philosopher, the Spirit. For Luther the law could only lead people to despair. Faith in Christ, the believers' union with Christ (Gal. 2:20), liberated them from the tyranny of the law and freed them to become sons of God. But with Calvin comes a different reading. Paul, he argues, is here talking about the functions of the law before Christ came. These functions still hold good for those who have not yet come to faith. But for those who believe, they no longer hold. This, however, is not to say that the law ceases to be of importance altogether. For believers it has a new function, which is to act as the final arbiter in ethical disputes for those who 'flourish in the Spirit'. It is admittedly not possible to find such a view in Galatians, as Calvin acknowledges; but that is merely because Paul is here concerned with other matters. In Romans such views can be more easily supported. It is a key question for all interpreters whether they read Galatians in the light of Paul's other writings or whether they 'let Galatians be Galatians', reading it for what it says and not in the light of such thoughts on these matters as Paul might have had later. Such questions are particularly acute when it comes to interpreting Paul, precisely because of the multifaceted nature of his thought with its roots in the richly diverse culture of the first century CE.

THE RECEPTIVITY OF PAUL'S
READERS TO HIS LETTERS

All of these factors may well explain in a measure why Paul was so widely read and for so long, but they should not blind us to the fact that perhaps the main reason why he has been so popular and had such an impact is that he had a captive audience. The fact that his writings were incorporated into the canon of—very different—Christian communities meant both that they were read in their gatherings for teaching and for worship and that they were imbued with a particular kind of authority. These were writings which were officially recognized as containing all that was necessary for salvation, for one's eternal health, and for wisdom and well-being. But, again, this is true of a significant number of other books in the Christian church's canon, and does not wholly account for Paul's and, in particular, Galatians' influence. What was it about Paul and his letter that earned him such devotion?

In the first place, we should not overlook the simple fact that this letter, dictated in the heat of the moment, is full of metaphors, phrases, and sentences which are in need of further clarification, and which, in certain cases (as we saw with Gal. 5:17), are straightforwardly ambiguous. In any act of reading (beyond, perhaps, the most simple) there is a creative interpretative element, a filling in of gaps and clarifying of passages where the meaning is indeterminate; in Paul the need for such interpretative action is particularly great, and this means that the reader has greater opportunities to bring in his or her beliefs and experience to fill in and supplement what is missing. Within an ecclesiastical context, where Paul's writings have canonical status, such interpretative freedom is, it is true, somewhat constrained. Precisely because he is a figure whose authority is underwritten by the church, the expectation is that he will not be saying things which are contrary to the teachings of the church. Putting a book in the canon can change its meaning. The interpretative work of Paul's readers is done within a broad horizon of expectations set by the teaching of whichever part of the church they find themselves in. Nevertheless, at least the more scholarly interpreters are keenly aware of the history of interpretation and engage vigorously with the views of other interpreters.

Such socially embodied readings—embodied, that is, in a historically quite diverse family of ecclesial communities all of which accept Paul's writings as binding—seem as a matter of fact to have been the most influential. It is not that there are not other readings of Paul, both from those in other religious communities which do not acknowledge his authority—who may, indeed, have suffered at the hands of his followers—and from those with no particular religious allegiance at all. But even in such cases much of the influence may well be within the Christian communities in so far as they are willing to learn from voices outside their own communities. Perhaps the fact is simply that ecclesial readings have effect precisely because they may be taken up by and then shape the life of a community. And in that respect the letter form is particularly effective, if the community can, as it were, hear itself being addressed across the ages by Paul himself.

But that still leaves the question: what is it about Paul, about his thought, about the arguments that he is having in this particular letter, that has made such a deep impression on subsequent readers and communities of readers? Again, there are no single or simple answers to such a question. John Chrysostom, who admired Paul with a deep and all-consuming passion, found in him someone who embodied many of his own ideals, both as an interpreter of scripture and as an ascetic. Aquinas reads him ultimately as a thinker, someone whose thought and arguments he can expound and engage with and who will inspire and inform his own thinking. Luther sees him as the one who has above all experienced the grace and forgiveness of God and who can provide him with comfort and assurance in all the toils of his conscience. That kind of response has probably been the one that has inspired most people within the Protestant wing of the church: blessed assurance! But for Luther not only is Paul the preacher of forgiveness and assurance, he also proclaims a doctrine of freedom, of Christian emancipation from tyranny and servitude which has had enormous political implications both inside and outside the church. To be able to claim the support of such a canonically accredited theologian must too, in its way, have been reassuring as well as politically valuable.

For Paul's influence was by no means only restricted to the diversity of personal affinities which writers of very different character would discover they shared with him. As we saw above, he is able to speak to key figures at major junctures of cultural and political history, whether it is Chrysostom, Jerome, or Augustine at the beginning of the Constantinian era, Aquinas at the height of the Middle Ages, or Luther or Calvin at the Reformation. At one level, the reason for this is simple. Paul was one of the major authority figures in Christianity—after Jesus, perhaps the major authority—and anyone who wished to shape the world in the age of the church would need to come to terms with him and show that what he or she had to say could rightly claim his support. But at another level Paul is precisely the sort of thinker that anyone engaged in rethinking the cultural boundaries of their world would want to engage with, could learn from, precisely because this is what Paul is doing. He finds himself at a defining moment of human history and, in the concepts and mythologies and stories which he has learnt from the diverse cultures of his own age, he gives expression to that sense of the new, he resists fiercely those who fail to see, as he does, that here is a new world to be grasped, to be brought to birth. The great nineteenth-century New Testament scholar and church historian F. C. Baur saw this as clearly as anyone, before or since. Paul is the theologian of the new age which emerges when Rome establishes its rule over the western world, the prophet of a new universalism which transcends the ethnic and religious particu-larities of the old world of the Mediterranean, of the gods of the ancient world and of the divisions between Jews and gentiles. What Paul brings to expression is a new 'God-consciousness' which will, in time and after an intense battle within the church, replace the old cults and ethnic divisions. This is why it is so important for Paul to claim that what he has received is not 'from man' but was taught to him by a revelation of Jesus Christ (Gal. 1:12). His gospel is not authenticated by those who are still tied to the old world, however much that world may be a necessary precursor to the world which they are now entering. It comes from Jesus Christ, 'through whom the world is crucified to me and I to the world'. As scholars like Krister Stendahl, E. P. Sanders, and perhaps more pertinently, the Jewish scholar Daniel Boyarin have rightly pointed out, such a view of Paul effectively disqualifies Jews as belonging to the old world of ethnic *particularities*. And this is a conse-quence of the radicalness of Galatians that Paul is himself—later—to wrestle with and, in Romans 9–11 to deny. While there is no room here to debate these crucial issues, mention of them brings out precisely the sense in which Paul struggles to think through the nature and implications of the radically new world which he is entering.

Works Cited

Aquinas, Thomas, (1966), *Commentary on Saint Paul's Epistle to the Galatians*, trans. F. R. Larcher, OP, Aquinas Scripture Series. Albany, NY: Magi Books.

Augustine, (2003), *Augustine's Commentary on Galatians: Introduction, Texts, Translation, and Notes*, ed. Eric Plumer, Oxford Early Christian Studies. Oxford: Oxford University Press.

Baur, Ferdinand Christian (1878), *The Church History of the Three Centuries*. London: Williams & Norgate.

Boyarin, Daniel (1997), *A Radical Jew: Paul and the Politics of Identity*. Berkeley: University of California Press.

Calvin, John (1965), *The Epistles of Paul to the Galatians, Ephesians, Philippians and Colossians*, trans. T. H. L. Parker. Grand Rapids, Mich.: Eerdmans.

JEROME, *Commentatorium in epistulam ad Galatas*, libri tres, in Migne (ed.), *Patrologia Latina* 26. 331–468.

JOHN CHRYSOSTOM, *Galatians*. ANF 13: 1–48.

LUTHER, MARTIN (1953), *A Commentary on St. Paul's Epistle to the Galatians: Based on Lectures Delivered by Martin Luther at the University of Wittenberg in the Year 1531 and First Published in 1535. A Revised and Completed Translation Based on the 'Middleton' Edition of the English Version of 1575*. London: James Clarke.

SANDERS, E. P. (1977), *Paul and Palestinian Judaism*. London: SCM Press.

STENDAHL, KRISTER (1976), *Paul Among Jews and Gentiles*. Philadelphia: Fortress.

FURTHER READING

ALAND, BARBARA, (1992) *Marcion/Marcioniten. In Theologische Realenzyklopaedie*, 22. 89–101. Berlin: Walter de Gruyter.

BAUR, FERDINAND CHRISTIAN (1875), *Paul, the Apostle of Jesus Christ, His Life and Work, His Epistles and His Doctrine: A Contribution to a Critical History of Early Christianity*, Volumes 1 and 2. London: Williams & Norgate.

BETZ, H. D. (1979), *Galatians: A Commentary on Paul's Letter to the Churches in Galatia*. Hermeneia. Philadelphia: Fortress Press.

BORNKAMM, KARIN (1963), *Luthers Auslegungen des Galaterbriefs von 1519 und 1531*. Berlin: Walter de Gruyter.

BULTMANN, R. (1929), 'Geschichte der Paulus-Forschung', *Theologische Rundschau*, NF 1: 26–59.

FREDRIKSEN, P. (1986), 'Paul and Augustine: Conversion Narrative, Orthodox Traditions and the Retrospective Self', *JThS* 37: 3–34.

LIGHTFOOT, J. B. (1865), *St. Paul's Epistle to the Galatians: A Revised Text with Introduction, Notes and Dissertations*. Cambridge and London: Macmillan & Co.

LONGENECKER, R. N. (1990), *Galatians*, Word Biblical Commentary. Dallas, Tex.: Word Books.

MITCHELL, M. M. (2000), *The Heavenly Trumpet: John Chrysostom and the Art of Pauline Interpretation*, Hermeneutische Untersuchungen zur Theologie. Tübingen: Mohr Siebeck.

PERKINS, WILLIAM (1989), *A Commentarie, or Exposition Upon the First Five Chapters of the Epistle to the Galatians*, Pilgrim Classic Commentaries. New York: Pilgrim Press.

RICHES, J. K. (1993), *A Century of New Testament Study*. Cambridge: Lutterworth.

——(2001), 'Theological Interpretation of the New Testament and the History of Religions: Some Reflections in the Light of Galatians 5:17' in A. Y. COLLINS and M. M. MITCHELL (eds.), *Antiquity and Humanity: Essays on Ancient Religion and Philosophy presented to Hans Dieter Betz on his 70th Birthday*, 245–62. Tübingen: Mohr Siebeck.

——(2002), 'Readings of Augustine on Paul: Their Impact on Critical Studies of Paul, in D. Patte and E. Te Selle (eds.), *Engaging Augustine on Romans: Self, Context, and Theology in Interpretation*, 173–98. Harrisburg, Pa.: Trinity Press International.

——(2008), *Galatians Through the Centuries*, Blackwells Bible Commentaries. Oxford: Blackwell.

WEINANDY, T. G., KEATING, D. A., and YOCUM, J. P. (eds.) (2005), *Aquinas on Scripture: An Introduction to His Biblical Commentaries*. London: T. & T. Clark.

WILES, MAURICE (1967), *The Divine Apostle*. Cambridge: Cambridge University Press.

YOUNG, FRANCES (1997), *Biblical Exegesis and the Formation of Christian Culture*. Cambridge: Cambridge University Press.

CHAPTER 12

··

REVELATION

··

CHRISTOPHER ROWLAND

THE Book of Revelation, or the Apocalypse of Jesus Christ, to use the opening words of the book, is a collection of visions, some of which follow on from each other (e.g. chs. 5–6) while others begin a new visionary sequence (e.g. chs. 12–13). The very first word in Greek is the only reference in the book as a whole to it being an 'apocalypse' (elsewhere the book and its author are seen as prophecy and prophets respectively, Rev. 10:11; 22:9). The closest parallel to Revelation in the Bible is the Book of Daniel in the Hebrew Bible, in which dreams and visions, whether those of Daniel or interpreted by Daniel, as is the case with Nebuchadnezzar's dream (Dan. 2), dominate the text. The visionary nature of Daniel sets it apart from other prophetic books of the Hebrew Bible, which, although containing occasional visionary experiences (as in the case of Ezek. 1 and Isa. 6), are in the main records of words given to the prophet to speak to Judah or Israel outlining their wrongdoings and promising judgement and hope. Revelation similarly stands apart from the rest of the New Testament. While reference is made to visions in the context of narratives (Mark 1:10; Luke 10:16; Acts 10:11) and letters (2 Cor. 12:2–4), nowhere else do we find a sustained collection of visions which are to be communicated to humans, 'the seven churches' (Rev. 1:11), based on letters to the angels of each of those seven churches (probably a reference to their guardian angels, Rev.1:20 cf. Matt 18:10). In his vision John is privileged to see things in heaven, to behold the mysteries of what must take place hereafter (Rev. 1:1; 4:1), and to allow others to read the communications which he is commissioned to write to the angelic representatives of the churches.

Despite the variety of the visions in the Book of Revelation, there is a discernible thread running through it. In John's initial vision of heaven (ch. 4) God is acknowledged as creator (4:11) and honoured as such. This contrasts with the world below in which humanity is in rebellion (9:20–1). The inexorable over-coming of that rebellion through the chaos which follows the opening of the first seal by the Lamb (6:1) paves the way for the establishment of a messianic reign on earth (20:4–6), judgement (20:11–15), and ultimately heaven on earth (21:1–4) when the God hidden from all except the visionary (4:1) will be seen face to face (22:3–4).

THE OUTLINE AND STRUCTURE
OF REVELATION

I. 1:1–8, John introduces his book: the apocalypse of Jesus Christ.

II. 1:9–20, the vision of 'the son of man' who commissions John to write.

III. 2:1–3:22, John writes to the angels of the seven churches:
   A. 2:1–7, the Letter to the Angel at Ephesus;
   B. 2:8–11, the Letter to the Angel at Smyrna;
   C. 2:12–17, the Letter to the Angel at Pergamum;
   D. 2:18–29, the Letter to the Angel at Thyatira;
   E. 3:1–6, the Letter to the Angel at Sardis;
   F. 3:7–13, the Letter to the Angel at Philadelphia;
   G. 3:14–22, the Letter to the Angel at Laodicea.

IV. 4:1–11, a vision of heaven: a door is opened for the seer to see the divine throne which will appear on earth in the New Jerusalem (21:3; 22:1). The paean of praise acknowledges God's sovereignty in heaven.

V. 5:1–14, vision of the divine scroll and the Lamb: in contrast to what he hears in heaven about the conquering Lion of Judah, the seer sees a Lamb that is slain which is shown to be worthy to open the seals and to initiate the process of divine judgement and the reconciliation of God and humanity, heaven and earth, which reaches its climax in chs. 21–2.

VI. 6:1–17, John sees the seals opened: here begins the sequence of *seven* seals, trumpets, and bowls in which the process of eschatological judgement which must precede the establishment of the divine reign on earth is laid out.

VII. 7:1–17, the opening of the seals in chs. 6–8 is interrupted by a description of the sealing of the 144,000 that have been redeemed from mankind as first fruits for God and the Lamb, and the promise of ultimate vindication for those who are faithful in the period of 'the great tribulation' (7:14):
   A. 7:1–8, the 144,000 of Israel sealed;
   B. 7:9–17, the multitude from every nation;

This structure suggests several major themes. First and foremost, as we have seen, the book as a whole offers an account of the resolution of the contrast between heaven and earth, when the dwelling of God with humanity comes about and the New Jerusalem comes from heaven to earth. The whole of the apocalyptic vision points forward to this. The inexorable unfolding suggests an inevitability about the fulfilment of the divine purposes. There is a determined pattern to the divine purpose whose fulfilment in the last resort does not depend on human consent, even if humanity is given the opportunity to repent (2:16; 9:20–1; 16: 9, 11). The opposition to God means that a huge upheaval is required in order to bring about the establishment of heaven on earth. There are hints that there is a divine longing for repentance from humanity (e.g. 9:20), but elsewhere there is a grim demonstration of the cataclysm set in train before heaven comes to earth. The book stresses the imminence of the fulfilment of some (though not necessarily all) of what is glimpsed by John (4:1; 10:6). So the angelic letters emphasize that the *present* is a moment of opportunity for repentance and vigilance, and the vision of heaven and of the beast and Babylon (chs. 13 and 17) concern contemporary realities on earth, rather than some future state of affairs. But there can be no rushing the divine purposes. In this situation patience and endurance are important virtues (e.g.13:10; 14:12). The vision of what is to come seems to offer a means of carrying, on whether there be a threat to discipleship from persecution or from complacency.

The first three chapters of the book describe the call of John the seer, who is on the isle of Patmos 'because of the word of God and the testimony of Jesus' (1:9)— no explicit mention is made here of exile or imprisonment, though this was from early days a feature of the understanding of the context in which the book came to be written (Boxall 2002). That is followed by a series of letters to the angels of the seven churches in Asia Minor, in which the heavenly Christ offers reproof and encouragement, encouraging a steadfast witness and the arousal of the complacent from attitudes of compromise. Another dimension of the vision begins in 4:1, and John's heavenly vision reaches its climax with the coming of a Lamb to God to receive a sealed scroll (5:6). This initiates the process of judgement, beginning with the opening of seals (the first four of which herald the Four Horsemen of the Apocalypse) and culminates with the advent of a new heaven and earth.

The pattern of three sequences of sevens, starting with the letters to the angels of the seven churches, is followed by sequences of seven seals, trumpets, and bowls. The threefold 'sevens' largely concern the disasters which are to befall an unjust and unrepentant world and form a structure which encompasses a large part of chapters 6–19. Thus, the opening of the first six seals is followed by the seventh seal in 8:1 which leads to silence in heaven and the seven angels being given seven trumpets which are then blown (8:7–13). Both sequences are interrupted after the sixth in the sequence. In the seals sequence it is by the disclosure of the 144,000 sealed and the vision of the multitude which none could number (7:4, 9), and in the case of the trumpets sequence by the vision of the mighty angel (ch. 10) and the two witnesses (11:1–12). It is only after these visions and the declaration that the Second Woe has passed (11:14) that the seventh angel blows his trumpet (11:15). The sequence of bowls has a sense of finality (15:1). It is related without interruption before attention turns to the destruction of Babylon and its culture (17:1–19:10). So, within the sequence of sevens we have two passages (ch. 7 and chs. 10–15) which have as their theme the destiny of and the threat to the people of God (the promise of salvation to the persecuted in chs. 7 and 14, the need for a prophetic witness in chs. 10–11, the threat to God's people in chs. 13–14 and the song of deliverance in ch. 15).

The sequence of seven seals, trumpets, and bowls has been a crucial aspect of the interpretation of Revelation down the centuries. Thus, Joachim of Fiore (*c.*1135–1202) regarded the Apocalypse as a hermeneutical key to both the entire scripture and the whole of history, and the sequences of sevens are crucial for his interpretative approach. In the various sequences of seven, the sixth in the sequence assumes great importance. This preoccupation with the *penultimate* period is characteristic and relates closely to a feature of the text of Revelation where we find, as we have seen, an interruption on two occasions between numbers six and seven in two of the series of seven, the seals and the trumpets. For Joachim the penultimate age is the period of the Antichrist, which immediately precedes the fulfilment of the final age of the Spirit. Thus Joachim regards the sixth letter, to the angel of the church at Philadelphia (3:7–13) as a prophecy of the coming sixth age to begin soon after the year 1200. The opening of the sixth seal (6:12–16) begins a time of persecution and exile which would purify the church. The seventh era, begun by the opening of the seventh seal, would be the era of the Holy Spirit, when seeds sowed long before would come to fruition. Later, in the seventeenth century, Joseph Mede (1586–1638), in his *Clavis Apocalyptica*, interpreted the series of sevens as 'synchronisms', or recapitulations, relating to the same period of history as one another. His emphasis on 'synchronisms' anticipates interpretative approaches that have had wide currency in modern scholarship, whereby the sequences of seven are not read chronologically and sequentially but are taken to refer to the same set of eschatological realities.

We have already had a reason to note the significance of numbers in the book. This is nowhere better seen than in a verse which has been a happy hunting-ground for interpreters of the Book of Revelation: 13:18, which discloses the number of the beast. The significance of the number 666 is to be understood in the light of the fact that letters stand for numbers in both Hebrew and Greek, and Jewish interpreters were fond of working out the numerical value of letters (so a=1, b=2, etc.). In an interpretative technique called *gematria* Jewish interpreters worked out the numerical values of words (Fishbane 1985). In the light of this, the most probably interpretation of Nero Caesar is the sum of the Hebrew letters of נרון קסר. The Greek form of Nero Caesar written in Hebrew characters is equivalent to 666 whereas the Latin form of Nero Caesar is equivalent to 616, found in some ancient readings of the text of 13:18.

Within Revelation itself the number seven (used of angels, churches, seals, trumpets, and bowls) suggests completeness. The number 666, however, is three times over falling one short of the perfect number 7. The beast seems to be near perfection (it is, after all, a caricature of the Lamb who was slain in 13:3), but it is opposed to God in supposing that it has ultimate power and wisdom (13:4). This is consistent with the fact that there seems to be a preoccupation with the penultimate, the sixth, in the interrupted seals and trumpets sequences.

APOCALYPSE AND AUTHORITY

Two verses, one from the first chapter (1:1: 'The revelation of Jesus Christ, which God gave him to show his servants what must soon take place; he made it known by sending his angel to his servant John, who testified to the word of God and to the testimony of Jesus Christ, even to all that he saw') and the other from the concluding chapter (22:18–19: 'I warn everyone who hears the words of the prophecy of this book: if anyone adds to them, God will add to that person the plagues described in this book; if anyone takes away from the words of the book of this prophecy, God will take away that person's share in the tree of life and in the holy city, which are described in this book'), demonstrate the authority given to this book. Verse 22:18 gives the text a level of authority qualitatively different from any other New Testament book. There are attempts elsewhere in the New Testament to indicate why particular books have been written and why they should be regarded as authoritative (e.g. John 21:24–5 and Luke 1:1–4), but none places itself on a level of authority equivalent to that found in the Hebrew Bible in the way that Revelation does, through, for example, the allusion to Deuteronomy 4:2 in 22:18. Revelation is recognized by its writer as having its origin in heaven: it is after all the Apocalypse of Jesus Christ. This verse makes this text *the* archetypical prophetic text. The word 'apocalypse' encapsulates so much of the influence of the book down the centuries, whether in terms of the way in which it inspired later visionaries to write books of a similar cast, or has led to the application of Revelation's images to particular catastrophic events. This word has been the heuristic key which has enabled attempts to understand a wide variety of works from Judaism and Christianity (and indeed other religions: Collins, McGinn, and Stein 2000) which have affinities in terms of form and content. 'Apocalypse' denotes a particular literary type found in the literature of ancient Judaism, characterized by claims to offer visions or other disclosures of divine mysteries concerning a variety of subjects, especially those to do with the future ('eschatology'). When we find cataclysmic events described in these texts, they are often labelled 'apocalyptic' because they resemble the world-shattering events described in John's visions in the Book of Revelation. There is only one apocalypse in the Hebrew Bible, the Book of Daniel, though the discovery of fragments of an Enoch apocalypse among the Dead Sea Scrolls remind us that such visionary ideas were widespread in the Jewish religion which came to an end with the destruction of Jerusalem in 70 CE. Unlike Daniel, which contains a mixture of stories concerning the life of a Jewish elite in Babylon and their participation in discerning the mysterious dreams and signs which confront Babylonian kings, Revelation has only the briefest hint of context (1:9).

A later prophet in engagement with his or her own context, may, like John, interpret the beast and Babylon using John's imagery, just as John used the prophecies of Ezekiel and Daniel as the inspiration and language for his own vocation of a prophet. For many later visionaries (especially women—one has only to think of Hildegard of Bingen: Mack 1992) the Book of Revelation was an inspiration and licensed new prophecy. While the apostle Paul had instructed women to keep silent in the assembly (1 Cor. 14:34), he *had* allowed them to prophesy (1 Cor. 11:5). So the Book of Revelation was an obvious model, and as a result the imagery of Revelation was frequently the basis of such prophecy. Indeed,

William Blake believed that John on Patmos had *already* seen what he, Blake, the later prophet, had seen 1,800 years later and was writing about (*The Four Zoas*, book 8, lines 595–8). Just as Blake and others looked back to the Book of Revelation, a similar sense of continuity with earlier prophecy is evident in Revelation itself, whereby John's prophecy echoes many prophetic predecessors, Ezekiel (e.g. Rev. 4) and Daniel (Rev. 13) being chief among them. Such a prophetic tradition is found in the Bible in Deuteronomy 18:15 and in 1 and 2 Kings, where Elisha is said to have a double portion of his mentor's, Elijah's, spirit (2 Kgs 2: 9, 15).

JOHN AND HIS PROPHETIC PREDECESSORS

At many points Revelation echoes the writings of earlier prophets. John in his vision never explicitly states that he is quoting his prophetic predecessors. Rather, the prophetic words are the language of his own vision. For example, Ezekiel 1, Isaiah 6, and Daniel 7:9–13 merge in John's vision of God's throne in heaven in chapter 4: significant sources, as the first two of these texts constitute the two major accounts of visions of God in the Hebrew Bible. But what is surprising is that the description of the scene in heaven in Revelation 4, populated by angels and paeans of praise, introduces the image of a lamb that is slain (5:6). In doing so, John's visionary imagination also includes the contemporary Christian testimony about Jesus, the slain messiah, in a vision largely inspired by earlier biblical images. We might expect developments of this kind in a visionary text where themes and images previously learnt surface in the visionary imagination without any obvious evidence of deliberate literary artifice, the earlier images being transformed through the inventiveness of John's visionary imagination.

The relationship between Revelation and prophetic and other apocalypses is a complex matter. A neat distinction between them has sometimes been made along the lines that biblical prophecy foretold history which emerged from the present, whereas apocalyptic texts were about a future breaking into the present (Rowley 1947: 38). The apocalyptic texts we now possess differ little in their understanding of history, however. Where they differ from biblical prophecy is in the *form* in which the divine revelation takes place and in their authorship. In a text like Revelation, the prophets are rarely mouthpieces of the divine word (there is little of the canonical prophets prefatory words, 'Thus says the LORD', e.g. Isa. 66:1). Instead they depend on visions and angelic communications to mediate the divine purposes. The hope for the future is basically the same as that which we find in biblical prophecy, especially the development of prophecy we find in later biblical prophetic writings like the later chapters of Ezekiel (40–8) and Zechariah. What we have in the apocalypses is the form that prophecy took in Second Temple Judaism (Barton 1986). The veneration of written prophecy had the effect of marginalizing contemporary prophecy. While there is much debate as to why Jewish and many Christian apocalypses are pseudonymous, one plausible explanation for this is that the only way prophets could get a hearing for their visions and divinely inspired insights was to attribute them to some biblical worthy like Enoch, Abraham, or Ezra. John's apocalypse is different. It is presented in his own name, and not that of some hero of early Christianity: John of Patmos is almost certainly *not* John the son of Zebedee.

Luther rightly recognized that the form of Revelation set it apart to some extent from Daniel. In the latter, the obscure dreams have been rendered *more* comprehensible by angelic interpretations. Daniel's vision of the four beasts rising from the sea and the heavenly scene with the Ancient of Days and the Human Figure who receives divine authority (Dan. 7:1–13) are made a little less opaque by being related to the events of history (Dan. 7:19–22). There is little of that kind of explanatory gloss in Revelation (1:20, 4:4, and 17:9–12 being exceptions). Revelation's polyvalent imagery is almost always without explanation, meaning that it is a text which more than any other biblical text manifests open-endedness and lack of closure.

JOHN AND HIS VISIONARY EXPERIENCE

It is possible that we have in Revelation a carefully structured work which drew on apocalyptic and prophetic genres familiar to its author. There is a semblance of order and structure, which does yield a coherent pattern. This suggests that some attempt has been made to give the book shape and coherence, evident in the sayings and exhortations in 1:8 and 22:5–19. Revelation differs markedly from a Jewish apocalypse like 1 Enoch, which is a veritable jumble of heterogeneous material originating in different contexts and from different periods (perhaps John may have been aware of such a cumulative process of authorship—hence his warning in 22:18–19). John's book is, at first glance, an account of a visionary experience akin to a dream. If we take John at face value, what we find in the book came to him in some kind of dream-vision state ('in the spirit', 1:9), and there are many signs in the book itself of that dream-like quality in which the visionary not only sees but also is involved in the vision which he records (e.g. 1:12; 1:17; 5:4; 7:13; 11:1;17:3 cf. 1:10 and 21:10). There is a close relationship with earlier biblical books, indicating a knowledge which never manifests itself in the form of explicit quotation.

The most likely background to Revelation is to be found in the history of the interpretation of Ezekiel 1 (referred to simply as the *merkabah* in Jewish tradition, because what Ezekiel sees resembles a chariot, e.g. Ezek 1:15). In this tradition of interpretation the meaning of the text may have come about as the result of 'seeing again' what Ezekiel saw. John's imaginative visualization of, and engagement with, the prophecies of Ezekiel and others become the vehicle for his own prophecy. For John and his apocalyptic contemporaries in the first century CE, a prophetic text like Ezekiel 1 was probably not just the subject of learned debate but a catalyst for visionary experience. Interpreters of Ezekiel were not simply exegetes in the conventional sense; rather, their own imaginative engagement enabled them to see again what had appeared to the prophet, but in their own way and appropriate for their own time. David Halperin has captured this aspect of visionary exegesis well when he writes: 'When the apocalyptic visionary "sees" something that looks like Ezekiel's *merkabah*, we may assume that he is seeing the *merkabah* vision as he has persuaded himself it really was, as Ezekiel would have seen it, had he been inspired wholly and not in part' (Halperin 1988: 71; also Lieb 1991; Morray-Jones and Rowland 2009).

Such meditative practices have been a key part of religion down the centuries, and became the cornerstone of the religious life in the late medieval period. Medieval interpreters visualized biblical texts as they interpreted them (Carruthers 1998). In this process there could be no predicting how different images might come together and in what order. This is the most plausible background for understanding the use of the Bible in John's apocalypse. Meditative practice was the result of a sophisticated process of memorization of scriptural texts, in which the one meditating was able to recall and envision the content of those texts. The exercise of imagination, which might involve the visualization in the mind of objects, has long been an important part of the reading of scripture (Carruthers 1998: 68–9). So, ancient readers and hearers of texts could seek to visualize what they read (or heard), and that seeing or listening would frequently involve the creation of mental images. Biblical texts recalled in this way might yield new meaning by a process of spontaneous interconnection, through meditative recollection.

John also uses images which are familiar to us from elsewhere and have a fairly well-established meaning. Thus, the contribution of Daniel 7 to the political symbolism of Revelation 13 establishes a frame of reference which will inform (though not determine) the sense we make of that chapter. In John's interpretation of Daniel's vision of the beasts arising out of the sea we have a vehicle for a powerful political critique of the contemporary polity. In Revelation 13 the Danielic vision is interpreted synchronically rather than diachronically: it is not a succession of empires, therefore, but a fourfold imperial oppression. The importance for us is that the visionary experience, while conditioned by life under Roman dominion, is not determined by it. It is the beast and Babylon, not Rome and Caesar, which are the vehicle of John's message. As such, they have a wider appeal than a narrowly focused political analysis rooted in particular historical events.

THE FUTURE HOPE

In addition to being the only visionary text in the New Testament, the Book of Revelation has the most extensive and coherent account of the future hope (cf. 1 Cor. 15:20–8). This is distinctive and has had far-reaching effects in the history of interpretation. It is based on patterns which were firmly established in the Judaism of the first century CE, whereby a period of political and cosmic disturbance (often known as the messianic woes: Mark 13:8 and Romans 8:22, in both of which passages the woes are likened to birth-pangs) would lead to a messianic age on earth. The woes in Revelation (actually referred to on two occasions in Rev. 9:12 and 11:14—a third woe is promised but never mentioned) have a place within the sequence of sevenfold seals, trumpets, and bowls, with the last of the three sequences (Rev. 16) being a climax of the eschatological disasters. This leads to judgement on political arrangements opposed to God and the establishment of the messianic on earth (Rev. 17–19). Revelation 20:1–6 is a passage which describes a messianic reign on earth for a thousand years (hence the terms 'millennialism' and 'chiliasm', influenced by Latin and Greek words respectively). The text 4 Ezra 7:28, which is roughly contemporary with the Book of Revelation, has a messianic period of 400 years. In the Book of Revelation it should be noted that the millennium is depicted as a time of perfection when humanity is not subject to the ravages of evil, as Satan is bound for the duration (20:2–3). What is distinctive about belief in a millennium is that it is very much 'this-worldly', and it is this feature which has pervaded discussions in both a religious and a secular context. As in 4 Ezra the messianic kingdom is followed by a final judgement and a final, eschatological, era. In Revelation the millennium is not the end-point of the divine purposes: that takes place when the New Jerusalem comes down from heaven to earth (cf. Isa. 65:17 and 66:22). At that time, the divine dwells with the human (Rev. 21:3; 22:3) and the Last Things are linked with the First Things as the new age is seen as the Garden of Eden (22:1–2). The literal expectation of a period of a thousand years has been an inspiration for revolutionary theology in Western Christianity (Cohn 1957). Of all books in the New Testament, Revelation has challenged a view of hope which sees the future consummation being about life in heaven, and, as we have seen, presents a pattern of hope that focuses on *this* world.

One feature of the Book of Revelation which has contributed in an extraordinary degree to theological interpretation in subsequent centuries is the theme of the Last Judgement. Revelation is not the only book where this theme is to be found and later visual and textual evidence is not solely dependent on the Last Judgement in Revelation 20:11–15. Matthew 25:31–45 offers another extended example of the Last Assize in the New Testament, and there are other passages, such as Romans 14:10 and 2 Corinthians 5:10, indicating that there was an expectation of a final divine tribunal, when the eternal destiny of the whole world would be judged. Revelation

20:11–15 and Matthew 25:31–45 both emphasize the importance of good works as criterion for eternal life rather than faith (Rev. 20:12; Matt. 25:40; cf. Matt. 7:15–23). The roots of this lie in the prophetic message of judgement against a disobedient nation (e.g. Isa. 10). In most of those texts the judgement came through history rather than through a final, supernatural event when the sheep would be separated from the goats. There are other passages in the rest of the New Testament, such as John 5:24, where this event is brought into the present in line with the present actualizing of eschatological hope (e.g. the raising of Lazarus from the dead in John 11).

WORKS CITED

AUNE, D. E. (1997–8), *Revelation*. Word Biblical Commentary 52, Dallas: Word.

——(1993), *Prophecy in Early Christianity and the Ancient Mediterranean World*. Grand Rapids, Mich.: Eerdmans.

BOXALL, I. (2002), *Revelation: Vision and Insight: An Introduction to the Apocalypse*. London: SPCK.

CARRUTHERS, M. (1990), *The Book of Memory: A Study of Memory in Medieval Culture*. Cambridge: Cambridge University Press.

——(1998), *The Craft of Thought: Meditation, Rhetoric, and the Making of Images, 400–1200*. Cambridge: Cambridge University Press.

——(2002), *The Medieval Craft of Memory*. Philadelphia: University of Pennsylvania Press.

CHARLESWORTH, J. H. (1983), *The Old Testament Pseudepigrapha*, vol. 1. New York: Doubleday.

COHN, N. (1957), *The Pursuit of the Millennium*. London: Paladin.

COLLINS, J. J. (1984), *The Apocalyptic Imagination: An Introduction to the Jewish Matrix of Christianity*. New York: Crossroads.

——McGINN, B. and STEIN, S. (2000), *The Encyclopedia of Apocalypticism*, 3 vols. New York: Continuum.

FISHBANE, M. (1985), *Biblical Interpretation in Ancient Israel*. Oxford: Clarendon Press.

HALPERIN, D. J. (1988), *The Faces of the Chariot: Early Jewish Responses to Ezekiel's Vision*, TASJ 16. Tübingen: Mohr–Siebeck.

KOVACS, J. and ROWLAND, C. (2004), *Revelation: The Apocalypse of Jesus Christ*. Oxford: Blackwell.

LIEB, M. (1991), *The Visionary Mode: Biblical Prophecy, Hermeneutics, and Cultural Change*. Ithaca, NY: Cornell University Press.

MACK, P. (1992), *Visionary Women: Ecstatic Prophecy in Seventeenth Century England*. Berkeley: University of California.

ROWLAND, C. (1982), *The Open Heaven*. London: SPCK.

——(1998), *Revelation New Interpreter's Bible*, vol. 12. Nashville, Tenn.: Abingdon.

——and MORRAY-JONES, C. (2009), *The Mystery of God: Early Jewish Mysticism and the New Testament*. Leiden: Brill.

ROWLEY, H. H. (1947), *The Relevance of Apocalyptic: A Study of Jewish and Christian Apocalypses from Daniel to the Revelation*. London: Lutterworth.

FURTHER READING

BARTON, J. (1986), *Oracles of God: Perceptions of Ancient Prophecy in Israel after the Exile*. London: Darton, Longman & Todd.

BURDON, C. (1997), *The Apocalypse in England 1700-1834: The Apocalypse Unravelling*. London: Macmillan.

CAREY, F. (ed.) (1999), *The Apocalypse and the Shape of Things to Come*. London: British Museum Press.

McGINN, B. and EMMERSON, R. K. (eds.) (1992), *The Apocalypse in the Middle Ages*. London: Cornell University Press.

MEDE, J. (1643), *The Key of the Revelation*. London.

PRIGENT, P. (2001), *Commentary on the Apocalypse of St. John*. Tübingen: Mohr.

REEVES, M. and HIRSCH-REICH, B. (1972), *The Figurae of Joachim of Fiore*. Oxford: Oxford University Press.

ROWLAND, C. (2007), 'Apocalyptic Literature', in A. Hass, D. Jaspers, and E. Jay (eds.), *The Oxford Handbook of English Literature and Theology*, 342–62. Oxford: Oxford University Press.

VAN DER MEER, F. (1978), *Apocalypse: Visions from the Book of Revelation in Western Art*. London: Thames & Hudson.

PART II

CHAPTER 13

....

THE BIBLE AND ICONOGRAPHY*

....

ALBERT C. LABRIOLA

In line with its Greek etymology, 'iconography' refers to all forms of visual images, including any material means of artistic representation. Religious iconography typically refers to visual images of personages, events, and objects in the Bible. As such, religious iconography is a means of investigating how the Bible was received and interpreted in various eras. Included in religious iconography are the following: illustrated Bibles, manuscript illuminations, books of hours, missals, sacramentaries, lectionaries, paintings, sculptures, murals, frescos, mosaics, metalwork, stained glass, and the like. In short, religious iconography appears inside or outside the pages of the Bible.

Widespread use of religious iconography developed in the Christian Middle Ages and continued through the Renaissance. In their illuminations, medieval manuscripts provide insightful and sophisticated interpretations of the Bible. Sometimes the illuminations juxtapose images from the Old and New Testaments, the former supplying prefigurations, foreshadowings, or types of the latter. Called biblical typology, this method of interpretation relates personages, events, and objects from

* For the present chapter, permissions have been kindly granted to refer to some of the illustrations and descriptions of them from my previous essays: '"God Speaks": Milton's Dialogue in Heaven and the Tradition of Divine Deliberation', *Cithara: Essays in the Judaeo-Christian Tradition*, 25/2 (1986), 5–30; 'Biblical Typology and the Holy Spirit: The Tree of Jesse and the Crucifixion', ibid. 39/1 (1999), 3–12; 'The Annunciation and Its Hebraic Analogues', ibid. 40/2 (2001), 27–35; 'The Holy Spirit in Selected Manuscript Illumination', ibid. 42/1 (2002), 13–25; 'The Holy Spirit in Art', *Proceedings of the Fifty-first Annual Convention of the Catholic Theological Society of America*, 51 (1996), 143–62.

the Old Testament with counterparts from the New Testament. On the one hand, medieval iconography emphasizes how and why the redemptive ministry of Jesus Christ fulfils both the prophecies concerning, and prefigurations of, the Messiah in the Old Testament. On the other hand, medieval illuminations often dwell primarily on the Old Testament, but they integrate Christian significance and interpretation into the iconography. In images of the Creation, for instance, medieval illuminations often include the three Divine Persons, individually rendered but interactively deliberating on the Creation, thereby affirming Trinitarian theology central to Christianity.

In what follows, I aim to survey religious iconography by emphasizing medieval illuminations from the tenth through the sixteenth centuries, the seedbed of religious imagery. Religious iconography in the Middle Ages, moreover, profoundly affected art in the Renaissance and afterwards, examples of which I will cite. To pursue this aim, I will focus on selected but representative personages, events, and objects from the Old and New Testaments.

When depicted as a dove in scenes of the Creation in which the Father and the Son are anthropomorphically rendered, the Holy Spirit may hover at a body of water below while the other Divine Persons are enthroned above. This deployment characterizes the Spirit not as subordinate to the Father and the Son but as the overseer of the Creation, acting on behalf of all three Divine Persons. In a variation of this image, the Holy Spirit as a dove may remain at the throne of the triune godhead, between the Father and the Son who face each other. Uniting them is the dove in a cruciform attitude: head upright and facing the viewer, tail downward, and wings extended horizontally toward the Father and the Son. The tip of the one wing is at the mouth of the Father, and the tip of the other reaches into the mouth of the Son.[1]

Another option, which combines the two cited above, portrays the Holy Spirit between the Father and the Son. With outstretched wings whose tips extend to the Father and the Son, who are seated together on the same heavenly throne, the Holy

---

[1] Most of the artistic representations cited are from illuminated manuscripts in The Pierpont Morgan Library, 29 East Thirty-sixth Street, New York, New York 10016. Pierpont Morgan Manuscripts (PMM) are listed by their shelf numbers, followed by folio numbers for the illuminations (as rectos, unless versos are stated). Some other relevant information will be provided: author, text, language of the manuscript, place of production, the date, scribe, illuminator, patron, the names of masters, their workshops, and their followers. Sometimes such information is controversial and speculative, and further research may lead to more certain attributions, dates, and localizations.

For iconography of the Creation, see PMM 110, 3A11 79v, from a Bible in Latin, France, c.1260; PMM 132, 3B2 158, from Guillaume de Lorris and Jean de Meun, *Roman de la rose*, in French, c.1380, perhaps by the Boqueteaux Master; PMM 893, 14B9 195, from the Warwick Hours, England, c.1430–40, attributed to William Abell. See also Didron 1965: 1. 213–14 and fig. 59, which reprints a French miniature from the early thirteenth century; ibid. 2. 64 and fig. 143, which reprints a French miniature of the Trinity from the 16th-c. *Cité de Dieu*, in the Bibliothèque de Saint Geneviève; and PMM 791, 12F3 4v and 12F4 4v.d1, from the Lothian Bible in Latin, Abbey of St Albans, c.1215–20. See PMM 69, 2A6 59v, from a Book of Hours in Latin, Rome, 1546, written by Francesco Monterchi, signed by the illuminator Giulio Clovio, for Cardinal Alessandro Farnese.

Spirit while facing the viewer unites the First and Second Persons. In such illuminations, the Third Person sometimes also appears below, figured as a dove over water. Appearing twice in the same illumination, the dove dramatizes the ongoing presence of the Third Person in the midst of the Father and the Son and also the Holy Spirit's role in overseeing the Creation on behalf of the triune godhead. By simultaneously depicting the Holy Spirit integrated with, and also away from, the Father and the Son, this multiphasic or bilevel image conveys the mystery of three distinct Persons in one godhead.

One such depiction from the Lothian Bible of the early thirteenth century shows the Father and the Son enthroned on high, the former to the left of the viewer, the latter to the right. The Father is an adult with a beard, the Son an adolescent without one. Between and partly behind them is the dove, head upright and facing the viewer with wings partially extended so that their respective extremities touch the temples of the Father and the Son, who face one other. Each Divine Person, including the dove, has a cruciform nimbus, though only the Son's is red to signify his eventual bloodshed. The Third Person is between the other two Divine Persons but slightly elevated above them. In some illuminations where the Holy Spirit is elevated in this manner, he becomes the apex of a triangle, an inveterate symbol of the Trinity. Lines radiating from him descend onto the Father and the Son, who are connected, in turn, by the base of the triangle.

Analogously speaking, the apex of a triangle functions like the keystone of an arch, the principle of cohesiveness in a structure or interrelationship. While facing the Son, the Father extends his right arm horizontally away from the Second Person, and the palm of his hand is open and upward. He outstretches his left arm horizontally across the upper back of the Son from shoulder to shoulder, his left hand, palm open and upward, visible beyond the left shoulder of the Second Person. The Father's left arm and hand, though not embracing the Son, still envelop him from behind. Not merely next to the Father, the Son is actually seated on his lap or on his left leg. The Son's hands are uplifted and partially outstretched in the attitude of praying and of crucifixion. In this visual image, all three Persons assume the cruciform attitude that the Son will bloodily enact during his most intense suffering on earth.

Surrounding the Father and the Son is a red mantle that they share, which runs behind their backs, as high as the napes of their necks, while in the foreground it does not cover their chests, but loops across their waists and drapes downward until it falls below the knees of the Father. Only the Father's lower legs and feet appear below the mantle. Because he is an adolescent of shorter stature than the Father on whose left leg he is seated, the Son is concealed from the waist downward by the flowing garment. Encased in a quatrefoil design, the enthroned Divine Persons are flanked by angels deployed in hierarchical or vertical tiers.

Immediately below the throne of the Trinity and outside the quatrefoil are the fallen angels, who descend headlong after their expulsion from proximity to

Fig. 13.1. PMM. M.791, fol. 4 verso, Trinity and Creation of the World, Lothian
Bible, in Latin, Abbey of St Albans, c.1215–1220.

the godhead. Also below the Trinity are seven roundels, each with a scene from the Creation. In the first and highest roundel is the Holy Spirit figured as the dove hovering over water, thus depicting Genesis 1:2, which recounts the formlessness, darkness, and winds before the Lord decreed, 'Let there be light' (Gen. 1:3). Six angels, symmetrically arranged (in two groups, each composed of three angels), surround the circular periphery of the water as witnesses of the presence of the dove, the executor of the triune godhead. That is to say, some of the angels who usually are worshipping at the throne of the godhead accompany the dove-like Holy Spirit as the Creation is being initiated. The deployment of the angels in three-member groupings may numerologically signify that the Trinity is present at the Creation despite the visible manifestation of only one Divine Person. Furthermore, the six angels may anticipate numerologically the remaining six roundels, each depicting one of the days, the Sabbath excluded, of the Creation. Inside each of the six roundels, God the Father himself appears on behalf of the Trinity to bless each day of the Creation.

Such illuminations, which accommodate the Divine Persons to human comprehension, stress the Trinitarian relationship among the Father, the Son, and the Holy Spirit at the Creation. In the Lothian Bible, for instance, which features the interaction of the Divine Persons, the Holy Spirit, while figured as a dove, may be interpreted as the kiss of the Father and the Son, the breath of their love, the mediator of their mutual relationship, and the issuance, offspring, or manifestation of their interaction. Despite the zoomorphic representation of the Holy Spirit, the illumination in the Lothian Bible seeks to humanize the godhead, to invest the Divine Persons with human attributes, to ascribe human psychology to the Trinity, not to mention the emotions that characterize the human personality. The illumination in the Lothian Bible achieves these purposes by augmenting the scene of the Creation with explicit reference to other events in Scripture: the expulsion of the fallen angels, who are pictured as they plummet downward from heaven, and the Crucifixion. Interrelating the expulsion of the fallen angels and the Crucifixion becomes significant. For the Crucifixion emerges as the means by which fallen humanity, in contrast to the fallen angels, can elicit a judgement of mercy from the enthroned godhead, not a decree of damnation. From the lap of the Father, the Son oversees the creation of humanity shown in the last roundel. Anticipating the downfall of humanity and his sacrifice on their behalf, the Son foreknows, as well, that some of them will reject his offer of salvation though he continues to reaffirm it lovingly.

Sitting on the Father's lap, the Son in an attitude of prayer foresees that he will ascend heavenward after his Crucifixion. When he does resume his position on the throne of God, he will plead for merciful judgement for regenerate humanity but not for the reprobate. By assuming a cruciform attitude when he envelops or embraces the Son, the Father signifies that he is sympathetically present at the Redemption. At the Son's Crucifixion, the grief-stricken Father will suffer a sympathetic death by heartbreak. And the position of the Son on the lap of the heavenly Father foreshadows this very role of the latter as *pater dolorosus* or the sorrowful father, the heavenly counterpart of *mater dolorosa* or the grieving Virgin mother on earth, who is rendered in numerous works of art; foremost among them is Michelangelo's *La Pietà* (1499). The cruciform attitude of the Father not only prefigures his loving embrace of the Son after he fulfils his temporal ministry but also signifies the efficacy of the Redemption that extends to humankind across the expanse of the Creation. If, therefore, the arms of the Father reach toward the Creation (in the various roundels) to offer benediction, his arms and those of the Son will do likewise during Redemption and at merciful judgement on Doomsday. And the red mantle surrounding the Father and the Son implies their collective or interactive participation in the Creation, the Redemption, and merciful judgement. They are 'wrapped together' throughout the foregoing events in Scripture: from Genesis, through the Gospels, to the Apocalypse.

Equally important is the Holy Spirit who, figured as a dove, appears at the significant points of affinity between the Father and the Son: their heads, their faces, their eyes, their mutual transpiration. Considering, moreover, that the eyes are the windows of the heart and soul, a philosophical truism that informs Platonism and Neoplatonism, a viewer perceives the Father and the Son engaged in what is tantamount to a dialogue of one in their minds and their hearts, including their mutual sympathy for one another (each for the plight of the other) and their collective sympathy for humanity. Reflected in the mediation of the Third Person, this profound sympathy of the Father and the Son for each other and for humanity enables them to resolve a conflict in favour of humanity. For humanity, they will experience the sorrow of separation; the Father will consent to the suffering of his Son; and during the Crucifixion, the Son will express anguish that the Father has forsaken him, perhaps doubting the expectation of heavenly reunion with him.

Though more unusual than zoomorphic representations, anthropomorphic depictions of the Third Person at the Creation supplement and enrich our understanding of the Divine Persons, who in medieval iconography are sometimes pictured identically and enthroned alongside one another. They deliberate on the creation of humanity or, in particular, the creation and animation of Adam. One, two, or three of the Divine Persons may animate Adam by gazing into his eyes, by inbreathing, by surrounding him with mist or dew, or by uplifting him from the earth, a means of representation in which the godhead becomes a gardener and Adam a plant or tree.[2]

One of the most compelling anthropomorphic renditions of the triune godhead deliberating on the creation of Adam occurs in *l'Hortus Deliciarum*, a twelfth-century

---

[2] For images of the creation of Adam, see Didron 1965: 1. 201–3 and fig. 52, which is a Greek miniature from the 10th c., and ibid. 1. 240 and fig. 65; 2. 41–2 and fig. 137. See also Cames 1971: 7, 13–15, 128, and pl. III. For commentary on divine deliberation, see Schiller 1971–2: 1. 9–11, 145–52; 2. 122–4, 137–40; Didron 1965: 2. 15, 42–3, 63–72, 81; Traver 1907: 5, 104–5; Chew 1947: 37, 46–7, 59–60, 163. For commentary on, and illustrations of, the Holy Spirit represented as a man, see Didron 1965: 1. 467–74.

Fig. 13.2. PMM. M.644, fol. 79 recto, Noah's Ark, Beatus of Liebana, Spain. For a monastery dedicated to St Michel, middle of tenth century.

Latin manuscript that pictures the Divine Persons as identical in nearly all details (physical appearance, attire, accoutrements), enthroned, and holding a scroll. Written across the scroll is the text of Genesis 1:26: *Faciamus hominem ad imaginem et similitudinem nostram* ('Let us make man in our image and likeness'). This text is joined, in turn, with the text of Genesis 2:7: *et inspiravit in faciem eius spiraculum vitae et factus est homo in animam viventem* ('and he breathed into his creation the breath of life and man became a living being'). From this perspective, humanity becomes the alter ego or self-image of the godhead. If the Divine Persons are often depicted alike in order to dramatize the godhead interacting with and within itself, the deity in perceiving its image in humanity, whether originally imparted at the Creation or restored by redemption and sanctification, may experience self-recognition. Accordingly, the sanctified soul, like Adam at the Creation, will be as intimate with the deity as the Divine Persons are with one another. Such intimacy includes eye-to-eye and breath-to-breath interaction, so that the deity will view itself in the 'looking glasses' or in the eyes of, and transpire interactively with, beloved humanity.

In the illumination that I cite above, the one detail that distinguishes the Son from the Father and the Holy Spirit is the presence of the stigmata at the feet. Thus identified, the Son is the central Divine Person, flanked by the Father and the Holy Spirit, who are indistinguishable in attire and in appearance. Another detail may provide the interpretive key to distinguish the Father from the Holy Spirit, notably the scroll held by the Divine Persons. As the texts of Genesis unfold, the central figure of the Son holds the scroll at the word *similitudinem*, presumably because in his Incarnation he will bear the likeness of humanity. From a related perspective, the figure at the viewer's left grasps the scroll at the word *Faciamus*, which may identify the Father as the maker of humankind; and the word *animam* on the scroll, borne by the figure at the viewer's right, may distinguish the Holy Spirit as the breath of life. If such interpretation is correct, the anthropomorphic depictions of this illumination may identify the Father as making, the Son as being or becoming, and the Holy Spirit as breathing into humanity. But such distinctiveness is of lesser significance than the simultaneous and conjunctive involvement of the Father, the Son, and the Holy Spirit in all deliberations and activities.

Another illumination that drives home the simultaneous and conjunctive involvement of the triune godhead appears in a Book of Hours (1546). Of the Divine Persons, only the Father is depicted in the firmament during the Creation, with his long white hair, flowing white beard, and arms extended horizontally. His muscular arms and cruciform attitude indicate a younger man, presumably the Son. The same cruciform attitude, especially when accentuated by his sleeveless white garment, the bright clouds below him, and the sunlight in the background, all dramatize his resemblances to an outstretched dove, head upright and wings extended. In addition to the more tightly fitting white garment, which is visible from his shoulders to his waist, he has a red mantle wrapped across the front and back of his legs, from the upper thighs to his ankles. Only his feet are visible below

Fig. 13.3. Rare Book 108798, Catholic Church, *Book of Hours*, 1511 [c3ᵛ–c4ʳ].

Reproduced by permission of The Huntingdon Library, San Marino, California.

it. The same red mantle unfurls at his waist; behind him, it billows upward against the golden sunlight. The viewer thus engages the cruciform figure in a white sleeveless garment behind which the red mantle unfurls against the golden sunlight. Though depicting the Father at the Creation, the figure evokes various images of the Son: at the Transfiguration, the Crucifixion, the Resurrection, the Ascension, and in his 'power and glory' at the Second Coming. Likewise suggested are images of the Holy Spirit as a dove hovering at the Creation, at the Baptism of the Lord, and at Pentecost. This kaleidoscopic interplay of the Divine Persons anticipates images of the triune godhead at the re-genesis after the Deluge.

In such images of the re-creation, the Holy Spirit figured as a dove is released by Noah from the ark, to which it returns with an olive-sprig in its beak.[3] In numerous medieval illuminations of the biblical Deluge, the dove alights at the top of the ark,

---

[3] For representations of Noah's ark, see PPM 739, 11E12 10 (13th-c. Book of Hours); PMM 644, 8G2 79 (10th-c. Beatus of Liebana, from Spain); PMM 338, 4F5 122 (Psalter, *c*.1200, by the Ingeborg Psalter Workshop in Belgium, probably Tournai); PMM 43, 1D5 9 ('Huntingfield Psalter', in Latin, *c*.1215).

from which Noah, emerging from the enclosure, moves to grasp it. Or the dove alights into the outstretched and cupped hands of Noah, who has already emerged to welcome its return. The whiteness of the dove, its gentleness, and the olive-sprig respectively signify purity and innocence, a temperate or mild godhead, and the restored peace and harmony between the godhead and humankind, heaven and earth. But the dove, while figuring the Holy Spirit, signifies concurrently all three Divine Persons: purity and innocence are the virtues of the Son in his sacrificial ministry, virtues that through his merits he transposes to humankind; mildness distinguishes the Father when his anger is mollified and after justice is satisfied by the Son's sacrifice on behalf of humankind; and peace and harmony between the godhead and humankind are restored as the Holy Spirit, a gentle dove with an olive-branch, returns to Noah when the tempest-tossed Deluge subsides. These traits of the triune godhead, whom the Third Person represents, are consonant with human nature and divine deliberation.

In the illuminations referred to above, the dove sometimes is contrasted with the other bird released by Noah, the glossy black raven, a 'ravenous' predator with a long and pointed bill. The raven is visible in the background or in a marginal miniature, usually atop a hill and pecking at carrion. Such depictions suggest that as the waters rose during the Deluge people presumably fled to safer ground on high, but even the peaks were inundated. When the waters receded and as the peaks again became visible, they were littered with the carcasses of the victims of the flood. Its prey thus exposed, the raven does not return to the ark. As such, the raven signifies the mouth and jaws of hell, in which the reprobate are confined and through which biting and mastication punish numberless victims and feed an insatiable appetite. And the Deluge, with its steep cataracts that inundated the reprobate, anticipates another cataclysm, the tumultuous lake of sulphurous fire in the Apocalypse, presumably where the damned will undergo eternal punishment. The Deluge and the raven thus signify the hellish torment to be endured by the reprobate; whereas the receding waters, the calmness after the Deluge, and the appearance of the dove reflect the pacific relationship of the triune godhead with humankind and heavenly approval of the regenerate.

In some illuminations Noah's ark resembles a church or temple. That is, the structure is upright and rectangular, with a peaked roof, at the top of which the dove alights. With its head upright and an olive-sprig outstretched horizontally at the mouth, the dove projects a cruciform appearance akin to a cross or crucifix surmounting a church. In this attitude or posture, the dove is a Christ-like figure. Or the ark may have an opening at its peak, an aperture through which Noah launches the dove and from which he reaches upward to welcome its return. But when such illuminations also depict the interior of the ark with hierarchies of creatures at various levels, the overall structure simulates a microcosm of the Creation, at the top of which the Holy Spirit, dove-like but resembling Christ crucified, oversees the second Creation that issues from the ark and from which propagation will begin anew after the Deluge. In this same attitude, as well, the dove recalls the Father at the first Creation.

Accordingly, the Holy Spirit signifies the triune godhead in the attitude of divine deliberation: bringing into existence the Creation of the world and of humankind; making redemption possible after humanity has fallen; and foreseeing Doomsday and the judgements of salvation or damnation. This chronology proceeds from the past, through the present, and toward the future: the tripartite division typical of human perception. Interpreting all three temporal states simultaneously through the one work of art enables humankind to approximate, albeit imperfectly, the transcendent view of the godhead, whose outlook is *sub specie aeternitatis.* Divine deliberation thus becomes a process simultaneously encompassing the plan of the triune godhead to create humanity, the deific prescience that acknowledges their eventual fallen state, the intent to offer redemption, and the prospect of merciful judgement at Doomsday.

The foregoing explanation highlights how and why the triune godhead simultaneously creates and redeems or, to put it another way, creates and re-creates at the same time. When the simultaneity of divine deliberation is reformulated to become accessible to humanity, the results appear illogical and incredible, if not absurd. For the deity, in effect, repurchases its own creation, pays twice for the same thing, or continues to express self-sacrificing love, which has been, is being, and will finally be rejected in many instances, the final rejection already foreknown to the Divine Persons though not yet enacted by humankind. Accordingly, the Holy Spirit figured as a dove (in its purity, innocence, and gentleness and by its role as a sacrificial offering in Scripture) dramatizes that the deity, having rightfully levied on humankind the strict demands of justice, will then mercifully intercede to fulfil these very expectations. Foremost among the constellation of virtues that distinguish the Divine Persons are justice and mercy and their interrelationship.

Other illuminations of the re-creation after the Deluge emphasize the interaction of the heavenly and earthly realms. An opening through the top of the ark or at one of its upper ports or hatches signifies the conduit between earth and heaven, as well as communication between humankind and the godhead. The return of the dove and the descent of light onto and inside the ark re-enact the process of the Creation, beginning with the primal decree that resulted in the issuance of light.

The ensuing stages across the so-called days of the Creation are re-enacted after the Deluge when the various animals exit the ark and as Noah and the seven members of his family also emerge. Instructing Noah after the manner of his earlier enjoinder to Adam, God emphasizes that humanity should increase and multiply and that the animals of the earth, all under the governance of Noah, his family, and their descendants, will serve as food and sustenance. In fact, Noah's progeny who settle the earth anticipate the worldwide evangelization by the Apostles, whose minds are enlightened and hearts emboldened by the descent of the Holy Spirit at Pentecost. The egress of the disciples from the upper room resembles in several ways the emergence of Noah and his family from the ark. In both instances (after the Deluge and at Pentecost) the dove predominates as the representative of the Divine Persons.[4]

Having been liberated, in other words, the Apostles serve as liberators of others. That is, the heavenly light at Pentecost and the presence of the Holy Spirit liberate them from ignorance and diffidence. By enlightening and emboldening others, the Apostles become agents of the Holy Spirit. Dramatized by the Apostles in their ministry (particularly as recounted in Acts of the Apostles), the evangelizing light that they impart to others re-enacts their own Pentecostal experience. Consequently, the plenitude of the Creation anticipates the multitudes of people in the worldwide church, their diversity, and the geographic expansiveness of the ecclesial community. And the re-creation after the Deluge foreshadows the regenerate community whose rectitude does not waver and whose faith has been tested and strengthened by threats of darkness and destruction.

In addition, the image of rebirth after the Deluge anticipates other episodes from the New Testament that generate ecclesial significance: the Crucifixion, Christ's harrowing of hell, and Christ's Resurrection. When the dove with wings extended stands atop or hovers above the ark, this cruciform image signifies the opposite states of humiliation and exaltation or, more properly speaking, the transition from the one state to the other. The ark of wood and the wood of the cross converge in their various suggestions of humiliation and suffering. Whether enshrouded by darkness and confined in the ark or overcome by death on the cross and afterwards enclosed in a tomb, the family of Noah and Christ, respectively, suffer profoundly. Upright at its centre and transverse along its extremities, the ark projects a cruciform image, particularly when the dove (head upward, wings outstretched, and surmounting the vessel) serves as its insignia. Illuminators correlate the wood of the ark and the cross of Christ, the virtual rack on which he was placed for suffering.

Termed an instrument of the Passion, the cross of suffering inflicts pain on its bearer, Christ, and fear in his community of followers. After it becomes the site of the death of Christ and the nadir of his humiliation, it begins to be transformed into a cross of triumph. In its resemblance to outstretched wings, the transverse

---

[4] For illuminations of Pentecost, see PMM 275, 4A7 9 (13th-c. Psalter, Augsburg); PMM 710, 10D9 64v (Missal, Weingarten Abbey, Germany, c.1200–32); PMM 743, 11G3 88 (Book of Hours, Lucon Master Workshop, c.1415); PMM 641, 8E4 80v (Sacramentary, Mont-Saint-Michel, c.1060); PMM 905. II, 14C9 194 (Gradual, Nuremberg, dated 1510, signed by the scribe Friedrich Rosendorn and by the illuminator Jacob Elsner); PMM 495, 7B11 59 (Missal, Tours, end of 15th c.); PMM 69, 2B1 106v (Book of Hours, Rome, dated 1546, signed by the illuminator Giulio Clovio); PMM 781, 12E8 215v (Gospels, Monastery of St Peter, Salzburg, first half of the 11th c.); PMM 92, 2F8 11v (Book of Hours, Paris, c.1230); PMM 780, 12D9 51 (Gospel Lectionary, Monastery of St Peter, Salzburg, second half of 11th c.); PMM 493, 7A11 18v (Book of Hours, Bruges, workshop of the Master of Anthony of Burgundy, c. last third of the 15th c.).

beam of the cross signifies that Jesus will be elevated to a state of exaltation after humiliation. Even the inscription at the summit of the cross, which derisively identifies Jesus as 'king', will come to designate reverently his transcendent majesty. From an instrument of the Passion that tortures *Christus Patiens* or the suffering Christ, who exemplifies patience and fortitude under adversity, the cross becomes transformed into a lance-like weapon held aloft by *Christus Victor* or the triumphant Christ.[5]

By deploying the *crux invicta* or triumphal cross against his adversaries in the harrowing of hell, Jesus enters into the mouth of hell, often visualized as the jaws of a voracious beast (whether a sea-monster called Leviathan, a dragon, a crocodile, or another predator), after which he, the liberator, exits with a multitude of followers. In short, Jesus leads the members of his church behind him. From the top of the triumphal cross a white pennon, sometimes emblazoned with a red cross, typically flutters. The fluttering pennon usually has a swallow-tail or forked points at the end. Resembling the dove in flight, the white pennon signifies the transcendent power that enables one to escape humiliation and to attain to exaltation by surmounting previous limitations of darkness and enclosure.

Imprinted with the cross, the pennon dramatizes the metamorphosis of that very image from a sign of humiliation to an emblem of triumph. When borne by the risen Christ at or above his tomb, the triumphal cross, its white pennon unfurled above the place and powers of darkness, interrelates by its multiple significance the Second and the Third Persons. And to reinforce the interrelation of the Second and Third Persons at biblical events more often associated with the former, the white pennon sometimes bears the image of the *agnus dei* or lamb of God. Like the dove, the lamb is a sacrificial animal in Scripture. Though the lamb is white and gentle like the dove, the airborne nature of the latter enables it to escape from the earthly condition. Such is the legend of the dove, especially after its sacrifice. Like the fabulous phoenix, the heavenly ascent of a dove from the site of flaming immolation, such as the pyre of a martyr, designates the release of one's higher nature, or one's soul, heavenward. Indeed, the Psalmic vision of ascending on the wings of a dove also comes into play here.

---

[5] For various depictions of the Crucifixion and the involvement of the three Divine Persons, see PMM 677, 9F3 190 (Book of Hours, in Latin, France, probably Bourges, c.1480–85, by Jean Colombe and his workshop, probably for Anne de France, dame de Beaujeu). See Didron 1965: 2. 66–72 and figs. 144–6; Schiller 1971–2: 2. 22–124 and pls. 411–14; PMM 710, 10E8 132v (Missal, Weingarten Abbey, Germany, c.1200–32); PMM 324, 4E3 145 (Guillaume de Lorris and Jean de Meun, *Roman de la rose*, in French, middle of 14th c.; PMM 945, 14G3 77v ('Hours of Catherine of Cleves', Utrecht, c.1440, by the Master of Catherine of Cleves, for Catherine of Cleves, duchess of Guelders); PMM 421, 5G4 15v (Book of Hours, in Latin, Belgium, probably Tournai, c.1445).

For iconography that highlights (1) the transformation of the cross of suffering into the cross of triumph, (2) the fluttering streamer on the cross of triumph, and (3) the resemblance of Jesus to the lamb, see Didron 1965: 1. 292–337, 374–405, and esp. figs. 77, 82, 85, 86, 97.

After the death of Christ on the cross, his reappearance as *Christus Victor* dramatizes his exalted and glorified state: the triumphal cross aloft, its fluttering pennon representing the dove in flight, and the white-and-golden light behind him, if not contracted into an aureole or mandorla surrounding him. Emerging from death, like the dove in flight, Jesus triumphs over the forces that claimed him: *Christus Patiens* gives way to *Christus Victor*. Consistent with the larger ecclesial significance of such iconography, the lamb on Christ's pennon signifies the Church Militant, whose members will also suffer, while the windswept pennon unfurling on extended wings, like a dove aloft, betokens the Church Triumphant, whose members will be elevated heavenward.

But the saga of Noah has further significance to an understanding of the sacrifice of Jesus. While unclothed, Noah falls asleep after having become inebriated in his vineyard. In one of fifty decorated initials from a Latin Psalter (*c.*1200), Noah slumps on the ground in his vineyard. Above him are clusters of grapes; and while Ham points to his father's nakedness, the other two brothers, Shem and Japheth, move to cover Noah with a fluttering white garment. Billowing as it spreads over the recumbent Noah at his mid-section, the white garment is swallow-tailed at its extremities, forming a virtual canopy.

If, with the dove overhead, Noah emerging from the darkness and confinement of the ark anticipates the resurrection of Christ from his tomb, the unconscious and exposed patriarch, perhaps soiled by excessive wine, prefigures the faint, bloodied, and naked Jesus at his scourging. And the white garment, similar to a canopy gently billowing over Noah, signifies the dove hovering above Jesus, who continues to be overshadowed by the Holy Spirit not only at such moments as the Baptism of the Lord and the Transfiguration but also throughout his temporal ministry. Indeed, the swallow-tailed extremities of the garment over Noah, its whiteness, and its appearance of being wafted on a gust of air all converge as signs of the Holy Spirit. Depicted in this manner, the Holy Spirit highlights the typological resemblances between Noah and Jesus. By their association with the fertility of the vineyard, Noah, his progeny, and their settlement of the earth establish the context for genealogical catalogues in Genesis that cite the descendants of Shem, Japheth, and Ham.

One of Shem's descendants was Abram, whom God later renamed Abraham, similar to the Hebrew expression for 'father of many', and to whom God promised that he would become 'father of a multitude of nations' (Gen. 17:1–6). At the outset of Matthew's Gospel catalogues recur, which centre on the ancestors of Jesus who are the descendants of Noah. In other words, the catalogues in Genesis of Noah's descendants, which recur, in part, in Matthew's Gospel, become the genealogy or family tree of Jesus. The Gospel, which begins in the following way: 'A genealogy of Jesus Christ, son of David, son of Abraham' (Matt. 1:1), cites the Hebrew king and the Hebrew patriarch as the two most significant ancestors of Christ, both of whom, including David's father, Jesse, are descendants of Noah's son Shem.

Kingship and patriarchy, therefore, enrich our understanding of the ministry of Jesus. Like David, Jesus is a powerful king, though his realm is heavenly rather than earthly; like Abraham, Jesus is a patriarch and a progenitor, the creator of humanity anew after the Fall, when multitudes of the redeemed will dwell in the eternal afterlife.

Descendants of Noah and ancestors of Jesus appear together in illuminations of the Tree of Jesse.[6] In the Latin Vulgate, Isaiah 11:1–5 reads in the following way: *Egredietur virga de radice Jesse et flos de radice eius ascendet* ('a rod or shoot will emerge from the root or stump of Jesse, and a bloom will rise from his root'). The illuminations to which I refer simultaneously visualize this biblical text from Isaiah 11:1–5 and the genealogical catalogue in Matthew's Gospel. Or to put it differently, through visual imagery the one text is superimposed on the other. Thus, Jesse, recumbent and asleep on the ground, has a dream-vision, for which Jacob's dream (Gen. 28:10–19) is an analogue. Jacob dreams of a ladder of intercourse between heaven and earth, between the godhead and humanity. From Jesse's torso, which resembles a stump or root, a tree emerges; and as it rises, naturally it becomes more attenuated at the top. From a branch toward the top of the tree, a bud or blooming flower grows. Thus, the Tree of Jesse, which acknowledges the godhead of Jesus, features his human ancestry, the tree being his *scala* or ladder for descending to earth and returning to heaven. In short, the tree is a metaphor to suggest the entry of the Son into the human condition and his eventual return to the transcendent realm.

Illuminators associate the branch (*virga*) with the Virgin (*virgo*) and liken the bud or blooming flower to Jesus. Mary and the Christ child, whom she holds and with whom sometimes she is enthroned, appear at the summit of the tree. Or mother and child together appear against the backdrop of a flower, whose petals, the corolla, resemble rays of the sun. When the tree bears a flower and fruit, the Virgin is likened to the former and Christ to the latter, particularly because of his association with Eucharistic repast. And if the depiction stresses the adulthood, rather than the infancy or childhood, of Christ, he alone will be at the summit, while the Virgin is enthroned immediately below him. To depict other features of the Tree of Jesse, most illuminators superimpose Matthew's Gospel onto Isaiah's text. To the superstructure of the Tree of Jesse they add visualizations of Christ's ancestors from Matthew's Gospel: patriarchs, prophets, and kings whose full-length figures, busts, or heads appear in the branches of the 'family tree' of Jesus.

---

[6] The Tree of Jesse is often rendered in stained glass. Manuscript illuminations include PMM 710, 10E4 112 (Missal in Weingarten Abbey, Germany, *c*.1200–32); PMM 440, 6B7 7v (Psalter and Book of Hours, *c*.1240); Book of Hours (Paris, 1511), C3v–C4r, Henry E. Huntington Library, San Marino, California (HEH 108798). For portrayals of Jesus near a lattice that props up grapevines and of him in the winepress of the cross, see PMM 917 14D10 (fol.161), 14D3 (fol. 121), ('Hours of Catherine of Cleves', Utrecht, *c*.1440, by the Master of Catherine of Cleves, for Catherine of Cleves, duchess of Guelders).

Scrolls imprinted with their names designate these ancestors of Jesus. Or their accoutrements and trappings identify them. For instance, David may hold a harp, Solomon, a sword.

If the account of illuminations of the Tree of Jesse has focused chiefly on the Virgin, Jesus, and their ancestors, not to be overlooked is the significance of the Third Person in the overall scheme. Isaiah 11:2 recounts that 'the Spirit rests' on Jesus. Elaborating on this statement, the biblical passage cites seven virtues or gifts that the Holy Spirit infuses into Jesus: *sapientia, intellectus, consilium, fortitudo, scientia, pietas, timor* (wisdom, understanding or insight, counsel, fortitude, knowledge, piety, and fear of God). In two principal ways, illuminations show the presence of the Third Person and the virtues or gifts that he imparts. The one way portrays a single dove; the other way, multiple doves, usually seven but sometimes twelve. The single dove over the head of Jesus may be upright with wings outstretched, or it may be descending so that its bill makes contact with the nimbus of Jesus. And the dove's bill touches directly onto the apex of the cross imprinted inside Christ's nimbus.

Above the Tree of Jesse, the Holy Spirit overshadows Jesus. This Old Testament image prefigures the Baptism of the Lord, when Jesus, before entering the wilderness for forty days, is infused with the virtues or gifts of the Holy Spirit. There, because of these virtues or gifts, Jesus endures suffering and rejects temptations. If these adversities are perceived as a prelude to, if not preparation for, the Passion and Crucifixion, then the Holy Spirit, in effect, will revisit Jesus during the consummate ordeal, enabling him to endure the suffering and the sense of abandonment that challenge his faith in the Father and his hope for his followers. This visitation by the Holy Spirit at the Passion and Crucifixion also recalls the visual imagery of the Tree of Jesse. Overshadowed by the dove, Jesus at the summit of the Tree of Jesse prefigures his elevation or enthronement on the cross.

Through the mediation of the Holy Spirit, another linkage in the visual imagery between the Tree of Jesse and the Passion and Crucifixion of Christ also emerges. The suffering and abandonment experienced by Jesus may produce doubt, but not a lapse in faith. After an earlier expression of doubt ('Why have you forsaken me?'), Jesus immediately before dying affirms faith in the Father: 'Father, into your hands I commend my spirit.' Jesus undergoes the very anxiety and anguish of humanity in order to exemplify that one may endure, ultimately prevail, and be exalted when overshadowed by the Holy Spirit and infused with his virtues or gifts, all signified by the pennon at the summit of the cross. Other illuminations highlighting the Holy Spirit at the Tree of Jesse use multiple doves, often seven of them to signify the number of gifts or virtues infused by the Third Person. One of the most memorable renditions of this popular design appears in the stained glass of Chartres Cathedral, whose windows, as well as those in other Gothic cathedrals especially in the thirteenth century, were greatly influenced by illuminated manuscripts. Called *Vitrail de l'Arbre Jesse*, this thirteenth-century stained-glass window features one dove in headlong descent toward Jesus, who is enthroned at the summit of the tree. Thus overshadowing Jesus, the dove initiates multiple contact because its downward bill, the first point of contact, touches concurrently the top of Christ's head and the apex of the cross inside his nimbus.

This same design, whether in illuminated manuscripts or in stained-glass windows, portrays the other six doves, three at the left and three at the right, surrounding Jesus from top to bottom. Flanking him are pairs of doves close to his ears or shoulders, along his arms, and near his lap or upper legs. If deployed toward his ears, the doves come close to making contact with the extremities of the transverse bar in Christ's nimbus. That configuration results in two congruent triangles: the first composed of three doves, the one overhead and the other two at the ears of Jesus; the second demarcated by the apex and the lateral extremities of the cross in Christ's nimbus. While the triangle is an inveterate symbol of the Trinity, the congruent triangles described above highlight the role of the Holy Spirit. Inside Christ's nimbus, three doves appear, outstretched and facing the viewer: the one at the apex of the cruciform image and one at each of the lateral extremities. The effect is to compound the one cruciform image inside the nimbus. The iconographic interpretation that results from this deployment of the doves stresses the involvement of the Third Person with the ancestors of Jesus. Their Providential selection to be members or branches of the family tree or consanguinal family of Christ appears to have been overseen by the Holy Spirit, the representative of the Divine Persons.

Variations of the more traditional depictions of the Tree of Jesse occasionally feature Mary in the Tree, but without Jesus or any of his ancestors. Mary, however, is surrounded by seven doves to signify that she and the babe whom she is to conceive will receive the gifts and virtues of the Holy Spirit. This rendition of the Tree of Jesse, therefore, anticipates that the Holy Spirit will overshadow Mary at the Annunciation, when the virginal conception of Jesus actually takes place to fulfil the prophecy of his coming, a prophecy associated not only with Isaiah 11:1–5 and the Tree of Jesse but also with Isaiah 7:14, a biblical text addressed to the House of David: 'The Lord himself . . . will give you a sign. It is this: the maiden is with child and will soon give birth to a son.' Whether descending onto Christ and the Virgin together or onto the one figure that may be depicted without the other, the presence of the Holy Spirit anticipates later involvement in the Incarnation of Jesus, which is initiated at the Annunciation and consummated in his death at the Crucifixion.

Another design, common in rose windows of Gothic cathedrals of the thirteenth century, situates the Virgin and the Christ child, who is seated on her lap, at the centre of a large *rota-rosa* or wheel-rose. A single enormous rose with petals unfolding from the centre is the overall design. Immediately surrounding the enthroned Virgin and the Christ child are twelve doves. As the petals of the rose begin to radiate from outside the circle of doves, the ancestors of Jesus are portrayed in them. Each layer of petals is also circular, so that the Virgin and the Christ child are enclosed in concentric rings. Order and design, in other words, issue from the central presence of the rose, implying that biblical history is Christ-centered. The Hebraic Scriptures prefigure the coming of Christ; the Christian Scriptures narrate his temporal ministry, celebrate his Ascension, and anticipate his Second Coming. The cycle of unfolding and enfolding also comes into play as the Son issues from the godhead to become incarnate. Afterwards, he returns heaven-ward to be enfolded with the godhead. The rose is significant for other reasons: Mary is called the rose of the tribe of Judah; and Jesus is likened to the rose whose petals are pressed for their fragrance, which pervades the atmosphere. In similar fashion, Christ sheds his blood for all humanity, so that the efficacy of his redemptive act becomes omnipresent and ubiquitous. Not to be overlooked are the two colours that predominate in rose windows, red and blue. Red signifies Christ's bloodshed; and blue, the colour associated with Mary, suggests a pacific temperament in the Father, whose anger is mollified and whose demand for justice is fulfilled because of the sacrifice of his Incarnate Son, who has entered the human condition through the virgin birth.

A highly imaginative rendition of the Tree of Jesse, for which a Book of Hours of the mid-fifteenth century serves as a prime example, features the Virgin and the adolescent Jesus under a grape arbour, which encloses them at the back, along two sides, and overhead. The enclosure is open at the front. At the centre the Virgin sits as she reads a book, while Jesus in a corner at the background leans against the wooden lattice, calling attention to clusters of grapes, as if he intends to harvest them. Two angels are dressing vines and tendrils and harvesting grapes at the wooden lattice on the side opposite Christ. This version of the Tree of Jesse as a grape arbour recalls the significance of Noah in his vineyard, whose unconscious-ness, nakedness, and skin reddened with the overflow of wine glance toward the Passion of Jesus. And this illumination likewise adapts the visual image of the Tree of Jesse, so that the fruitful bounty of the grape arbour implies the effusion of Christ's blood that will vitalize the multitudes whom he redeems.

In this rendition of the Tree of Jesse, moreover, the Christ child appears virtually trapped inside the wooden lattice, which resembles a barred enclosure. His physical contact with the wooden lattice and with the grapes transforms the Tree of Jesse into an *arbor vitae* or tree of life. The fruit of this transfigured Tree of Jesse becomes associated with the Eucharistic drink, and the wooden lattice and child's entrapment inside it foreshadow visual images of Christ as a stalk of grapes being crushed in the winepress of the cross. In fact, another image in the same Book of Hours shows Jesus in a winepress. The crosspiece at the top, which resembles the upper jaw of a vise, lowers onto Jesus so that his shoulders and back are slumped. Both armpits clamp downward around the handles of whips, which are drawn next to one another against his chest. The lashes of the whips, which are red with the blood of Christ after the scourging, extend horizontally beyond the sides of his body, suggesting thereby the transverse bar of the cross. His bleeding forearms, bound with a rope, project a cruciform image as the one crisscrosses behind the other. With his feet firmly planted in a trough, his blood, like wine from a press, flows through a conduit and into a golden chalice, so that sacrificial and sacramental symbolism predominates.

In this illumination, the attitude of Mary resembles typical portrayals of her at the Annunciation, when she is also reading, presumably Old Testament prophecies from Isaiah, in which the virgin birth of Christ is emphasized. Furthermore, the folds of her garment are gently billowing, as if a breeze overtakes Mary, a sign of the presence of the Holy Spirit. Hovering above and behind Mary is an angel. Head upright and arms outstretched horizontally, this angel, in an attitude typical of the Holy Spirit, overshadows Mary. Held by the angel and facing the viewer is a banderole that flutters as if wafted on a breeze. It bears the following inscription: *Salve sancta parens enixa puerpera regem* ('Hail, Holy Mother, you who brought forth the king'), an utterance that the angel seems to be addressing to Mary, comparable to Gabriel's greeting at the Annunciation and indicative of the royalty of Jesus portrayed in visualizations of the Tree of Jesse.

Illuminations of the Annunciation, in fact, provide a confluence of the imagery previously discussed.[7] Luke's narrative is the only Gospel that recounts the presence and participation of the Holy Spirit at the Annunciation. The angel indicates to Mary that the 'Holy Spirit will come upon [her]' and that 'the power of the Most High will overshadow [her]' (Luke 1:35). Luke thereby emphasizes that the Holy Spirit interacts with Mary in the virginal conception of Jesus and that the Third Person acts as the agent, representative, and efficient cause of 'the power of the Most High'. This Gospel account of the virginal conception of Jesus exercised profound impact on the imagination of illuminators.

By choosing particular visual images to depict Luke's Gospel, illuminators serve as interpreters of the scriptural text. Two examples will make the point. Whereas Luke states that the Holy Spirit 'will come upon' Mary and that the 'power of the Most High' will 'overshadow her', illuminators of the Annunciation usually render that passage by depicting the Third Person as a dove that descends toward the Virgin. And rather than casting a shadow (whether darkness or near darkness, respectively umbra or penumbra) over the Virgin, the dove descending projects rays of light. Through such visual imagery, illuminators interpret 'shadow' to mean proximity, not darkness. In other words, the *mysterium tremendum* will illuminate Mary because of its proximity to her. Illuminators who imaginatively select and artistically deploy these and other visual details render the Annunciation not only as a tableau of the virginal conception of Jesus but also as a focal point for interpreting biblical events from the Creation to Doomsday.

Depictions of the Annunciation promote historical recollection of at least three accounts in the Hebraic scriptures: the Creation, the re-genesis after the Deluge, and

[7] Commentary on, and illustrations of, the Annunciation may be found in Schiller 1971–2: 1. 33–52, figs. 66–129. See also Labriola and Smeltz 1990: 15, 57, 99, 143–5.

the ancestry of Jesus in the Tree of Jesse. In typical scenes of the Annunciation, the Holy Spirit figured as a dove descends along a diagonal axis: from the viewer's upper left toward the lower right. At times the Holy Spirit represents the triune godhead, for no other Divine Person may appear in the scene. Or one ray of light, which emanates from on high, though its source is not pictured, may trail behind the Holy Spirit's diagonal descent; or the diagonal ray may enter from the upper left and travel downward both behind and in front of the dove, which appears somewhere along this axis. However the dove and ray(s) of light are visualized, they head toward the Virgin Mary and approach or touch against her head, breast, or womb, respectively imprinting her mind, heart, or procreative faculty with the Logos.

By associating the dove with radiant descent, scenes of the Annunciation recall the primal Creation, especially as it is initiated by the onset of light, a sign of God's presence. When, in depictions of the Creation, the abyss is enshrouded in darkness, the Third Person figured as a dove becomes a source of light and warmth from above, which are radiated, in turn, to the waters below. By imparting light and warmth, first, to the waters that will recede and, then, to the emergent earth that will abound with life, the Holy Spirit is an agent of insemination, after which gestation and birth ensue.

Similarly, portrayals of the Annunciation that represent the dove as heavenly light epitomize fertility because a vase with water and flowers usually appears in the foreground or somewhere near the centre of most illuminations. In the background, furthermore, one may see a luxuriant outdoor landscape, visible through a window or door, either ajar or open. The transition from the background to the foreground, from the expansive outdoors to the circumscribed enclosure, signifies the willingness of the godhead to enter the confines of the human condition; and the contrast between the brightness outside and the lesser light inside portends that the godhead will be enshrouded by the darkness of the Virgin's womb.

In other words, natural fertility in scenes of the Annunciation recalls the emerging earth that becomes fecund while the waters of the Deluge recede under the light and warmth of the sun and when Noah perceives the dove with an olive-sprig as a sign that the earth should begin to be reinhabited. In particular, the fertility depicted at the Annunciation enhances the verbal image of the 'fruit' of the Virgin's womb (Luke 1:42), which is Elizabeth's reference to the Christ child during the Visitation by Mary. When consumed, that 'fruit' becomes the Eucharistic repast for all humanity; when pressed, it produces the sacramental drink. The larger implications, therefore, of the natural fertility associated with the Annunciation point to the abundant grace that humanity will receive by Christ's ministrations.

In scenes of the Annunciation, often a lily issues from atop the rod or sceptre held by Gabriel at the Annunciation. The flower usually has three petals: the central one upright and the other two splayed horizontally left and right. The cruciform image thereby suggests the dove with wings extended and Christ crucified. That is, the dove and its rays graphically represent divine insemination of the Virgin, and the Crucifixion is the means by which Mary's child, who is conceived at the Annunciation, will die.

Though artistic representations of the Annunciation thus feature the Divine Persons in various ways, the common emphasis is that the site of their presence is a holy place. Accordingly, the Annunciation is visualized as having taken place in a virtual inner sanctum or *sanctum sanctorum*. Whether in a room, a chapel, oratory, cathedral, or the like, Gabriel enters while the Divine Persons manifest their presence symbolically. Such enclosures, usually with a door or window either open or ajar, signify that access occurs only under the aegis of the godhead. When a closed door (*porta clausa*) appears in the scene, the implication is that it remains locked except to the godhead or a delegated emissary, such as Gabriel.

Reinforcing this interpretation in many scenes of the Annunciation, Mary is reading a book, or an open book is on a table or lectern nearby, when she is greeted by the angel. Presumably, the text that she reads or that appears on the open pages includes scriptural prophecies of the coming of the Lord, the fulfilment of which occurs at the Annunciation. Furthermore, for scenes of the Annunciation that occur in an ecclesial setting (chapel, oratory, or cathedral), the book that Mary reads or that is nearby may include passages from the Old Testament, including Isaiah, that anticipate the birth of the Messiah. In addition, the ecclesial setting implies that liturgies and devotional exercises enable participants also to be imprinted with the Divine Word after the manner of Mary at the Annunciation.

In a few portrayals of the Annunciation the dove and rays of light descend diagonally from the Father, whose face is visible in the upper left. And the Christ child accompanies the dove. In tandem, the dove leads the way, after which the burning babe who descends headlong carries a flaming cross against his shoulder, suggesting that his eventual crucifixion is akin to immolation and a burnt offering. Whether titled the Annunciation or the Trinity, such depictions highlight the interaction among the Divine Persons, as well as the triune godhead's impregnation of the Virgin. When the babe descends already fully formed, the role of Mary in parthenogenesis is somewhat diminished; for Jesus as the homunculus or 'little man' issues from the triune godhead and only abides in the womb of the Virgin until his birth.

One of the most memorable artistic representations of the Annunciation is a stone sculpture in the portal of the Virgin's Chapel in Wurzburg, built between 1377 and 1479 in the late Gothic style. The Father, while enthroned on high, holds a tube into which he breathes. The end of the tube inclines toward the ear of the Virgin, whom Gabriel greets. From the tube and into the Virgin's ear issues the breath of the Father. At its middle (that is, between the one end held by the Father and the other end at the Virgin's ear) the pneumatic tube resembles a sack, indeed a placenta atop which the homunculus descends headlong. Between the Virgin and Gabriel is a lily, with the Holy Spirit on top of it. The Third Person is figured as a dove, head upright and wings extended. The vase containing the lily resembles an hourglass, signifying the imminent fulfilment of prophecies of the coming of the Messiah. Gabriel's greeting of Mary is inscribed on a scroll, which the angel uplifts in his left hand while he extends his right hand in benediction toward Mary. The scroll held by Gabriel is configured like the Greek *rho*, the second letter of 'Christ' in Greek, signifying *Christos*, the anointed one (in Hebrew, the Messiah). Lit tapers rest on an altar behind the Virgin, suggesting the wondrous mystery of her impregnation but unviolated chastity. The tapers are burning, but unconsumed, similar to the burning bush in the theophany at Horeb (Exod. 3), a wonder that typologically prefigures the mystery of the virginal conception of Jesus. The images in this sculpture reinforce the presence of the Holy Spirit in at least three ways, combining polymorphic and zoomorphic representation: the breathing from the Father that wafts the babe below, the dove that alights on the lily, and the flames of the tapers, not unlike tongues of fire.

Comparable to such depictions of the triune godhead at the Annunciation are portrayals of all three Divine Persons at the Nativity. In an early fifteenth-century Book of Hours, *Très riches heures* (the manuscript is in the Musée Conde, Chantilly, France), prepared under the patronage of Jean, duc de Berri, a rendition of the Trinity is integrated into the scene of the Nativity. On high is the Father, from whose face and mouth rays of light descend, in the midst of which the dove heads toward the Christ child. The babe lies in a manger, flanked by Mary to his left and Joseph to his right. Artistic renditions of other New Testament events in which the Divine Persons play a major role include the Baptism of the Lord, the Transfiguration, and Pentecost. At the beginning of his public ministry, Jesus, when baptized, is proclaimed and identified as the Son by the voice of the Father (who in some artistic representations, such as *Très riches heures*, is often enthroned on high), while the Holy Spirit imaged as a dove descends toward the Son or overshadows him. At his Baptism, in other words, the Son and the other Divine Persons become integrated in a theophany. Thereafter, as Scripture recounts, the Holy Spirit impels Jesus into the wilderness for forty days, during which he withstands adversity and resists temptation by exercising the virtues and gifts imparted to him at his Baptism. Forty days in the wilderness may be interrelated typologically with Noah's experiences for the same period of time, when he was enclosed in the ark, emerged from it, released the dove that had been with him during the Deluge, and received the dove at its return. Furthermore, the travails of Jesus in the wilderness may be likened to the sojourn of the Chosen People, who were accompanied by the Holy Spirit, manifested alternately as a pillar of fire by night and a cloud by day. Such manifestations of the Holy Spirit, recounted in Scripture and rendered in art, underscore the Third Person's accompaniment of 'the chosen people', whether Noah and his family, the Israelites, or the Messiah and his followers.

Like the Baptism of the Lord, the Transfiguration is another episode in which all three Divine Persons are manifested to humankind because the Father voices his affirmation of the divinity of Jesus, who is also overshadowed by a cloud that signifies the presence of the Holy Spirit. Iconography of the Transfiguration situates Jesus on Mount Tabor encompassed by light, an aureole with sun-like emissions or a mandorla. Flanking Jesus are Moses and Elijah, while Peter, James, and John, the same three disciples who will witness his anguish in Gethsemane, fall prostrate at his feet. Illuminated manuscripts, illustrated bibles, paintings, mosaics, and frescos portray Jesus simultaneously in the states of humiliation and exaltation, suffering and triumph or, in effect, as *Christus Patiens* and *Christus Victor*. His numinous appearance and attitude anticipate his imminent Resurrection and Ascension, not to mention his eventual return in 'power and glory' at the Second Coming. But visible, though inconspicuous, signs, such as the stigmata, remind the onlooker that humiliation and suffering will precede the triumph of Jesus. Raphael's oil painting of the Transfiguration in the Vatican (*c*.1517–20) shows Jesus with the wounds of his suffering but in a state of levitation and against the vault of the heavens. By such a depiction Raphael anticipates, on the one hand the Crucifixion, and on the other, later glorious events: the triumph of Jesus at the Resurrection, his travel heavenward at the Ascension, and his return in 'power and glory' at the Second Coming. Similarly, Fra Angelico's fresco of the Transfiguration (*c*.1437–46) in the convent of San Marco in Venice shows Jesus in a full white garment, arms extended horizontally and his entire figure radiating light. This attitude simultaneously suggests both the Crucifixion and the Resurrection, as well as the extended wings of the Holy Spirit.

While the Holy Spirit at the Transfiguration is figured as a luminous cloud over the head of Jesus, the Third Person at the Resurrection artistically appears as the rays of the rising sun and bright clouds, at the Ascension as the effulgent heavens into which Jesus enters, and at the Second Coming as the resplendent firmament against which Christ will be highlighted. The foregoing artistic motifs converge in representations of certain appearances of Jesus after the Resurrection. In John's Gospel, Jesus breathes on the disciples, thereby impelling them into travail then triumph, in the manner that he was guided and accompanied in his temporal ministry by the Holy Spirit. Likened to the animation of Adam at the Creation, this intervention of Jesus causes the disciples, in effect, to be 'born again' of the Holy Spirit.

Soon afterwards they witness a theophany at Pentecost. In most artistic renditions of the Pentecost, the Virgin Mary, reading a book, is in the midst of the disciples, so that the rays of light or tongues of fire and the descent of the dove recall the Annunciation. If at the Annunciation the Virgin Mary was imprinted with the Divine Word in her mind, heart, and soul and impregnated with it, at Pentecost the disciples undergo a comparable experience. The heavens having opened above them (from which placid waters appear, fire and wind issue forth, and the dove descends), the disciples also receive a veritable baptism and accept divine indwelling, becoming pregnant with the Holy Spirit or suffused with his gifts and virtues.

In *The Bible of the Poor*, a fourteenth-century block-book that visualizes 120 scenes, the depiction of Pentecost is juxtaposed with a portrayal of Moses and the tablets on which the Divine Word was inscribed. Accordingly, the disciples, in the company of the Virgin Mary, become the living temples surmounted by the dove and bear the Divine Word inscribed on the tables (or tablets) of their hearts, largely because of the indwelling of the Holy Spirit. The tongues of fire signify the ardour and zeal of the disciples who, when fortified with the gifts or virtues of the Holy Spirit, impart or breathe the Divine Word as part of their worldwide evangelical ministry. Various renditions of Pentecost recall artistic representations of the temple-like ark on which the dove alights or into which it enters, as well as of Noah who represents a living temple bearing the Divine Word. In some renditions of Pentecost, Jesus oversees the event from the vault of the heavens, while the Holy Spirit below him is represented by rays, occasionally red to signify the issuance of blood, descending onto the Apostles. Or Jesus is ascending heavenward, visible only from the waist downward; but as he ascends out of sight, the dove appears at his feet, descending into the midst of the Apostles. Or the Trinity enthroned in heaven (the Father and the Son anthropomorphically depicted, and the Holy Spirit portrayed as a dove) oversee the Apostles and the Virgin Mary below.

Precisely here at Pentecost is the so-called birth of the Christian church. Its members through time, the Church Militant, by recourse to Scripture itself and to religious iconography, receive a view of history that may be deemed Christ-centered. Situating themselves along the continuum of biblical history and aided immeasurably by the art that they view, members of the Church Militant learn how and why their lives are to be oriented religiously. In their memory and mind's eye are visualizations of events in the redemptive ministry of Jesus, prefigured in the Old Testament and enacted in the New Testament. Applicable to each and every one of the members of the Church Militant, the redemptive act by Jesus supplies the means by which transition and translation heavenward will occur. The multitude of the faithful on earth will then become members of the Church Triumphant in the blissful afterlife.

WORKS CITED

CAMES, G. (1971), *Allegories et symboles dans l'Hortus deliciarum*. Leiden: E. J. Brill.

CHEW, S. C. (1947), *The Virtues Reconciled: An Iconographic Study*. Toronto: University of Toronto Press.

DIDRON, A. N. (1965), *Christian Iconography*, trans. E. J. Millington, 2 vols. New York: Frederick Ungar Publishing Co.

LABRIOLA, A. C. and J. W. SMELTZ (1990), *The Bible of the Poor [Biblia Pauperum]: A Facsimile and Edition of the British Library Blockbook C.9 d.2.* Pittsburgh: Duquesne University Press.

SCHILLER, G. (1971–2), *Iconography of Christian Art*, trans. Janet Seligman, 2 vols. Greenwich, Conn.: New York Graphic Society.

TRAVER, H. (1907), *The Four Daughters of God*. Bryn Mawr, Pa.: Bryn Mawr College Monographs 6.

FURTHER READING

For numerous and diverse examples of Christian iconography, see the following:

GRABAR, A. (1968), *Christian Iconography: A Study of Its Origins*. Princeton: Princeton University Press.

MÂLE, E. (1958), *The Gothic Image: Religious Art in France of the Thirteenth Century*, trans. Dora Nussey. New York: Harper & Row.

MOREY, C. (1935), *Christian Art*. New York: W. W. Norton.

RÉAU, L. (1955–9), *Iconographie de l'Art Chrétien*, 3 vols. Paris: Presses Universitaires de France.

ROTHE, E. (1968), *Mediaeval Book Illumination in Europe*. New York: W. W. Norton.

STRACHAN, JAMES (1957), *Early Bible Illustrations*. Cambridge: Cambridge University Press.

CHAPTER 14

....

LINGUISTIC AND CULTURAL INFLUENCES ON INTERPRETATION IN TRANSLATIONS OF THE BIBLE

....

DAVID J. CLARK[1]

INTRODUCTION

....

The earliest probable reference to the translation of scripture is in Nehemiah 8:8. There the book of the law was read 'with interpretation' by a group of Levites, with the comment 'they gave the sense, so that the people understood the reading' (NRSV: all Bible quotations are from the NRSV unless otherwise stated; abbreviations of Bible versions are listed at the end of the chapter). 'Interpretation' here may mean 'translation' from Hebrew to Aramaic (cf. GNT, NJB, NJPS), or perhaps something more like exposition (cf. NIV, REB). At any rate the aim of the exercise

[1] I am grateful for the help of my friends and colleagues Dr Stephen Pattemore and Mr Vitaly Voinov in checking the accuracy of various statements in this chapter.

was explicitly that the people should understand the scripture, because understanding was a prerequisite for obedience.

The motive that the text should be understandable to the reader or hearer has been an essential element in most subsequent Bible translation work, both Jewish and Christian. The need to give meaning priority over form, understood intuitively by competent Bible translators for many centuries, received a comprehensive theoretical underpinning only in the 1960s (Nida 1964, Nida and Taber 1969, updated in de Waard and Nida 1986). A more recent evaluation of this theory in a wider context appeared in Wilt (ed.) 2002. The need for intelligibility is the foundation for recognizing that the intended audience must have some influence on the form of the translation. This chapter will survey some of the ways in which the needs of the receptors have influenced some modern Bible translations. 'Interpretation' is not something that affects only theology. It is in fact much more pervasive, and affects many very mundane matters that translators have to handle. These are what will be in focus in this chapter.

We all view the Bible through the prism of our own geographical, ecological, historical, educational, linguistic, cultural, and religious backgrounds, and may fail to realize that members of every other language group do the same. As western readers, even as scholarly readers, we may be unaware of the extent to which our background influences our interpretation, and therefore fail to appreciate the influence that their background has on translators working in other languages. My approach will be to illustrate the typical problems encountered in Bible translation projects in various receptor languages. Examples will be drawn primarily (though not exclusively) from two very different countries in which I have extensive personal experience, namely Thailand and Russia. Thailand and Russia are alike in that there is one undisputed primary 'official' language in each country, namely Standard Thai, and Russian. There are other languages that are prominent in a given area (secondary languages), and yet others spoken by smaller and sometimes scattered groups often in remote areas (tertiary languages). The relative status of the receptor language may influence the attitude of its speakers towards written material in their own language, but such considerations fall outside the scope of this chapter.

This study will deal with translations into minority languages in both countries, and is based on my own field notes in working with each of the languages mentioned. For reasons of space, only the briefest linguistic and traditional religious background information can be provided. In Thailand the languages and religions are Akha (north Thailand and Burma: animism), Mien (north Thailand and Laos: animism and Taoism), Pwo Karen (north-west Thailand and Burma: animism and Theravada Buddhism), Kuy (north-east Thailand: Theravada Buddhism with animist substratum), Urak Lawoi (west coast of south Thailand: animism), and Pattani Malay (east coast of south Thailand: folk Islam). Pattani Malay is a secondary language spoken by around a million people, and the other languages are all tertiary languages with much smaller numbers of speakers.

In Russia the languages and religions are Yakut (eastern Siberia: Orthodoxy with shamanistic substratum), Khakas (southern Siberia: Orthodoxy with shamanistic substratum), Tuvan (southern Siberia: Tibetan Buddhism and shamanism), and Kalmyk (southern Russia, west of the Caspian Sea: Tibetan Buddhism). These are all secondary languages. Occasionally examples will be drawn from other areas within my experience, and problems will also be illustrated from English versions.

Geographical and Ecological Influences

Almost all the events recorded in the Bible took place in the eastern Mediterranean, with its specific geology, land forms, climate, and ecosystems. Inhabitants of the temperate zone in northern Europe are close enough to this setting that it is not unimaginable for them, even though it may be unfamiliar. But both tropical Thailand and most of continental Russia are much further removed from the Mediterranean, and for minority language groups with little or no background knowledge of that area, some of the basic features of Mediterranean life may seem very strange. For instance, in terms of geography, how will the term 'desert' be understood? In several of the tertiary languages of the hill peoples in north Thailand, terrain is generally divided into two categories, the cultivated and the uncultivated, and their lexical resources usually offer no other simple choice. Biblical deserts were certainly not cultivated, but neither were they uncultivated in the north Thailand sense, for there uncultivated land normally consists of mountainous jungles. Thus, for readers with such a background it may often be necessary to give an expanded description of a biblical desert in a footnote or glossary entry. In any specific context it may be essential to mention whatever feature of the desert is in focus there, such as the lack of water, the lack of vegetation, the absence of people, or whatever it may be.

A very different problem faces the Yakut people, who live in a vast area that is largely permafrost and in which only a few root vegetables can be grown. But despite the infertility of the land, for them in a sense nothing is desert, because they have lived off it for centuries. Again translators may have to resort to footnotes or glossary entries to give an adequate explanation.

At the other end of the scale are the Berber languages of North Africa, where the people are familiar with the Sahara and have well-developed vocabularies for different types of desert. So they constantly demand to know what kind of desert is in view in any particular context: flat or hilly, stony or sandy, with or without scrub vegetation, and so on. Probably most English readers think of a desert primarily in terms of sand. It may come as a surprise to realize that the Bible nowhere mentions sand in connection with a desert. Sand normally refers to the sand of the seashore and is mentioned almost always metaphorically. So from a biblical perspective our English perception may not be as accurate as we imagine.

In terms of directions, the normal order in English is 'north, south, east, west', but this is by no means universal. In Akha south has to come before north (Ps. 89:12), and in Mien the expected order is east, south, west, north. To depart from the normal order would make the translation sound as unnatural as saying 'butter and bread' in English.

In the sphere of climate, a simple example must suffice. The biblical lands normally experience a year with four seasons, spring, summer, autumn, and winter. Temperate Europe is much the same. However, most of Thailand experiences only three seasons, the wet season (roughly June to October), the dry season (November to February), and the hot season (March to May). This is obviously not commensurate with such phenomena as summer and winter (Gen. 8:22), or 'the early rain' and 'the later rain' (Joel 2:23), and inevitably creates problems of interpretation for translators. In Siberia the seasons are dominated by winter, which in Yakutia may last for seven months, with temperatures in some areas at −40 degrees C for weeks on end. Summer is short and can be very hot, and spring and autumn are brief. Translators again have a hard job interpreting biblical seasons and weather patterns in terms that are understandable to their readers.

In such very different environments, the flora and fauna are of course very different from those in the Bible, and this creates both superficial problems and deeper ones. The basic crops of the Holy Land are wheat, barley, olives, and grapes. Of these none is indigenous to Thailand, though vines have been introduced in the twentieth century and there is now a fledgling wine industry. The staple food is rice, in the plains paddy rice and in the hills dry rice. In some biblical contexts where 'wheat' or 'bread' stands for food in general (as in the Lord's Prayer), it may be possible to substitute 'rice' in a translation, but this is not appropriate everywhere, for instance in the accounts of specific events such as the Last Supper. Again, tropical fruits are different from those of the Mediterranean. Thailand has a wide variety of delicious fruit, but mangos and rambutans are not the same as figs and pomegranates (Deut. 8:8). In some places a generic term for 'fruit' can be used, but not everywhere. Therefore translators may have to choose between making a less than fully satisfactory substitution of a local item for a biblical one, and rendering a biblical fruit by a foreign word that may not be understood. The degree of familiarity with the outside world varies from one minority language to another, so there can be no one-size-fits-all solution.

In Siberia this problem is even more acute. In large areas there is no fruit except wild berries, so the whole notion of fruit cultivation is very alien. In the Bible the generic term 'fruit' is often used in a figurative sense (e.g. Prov. 1:31; 8:19; Matt. 7:20; Gal. 5:22), but this is very unnatural in Siberian languages like Khakas. So all such metaphors are necessarily lost in translation, and have to be replaced by a more prosaic term such as 'result'.

As for examples of fauna, vultures are not found in the Kalmyk, Tuvan, or Yakut areas of Russia, so they become 'kites' in Kalmyk and 'scavengers' in Yakut and Tuvan. Scorpions do not exist in Yakutia, so in Luke 11:12 in Yakut they become 'poisonous spiders'.

A further influence in this general area is the existence of folk taxonomies which are not in line with modern scientific classification. The lion is not found in Thailand, though people are often familiar with the name of the animal through traditional stories, in much the same way as English children may 'know' about unicorns through stories. In Kuy the lion was 'known' as a name but was classified not as a kind of tiger (which an English reader might have expected) but as a kind of bear. This is hardly a translational disaster, but it does illustrate how inescapable elements of the receptor context impose an indigenous flavour on the translated text.

HISTORICAL AND EDUCATIONAL INFLUENCES

Some parts of the Old Testament presuppose a familiarity with the history narrated in the earlier books, but such familiarity cannot be taken for granted among most modern western readers, let alone among first- or second-generation Christians in distant minority groups. To give a single example, Micah 6:5 calls on people to remember 'what King Balak of Moab devised, what Balaam son of Beor answered him, and what happened from Shittim to Gilgal'. The story of Balak and Balaam in Numbers 22–4 may be moderately familiar to the average churchgoer in the West, but how many would have any idea that 'what happened from Shittim to Gilgal' was the crossing of the Jordan in Joshua 3–4? Should translators leave the text sounding entirely mysterious, or include some clue to the event referred to? If the latter, should the clue be incorporated into the text (cf. REB, 'the crossing from Shittim to Gilgal'), or into a footnote (cf. GNSB, NJB)?

On a wider scale, the New Testament takes for granted a familiarity with both the history and the cultic practices of the Old Testament, but such familiarity is completely absent in many cultures. Various parts of the New Testament text will be particularly baffling for readers whose languages do not yet have a translation of the Old Testament. The genealogy in Matthew 1:1–17, coming as it does right at the beginning of the New Testament, can be very intimidating. Stephen's speech in Acts 7, or the references to Old Testament ritual in Hebrews, can also leave first time readers floundering. In the vast majority of cases they have no access to commentaries and other aids to understanding.

The amount of information that can be included to help them will vary according to many factors. How much more of the Bible is likely to be translated into this language? Will the readers ever get the Old Testament? Is the Bible available in some national language or trade language that at least church leaders have access to? How much are people likely to be willing to pay for a New Testament? The more information included in a New Testament by way of notes, glossaries, maps, historical charts, and so on, the higher the unit cost and therefore the smaller the potential market. What about standards of literacy? The ability to read a relatively straightforward narrative text is no guarantee that the reader will be able to follow the complexities of the Epistles, much less handle footnotes, or understand maps and charts. In this respect, the literacy skills among minority language groups in Russia are in general likely to be higher than among minority language groups in Thailand, though literacy in a national language does not transfer automatically into literacy in a vernacular, especially if the vernacular has a more complex orthography. Thus the influences on interpretation in the widest sense include matters of education and economics which are generally beyond the control of any translation team.

LINGUISTIC INFLUENCES

Differences between languages may affect linguistic structure in any of its elements, such as phonology, vocabulary, morphology, syntax, or discourse structure. Differences in phonology are especially noticeable in the transliteration of personal and place names. The absence of any equivalent in roman script to the Hebrew letter *ayin* leads to such odd-looking names in English Bibles as Canaan, Baal, and Naaman, though long familiarity has desensitized most readers to the fact that spellings with –aa- are not normal in English. The problem is vastly compounded in a language like Akha which does not tolerate any syllable-final consonants and does not differentiate l and r. The contrasts between Balaam, Baal, Balak, and Barak have to be carried instead by arbitrary tonal distinctions.

A different problem arises in Russia in areas where there is a long Orthodox tradition. Many biblical names have become familiar in a Russianized form, and even if this does not fit the phonological patterns of, say, Yakut or Khakas, people want to keep the familiar form to avoid confusion. The result is a different kind of anomaly, with Hebrew and Greek names passing through the filter of Russian orthographic tradition before reaching the minority language. To some extent we find a similar feature in English, where some Hebrew names in the New Testament have passed through a Greek filter before coming into English. This has given rise, especially in older English versions, to confusing variations in the form of the same name, such as Hannah/Anna, Zechariah/Zacharias, Judah/Judas/Jude, and of course Joshua/Jesus.

Vocabulary differences are to be encountered in any translation process, and it is widely recognized that they lead to problems. In English, for instance, no one root can produce forms that cover the wide area of meaning of the Greek root *dikaio-*, so English has to use the two roots 'righteous' and 'justify'. The cohesive links in the Greek in a passage like Romans 3:21–6 are thus lost in most English versions. The problem is perhaps most acute with plays on words. Two examples found in many languages, including English, are that there is no single term meaning both 'wind' and 'spirit' and no single term meaning both 'again' and 'from above', so that in John 3:5–8 the recursive links in the Greek account of the conversation of Jesus and Nicodemus are far from clear. This can be resolved by means of footnotes, but a greater problem arises where the lexical structure of a receptor language has obligatory categories that are absent from Hebrew and Greek. This difference can force translators to make exegetical decisions for which the source text does not supply adequate information. One such case that occurs widely is an obligatory distinction between older and younger siblings. Thus every time the words 'brother' and 'sister' occur, the translator has to decide which brother or sister is older. The situation is especially complicated in the case of Mary, Martha, and Lazarus. Their relative ages were of no interest to the Gospel writers, but if they have to be stated, translators must make more or less arbitrary decisions, and must remember that it is more important to be consistent than to be right. In the case of the 'brothers and sisters' of Jesus in Mark 3:32, the translator's decision carries theological freight, especially in situations where Orthodox or Catholic communities exist.

The problem of obligatory categories extends to morphology as well. For instance if a language makes an obligatory distinction between inclusive and exclusive first-person plurals, then the translator cannot avoid deciding whether or not the addressee is included every time a first-person plural occurs, whether as a verb, a pronoun, or a possessive. In Galatians 5:5, for instance, when Paul says 'we eagerly wait for the hope of righteousness', was he including his readers or not? In the light of the rebuke in the previous verse, the translators in Urak Lawoi decided he was probably not, so used an exclusive form. In many Malayo-Polynesian languages there is no passive voice, and this means that every passive verb has to be restructured somehow. A verb like 'be baptized' may be expressed as 'receive baptism', but very often a subject has to be stated, and this entails more exegetical decisions, for instance in Matthew 7:1, 'Do not judge, so that you may not be judged'. Many English versions retain the ambiguous passive, though GNT bites the bullet and says clearly 'Do not judge others so that God will not judge you' (cf. CEV). Many other languages, such as Urak Lawoi, have followed this example.

In terms of syntax, almost every other language finds the long Greek sentences in the Epistles indigestible. A literal translation will inevitably sound highly unnatural, as the KJV demonstrates frequently in English. To give a brief example, in Kalmyk the head word in a phrase or clause has to come last, with subordinate material preceding it. Thus, in the Kalmyk rendering of 2 Timothy 2:8 ('Remember Jesus Christ, raised from the dead, a descendant of David . . .') the verb 'remember' has to come last, and 'raised from the dead' must precede 'Jesus Christ' or else it will be taken to apply to David. The end result is: 'David-from descended the-dead-from risen Jesus Christ remember.'

In the Turkic and Altaic languages that spread across Central Asia and Siberia the default pattern is for subordinate clauses to precede the main clause in a sentence, whereas in Greek they normally follow it. This difference is in itself sufficient to change the flow of information through a paragraph, and requires that translators take great care to maintain cohesion and coherence in a paragraph according to the natural patterns of the receptor language. The ramifications of this are many. Even in relatively simple narrative, keeping clear track of the participants may require significant adjustments in choosing whether to use nouns or pronouns or neither.

The decision where to start a new paragraph is by no means as straightforward as might be imagined. In the New Testament, even the fourth edition of the UBS Greek Text and the twenty-seventh edition of Nestlé-Aland, which claim to offer the same text, differ frequently in their punctuation and paragraph-breaks, and it is clear that neither is based on a serious discourse analysis of the Greek. But even if translators had access to an agreed set of linguistically well-founded paragraph-breaks in the Greek text, they would still have to make adjustments to fit the paragraph structure of the receptor language.

A further area where there is significant mismatch between languages is figures of speech. What is perfectly natural in one language may sound absurd or even offensive in another. In Greek the word for intestines is used as a metonymy for sympathy, but not in English. Thus the KJV rendering in Philippians 2:1, 'bowels and mercies', sounds ridiculous in modern English, so even a translation like ESV that claims to be 'essentially literal' drops the metonymy here and translates as 'compassion and sympathy'. Similarly in other languages, some figures of speech are unavoidably lost in the translation process. Figures based on universal human experiences generally cross language barriers more readily than those which are culture-specific. Thus, a metaphor like 'our God is a consuming fire' (Heb. 12:29) can often be translated literally without distortion of meaning.

In many cases the receptor language uses a different figure to convey the same meaning, so the proportion of figurative language in a given book is not always reduced. An example in English is the use in the REB of the phrase 'wipe out' in Zephaniah 1:3, where the Hebrew has literally 'cut off'. 'Wipe out' is so natural in English that most readers would not notice that it is figurative. Similarly in the Hebrew of Genesis 4:5 Cain's face 'fell', but in Kuy it was 'sour' and in Mien, where couplets are common, it was 'blind and dark'. In other situations the receptor language may offer a natural figure of speech where the Hebrew or Greek uses plain language, and provided that the figure does not introduce anything that would be historically or culturally anomalous, it may be suitable. An example in English would be to say in Mark 7.6, 'Isaiah hit the nail on the head when he said . . .', though no version I am aware of does this. However, in Pattani Malay the rebuke given by Wisdom in Proverbs 1:25 becomes 'my advice you would not wear', and in Proverbs 17:23 the wicked 'eat a bribe'. In Yakut in Romans 1:18, 'suppress the truth' is expressed as 'stifle the truth', and in 2 Timothy 3:3 'inhuman' is rendered by a climate-related figure as 'icy-hearted'. In Matthew 13:15, quoting Isaiah 6:10, Jesus says, 'this people's heart has grown dull, and their ears are hard of hearing, and they have shut their eyes'. In Tuvan this is expressed very vividly and idiomatically as 'their hearts are like stone, their ears are full of sand, and their eyes are curtained'.

It is an inherent feature of language that it carries not just information but also implications. The same piece of information, however, may carry different implications in different languages. In Acts 21:9 the statement is made about Philip the evangelist that 'he had four unmarried daughters who had the gift of prophecy'. In English, as in Greek, this is a simple statement of fact, but in Iai, a language of the Gulf Province of Papua New Guinea, the statement that the daughters were unmarried carried unwanted implications. In a society in which everybody marries, the fact that these women were not married raised in the minds of readers a question that was not intended by the original writer: what was wrong with them? Were they too young to marry? Were they too lazy, so that nobody wanted to marry them? But if either of these possibilities were true, would God have given them the gift of prophecy? Or were they so ugly that nobody found them attractive? Such speculations were a distraction to the readers' understanding. The implication that there was something wrong with Philip's daughters had to be excluded without distorting the text, and in this case there was an easy solution. The translation was adjusted to say that they were 'not yet married'. This conveys the basic fact, but leaves open the possibility that at some later stage these women conformed to the expectations of the receptor culture. The readers were no longer distracted by an irrelevance.

In Galatians 5:17 Paul writes that the Spirit and the flesh 'are opposed to each other, to prevent you from doing what you want'. The Pwo Karen translators asked whether this implied that the Spirit prevented you from doing the bad things you wanted to do, or the flesh prevented you from doing the good things you wanted to do. Both interpretations are, after all, true to Christian experience. In favour of the first possibility is that it matches up well with the previous verse, 'Live by the Spirit, I say, and do not gratify the desires of the flesh'. In favour of the second possibility is that the closest parallel statement in Romans 7:15–19 focuses on failing to do good things. It seems unlikely that Paul intended to be ambiguous, so it is better that translators should indicate their preference than that they should pass on the problem to their unsuspecting readers, as NRSV has. An alternative rendering can be supplied in a footnote.

Apart from logical implications, individual words or phrases may carry connotations that are not present in the Greek or Hebrew. On rare occasions unwanted connotations can even affect textual decisions. In Matthew 15:39 the oldest manuscripts have a place name Magadan, and this is the form given in NRSV and most modern versions in English. In Yakut the problem is that there is a modern town with this name on the Pacific coast of Russia, on the Sea of Okhotsk, not so far from Yakutia. It had a bad reputation as a prison city in Soviet times, and the appearance of this name in a Bible translation would bring unfortunate connotations to the minds of the readers. Since the name occurs only once in the New Testament and is not crucial to the story, in this case the translators chose to follow the alternative reading Magdala. This is also the reading in the Russian Synodal version, widely used by both Orthodox and Protestants, so it has the added virtue of familiarity.

CULTURAL AND RELIGIOUS INFLUENCES

Culture is notoriously difficult to define (van der Jagt 2002: 2–4). Here the word is used in a very general sense to include both the material aspects of life in society and the value systems and attitudes of societies, including the way people interact and the linguistic markers that show their relationships. If missionary translators who are not native speakers of the receptor language are involved in a project as translators, it is likely that at some point their third culture and its baggage will come between the source language and culture and the receptor language and culture, and make the situation even more complex. However, this section will assume the increasingly common situation in which the translators are native speakers, with no more than exegetical help from foreign colleagues.

On the material level, the nautical vocabulary in Acts 27 may present many problems to people who live far from the sea, for whom ships may be remote from daily experience and appropriate vocabulary non-existent. So suitable adaptations may be required: for instance, the prow of the ship in Khakas is expressed as 'the nose'. By contrast, the Urak Lawoi people, who depend on the sea for their entire livelihood, have a rich nautical vocabulary, and in the storm narratives in the Gospels they needed to decide whether the boat was heading into the wind, running before it, or tacking, because different words would be used of the action of the water in each case.

An area where all translators face difficult decisions is that of weights and measures. If the original terms are retained, especially in the Old Testament, there will be a significant number of unknown terms. Yet if modern (nowadays usually metric) terms are substituted, there is an unavoidable element of anachronism. But in many modern situations where receptors are unfamiliar with any other terms, they are unlikely to notice the anachronism, so in the overriding interest of intelligibility translators generally choose modern terms over unknown ones. This solution has its difficulties in contexts where the actual numbers of the ancient units carried some symbolic significance which is lost when the metric measures are worked out (cf. Rev. 14:20; 21:16–17). However, such situations are not too common, and footnotes can help to restore these losses. GNT has a footnote at Revelation 21:17, but not at 14:20.

Moving on to sociological and sociolinguistic matters, all societies are structured in some way (as monarchies, republics, tribes, clans, age-sets, and so on), and have vocabulary appropriate to their own social units. The Bible nowhere gives a detailed description of the social structures of the people-groups it mentions, though a good deal of information is implicit in different places, for instance about Persian court practices in Esther, or about Roman citizenship in Acts. Nowhere is a hierarchy of social units plainer than in Joshua 7:14–18, where tribe, clan, and family are identified as units of descending size. There is nothing really parallel to this in modern western societies, where there is no automatic membership of any intermediate unit between the family and the nation, so that terms like 'tribe' and 'clan' carry overtones of the exotic, and lack the emotive impact of 'family'. In some language groups the social structure is much closer to that of ancient Israel, and the parallel terms carry a higher emotive impact than they do to English readers.

In many societies age carries prestige and requires deference, and this is often shown by the terms used, either pronouns or descriptive terms, usually kin terms. For instance, the boy Samuel has to address Eli as 'uncle' in 1 Samuel 3:5 in Kuy, and in Pattani Malay in Genesis 47.8 even Pharaoh has to question the aged Jacob respectfully in the third person with the kin term 'grandfather'. Politeness is often conveyed by the presence or absence of vocatives in a way that is different from the usage in Hebrew or Greek. This means that a translation may need to include a vocative in direct speech where the source text does not have one, because the absence of a vocative would convey the false impression that rudeness is intended. Of course, the vocative chosen has to fit unobtrusively with the social expectations of the receptor culture. This is an area of translation where it is all too easy to be unthinkingly literal without taking sufficient account of the sociolinguistic implications of a literal rendering.

At the other end of the scale, there are different ways of showing scorn, contempt, or just plain rudeness. In the Old Testament the most frequent way is to address or refer to someone not by his personal name, but as 'son of x', as for instance in 1 Samuel 20:27, 30, 31; 22:7, 8, 9, 12, 13. To retain this form literally in an English translation, as many versions do, sounds rather odd but fails to convey the interpersonal overtones of the Hebrew. Among English versions the derogatory nuance is captured most effectively by CEV with the expressions 'that son of Jesse' (1 Sam. 20:27, 30, 31; 22:7, 8, 9, 13) and 'you son of Ahitub' (22:12).

Sometimes the value system of the receptor culture can legitimately influence exegetical decisions where the evidence is otherwise evenly balanced, and one such place is Galatians 5:12, where the meaning of the Greek verb *apokopsontai* may be either 'cut themselves off' in the sense of 'separate themselves', or else 'castrate themselves'. The latter meaning presents no problems in areas such as North Africa or Kalmykia where there is a folk memory of harems under the charge of eunuchs, but in areas where castration has never been practised to mention it could involve either a lengthy periphrasis that may not be understood, or a more vulgar expression that would render the passage unreadable in public worship. In Thailand the culture of the Pwo Karen is outwardly somewhat prudish, and for this reason the meaning 'separate themselves' had to be chosen.

The religious background of the receptors may influence their response to the biblical text in diverse ways. The religious background of the receptors is often not homogeneous anyway: popular Buddhism or Islam may be mingled with animism, or popular Orthodoxy with shamanism. For people with a Theravada Buddhist background, in which there is no creator, the opening chapters of Genesis represent a major divergence from their own traditions. Stories in the Gospels involving spirit possession evoke very different responses from readers with animistic or shamanistic cultures and from those with materialist, urban, industrial backgrounds in western Europe. In groups influenced by Chinese culture (as some in north Thailand have been) the dragon in Revelation 12 will probably be seen as a positive rather than a negative symbol.

The translation is sometimes influenced by the religious context of the readers. Differences between the religious presuppositions of the source text and those of the receptors came to the surface frequently in the Pattani Malay translation, no doubt because the background there is Islamic and has its own well-defined theology. One of the common problems was that no anthropomorphisms were acceptable in connection with God, so that in all such places the meaning behind the figure had to be expressed, for instance 'the power of God' for 'the finger of God' in Exodus 8:19. Because God can have no equal, it was not possible for the Lord to say to Moses in Exodus 7:1, 'I have made you like God to Pharaoh'. This was rendered as 'I will cause you to be my voice to Pharaoh', a voice being considered sufficiently incorporeal to be attributed to God. In Kalmyk, with its Tibetan Buddhist worldview, New Testament references to 'new life' had to be framed very carefully to avoid any implication of reincarnation.

CONCLUSION

The original message of the Bible was conveyed in and through the social and linguistic phenomena of specific ancient cultures. It was therefore inevitably clothed in the 'garments' of those cultures, many of which appear exotic and even shocking in modern settings, not only non-western but also western. A certain measure of what some translation theorists call domestication is therefore essential if the message is to remain intelligible, and to bring to its modern readers or hearers a challenge that is at all comparable with the challenge that the original text brought to its readers or hearers. This chapter has attempted to demonstrate some of the ways, often unexpected, in which the culturally conditioned understanding of the modern reader has to be taken into account in formulating a translation adequate to fulfil this purpose.

ENGLISH BIBLE VERSIONS

CEV: Contemporary English Version.
ESV: English Standard Version.
GNSB: Good News Study Bible
GNT: Good News Translation
KJV: King James Version
NIV: New International Version
NJB: New Jerusalem Bible
NJPS: New Jewish Publication Society Translation
NRSV: New Revised Standard Version
REB: Revised English Bible

WORKS CITED

VAN DER JAGT, KRIJN (2002), *Anthropological Approaches to the Interpretation of the Bible.* UBS Monograph Series, no. 8. New York: United Bible Societies.
NIDA, EUGENE A. (1964), *Towards a Science of Translating.* Leiden: E. J. Brill.
——and CHARLES R. TABER (1969), *The Theory and Practice of Translation.* Leiden: E. J. Brill.
DE WAARD, JAN and EUGENE A. NIDA (1986), *From One Language to Another: Functional Equivalence in Bible Translating.* Nashville, Tenn.: Nelson.
WILT, TIMOTHY (ed.) (2002), *Bible Translation: Frames of Reference.* Manchester, UK and Northampton, Mass.: St Jerome Publishing.

FURTHER READING

CLARK, DAVID J. (2004), *Anthropology and the 'End User': The Influence of Receptor Cultures on the Translation of the Bible,* in Louise J. Lawrence and Mario I. Aguilar (eds.), *Anthropology and Biblical Studies: Avenues of Approach*, 62–76. Leiden: Deo Publishing.

——(2004), *Minority Language Biblical Translation Work in Russia: Then and Now*, in Stephen Batalden, Kathleen Cann, and John Dean (eds.), *Sowing the Word: The Cultural Impact of the British and Foreign Bible Society 1804–2004* (*Bible in the Modern World*, 3), 217–33. Sheffield: Sheffield Phoenix Press.

....

CHAPTER 15

MEMORY, IMAGINATION, AND THE INTERPRETATION OF SCRIPTURE IN THE MIDDLE AGES

....

MARY CARRUTHERS

IN one of the most moving acts of his reign, when Charlemagne decided to collect a great library to build up the palace school of his court in Aachen, he did so first by bringing over from England a person, Alcuin of York. Alcuin in turn collected a group of scholars about him, to form the palace school and thus to create the palace library. Of course they brought books with them, but mostly they brought their learning, stored away in the treasuries of their memories. In doing so, Charlemagne, wittingly or not, was realizing an antique and early Christian trope (and reality) that one finds articulated in Jerome and in Cassiodorus, among others—that of the learned person as a living library, one who makes for him- or herself a mental chest of memorized texts and materials, which are then always ready as a reference and meditation tool.

In his sixtieth epistle, Jerome wrote how 'by constant reading and [continual] meditation,' a young cleric 'had made his mind a library of Christ' (Letter 60.10).[1] Two centuries later Cassiodorus described a blind Greek scholar named Eusebius, who had come to the monastery at Vivarium at Cassiodorus' invitation. This Eusebius had been blind since childhood, yet 'he had hidden away in the library of his memory (*in memoriae suae bibliotheca*) so many authors, so many books, that he could assuredly tell others who were reading in what part of a codex they might find of what he had spoken' (Cassiodorus, *Institutiones* 1.5.2). Another example known to Cassiodorus was that of the scriptural expositor Didymus of Alexandria, a man whose commentaries were renowned for their comprehensiveness and subtlety, yet who had been blind from birth and thus could read only by means of his memory. There are also examples of scholars from the later Middle Ages, including Aquinas, Ockham, Wyclif, and Petrarch, whose reading and compositional habits make clear that the goal of making a library of one's memory was by no means dimmed in an age when written books were far more plentiful, at least to scholars.

Two questions at once present themselves. Most intriguing perhaps is how one might go about making oneself into a library (whether of Christ or not). But this question depends on a prior one: why would want to make oneself into a library? The bulk of this chapter will be concerned with the question of how, but only after we have addressed the question of why. A common explanation of 'why' is that oral societies rely on memory because they lack access to writing and written sources. But this is not the case in Mediterranean antiquity, for scrolls and codices were not particularly scarce in those societies, and learned authors had plentiful access to books. It is Didymus' profession of commentator which provides us with the correct answer. Didymus had made himself into a library not because he was blind and could not see to read, but because he was a composer of new thoughts and learning about the biblical text. Many scholars with normal vision also made themselves into libraries, because doing so enables the kind of richly concording and paralleling style of interpretation that we associate particularly with patristic and medieval exegesis.

Here is an example, from a text typical not only in its formal properties but also in having an uncertain author. It is part of a commentary on the Penitential Psalms attributed to Pope Gregory I in some early editions of his work. No scholar that I know of now accepts it as authentic, mainly because Gregory nowhere mentions commenting on these Psalms in his extensive letters. Yet the style of this commentary is of a piece with that in Gregory's authentic work. And indeed, what is important in the context of my chapter is not who wrote it but its very conventionality as a piece of 'Gregorian' commentary (his text is Ps. 50:1):

---

[1] The letter is Jerome's eulogy for the young priest and bishop, Nepotian, addressed to his 'episcopal uncle', Jerome's great friend Heliodorus.

Let us place before the eyes of our mind someone gravely wounded and scarcely drawing his last gasps of vital air, who both lies naked on a dungheap [cf. Job 2:8; Ps. 112:7], and displays a wound not yet dressed, is overwhelmed by desire for the coming of a physician and when recognized, begs that he take pity on him. For his wound is the sin of his soul, concerning which is said: 'wounds and bruises and swelling sores: they are not bound up, nor dressed, nor fomented with oil' (Is. 1:6). O wounded man, acknowledge inwardly your physician, and reveal to him the wounds of your sins. Let him hear the groan of your heart, to whom the secret of your thought lies entirely open. Let your tears move him, and with some importunity seeking him, always bring forth to him deep sighs from the bottom of your heart; let your grief penetrate to him, that it may be said also to you: 'The Lord also hath taken away thy sin' (2 Kings [2 Sam.] 12:13). Cry out with David; see (*vide*) what he said: *Miserere mei Deus secundam magnam misericordiam tuam*. As though he should say: I am in danger from a mighty wound, such that none of the physicians has the power to cure, unless that physician who is omnipotent gives prompt aid. Indeed to the omnipotent physician nothing is incurable; who, as he heals without a fee, so restores health with his word. I should despair therefore of my wound, did I not count on his omnipotence. *Miserere mei Deus secundam magnam misericordiam tuam*. Let them seek mercy who ignorantly incur guilt. But as I have gravely fallen, so too I knowingly sinned. But you, omnipotent physician, correct those who are contemptuous, you instruct those who are ignorant, and you forgive those who confess. Lord Jesus, would that you, moved by your mercy, should deign to come to me, who going down from Jerusalem to Jericho, that is to say rushing from the heights to the deep, from health to sickness, have fallen among the angels of darkness, who not only have taken away from me my garment of spiritual grace, but indeed beaten me and left me half-alive [cf. Luke 10:30]. Would that you should bind up the wounds of my sins, and give me assurance of recovering my well-being, lest they rage more savagely if they despair of being healed. Would that you should apply to me the oil of remission, and pour out the wine of your compunction [cf. Luke 10:34; Ps. 22]. But if you place me on your beast of burden (*iumentum*) [Luke 10:34], you will raise up the needy man from the earth, the poor man from the dunghill [Ps. 112:7]. For it is you who have borne away our sins, who have paid for what you had not snatched off [1 Pet. 2:24; 2 Kgs 12:13; Ps. 68:5]. If you lead me into the stable (*stabulum*) [Luke 10:34] of your Church, you will feed me with the refreshment of your body and blood. If you will take care of me, I will neither neglect your commandments, nor incur the rage of roaring beasts. I stand in need of your protection for as long as I carry this corruptible flesh. Wherefore hear me, O Samaritan, robbed and wounded, weeping and groaning, calling on you, and with David, crying out: *Miserere mei Deus secundam magnam misericordiam tuam*.   ([Gregory the Great], *PL* 79.582–3)[2]

This is not what we would call the exposition of a text; indeed it is quite the opposite of our standard of neutral, factual scholarship. We might call it a

---

[2] The work is printed with others of uncertain Gregorian authorship. I have given references for only some of the more obvious allusions made in this passage; there are others. The *frementium rabies bestiarum*, 'rage of roaring beasts', is only indirectly biblical; a search of the online *Patrologia Latina* reveals the same phrase (with an appropriate change of case) in a sermon of Leo the Great (d. 461), in reference to Daniel in the den of lions. Searches of other words in this Gregorian text would undoubtedly reveal many more such allusions.

'meditation', and expect it in a sermon. Yet its mode of discourse is a blend we find curious now, of the intimate, the exemplary, and the instructional. It focuses on Luke 10, the Good Samaritan parable, without ever citing it directly; evidently the composer of these words saw no need for that with the audience he had in mind. The type of analysis practised is what came to be called *tropological*, an interpretation of the literal words that 'turns' their sense towards the ethical and psychological situation of a listener, and also invites that listener to make more turns upon the literal words, in an exercise of spiritual invention that is grounded in basic rhetorical method, as its designation conveys.

The listener is required to experience the scene in a way deliberately engaging imagination, emotion, memory, and rational investigation. The verse in Psalm 50 is encountered not as words but as a picture placed before the eyes of the mind. The invitation to place something that is conceptual and verbal as though it were instead an image or a picture before the eyes of the mind, or of the heart, or even the eye of cogitation is a common idiom in patristic and later exegesis. Being required to make a mental picture immediately engages the listener in a rational activity. Sometimes, when the text itself is a verbal picture, an ekphrasis, mental painting augments the words: this is common in exegesis of the great biblical ekphrases, such as the Ark, the Tabernacle, the Temple and its vessels, Aaron's breastplate, the prophetic sights of Ezekiel, Isaiah, Daniel, and Revelation. Mental picturing in these cases becomes itself an elaborate exercise in composing, for in rhetoric artful augmentation (*dilatatio* or *copia dicendi*) is a fundamental method of invention. The meticulously experienced imagining of the Passion and related matters is a similarly elaborated mental discipline. Because these pictures are elaborated from texts (though later in the Middle Ages of course also from material images), they have often been explained as illustrations or mental aids, pictures of the words they serve, addressed mainly to the 'illiterate'.

But in this case, the picture asked for is not an illustration or representation of the literal content of Psalm 50:1, of the sort which might help an illiterate or ignorant person to grasp words he cannot otherwise read. It is a vigorous and quite unexpected picture of a man lying in a dungheap, seriously wounded and begging for a physician. Nothing in the actual words of Psalm 50:1 suggests such a figure. What the image does in its deliberately considered way is to link the psalm text with the exegesis to come in a manner that requires the full attention of the listener, not only imaginatively but intellectually. This mental image is the basis of the commentary to follow, and unless one undertakes the exercise of making the image for oneself, one will be unable to comprehend the rest of the commentary, because the incident of the Samaritan is never quoted from specifically in the text. Even less identified is the story of Job on his dungheap (Job 2:8) and the story of David confessing his sin to Nathan (2 Kgs 12:13). And yet this whole passage is as much commentary on these incidents, though especially of course the Samaritan story, as it is exegesis of Psalm 50. The mental picture which one is asked to make brings these three texts together in a single site. It is not an illustration deriving from something else, it is the essential commentary itself.

In the language of that contemplative discipline which the monks called *mneme theou* or *memoria spiritalis*—remembering God—such an image was regarded as an *imago agens*, an agent image. It fulfils the basic requirements for mnemonically successful images described in connection with the *memoria* of rhetoric by a well-known ancient handbook, the *Rhetorica ad Herennium* (*c.*85 BCE), but the practice was by no means confined to ancient schools of rhetoric. Its practical function in this psalm commentary is not to recall the main points of a speech one needs to give, but rather to initiate meditation on a particular text. Yet the two activities are not so dissimilar. Rhetorical *memoria* was learned and practised as a device of composition, the basis for someone speaking extemporaneously to recollect the subject-matters he would need to develop whilst he spoke. The function of this image is also inventive, to start off a meditative composition upon the theme text.

And the textual ex-position is conceived of strictly as a com-position, bringing together materials into one place, according to the method taught in ancient schools. The foundational text, incorporated and given form in a vividly active image taken from a completely different and uncited pair of texts, is then made into a gathering-place for many other materials, some directly quoted, most not. In this brief section of commentary on the single verse of a psalm, over a dozen other biblical texts and episodes are alluded to or paraphrased, often only by a word or two or a shared image (Job, for example, is linked solely by the image of one naked on a dungheap, *nudus in sterquilinio*). *Sterquilinius* in turn calls in Psalm 112:7, 'suscitans a terra inopem, et de stercore erigens pauperem', though this verse, never directly quoted or identified, is not alluded to until much later in the composition. The goal is not to clarify or define the meaning of the words of Psalm 50, but to produce a cornucopia of allusions, like a net or web collecting up ever-greater numbers of matters, and inviting a listener to supply yet more than those given, supplementing and augmenting the bones supplied by the bit of text. The listener is required to be the active agent of this commentary ('ponamus'), not a passive receptacle into which material is poured. Creating this tissue of allusions is a rich mental game, for none is identified by the author, whoever he was: yet we are plainly being invited to play the game as well, as we recognize the texts and images used, and augment them ourselves. Such commentary is designed to draw us in.

It is common to say that such a procedure makes the texts present to the listener. Yet this is not really so. Nor can one say that the reader is carried away from his or her actual moment into a transcendent moment. The reasoned, deliberate experience of making the commentary up as one is thinking, gathering texts together in the accretive method so typical of medieval commentary certainly occurs in present time. But the traditional authority of the text is not compromised by an effort to make it 'relevant to me' (as is now so frequently the case). Rather, the listener is invited to participate in the constantly creative dialogue with the basic text. Psalm

50:1 is repeated several times in this brief paragraph, each time in a somewhat different context, rather like a refrain in poetry. The creative aspect of the exercise lies precisely in this procedure of finding new contexts by making new links among a great variety of materials. And the intellectual agents for doing this are recollection and imagination, working with a well-stocked memory. The procedure assumes that new thoughts are created from the materials of old ones, held most conveniently and usefully in the thinker's own prepared mind.

The mnemonic range and flexibility expected of orators (and ideally bestowed on anyone completing a proper education) is characterized many times in antiquity. One of best is Augustine's discussion of memory in Book 10 of his *Confessions*. Master of rhetoric as he was, Augustine knew the procedures of the schools perhaps even better than what he had read in his Platonic books, and not all of his discussion of memory is grandly theoretical. His description of recollection is a case in point:

Sojourning there [in my memory] I command something I want to present itself, and immediately certain things emerge, while others have to be pursued for some time and dug out from remote crannies. Others again come tumbling out in disorderly profusion, and leap into prominence as though asking, 'Are we what you want?' when it is something different that I am asking for and trying to recall. With my mental hand I push them out of the way of my effort to remember, until what I want becomes clear and breaks from cover [like a hunted rabbit]. Then, there are remembered items that come to hand easily and in orderly sequence as soon as they are summoned, the earlier members giving way to those that follow and returning to their storage-places, ready to be retrieved next time I need them. All of which happens when I relate (*narro*) anything from memory.   (*Confessions* 10.12–13)

What Augustine's analysis stresses is memory as *techne*, the procedures and processes of recollection, and not the truth-content or accuracy of its images. As an art of invention, *memoria artificialis* was cast in the Middle Ages as a procedure of reasoning with links as close to dialectic's task of 'inventing arguments' as to rhetoric's task of composing. When the ancient texts of the *Rhetorica ad Herennium* (and somewhat later Aristotle's *De memoria* treatise) came to be taught in the twelfth century, they seemed to confirm and deepen an understanding that was already present in monastic schools, which regarded recollection as rational investigation with procedures and methods akin to those of dialectic. The purpose of such memory-craft is primarily invention, enabling the activities designated by both English words which derive from Latin *inventio*: making and stocking an 'inventory' of materials, and with it creating newly composed 'inventions'. Both senses are germane to the role played by mnemonic structures, often architectural in form, as primary instruments for inventing new work.

And how did medieval scholars manage such memories? It is clear that, while the accomplishment of men like Didymus and Eusebius is the occasion of near-incredulity for Cassiodorus, it is not the fact of their having vast memories that amazes him, but that they accomplished this feat without eyes to see their books.

And yet the blind Eusebius was able to tell a questioner precisely where in a codex to locate the text he desired. This seemingly pointless accomplishment indicates to us in fact the key to Eusebius's success. His memory was *designed* in accordance with those basic principles of locational memory taught in ancient schools, and augmented in the practices of monastic meditation.

In the arts curriculum, rote memorization was particularly associated with initial schooling in reading, the curriculum of 'language arts', as this is now called. It was instilled through the common exercise of *recitatio* or 'recitation', as indeed it is to this day. *Memoria rerum*, or compositional memory, was learned in the two more advanced paths of study: dialectic, or the study of the topics and seats of argument and the relationships of propositions; and especially, the study of rhetoric, the invention of new compositions. It was especially to the investigative and inventive tasks of dialectic and rhetoric that mnemonic art was addressed. Thus, as grammar provided the foundation upon which the trivium built, so memorized texts were thought to provide the exemplars and the materials for new composition. Because *memoria* is to such an important extent the basis of an art of composition, the primary goals when preparing material for memory are flexibility, security, and ease of recombining matters into new patterns and forms. Basic to this are the paired tasks of division and collection.

As conceived in rhetoric, to divide up complex material into summary packages (called *distinctiones* or *divisiones*), in order to preach or prepare other composi-tions, is not so much a method for classification as a means for easily mixing and mingling a variety of matters, and to be able to know where you are in your composition. A simple, rigorous ordering scheme is critical to the practice of oratory, for it cues the route (*itinerarium, via*) of a speaker's principle points, in a manner similar to that of any outline, but with the greater flexibility needed for oral performance. It enables a speaker readily to enlarge a point, to digress, and to make spur-of-the-moment rhetorical side trips of all sorts, because one can always be sure of where one is in the composition—not in the manner of a parrot (which, reciting mindlessly, has no need to know where it is), but in the manner of a pilot who understands his location relative to his goal from distinctive markers in the water and on the horizon.

Figure 15.1 shows some uses of the original digital computer, the hand. These drawings of a left hand (right hands are sometimes also drawn, but far less often) diagram how to compute solutions to three entirely different problems. One is the liturgical calendar: how to reckon moveable feasts throughout the year (fig. 15.1*a*). One is for learning and recalling musical relationships (though of what sort we remain unsure), including melodies unheard before (fig. 15.1*b*). And one is for a meditation on penance, sin, and virtue (fig. 15.1*c*): it alone is usually diagrammed on both hands, one for night-time (sins) and one for morning (blessings). The methods diagrammed on these various hands are complex, and no one to my

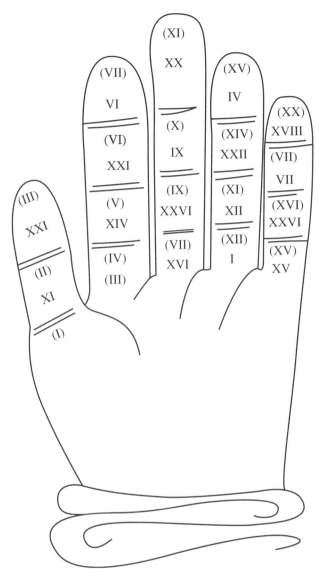

Fig. 15.1(a). The 'heavenly hand' used to calculate the liturgical calendar; redrawn from Oxford, St John's College MS 17, fol.98v (after F. Wallis, *Bede: The Reckoning of Time*).

knowledge has quite worked every system out (even though they sometimes came with an instruction manual).

These calculation hands share certain basic characteristics. The thumb is in each case drawn with three segments, but a human thumb has two. So none of these figures should properly be termed drawings of a hand; rather, each is conceived as a schematic for making particular sets of calculations. Each diagram makes use of

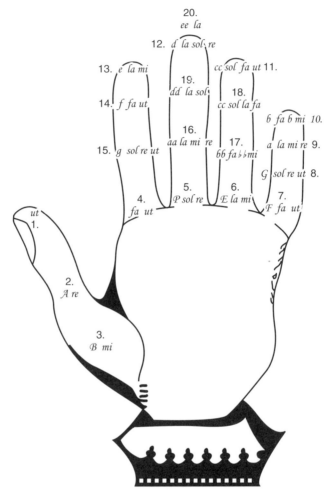

20.
ee la

12. d la sol re

13. e la mi   cc sol fa ut 11.

     19.
     dd la sol   18.
14. f fa ut   cc sol la fa

                               6 fa 6 mi 10.

     16.
     aa la mi re   17.   a la mi re 9.
15. g sol re ut   66 fa 6 6mi

                               G sol re ut 8.

     5.   6.
     P sol re   E la mi
4.   7.
fa ut   F fa ut

ut
1.

2.
A re

3.
B mi

Fig. 15.1(b). The Guidonian hand; redrawn from Ghent, University Library MS 70 (71), fol.108v (after K. Berger, 'The Guidonian Hand').

nineteen locations projected onto the hand, three on the thumb and four on each finger. These same nineteen places are drawn for the penitential hand as well, though it does not appear that there is any numerical need for nineteen dictated by the content being displayed. So these various hands employ a basic scheme adapted to a variety of content and uses, rather than something designed uniquely for each task. Instead of thinking of such a diagram simply as the representation of some other and prior content, or as a substitute 'calculator' in our sense, we should conceive of it as a highly versatile locating tool. There are three sections on the thumb because three places are needed there for calculating something's position, just as in our own base-ten algorithmic scheme only nine digits can go into a single column of places—when filled up, each ten then 'carries over' into the next column

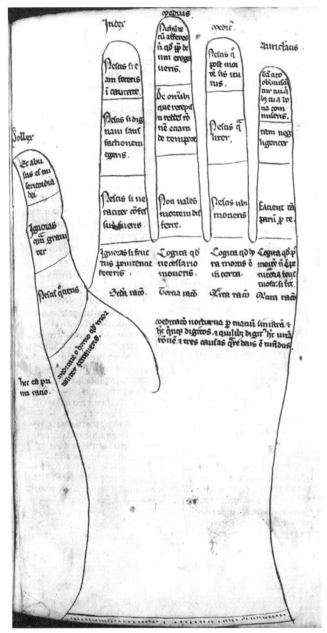

Fig. 15.1(c). The 'hand of meditation' (for examination of conscience): British Library MS. Harley 273, fol. 111. Photo ©The British Library Board.

to the left. Calculation performed on the hand is visual and tactile, but most important it is spatial. Each of those numbers, for the purposes of a calculation, occupies one of the locations that we imagine as though having spatial characteristics and boundaries.

When content is conceived in this way it can be moved about, like a counter, within the calculation grid. Rather than being affixed like a label, a counter can operate in a variety of mnemonic and investigative contexts. One can move in several directions from each place, or skip around, or go backwards, not just in one way. Locational schemes like this build such flexibility into themselves. They are random-access, or multiple-access, schemes.

In both antiquity and the Middle Ages, the commonest model for human memory likened it to a tablet or a parchment page, upon which a person writes. This model is extremely old and widespread, and it is very interesting that even in antiquity, when actual books were written in rolls, the model for memory is that of a flat, rectangular surface which can be taken in with a single mental 'look.' This page can become quite complex. Figure 15.2 reproduces one such page of memory, in this case a Psalter with several commentaries. The mise-en-page of this book illustrates many basic principles of the arts of memory. The Psalms was one of the fundamental texts of medieval culture, one book every educated person learned by heart as an aspect of learning to read. It was considered foundational not just to literacy and moral character but to rational thought itself. Scholars like Hugh of St Victor thought by means of the Psalms.

In order to memorize such a long work, it was cut up into brief segments, and then 'placed' mentally into an orderly scheme. This order could be anything, so long as it was clear and readily recoverable. Numbers and the alphabet were two obvious schemes that fit these requirements, although there were others in use as well. The scheme of divisions into chapters and verses imposed on the Bible today was largely in place by the fourth century, even though it was not fully written out in books until the sixteenth century. Figure 15.2 shows the textual divisions of Psalm 58 written in a large script. Each is marked by a painted initial and written in a large script. By building chains of such segments in one's memory, a very long work—such as all of the Psalms or the whole *Aeneid*—can readily be retained and securely recovered, either in its original order or rear-ranged and extracted to suit a new composition, simply by rehearsing various numerical sequences. Each division of the main text is treated as though it were a separate place in the order, and the commentary is then written into the margins, in a different and smaller script. The segments of commentary are linked to the main text to which they refer by a common initial or, in some cases, a shared figural drawing. Surrounding the main commentaries are margins containing yet other commentary, and in the outermost margins brackets indicate the sources of the texts: Augustine, Cassiodorus, Jerome, and others. They also indicate correc-tion and disagreement: in the lower left 'Augustinus' points to commentary and says 'non ego'.

The page shown here was intended for study and meditation: it was not to be used by beginning readers. Indeed, this manuscript is not a single work but a whole library of materials, an encyclopedia of related knowledge gathered into its pages. Its locations are conceived and used like boxes or rooms, cells like those in a

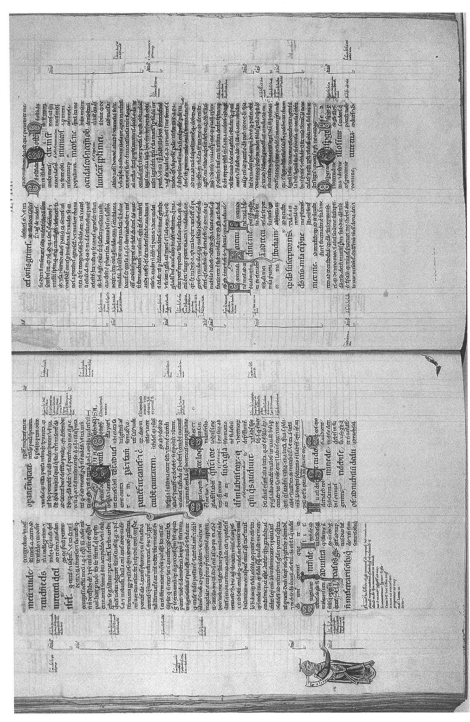

Fig. 15.2. Glossed Psalter of Herbert of Bosham, Psalm 58 (Cambridge Trinity College Library, B. 5.4, fols. 146v–147). Photo reproduced with permission of the Master and Fellows of Trinity College, Cambridge.

beehive. This page is indeed an early version of 'hypertext', its links and networks securely fashioned for ready reference and recollection.

The locational schemes used in monastic contexts to organize memory varied greatly. One could choose among using an architecturally modelled plan and section of a large though entirely literary building (for example Noah's ark); the feathers on the six wings of a seraphic angel; a five-storey, five-room section of a house; the stones in the wall of a turreted castle tower; the rungs of ladders;—or a world map. Gardens were also popular, the medieval sort of garden, with orderly beds of medicinal plants and fruit trees, separated by grass and surrounded by a wall. We now would never think to organize an encyclopedia of knowledge on a world map, but for a clerical audience to whom this picture was as familiar as the order of the alphabet is to us—why not? It provides a simple, clearly arranged composition site, containing many useful compartments with multiple routes among them, and thus can serve as a foundational map to use in arranging one's subjects and materials, gathering them into the location of a new composition from the networks of one's prior experiences, including of course all one's experiences of books, music, and other arts. Thus, in the course of an ideal medieval education, in addition to acquiring a great many segments of scriptural and classical texts, one also would acquire an extensive repertoire of picture-schemes in which to put them, both 'to lay them away' and 'to collect them' in new arrangements on later occasions.

Perhaps the best-known medieval recollective schemes involve architecture, imagining a building in one's mind. The ancient *auctor ad Herennium* is quite specific about what sort this should be: a Roman house or an arcade, with recesses and niches. One should pick a place that is familiar and can often be revisited to refresh its details. Into the compartments formed by such features one places those vivid agent images, the *notationes*, that are linked to specific material. The images are made and erased according to each new task, but the backgrounds are stable and lasting. The analogy the *auctor* makes is to writing on a wax tablet, for the images are like the letters which one erases after each use, but the backgrounds are like the supporting surface of the waxed tablet. It is clear from what the author says here that he is thinking of a situation of frequent new composition, not one of stable, archival storage; we should not confuse these two tasks.

More standard advice was given about the mnemonic places: they must always have a coherent, easily recognized order among themselves; that is, a mnemonic background is always conceived in relation to other backgrounds, and not by itself. Placing memories also spatializes them; they occupy relative locations. And these places have other characteristics that make them distinct. They have a clear internal order: for example, every fifth or tenth place might be specially marked. In the preface to his chronicle of biblical history, Hugh of St Victor takes pains to caution that each mental location containing the text of a psalm should carry its number prominently as well as its *incipit*, rather as though one were looking at the shelf-marks and titles of books in a library case.[3] The backgrounds must be immediately visible: they must be moderately lighted, not too dim nor too bright for the eye of the mind to perceive them in one *conspectus*. 'Crowding' a location is a fault producing recollective confusion, so not only must there be no more images in any single place than one can readily and distinctly take in as a group, there must be space between the locations as well, optimally (it was said, by Peter of Ravenna)[4] five or six feet. And how long would six mental feet be? Far enough that one can actually walk in imagination from one place to another. The places must also be three-dimensional, like a box or a room, and moderate in size: Peter of Ravenna says that a grown man stretching out his arms should be able to touch the ceiling and the sides. Most earlier writers, including the *auctor ad Herennium*, do not imagine themselves in their mental rooms but standing before them and gazing from a distance of about thirty feet.

Roman Republican architecture is the one most often associated now with mnemonic *techne*, but a far more lastingly influential architecture for memory work developed in the meditational practices of classical Judaism and Christian monasticism. This was based on an ideal architecture, those great buildings described, often in elaborately measured detail, in the Bible: Noah's ark, the Tabernacle of Exodus 25ff., the temple built by Solomon in 1 Kings, the great visionary re-creation of the temple complex in Ezekiel 40ff., the Heavenly City imagined by John as measured out in Revelation 20. These structures served as the basis of meditations themselves and also as ordering devices for other compositions, in the manner of the *memoria rerum* scenes counselled in ancient rhetoric for the situation of *ex tempore* speaking, but differently, more encyclopedically imagined.

Hugh of St Victor composed an ekphrastic reconstruction of Noah's ark, the *Libellus de formatione arche*. He requires his readers to use this *descriptio* (the Latin translation of ekphrasis) in ways that fully realize the imaginative potential of this rhetorical figure as an engine of invention. He begins:

First, in order, to show in a figure the religious meanings of Noah's Ark, I find the center of the plane on which to depict the Ark and there I fix a point. Around this point I make a small square, which is like the cubit by which the Ark is measured out. And around this square I draw another one, slightly bigger. . . . I paint a cross in the inner square, so that its arms touch each side of the square, and I paint over it in gold. . . . And in the middle of the golden cross which I made, I paint a yearling lamb standing upright. (Weiss 2002: 45)

[3] Hugh makes a point of using the psalms' numbers in his mental scheme, though few Bible manuscripts at this time included them, and the psalms were most commonly referenced by *incipit* only (Carruthers 2008: 106–35).

[4] Peter of Ravenna (also called Petrus Tommai) was a master of law and author of a popular memory treatise, *Fenix*, published in 1491, with many Latin reprintings, and translations into vernacular languages including, eventually, English.

A great many other figures and devices are imagined by Hugh in this diagram as his description proceeds, so many that they cannot all be encompassed in a single, manuscript-sized drawing. Moreover, at one point Hugh says that the whole plan must be imagined as elevated, the square with the cross being drawn upwards in the mind's eye so that it forms a central column of the ark. In fact it is clear that this ekphrasis is of an imaginary construction, for all the verbs Hugh used are in the present tense, *pingo, depingo,* and *fingo,* verbs used also in medieval advice about making *imagines agentes* for use in memory work. The various diagrams and figures which Hugh places in his ark—genealogies, histories, a Bible catalogue, a mappamundi, trees of vices and virtues, a geographia, a cosmologia, an angelology, and many others—form an encyclopedia of images that mark content pertinent to all aspects of monastic virtue and contemplative life. Hugh's imaginary picture of the ark is like nothing so much as the complex sculptural programmes of a major cathedral—one perhaps like St Denis, with whose encyclopedic programme Hugh is thought by some historians to have been associated.

But, unlike the pictures which accompany the exegesis of Ezekiel composed by his contemporary at St Victor, Richard, no pictures accompany Hugh's book. Others of his works do have diagrams, faithfully copied; notably the diagram Hugh made for his universal chronicle of biblical history. The lack of illustration in the many manuscripts of *De formatione arche* is telling evidence that the picture of the ark which Hugh paints is a rhetorical ekphrasis, not the description of an actual object. It is designed to raise up pictures for the eyes of the mind, pictures of a highly rationalized sort. Hugh's 'ark' is not a representation but a schematic library of the whole Church, its doctrine, its history, its present and future.

It was composed as a picture *summatim,* 'in summary fashion', the last section of a much longer moral treatise that Hugh composed on the ark of Noah. The two works, separated in Migne's *Patrologia Latina,* belong together, and they have at last been published that way in the Corpus Christianorum edition. A paragraph joins them, as follows: 'Now I will offer an exemplar of our own Ark, as I have promised. I depict as though it were an actual object, so that you may learn outwardly what you should do inwardly, and so that, once you imprint the form of this example in your heart, you will be glad that the house of God has been built inside of you' (Weiss 2002: 45).[5] Complex as this mental picture is, it recognizably uses the method of collecting vivid images linked to various content into structured sets of places that is the hallmark of *memoria rerum.*

The meditation on imaginary biblical edifices is an exercise commonly performed throughout the Middle Ages. Jerome's commentary on Ezekiel is filled with ekphrastic amplification of the visionary 'pictures', and he incorporated earlier

---

[5] The *Libellus* is called *De arca Noe mystice* in *PL;* the longer piece, there called *De arca Noe morali* has been retitled *De Archa Noe* and shown to be the work for which the *Libellus* was intended: see the introduction to Sicard's edition.

commentary by Origen. Bede commented on the Temple and its furniture; Gregory the Great composed a set of sermons on Ezekiel that moralize the structures of the Temple vision; Adam Scot of Dryburgh, a contemporary of the great Victorines, commented on the Tabernacle, including an ekphrastic picture as part of his commentary. In this very long tradition the structures tend to be conflated, conceived as exemplars of one another; as indeed the Bible itself presents the sequence of Noah's ark, the Tabernacle, First Temple, the imaginary Ezekiel Temple-in-exile, the Heavenly City. The exemplary nature of the biblical structures is always stressed, but so is the merit of 'measuring' them precisely, seeing them inwardly in full detail. Measuring the Temple in Ezekiel is presented specifically as a penitential exercise; this also carried over into monastic traditions.

The famous Carolingian drawing (fig. 15.3) known as the Plan of St-Gall (somewhat misleadingly, as it wasn't made at St-Gall, and it isn't a plan of the actual abbey at all) comes out of this tradition of meditation. Some architecture historians have thought it was offered as the plan for a real monastery, but most now believe it was not—that it was what its composer said it was, a device for meditation. Abbot Heito of Reichenau wrote to Gozbert of St-Gall: 'I have sent you, Gozbert my dearest son, these few designs (*exemplata*) for the lay-out of a monastery (*de positione officinarum*), by means of which you may exercise your wits . . . [D]o not think that I have elaborated it because we considered that you need our instructions, but believe that it was drawn in God's love for you alone to scrutinize' (Braunfels 1972: 46).

As Wolfgang Braunfels commented, 'the Plan is to promote meditation upon the meaning and worth of the monastic life' (ibid.).[6] By calling it a plan for the disposition of the various buildings of monastic life and the services (*officinae*) performed within them, Heito would seem to be emphasizing its idealized and moralized function, the role played by the Temple in Gregorian meditations on Ezekiel 40 ff., as affording the *dispositio*, the structure, of the composition and thus also the ways through which one might make one's intellectual journey. Later in the ninth century a commentator labelled the church in this drawing the *templum*. This is not an unusual usage when referring to churches, but in this particular context it does have some added significance. The entrance-way, which is also the route into all the *officinae* of monastic life, was given the legend: 'This is the way (*via*) to the holy Temple for the multitudes, by means of which they conduct their prayers and return in joy.' All architecture implies movement. Notice how the drawing includes indications of doorways—one must imagine not just a material construction but the routes created through it.

---

[6] In 1523 a physician from Strasbourg, Laurent Fries, counselled using Strasbourg Cathedral for an invention device, placing subject-matters on locations within it and mentally walking through them (Massing 1984; also Carruthers 1998: 228–54).

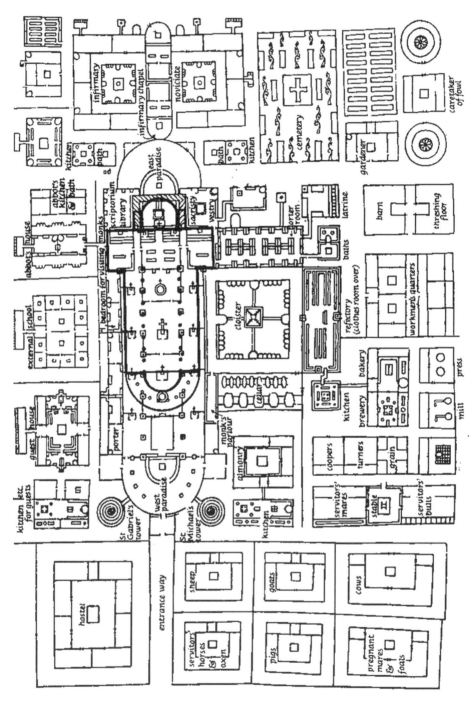

Fig. 15.3. 'The Plan of St Gall', redrawn from stiftsbibliothek St. Gallen, cod. Sangalensis 1092 (after W. Braunfels, *The Monasteries of Western Europe*).

In a letter to Bishop Paulinus of Nola, St Jerome listed the most difficult parts of the Bible, properly to be studied only by those over 30 who by then have acquired the learning and experience to do so. These include the last chapters of Ezekiel, with related visions in Isaiah and Daniel, and the Apocalypse (Letter 53). It is noteworthy that these are also parts of the Bible which attracted some of the earliest known Christian painted pictures, from the time of Constantine. These pictures were not made primarily as helps for the ignorant and illiterate. Figure 16.4 shows a representative page from a manuscript of the Apocalypse now in the Pierpont Morgan Library in New York. This book was made by a northern Spanish monk named Maius sometime about 945. The text is the commentary made by Beatus of Libana in 776, also in northern Spain. Maius comments on the role of the pictures in his book, and his reasons for making them, in language that clearly indicates their purpose. Maius' colophon reads: 'Part of its ornamental order are the picture-making words of its stories, which I have painted in their order [in the text], so that they may inspire fear of the coming of the future judgment at the world's end for those who are learned (*scientibus*)' (Williams and Shailor 1991: fol. 293). In a tradition going back at least to Augustine, meditation begins most effectively with the emotion of fear—the chilling terror that raises prickles on our flesh to make us stick tight when we throw ourselves upon the redeeming cross (Augustine, *De doctrina christiana* 2.7.9). Augustine and Maius both wrote for the learned, *scientes*, 'those who have knowledge'.

Maius says he painted the pictures which are in the words of the *storiae*, as Beatus called the sections, each a few verses long, into which he divided the narrative of St John's vision. *Verba mirifica* are words which make images to be looked at in the mind: they are marvellous, but what makes them so are the wonderful sights, the imaginings (*mir-*, 'gaze with wonder') which they fashion (*fac-*, the root of *fica*). These are what Maius says he has depicted. In medieval Latin, *pingere* is commonly used for the scribal task of lettering (Carruthers 2008: 224–6). The verb *depingere*, an intensive form, serves a dual purpose in this sentence, for it refers to both the letters of the *verba* which Maius wrote and also to the *mirifica* pictures which these words raise up in his mind and, through his brush, are translated as paintings to the book.

The union of words and pictures is apparent in the layout of the Beatus commentary. Figure 15.4. shows the section of the text which describes the sixth angel pouring out his bowl. Notice that the complete book chapter is comprised of the *storia*, a short segment of Revelation (16:12, in this case), written immediately under the 'incipit' in the left-hand column. As one reads the chapter from beginning to end, one then must immediately continue on to the picture of the sixth angel, pouring his vial into the River Euphrates so that it dried up. This picture is framed, a device that seems to be Maius' contribution to the Beatus tradition (Williams 1994–2003: 1. 77–8). And it has a title which identifies the scene, written in the right-hand part of the L-shaped frame. The commentary on the

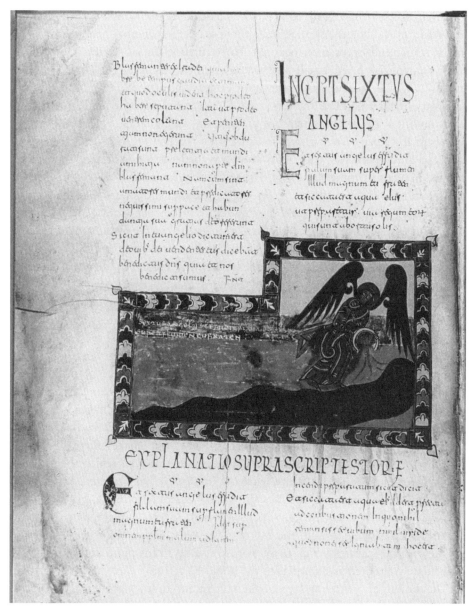

Fig. 15.4. The 'Morgan Beatus', sixth angel: J. Pierpont Morgan Library, MS M. 644, fol. 190v. Photo reproduced with permission, ©The Morgan Library and Museum.

Apocalypse text is then written within the frame below the picture. Notice that it begins in the right-hand column, following directly upon the picture. And notice particularly that it is introduced as 'the explanation of the above-written *storia*'. A reader must proceed through both the written Bible verse and the picture in order to get to their gloss, or *explanatio*. One historian has characterized these pictures as 'a surrogate' for the text, mediating 'between the text and the reader's imagination' (Williams 1992: 227). Another has called them a translation of the literal text into 'a dense sequence' of equally literal 'tableaux' (Werckmeister 1978: 169). I would go further than either of these statements to suggest that word and picture together make up, equally, the subject of meditative reading. Neither surrogate nor translation, word and picture equally and together constitute 'the above-written *storia*'. Together they make up the marvellous-picture-forming words of the stories (*uerba mirifica storiarum*) which Maius has painted in full, a concept emphasized by the frame Maius has painted around it. The ornaments of Maius, like the words of Beatus, can be dilated and expanded in the ways verbal texts can be, by procedures of shuffling, collating, gathering in—devising and composing meditation.

An influential medieval manual of rhetorical composition, *Poetria nova*, written by the Parisian master Geoffrey of Vinsauf (*c.*1210), proposes three models for the activity of composing: architect, mapmaker, and conjurer—*praestigiatrix*, someone who juggles and practices sleight-of-hand. The artist plays with his material, moving it about, changing it around, constantly inventing during the procedure of disposing its various parts. Geoffrey describes it as a kind of game-playing, mental calculating of a sort that involves shifting counters from one place to another, and thereby 'causes the last to be first, the future to be present, the oblique to be straight, the remote to be near; what is rustic becomes urbane, what is old becomes new' (ll. 121–5). Medieval invention is thought of in part as placement and re-placement of materials, collection and recollection of subject-matters, all enabled by the spatial and locational nature of investigative *memoria* and vivid imagination, its primary engines.

WORKS CITED

AUGUSTINE, ST. *The Confessions*, trans. M. Boulding. Hyde Park, NY, 1997.
——*De doctrina christiana* (*Teaching Christianity*), trans. E. Hill. Hyde Park, NY, 1996.
BERGER, KAROL, 'The Guidonian Hand', in M. Carruthers and J. Ziolkowski (eds.), *The Medieval Craft of Memory*. Philadelphia, 2002, pp. 71–82.
BRAUNFELS, WOLFGANG, *Monasteries of Western Europe: The Architecture of the Orders*, trans. A. Laing. London, 1972.
CARRUTHERS, MARY, *The Book of Memory*, 2nd edn. Cambridge, 2008.
——*The Craft of Thought: Meditation, Rhetoric, and the Making of Images 400–1200*. Cambridge, 1998.
CASSIODORUS, *Institutiones* I. 5. 2, ed. R. A. B. Mynors, Oxford, 1937; trans. L. W. Jones, *An Introduction to Divine and Human Readings*, New York, 1946.
GEOFFREY of VINSAUF, *Poetria nova*, trans. M. F. Nims. Toronto, 1967.

[GREGORY THE GREAT], *Expositio psalmi quarti poenitentialis*. *Patrologia Latina* 79, cols. 582–583.

JEROME, ST. 'Letter 60', trans. F. A. Wright, *Jerome: Selected Letters*. Loeb Classical Library. London, 1963.

——'Letter 53', ed. I. Hilberg. Corpus scriptorum ecclesiasticorum latinorum 54 (corrected edition). Vienna, 1910, 1996.

LIEB, MICHAEL, *The Visionary Mode: Biblical Prophecy, Hermeneutics, and Cultural Change*. Ithaca, NY, 1991.

MASSING, JEAN MICHEL, 'Laurent Fries et son "ars memorativa": la cathédrale de Strasbourg comme espace mnemonique', *Bulletin de la Cathédrale de Strasbourg*, 16 (1984), 69–78.

SICARD, PATRICE (ed.), *Hugonis de Sancto Victore de Archa Noe* and *Libellus de formatione arche*. Corpus Christianorum continuatio medievalis 176–76A. Turnhout, 2001.

WALLIS, FAITH, *Bede: The Reckoning of Time*. Liverpool, 1999.

WEISS, JESSICA (trans.), 'Hugh of St. Victor: *Constructing Noah's Ark*', in M. Carruthers and J. Ziolkowski (eds.), *The Medieval Craft of Memory*. Philadelphia, 2002, pp. 41–70.

WERCKMEISTER, O. K., 'The First Romanesque Beatus Manuscripts', *Actas del Simposio para el Estudio de los codices del 'Comentario al Apocalypsis' de Beato de Liébana*, 3 vols. Madrid, 1978: vol. 2, pp. 167–200.

WILLIAMS, JOHN. *The Illustrated Beatus: A Corpus of Illustrations of the Commentary on the Apocalypse*, 5 vols. London, 1994–2003.

——'Purpose and Imagery in the Apocalypse Commentary of Beatus of Liébana', in R. K. Emmerson and B. McGinn (eds.), *The Apocalypse in the Middle Ages*. Ithaca, NY, 1992: 217–33.

——and BARBARA SHAILOR (eds.), *A Spanish Apocalypse: The Morgan Beatus Manuscript*. New York, 1991.

FURTHER READING

CLANCHY, MICHAEL T., *From Memory to Written Record, England 1066–1307*, 2nd edn. Cambridge, Mass., 1993.

COOLMAN, BOYD, T., *The Theology of Hugh St. Victor: An Interpretation*. Cambridge, 2010.

EMMERSON, RICHARD K. and BERNARD McGINN (eds.), *The Apocalypse in the Middle Ages*. Ithaca, NY, 1992.

GAVRILOV, A. K., 'Techniques of Reading in Classical Antiquity', trans. with a postscript by M. F. Burnyeat, *Classical Quarterly*, 47 (1997), 56–76.

KNOX, BERNARD. 'Silent Reading in Antiquity', *Greek, Roman, and Byzantine Studies*, 9 (1968), 421–35.

KOVACS, JUDITH and C. ROWLAND, *Revelation: The Apocalypse of Jesus Christ*. Blackwell Biblical Commentaries. Oxford, 2004.

ROWLAND, CHRISTOPHER, *The Open Heaven: A Study of Apocalyptic in Judaism and Early Christianity*. London, 1982.

THOMAS, ROSALIND, *Literacy and Orality in Ancient Greece*. Cambridge, 1992.

CHAPTER 16

THE ORIGINS, SCOPE, AND SPREAD OF THE MILLENARIAN IDEA

PETER CLARKE

THIS chapter looks at the origins, force and scope of millenarianism, sometimes referred to as millennialism or messianism, and offers some idea of how widespread the belief has become. The conclusion speculates about the reasons for its vitality, appeal, and persistence. Often associated exclusively with Christianity, the belief in paradise on earth has a long history and is found in many religious traditions, including Zoroastrianism, Islam, and forms of Hinduism and Buddhism. While the origins of millenarian belief pre-date Christianity, the Christian tradition very soon after its beginnings in the first century CE became and has remained the main vehicle for its dissemination worldwide.

In Christianity the term millenarianism assumed a narrow, precise meaning and relied for support on scriptural texts, one of the most important being that of the Book of Revelation (Rev. 20:4–6), which speaks of the martyrs and faithful followers of Christ reigning with him for a thousand years. This thousand-year reign would be a blissful age that would bridge the gap between the end of life on earth and the final resurrection, and is referred to as the 'first resurrection'.[1] The idea of the millennium is present not only in the Book of Revelation but is also found a number of the Epistles, including 1 Peter 1:11–12, 1 Corinthians 10:11, and Hebrews 1:1–4, all of which speak of the present age or dispensation as the *kairos* or most critical juncture in history, and of the Kingdom of God on earth as being close at hand.

The belief in the establishment of a messianic kingdom on earth ruled over by Christ, when further unpacked and widened beyond the precise sense given to it in the New Testament, refers to the imminent and total transformation of the present world through divine intervention, a transformation that will involve the total destruction of the present terrestrial conditions of existence with all their limitations, physical, material, and spiritual, and the creation of paradise on earth.

Cohn (1993) speculated that the origins of the concept can possibly be traced back to the prophecies of the Persian priest and reformer Zoroaster (also referred to as Zarathustra, who probably lived and ministered in the eastern part of what is today widely referred as Iran/Persia sometime between 1500 and 1200 BCE. Zoroaster is often credited with changing the way the worshipper began to perceive the deity by portraying him/her as a partner rather than the more traditional distant and alien being. This new way of thinking of the deity as partner becomes evident too in Israel in the prophetic tradition that follows the Babylonian Exile.

Zoroaster is also credited with having introduced into Persian religion another innovative idea, the monotheistic idea of a single deity in the form of the Most High God, known as Ahura Mazda (the Lord of Wisdom), who was believed to be eternal and the first cause of everything in the universe. Following on this came the equally revolutionary notion of time as linear rather than cyclical, as a process that began at creation and moved towards its end (eschatology). This idea came to influence many diverse peoples, including Indo-Iranians, Egyptians, Babylonians, Sumerians, Canaanites, and pre-exilic Israelites, as well as the descendants of all of these and others. Zoroaster also broke with the commonly accepted view that the world was static and immutable, and importantly spoke of a final victory of good over evil, of order over chaos, that would be followed by the 'making wonderful' or total transformation of the world. Cohn (1993) is persuaded that the Zoroastrian belief in the imminent advent of a world without evil and want deeply influenced Old and New Testament writing, albeit in different ways. It is worth noting that, by contrast with early Christianity where it is mostly conceived of in spiritual terms, the messianic age as a phase of the 'end of days' represents more what might be termed the fulfillment of the earthly strands of Jewish eschatology grounded in the Hebrew scriptures. It looked to the restoration of an Israelite kingdom (Collins 1997: 90). A version of millenarianism is also found in the Dead Sea Scrolls (Collins

---

[1] Biblical references are to the 1966 edition if the Jerusalem Bible.

1997), and from there came to influence both the Old and New Testament concept of the millennium, as did the so-called apocalyptic literature of the period *c.*200 BCE–*c.*100 CE.

APOCALYPTICISM AND ARMAGEDDON

Closely associated with the notion of the millennium in Jewish and Christian scriptures is the concept of apocalypticism, an idea which derives from the Greek term *apokalypsis* meaning the 'opening' or 'uncovering' of secret knowledge about such things as the workings of the heavenly world and the interrelated issue of the destiny of humanity. The argument found in this genre of thinking is that if the total transformation of life on earth is imminent then this is so because heaven has decreed that it should happen. Chapters 2 and 7 of the Old Testament Book of Daniel contain apocalypses the content of which is thought to have been revealed, significantly, in a vision to its author while on the banks of the River Tigris, in Mesopotamia. This part of the world was, historically, an important centre for specialists in astronomy, meteorology, and the geography of the known world and of the mythical world of paradise.

Apocalyptic literature, often written in response to one kind of catastrophe or another and to the humiliating and unacceptable occupation by foreign rulers, proposes that there will be divine intervention in human affairs that will annihilate demonic forces and lead to the ending of human history and its replacement with the age of everlasting salvation. This is the apocalyptic answer to seemingly intractable problems of a moral, social, spiritual, political, and material kind.

That the term apocalypticism has come to connote a catastrophe of cosmic proportions is due in large measure to the last book of the New Testament, the Apocalypse or Revelation of St John. This book speaks of the coming final battle or 'War of the Great Day of God the Almighty' (Rev. 16:16) at Armageddon, resulting in cosmic destruction. This historic and defining battle is to be followed by the resurrection and judgement of the dead and the promise of a new heaven and a new earth, 'for the first heaven and the first earth had passed away' (Rev. 21:1). The word apocalypse, thus, comes to refer not only to any catastrophe of cosmic proportions that appeared to jeopardize life on earth, but also to the end of the world as it presently existed.

Millenarianism, then, probably had its theological and philosophical origins in Zoroastrianism and was developed and elaborated in Jewish and early Christian writings and, as in the case of Zoroaster and his followers, formed an integral part of the response of communities, both Jewish and Christian, to the experience of profound crisis.

PRE- AND POST-MILLENARIANISM

In the case of Christianity, an important distinction is often made by scholars between pre-and post-millenarian movements, which essentially concerns the different ways in which the transformation of the world is envisaged. Movements termed pre-millennial emphasize the importance of human action alongside divine assistance in transforming the world, and resemble the *reformist* sect or new religion as described by Wilson (1970). Such a movement is commonly thought of as presenting a dramatic, stormy, explosive vision of a new age, and as being disposed to use violent means to bring about this vision. Of course, not all such movements have recourse to violence. The post-millenarian movement, by contrast, is *utopian* (Wilson 1970) in the sense that it waits patiently in what is seen as a community of the saved, usually situated away from the rest of society, for divine intervention to bring about the new world. I have suggested elsewhere that the Rastafarian movement is a post-millenarian movement in this second sense (Clarke 1987).

MILLENARIAN MOVEMENTS: SOME COMMON CHARACTERISTICS

While, as we have seen, millenarianism is mostly associated with the Judeo-Christian tradition, it is also the case that if seen as a datum of popular religion the principal characteristics of millenarianism can also be found in numerous religious movements of Islamic, Buddhist, and Hindu origin, in some of the traditional religions of the world, and in secular ideologies. In some of these religions the Judeo-Christian Bible has been one source of this idea or has acted as a catalyst in shaping its form and content. For example, it is highly probable that biblical apocalyptic ideas, while they did not give rise to it, nevertheless influenced the development of the millenarian tradition which became an important theme in Chinese Daoism from as early as the second century CE (Kohn 1998). The Bible has also shaped in medieval (Cohn 1970) and modern times countless other millenarian movements of Christian origin, or claiming to be so. The Rastafarian movement (Clarke 1987) is but one example of a modern millenarian movement greatly influenced by biblical notions of the advent of heaven on earth. Lanternari (1991) is convinced that Christian missionary teaching and preaching were the source of the millenarian ideas that inspired the nineteenth- and twentieth-century outbreaks of Melanesian 'cargo cults' in Papua New Guinea and the South Pacific more generally. In South Africa the nineteenth century saw the outbreak of millenarianism in the form of the Xhosa cattle killings, and once again

Christian notions of the millennium made an important contribution to these, as Peiris (1989) has shown. Biblical notions of the kingdom of heaven of heaven on earth have also helped form, as will be shown below, the apocalyptic and millenarian worldviews of numerous nineteenth- and twentieth-century Japanese and Korean millenarian movements, some of which displayed the characteristics associated more generally with Green millenarianism—the linking by some Christians of the eschatological hope found in, for example, Rev. 21:5 with the transformation of the present creation (Clarke 2006).

While the core of millenarian belief is the sudden and imminent realization of paradise on earth, the form, location, content, and inhabitants of that paradise can mean one thing to people of one age and culture and something else to those of another. Millenarians in medieval Europe held different notions of paradise on earth. For the marginalized, landless peasants as well as for the urban journeymen and unskilled workers constantly threatened with unemployment, the advent of the millennium meant more than anything else the advent of a world of security and social support and solidarity. The thirteenth-century lay movement the Franciscan Spirituals, or Fraticelli as they were known, who were most active in the north of Italy and the south of France, saw the millennium essentially in terms of themselves as the foundation-stones of the new order. They would replace the Church of Rome and lead the world into the Glorious Age of the Spirit, thereby fulfilling the spiritual vacuum left by the rampant pursuit of materialism and the established church's search for political influence.

The theme of the advent of the millennium motivated and inspired the fifteenth-century voyages of discovery. Christopher Columbus was convinced that paradise on earth was situated close to the territories of the West Indies, and wrote of the island of Haiti as unique in its charm, beauty, and tranquillity. Others saw Brazil as paradise on earth. Among the indigenous inhabitants of parts of South America, including the Tupi Guarani, paradise on earth consisted of the search for the Land-Without-Evil, understood to be a place where there would no longer be any need to labour on the dry, barren lands to produce crops since these, it was believed, would grow by themselves. The Rastafarian idea of the millennium sees world transformation in terms of a profound shift from the artificial, unnatural way we live to living naturally and/or according to the laws of nature. Paradise on earth will be located in Africa, away from the influence of 'Babylon' or White society. By way of contrast, the above-mentioned cargo cultists of Melanesia believed that paradise on earth would arrive with the coming of European cargo in the form of modern technology and other products of convenience, making for what might be termed 'commodity' millenarianism.

There are also millenarian movements for which paradise on earth consists of freedom from human limitations of every kind, including physical, a theme evident the theology of the Church of Scientology which started in the United States in the early 1950s. The goal of this church is to enable everyone to become a 'clear', with the capacity to transcend all human obstacles to full spiritual and human growth.

Millenarian belief has the capacity both to inspire great revolutionary zeal and induce the most deadening kind of passivism. The latter state of mind can paradoxically have profoundly disturbing consequences for the existing economic, social, and political order by, among other things, encouraging the abandonment of all kinds of activities and even the complete cessation of agricultural and factory work and the performance of essential community services. It has also resulted in mass migration, as in medieval Europe (Cohn 1970) or during colonial rule, as in Northern Nigeria and the Sudan (Clarke 1995). It can also inspire innovation in the form of new inventions and new and relevant designs, as in the case of the Shaker movement whose furniture products have come to be highly prized for their many qualities, including simplicity and compactness.

In the hands of prophets and founders of religions millenarianism has been fashioned into the most effective of recruiting sergeants, and, as the medieval Muslim statesman, jurist, and historian Ibn Khaldun (1332–1406) noted, into a most effective means of creating *asabiyya* or group solidarity in the Muslim world (1967: 2. 196). It is difficult to find a single example of a religion that has gone on to survive for any considerable period of time that has not been in its early years stridently millenarian, only to tone down this disturbing and potentially destabilizing belief in the imminent transformation of the world as it becomes more established.

Thus, while some millenarian preoccupations are, as history shows us, enduring—the pursuit of authenticity, equality, harmony, meaningful work, and a world free of sickness and human want, for example—others are transitory and passing. The utopian dreams of one age or generation tend to become the commonplace aspirations, and sometimes expectations, of the next. As for millenarianism's enduring and widespread appeal, this can be attributed, I suggest, to its plasticity as a concept and to its innate capacity to induce so many different, and at times seemingly contradictory, attitudes and responses to the world. But like authentic charismatic power, its dynamism tends soon to evaporate.

Different though they may be in so many respects, millenarian movements share the following general features which, as Cohn (1970: 13) suggested, allow them all to be classified as millenarian: the belief that the benefits of paradise are to be enjoyed by all the faithful as a collectivity; that this paradise is terrestrial in the sense that it is to be established on earth and not in some otherworldly heaven; that it is imminent and will come suddenly; that it is total, in that it will utterly transform life on earth and bring perfection itself and not just improvement; and that it is miraculous, in that it is to be accomplished by, or with the help of, supernatural agencies. Not all of these conditions are always present in their ideal form in every millenarian movement, but all such movements display all of these characteristics to at least some degree. I will briefly illustrate this point by reference to a number of such movements from different religions and different parts of the world, beginning in Korea with the Tonghak/ Ch'ondogyo movement.

THE TONGHAK/CH'ONDOGYO MOVEMENT

In Korea, as in China, in other parts of Asia and globally, millenarianism, has often been a core belief of many of the modern as well as the historical religions. Hard pressed, under severe strain, and greatly resentful and alienated, historically the peasantry in Korea under the leadership of local prophets turned to such well-known sources of divination as the book of Omens (*Chonnggamnok*) for some indication of a better future. Not unexpectedly, predictions of the fall of one of the world's longest-standing dynasties, the Choson and/or Yi dynasty (1392–1910) were given great credence.

The social, economic and political circumstances in which Eastern Learning (Tonghak) was founded by Ch'oe Che-u (1824–64) in 1860 did not differ greatly from those in which the new and highly influential religion Omoto (Great Origin) (Berthon 1985; Ooms 1993) came into existence in Japan in 1892. Both movements arose as modernization programmes began to be implemented with little concern for the interests of the rural population. Ch'oe Che-u, son of a well-known Confucian scholar but regarded, nonetheless, as lower-class on account of his mother's position as a concubine, despaired of finding an answer to society's ills in the traditional teachings of Buddhism, Confucianism, Daoism, Christianity, and Folk Religions, and instead sought a remedy for these in a new form of Eastern Learning (Tonghak) (Grayson 1989).

The movement was particularly critical of Christianity's concept of a transcendent God who was understood to stand apart from humanity and the natural world. God, Ch'oe Che-u believed, was the Great Totality innate in human beings, the 'Great I' to which everyone could aspire. Claiming that he had been commissioned by the Lord of Heaven, the Great Totality, the ultimate energy (*chigi*), to save humanity from destruction Choe Ch'eu devised the following mantra which encapsulated the movement's basic teachings: 'Infinite Energy being now within me, I yearn that it may pour into all living beings and all created things. Since this Energy abides in me, I am identified with God, and of one nature with all existence. Should I ever forget these things all existing things will know of it' (citation from Chryssides 1991: 85).

In terms of its millenarian belief, Tonghak taught that heaven and hell were not places that souls departed to after death but states that could be realized on earth, depending on behaviour. It was widely believed that Chongdoryong ('the one with God's truth'), would proclaim from his position on Mount Kyerong the *chongdo* or right way for the new heaven on earth in which all nations, laws, and teachings would be united. Unification was a constant theme in most nineteenth-century Korean new religion and is at the centre of the theology of its most widely known twentieth-century movement the Unification Church (UC; see below).

Tonghak's description of paradise on earth displays a deep concern for the plight of the poorest, with the inconveniences and even intractable problems created by climate, and by the forces of Nature generally, and with equality, and with a desire to escape from disease and attain immortality. Also evident is deep concern over the profound disruption to social and economic life and culture resulting from the introduction of a new form of exchange based on money, a new system of taxation, and the threat to the Korean language posed by the opening up of the country to the West. In the new world, the movement proclaims:

there will be no cold or hot weather, no poor harvest, no flood, no typhoons, and no diseases. Man will live as long as he wants . . . till 500 years of age at the medium, and till 300 years at the minimum . . . There will be things to eat and clothes. There will be no poor and rich. There will be no need for money. All transactions will be by barter. The international language will be the Korean language and its alphabet . . . At Mount Kyerong there will be built a palace of precious stones and a bank of all nations. In the new world there will be no tax. (Citation from Chryssides 1991: 89–90)

Though its teachings were contrasted with Western Learning/Christianity (*Sohak*), this religion, like the Vietnamese movement Cao Daism and many Japanese new religions or shinshukyo, was influenced by ideas and practices derived not only from Confucianism, Buddhism, Daoism, and Folk Religion but also from Christianity.

Tonghak's millenarianism and its core idea that all individuals possessed a God-like nature—or the doctrine that humans and God are one but different (*In Nae Chon*) and were, therefore, equal in dignity and worth—had obvious revolutionary implications, as did its prediction that the oppressive old order would be destroyed by an invading forces, a fate which Tonghak members could avoid by the use of incantations and magical means, and as immortal beings enjoy everlasting bliss in an earthly paradise (*Chisang Chonguk*).

Under the leadership of Chou Pong-jun, succcessor to Ch'oe Che-u, the Tonghak movement staged a rebellion against the government to eradicate injustice and inequality, which was quashed only with the assistance of Japanese and Chinese forces. The outcome of such forceful repression was a change of name from Tonghak to Ch'ondogyo in 1904, principally for the purpose of convincing the government that it was now a non-political, purely religious body.

WON BUDDHISM

There are several interesting parallels between Tonghak/Ch'ondogyo beliefs and those of another Korean millenarian movement Won Buddhism. Won Buddhism, while also emphatically millenarian in outlook, offers the version of paradise on earth that is less ambitious in terms of the transformation it anticipates, and more pragmatic, utilitarian, and small-scale than that envisaged by Tonghak/Ch'ondogyo.

Founded in 1916 by Pak Chungbin (1891–1943), who is also known by his literary name Sot'aesan (Park 1997), Won Buddhism was one of several new forms of Buddhism that began to emerge in Korea with the collapse in 1910 of the Choson (also known as the Yi) dynasty. Like much of the new Buddhism in Asia and elsewhere, Won Buddhism is primarily concerned with modernizing the image of the religion, and to this end it uses more-contemporary language than conventional Buddhism. For example, while the latter understands the nature of ultimate reality through the Threefold Learning, *samadhi* (meditation), *prajna* (wisdom), and *sila* (morality), these concepts are expressed by Won Buddhism in more-contemporary language as 'the cultivation of spirit', 'the study of facts and principles', and 'choice of conduct'.

An important difference between Won Buddhism and traditional Buddhism can be seen in the former's abandonment of the traditional understanding of liberation as nihilistic and its replacement of it with the idea of a paradise on earth in which people develop their talents and abilities. It insists that there is no difference between this world and Truth or essential reality. The purpose of life, as Won Buddhism understands it, is to realize the Truth or one's innate Buddha nature, and to serve others with a view to saving all sentient beings. In serving others one not only helps them to find the Truth, but also contributes to the process of making connections between all sentient life, of bringing the world together.

Won Buddhism's earthly paradise is unusual not only in relation to Buddhist notions on this subject but also when seen in a wider comparative framework. It promises nothing truly spectacular or idyllic, but simply that basic facilities necessary for ordinary living will be readily available and thereby help resolve some of the more serious emotional, social, and economic consequences of modern life. From the standpoint of some—the most indigent—the provision of such facilities would, of course, amount to a total transformation of the world:

In the coming world...more employment agencies will serve those who are looking for jobs, and marriage bureaus will assist those who wish to get married; a day nursery will be established in many places so that mothers can go out to work and not worry about their children. Old people without a protector will live comfortable lives without anxiety at homes for the aged which will be established by the government, by organizations, or by social and charitable workers...Life in even the remotest places will be surrounded by the most convenient cultural facilities, a fast food cafeteria will provide us with food adequate for our needs, so that we may not have to cook all the time at home; there will be many tailors, dressmakers, and laundries to help people in making their clothes and doing their laundry. (Citation from Chryssides 1991: 90)

Different from the rather dreamy versions one sometimes encounters, Won Buddhism's millenarianism is of a practical kind. Moreover, like other versions of this kind, it clearly mirrors the emotional, psychological, economic, and social concerns of many in society.

UNIFICATION CHURCH (UC) (T'ONGIL-GYO) A.K.A. THE MOONIES

Perhaps the most widely known of all Korean millenarian movements, at least in the West, is the previously mentioned Unification Church more widely known as he Moonies. Here space permits only the briefest account of the history and main beliefs of this controversial and complex movement.

The Unification Church (formerly the Holy Spirit, or more accurately the Spiritual, Association for the Unification of World Christianity) was founded in Korea in May 1954 by the Revd Sun Myung Moon (hence the name Moonies). Moon was born into a Christian, Presbyterian family in 1920 in what is today North Korea. Like Tonghak/ Ch'ondogyo and Won Buddhism, the UC is also strongly millenarian in orientation, believing that in these last days the Lord of the Second Advent will appear to complete the mission left unfinished by Christ and establish the Kingdom of Heaven on Earth.

Rejected as heretical by Christian groups in the South, Moon moved to North Korea to preach his message of the imminent arrival of the Lord of the Second Advent and the establishment of the Kingdom of God on earth. In 1960 the movement reached a defining point in its development with the marriage of Moon to the 'true mother' Hak Ja Han. As Chryssides (1991: 158) points out, this decisive event is held to have restored Eden, and marked the origin and source of new life for all humankind. Together the couple are believed to constitute the 'True Parents', and to mark the occasion a holy day known as Parents' Day was instituted.

The principal task of the Lord of the Second Advent is to accomplish through Moon and his wife and family, and the new families they will form, the physical salvation of human beings which Jesus allegedly failed to accomplish, by the creation of a sinless new family from which the Kingdom of God on earth will emerge. Heaven and earth meet symbolically at the movement's main shrine at Chungpyung Lake Training Centre to the north of Seoul. The shrine includes a holy site with an abundance of sacred trees and healing springs. The understanding of millenarianism found in other cultures differs in substance from this, as we shall see from a brief consideration of the Rastafarian movement and of Islamic millenarianism.

RASTAFARIANISM

Although number of its key concepts are older, the formal beginnings of the Rastafarian movement date back to Jamaica in the 1930s, a time of deep economic depression that further lowered the standard of living of a colonized and culturally alienated people. Many of those of African descent began to seek liberation and salvation in their African and African-Christian beliefs, particularly the biblically inspired belief in the imminent destruction of the oppressor 'Babylon' or white society and its replacement in Africa with a black earthly paradise where all black people would live naturally, with dignity and in harmony (Clarke 1987).

The Rastafarian response to colonialism and social and economic oppression, while in several ways unique, was also part of a long history of African-Christian rebellion against slavery and the plantation system in the Caribbean. For example, its philosophy of Ethiopianism based on the idea of Ethiopia as an ancient and sophisticated African society that had never been formally colonized, and as symbol of a free, self-sufficient and independent Africa, echoes that of the former slave and Baptist pastor the American George Liele, who worked in Jamaica. Attempts to apply that philosophy have resulted in the establishment of Rasta settlements in Africa, including the Rastafarian model of an earthly paradise at Shashamane in Ethiopia. The tradition of African-Christian rebellion to which Rastafarianism is an heir is also a long one, and included the extremely violent myalist- a syncretistic Jamaican millenarian movement- inspired Tacky Rebellion of 1760 against slavery, the 1831 rebellion led by Baptist deacon Sam Sharpe, known as daddy, also against the institution of slavery, and the Morant War for independence of 1840 waged by Paul Bogle and 400 black Caribbeans.

An African-Christian preacher more directly linked to the beginnings of Rastafarianism was the founder of the Baptist Free Church in Jamaica, Alexander Bedward (1892–1930), who foretold that a holocaust was imminent in which all whites would be destroyed and all blacks saved. However, Bedward, whose ideas were to have a profound impact on Rastafarian thinking, differed from Sharpe, Bogle, and other opponents of colonialism including Marcus Garvey (1887–1940), by insisting that liberation would come through supernatural intervention and not by taking up arms or any other form of human endeavour.

Marcus Garvey, recognized as one of the most important of Rasta prophets, stressed the necessity for black people to save themselves by their own efforts rather than rely solely on faith and hope, a worldview that not all Rastafarians accept. Printer, activist, and inspirational black nationalist, Garvey founded in 1914 the Universal Negro Improvement Association (UNIA) whose rallying-cry was 'Africa for the Africans', and the first line of whose anthem was 'Ethiopia, Thou land of Our Fathers'. Revered by Rastas as a prophet, Garvey frequently referred to Psalm 68:31—'Princes shall come forth from Egypt, Ethiopia shall stretch forth her hands to God'—as clearly predicting Africa's liberation.

The clearest sign of this was the crowning of Ras Tafari, Haile Selassie (1892–1975), as emperor of Ethiopia in 1930. Haile Sellassie claimed to be the 255TH in the line of Ethiopian kings who descended in unbroken succession from the time of King Solomon and the Queen of Sheba. The first person in Jamaica to claim divinity for Haile Selassie was Leonard Percival Howell, who on returning from labouring in North America in 1931 began preaching to the descendants of Central Africans (Congolese) who had arrived in the country in the second half of the nineteenth century as immigrant labourers, and who had plans to return home. Howell and others, drawing on the King James' version of the Bible, were convinced that scripture provided proof of Haile Selassie's divinity and of the special role the African race was to play in God's plans. One such passage was Ezekiel 37:19–23, which Rastas interpret to mean that under a new king Africans from everywhere would come together on their own soil and be united. The Jamaican Leopold Howard was one of the most active exponents of this belief, and of the idea that Africans who had been enslaved by the whites, the agents of Babylon, were the true descendants of Israel. A great deal of effort has been expended by, among other Rasta bodies, the Twelve Tribes (see below) on establishing the physical and mystical links between the Rastas and the Israelites.

For several decades Rastas adopted an essentially quietist approach to change and waited patiently for the divine intervention that would destroy Babylon, the term for the white oppressor who had enslaved and exploited the black race. However, the movement became increasingly politicized and militant from the 1960s. Rastafarian themes of black consciousness and the elimination of colonial influence became closely associated with the Jamaican People's National Party led by Michael Manley, who would later become prime minister of Jamaica. Rastafarian ideas also influenced the intellectual debate among black people regarding how they ought to respond to the continuing impact of colonialism and neo-colonialism on African societies. The thinking of the Guyanese Black Power activist, the historian Dr Walter Rodney (1942–80), who was eventually assassinated for his political radicalism, was partly inspired by the Rastafarian critique of colonial and post-colonial African societies in the Caribbean and elsewhere.

The 1970s saw a tremendous growth in the numbers of Rastas and Rasta sympathizers worldwide, a growth that was greatly assisted by the music and charisma of Bob Marley, who personified Rasta thought and became its most effective emissary. Marley, who was introduced to the movement by his wife Rita and became a member of the Rasta organization known as the Twelve Tribes, was widely believed to have been gifted with special powers by the deity. His songs spoke of the evil of slavery, of how it had destroyed the African personality, of the need to reconstruct a true sense of self, of the inequalities of Babylon, the white power system, and—as in the song 'Exodus' (1977)—of the movement of African people from Babylon to their 'Father's Land', which came increasingly to mean the psychological transformation in black self-understanding rid of colonial interpretations rather than an actual return to Africa.

The movement gives symbolic expression to all of these themes through its manner of communicating, relating, and living. Rastafarian colours, for example, taken over from Garvey's UNIA of red, green, and black symbolize respectively the blood of African people spilt in slavery, the colour of nature whose rules Africans should live by, and the colour of the African people. Their wearing of dreadlocks is based, it is claimed, on scripture (Lev. 19:27, 21:5, and Num. 6:5) and symbolizes their dignity as black people, while the language they have constructed likewise serves the same end. The pronoun 'we', for example, is replaced by 'I and I', to counter the damaging psychological effects of slavery and colonialism which reduced Africans to units of labour and to create awareness that each and every black person is a unique and special individual. Rastafarians follow many of the dietary laws of the Jews, which include abstinence from pork, and prefer 'natural' food which is specially prepared. Alcohol, grapes, currents, raisins, and processed foods should not be consumed.

Mahdism

The scope and force of the millenarian theme will be further illustrated by the following a brief account of Mahdism, the Islamic version of the idea. The frequency of millenarian belief has been witnessed perhaps nowhere more than in the Islamic world in the form of Mahdism. Ibn Khaldun, the jurist and historian already referred to on this topic, wrote in his *Muqaddimah* or Introduction to World History:

It has been well known and generally accepted by all Muslims in every epoch, that at the end of time a man from the family of the prophet will without fail make his appearance, one who will strengthen the religion and make justice triumph . . . He will be called the Mahdi (God-guided one). Following him the Antichrist will appear together with all the subsequent signs of the Day of Judgement. After the Mahdi Isa (Jesus) will descend and kill the Antichrist. (1967: 156)

Prior to Ibn Khaldun, the Persian Muslim scholar and mystic Muhammad Al-Ghazali (1058–1111 also regarded the Mahdi figure as a popular construct. It was a concept which, he wrote, 'was nurtured and cultivated by the multitudes' who saw in the Mahdi an instrument against oppression (Clarke 1995).

Despite the lack of support for the notion in the Qur'an and in sound *hadith* or tradition, there have been countless Mahdis throughout Islamic history in both Sunni and Shi'ite Islam. Two of the most prominent and widely known are Ubaydulah al-Mahdi (d. 934), founder of the Fatimid dynasty that ruled in North Africa in the tenth century, and Muhammad ibn Tumart (d. 1130), founder of the Almohad movement in the Maghrib in the twelfth century. The nineteenth century proved to be a time of unprecedented millenarian expectancy in the Muslim world, much of it triggered by the pressures of colonialism. India saw the rise of self-proclaimed Mahdis who, it was hoped, would lead Muslims to final victory over the British. Similar Mahdist movements, many of them short-lived, emerged in Afghanistan and throughout Africa during colonialism. A Mahdist revolt broke out in Upper Egypt in 1865 and others occurred elsewhere in Africa, including the Sudan, where Muhammad ibn Abdullah (d. 1885) founded a Mahdist state in the late nineteenth century.

Although at the popular level all Muslims share an almost identical understanding of the Mahdi in terms of his status and role, the Mahdi idea is a much more central feature of official Shi'a Islam. In Ithna'asharite or Twelver Shi'ite Islamic theology the Mahdi, who is known as the Hidden Imam—the twelfth and last of the Imams: hence the name Twelvers—is seen as an infallible and indispensable guide. The Hidden Imam, it is believed, will rule personally and by divine right. It is he who provides certainty concerning the meaning of the divine revelation and not the qualified scholars or *mudjtahids*. In Sunni Islam, by contrast, the people are the ultimate interpreters of the revelation given by God through the Prophet Muhammad, and the belief in the Mahdi in the Sunni tradition thus finds its support primarily in the heart of the believers and is not an essential part of its 'systematic' theology.

Marxism as Secular Millenarianism

Millenarianism is found not only in religions but also in secular ideologies, some of which were undoubtedly influenced by religion. Space allows for only the shortest summary of one such secular millenarian ideology, Marxism.

While secular versions of the millennium such as that presented by Marxism have much in common with religious ones, along with significant differences, Karl Marx (1818–83) himself was strongly opposed to millenarian thinking and rejected outright any suggestion that there were similarities between his own thoughts about the future condition of human society and those of millenarians. His concern, he insisted, was with the dynamics of change that would see the proletariat liberate itself from oppression. Millenarians and utopians, by contrast, simply willed things to happen.

Notwithstanding Marx's absolute refusal to acknowledge any hint of millenarian thought in his writings, it is clearly present in some of these and in those of his lifelong friend and collaborator Friedrich Engels (1820–95). Some—for example Kumar (1991: 55)—would claim that Marxism presents a vision of society 'that in outlines at least is as grand as anything found in the whole utopian tradition'. Marxism paints a picture of life on earth after the ending of exploitation, particularly economic exploitation, and the transformation of the world by revolution, as one of harmony and goodwill. Justice and peace will reign and all that humans require to enable them to achieve full self-realization will be readily available at this end-stage of human history. Distinctions between people would be dissolved, as would class structures, and bureaucracy, the forces of law and order, and eventually the whole apparatus of the state would wither away.

Engels was persuaded that once society had risen up and taken over the means of production from exploitative capitalist entrepreneurs then for the first time in history human beings would become truly human, truly themselves and distinct and separate from the beasts of the animal kingdom. They would be the lords of Nature and masters of their social organization. These views on the relationship of human beings to nature are best described in contemporary environmentalist language as anthropocentric.

Furthermore, in this secular paradise on earth there would be no constraint of any kind, as everything would be the result of free action. What humans intended would actually happen, and thus they would make their own history. In sum, the successful overthrow of the bourgeoisie would see human beings pass from the kingdom of necessity to the kingdom of freedom.

While this is not unlike the Christian and Mahdist pictures of the millennium, at least in some of their essentials, it differs from them in a number of ways, including its lack, at least in theory, of a messianic figure, although some consider Lenin, Stalin, or even Marx himself to be such a figure. Marxism, positivist and materialist as it is, sees the prophet or messianic figure as irrelevant, or as an ambiguous personality who at the very most might act as a catalyst but without whom the march of history toward full human liberation would continue, and probably more rapidly and effectively. While, then, differences exist between it and religiously inspired millenarian movements, Marxism ultimately holds out much the same promise as these movements.

CONCLUSIONS

The millenarian idea, then, is found in diverse religious and secular traditions. Much of its popularity can be explained by reference to one kind of deprivation or another. Opinions vary greatly regarding the achievements and impact of movements driven by millenarianism. A common view of such movements is that they fail to identify and provide remedies for the injustices and inequalities, social and otherwise, that give rise to them and often induce extreme abandonment, passivity, and resignation. This notwithstanding, there is very often a compelling situational logic about millenarian responses, as the studies on millenarian movements by

Worsley (1968), Burridge (1971), Wilson (1973), and Clarke (1995), among others, have shown. This does not, however, mean they are effective methods of solving problems. Douglas, who sees witchcraft as carrying a millenarian possibility in its promise to end evil and suffering, is persuaded that millenarian movements change nothing. She writes (1973: 147): 'But like the millennial movements the witch cleansing movement comes and goes and leaves the community as it was, still prone to witch beliefs, still awaiting a new, more effective movement which will kill off or immobilise witches forever ...'

Others have reached more positive conclusions about the effects of millenarianism than this, seeing it as one of the few effective weapons at the disposal of the oppressed which historically the oppressor has greatly feared. This belief not only generates cohesion or *asabiyya*, as Ibn Khaldun observed, but also deep emotion, fervour, commitment, dedication, and enthusiasm, as many a 'prophet' who has used it to mobilize mass support has discovered, and as Arjomand (1984) has shown in the case of Shi'ite Iran. Focusing on endings can be, as Kermode (1967) suggests, as determinant as beginnings in sustaining actions and motivations, and in shaping the dispositions of humans as they strive to make sense of the world they live in and their brief span of life on earth.

Accounting for millenarianism is no easier than evaluating its impact and achievements. One of the more common types of explanation is psychopathological. From this perspective millenarianism is defined as a form of collective fantasizing which attracts those who cannot cope. Another, not entirely dissimilar, explanation attributes it to the state of collective anomie or loss of a sense of direction and of meaning that results from rapid social change. While acknowledging that millenarianism—like religious fundamentalism, whose literalism and strict and undeviating approach to scripture it lacks—can provide great emotional and intellectual security, such psychological and social-psychological explanations are incomplete. What the study of millenarian movements shows is that their members come from very different social and economic circumstances and from very different ways of life. We know, for example, from Cohn's (1970) study of medieval millenarian movements in Europe that they attracted women of high status and wealth as well as women from poor, low-status backgrounds.

Regarding rapid social change as an explanation, the point, though obvious, needs to be made that change, even rapid change, is by no means always problematic in itself, and certainly not for all those affected by it. Social change, however rapid, does not necessarily destroy or undermine confidence or create deep-seated anxiety, or a yearning for the stability of the past. It can also be a liberating experience. Change can, of course, be profoundly disorientating, especially that kind of change that seeks to take away the power of individuals and communities to control what is happening to their world. This tends not only to bewilder but also to incapacitate. However, the lack of the means and the felt powerlessness to effect radical change of a political, economic, or social kind can have the same emotional consequences. Both experiences can generate millenarian fervour.

While there is no satisfactory general explanation of millenarianism, research shows it to be one of the most widely held beliefs across the ages and across cultures, and a belief that is attractive to many regardless of socio-economic and intellectual background. It is a belief, moreover, that seems most likely to appeal in its dynamic form to those who are frustrated by marginality in one or more of its various guises and with no effective means of voicing this experience.

Works Cited

ARJOMAND, S. A. (1984), *The Shadow of God and the Hidden Imam: Religion, Political Order and Societal Change in Shi'ite Iran from the Beginning to 1890.* Chicago: Chicago University Press.

BERTHON, JEAN-PIERRE (1985), *Esperance millenariste d'une nouvelle religion Japonaise.* Paris: Cahiers d'etudes et de documents sur les religions du Japon, no.6, Atelier Alpha Bleu.

BURRIDGE, K. (1971), *New Heaven, New Earth.* Oxford: Basil Blackwell.

CHRYSSIDES, GEORGE D. (1991), *The Advent of Sung Myung Moon: The Origins, Beliefs and Practices of the Unification Church.* Basingstoke: Macmillan.

CLARKE, P. B. (1987), *Black Paradise: The Rastafarian Movement.* Wellingborough, Northants: Aquarian Press.

——(1995), *Mahdism in West Africa: The Ijebu Mahdiyyat Movement.* London: Luzac Oriental.

——(2006), *New Religions in Global Perspective.* London: Routledge.

CLASTRES, H. (1995), *The Land-Without-Evil,* trans. from the French by Jacqueline Grenez Brovender. Urbana and Chicago: University of Illinois Press.

COHN, N. (1970), *The Pursuit of the Millennium.* London: Paladin.

——(1993), *Cosmos, Chaos and the World to Come: The Ancient Roots of Apocalyptic Faith.* New Haven and London: Yale University Press.

COLLINS, J. J. (1997), *Apocalypticism in the Dead Sea Scrolls.* London: Routledge.

DOUGLAS, M. (1973), *Natural Symbols.* Harmondsworth: Penguin Books.

GRAYSON, JAMES H. (1989), *Korea: A Religious History.* Oxford: Oxford University Press.

KERMODE, FRANK (1967), *The Sense of an Ending: Studies in the Theory of Fiction.* Oxford: Oxford University Press.

IBN KHALDUN, ABD AR RAHMAN (1967), *The Muqaddimmah: An Introduction to History,* edited and abridged by N. J. Dawood, trans. from the Arabic by F. Rosenthal, vol. 2. London: Routledge & Kegan Paul, 1958.

KOHN, LIVIA (1998), 'The Beginnings and Cultural Characteristics of East Asian Millenarianism', in *Japanese Religions,* 23/1 and 2 (Jan.), 29–53.

KUMAR, K. (1991), *Utopia and Anti-Utopia in Modern Times.* Oxford: Blackwell.

LANTERNARI, V. (1991), 'Melanesian Religions', in S. R. Sutherland and P. B. Clarke (eds.), *The Study of Religion: Traditional and New Religion,* 85–95. London: Routledge.

Ooms, E. Goszos (1993), *Women and Millenarian Protest in Meiji Japan: Nao Deguchi and Omoto*. Ithaca, NY: Cornell University East Asia Program.

Park, Kwangsoo (1997), *The Won Buddhism (Wonbulgyo) of Sot'aesan: A Twentieth Century Religious Movement in Korea*. San Francisco: International Scholars.

Peiris, J. B. (1989), *The Dead Will Arise*. London: James Curry.

Wilson, B. R. (1970), *Religious Sects*. London: Weidenfeld & Nicolson.

——(1973). *Magic and the Millennium*. London: Heinemann.

Worsley, P. (1968), *The Trumpet Shall Sound*. St Albans: Paladin.

FURTHER READING

Bloch, Ruth H. (1985), *Visionary Republic: Millennial Themes in American Thought 1756–1800*. Cambridge: Cambridge University Press.

Bull, Malcolm (ed.) (1995), *Apocalypse Theory and the End of the World*. Oxford: Basil Blackwell.

Clarke, Peter B. (ed.) (2000), *Japanese New Religions: In Global Perspective*. London: Curzon.

Delumeau, Jean (1995), *Mille Ans de Bonheur*. Paris: Fayard.

Desroches, Henri (1979), *The Sociology of Hope*. London: Routledge & Kegan Paul.

Harrison, J. F. C. (1979), *The Second Coming*. London: Routledge & Kegan Paul.

Hatch, Nathan O. and Mark A. Noll (eds.) (1982), *The Bible in America: Essays in Cultural History*. Oxford: Oxford University Press.

Hill, Christopher (1970), *God's Englishman: Oliver Cromwell and the English Revolution*. London: Weidenfeld & Nicolson.

Manuel, Frank E. and Fritzie P. Manuel (1979), *Utopian Thought in the Western World*. Oxford: Basil Blackwell.

O'Leary, Stephen D. (1994), *Arguing the Apocalypse: A Theory of Millennial Rhetoric*. Oxford: Oxford University Press.

Scholem, G. (1971), *The Messianic Idea in Israel*. New York: Schocken.

Weber, Timothy P. (1979), *Living in the Shadow of the Second Coming: American Pre-millennialism 1875–1925*. Oxford: Oxford University Press.

CHAPTER 17

NON-RETALIATION AND MILITARY FORCE: THEIR BASIS IN THE BIBLE

RICHARD HARRIES

GANDHI was not alone in finding something distinctive and compelling in the teaching and example of Jesus about violence. This aspect of his life and work has been universally admired, and it is difficult to see how anyone could call themselves a Christian without being haunted by it.

Jesus taught that we are to love our enemies and pray for those who persecute us. (Matt. 5:44). He said we were not to resist those who wrong us, but if hit on one cheek we are to turn the other (Matt. 5:39). When he was arrested in the Garden of Gethsemane and one of his followers cut off the ear of the high priest's servant, Jesus healed it and told them to put their swords away. On the cross he prayed for the forgiveness of those who were responsible. As Simone Weil put it: 'All the criminal violence of the Roman Empire ran up against Christ and in him became pure suffering... the false god changes suffering into violence. The true God changes violence into suffering.'[1]

It is this picture which left an indelible impression on the first Christians and inspired them to emulate it. Paul says that Christians are never to pay back evil for

---

[1] Simone Weil, *Gravity and Grace* (Routledge, 1952), 65.

evil. On the contrary, we are even to give food and drink to our enemies if they need them: 'Do not let evil conquer you, but use good to conquer evil' (Rom. 12: 21). Another writer urges his readers to submit to hardship whether or not it is justified: 'It is your vocation because Christ himself suffered on your behalf, and left you an example that you should follow in his steps . . . When he was abused he did not retaliate, when he suffered he uttered no threats, but delivered himself up to him who judges justly' (1 Pet. 2:21–3).

Yet this is not the only strand that relates to the issue of violence in the New Testament, let alone the Bible as a whole. For example, John the Baptist appears to have accepted military life as a legitimate vocation and Jesus is reported to have had a positive attitude to centurions, who were soldiers of an occupying power. St Paul, like other writers, sees the coercive power of the state as having a legitimate role. It is not surprising that these features have also been appealed to by Christians down the ages.

This chapter is not a history of how these texts have been interpreted, nor is it a history of the changing circumstances in which force has been used or a history of the Just War tradition. It is an attempt to show how there has been a tension throughout Christian history between these two strands in the New Testament, a tension, or at least a contrast, which is inescapable, if justice is to be done to the New Testament. Nevertheless, it is not possible to consider this tension without also being aware of the changing circumstances in which force has been used, how the key texts have been interpreted, and the developing tradition of Christian thinking about the criteria which must be met if war is to be waged on a moral basis. The church has never been easy with this tension, and has tried to ease it or dissolve it altogether in different ways; and it has been expressed differently depending on whether most weight has been put on the teaching and example of Jesus about non-retaliation, or on the apparent need for state-sanctioned force to maintain order both within a state or empire or, reflecting a later period, between states.[2] How this tension is rooted in the New Testament and why it is inescapable is taken up again at the end of the chapter.

The first evidence of Christians joining the army dates from the late second century, and even then they may at first have joined sections corresponding to our police or ambulance services. Before then there was a reluctance to join for a variety of reasons, including fear of idolatry. But a famous saying of Tertullian (c.160– c.225) clearly spoke for many: 'For even if soldiers came to John and received advice on how to act, and even if a centurion became a believer, the Lord, in subsequently disarming Peter, disarmed every soldier.'[3] The church at that time was a small,

---

[2] The most lauded recent pacifist reading of the New Testament is Richard Hays, *The Moral Vision of the New Testament* (T. & T. Clark, 1996), ch. 14. There is a critique of this by Nigel Biggar, 'Specify and Distinguish! Interpreting the New Testament on "Non-violence"', *Studies in Christian Ethics* (2009).

[3] Tertullian, *Treatise on Idolatry* 19; *Ante-nicene Fathers* 3.73.

spasmodically persecuted community, concerned for the highest standards in the life of its own community and, in our terms, a counter-cultural sect. At the same time Christians accepted the legitimacy of secular coercion, even though they themselves suffered at its hands. In these circumstances, though both strands of the New Testament are present, it is easy to see why priority should have been given to the teaching and example of Jesus about his followers not using violence under any circumstances.

With the conversion of Constantine and the official recognition of Christianity, Christians found themselves in positions of responsibility in the empire. This remains today a controversial turning-point in the history of the church, viewed as either the great betrayal or the assumption of a proper responsibility for ordering the affairs of the world. It led to an acceptance that Christians could fight in wars if certain moral criteria had been met. Augustine is the decisive figure here, though he drew on the work of others, such as Ambrose, and his thinking stands in the tradition of Roman thinkers such as Cicero.[4]

Although Augustine argued that our true citizenship belongs with the Kingdom of God, whilst on this earth we have to work with others to maintain the fabric of society with a degree of order and justice. This led him personally to bear significant responsibilities as a magistrate, and also to write to Count Boniface, the Roman governor of North Africa, urging him to stay at his post and see his Christian vocation as helping to defend the empire rather than withdrawing to a more contemplative form of existence. But in stressing Christian responsibilities for the right ordering of a violent world, he did not lose sight of the other strand in the New Testament, the distinctive teaching and example of Jesus. First of all he saw it as an essential aspect of our love of the enemy that we do not let bullies get away with their bullying. We show our love for them by stopping them. But force should only be used as a last resort, and even then with a profound sense of regret and sadness. It should always be used with the spirit of moderation and kindness, with the aim of establishing peace.[5] Perhaps most significantly of all, Augustine rejects the idea of a right of self-defence, which Aquinas did later allow. The basis of Augustine's approach to the use of force is not the right of self-defence but the obligation of love to protect the innocent.

Between Augustine and Aquinas, the next great architect of the tradition, the crusades began. These have become a byword in the modern world for all that has been wrong in the church's attitude to war, and they are not to be justified. But they do need to be understood in the context of their own times, and recent scholarship

---

[4] *The Ethics of War: Classic and Contemporary Readings*, eds. Gregory M. Rechberg, Henrik Syse, and Endre Begby (Blackwell, 2006), is now available as an invaluable resource for this subject, though not all the texts cited in this essay are to those in that book.

[5] St Augustine, letter 138 to Marcellinus, *Letters*, vol. 3 (Catholic University of America Press, 1953), 47. See also *Contra Faustum* 19.7; 12.74; and *Epistle ad Bonifacium* 189.6.

has shown how their proponents appealed with some legitimacy to criteria of justice.[6] But the aspect of the crusades that matters from the standpoint of this chapter is that whatever criteria might or might not have been met, they were seen as a holy war, a war for God against God's enemies. On that basis the wars in the Old Testament could be appealed to as setting a precedent. In this respect a crusade mentality is to be distinguished from the approach of someone who stands in the Just War tradition, a point taken up towards the end of the chapter.

Thomas Aquinas (1225–74), building on the work of his predecessors, especially Augustine and the canonist Gratian (d. c.1160), set out the rudiments of the Just War tradition in a brief, clear, and characteristically balanced way that has been hugely influential on subsequent thinkers.[7] From the point of view of the theme of this chapter, it is fundamental to note that his consideration of war occurs as part of a wider discussion of sins against charity. This is of contemporary relevance, for in the debate over the moral legitimacy or otherwise of the invasion of Iraq, some American Roman Catholic Just War theorists, such as George Weigel, accused the United States Roman Catholic bishops of regarding the Just War criteria as carrying a presumption against war which, they said, was not there. But the Catholic Bishops were right. Our human striving for such *pax-ordo-iustitia* as this world allows is always subject to the call and judgement of God's ultimate will for universal peace. War, like strife and sedition, which are also discussed in the same section by Aquinas, is contrary to peace, except under some circumstances when special criteria have been met. These are, first, that it must been authorized by the highest authority—that is, the one above which there is no court of appeal for a peaceful resolution. At the time of developing feudal monarchies in Europe, this was the sovereign. Then, the cause must be just and there must be a right intention. For Aquinas this refers primarily to what we would term the spirit in which military action is engaged. Following Augustine, it must be with a view to peace, with the spirit of a peacemaker; that is, without cruelty, excessive violence, the desire for revenge, the lust for power, and so on. If these are not present, a cause which might otherwise be regarded as just becomes immoral.

In short, the very existence of conditions that must be met if a military action is to be regarded as morally legitimate indicates a presumption against war. If they are not met, it constitutes a sin against peace and charity.

In addition to the basic framework of charity within which Aquinas places his discussion, and the need for the spirit of a peacemaker, already mentioned, there are two other aspects of his teaching on war that indicate an awareness of the

---

[6] Jonathan Riley-Smith, *What Were the Crusades?*, 2nd edn. (Macmillan, 1992), 8. Though a crusade is a holy war, it 'must conform to the criteria of the just cause, the authority of the prince and right intention'.

[7] *Summa theologica*, II-II, q. 40.

tension inherent in the Christian approach to war, even if it is being argued that it is justified under certain circumstances.

The first is the indication, in his discussion on whether religious orders (like the Templars) can have a proper vocation to engage in war, that it might be properly Christian to set aside the right of self-defence.[8] On the whole Aquinas allows the right of self-defence, if it is proportionate and not primarily directed to killing, as opposed to simply stopping, the attacker.[9] But in this discussion he distinguishes injuries to oneself from injuries done to others. It may be right not to resist evil, for 'it may pertain to perfection, when it is expedient to act thus for the spiritual welfare of others'. But to tolerate wrong being done to others when it is in our power to defend them is certainly an imperfection and may be a vice.

The second example is his refusal to allow clerics and bishops to fight even in a just cause. Various reasons are given, but the prime one is their ministry at the altar: 'Wherefore it is unbecoming for them to slay or shed blood, and it is more fitting that they should be ready to shed their own blood for Christ, so as to imitate in deed what they portray in their ministry.'[10] He allows clerics and bishops to travel with their armies, to pray for them and to minister to them spiritually, but not to bear arms. This is an important distinction that has been carried forward into the armies of Christian countries to this day. It is a powerful, symbolic statement that, though bearing arms may be necessary in the actual world in which we live, it is still contrary to the ultimate purpose of God, which will be fulfilled in his universal kingdom of justice and peace.

So although Aquinas has done more than anyone to make war seem, under certain strict conditions, morally legitimate, it is important to note that he regards war in principle as a sin against peace. Then, in at least three ways—in his stress on right intention, his teaching on self-defence in relation to the military orders, and his forbidding of clerics and bishops to fight—he witnesses to what will ultimately be the case when God's rule prevails over all things.

The situation to which Fransisco de Vitoria (1480–1546) responded in his lectures and writing was the Spanish conquests in what is now Central and South America. He said that the reports of what was happening there 'made my blood run cold'. Although he had important things to say about the conditions under which military force could be used in the first place, his significance for the tradition lies primarily in what he taught about the just conduct of war. Although he did not use the terminology, it is in what he said about the latter (*ius in bello*) rather than in what he said about the former (*ius ad bellum*) that will be considered here. First, like Aquinas, he said that the *innocentes* were not to be the direct object of military attack. This principle, sometimes called the principle of discrimination and

---

[8] Ibid. q.188, a.3.   [9] Ibid. q.64, a.7.   [10] Ibid. q.40, a.2.

sometimes non-combatant immunity, was not a new teaching. The church's attempt to limit the ravages of war in the tenth and eleventh centuries through the Peace of God and the Truce of God listed categories of people who were not to be attacked. These categories passed into the canon law of the church, especially as put together by Gratian. They were implemented on the battlefield in the codes of chivalry and the ideal of a chivalrous Christians knight. Vitoria brought together the idea of the innocent with these categories of people, arguing that if someone was not carrying a weapon or otherwise posing a threat they were innocent and therefore not to be killed. The key consideration was if they were injurious. If they were not, they were not to be attacked, and this included soldiers after a victory. Furthermore, people could not be attacked just on the grounds that they might be a threat in the future.[11] It did not need the teaching of Jesus to ground this, for it is simply one particular instance of obedience to the commandment that we are to do no murder, and in that sense it belongs to natural law or the shared morality of humanity. However, Paul Ramsey argued that the specifically Christian basis of this teaching is to be found in the teaching of Augustine.[12] Although the principle of non-combatant immunity as such is not to be found in Augustine, the logic of a love that leads people to use force to protect the harmless leads us at the same time to put a ring of protection around the harmless on the side of the enemy.

In addition to the principle of discrimination the other key notion of *ius in bello*, the principle of proportion, is also to be found in Vitoria. He argued that whilst it might be morally legitimate in principle to attack a military target if in doing so great destruction results, this could outweigh any good that might be achieved by the attack. If this is the case, the attack becomes unjust. What is interesting is that he does not limit an assessment of the damage to one side, but considers the wider good of the church, Christendom, and the world which will result.[13]

In the modern world it has sometimes been suggested that in war 'anything goes', and once war breaks out there are no restraints. The Christian tradition has always been quite clear, at least in theory, that this is not the case. War can be waged only to uphold a moral order, and it must be waged in obedience to that moral order.[14] The conduct of the war matters as much as the cause.

The work of Vitoria was put in more systematic form by another Spaniard, Francisco de Suarez (1548–1617). Like Aquinas, his teaching on war is discussed in the context of charity. He is also interesting in what he says about not going to war unless there is a reasonable chance of success, which is in fact a logical implication of the principle of proportion but in Suarez becomes a more formal principle. His

[11] *De Indis et de iure belli relectiones*, 36. English trans. by J. P. Bates and E. Nys (Scott's Classics of International Law, NY, 1964).

[12] Paul Ramsey, *War and the Christian Conscience* (Duke University Press, 1961), ch. 3.

[13] *De potestate civile.* An English translation is given in the appendix to the book cited in n. 6.

[14] A point strongly urged by Grotius and today by Oliver O'Donovan in *The Just War Revisited* (Cambridge University Press, 2003).

argument is that to do so, causing destruction to both sides without achieving the moral goal sought, is a sin against both charity and justice. This brings out the point which is a feature of so much of this tradition, that there is often a coalescing of what we might call distinctively Christian elements and considerations of natural prudence and justice which all rulers might be expected to affirm.

This is especially true in the work of Hugo Grotius (1583–1645), who systematized the teaching of Just War thinkers before him and laid the foundation for international law. Grotius, primarily a jurist, was a classicist, philosopher, and theologian as well, and unites in himself many strands of thinking, not least the distinctive teaching of Jesus. He urges that we are to pay attention not just to what the laws permits but what mercy enjoins us to do or refrain from doing, sparing death and destruction wherever possible, even in the case of those who deserve it.[15] Sydney Bailey sums up this aspect of his teaching:

Grotius does not fail to remind his readers of the perfectionism of 'Sermon on the Mount' Christianity...here was Grotius, a Christian and a humanist, a man of the world, a professional bureaucrat, formulating a theory of international law 'from an entirely secular point of view' and yet constantly reiterating the need to love the enemy, to give him the benefit of the doubt, to be killed rather than kill.[16]

The terrible carnage in the trenches of World War I led in Europe to a radical reappraisal of attitudes to war, nationalism, and patriotism. Through the work of poets, especially Wilfred Owen, whose theme was 'the pity of war', this has been influential up to our own times. Between the two world wars of the twentieth century this resulted in the coalescence of a number of movements: a new internationalism expressed in the formation of the League of Nations; a conviction that poor social conditions, that so often give rise to war, can and ought to be changed for the better, which in the churches found expression through the social gospel; and a new emphasis on Christian pacifism which found expression in hundreds of tracts and booklets, as well as the Peace Pledge Union, which expanded to 100,000 members. This pacifism contained both a principled pacifism, the conviction that we should not resist whatever the consequences, and a pragmatic pacifism which, without denying the principled form, believed that a non-violent approach could win over those regarded as enemies.

When war with Hitler became inevitable this pacifism tended to melt away in a reluctant acceptance that he could only be stopped by the force of arms. There was little Just War theorizing, simply a weary but determined acknowledgment that Hitler must be resisted, and most people today share the judgement that if there can be such a thing as a just war, then military opposition to the Nazis was one. There was at least one Christian thinker who did not go along with either the

[15] Hugo Grotius, *De iure belli et pacis*, book. 3, ch. 11, secs. 7 and 8.
[16] Sydney D. Bailey, *Prohibitions and Restraints in War* (Oxford University Press, 1972), 35.

pacifism (or crypto-pacifism) of the churches, or with the optimistic view of human beings implied by both it and the proponents of the social gospel. Reinhold Niebuhr saw what was happening to the Jews in Germany in the early 1930s and urged the United States to enter the war. A Christian realist in the tradition of Augustine, he argued that we have to take into account the fact that human beings are not only made in the image of God, they are also crucifiers of Christ, and any attempt to achieve even a rough-and-ready justice in the world means taking power seriously.[17]

During World War II there were a few who criticized the Allies' policy of obliteration bombing and, later, the dropping of atomic bombs on Hiroshima and Nagasaki, such as Bishop Bell in Britain and Father Ford in the United States, but the moral challenge posed by nuclear weapons really began to be faced from the end of the 1950s. It was during this time that the two key principles of *ius in bello*, discrimination and proportion, came into their own. A new position, nuclear pacifism, emerged, held by those who regarded any use or threatened use of nuclear weapons as inescapably immoral. For they could not help being directly aimed at civilians—or, to be more precise, people who were not directly contributing to the military aspect of the war effort—for they would inevitably kill millions of civilians even if a military installation was being targeted, an outcome which would be disproportionate to any possible good.

Those who argued in favour of retaining nuclear weapons maintained that nuclear deterrence was essentially stable, because for the first time in human history it could not conceivably have been in the interest of either superpower to go to war. Further, they maintained that it was in principle possible still to direct weapons to military targets, and the threat of escalation, a key factor in maintaining deterrence, was not in itself immoral. Those who argued against this maintained to the contrary that deterrence was not inherently stable, accidents and misunderstandings happen, that any use of weapons could not help being both indiscriminate and disproportionate, and that to threaten what is immoral is itself immoral. The debate reached a high level of sophistication amongst those using Just War categories on both sides of the Atlantic, and involved both Christian Ethicists and those from departments of politics and international affairs.[18]

The nuclear stalemate ended with the end of the Cold War, yet the world is arguably an even more dangerous place now, with nuclear weapons in the hands of

---

[17] Reinhold Niebuhr, 'Why the Christian Church is Not Pacifist' in *Christianity and Power Politics* (Scribners, 1940). For a reply to Niebuhr see G. H. C. MacGregor, *The Relevance of the Impossible: A Reply to Reinhold Niebuhr* (The Fellowship of Reconciliation, 1941). For an assessment of the different strands within Christian Pacifism see Richard Harries, 'Niebuhr's Critique of Pacifism and his Pacifist Critics', in Richard Harries (ed.), *Reinhold Niebuhr and the Issues of our Time* (Mowbray, 1986).

[18] Richard Harries, 'Application of Just War Criteria in the Period 1959–89', in Richard Sorabji and David Rodin (eds.), *The Ethics of War* (Ashgate, 2006). See also Richard Harries, *Christianity and War in a Nuclear Age* (Mowbray, 1986).

a number of states, and the problem of proliferation not solved. The moral issue posed by their existence has not gone away.[19] There is also, of course, the threat posed by terrorists willing to commit suicide, who are not deterred by any threat of force against them.

At a more public level, the Campaign for Nuclear Disarmament (CND) became a mass organization, with a number of Christians playing a prominent role. Some of the Christians who supported it described themselves as nuclear pacifists, whilst others regarded themselves as pacifists per se. Overall the issue of nuclear weapons resulted in a new interest in Christian pacifism, both in its principled form and its political possibilities. One expression of this was a conviction amongst some that non-violent resistance was not only the morally right course of action, but could be the most effective method of achieving a desired political goal. The success of Gandhi in the struggle for Indian independence was held out as a model, and this approach still remains a key element in the thinking of some, with later successes including Corazon Aquino's overthrow of the corrupt Philippine dictatorship of Marcos by non-violent methods in the 1980s. Sceptics doubt whether such methods would have had much effect on Hitler or Stalin.

At the same time as the debate over the morality of nuclear weapons was continuing there was another equally contentious discussion over whether Christians should support revolutionary violence. In many parts of the world liberation movements against colonial regimes were achieving success, whilst in Latin America liberation theology was seeking to empower the poor to achieve social justice. Liberation theology often was accompanied by a Marxist analysis of society, and some of its proponents were attracted by the analysis of violence of Franz Fanon. Amongst Christians there were those who advocated only peaceful means in the overthrow of despotic regimes responsible for economic oppression and exploitation, but others, such as the Colombian priest Camillo Torres, said that the Christian who is not a revolutionary is living in sin, and it is the job of the revolutionary to make the revolution.[20]

In all this debate there was an extraordinary lack of historical awareness. For there is in the Christian tradition a theory of justified tyrannicide, as well as a theory of just revolution in Catholic theology, and of justified overthrow of governments in Calvinistic thinking.[21] Two key issues emerge for those who are not pacifists. One is the question of obedience to the state, so strongly enjoined in the New Testament. How can an overthrow of the government ever be justified in the light of that teaching, and of the first of the Just War criteria that war can only

---

[19] Brian Wicker and Hugh Beach (eds.), *Britain's Bomb: What Next?* (SCM, 2006).

[20] This debate helped to clarify a distinction, not always supported, between force, which is the legal, moral and proportionate use of coercion, and violence which is its illegal, immoral, and disproportionate deployment.

[21] Richard Harries, *Should a Christian Support Guerillas?* (Lutterworth, 1982).

be authorized by legitimate authority? The German theologian Thielicke, having in mind both the Nazi state and the Soviet system, argued that Romans 13 must be balanced by Revelation 13. In the latter the state has usurped the function of God and has therefore become demonic. It is no longer the state referred to by St Paul, and it has therefore no claim on our obedience. Others, drawing more on political philosophy, argued that all governments depend in the end on the consent of the people, and it is possible for a government to appear to govern, as in Iran under the Shah, who had the full panoply of army and secret police, when in fact the people had withdrawn their consent.

The other issue is that of success. The Just War tradition lays down that there must be a reasonable chance of success, but liberation forces cannot usually win military victories. This forces a re-examination of what is meant by success in different contexts. Success for a liberation force was possible if it stayed in existence long enough and was enough of a nuisance to achieve its political goals. It succeeded in doing this if it won and retained the loyalty of the constituency in whose name it sought to act. This is an issue with a renewed relevance in the struggle against terrorism.

Whereas the debate over nuclear weapons was dominated by considerations drawn from *ius in bello*, with the end of the Cold War and the increasing frequency of conventional wars, together with a new stress on humanitarian intervention and the obligation to protect, there has been a renewed emphasis on the criteria drawn from *ius ad bellum*. These have been to the fore in thinking about the Falklands War (1982), the expulsion of Saddam Hussein from Kuwait (1991), the Kosovo campaign (1999), and the invasions of Afghanistan (2001) and Iraq (2003).[22]

A frequent criticism of Just War thinking in recent decades has been that the conditions of modern warfare and the weaponry have changed so much that it is no longer relevant. Just the opposite is true. In the discussion of nuclear weapons, for example, it was the *ius in bello* principles that both nuclear pacifists and supporters of nuclear deterrence used in their arguments. A recent high level UN report adopted by the Assembly has come up with a set of criteria that must be met for military intervention which is virtually identical to those of the Christian tradition.[23] This is a remarkable tribute to its contemporary applicability. It is also important to note, however, as has also emerged in the discussion so far, that the criteria are not to be applied in a static, wooden way. They need to take into account the changing circumstances in which military action is used, as was instanced in the case of force used to overthrow manifest and long-standing

---

[22] For a succinct modern statement of the tradition in relation to these conflicts, see Charles Guthrie and Michael Quinlan, *Just War—The Just War Tradition: Ethics in Modern Warfare* (Bloomsbury, 2007).

[23] *Report of a High-Level Panel on Threats, Challenges and Change, a Report to the UN General Assembly* (Dec. 2004).

tyranny above. The criteria have been set out in various ways over the years, but the list below is one way, with points noted that particularly have to be taken into account today in the application of *ius ad bellum*:

1. Military action must be authorized by the highest possible authority. This is because disputes at a level below this will always have a higher authority to which appeal can be made to adjudicate and resolve the issue without recourse to force. In the modern world most Christians would argue that we now have the basis for an authority above that of a single nation-state in the United Nations, and no military action should be initiated without that authority except in the most extreme circumstances. Some Christians have argued that Kosovo did provide an example of such circumstances but the 2003 invasion of Iraq did not.[24]

2. There must be just cause. Article 51 of the UN Charter reserves to every member state the right of self-defence, but the recent high-level panel report argues that in every other instance specified approval from the UN must be obtained. It does allow for the possibility of pre-emptive attacks, as did Grotius when the threat was immediate and serious, but argues that such an attack must be authorized by the UN.

   A recent important development of just cause has been the agreement by the UN that not only individual states but the UN itself has a 'Responsibility to protect populations from genocide, war crimes, ethnic cleansing and crimes against humanity' (paras. 138–40 of the 2005 World Summit Outcome, 15 September 2005).

3. Every peaceful method of resolving the dispute must first have been tried and found wanting. This cannot in fact mean waiting for ever or even a very long time, for an enemy occupier, for example, will be more firmly entrenched the longer they are allowed to remain and the human cost of removing them that much more difficult.

4. There must be a reasonable expectation that the ill unleashed by the military action will not outweigh any possible good. This is the kind of political calculation that statesmen have to make, but it is also important to note that it is a fundamental feature of Christian moral thinking. For a cause might be just in principle, but the proportion of evil to good so great, that military action would have to be judged disproportionate and therefore immoral.

5. There must be a reasonable chance of success. In some instances what counts as success is clear enough—the expulsion of the Argentinians from the Falklands, for example, or of Saddam Hussein from Kuwait. But in counter-terrorism a more sophisticated answer is necessary, as was the case for both revolutionary and counter-revolutionary struggles, whose example is relevant here. Extremist

---

[24] Charles Reed and David Ryall (eds.), *The Price of Peace: Just War in the Twenty First Century* (Cambridge University Press, 2007).

terrorists cannot win great military battles. What they can do is be enough of a threat and stay in existence long enough until they have achieved their political goals. Whether or not they succeed in doing this will depend on whether they can win and retain the loyalty of the constituency in whose name they are using terror. This means that a sound counter-terrorist strategy must always bear in mind that this is primarily a struggle of hearts and minds, a struggle for the allegiance of the constituency in whose name the terrorists say they act. That is why the phrase 'war against terror' is so damaging. It implies that the main means to be used is military. Military means are very likely to have to be used, but the strategy is not primarily about winning military victories.[25]

The expression 'Just War' is an unfortunate one in many respects, so it is important to state what it does and does not imply. It is very different, for example, to a crusade mentality or belief that a holy war is being fought. A crusade is based on the belief that one side is fighting for God against God's enemies. A crusade mentality can arise even if a crusade has not been formally declared, as when (so it is alleged) during the Cold War stickers and badges were seen in America bearing the slogan 'Kill a commie for Christ'. In contrast to this, those who take part in a way that they believe meets the traditional criteria will still be conscious that sin lies on both sides. This need not and should not lead to a moral relativism. A choice still has to be made, but it is made in the awareness of universal human frailty and sin. This attitude is well expressed in some of the prayers that Reinhold Niebuhr wrote for use during World War II, with sentences like: 'We pray for wicked and cruel men, whose arrogance reveals to us what the sin of our own hearts is like when it has conceived and brought forth its final fruit'; and again: 'Help us to recognize our own affinity with whatever truculence or malice is confronting us that we may not add to the world's woe by the fury of our own resentments.'

This means that in war there will always be a sense of failure and tragedy that it has come to this, even when the cause is manifestly a just one. The Duke of Wellington expressed the spirit well when he remarked that: 'There is only one thing sadder than winning a military victory.' Only one thing.

The tradition of Christian pacifism based on the distinctive teaching and example of Jesus, which found expression in the early church, which was strongly advocated by some Reformation sects, and which became a powerful influence between the two world wars of the twentieth century, remains in existence today and continues to act as a witness to one aspect of the totality of Christian truth. Most pacifists, however, are not content simply with teaching the principle of non-resistance. They will encourage resistance of a non-violent kind. They will work for the strengthening of the United Nations. They will be active in peacemaking and

[25] *Countering Terrorism: Power, Violence and Democracy Post 9/11*, Report of a Working Group of the Church of England's House of Bishops (Church House Bookshop, SW1, 2005).

conflict-resolution. In all this they may be working alongside many who do not define themselves as pacifists. Those with both approaches will regard themselves as bringing to bear on the world the example and teaching of the Prince of Peace who said: 'Blessed are the peacemakers, for they shall be called the children of God.'

That said, there nevertheless remains a fundamental contrast between those who think the teaching and example of Christ calls for an obedience of not resisting violence with violence in every aspect of life, public as well as private, and those who think that under the conditions of finite, sinful existence, the conditions and restraints of the Just War tradition are the best way of balancing the different moral claims upon us. I believe that some kind of contrast is inescapable and goes back to the New Testament itself.

The church has had different ways of living with this double perspective. There was a time when it was thought there were two classes of Christians, those who married and had children and could legitimately join the army, and those who became priests and, better still, monks. Luther rightly rejected this idea of two classes of Christians, but came up with his own way out of the difficulty by differentiating between what might be morally permissible in a public role and what was permissible as a private citizen. Although there is some truth in this, there cannot be a total dichotomy, for Jesus' ethic of the Kingdom of God bears upon the totality of life, public and private.

There are those who totally reject these attempts at accommodation and argue that the ethic of the Kingdom has to be applied to all aspects of life in total obedience. As Ronald Sider and Richard Taylor have written: 'We do not believe God has a double ethic. We do not believe God ordains a higher ethic for especially devout folk and a lower ethic for the masses. We do not believe that God intends Christians to wait until the millennium to obey the Sermon on the Mount. We do not believe God commands one thing for the individual and another for the same person as a public official.'[26] What this does not take into account, however, is that Christians in the New Testament were conscious of living between the times, between the time of Christ's rising and the time of his coming again in glory.

Jesus lived and taught non-retaliation, and called his close followers to live this out as part of their life in the new milieu of God's rule on earth. This is the clear, ineradicable impression left on the whole New Testament. It was particularly applicable to the context of the early Christians, with their sense of being threatened by both Jews and gentiles At the same time, according to the Gospels, Jesus respected Roman centurions and did not call on them to leave their positions. Furthermore, the writers of the Epistles have a positive role for the use of coercion by rulers. Whilst this may in part reflect the attitude of the early church to authority, as an expression of their desire for a low profile as loyal citizens, it

---

[26] Ronald J. Sider and Richard K. Taylor, *Nuclear Holocaust and Christian Hope* (Hodder & Stoughton, 1983), 152.

seems to reflect the genuine attitude of Jesus himself. Both his teaching on non-retaliation and this positive attitude to secular authority have to seen against the background of the imminent arrival of the Kingdom, which Jesus proclaimed and ushered in. In this new order all would be transformed and God's universal reign of peace and justice established. There would be no need for the use of military force.

Because of the imminent arrival of the rule of God in human affairs, when the old order would pass away, the first Christians were not particularly conscious of the tension between the teaching of Jesus on non-retaliation, which they sought to put into practice in their personal lives, and his attitude to the Roman military. Nor did it trouble the church for nearly another 150 years, for they were a counter-cultural sect who sought only to be left in peace to worship God and witness to their faith. However, the context changed dramatically in the fourth century when Christians found themselves in positions of authority in the state responsible for exercising power. Then it was clear, whether or not it had been before, that the non-retaliation which they were still urged to practice in their personal lives was not applicable in the ordering of public life. It seemed to them that the use of coercion in the service of public order was in accord with the will of God.

So long as we live on this earth we are conscious of a contrast, even a tension, between the use of force which is necessary for civic and international order and principled non-retaliation, which can point to that ultimate state of affairs when suffering love has triumphed over all evil. This contrast is ineradicable for as long as we must remain here, poised between the time of Christ's rising and his coming again in glory. We have a responsibility to share in what is necessary to maintain the just order of the world, including the use of moral, legally authorized, and proportionate coercion, but this proximate will of God is always open to the challenge and judgement of God's ultimate purpose, the Kingdom which Jesus set before us, that transformed order in which coercion has no place.

FURTHER READING

GREGORY M. REICHBERG, HENRIK SYSE, and ENDRE BEGBY (eds.), *The Ethics of War: Classic and Contemporary Readings*. Oxford: Blackwell, 2006.
RICHARD HARRIES and STEPHEN PLATTEN (eds.), *Reinhold Niebuhr and Contemporary Politics: God and Power*. Oxford: Oxford University Press, forthcoming.

CHAPTER 18

THE BIBLE AND ANTI-SEMITISM

TOBIAS NICKLAS

'The Bible and Anti-Semitism' is a prima facie case of connecting two worlds that seem repugnant to each other: How can there be a connection between Anti-Semitism and the Bible, when the first part of the latter (the Old Testament) deals with the salvific history of the people of Israel and the second part (the New Testament) narrates the story of Jesus of Nazareth, his disciples, and Paul—all of them Jews (and probably remaining Jewish for their whole lives)?

Even so, and with good reason, an elaborate discussion has been going on for decades over whether, and if so, to what extent, some passages, in particular of the New Testament, are anti-Jewish or admit anti-Jewish interpretations. Especially 1Thessalonians 2:15–16; John 8:44, or Matthew 27:25 come to mind—but the array of examples could be well extended. The polemic usage of biblical passages in anti-Jewish homilies or ancient tracts can be adduced as another instance—particularly well-known are texts like the Epistle of Barnabas, Melito of Sardis' sermon 'On the Passover' (*Peri Pascha*), or John Chrysostom's homilies 'Against the Jews'.

This field, however, is not the issue here. First of all, the terms 'anti-Judaism' and 'anti-Semitism' have to be distinguished from each other: whereas the usual term for religious motifs leading to hostility toward Jews is anti-Judaism, the term 'anti-Semitism' should only be used when said hostility is motivated by nationalistic and economic ideas, but most of all by scientific racism. Although it is difficult to distinguish both phenomena from each other with complete selectivity, 'anti-Semitism' (or even 'racial anti-Semitism') in the narrow sense of the word cannot be made out earlier than the nineteenth century. Another phenomenon is closely related to this: interestingly enough, in nineteenth- and early twentieth-century Germany an 'Aryan Christianity' developed, and in the course of this development a peculiar relation emerged between religion and anti-Semitism motivated by scientific racism. Saul Friedländer names this phenomenon 'salvific anti-Semitism' (Friedländer 1998: 101). One of this phenomenon's aspects in particular shall be the centre of the present chapter: the misuse of biblical texts in order to underpin the ideology of an 'Aryan' or 'German Christendom' (see Bergen 1996, as well as Meier ²2001).

Therefore, the topic of the present chapter can be specified as follows: seen against the backdrop of anti-Semitic ideologies, to what extent were biblical texts of the Old and New Testament misused in order to uphold anti-Semitic ideas or within the framework of anti-Semitic propaganda? In the present case there is, of course, no room for the intention of being exhaustive. Besides, it does not seem reasonable to provide an overview which orientates itself predominantly by historical developments (for such an overview see Fenske 2005).

In what follows I intend to choose a different approach and point towards typical, regularly appearing motifs, which can be encountered in anti-Semitically motivated exegesis, especially in the National Socialist milieu. The same exegesis reappears—fatally enough—in the form of stereotypically reiterated statements among authors who can by no means be reproached with an anti-Jewish or anti-Semitic mindset. The case becomes even more precarious once said stereotypes catch on in wide circles of the church and society—to break through them after their acceptance involves an immense struggle and strain.

FUNDAMENTALS

Several differing variations on the fundamental type of anti-Semitically motivated exegesis exist. This exegesis often rests on the following cornerstones, which then lead to further derivations: (1) a dissociation of Jewishness that can take different shapes is attributed to Jesus of Nazareth. Its most extreme form attempts to prove Jesus' 'Aryan' origin; other cases distance Jesus from the Judaism of his time and try to preserve at least parts of the Old Testament for Christianity.

Both cases are accompanied by (2) a general devaluation of the Judaism at the time of Jesus, calling it 'late Judaism'. The second point implies the following differentiations: the devaluation of Jewish literature, from the period of the Second Temple onwards (this includes a rejection of apocalyptic literature in particular, dismissing it as eschatological enthusiasm that bears no reference to revelation), and the construction of a historical distortion of an alleged pharisaic-rabbinic reign of terror that displays almost totalitarian characteristics. Again and again, this idea is combined with the conception of ancient Judaism already attempting to achieve world dominion by hook or by crook (see mainly Bertram 1940 and 1943). Eventually, the blame for Jesus' execution is solely put on 'the Jews' at the time of Jesus, whereas the role of Pontius Pilate is repressed. Associated with this is the lack of appropriate consideration of early Jewish and rabbinic sources in the course of the argumentation; instead, only excerpts of these texts are called on in order to support blanket judgements, without further enquiries about their historical classification, plausibility, and significance.

However, Jesus' dissociation from Jewishness means that Jesus has to be distanced also from the holy scriptures of Israel, the Old Testament. There are different ways of accomplishing this dissociation (see also Nicolaisen 1966 and Kusche 1991): (1) with the aid of a flat devaluation of the Old Testament, declaring it a text that reveals a sinister image of God, which has nothing in common with the true God who reveals himself in the New Testament; or (2) by means of a (mostly) strict separation of pre-exile and post-exile Judaism; or (3) by detecting two different tendencies in the Old Testament—one is alleged to be 'Jewish' and is devalued, while the other part is said to criticize Judaism and its practice of religion. While the Torah is most often regarded as an example of the first orientation, the prophetic texts are usually attributed to the second tendency.

The first of these 'solutions' has occupied Christianity ever since Marcion. Fatally enough, not only self-confessed anti-Semites but also authors like the distinguished church historian Adolph von Harnack paid influential attention to this 'solution' in the early twentieth century (Harnack ²1924: 217). Their contributions have been frequently cited up to the present day. Some of their worst spin-offs are to be found in the writings of one of the chief ideologists of National Socialism, Alfred Rosenberg (1893–1946), author of *Der Mythus des 20. Jahrhunderts* ('The Myth of the Twentieth Century'), a book in which he calls for the abolition of the Old Testament so that 'the unsuccessful attempt of the last thousand and a half years to make us spiritually into Jews' would cease. As a substitute 'for the Old Testament stories of pimps and cattle dealers' he intended to let 'the Nordic sagas and stories appear, at first simply told, later as symbols' (Rosenberg, ²1941: 603 and 614).

The second and more moderate variant affiliates with the concept of Israel diverging from its original revelation and with its alleged evolvement into late Judaism or rabbinic Judaism, whereby the critical dividing-line between 'Israel' and 'Judaism' is mostly placed in the exilic period (see already De Wette 1813). At least this alternative still tolerates the concept of Jesus being a Jew, although his ideas are said to have clearly differed from those of his contemporaries.

Finally, the theory of two different tendencies in the Old Testament could be expressed in various ways (cf. Fenske 2005: 194–8). Beside the approach of differentiating between 'Israelitism' and 'Judaism', there was the effort of making a distinction between divine revelation and traditional thinking, or putting the emphasis on the prophets' contraposition towards the Jewish people.

In addition, in this process the early Christian sources have to be reassessed as well, and texts that portray a Jewish Jesus tend to be devalued: it was supposed that early Christianity, still under a strong Jewish influence, barely understood the religious genius Jesus of Nazareth—some authors even go as far as to claim that a proper comprehension of Jesus' nature could have only been possible in an 'Aryan'—Germanic—context. Surprisingly enough, the Gospel according to Matthew (which is repeatedly criticized nowadays because of its anti-Jewish potentialities) was rejected by several authors due to its alleged tendency to turn him back into a Jew, whereas the Gospel according to John became the focus of interest. Artur Dinter (1876–1948), for example, went so far to call John's Gospel the 'most virulent anti-Semitic writing that has ever been produced' (Dinter 1922: 92).

THE 'ARYAN JESUS'

As Albert Schweitzer testifies in his book *The Quest of the Historical Jesus* (first edition 1906, second edition 1923), most of the important nineteenth-century biographies of Jesus reveal more information on the ideals of the author writing them than on the historical Jesus himself (cf. Schweitzer ⁹1984). Schweitzer writes that the authors involved in the 'quest for the historical Jesus' did not sketch an 'objective picture' of the historical Jesus; rather, they projected themselves into their images of Jesus (more or less unconsciously so). As we know today, Schweitzer's observations held a core that is of abiding, categorical validity, applicable not only to the nineteenth-century writings he criticized: it is impossible to objectively reconstruct 'history' because the past is beyond reach and only to some extent mirrored in sources which again are selective and composed from a subjective perspective. First of all, the available sources have to be inspected in a methodically immaculate manner to determine if and to what extent they are mirroring 'facts'. The facts on their own do not constitute 'history', for it cannot be 'constructed' before the 'facts' are sensibly interconnected and interpreted. Of necessity, the interpreter always plays a part in this process. That is to say, there will never be a perfectly 'objective' portrayal of the historical Jesus of Nazareth. However, this does not mean that the scholar working in historical terms is delivered from his responsibility, or that there are no 'limits of interpretation' of the material. Whenever the contents of the sources fade into the background, when they are handled without methodical correctness or with a lack of responsibility, and especially when their only remaining purpose is to be misused as a prop for the ideology supported by the interpreter, then it is clear that these limits have been exceeded. This turns the historian's work into a balancing act which requires a high degree of constant self-reflection. The evaluation of Jesus of Nazareth not only determines 'the' Christian faith, but is also connected to ancient gulfs between confessions and between various possibilities of ideologization. So, when it comes to a figure like Jesus of Nazareth, a theologian researching in the historic field carries a particularly heavy responsibility. At the same time, the danger of ideological appropriation is particularly great. How dangerous such a violation of the 'limits of interpretation' can be is made manifest in the attempts to detach Jesus from his Jewish origin in order to make him agreeable to 'German Christianity' against the backdrop of National Socialist ideologies.

The most extreme attempts to separate Jesus and Jewishness from each other completely denied Jesus' Jewish origin and tried to prove his alleged Aryan origin instead. However, to achieve this all kinds of methodically unjustifiable tricks and dodges had to be applied. First was the idea of two different 'racial' tendencies in Judaism, that dates back to the nineteenth century and is a resumption of the aforementioned concept of two tendencies within the Old Testament (cf. Fenske 2005: 32, 194–8). Among other things it represents the thesis that even before the Jews established themselves in Israel there would have been Aryans or Teutons residing in the area. This kind of a thesis permits the detection of 'Aryan' thinking in at least some parts of the Old Testament; at the same time it also allows one to imagine that Jesus was an Aryan who was misunderstood by his Jewish contemporaries (and that centuries later other 'Aryans' like Meister Eckhart or Martin Luther have rediscovered his true significance).

Secondly, the Galilean parentage of Jesus of Nazareth is frequently turned into the jumping-off point for arguing that the Galilean area was characterized by heathenism to a great extent, or was forced to adopt Judaism, at best. It is claimed that the native people, a group to which Jesus' parents belonged, were mostly Aryan Galatians. Ernest Renan's famous and influential *Leben Jesu* ('The Life of Jesus', 1863) proceeds on the assumption that there was basically a mixture of various peoples residing in Galilee, and whereas Hermann Freiherr von Soden (1852–1914) wrote that Galilee at the time of Jesus was 'still perhaps half occupied by non-Jews' (Soden 1909: 113–14; see also Fenske 2005: 124), he did not link this with a precise statement about Jesus' parentage. The long-time (1933–45) dean of the Göttingen Faculty of Theology, Emanuel Hirsch, took a bold step further in 1939: 'the probability of a Galilean in the time of Jesus not having a single drop of Jewish blood must be 9 to 1' (Hirsch 1939: 161; cf. also Fenske 2005: 226). It goes without saying that no evidence whatsoever is given for numbers like these.

Thirdly, in order to prove that Jesus' father (or grandfather) was not of Jewish but of Greek descent, authors frequently refer to the rather obscure 'Panthera tradition' (Fenske 2005: 14–16, 144–5). In his *Contra Celsum* Origen quoted probably the oldest-known evidence of the tradition of Jesus being the illegitimate child of a soldier called Panthera (*Cels.* 1.32). The tradition re-emerges in various alternate forms in some passages of rabbinic literature and eventually in the Jewish 'anti-Gospel', the *Toledot Yeshu*. The origin of the tradition is obscure—it might derive from a play upon the Greek word for 'virgin' (*parthenos*) and the name of the alleged father of Jesus, called *pantheros* or *panthera* in the texts (Maier 1978: 267 and 314, n. 625). In these late sources the information is given in order to sully even the circumstances of Jesus' birth as much as possible, but there were circles that did not wish to accept a Jewish Jesus and went to any lengths to turn Jesus into an Aryan—so they seized on the idea and attempted to justify it. Walter Grund-mann, who became very influential from 1939 onwards in his position as the academic director of the Institute for Research into and Elimination of Jewish Influence in German Church Life (based in Eisenach), made an effort to prove that Mary was 'a Galilean non-Jew' in his book *Jesus der Galiläer und das Judentum* ('Jesus the Galilean and Judaism', Grundmann 1940: 196). As a consequence, the same campaign had to be conducted with regard to Jesus' paternal bloodline. To achieve this, he referred to the purported antiquity of the Panthera tradition and at the same time disavowed the words of the Synoptics as 'apologetical'. Interestingly enough, even the assertions made in the Panthera tradition are not taken seriously; instead the father of Jesus is turned into his grandfather—the distorting of the source material could hardly be more extreme. Grundmann writes (ibid. 198–9):

[But Panthera] is an altogether un-Jewish name. It is impossible for it to have been the name of one of the descendants of David. The logical conclusion is that the name belongs to a Galilean who himself, under the influence of very strong Judaizing, assumed or retained a second name, and who also gave his children names from the Old Testament. If we assume that Jesus' mother was in all probability of Galilean non-Jewish origin, then on the basis of various observations we are compelled to follow the same reasoning for his father . . . In the Christian community it was held that the Jewish tradition, however, made the son of Panthera's son himself Panthera's son, and later this Panthera was turned into a soldier who seduced Mary and fathered Jesus.

The image of the Aryan Jesus is often linked with the idea that Jesus was living in a deadly controversy with Judaism. For instance, Georg Bertram, who acted as Grundmann's successor in the post of director of the above-mentioned Institute from 1943 onwards, attributes the Occident's rescue from Jewish claims to world domination to Jesus (1943: 88–9): 'In actual fact though, the power [of Judaism] was broken after Jesus of Nazareth set an axe to the root of Jewish aspiration for power and thus protected the West from subjugation to the Jewish cult of Mam-mon. . . . Jesus of Nazareth's message protected the West from Judaism.'

A wider distribution than such so-called 'scholarly' books was achieved by works addressed to a more general clientele—these writings adopt the same concepts but their expression is much more drastic in some cases. One example is the *Anti-Semitic Christian Compendium* (dedicated to Julius Streicher!), published in 1935 in Vienna and Dresden. In pithy terms it describes Christ as the 'most ardent anti-Semite of all time' (for further information cf. Schenk 2002: 226–7; Heer 1981:

365–76). Some popular writings published by the aforementioned Institute were produced in vast numbers. Not only *Die Botschaft Gottes* ('The Message of God', a version of the New Testament deleting, as far as possible, all reference to the Jewish roots of Jesus and the Early Christian church) was issued from the Institute, but also a 'de-Judaicized' hymnbook and the catechism *Deutsche mit Gott: Ein deutsches Glaubensbuch* ('Germans with God: A German Confessional', 1941), which says, among other things (Grundmann 1941: 46, adapted from Heschel 2002: 78–9):

Jesus of Nazareth in Galilee demonstrates in his message and conduct a spirit that is in all respects opposed to Judaism. The struggle between him and the Jews became so relentless that it led to his crucifixion. So Jesus cannot have been a Jew. Until this day the Jews have persecuted Jesus and all who follow him with implacable hatred. By contrast, Aryans in particular found in Jesus the answer to their most private and deeply felt questions. So he became the Saviour of the Germans.

Further comment on these sentences—published in 1941 in Weimar in an edition of more than 100,000 copies—is unnecessary.

PAUL

The points mentioned so far have focused mainly on the portrayal of Jesus of Nazareth, on the exegesis of the New Testament Gospels, and on theses about the Old Testament that were motivated by the former two topics. Compared with this, Paul of Tarsus fades into the background. Nevertheless, it is intriguing to observe what kind of exegeses of Paul's writings anti-Semitic authors of the nineteenth and twentieth centuries undertook. Nowadays we would consider the Jew Paul as probably the leading historical personality in the opening-up of Christianity for the 'nations', thus providing a vital basis for its global implementation. Many anti-Semitically minded authors, however, tended to reject him as 'too Jewish' (see information by Bell 2005: 355–64).

Paul is blamed for the alleged 're-Judaicizing' of Christianity. The Göttingen Orientalist scholar Paul de Lagarde (1827–91), for example, accuses Paul of being to blame for the church's adoption of the Old Testament, under 'the influence of which the Gospel, in so far as this is possible, has been ruined' (De Lagarde 1934 [1873]: 68). Another group of authors envisions Paul as being in two minds about his Jewish background, which he never abandoned, even after he became a Christian: typically of this ambivalent, but altogether hostile attitude towards Paul is an essay written in 1943 by the aforementioned Georg Bertram. Bertram poses the question to what extent Paul, 'who was once sent to Damascus by the Jewish central authority,' remained 'deep in his own mind a Jewish envoy, even as a Christian apostle' (Bertram 1943: 90). Unlike Jesus, Paul, 'a real Jew by origin' (ibid.), is identified as such: although Paul had understood Jesus' major ideas at least, he was never able to wholly cast off Judaism. Bertram tries to attest this circumstance by commenting on Paul's attitude towards the state, his alleged support of the centrality of Jerusalem, his alleged syncretism, and several other points. He adds that, for all these reasons, the Christianity promulgated by Paul is a 'judaicized' Christianity, with negative effects only. In accordance with this, Bertram accords a certain historical significance to Paul but scorns him nevertheless as 'too Jewish', because Bertram's ideal is, of course, a Christianity purified of any Jewish influence.

Apparently, Bertram was not alone in this opinion. In her study on the Institute for Research into and Elimination of Jewish Influence in German Church Life of Eisenach, Susannah Heschel writes (2002: 81–2):

> In their discussions on how Christianity could be 'de-Judaized', the members of the Institute also talked about how 'Judaism' should be defined. Eisenhuth [i.e. Heinz Eisenhuth, Professor of Systematic Theology, Jena] was of the opinion that the entire 'Old Testament' including the Books of the Prophets ought to be eliminated; while the 'New Testament' should be cleansed of all texts except for the four Gospels—he considered Paul a Jewish theologian.

AFTER-EFFECTS

Although some prominent names have already been mentioned in connection with the major conceptions of anti-Semitic Christianity, it is important to emphasize that these few were neither isolated cases nor did these scholars (at least the ones discussed here) promulgate their theses out of fear of the regime—instead, one has to assume that many authors wrote as they did out of conviction, including at least some who wielded considerable influence even after World War II. It is important to recognize that many of these authors were able to propagate their ideas in publications that had continuing effects even after 1945. Most notably, however, it becomes apparent that at least in some cases ideas with an anti-Jewish or anti-Semitic background developed a momentum of their own and turned into 'scholarly legends': repeated stereotypical opinions that are held, and will continue to be held, by even well-intentioned exegetes and theologians of the latest generation.

The most specific and best-known example, which still exerts immense influence, is the famous *Theologische Wörterbuch zum Neuen Testament* ('Theological Dictionary of the New Testament', henceforth *ThWNT*)—a resource that has been frequently called on up to the present day to answer questions on New Testament exegesis. Not only was its first volume released in 1933—the year of Adolf Hitler's *Machtergreifung* ('seizure of power')—but it was initiated and directed until the end of the war by Gerhard Kittel, who had been a member of the NSDAP since 1933. Certainly, Kittel's attitude does not imply the nature of his whole staff's mindset: whereas, apart from Kittel, several staff members of the *ThWNT* held leading positions at the aforementioned Eisenach Institute (e.g. W. Grundmann, K. G. Kuhn, G. Bertram, H. Odeberg, C. Schneider, H. Preisker, und G. Delling) and some others, like Ethelbert Stauffer, supported the 'German Christianity' movement, there were others again who, like Rudolf Bultmann, repudiated National Socialist ideology in the strongest terms (cf. Vos 1984: 91). Karl Ludwig Schmidt (1891–1956), who had been teaching in Bonn since 1929, contributed no fewer than four articles to the first volume, but in 1933 he was already about to be removed from his post by the National Socialists—in the very same year he had sought a public dialogue with Martin Buber (Johnson 1986: 20–3). It would, however, be inaccurate to conclude that the first-named authors' articles are full of awkward anti-Semitisms whereas other texts are completely free of concepts which could be at least potentially construed as anti-Jewish. At any rate, there is certainly no blatant example of anti-Semitism in Kittel's articles (Vos 1984: 93). All the more dangerous, however, are those passages which are based on an anti-Jewish argument that is not immediately recognizable as such: particularly extreme examples can be found in some of the contributions of Walter Grundmann and Georg Bertram (cf. Casey 1999: 286–9). The article κάκος in the third volume has to be attributed to W. Grundmann (1938*d*), the passages corresponding to the Septuagint, however, have been reworked by Bertram: in the paragraph titled 'τὸ κάκον als ethischer Begriff' appear some familiar anti-Semitic stereotypes concerning 'late Judaism'. It says, for instance (pp. 479–80): 'What was in the prophets a living interpretation of history, that issued from the living faith in God, has here [in what was later called Wisdom literature] become a frozen and distorted pattern into which everything is forced'; and a little later: 'The moral judgement of the Judaism of that time is as superficial and formulaic as that of the translator of Pro. [the Book of Proverbs in the Septuagint]. . . . It perfects the inflexibility of the moral and religious attitude that is typical of the legalistic piety of Judaism.'

There are similar phrases to be found in Rudolf Meyer's article καθαρός κτλ., also in the third volume (Meyer 1938): after certifying 'remnants of primitive thought' in relation to issues of purity and impurity in the concepts of the 'Old Testament religion' (p. 419), he labels the prophets 'the ones who paved the way for the religion of Jesus' (p. 420) because they demand ethnical purity, and later continues: 'It became the shortcoming of the late Jewish official religion that it granted the requirement of cultic purity excessive predominance over the innermost concerns of the religion, and it was incapable of rejecting the primitive. Both led to a disastrous distortion and petrification of the Jewish religion' (p. 420).

Whereas in the abovementioned examples the authors' ideological background leads to extremely distorting broad-brush presentations, there are, at the same time, even examples in which the New Testament texts are blatantly misinterpreted in order to make them useful to anti-Semitical exegeses. In this connection, Carl Schneider's article μέτωπον in the fourth volume can be mentioned (Vos 1984: 100–1). In his interpretation of Revelation 13:16; 14:9, and 20:4 Schneider writes (1942: 639):

In all three passages the sign of the beast is clearly an allusion to the tephillin, as the forehead and the hand are named. This would indicate an anti-Jewish way of thinking in the book of Revelation, and Rev. 13:16 therefore means: He who does not bear the tephillin will be boycotted by the Jews. In the Roman empire even at the time of Revelation one of the driving forces behind the persecution of Christians was the highly influential world Jewry at the Roman court since the days of Nero.

Many other statements made in the *ThWNT* and its absorption could be used to demonstrate the continuing effects of anti-Semitically motivated exegesis—but it is anything but a solitary case.

Grundmann published a number of books even after World War II, and these found a ready market—he wrote commentaries on the Synoptics, studies on the second quest for the historical Jesus, and several other contributions. Other authors kept active as well: Ethelbert Stauffer (1902–79) was not a member of the NSDAP but he sympathized with the 'German Christians' for a long time, and as early as 1933 came forward with a contribution entitled *Unser Glaube und unsere Geschichte: Zur Begegnung zwischen Kreuz und Hakenkreuz* ('Our Faith and Our History: Towards a Meeting between Cross and Swastika', Stauffer 1933). Stauffer's position during the time of the 'Third Reich' is certainly much more ambivalent than the attitude of Grundmann or Bertram; after all, he was removed from his post as vice-dean of the faculty of Bonn University in January 1943 because of anti-fascist statements made in a lecture on 'Augustus and Cleopatra'. But the extent to which his thinking was influenced by the stereotypes of anti-Semitic exegesis, even after World War II, is indicated, for example, by an overview article about Jesus of Nazareth. This article of more than 100 pages appeared in the prestigious standard work *Aufstieg und Niedergang der römischen Welt* ('Rise and Decline of the Roman World' (*ANRW*), 1982). In a staggeringly forthright manner Stauffer repeats in this contribution a whole raft of stereotypes of anti-Semitically motivated exegesis.

In Stauffer's discussion of the second quest for the historical Jesus, he claims that an image of Jesus evolves that is the image 'of a non-conformist ... an agent provocateur. This image has the advantage of making two historical facts intelligible to us: first the deadly hatred of Jesus prevalent in contemporary Judaism (which led to Jesus' crucifixion), and then the efforts of the early Church (manifested in the Gospels) to achieve a theology of intercession' (Stauffer 1982: 9). Therewith Jesus is detached as much as possible from his Jewish environment—in the immediate connection Stauffer only speaks about '*any possible* common ground between Jesus and late Judaism' (ibid., emphasis added).

Stauffer paints this negative picture of the Judaism of Jesus' time in lurid colours. In his contribution the reader meets with prejudices at every turn: not only does he characterize Pharisees as hypocrites, as the 'super pious' whose pastoral care he calls that of 'a belief mafia', he also does not shy away from calling them 'an abomination to God and Man' (ibid. 55). Most notably, however, he paints a picture of a Judaism that is oppressed by blinded Torah zealots, and leaders who had established a monitoring and spying system that evokes the actuality of totalitarian states in the twentieth century. Of course, this has nothing to do with the actual conditions in Jesus' day (see mainly ibid. 98–102). The question of how the editorial board of an international standard work could have allowed such a contribution to appear in print arises constantly while reading.

Conclusion: Aspects of the Contemporary Situation

A satifactory overview of the situation today is hardly possible—especially in only a few sentences. In many respects, the data necessary for scholarly investigation are missing—not surprisingly, as the topic is all-too-hotly disputed and it is easy enough to burn one's fingers. What is most important, however, is to differentiate between what emerges from scholarly round-table discussions and those bits of information which are actually reaching the governing body of the churches, the parishes, and public discourse. The following observations can only serve as examples of changes that have occurred over the past decades and can be interpreted as signs of a tendency that has an impact which is presently difficult to assess.

At least the concept of a 'late Judaism' outlined above now seems to be almost a thing of the past in scholarly circles. It was this concept that mostly went hand in hand with a lack of interest in or an obvious depreciation of the Jewish literature of Graeco-Roman times. It is mostly thanks to Karlheinz Müller that many of the related theories were consequently disposed of in the German-speaking area (1983: 103–17). Even after 1945, these theories made it easy to describe Jesus of Nazareth as a kind of misunderstood genius, who should not be imagined as a 'Jewish person'. The positive signals of a movement towards a clearly more balanced attitude are obvious: nowadays there is barely a scholarly publication using the term 'late Judaism'—a high degree of sensitivity has developed towards what the choice of this term might imply, and as a result the terms used in the discussion have changed to phrases like 'Early Judaism' or 'Middle Judaism', 'Judaism of the Second Temple' or 'Judaism of the Graeco-Roman Period'.

The tendency to dissociate the New Testament from the Old Testament has almost vanished from scholarly works, but it remains present in public awareness. One piece of evidence for this is (in the German-speaking area) the frequent omission of Old Testament lections during church services and the rarity of sermons pertaining to Old Testament texts. In most of these cases no one realizes that by this process the New Testament is deprived of its historical and literary roots and, like a 'plant without roots', it becomes stunted.

The 'double criterion of difference' developed by Ernst Käsemann has become a thing of the past by now, at least within the scope of the scholarly dialogue. This criterion located the core of our gainable knowledge of the historical Jesus just where the sources of statements on Jesus are not derived from his Jewish background, nor from the developments in the early parishes (which were still intensely characterized by Judaism). Among some authors of the so-called 'Third Quest', however, this does not rule out a new tendency to portray a historical Jesus with little connection to the Palestinian Jewishness of his time (cf. Pearson 1995).

In spite of these changes, of which at least some have set a trend which even reaches into official church documents, the relation of anti-Semitism and exegesis still remains potent. The material of anti-Semitic exegesis, its ideological background, and its direct and indirect consequences remain newsworthy—the problem is not a mere issue of the past, it is indeed 'historical' in the true sense of the word, as a problem posed by a past that still concerns us today. It is this topicality and relevance that make it a persistent challenge not only for historians, exegetes and theologians, but also for churches and society.

BIBLIOGRAPHY

BELL, R. H. (2005), *The Irrevocable Call of God. An Inquiry into Paul's Theology of Israel.* WUNT 184. Tübingen.

BERGEN, D. (1996), *Twisted Cross: The German Christian Movement in the Third Reich,* Chapel Hill, NC.

BERTRAM, G. (1940), 'Philo und die jüdische Propaganda in der antiken Welt', pp. 79–105 in *Christentum und Judentum. Studie zur Erforschung ihres gegenseitigen Verhältnisses,* ed. W. Grundmann. Leipzig.

——(1943), 'Paulus, Judensendling und Christusapostel', pp. 83–136 in *Germanentum, Christentum und Judentum. Studien zur Erforschung ihres gegenseitigen Verhältnisses,* ed. W. Grundmann, Leipzig.

CASEY, M. (1999), 'Some Anti-Semitic Assumptions in the *Theological Dictionary of the New Testament*', *Nov.T* 41: 280–91.

DE LAGARDE, P. (1934 [1886]), 'Die Religion der Zukunft', pp. 279–318 in *Deutsche Schriften 1*. Munich.

——(1934 [1873]), 'Über das Verhältnis des deutschen Staates zu Theologie, Kirche und Religion. Ein Versuch, Nicht-Theologen zu orientieren', pp. 45–90 in *Deutsche Schriften 1*. Munich.

DE WETTE, W. M. L. (1813), *Biblische Dogmatik Alten und Neuen Testaments. Oder kritische Darstellung der Religionslehre des Hebraismus, des Judenthums und Urchristentums*. Berlin.

DINTER, A. (1922), *Die Sünde wider die Liebe*. Leipzig and Hartenstein.

FENSKE, W. (2005), *Wie Jesus zum 'Arier' wurde: Auswirkungen der Entjudaisierung Christi im 19. und zu Beginn des 20. Jahrhunderts*. Darmstadt.

FRIEDLÄNDER, S. (1998), *Das Dritte Reich und die Juden. Die Jahre der Verfolgung 1933–1939*. Munich.

GRUNDMANN, W. (1938*a*), *Die Gotteskindschaft in der Geschichte Jesu und ihre religions-geschichtlichen Voraussetzungen*. Studien zu deutscher Theologie und Frömmigkeit 1. Weimar.

——(1938*b*), κράςω κτλ., *ThWNT* 3: 898–905.

——(1938*c*), καρτερέω κτλ., *ThWNT* 3: 619–22.

——(1938*d*), κάκος κτλ., *ThWNT* 3: 470–87.

——(1940), *Jesus der Galiläer und das Judentum*. Leipzig.

——(1941), *Deutsche mit Gott. Ein deutsches Glaubensbuch*. Weimar.

——(1956), *Die Geschichte Jesu Christi*. Berlin.

——(1975), *Jesus von Nazareth. Bürge zwischen Gott und Menschen*. Göttingen.

HARNACK, A. VON (²1924), *Marcion: Das Evangelium vom fremden Gott*. Leipzig.

HEAD, P. M. (2004), 'The Nazi Quest for an Aryan Jesus', *Journal for the Study of the Historical Jesus*, 2: 55–89.

HEER, F. (1981), *Gottes erste Liebe. Die Juden im Spannungsfeld der Geschichte*. Munich.

HESCHEL, S. (2002), 'Deutsche Theologen für Hitler. Walter Grundmann und das Eisena-cher "Institut zur Erforschung und Beseitigung des jüdischen Einflusses auf das deutsche kirchliche Leben"', pp. 70–90 in *Das missbrauchte Evangelium: Studien zu Theologie und Praxis der Thüringer Deutschen Christen*. Studien zu Kirche und Israel 20. Berlin.

HIRSCH, E. (1939), *Das Wesen des Christentums*. Weimar.

IMENDÖRFFER, B. *et al.*, eds. (1935), *Israel und die Völker*. Vienna (= Köber 1935).

JOHNSON, M. D. (1986), 'Power Politics and New Testament Scholarship in the Nationalist Socialist Period', *Journal of Ecumenical Studies*, 23: 1–24.

KITTEL, G. (1933), ἀββᾶ, *ThWNT* 1: 4–6.

KÖBER, R., ed. (1935), *Antisemitismus der Welt in Wort und Bild*. Dresden (= Imendörffer 1935).

KUSCHE, U. (1991), *Die unterlegene Religion. Das Judentum im Urteil deutscher Alttestamen-tler: Zur Kritik theologischer Geschichtsschreibung*, Studien zu Kirche und Israel 12. Berlin.

MAIER, J. (1978), *Jesus von Nazareth in der talmudischen Überlieferung*. EdF 82. Darmstadt.

MEIER, K. (2001), *Kreuz und Hakenkreuz. Die evangelische Kirche im Dritten Reich*. Munich.

MEYER, R. (1938), καθαρός κτλ., *ThWNT* 3: 416–27.

MÜLLER, K. (1983), *Das Judentum in der religionsgeschichtlichen Arbeit am Neuen Testament. Eine kritische Rückschau auf die Entwicklung einer Methodik bis zu den Qumranfunden*. Judentum und Umwelt 6. Frankfurt, Main, and Berne.

——(1991), 'Die frühjüdische Apokalyptik', pp. 35–173 in his *Studien zur frühjüdischen Apokalyptik*. SBB 11. Stuttgart.

NICOLAISEN, C. (1966), *Die Auseinandersetzungen um das Alte Testament im Kirchenkampf 1933–1945*. Hamburg.

PEARSON, B. (1995), 'The Gospel According to the Jesus Seminar', *Religion*, 25: 317–38.

RENAN, E. (1981 [1863]), *Das Leben Jesu*. Zürich.

ROSENBERG, A. (^{2}1941 [1930]), *Der Mythus des 20. Jahrhunderts. Eine Wertung der seelisch-geistigen Gestaltenkämpfe unserer Zeit*. Munich.

SCHENK, W. (2002), 'Der Jenaer Jesus', pp. 167–279 in *Das missbrauchte Evangelium: Studien zu Theorie und Praxis der Thüringer Deutschen Christen*, ed. P. von der Osten-Sacken. Studien zu Kirche und Israel 20. Berlin.

SCHNEIDER, C. (1942), μέτωπον, *ThWNT* 4: 638–40.

SCHWEITZER, A. (^{9}1984), *Die Geschichte der Leben-Jesu-Forschung*. Tübingen.

SODEN, H. VON (^{2}1909 [1904]), *Die wichtigsten Fragen im Leben Jesu*. Berlin.

STAUFFER, E. (1933), *Unser Glaube und die Geschichte. Zur Begegnung zwischen Kreuz und Hakenkreuz*. Stimmen aus der deutschen christlichen Studentenbewegung 86. Berlin.

——(1938), 'Die urchristliche Gottestatsache und ihre Auseinandersetzung mit dem Gottesbegriff des Judentums', *ThWNT* 3: 91–3.

——(1982). 'Jesus, Geschichte und Verkündigung', *ANRW* II.25.1: 3–130.

VOS, J. S. (1984), 'Antijudaismus/Antisemitismus im theologischen Wörterbuch zum Neuen Testament', *Nederlands Theologisch Tijdschrift*, 38: 89–110.

CHAPTER 19

DANTE AND THE BIBLE: A SKETCH

PIERO BOITANI

DANTE's *Commedia* is the poem which, in the author's own intentions, comes closest to the Bible and, more even than Milton's *Paradise Lost*, constitutes a re-Scripture. What I am going to offer here is a mere sketch of this rewriting, which focuses first on some general structural problems and then on selected passages of the poem.

I begin at the very beginning, with the *Commedia*'s *incipit*, 'nel mezzo del cammin di nostra vita' ('in the midst of the path of our life'). The first line of the poem is precisely modelled on Isaiah 38:10, when the prophet announces he is about to die and reach the gates of hell: 'in the cutting off of my days, I shall go to the gates of the grave' (AV). The Vulgate from which Dante drew is much closer to the *Inferno*: 'in dimidio dierum meorum vadam ad portas inferi.' There is daring closeness, here, to the sacred text, and Dante's identification with Isaiah is immediately striking, for indeed the poet implicitly proclaims himself to be a prophet and at the same time boldly rewrites the biblical text by replacing 'my' (*meorum*) with 'our' ('*nostra* vita'). For what is happening to Dante the pilgrim, the poem's protagonist, is part of a more general pattern which involves the whole of mankind, its—our—life. The poet and the prophet are each but a man, the representative of all human beings.

What we have at the very beginning of the *Commedia* is thus a prime example of the way in which Dante rewrites the Bible. The poem is not a re-Scripture structured like the Christian Bible itself, that is to say, a narrative of salvation which begins with Creation and ends at the end of time (with Revelation), going through the history of the patriarchs, of Israel, and of Jesus of Nazareth and his apostles, but an oblique rewriting in which the poet bends the original text to his own needs and aims. Parallels to the biblical sequence are indeed relevant to Dante's itinerary—and I shall point out some of them here—but they are always transformed by Dante.

To give but one example, the second biblical allusion in the poem is precisely to the Creation, when the protagonist has put the dark wood behind him and finds himself at the foot of the hill of virtue, where he is stopped by the leopard of lust. We are immediately given the hour of the day and season of the events about to unfold: a spring morning with the sun in the constellation of Aries, that is, the spring equinox, precisely the time of year when, according to medieval tradition, God had created the universe 6,498 years before:[1] when the sun 'was mounting with those stars which were with it when Divine Love first set in motion those fair things' (*montava 'n su con quelle stelle | ch'eran con lui quando l'amor divino | mosse di prima quelle cose belle*).

For one moment, as the sun of this first spring lightens the landscape, external and internal, the terror which had seized Dante in the dark wood seems to give way to hope. Light and hope are shot through with longing, made explicit in the two past tenses of the verbs, enacting the distance between the world's Beginning and its present. Dante clearly feels this nostalgia for the Beginning as some essential aspect of his own self: a feeling which is both sensual and intellectual. The idea of the beginning of all things allows him, imaginatively, to see and enjoy the sun and stars as 'cose *belle*', *fair* things, and not simply 'good', as Genesis has it. This first firmament possesses a *pulchritudo* of intimate and pristine aesthetics, like the dawn and the aura which the 'things' shed on everything surrounding them.

What this introductory Canto of the *Inferno* is also doing is attributing the Creation to divine 'love', in an operation which is both poetic and evangelical. Dante is possibly thinking of Thomas Aquinas's commentary on Aristotle's *Metaphysics*, where he states that the poet Hesiod, 'before the time of the philosophers', had placed love as 'principium rerum'.[2] The act of Creation is then envisaged by Dante, following Aristotle, as a first, primordial (*di prima*) impulse to the movement imparted by the Prime Mover to the celestial bodies, setting time and space in motion. The verb *mosse* in line 40 is a precise philosophical term which, followed by *cose belle*, is also perceived as an effortless gesture, as if God had given a light flick at some slender circle of light which, however, supported the entire weight of gravity of the universe. Genesis's 'Fiat lux', 'fiat firmamentum', and 'fiant luminaria' are thus translated from words into one silent, luminous touch, reflected by the light of the sun and the stars.

---

[1] For the precise date, 5200 BC, see *Paradiso* XXVI, 118–23; Genesis 5. 5; *Purgatorio* XXXIII, 61–3 and Eusebius, *Chronica*, in *Patrologia Graeca* 19, 530.

[2] 1 John 4.8: 'Deus est charitas'; Thomas Aquinas, *In Duodecim Libros*, p. 29.

It is difficult, then, to maintain that Dante has no specific poetics of Creation when these verses begin the wonderful rainbow which is completed in the very last line of *Paradiso*: *l'amor che move il sole e l'altre stelle*. Here, the 'desire and will' that Dante speaks of three lines before the end are finally fulfilled by the vision of God, and are directed by that same 'love which moves the sun and the other stars'; here Dante himself becomes, with the *cose belle* of *Inferno* I, an object of the Creation—of a Creation in whose end is its new and present Beginning.

The theme of Creation runs through the whole *Comedy*, down to Canto XXIX of *Paradiso*. Yet one would have to add immediately that the beginning of the journey is linked to a specifically Christian calendar as well. It is clear from various references in the poem (*Inferno* XXI, 112–14; *Inferno* I, 1; *Purgatorio* II, 97–9)[3] that the journey starts on the eve of Good Friday 1300, the year of the first Jubilee proclaimed by Boniface VIII. In other words, the story of the *Comedy* is tied to Christ's Passion, the crucial moment of the Incarnation, which is itself the central time in the history of Salvation. At the same time, that story takes place at a time when the first Holy Year proclaims general forgiveness for all sins and thus becomes part of actual, present history.

The descent to hell begins, as the opening of *Inferno* II suggests, at sunset on the eve of Good Friday. Dante's protestations to Virgil at that moment are also highly significant, because he tells his guide that he does not feel he is either Aeneas or Paul, who embarked on the journey to the other world before him. The reference is to *Aeneid* VI and to 2 Corinthians 12. A modern reader will probably be struck by the superimposition of these two stories, Aeneas' descent to Hades in the pagan poem by Virgil, and the Christian apostle Paul's *raptus* to paradise. Dante, on the other hand, tries to combine the classics and the Bible as much as possible and will often adopt two models, or two images—one from classical antiquity, one from Scripture—to clarify his meaning. I shall come back to this point presently. But before doing so, it might be opportune to note that in fact Dante does present himself as an Aeneas and a Paul. The first five Cantos of the *Inferno* brim with quotations from the *Aeneid*, and characters such as Charon or Minos stem straight out of Book VI of that poem. Nor does *Aeneid* VI stop radiating in Dante's mind in the *Inferno*. Its presence is still central in *Purgatorio* XXX, when Virgil disappears and Beatrice finally comes upon the scene, and in the poem's last Canto, *Paradiso* XXXIII, when the Sibyl's leaves are invoked. And the moment comes, in *Paradiso* XV, 25–7, when the answering of Cacciaguida's light to his descendant, Dante, is compared precisely to that of Anchises to his son, Aeneas, in *Aeneid* VI: 'Sì pia l'ombra d'Anchise si porse, | se fede merta nostra maggior musa, | quando in Eliso del figlio s'accorse' ('So piously the shade of Anchises offered itself, if we are to credit our greatest muse, when he recognized his son in Elysium'). Dante, then, *is*

---

[3] Baranski, '*Commedia*', p. 183.

Aeneas. And Paul. When he finally reaches paradise, the first thing he does as a poet is to repeat what Paul had written in 2 Corinthians 12: 'I knew a man in Christ above fourteen years ago, (whether in the body, I cannot tell; or whether out of the . body, I cannot tell: God knoweth;) such an one caught up to the third heaven . . . How he was caught up into paradise, and *heard unspeakable words, which it is not lawful for a man to utter.*'

> La gloria di colui che tutto move
> per l'universo penetra, e risplende
> in una parte più e meno altrove.
>   Nel ciel che più de la sua luce prende
> fu' io, e *vidi cose che ridire*
> *né sa né può chi di là sù discende.*
>
> (*Paradiso* I, 1–6)

Dante, then, *is* Paul—in fact, he is more than Paul, because three lines later he proceeds to declare that he will now sing what he has kept in his mind of the holy kingdom, of paradise. Paul was unwilling or unable to recount his heavenly vision; Dante thrusts forth with the help of all the nine Muses, Apollo the Word, and the Divine Wisdom of Minerva. In *Purgatorio* XXIX he had already proclaimed with unprecedented boldness that 'John is with *him*', and through the *Paradiso*, when he calls his poem 'sacro', he identifies with John and the 'scrittor de lo Spirito santo', in particular with David and his 'teodia' (*Paradiso* XXV, 1 and 73; XXIX, 41).

While the complex procession which unfolds at the top of the mountain of purgatory allegorically and hieratically re-enacts the entire history of salvation—including all the books of the Old and the New Testament, Christ the griffin, the animal-like evangelists, the Church in the form of a chariot—there is a sequence of biblical events which has particular relevance to the *Commedia*. This is the story recounted in Exodus. The souls of the penitent arriving at the island of purgatory on the boat guided by the angel sing Psalm 113 in the Vulgate, *In exitu Israel de Aegypto* (*Purgatorio* II, 46–8; the whole of the *Purgatorio* resounds of the singing of Psalms, and in particular of Psalm 50, the so-called *Miserere*). They thus signal their liberation from the chains of the flesh and of sin and their future entrance into the Promised Land, the glory of heaven which is Celestial Jerusalem. But the events of Exodus are precisely recalled in the opening scene of the poem, and Dante (or someone very close to him) has in fact provided an explanation for his work as a whole which rests on *In exitu Israel*. In maintaining that the meaning of the *Commedia* is not just one, but multiple (*polysemous*), the author of the Epistle to Cangrande specifies that there are four different 'senses'. He then adds (7):

And this mode of treatment, for its better manifestation, may be considered in this verse: 'When Israel came out of Egypt, and the house of Jacob from a people of strange speech, Judaea became his sanctification, Israel his power'. For if we inspect the letter alone the departure of the children of Israel from Egypt in the time of Moses is presented to us; if the allegory, our redemption wrought by Christ; if the moral sense, the conversion of the soul from the grief and misery of sin to the state of grace is presented to us; if the anagogical, the departure of the holy soul from the slavery of this corruption to the liberty of eternal glory is presented to us.

In short, the entire *Commedia* is an Exodus, and in *Paradiso* XXV Beatrice duly tells Saint James that Dante has been 'allowed to come from Egypt to Jerusalem in order for him to see' (55–7).

Let me concentrate now on a few particular passages to show how Dante uses the Bible locally. I will begin with *Inferno* XXVI, which everyone knows as the Canto of Ulysses. In his presentation of the scene, Dante works like a film director. First, he sketches in the general landscape of the bolgia (by means of the famous simile of the peasant resting at the top of the hill on a summer evening and looking down on the many fireflies), then closes in to concentrate on the flames which envelop the fraudulent (these had been identified as the 'fireflies' before), and finally focuses on one of them, which looks so 'divided' as 'the pyre on which Eteocles was placed with his brother', Polynices. The second movement of the sequence is explained by means of a biblical simile:

> E qual colui che si vengiò con li orsi
> vide 'l carro d'Elia al dipartire,
> quando i cavalli al cielo erti levorsi,
>   che nol potea sì con li occhi seguire,
> che'el vedesse altro che la fiamma sola,
> sì come nuvoletta, in sù salire:
>   tal si move ciascuna per la gola
> del fosso, ché nessuna mostra 'l furto,
> e ogne fiamma un peccatore invola.
>
> (*Inferno* XXVI, 34–42)

The passage Dante has in front of him and which his simile extends is 2 Kings 2 (1 and 11–12):

And it came to pass, when the Lord would take up Elijah into heaven by a whirlwind ... (*Factum est autem cum levare vellet Dominus Eliam per* turbinem *in caelum...*) that behold, there appeared a chariot of fire, and horses of fire, and parted them both asunder; and Elijah went up by a whirlwind into heaven (*ecce currus igneus, et equi ignei diviserunt utrumque: et ascendit Elias per* turbinem *in caelum*).

I shall return to the 'whirlwind' in a minute. The simile is on the whole fairly straightforward, if at the same time daring (for the flame of Elijah's chariot is an upward, and indeed Ascensional, movement, whereas the movement of the flames is even), except for the rocket-like effect of seeing the flame rise up 'like a small cloud'. These are, as we should have expected, Dante's own additions to the biblical text.

What should be noticed in passing, however, is how the 'sundering' of Elijah and Elisha by the fire of chariot and horses anticipates (and possibly, in the writerly stream of consciousness, surpasses) the next mythical shade, the cloven pyre of Eteocles and Polynices, which concludes all the 'matter' regarding Thebes, and which Dante has adapted from Statius' *Thebaid* and/or from Lucan's *Bellum Civile*.

A biblical simile and a classical allusion are, as usual in Dante, joined. But there are two further points where the Bible conditions Dante's imagination in this Canto—and crucial points at that. The souls of the fraudulent counsellors punished in the eighth bolgia are enveloped by fires, and indeed use the tip of the flames as tongues. The two models in Scripture are no less than the Burning Bush of Exodus and the tongues of flame of Pentecost (Exod. 3:2 ff.; Acts 2). There even is a more general, and poignant, parallel, which Maria Corti was first to point out.[4] In the Epistle of James a metaphorical cluster of ships, tongue, fire, and hell appears, which is of course the same stuff the Ulysses story is made of:

Behold also the ships, which though they be so great, and are driven of fierce winds, yet are they turned about with a very small helm, whithersoever the governor listeth. Even so the tongue is a little member, and boasteth great things. Behold, how great a matter a little fire kindleth! And the tongue is a fire, a world of iniquity: so is the tongue among our members, that it defileth the whole body, and setteth on fire the course of nature; and it is set on fire of hell. (Jas. 3:4–6)

The story of Ulysses, which occupies the second, and more substantial, section of the Canto, regards an ancient pagan hero. But in the closing lines of the episode Scripture comes back (literally) with a vengeance. The Ulysses episode opens, as we have just seen, with an allusion to Elijah's ascending into heaven: 'cum levare vellet Dominus Eliam *per turbinem*.' A disturbed echo of Genesis is heard again mid-Canto: 'fatti non foste' ('you were not made'). Now, Ulysses' voice and whole adventure begin to fade with the whirlwind, *turbo*, rising up from the 'dark mountain'. It is difficult not to read this whirlwind as reference to the words of Jeremiah (23:19) against false prophets and the wicked generally: 'Ecce *turbo* Dominicae indignationis egredietur, Et tempestas erumpens *super caput* impiorum veniet' ('Behold, a whirlwind of the Lord is gone forth in fury, even a grievous whirlwind: it shall fall grievously upon the head of the wicked'), and, eschatologically, upon all peoples:

Haec dicit Dominus exercituum: Ecce afflictio egredietur de gente in gentem, Et *turbo* magnus egredietur a *summitatibus terrae*. Et erunt *interfecti* Domini in die illa, A summo terrae usque ad summum eius.

Thus saith the Lord of Hosts, Behold, evil shall go forth from nation to nation, and a great whirlwind shall be raised up from the coasts of the earth. And the slain of the Lord shall be at that day from one end of the earth even unto the other. (25:32–3)

---

[4] Corti, *Percorsi*, pp. 143–4.

To understand Ulysses' *altrui* we must listen to Yahweh's terrifying *se'ara*. It is from this, *de turbine*, that Yahweh answers Job and Dante's Ulysses, in absolute, incomprehensible, transcendent, and primitive alterity:

> Ubi eras quando ponebam fundamenta terrae?
> Indica mihi, *si habes intelligentiam.*
> Quis posuit mensuras eius, *si nosti?*
> [. . .]
> Numquid ingressus es *profunda maris?*
> Et in *novissimis abyssi* deambulasti?
> Numquid apertae sunt tibi *portae mortis,*
> Et ostia tenebrosa vidisti?
> Numquid considerasti *latitudinem terrae?*
> Indica mihi, *si nosti*, omnia.

> Where wast thou when I laid the foundations of the earth?
> Declare, *if thou hast understanding.*
> Who hast laid the measures thereof, *if thou knowest?*
> [. . .]
> Hast thou entered into the *springs of the sea?*
> Or hast thou walked in the *search of the depth?*
> Have the *gates of death* been opened unto thee?
> Or hast thou seen the doors of the shadow of death?
> Hast thou perceived *the breadth of the earth?*
> *Declare if thou knowest* it all.

(Job 38:4–18)

Of course, evoking the divine '*turbo*' of Elijah, Jeremiah, and Job to get some idea of the nature of the Ulysses episode in Dante means *ipso facto* recognition that it contains enormous problems, a massive mystery which can be answered (and Dante makes no answer to the flame) with neither romanticism, nor direct exegesis, nor mere classical, patristic, or Thomistic parallels, nor simple or complex deceit, nor pagan/Satanic hubris. The only response is to allow the whirlwind to take over one's entire existence, and become 'quella cui vento affatica', 'wearied by the wind'.

In the episode of Ugolino in *Inferno* XXXIII the Bible is again central. I have shown elsewhere how the story unfolds as a reverse of the Creation, of the Eucharist, and of the Crucifixion.[5] The agony of Ugolino's sons and grandsons lasts six days, exactly as many as the Creation, and is thus presented as an Undoing. The 'children' ask their Father for bread in a sort of *Pater noster*, he responds by turning to stone within and thus picking up 1 Kings and the Gospels (Matt. 7 and, above all, Luke 11:9–13). The children's offer of their flesh to their father ('Padre, assai ci fia men doglia | se tu mangi di noi: tu ne vestisti | queste misere carni, e tu le spoglia') resembles Job's verse at 1:21,

---

[5] Boitani, *Tragic and Sublime*, pp. 20–55.

and of course Jesus' offer of his own body for the sacrifice. Line 69 of *Inferno* XXXIII, Gaddo's 'Padre mio, ché non m'aiuti?', clearly echoes Christ's words on the cross ('Eli, Eli lama sabactani'), and in his invective against Pisa later in the Canto, Dante punctually maintains that the city should not have put innocent children 'a tal croce'. Finally, after the death of his children, Ugolino goes blind because of hunger, an image which derives from Deuteronomy 28:29 and Isaiah 59:9–10. Ugolino's story, which is framed by references to Statius' *Thebaid* (*Inferno* XXXII, 130–2, cf. *Thebaid* 8.751–61), thus presents us with an overall upside-down, devilish parody of Scripture. It is not by chance that the Canto of the ultimate human traitor, Ugolino, opens with a word, 'bocca', which shadows forth the three mouths of Lucifer, the supreme Traitor, the primeval inversion of Go(o)d, Evil.

Equally astonishing, but more quietly sublime, is the biblical echo throbbing through Dante's awakening in *Purgatorio* XXXII. This time the simile is taken from the end of the episode of the Transfiguration in Matthew's Gospel. Peter, James, and John have been brought to see the *fioretti del melo*, the 'apple-blossom', that is, the transfigured Christ. Stunned at the sight, they are just beginning to regain possession of themselves at the sound of Christ's voice, which had, of course, famously roused others from far deeper sleep. They find themselves alone, without Moses or Elijah, the blinding white of Christ's robes having now returned to normal. The passage thus evokes both John's powerful 'Lazarus, come forth', and the image of the wedding-feast indicating the kingdom of God and his glory:

> Quali a veder de' fioretti del melo
> che del suo pome li angeli fa ghiotti
> e perpetue nozze fa nel cielo,
>   Pietro e Giovanni e Iacopo condotti
> e vinti, ritornaro a la parola
> da la qual furon maggior sonni rotti,
>   e videro scemata loro scuola
> così di Moisé come d'Elia,
> e al maestro suo cangiata stola;
>   tal torna' io . . .
>
>   (*Purgatorio* XXXII, 73–82)

An even more effortless party-trick is the sudden appearance of the shade of Statius behind Virgil and Dante in *Purgatorio* XXI, described in terms of the apparition of the risen Christ behind the two disciples on the road to Emmaus, as recounted in Luke's Gospel:

> Ed ecco, sì come ne scrive Luca
> che Cristo apparve a' due ch'erano in via,
> già surto fuor de la sepulcral buca,
>   ci apparve un'ombra, e dietro a noi venìa . . .
>
>   (*Purgatorio* XXI, 7–10, cf. Luke 24:13–17)

I define it as a 'party-trick' simply to defamiliarize it for the modern reader: but what easy familiarity it reveals of the foundations of Christianity (as, elsewhere, of pagan myth), absorbed and effortlessly re-elaborated with precise, beguiling aesthetic trickery.

The climax in this kind of re-Scripture is reached in *Purgatorio* XXX, when Dante stages the appearance and recognition of Beatrice. During the procession in Earthly Paradise one of the old men representing the books of the Old Testament three times intones '*Veni, sponsa, de Libano*'. In the Song of Songs (4:8) this verse refers to the bride, who is traditionally identified with the Church or with the human soul. Following his exposition in the *Convivio* (II, xiv, 20), Dante sees the bride as celestial Wisdom, divine science. Thus, Beatrice 'signifies' Theology, the bride of Christ. Immediately afterwards, a thousand angels respond to the old man's chant by singing '*Benedictus qui venis*' and '*Manibus, oh, date lilia plenis*'. The former, of course, is the cry with which Jesus is greeted as he enters Jerusalem on Palm Sunday (Matt. 21:9), itself repeating the invocation of Psalm 117 (v. 26). It is also what the Mass proclaims in the *Sanctus*, just before the Consecration. Thus, Beatrice is the shadow of the Messiah. The latter Latin chant comes, however, from the *Aeneid*, where, once more in Book VI (v. 883), Anchises praises young Marcellus, Augustus' nephew and would-be heir. A pagan, Virgilian celebration is added to the Christian ones, only a few moments before Virgil himself leaves the scene for good. At this regard it should be remembered that in a few instants Dante the pilgrim will in fact turn to Virgil, unaware that he has disappeared, to tell him he again feels within himself the fire of the old love for Beatrice, and that he does so by quoting to him a line of the *Aeneid*, '*adgnosco veteris vestigia flammae*': 'conosco i segni de l'antica fiamma.' It is what Dido told her sister Anna when she recognized the symptoms of the love she once had felt towards her husband Sychaeus being rekindled in her now for Aeneas (*Aeneid* 4.23). This most crucial moment of the *Comedy* is signalled by an expression which had already been used for the 'maggior corno de la fiamma antica' of *Inferno* XXVI—Ulysses.

Scripture, Virgil, and Ulysses are summoned to describe the epiphany of the beloved. On the very same level Dante places his own works. For if the colours of Beatrice's dress and wreath here in the *Purgatorio* have sacred connotations—white, green, and red, symbolizing the three theological virtues of faith, hope, and charity—they are also the colours Beatrice wears in the *Vita Nuova*. And the *Vita Nuova* is referred to, and actually mentioned, at least twice in *Purgatorio* XXX: 'questi fu tal,' Beatrice says to the angels after haranguing Dante, 'ne la sua vita nova | virtualmente.'

To conclude this brief sketch of Dante's use of the Bible in the *Commedia*, let me return to the theme of Creation with which I began. After variously treating it in *Purgatorio* XVI and XXV (creation of the human soul), and again in *Paradiso* VII and XIII, Dante touches upon it in the great Eagle sequence of *Paradiso* XVIII–XX. The image of the Divine Architect in Canto XIX (40–5) is absolute. This is the geometer 'turning His compass about the bounds of the world'. He fills it with any number of things, manifest and hidden, but without infusing them with His own *valore*—his power as the creating Father. Thus, He avoids making his idea and word (the Son) appear 'infinitely exceeding' with respect to the created world. In just two terzinas the Creation is evoked in all its theological and philosophical complexity (with the whole structure of the universe, in which all things visible and invisible are contained, in discrete order), with the great biblical image from Proverbs (8:27–9, already employed in *Convivio*, III, xv, 16) of the compass as a beguilingly visual introduction which 'encompasses' the reader and stuns him into acceptance of the difficult cosmic ride ahead. This is Dante's Sapiential rewriting of the beginning of Genesis and John's Gospel:

> Poi cominciò: 'Colui che volse il sesto
> a lo stremo del mondo, e dentro ad esso
> distinse tanto occulto e manifesto,
> non poté suo valor sì fare impresso
> in tutto l'universo, che 'l suo verbo
> non rimanesse in infinito eccesso . . .'
>
> (*Paradiso* XIX, 40–5)

The theme surfaces again in *Paradiso* XXIX, where Beatrice offers the final explanation Dante needs. It is in fact in this Canto that Dante's long consideration of the divine Creation ends: a meditation which is not without reason, since creation by God of all that exists represents the central foundation, the intellectual pivot, of a religious understanding of the cosmos. This Canto contains all his impassioned analysis of the theme in passages which encompass a number of philosophical traditions and hover at the threshold of the ontologically unutterable. As soon as Beatrice starts speaking in the opening lines of *Paradiso* XXIX, she moves to the absolutes of beyond-time, beyond-space. She leaps towards the eternity which is God's, beyond any need and any desire to increase: 'not to gain any good for Himself.' For the pure pleasure of it, and according to His desire (*come i piacque*), 'the Eternal Love unfolded Himself in new loves'. God's only aim is to multiply existence into new, self-conscious lives, 'that His splendour, shining back, might say *Subsisto*'. This Latin verb which Beatrice uses includes not mere existence, of course, but the whole and complete state of Being, a Scholastic echo of the *Ego sum qui sum* through which God reveals His being to Moses, concealing it in absolute mystery (Exod. 3:14).

The creation of the angels—which constitutes Beatrice's first theme here—is a reflection of light, an opening out of Love into new loves, a blossoming and 'breaking', as the last lines of the Canto will have it, of the 'Eternal Goodness' into 'so many mirrors', 'remaining in itself one as before'. This, of course, is the Neoplatonism of Pseudo-Dionysius the Areopagite, but with an aesthetic consistency lacking in its models: a powerful affirmation of being requiring no divine hand (unlike, for example, *Purgatorio* XVI), nor, surprisingly, John's Logos or Word. When Goethe's wretched Faust attempts to translate the *incipit* of the Fourth

Gospel, 'In the beginning was the Word', he tries out four different expressions to render into modern thought-systems the *Verbum* which was already an adaptation, *via Logos*, of the Hebrew *dabhar*: *Wort, Sinn, Kraft*, and *Tat*. Dante, for his part, is having nothing of semantic speculations: he goes confidently to tradition and in the place of Word, Sense, Might, and Action consecrates Love: supreme Eros and Charity, which, as such, was never inactive, but had always (*né prima né poscia*, since time only came into existence after the Creation) proceeded as a *discorrer di Dio sovra quest'acque*, as God's moving over the face of 'these' waters.

I intend to stop here for the moment and examine Dante's moves more closely. When, in the Bible, God creates the heaven and the earth, the earth is 'without form, and void', and darkness is 'upon the face of the deep'. The Spirit of God 'moves' (in the Vulgate, *ferebatur*) 'upon the face of the waters'. God then says, 'Let there be light'. Immediately afterwards, He divides light from dark, which He calls day and night: 'and the evening and the morning were the first day.' Dante eliminates all this. He also considerably alters the one biblical phrase he quotes, 'and the Spirit of God moved upon the face of the waters'. In the first place, the waters become '*these* waters'. Following a tradition gaining considerable currency in the thirteenth century, he takes them as the waters above the firmament, those of the ninth heaven above the stars, in the Crystalline or Primum Mobile. Beatrice and Dante are now above the same primeval waters over which the divine Spirit of the Beginning moved: *these* waters; and from this giddy height Beatrice (i.e. Dante) dares to re-script the Holy Scriptures.

Secondly, Dante boldly cuts across centuries of controversy over the expression 'Spirit of God' by simply attributing the action to God Himself. Lastly, he eliminates the neutral form of the verb *ferebatur* of the Vulgate, ignores the *incubabat* and *fovebat* (i.e. the incubating and brooding which, for instance, are the origins of Milton's version), and, jettisoning the various connotations of *volitabat*, opts for a verb which is simultaneously powerful and delicate, *discorrer*, the signified of movement (*irruebat* is another translation) which is in the English noun and verb 'course'. In both classical and medieval Latin *discurrere* also stands for the orator's exploring the ramifications of an argument (as in 'discourse'). The former would agree with the opening of Eternal Love into new loves; the latter would refer indirectly to the action of God's word, which is fundamental to Genesis and John but notably absent from *Paradiso* XXIX.

In the Vulgate the spirit of God is carried or proceeds (*ferebatur*) above the waters. A tradition going from Augustine to Thomas Aquinas, and aptly summarized by Peter Lombard, interprets this as the will of the creator which 'passes above' the matter it wishes to shape.[6] Dante, who was certainly at home within this tradition, is thus describing the action whereby the supreme Agent-Artisan-Artist is preparing to give shape to shapeless matter, to the *res fabricandae*, the things to be created.

6 Augustine, *De Genesi contra Manichaeos*, I, vii, 12; Peter Lombard, *Sententiae in IV Libris Distinctae*, II, XII, c. 3; Thomas, *Summa Theologiae* I, q. 66, I ad 2.

In short, Dante's is a complete re-writing of Genesis. In the Bible, Creation continues for six full days. But Dante subverts this too, replacing the temporal sequence by the single moment. The Divine Being *raggiò insieme tutto sanza distinzione in essordire* and *senza intervallo*: that is, the Creation of the universe was both simultaneous and instantaneous. The point is that Dante—who knows perfectly well the troubles which the opening chapter of the Bible creates for the philosopher and the theologian[7]—rejects the anthropomorphic imaginary which dominates the account in Genesis and so many other myths of creation to start a philosophical *mythos* of his own. Dante is not interested in the single creatures, species, or types (trees, fish, reptiles, etc.), but the prime essences, created directly, immediately,[8] by God, which Dante then collects under philosophy's capital letters of Form and Matter, and analyses within the context of the equally upper-case categories of Act and Potency.

In short, to describe the Creation Dante employs Neoplatonist and Aristotelian concepts and images while producing his own re-Scripture of Genesis. Not 'in principio' but 'in sua etternitá, di tempo fore'. Not 'God created', but 's'aperse in novi amor l'etterno amore' and 'usciro ad esser'. Not God's words, 'Let there be light', but Love radiating, emanating, shining forth, 'ri-splendendo'. It is indeed this Love that, at the beginning of the poem, 'first moved these fair things'. It is this Love that, at the poem's end, turns the desire and will of the poet, 'sì come rota ch'igualmente è mossa', in the same way it moves the sun and the other stars.

WORKS CITED

Dante is cited from *La Commedia secondo l'antica vulgata*, ed. G. Petrocchi (Florence: Le Lettere, 2nd edn. 1994); English trans. by J. D. Sinclair (New York, Oxford University Press, 1939); and the *Epistle to Cangrande*, in *The Latin Works of Dante* (London: Dent, 1940), 347–8.

THOMAS, AQUINAS, *In Duodecim Libros Metaphysicorum Aristotelis Expositio*, I, 4, 984b 29, *lect.* 5, 102 (Turin and Rome: Marietti, 1964).
Z. BARANSKI, 'Commedia', in R. Lansing (ed.), *The Dante Encyclopedia* (New York, Garland, 2000).
P. BOITANI, *The Tragic and the Sublime in Medieval Literature* (Cambridge: Cambridge University Press, 1989).
M. CORTI, *Percorsi dell'invenzione* (Turin: Einaudi, 1993).

[7] For which it will be enough to recall Augustine's discussion in the *Confessions*, Book XII, and in the *De Genesi ad litteram*, particularly in Book IV.
[8] *Paradiso* VII, 67 states: 'sanza mezzo'.

Further Reading

G. Barblan (ed.), *Dante e la Bibbia* (Florence: Olschki, 1988).

P. Boitani, *The Bible and its Rewritings* (Oxford University Press, 1999).

——'The Poetry and Poetics of the Creation', in R. Jacoff (ed.), *The Cambridge Companion to Dante*, 2nd edn. (Cambridge: Cambridge University Press, 2007), 218–35.

——*Winged Words: Flight in Poetry and History* (Chicago: University of Chicago Press, 2007), 125–48.

P. Dronke, 'L'amor che move il sole e l'altre stelle', in *The Medieval Poet and his World* (Rome: Edizioni di Storia e Letteratura, 1984), 439–75.

J. Freccero, *Dante: The Poetics of Conversion*, ed. R. Jacoff (Cambridge, Mass.: Harvard University Press, 1986).

P. Hawkins, *Dante's Testaments: Essays in Scriptural Imagination* (Stanford: Stanford University Press, 1999).

D. H. Higgins, *Dante and the Bible: An Introduction* (Bristol: University of Bristol Press, 1992).

C. S. Singleton, '*In Exitu Israel de Aegypto*', in J. Freccero (ed.), *Dante* (Englewood Cliffs, NJ: Prentice Hall, 1965), 102–21.

C. Lund-Mead has edited a complete, commented catalogue of Dante's biblical references by the late Amilcare Iannucci: *Dante and the Vulgate Bible* (Rome, Bulzoni, 2010).

....

CHAPTER 20

GEORGE FRIEDRIC HANDEL AND *THE MESSIAH*

....

JOHN BUTT

'PRACTICALLY alone among Handel's English oratorios, [*Messiah*] has a New Testament subject and a text . . . drawn largely from the Gospels.' Thus runs the *New Oxford History of Music,* written by one of the most talented and incisive music historians of the early twenty-first century (Taruskin 2005: 325). In fact, the Gospels account for only ten of the eighty biblical verses that constitute *Messiah*'s libretto (Smith 1995: 152); rather more material (particularly towards the end) comes from later NT books, but the majority of the text is from the Old Testament. Yet the error in the *NOHM* is both understandable and illuminating: when we hear the oratorio we surely come away with a definite sense that Jesus is indeed the focal point of the work, and we could therefore easily assume that it relied on the principal body of evidence for Jesus' earthly ministry, the Gospels.

What Handel and his librettist, Charles Jennens, have done is to provide a rounded and convincing impression of Jesus as Messiah through textual and musical allusion and resonance. Part of the potency of the libretto lies in its 'blanks', what it leaves unsaid (and unsung), thus inviting the listener to construct the necessary connections. The word 'Christ' is used sparingly, owing to the preponderance of OT text, and the word 'Jesus' appears very late in the work—and only once— in the penultimate chorus, 'But thanks be to God'. This very delay makes the Christian claim for Jesus that much more convincing, as if everything up to this point has been designed to point towards this name (see Smith 1995: 152). The music provides 'harmony' in more than just its musical sense, melding OT prophecy to the Christian perspective in a way that exceeds what the texts can do on their own. Scraps of biblical text, only sporadically continuous, are somehow rendered part of the one work, or rather the one experience that the listener witnesses in a single performance. Music thus functions as a form of rhetoric, rendering a message convincing through emphasis, repetition, elaboration, and a rich array of emotional constructs that can capture the listener's attention over the span of time delineated by the musical forms. Moreover, Handel's music is strongly contrapuntal, by which lines of music are combined in various ways with one another simultaneously (most obviously in fugal movements, such as the fast section of the opening overture ('Sinfony') or the chorus 'And He shall purify'). This simultaneous combination of lines works as a musical analogue (vertically) to the way different texts are combined in linear sequence (horizontally). Hearing the ease with which Handel combines musical lines may well predispose us towards hearing the different types of text as belonging together, even if they are not heard simultaneously.

The music also seems to provide a sense of trajectory, taking us from the time of prophecy, through the Incarnation, Passion, and Resurrection of Christ, to the triumph of the church, the redemption of mankind, and the end-times—all within the span of a single oratorio. It is difficult to name any other musical work that covers such a broad temporality, enclosing the linear time-span of Jesus' life and our own 'local' position within an overarching godly plan. Yet there is never a sense of sublime terror at being marooned in a cosmology that totally transcends the human; the oratorio is very much of its age in presenting a sense of genial order, satisfying and moving, and overwhelming only in its cumulative power. The music renders the text and its allusive imagery accessible on a variety of levels, so that different types of listener are likely to be able to relate to it in some respect. Thus someone bringing the 'right' topological approach for the Christian reading of the Old Testament as the harbinger of the New, will find that the parallels and connections seem to work perfectly, any theological provisos notwithstanding (such as those concerning the meaning and authorship of the passages from Isaiah). Again, the function of the music is truly that of rhetoric: a means of rendering convincing that which could be questioned intellectually. Perhaps music in general shares something with faith as a mode of thought. Yet the allusions in the text are sufficiently understated that the cultural or theological concerns of librettist or composer are not automatically apparent. Very little about the text is likely to put the listener on the defensive. Unlike Bach's Passions, which continually emphasize both the sinfulness of the individual and the need to cultivate the necessary intensity of faith, salvation in *Messiah* is a communal affair and the audience is never accused of anything that could jeopardize an assured salvation ('the Dead shall be rais'd incorruptible, and We shall be chang'd'). There is none of the traditional Calvinist or Lutheran contrast between the worthlessness of earthly life and heavenly bliss, but a sense that the pleasure and benefits of God's grace are at least partly available in the present (Smith 1995: 357–8). This sense of a 'realized eschatology' perhaps goes some way towards meeting the progressive spirit of the modern age—the notion that this world is worth improving and enjoying—and renders *Messiah* more attractive to those who might not necessarily share its theological predispositions. If the inescapable sin of the human condition after the Fall is implicit in the chorus 'All we, like Sheep, have gone astray, we have turned ev'ry one to his own Way...', Handel's music (adapted from a secular Italian duet) seems to be the most delightful and witty he could muster.

CHARLES JENNENS AND THE LIBRETTO FOR *MESSIAH*

Charles Jennens had been attracted to Handel's music since the mid-1720s and may well have been the compiler of the text for Handel's other oratorio based entirely on scripture (albeit entirely OT), *Israel in Egypt*, first performed in 1739. He was also the librettist of *Saul*, from the same year, and clearly enjoyed a close, if sometimes stormy, relationship with the composer (Burrows 1991: 9–10). Jennens's background as a highly learned upholder of Anglican orthodoxy is itself a fascinating object of study (see Luckett 1992: 69–85; Smith 1995; Marissen 2007; Erhardt 2005). Most striking is the fact that, although orthodox, he hardly belonged to the establishment, since he was an Anglican 'non-juror', someone who refused to swear allegiance to the House of Hanover, yet was also hostile to the Roman Catholicism of the remaining Stuarts. Seemingly embattled on all sides, he rejected most other forms of Protestantism and was particularly vehement in counteracting the rationalist demystifications of the Deists. Much of *Messiah*'s text, with its unrelenting stress on the divinity of Christ and the power of mystery, can be read as a form of propaganda against the Deist position. This is evident even in the epigraph at the head of the 1743 libretto, the opening of which is derived from 1 Timothy 3:16: 'And without Controversy, great is the Mystery of Godliness: God was manifested in the Flesh...' Jennens's wager was perhaps that Handel's music would prove sufficiently enticing to render dreary the lean rationalizations of modern thought.

Jennens was by no means unusual in constructing a typological amalgam of OT and NT texts. He was clearly influenced by Virgil's 'Pollio', *Eclogue* IV, which had long been seen as a 'heathen' analogue to the Old Testament in prophesying the coming of Christ. Jennens drew from this the motto at the head of the 1743 wordbook for *Messiah*, 'Majora canamus' ('we sing a grander [strain]', see Burrows 1991: 85; Luckett 1992: 70). Virgil provided the direct model for the most significant poem about the 'Messiah' in the early eighteenth century, Pope's *Messiah. A Sacred Eclogue, Compos'd of several Passages of Isaiah the Prophet. Written in imitation of Virgil's Pollio* (1712; Smith 1995: 118). Ruth Smith has shown that, under the renewed influence of 'Longinus', the concept of the sublime had recently become central to literary composition and criticism, with the Bible seen as the archetypal source of sublime writing. Moreover, some of the passages from Isaiah that Jennens later incorporated into his *Messiah* libretto, such as 'For unto us a child is born', were those that drew specific admiration (Smith 1995: 108–18).

There was no shortage of theological writing presenting tables of parallels between the two testaments, particularly in the wake of Deist scepticism of anything but an accidental similarity. Jennens's library was both extensive and up-to-date, particularly in its theological content (see Erhardt 2005). The most obvious source for his Messiah theme is Bishop Richard Kidder's *A Demonstration of the Messias. In which the Truth of the Christian Religion is proved* (1726), the list of contents for which, as Smith observes, 'reads like a blueprint for the libretto of *Messiah*'; it cites over half the verses that Jennens later employed (Smith 1995: 148–50). Michael Marissen notes that Kidder's title continues: '. . . *is proved, against all the Enemies thereof; but especially against the JEWS*' (Marissen 2007: 169). Thus, Marissen believes, it is possible to read the 'other' against whom 'we' achieve salvation in the course of *Messiah* as the Jew who does not recognize Jesus as the Messiah. By tracing Jennens's reliance on the 1653 biblical commentary of Henry Hammond, Marissen suggests that his use of Psalm 2 in the latter section of Part 2, leading up to the Hallelujah chorus, refers to God's rejection of Judaism for failing to recognize Jesus. Indeed, Kidder and other eighteenth-century Anglicans relate the destruction of the Temple in 70 CE specifically to God's verdict on the Jews, so the Hallelujah chorus could have carried such connotations for some listeners who were familiar with contemporary English theological literature (Marissen 2007: 172–4). Marissen's suspicions about Jennens would seem to be strongly corroborated by a letter that his lifelong companion, Edward Holdsworth, wrote in the wake of Jennens's initial disappointment with Handel's setting: 'I am sorry to hear yr. friend Handel is such a jew. His negligence, to say no worse, has been a great disappointment to others as well as yrself . . . I hope the words, tho' murther'd, are still to be seen' (Burrows 1991: 24). But, as Ruth Smith has observed, Jennens's reply hardly substantiates a vitriolic anti-Judaism: 'You do him too much Honour to call him a Jew! A Jew would have paid more respect to the Prophets' (Smith 2007).

Whatever the anti-Judaic background to the text compilation for *Messiah*, it remained entirely unnoticed before the recent work of Marissen (and, as several observe, his is a very selective reading of all the possible literature). This suggests that neither text nor music has an unequivocal meaning enduring from one historical context to another. Indeed, it may well be the very 'generosity' of the music in its elaboration of the sense and emotion of the text that has rendered *Messiah* so appealing and influential throughout its reception. One other thing that recent studies of the libretto have shown is the degree to which Jennens adapted the text (or chose specific translations or commentaries) to focus it on the person of Jesus. Thus, first-person utterances are altered into third-person ones: 'Come unto me, all ye that labour . . .' becomes 'Come unto Him, all ye that labour . . .', 'For my yoke is easy, and my burden is light' becomes 'His Yoke is easy, his Burthen is light', and 'I gave my back to the Smiters' becomes 'He gave his Back . . .', while 'Behold, and see, if there be any sorrow like unto my sorrow' now reads '. . . like unto his Sorrow!' (Marissen 2007: 179–80, Luckett 1992: 74). Whenever it is crucial to maintain the sense of temporal trajectory—that is, Christ's Passion was in the past, our faith in salvation is in the present, our bodily resurrection is in the future—the tense of the biblical quotation is moved from present to past ('He was despised and rejected').

In basing his text on both the King James Version of the Bible and the 1662 *Book of Common Prayer*, Jennens was already aiming for what he considered the best overall resonance of text (traditional Anglican churchgoers would, after all, have been used to combining Coverdale's psalm translations in the *BCP* with the remainder of the Bible from King James). Indeed, Jennens's use of the *BCP* goes beyond the psalms, since he chooses the text 'I know that my Redeemer liveth' from the funeral sentences in the *BCP* rather than from the King James text of Job 19:25. Moreover, if the King James Version offers a subsidiary reading that is more suitable for his purposes, Jennens adopted that. The focus of the line 'O thou that tellest good Tidings to Zion' fits the notion of Jesus as Messiah more than 'O Zion, that bringest good tidings' (Luckett 1992: 73, Marissen 2007: 167–8).

Part of the cumulative effect of these choices and changes is to create a very strong sense of third-person reference in the first two parts. By avoiding any representation of the direct voice or internal feelings of Jesus he is magnificently objectified, coterminous with God himself. *Messiah*'s Jesus is created through the very authority that third-person narrative evokes. After all, in fictional narrative third-person statements are necessarily true within the world to which they relate (if they are inaccurate, the very existence and integrity of that world is threatened), while first-person statements might be flawed or misleading, at least within that same world. So there is no reason why the same principles might not apply to the way biblical text can work: the third person conveys a particular aura of authority. Moreover, in *Messiah* the occasional bursts of first-person speech are rendered supremely effective through their very rarity. The voice of God in the recitative 'Thus saith the Lord, the Lord of Hosts, Yet once a little while, and I will shake the heav'ns and the earth', has none of the existential authority of the third-person mode (which is used to conjure up his voice, with 'Thus saith the Lord'), but every sense of the presence and authority of God. A little later in Part 1, the angel addresses the shepherds directly in the first person in a short and vivid section that is the only active scene representing events in real time within the entire text.

Again, the use of the first person ('I bring you good Tidings of great Joy') gives a sense of real presence partly through its very isolation. Third-person narrative is all but absent in Handel's operas and only sporadic in his oratorios, so *Messiah* (together with the equally biblical *Israel in Egypt*) stands out for the sense of authority its text seems to carry, perhaps subtly inflecting the way we hear the music as a narrative authority of its own. One absolutely overt result of the predominance of third-person narration is the total change of mood at the beginning of Part 3, when the first person immediately brings us to the believer's 'now'. 'I know that my Redeemer liveth' provides a striking sense of the significance of all that has gone before for the believer, right now in the present.

While Jennens was not at the premiere of *Messiah*, on 13 April 1742, it seems that he made a particular effort in preparing the libretto for the first London audiences the following year. Unique to 1743's libretto is the division of the text into 'scenes' which delineate the topics to which the textual patchwork relates (Burrows 1991: 85–100). More often than not these also correspond to discrete musical scenes, integrated by their closely related keys and sometimes a flow from one musical number to another. Certainly, this had long been Handel's practice as an opera composer, and there is nothing to suggest that he treated his oratorio libretti any differently.

Scenic divisions of the *Messiah* text (1743 libretto, see Burrows 1991: 85–100, for the full text)

Part 1

1.1: Prophecy of Salvation (Isa. 40:1–5), 'Comfort ye' to 'And the glory of the Lord';

1.2: Prophecy of Jesus' coming and his cataclysmic purifying effect of the earth (Hag. 2:6–7 and Mal. 3:1–3), 'Thus saith the Lord' to 'And He shall purify';

1.3: Prophecy of Jesus' birth by a virgin, the move from darkness to light and the coming of the Prince of Peace (extracts from Isa. 7:14, 40:9, 60:1–3, 9:2, 9:6, Isa. 7:14 being duplicated by Matt. 1:23), 'Behold, a Virgin shall conceive' to 'For unto us a Child is born';

1.4: Angels bring the good tidings to the shepherds (Luke 2:8–11, 13–14), 'There were Shepherds abiding in the Field' to 'Glory to God in the Highest';

1.5: Jesus' effect on earth in miracles and the comfort of redemption (Zech. 9:9–10, 35:5–6; Isa. 40:11; Matt. 11:28–30).

Part 2

2.1: Redemptive power of Jesus' sacrifice, the indignities he suffers at the hand of sinful mankind (John 1:29; Isa. 53:3, 50:6, 53:4–6; Ps. 22:7–8; 69:21; Lam. 1:12), 'Behold the Lamb of God' to 'Behold, and see, if there be any Sorrow';

2.2: Jesus' descent into hell and resurrection (Isa. 53:8; Ps. 16:10), 'He was cut off out of the Land of the Living' to 'But Thou didst not leave his Soul in Hell';

2.3: Jesus' ascension and entry in to heaven (Ps. 24:7–10), 'Lift up your heads, O ye Gates';

2.4: God discloses Jesus' identity to the angels (Heb. 1:5–6), 'Unto which of the Angels said he at any time' and 'Let all the Angels of God worship Him';

2.5: The gifts of Pentecost and the spreading of the word (Ps. 68:18, 11; Rom. 10:15, 18), 'Thou art gone up on High' to 'Their Sound is gone out into all Lands';

2.6: The rejection of the Gospel by the world and its corrupt rulers (Ps. 2:1–3), 'Why do the Nations so furiously rage together?' and 'Let us break their Bonds asunder';

2.7: God's triumph over the ungodly (Ps. 2:4, 9; Rev. 19:6, 11:15, 19:16), 'He that dwelleth in Heaven shall laugh them to scorn' to 'Hallelujah! For the Lord God Omnipotent reigneth'.

Part 3

3.1: The knowledge of the bodily resurrection and the redemption of Adam's fall in Christ (Job 19:25–6; 1 Cor. 15:20–2), 'I know that my Redeemer liveth' and 'Since by Man came Death, by Man came also the Resurrection of the Dead';

3.2: The day of judgement and the resurrection of all (1 Cor. 15:51–4), 'Behold, I tell you a Mystery' and 'The Trumpet shall sound';

3.3: Victory over death and sin (1 Cor. 15:54–7; Rom. 8:31, 33–4), 'Then shall be brought to pass the Saying that is written' to 'If God be for us, who can be against us';

3.4: Glorification of Jesus as victim and Messiah, sitting on the throne of heaven (Rev. 5:12–14), 'Worthy is the Lamb'.

The text is striking for the almost total absence of narrated events. Only the scene taken from Luke presenting the visitation of the angels to the shepherds relates events as they might happen in most operas and oratorios. Handel's alternation of 'secco' and accompanied recitative (with glistening string patterns), leading into the chorus 'Glory to God' (which is the first time the two trumpets are used in the entire oratorio), capitalizes on his dramatic instincts. It may well be that Jennens anticipated that he would employ similar quick-fire changes of musical texture and mood in Part 2, so that we can use the music to synthesize a similar sense of narrative out of the various OT texts (particularly Psalms, which already bring a vivid descriptive energy). Thus we might intuit the events of the Passion, Resurrection, and Pentecost as if they had been taken directly out of the Gospels and Acts. One productive device is to change the person of the narrative voice at one point ('He trusted in God, that he would deliver him'), the only instance of a narrating voice that is not on the 'side' of the believing Christian. This lends the sequence of Part 2 a degree of character contrast, which helps generate the realism of events passing in time. Similarly, the use of antithesis in Part 3 ('Since by Man came Death/For as in Adam all die—by Man came also the Resurrection of the Dead/even so in Christ shall all be made alive'), prepares us for the actual event of sudden change in the next text ('we shall all be chang'd, in a Moment, in the Twinkling of an Eye'), even though this is to happen far in the future. Already, then,

Jennens's choice and manipulation of biblical text have a sense of pacing appropriate to the functions of each of the three parts, perhaps an attempt at stimulating a celebrated dramatic composer to turn his abilities to a more lofty form of persuasion.

HANDEL AND THE MUSICAL SETTING
OF THE *MESSIAH* TEXT

The view of Handel as a composer of the utmost piety and noble sentiment began in the later eighteenth century, and was fueled by the various religious revivals of the nineteenth. For the pious, this view was partly opportunistic—Handel did indeed write moving music on religious texts, not least in *Messiah* itself, so it was easy to reinvent him as a figure of profound piety—but it was also a matter of historical accident: most of the oratorios and virtually all of the operas were simply unknown. The newer, historicist view of Handel has, if anything, gone too far in the opposite direction: most of what is known of Handel's personality is as a superlative musical impresario (perhaps the first in history) who uncannily intuited the needs of the musical market and who generally benefited from the entrepreneurial risks he took. His particular strengths lay in his ability to convey drama in musical terms, but also to capture character and atmosphere in the musical language of the age.

In fact, it is clear that Handel was by no means uninterested in sacred music, and he wrote for the church throughout much of his career (see Burrows 2005). There are also two pieces of evidence to suggest that his knowledge of the Bible was rather more acute than would be assumed for such a master in the world of secular entertainment. According to Charles Burney, when 'the bishops' sent Handel the words to be set for the anthems for the 1727 Coronation of George II, he was offended and claimed 'I have read my Bible very well, and shall chuse for myself' (Burrows 2005: 257). The other piece of evidence for Handel's knowledge of the Bible comes from *Messiah* itself. This was first performed during the composer's Dublin residency, in 1741–2, far away from the clutches of Charles Jennens. At some point Handel abandoned the original version of the aria 'How beautiful are the Feet' which he had already composed (setting Romans 10:15, 18, including the text 'Their Sound is gone out into all Lands', which later became a chorus). He replaced this with a duet for two altos and chorus, setting a text that begins with the same line, but which in fact comes from Isaiah 52:7–9 (the opening musical material is very similar to the original 'How beautiful are the Feet' but it thereafter departs entirely, with the chorus section 'Break forth into joy'). That this movement was composed after Handel arrived in Dublin is suggested by the provenance of its paper (Burrows 1975: 319–34; 1985: 201–19). The alteration suggests that Handel had his own ideas about the biblical texts appropriate for an oratorio outlining the essence of Christian belief.

Looking further into Handel's background, it appears less surprising that he had a close knowledge of the Bible. He, like J. S. Bach, was brought up in the German Lutheran tradition, which was not only extremely thorough in its study of the Bible (together with its original languages) but which also had made the topological harmonization of Old and New Testaments a central plank of its theology. From this point of view, Handel's upbringing was even more conducive to the concept of *Messiah* than Jennens's. He would have attended the Gymnasium in Halle, in which study of both biblical and classical texts was extremely thorough. Moreover, as an area that had recently been absorbed into Brandenburg-Prussia, Halle benefited from a more cosmopolitan intellectual and spiritual environment than most cities in that part of Germany (Butt 1997: 13–14). It was during Handel's childhood that Halle steadily became the major centre of Lutheran Pietism, a movement lead in Halle by August Hermann Francke. This had begun as a reform and purification of Orthodox Lutheranism, but was soon to be seen as a separate wing, one that opened its own educational institutions and orphanages. Pietism was resolutely against complex music as a distraction from the immediacy of Scripture. While Handel was a student of the organist at Halle's main church (Lutheran Orthodox), there is no doubt that he would have been exposed to Pietism and the controversies it engendered. Its most fervent concern was with engaging the feelings in experiencing faith and Scripture (it was less concerned with theological details). Pietists stressed the need for a feeling of rebirth and a cultivation of the inwardness of the individual, both of which were meant to effect a real change in the world (and thus encouraging 'good works' more than the traditional Lutheran 'justification by faith alone' might imply). Whether in sympathy or antipathy to the Pietist cause, Handel may well have learned from it something of his ability to use music as a way of bringing real presence to a text, to create an actual event and encourage a change of heart in the present.

There might be a further strand in Handel's experience of church music, prior to his move to England in 1712. As Carolyn Gianturco has shown, Nativity cantatas were performed at the papal court in Rome (in which city Handel was intermittently resident during 1706–10), and these often involved the incorporation of OT prophecies of Christ (Smith 1995: 150; Gianturco 1992). While there is no evidence that Handel himself composed works of this kind, he was closely involved with the composers and patrons concerned. Given that these works were performed with tableaux, Handel may well have associated his religious music with the sort of visual images common in operatic practice, thus conditioning his musical view of each musical scene and the 'picture' summed up by each piece.

One of the primary musical means Handel had of giving a narrative backbone to Jennens's compilation was the system of tonality. The use of all twenty-four keys only became a reality in Handel's own lifetime, and it was only very recently that instruments were able to play in many (but still by no means all) of the more remote keys. Certain keys (particularly those with more sharps and flats) would have sounded quite bizarre and awkward, while the more common ones would have brought a sense of clarity and ease. One thing that was still more-or-less fixed in Handel's day was the key for the trumpets, which sounded most brilliantly in D Major. Thus the 'target' to which the piece led, even before Handel wrote a note, would have been the D Major of the final chorus, celebrating Christ's reign in majesty as predicted by Revelation. However, there was an immediate problem latent in Jennens's libretto: Part 2, which ends with the earthly success of Christ and the Church over the infidel, also ends with obvious trumpet music, the Hallelujah chorus. In terms of musical tonality, then, the piece seems to end twice, with the danger that the music of Part 3 could sound redundant after such a rousing 'Hallelujah' (to some listeners, perhaps it still does). A solution that Handel may have had in mind was to give the work a sort of double trajectory, which would reflect the victory of Christ in the worldly realm on the one hand, and his triumph at the end of time on the other. This would justify ending both Part 2 and Part 3 in the best trumpet key. However, this still left the problem of repetition, so it is quite striking that Handel approached the two D Major triumphal choruses in different ways.

Part 2 is characterized by the preponderance of flat keys. Beginning with the G Minor of 'Behold the Lamb of God', this shows an immediate contrast to the end of Part 1 ('His Yoke is easy' in B-flat Major). In other words, the two keys have the same array of notes, but the opening of Part 2 is the relative minor of the key that ended Part 1, as if both reflect the two sides to Jesus' earthly ministry (the comfort brought by his presence and miracles at the end of Part 1, and his suffering role as the Lamb of God at the beginning of Part 2). From now on the keys get flatter (a very palpable descent, which would have been reflected in the increasing discomfort to which Handel's instrumentalists would have been subjected). The choruses 'Surely He hath born our Griefs' and 'And with his Stripes we are healed' are both in F Minor, almost the flattest usable key ('All they that see Him', a little later, is flatter still, in B-flat Minor). The sequence of predominantly flat tonalities is finally broken in the course of the accompanied recitative 'Thy Rebuke hath broken his Heart', which dramatically modulates from F Minor to E Minor, the most striking change of key in the work. It is as if the music, already as flat as it can practicably be, can now only be expressive if it moves sharpwards in describing the agony and loneliness of Jesus (thus expression is found in the wrenching change rather than in any fixed symbolism of flat or sharp keys). The new, sharper tonality also provides a suitable vehicle for Jesus' resurrection ('But Thou didst not leave his Soul in Hell'). A change back to a flatter tonality articulates the change of scene to accompany Christ's entry into heaven ('Lift up your Heads', in F Major), and for the next few numbers the necessary contrast is provided by the alternation of sharper or flatter keys, or major and minor. The final approach to D Major begins with the B-flat Major of the Pentecost 'scene' ('The Lord gave the Word'), which moves via the 'neutral' keys of C Major and A Minor to the triumphal D Major of the Hallelujah chorus.

Handel does not devise an entirely rationalized flow of keys, but it is clear that he used their flow both to provide an overall trajectory and to give immediate contrast from one movement to another. Approaching the D Major at the end of the Part 3 involves the same sort of process, but most surprising of all is the E Major of the opening number, 'I know that my Redeemer liveth', the sharpest key he uses. This thus provides an unexpected contrast with the end of Part 2—instead of going flatwards again, the music begins in a sharper key, which, in the tuning of the day would have been a completely different sound world than the D Major of the Hallelujah chorus. In fact, E Major has appeared once before, as the key of the opening accompanied recitative and aria of Part 1 ('Comfort ye' and 'Ev'ry Valley shall be exalted'). Here it is used to provide striking contrast with the Overture, in E Minor (a key often associated with pain and strife in Handel's time), which seems to represent the state of the world before the optimistic prophesies from Isaiah. Returning to E Major at the opening of Part 3 thus suggests a parallel with these opening prophesies: first, it was associated with the prediction of the Messiah, long before our listening present; secondly, it is associated with our own present ('I know that my Redeemer liveth'), as the contemporary believer's faith in the bodily resurrection at some unspecified point in the future. This suggests a secondary, sharper trajectory, connecting our present hope to the earliest prophesies. It seemingly vaults over the flat-to-sharp trajectories of Part 2. Although D Major is soon to reappear in Part 3 (naturally, for 'The Trumpet shall sound', and later for the final chorus), the sound world has been 'recoloured' by the return of E Major.

Obviously, there is only so far any possible representational effect of keys can be pushed: Handel was not the sort of composer to indulge in multi-level abstractions, but he did have the most brilliant intuition into the attention-span of a listener, anticipating the way in which someone might notice the contrast of keys, modes, and moods. Moreover, it is clear that he did not think in strictly symbolist terms (such as that E Major must represent hope for the future, or D Major triumph), rather that there were pragmatic reasons for using these keys (such as the nature of the trumpets, reference to earlier tonalities, or simply a need for contrast) which as a by-product might have gained a sort of interpretative significance. The overall effect of his pacing of the music, including the spread, contrast, and relative duration of the keys, is to create the illusion of narrative cohesion.

Handel is particularly skilful at covering the seams between different fragments of text. The first striking melding of texts within a single movement comes with 'He shall feed his Flock', where the music is written in pastoral style in two identical blocks (like the two verses of a strophic song). The first half is the OT text (Isa. 40:11, 'He shall feed his Flock...') the second from the NT (Matt. 11:28–9, 'Come unto Him all ye that labour...', with the alteration to the third person to match the OT text). As originally composed, both halves were in exactly the same key (composed for soprano in B-flat Major, but sung by an alto in F Major at the Dublin premire). Thus the two texts are seamlessly harmonized, the identity of the two musical halves convincing us of the continuity of text. At a later date, Handel combined the two versions, beginning with the F Major version (alto) for the OT text, then making a very striking modulation to present the soprano in B-flat Major for the NT portion. The effect is to suggest a sort of transformation in the music as the text passes from Old Testament to New, like a living embodiment of the 'old law' transfigured by the new (this was a favourite topic of Luther, one that he himself described by the metaphor of musical transformation).

Another excellent example of the music unifying OT and NT texts is 'I know that my Redeemer liveth'. Here Handel plays with the conventions of baroque arias, by which the music of the beginning usually returns towards the end (in its stricter forms this is the 'da capo' aria). The opening strain returns as expected, although it is transposed into a higher register in the soprano's voice, giving a sense of the increasing intensity of her faith in Jesus' return. In the first section, a new, simpler texture introduces the text 'And tho' worms destroy this body', and a similar texture (with somewhat different notes) predictably appears towards the end of the last section. However, now the text is new: 'For now is Christ risen from the dead', thus an insertion of an NT text (1 Cor. 15:20) at a point in the aria where there would normally only be repetition of text from the first half. We might almost believe, having listened up to this point, that we must have heard this NT text in the earlier section—thus hearing the two texts as one and the same.

One final way in which Handel's musical thinking paralleled that of Jennens, using the Old Testament in the service of the New, lay in the reuse of his own music for new purposes. He had used the music that was to constitute five of the *Messiah* choruses (the particularly virtuosic ones, like 'For unto us a Child is born' and 'All we, like Sheep, have gone astray') as secular Italian duets, a year or so earlier. To Handel these intimate but intensely energetic pieces clearly suited the new purpose, lending a secular vibrancy to the sacred texts. In all, the net result of Handel's *Messiah* is itself a form of successful secularization—not secularization in the anti-religious sense, but in the sense of making the religious text very much part of *this* world, ever renewed in repeated performances. In an entirely palpable sense, the 'Messiah' that Handel creates in sound dwells among us through the very presence of the music.

Works Cited

Burrows, D. (1975), 'Handel's Performances of *Messiah*: The Evidence of the Conducting Score', *Music and Letters*, 56: 319–34.
——(1985), 'The Autographs and Early Copies of *Messiah*', *Music and Letters*, 66: 201–19.
——(1991), *Handel:* Messiah. Cambridge: CUP.
——(2005), *Handel and the English Chapel Royal.* Oxford and New York: OUP.

BUTT, J. (1997), 'German—Education and Apprenticeship', in D. Burrows (ed.), *The Cambridge Companion to Handel*, 11–23. Cambridge: CUP.

ERHARDT, T. (2005), '"A Most Excellent Subject": Händels *Messiah* im Licht von Charles Jennens theologischer Bibliothek', Ph.D. dissertation, University of Utrecht.

GIANTURCO, C. (1992), '"Cantate spirituali e morali", with a Description of the Papal Sacred Cantata Tradition for Christmas 1676–1740', *Music and Letters*, 73: 1–31.

LUCKETT, R. (1992), *Handel's* Messiah: *A Celebration.* New York and London: Harcourt Brace.

MARISSEN, M. (2007), 'Rejoicing Against Judaism in Handel's *Messiah*', *Journal of Musicology*, 24/2: 167–94.

SHAW, H. WATKINS (1965), *A Textual and Historical Companion to Handel's 'Messiah'.* London: Novello.

SMITH, R. (1995), *Handel's Oratorios and Eighteenth-Century Thought.* Cambridge: CUP.

——(2007), 'Ruth Smith on Handel's *Messiah*', *New York Times*, 25 Apr. 2007.

TARUSKIN, R. (2005), *The Oxford History of Western Music*, vol. 2. Oxford and New York: OUP.

FURTHER READING

The most authoritative general introductions to *Messiah* are Burrows 1991 and Shaw 1965. Erhardt 2005 is an indispensable study of the textual sources and Luckett 1992 is also particularly informative for its study of the text. The cultural conditions of Handel's oratorios are examined in detail in Smith 1995.

CHAPTER 21

ELIZABETH CADY STANTON'S *THE WOMAN'S BIBLE*

ANN LOADES

INTRODUCTION

The *New York Times* for 13 November 1895 reported on a splendid gathering which had been held the previous evening at the Metropolitan Opera House in honour of the eightieth birthday of Elizabeth Cady Stanton, in the beautifully decorated main auditorium. It was called a reunion of 'The Pioneers and Friends of Women's Progress'. It was as cosmopolitan and as representative of 'all classes and conditions' as was possible. Of course not everyone who hoped to attend could be present, not even the whole of Mrs Stanton's own family. The reunion was held under the auspices of the National Council of Women. Mrs Stanton herself would have preferred it to have been organized by the National American Woman Suffrage Association (NAWSA), the 1890 merger of two earlier organizations, of which she was for a time nominally president. Her age, absences from the United States, and divisions of opinion among the proponents of women's suffrage, not least between the 'pioneers' and younger women, had made the organizers opt for the National Council of Women as the lead organization for the great occasion. Unsurprisingly, women far outnumbered men, and parties of women had arrived without male escorts—a far cry from the days of public meetings when women had themselves been outnumbered, and if present, had been literally marginalized by seating arrangements, as well as never permitted to speak in 'promiscuous' (i.e. mixed) company.

The main set-piece was on the stage, on which a framework of flowers had been erected, surrounding a 'chair of state' for Mrs Stanton, instantly recognizable from the published portraits of her, with her benign face surrounded by white curly hair, and her particular way of framing her head by a delicate scarf arranged around her neck. The other principal guest was Mrs Susan B. Anthony, herself 75 years old, Quaker, and an equally formidable campaigner for social and political justice, known as 'Aunt Susan' or even 'St Anthony'. She was to succeed Mrs Stanton as president of NAWSA, which was to put her in a most difficult position on the publication of the first part of *The Woman's Bible*. Mr Job Hedges, secretary to the mayor of New York, 'not looking exactly in his element', delivered the mayor's welcome, beginning 'Gentlemen and Ladies', which, as the reporter commented, was 'manifestly not the happiest inspiration for the beginning of a speech on such an occasion', but everyone seems to have been in such a good humour for such verbal habits to be taken with a good grace, as they must have been all-too familiar to those present.

In her presidential address, Mrs Mary Lowe Dickenson referred to Proverbs 31, 'a marvellous picture of a great and useful woman', which concludes by stating that she shall be praised, 'though with great discretion fails to mention when'. Even that book, she commented, could not have predicted a day when women would gather 'to make their mutual recognition of each others worth and work', as well as bringing their tribute to the two great ladies and the other pioneers present. There were further addresses on education, and from the Revd Anna Shaw on 'Women's advance on religious lines'. This particular Methodist Protestant minister had a long track-record of commitment to the temperance as well as the suffrage movement, relying on the Protestant principle of 'reform' to quarry readings of the New Testament in the interests of such social changes as were undoubtedly needed (Kern 2001: 88). Advance in religion, in her view, was from 'blind faith' to 'honest doubt', from 'weak superstition' to 'the highest and sublimest love of God through love and service to humanity'. Yet another speaker deemed that 'naturally chaotic and brutal conditions' had given place to 'a higher civilisation', making possible 'individual existence in the body politic possible for women', other, that is, than as 'the mere producer and server of men'. Women's wisdom, careful judgement, delicate sense of justice, and intuition were indispensable to the welfare and progress of the world and its people.

Mrs Stanton herself was too incapacitated by age and weight to do more than introduce her own speech, which was to be read for her, but she had a word for the men present who might feel that 'the new woman' would crowd them off the planet. She urged them not to despair, since as long as they had mothers, sisters, wives, daughters, and sweethearts, these would look after their welfare. With this reassurance uttered, she too referred to what was for her a centrally important scripture (Gen. 1:27) on the creation of man, male and female, in God's own image, together with some appropriate lines on mutuality from Tennyson's poetry. As on every possible occasion, so on this one, she criticized the Christian churches for being so slow to accept the equality of female with male, precisely the criticism which was so problematic for the many women for whom church membership remained important in their struggles. If they could not find resources in the Bible, where were they to turn?

The record of the occasion is instructive in the light of what we know about Mrs Stanton from her own pen and from recent research. Her position was to be made unambiguously clear in her comments on *The Woman's Bible*, parts of which had been already serialized in a journal, but with the first section on the first five books in the press for publication just a fortnight later. In the first place, women of her generation were indeed pioneers, but however distinguished and reverenced, found themselves at odds with younger women, who were by no means necessarily as radical as they were in their approach to social and civic reform. Years of organizing meetings, passing resolutions, circulating petitions, travel, and lecturing had had some impact, but not enough. The combination of old age, long experience, limited energy, and increasing exasperation at the failure to precipitate change, and with little if anything to lose, was revitalizing Mrs Stanton, and she was not going to compromise her convictions, which she defended in print and correspondence until her death in 1902. In any case, she had no time for those who supported the suffrage movement in order to advance the case of religious tests for public office, legislation which would affect how people (especially the overworked poor) spent their Sundays, the removal of taxation from church properties, and religious instruction through the teaching of the Bible in schools. To all such proposals she was publicly and adamantly opposed.

Yet public speech by women to advance their interests was still couched in biblical allusion and phraseology and quotation. Mrs Stanton herself used biblical texts selectively when these articulated her convictions, not least to an audience which might otherwise disagree with her about the value of biblical teaching for them personally and for their society. Above all, however, she was known to hold firm to the Protestant emphasis on the priority of personal conscience, and in 1892 had several times delivered a subsequently printed speech on 'The Solitude of Self', the main point of which was that adult women had to be as 'self-sovereign' as men in taking responsibility for themselves. This was why women were asking for a voice in government and religion as well as in social and economic life. They simply must be capable of self-reliance. As the speeches at the birthday made abundantly clear, however, in the midst of these changes women were still to be associated with certain virtues, and still to be at the service of the men in their lives. Mrs Stanton provided reassurance for those concerned about significant shifts in the relationship between men and women, but she certainly wanted women to embrace what was for them the new virtues of self-reliance and self-sovereignty. They were both to embody the virtues associated with them when they were excluded from civic life, as well as those which would be required when they entered that life and sought to transform it. Not everyone had her courage, and no one could foresee that it would require generations of thought and experience to see that changes in women's legal status would not inevitably change the men whose civic and public life they wished to join. Such men, like themselves, 'native born' (emphatically not 'Native American'), mostly white Anglo-Saxons, were relishing freedom in the prevailing social and economic conditions, moving beyond the legacies of the appalling Civil War of 1861–5, still so vivid in memory, even if not all of them had shed habits of violence and intimidation associated for women with drink-fuelled intemperance (Elshtain 1981: 237–8). Mrs Stanton, however, was set to challenge the dependence of women's moral authority on biblical texts, and thus many were soon to distance themselves from her, having celebrated her achievements such a brief time before. She had to be true to what she had become in her eight decades of life, but the publication of *The Woman's Bible* was so controversial that when, in 1922, two of her children, Theodore and her beloved Harriot, published a carefully edited version of her autobiography, letters, and reminiscences, they omitted material on this, her last major publication. Only thus could her reputation be restored, and their tactic seems to have been successful (see the review in the *New York Times*, 24 September 1922). Mrs Stanton herself published her *Eighty Years and More* in 1898, as well as much else, and this document in particular illuminates just how it was that she had become such a courageous radical in her old age, and responsible for a book which was to become such a catalyst in a quite different context in the twentieth century, as well as galvanizing women and men both for and against in her own day.

ELIZABETH CADY STANTON

Born in 1815 (which in Europe marked the end of the wars precipitated by the French Revolution), she was one of a well-to-do family from Johnstown, New York. There were five boys and six girls born, only six of whom were alive at any one time. All the boys died young, with only one surviving to the age of 20, a brother nine years Elizabeth's senior. With the loss of this young man in 1826, Daniel Cady, her father, seems to have been so overwhelmed with grief that he could never quite regard her achievements as comparable to what his boys might have achieved. Somehow or other, through pregnancies, physical exhaustion, and the grief associated with dying and dead children, Margaret Cady, their mother, held the household together. That household included black slaves-become-servants, as it were. Britain had abolished its slave trade in 1807, with the bill for the abolition of slavery in British colonies put through parliament in 1824. The situation in the United States was complicated, since abolishing overseas slave trading by the US Congress in 1808 went alongside slave-holding gaining in strength in some states. New York State had in 1799 passed the Gradual Manumission Act, with further legislation in 1817 and 1827, appropriately enough to coincide with celebrations of 4 July. One slave, Peter, became a kind of surrogate parent to the children, giving them affection and mitigating their fear of parents and God. He could be said to have established the roots of Elizabeth's own self-confidence in later life. She was later to emerge from an experience of 'revival' which had played heavily on human fear of retribution from God, if not here then in the hereafter, and was thereafter to reject all such intimidation.

She also found a most important mentor in the Revd Simon Hosack of her own Scots Presbyterian church, who allowed her into the Greek classes he ran for boys, and in which she was a prize-winner. He was to honour her by leaving her his Greek lexicon, grammar, and commentary in his will. Her wits were further sharpened by the study of mathematics and chess with him, and she became physically tough, as a good horsewoman. She had a first-class education at the Troy Female Seminary in New York State, opened in 1821 by the remarkable Mrs Willard, who made no compromises in the range of topics in both the arts and the sciences for her female students. Beyond this school there was to be no college for Elizabeth, but she turned to books for information and education all her life. And from her early years, her lawyer father had let her into his office, and there, whether he intended it or not, she learned about the deplorable legal position of women as they came to him as clients.

Women's position under the law varied from place to place, whether enduring the extreme physical hardship of frontier life, or the crowding of cities and developing industrialization, not least as immigrants to the United States seeking new lives. Married women in many respects were worse off than those who never married or were widowed. New York State's Married Women's Property Act of 1848 (another revolution year in Europe) gave the well-off some control of their inheritance, since men of course did not want the risk of the provision they made for their daughters being squandered by feckless sons-in-law. It was not until after the Civil War that wage-earning women got control of their pittances. Until that point a husband could 'drink' those wages at the end of each week, leaving wife and children somehow to survive at the point of semi-starvation and disease. Elizabeth Cady Stanton lost support in the temperance movement for suggesting that a woman ought to be able to divorce a chronically drunken husband, but since on marriage a woman's legal existence was suspended, a divorce initiated by her was impossible. Nor had she redress against wife- or child-battering. Her husband had custody of her person and everything she possessed, including the last stitch of her personal clothing, and he had control and custody of the children and final decision in where they all lived. The promise to 'obey' him in marriage was taken to mean that she could not refuse him sexual intercourse, so she was constantly at the risk of the bearing of children who could hardly be reared. If she gave birth to a child out of wedlock, or was unmarried, given the conditions in which the birth might well occur, a child dead at birth or shortly thereafter put her at risk of accusation of 'child-murder', and hence of imprisonment if not hanging. 'He' in criminal legislation included 'Her', but not in the Constitution. She could not speak in court on her own behalf, nor could she be represented by a woman as a lawyer. Every person surrounding her in that context would be male. She could not sue or be sued, collect damages to her own person, make a contract or a will. She could have some claim on her husband's estate when he was alive, but if on his death his property went to his eldest son, who might or might not provide her with a home, she could end up in a situation where she could not even make provision for her own burial. The fundamental issue was that not only ecclesiastical but also civil law made women's existence problematic, because she was not deemed to be a person in her own right, since the whole conception and framework of her existence was deemed to be derived from 'the word of God'. Matters indeed changed slowly over time, but it was far from easy to persuade women themselves, some of whom could not conceive of a state of affairs in which they would be responsible agents in their own adulthood, that there was nothing either necessary or inevitable in the condition in which they found themselves. Some couples on both sides of the Atlantic used the occasion of their marriages to protest against the legal status of wives, and no doubt honourable men never exercised their legal powers, but the legal non-entity of their wives continued. This was wholly unacceptable.

Herself married on 1 May 1840 at the age of 24, seven years after leaving school and without the presence of her family, who disapproved of her choice of husband, Henry, largely on the grounds of his prospects, she omitted the word 'obey' from her marriage vows, as did others. Henry was an abolitionist, and by marrying him she was to cut her own political teeth, learning the important lesson that what appeared to be long-established social institutions could indeed be changed. On 12 May they sailed for the first world Anti-Slavery Convention, which opened on 12 June, and there she experienced a level of humiliation she never forgot. Women delegates were to be seated in a separate section of the hall, with the clergy the most vociferous in their objections to their very presence. Others present strongly supported the women, and as a result, although unable to speak, they were allowed to remain, even for the business meetings. And she discovered that although Henry Stanton fought for the abolition of slavery, he could not or would not put this goal in jeopardy by publicly supporting women's rights. Elizabeth herself came to opt for a multifaceted approach to reform, seeing one issue interlinked with another, not least given defensible analogies between the lot of slaves and those of women.

Most important from her attendance at the Convention was her new friendship with Mrs Lucretia Mott, American Quaker, trusting in her own conscience and in unmediated access to God, and reader of Mary Wollstonecraft's 1792 *A Vindication of the Rights of Women*. In due course, when Henry and Elizabeth had mended fences with the latter's family, lived as part of the large parental household, and had three children, they were to move out to a house at Seneca Falls, where Elizabeth, now aged 30, had never had to work so hard in her life, being responsible for the whole economic unit on which her household depended. She was extremely fortunate to give birth to seven children between 1842 and 1859 without damage to her own health, and to have all her children survive into adulthood. Notwithstanding her responsibilities, with visits from Mrs Mott, and with the support of the great William Lloyd Garrison who had backed the women in London, they held the famous 'Women's Rights Convention' in 19–20 July 1848 (the year of New York State's Married Women's Property Act). The Seneca Falls meeting resulted in a 'Declaration of Sentiments' and a list of 'Resolutions' by those present. Mrs Stanton insisted on the importance of including the demand for women's suffrage, well aware of the symbolic significance of the vote—that women had minds and wills of their own. The women present were sensitive to the criticisms to be levelled at them in their demands for changes in their legal status, access to education and employment, as well as to the horror expressed by the clergy at women who spoke in public, wrote essays and tracts, organized petitions, and generally moved into civic life, gaining valuable political experience (1 Tim. 2:12). Mrs Mott might well recollect the work of one of the founders of the Quaker tradition, Margaret Fell's 1666 *Women's speaking justified, proved and allowed of by the Scriptures, all such as speak by the spirit and power of the Lord Jesus. And how women were the first that preached the tidings of the resurrection of Jesus, and were sent by Christ's own command before he ascended to the Father John 20. 17*, and succinctly refer to Acts 2:17 and the Spirit's being poured out on daughters and sons alike. Others, like William Lloyd Garrison, thought the texts too problematic, since biblical texts had been cited not only in support of slavery but of many other human wrongs.

Seneca Falls was shortly followed by the Women's Rights Convention in Worcester, Massachusetts, in 1850, which launched the main campaign for women's suffrage. Harriet Beecher Stowe's *Uncle Tom's Cabin* (first published in serial form in 1851–2) familiarized her readers with at least some information about the reality of slave-life. Mrs Stanton learned of the reality through contacts with family and committed abolitionists protecting escaped slaves en route to safety, and in 1860 published her own *The Slave's Appeal* in which she adopted the voice of a black female slave turning the Ten Commandments against her oppressors (Stevenson-Moessner 1994). The mere existence of biblical texts had never prevented terrible injustices, not least the begetting of more children by white owners and estate managers on the bodies of black women, but here she attempted to use biblical texts in the interests of those most acutely vulnerable to such wicked behaviour. By

2 January 1863 freedom from slavery had at least been proclaimed in the states, and was ratified as the Thirteenth Amendment to the Constitution on 6 December 1865 at the conclusion of the Civil War. With literacy tests, poll taxes, and other hurdles, not to mention murderous physical intimidation, former slaves had future diffi-culties to surmount when, in addition, the Fourteenth Amendment of 9 July 1868 deemed male inhabitants only to be citizens of the United States, and not all adult inhabitants (over the age of 21). Women who had supported their side in the Civil War, and worked so hard for the abolition of slavery, found themselves jettisoned in their appeal for citizenship and therefore voting rights. Not until 1920 was their position to change, and Mrs Stanton for one was not alive to see it. In the meantime, the 'domestic tranquillity' of the introduction to the Constitution was not to be. Mrs Stanton left the American Equal Rights Association, since black men were deemed fit to join other men responsible for the legislature, but no women of any race. She helped to found the National Woman Suffrage Association in 1869, and travelled and lectured widely. One of her most powerful lectures was on the state of married women, including that of polygamous Mormon women—polyga-my being nowhere condemned in the Bible, as its readers could discover.

Apart from domestic support, Mrs Stanton could not have achieved half of what she did without the lifelong commitment of Susan B. Anthony, whom she first met in 1851, another formidable Quaker woman who stayed a friend and collaborator despite many difficulties and differences of opinion with Mrs Stanton. And togeth-er with the enthusiastic support of Mrs Stanton's youngest daughter Harriot (and from Mrs M. H. Gage) they put together the first large volume of a massive undertaking, the three-volume *History of Woman Suffrage*, the first volume of which came out in 1881 after a ten-year effort, with the remaining volumes published by 1886, the year when Mrs Stanton's husband died. Widowhood did not mean that she retired from public life. She had at least one other major publication in view—the book that was published as *The Woman's Bible*.

THE WOMAN'S BIBLE

As it so happened, in 1881 there was also published the first-stage revision of the Authorised Version of the Bible (the New Testament in 1881 and the Old Testament in 1885; the complete edition in 1888). This was the version used by Mrs Stanton and her collaborators. The fruit of a team effort instigated by the then archbishop of Canterbury, the scholars involved were largely from the United Kingdom, but with some American contribution by correspondence, and of course, no women. The Revised Version was as much criticized as applauded on publication, and it brought to the fore all sorts of issues about the interplay of translation and interpretation affecting the translation itself. Clearly, then, translators were not 'inspired', any more than were those who wrote the commentaries of the day. Quite apart from knowledge of relevant 'biblical languages', there was much debate about 'German' criticism, the relation of the texts to other ancient Near Eastern sources, developments in geology and astronomy, and a greatly extended time-line for human existence and development. There was considerable controversy and anxiety about the implications of 'Darwinism', both what Darwin himself had said, what he had meant by it, and what others made of his work. It certainly helped to dislodge the assumption that the first few chapters of Genesis were literally true, as had Thomas Paine's *The Rights of Man* (1791–2), in which Paine had done his bit to demolish biblical mythology. There were appeals to 'reason', to 'free thought' or 'new thought', not to mention Mary Baker Eddy's 'Christian Science' movement and her intelligent recasting of Eve's dealings with the serpent in line with other nineteenth-century women reformers. In addition, as ever, there were versions of Bible stories fit for children, Sunday School teachers, day-school teachers, ministers, and immigrant communities and congregations still struggling to learn American/English. Biblical texts could be handled in different ways. In that sense there were precedents for *The Woman's Bible*.

By this stage in her life Mrs Stanton had exhausted the usual range of actions available to advocates for change. Something new was called for, and in any case, with some notable exceptions, she had lost faith in the clergy and churches. She would not, however, focus on just one issue, such as women's suffrage, but as in her early days at Seneca Falls, opted for tackling a wide range of injustices, the foundation of which was a way of thinking about women and their place in the world. Central was to be women's new perception of themselves, and appeal to biblical tradition did nothing to help them change for the better, in her view. Moreover, she had largely lost patience with women who did not see things her way, and who still trusted their ministers and preachers. Since Harriot had in 1882 married an Englishman, Henry Blanch, and was an enthusiastic reformer in her own right, Mrs Stanton had a home in England to go to, as well as being able to rely on Harriot's expeditions back across the Atlantic. Journeys and visits to Harriot gave Mrs Stanton time to read and think, to meet with others in different contexts, and to be critical of the very slow pace of change in Britain, complicated as it was by the defence of aristocratic privilege in society and government. (It was not until the Life Peerages Act of 1958 that women could sit in the House of Lords.)

Mrs Stanton's last visit to England was in 1890, and she depended more and more on friends and on Harriot's visits back to the United States to further her projects. On one such visit Harriot, Stanton herself, and a friend (the Englishwoman Frances Lord, who was interested in the Theosophy movement) amused themselves by embarking on what Mrs Stanton provocatively referred to as 'The Woman's Bible'. This was not yet another 'great women of the Bible' production;

nor was it a commentary on the complete biblical text, with or without the Apocrypha (cf. Newsom and Ringe 1992). It was to be a commentary written by women on those parts of the Bible which explicitly referred to women, though some were excluded as unworthy of anyone's attention, for example the stories of Lot's daughters and of Tamar in Genesis. With the aid of a concordance and some cheap bibles to cut up, the three pasted cut-out texts onto blank pages (about one-tenth of the whole), and began their work, sometimes referring to Julia Smiths's 1886 translation (Stanton 1985: appendix to Part 1: 149–52). The original plan for completion was ambitious in the sense that Mrs Stanton wanted her team to include those with knowledge of 'biblical languages', textual criticism, skills in commentary work and interpretation, and knowledge of the history and context in which the texts had been written. She found it impossible to secure the team she had hoped for. Some of those approached had simply given up concern with the biblical text, pointing out that it could be read in a number of ways, as had the US Constitution in accommodating slavery and then abolishing it. Mrs Stanton's view was that since the Bible was so widely printed and circulated, and influential as 'the word of God', it simply had to be tackled. Far too many women still did not see that they had a major battle to fight in their own persons so long as they accepted biblically related and derived arguments for their civil and political degradation and understanding of themselves. Some possible contributors had other commitments; some pleaded that they did not have the skills she sought. Some did not want to associate themselves with so controversial a project, fearing that it would upset many 'evangelical' women in revival movements as well as in a range of denominations; and the majority of clergy were predictably hostile. Some, without saying so, may not have wanted to work with Mrs Stanton as the main editor, let alone without remuneration if they earned their living by writing.

The group who agreed to contribute could not in fact meet together as Mrs Stanton had first planned, for reasons which included poverty and age, so had to network by correspondence. The priority given to their commentary was immediately clear in the final production, with the biblical text in much smaller print than their own work. The text was to be treated as if written in plain English, though in the light of the fundamental question as to the way it had been used to subject women to men. The commentary, however, also made it abundantly clear that there could be more than one way of reading a text, since although the bulk of it appeared over Mrs Stanton's initials, other writers could and did offer alternative readings, frequently modifying their editor's more astringent views. Whilst she thought the texts were damaging in and of themselves, some of her collaborators clearly thought it was more a matter of the way the texts had been used that was the problem. Apart from that, it was clear that the writers accepted a view of the vastly expanded heliocentric universe of their own day, set in motion by 'our ideal great first cause', 'the Spirit of all good' (Stanton 1985: 1. 13, 61), the vastly expanded universe of modern astronomy (1. 125), and the importance of geology and archaeology (1. 25, 38). Inevitably, then, the commentary was critical of the anthropomorphism of the deity in the Pentateuch, 'a very contradictory character, unworthy of our love and admiration' (1. 47). The commentators drew on the work of Josephus, Eusebius, Lecky on rationalism, Andrew White on the 'warfare' between science and theology, and 'German' criticism' from De Wette onwards, which in Bonn had produced the thesis that the patriarchs were but 'mythical persons'. They knew of the contribution of Arab culture to architecture, science, astronomy, mathematics, and poetry, and knew too that a veil could be worn to protect a woman from 'premature or unwelcome intrusion', and not to indicate her humiliation (1. 49). One had studied the Jewish Kabbalah (2. 106–12), though the group had little appreciation otherwise of Judaism. They knew of the contribution of named women to the establishment and learning of the early church, including Paula's contribution to the production of the Vulgate. Bishop Colenso's work on the Pentateuch was clearly indispensable, especially because he had worked on it as a missionary among the Zulu, from whom he had learned so much. There was information available about the relationship of the biblical texts to those of Assyria and Egypt, and comparisons of biblical material with Greek and Roman fables, Norse and Mayan traditions, and those of the North American Indian peoples were all possible.

Turning to the actual biblical text, the commentary drew on source criticism, for instance the distinction between the strands that referred to the deity as 'Elohim' and Yahweh, and discussed whether the former term (a plural form in Hebrew) meant that the early Hebrews were polytheists or whether the word indicated the origin of the doctrine of the Trinity. In any event, since God made male and female in his image, the Godhead must represent the feminine as well as the masculine. In Mrs Stanton's view, the very first step in the elevation of women must be the address in prayer to God as Heavenly Mother as well as to a Father (1. 14), and in that case, even the New Testament also fell short of her ideal (1. 60). And she printed out in full a profound Zulu prayer from Colenso's work, which concluded with the words 'Thou art my Mother, Thou my Father!' (1. 136), language perhaps familiar from Shakers, but not from missionary endeavour. When it came to the human race, it was clear that woman was the 'crowning glory' of the whole, given with man dominion over all else, and certainly intended to be the head of her own household. Eve (Life) indeed was a character of courage, dignity, and ambition, while Adam was 'dastardly' in his whining attempt to shield himself at his wife's expense after the Fall (1. 24–7). The 'curse' then justified her subjection, though Mrs Stanton from her own experience argued that maternity was by no means the 'disability' spoken of by some churchmen, any more than was child-rearing, which required every possible skill (1. 82, 97, 114). She was rightly robust in her observations on how some women had refused to avail themselves of anaesthetics in childbirth, and how some orthodox physicians had refused to administer them, 'lest they should interfere with the wise provisions of Providence in making maternity a curse' (1. 31). So much for the admirable example of Queen Victoria (1. 78).

The commentary demolishes the examples of Sarah, Rebekah, and Rachel as models of virtue, describing them as being variously undignified, untruthful, and unkind, and lacking a sense of honour, though another commentator has them holding a dignified position in their families, with no hint of divinely intended subordination, saying that it was no accident, indeed, but of great significance, that Jacob, 'this most ardent and faithful of Jewish lovers should have deeper spiritual experiences than any of his predecessors' (1. 58). Mrs Stanton thought that Balaam's ass was a better example than the matriarchs of 'keen spiritual insight and the ready power of speech with which the female sex has been specially endowed' (1. 115). It was, of course, urged by others that the Hebrew scriptures taught tenderness to the vulnerable and generosity to the poor without robbing them of their dignity, as well as, 'rightly interpreted', the equality of the sexes (1. 142).

Notwithstanding the 'counter-voices' in the commentary, it is Mrs Stanton's polemic which makes her case throughout, from her 'Introduction' onwards. The Bible teaches that woman brought sin and death into the world, precipitated the Fall, was tried, condemned, and sentenced before the judgment-seat of heaven, that her marriage was to be bondage, maternity suffering and anguish, and she was to live in silence and subjection, utterly dependent on others for her material wants (1. 7). Mrs Stanton did not see how this 'mournful object of pity' could be transfigured into an exalted and dignified personage. She wanted neither the blessings nor curses of the Jewish God (1. 127), given that whenever women deferred to the clergy, having spotted the 'family resemblance' between scripture, canon, and common law, they were told that they owed their blessings and freedom to the Bible, but that their demands for political and civil rights were irreligious and dangerous to the stability of home, church, and state (1. 8). She attacked the clergy ('our Levites') and their financial and social privileges, not least their occupation of that 'coward's castle', the pulpit (1. 110), though she wanted more women to have access to it, as to other offices, synods, and conferences. She wanted women to free themselves of deference to the clergy and to cease pouring their energies into funding them and their churches (1. 130, 133). She urged self-development instead of self-sacrifice (1. 84). 'When people are in fortunate circumstances, the women are supposed, like lilies of the valley, to neither labour or spin, but when the adverse winds blow they suddenly find themselves compelled to use their own brains and hands or perish' (1. 95), putting middle-class women on a level with most others. Women must be in a position to protect both themselves and their children from 'desecration', never at the disposal of men, notwithstanding Numbers 31:35 (1. 120). No wonder that she urged visits to art galleries rather than reflection on scripture, since she claimed that there one could see how artists were associating women with virtue, with grace and science, far more reflecting the present and future than scripture could ever do (1. 132).

Mrs Stanton must have anticipated the furore which would result from the production even of this first part of *The Woman's Bible*, and in fact it was just what was needed in the long term. In the short term, however, the book was denounced as the work of Satan (not involved, as she tartly pointed out), and it played into the hands of anti-suffragists, not least since the contributors to the commentary were all known to have a long-standing commitment to the suffrage movement. It became easy to accuse suffragists of holding Mrs Stanton's opinions, which unfortunately was not the case, in her view. Even before the actual publication of Part II in 1898 (*Comments on the Old and New Testaments from Joshua to Revelation*), some of the very organizations to which she had given so much rapidly distanced themselves from her. The main case of this, which received maximum publicity, was the NAWSA meeting in January 1896, which proposed the following resolution: 'That this Association is non-sectarian, being composed of persons of all shades of religious opinion, and that it has no official connection with the so-called "Woman's Bible", or any theological publication.' In her capacity as president, Susan B. Anthony rose to her feet to argue for freedom of opinion in NAWSA rather than the revival of censorship. 'What you should do is to say to outsiders that a Christian has neither more or less rights in our Association than an atheist. When our platform becomes too narrow for people of all creeds and of no creeds, I myself shall not stand upon it.' She reminded them that at Seneca Falls in 1848 Lucretia Mott had thought Mrs Stanton mistaken in urging that women's suffrage be included in the demands of those present, but she had been proved to be right. Susan B. Anthony wanted to foster a 'broad and catholic spirit', or women would fail in government once they gained access to it. She was right to say that: 'This resolution, adopted, will be a vote of censure upon a woman who is without peer in intellectual and statesmanlike ability; one who has stood for half a century the acknowledged leader of progressive thought and demand in regard to all matters pertaining to the absolute freedom of women.' Notwithstanding her argument, the resolution was adopted by 53 to 41 votes; Susan B. Anthony stood her ground as president of NAWSA; and Mrs Stanton was so undeterred by what had happened that she printed the report of the meeting at the end of the second part of *The Woman's Bible* (2. 185–7).

Readers were frightened by the irreverent tone of the book; for example, Abraham, like 'many a modern millionaire', was not self-made but a wife-made man (1. 44); and 'If Miriam had helped to plan the journey to Canaan, it would no doubt have been accomplished in forty days instead of forty years' (1. 103). If Mrs Stanton's views were adopted, critics claimed, men would lose their reverence for Christian women. Quite what this meant or had meant for working women or black women remained unclear. At least one woman saw the point, on Mrs Stanton's side rather than on the side of her detractors, since 'when women who have had no property, no ownership of their children, no souls, no bodies, no clothes, and no place to lay themselves after death—their poor selves that have never belonged to themselves—it is no wonder that these poor creatures suddenly owning a Bible should shock conservatism'. Women wanted to find out for themselves just what the Bible did and did not have to offer them. 'We want to know if Paul meant all he expressed when he also tells us of the great help he had from women who preached with him. We want to tell the world all the Christ said to women, and how, when every disciple forsook him, woman was constant. She was last at the cross and first at the tomb.' Mary Seymour Rowell thus eagerly awaited the publication of Part II, urging women to beware of casting a blow against their own cause (letter to the *New York Times*, 1 March 1896).

When the shorter second part came out in 1898, it was quickly apparent to readers that Mrs Stanton was vigorously unrepentant. For instance, there was to be no easy dependence on the New Testament in repudiation of the Old, since the church had repeated everything in favour of women's subordination (2. 8). Some of her comments were predictable, as on Rahab (2. 12) and Deborah (2. 19–20), as well as on the Canaanite woman (2. 121) and the eminently 'wise virgins' (2. 123–8) in their self-reliance. Jephthah's daughter, belonging to the 'no-name series', should have opted for 'a dignified and whole-souled rebellion' (2. 25). For the first time in scripture, when we encounter Solomon's visit from the Queen of Sheba, we have an account 'of a prolonged rational conversation with a woman on questions of public policy', for 'he talked with her as one sovereign should with another' (2. 66–71). Elisha raises the dead indeed, and 'surpasses our Standard Oil Company in the production of that valuable article of commerce', though he cures one man of leprosy whilst inflicting it on his servant 'for being guilty of a pardonable prevarication' (1. 77). Huldah was a professor of jurisprudence, pondering law whilst 'her husband was probably arranging the royal buttons and buckles of the household' (2. 82–3); Deborah was commended for courage and military prowess, Esther for ruling, and Vashti for disregarding the Apostle's command to obey her husband, refusing to appear as an exhibit (2. 86–7). Isaiah 3 was useful for denouncing the distractions, the frivolities, and distractions of contemporary dress (2. 102, 161–2, 174–5), temptations which Eve had refused (1. 24). Part I had in fact included some reference to New Testament texts, not least those which were concerned with hair and the wearing of bonnets as signs of subjection (1. 104), now picked up in the second part (2. 156–7), and one interesting link was to be found in the comments on Miriam, prophetess, wise, leader of victory song, since Catholic writers represented her 'as a type of the Virgin Mary' (1. 103). Mrs Stanton was shrewd in pointing to the discrepancy between the honour paid to Mary and that paid to all other women, as well as on the way in which Jesus, the wise and virtuous son, was indebted to his mother. She was, however, thoroughly critical of his 'immaculate conception by the Holy Ghost' (2. 113). It could be hardly expected that Protestant women would grasp the difference between the virginal conception/birth of Jesus and the dogma of the Immaculate Conception of 1854, but in any case, as another of the commentators made clear, they saw both as slurs on 'natural motherhood' (2. 113–14). Jesus himself emerges as 'the great leading Radical of his age', and the apostles as responsible for teaching the inferiority of women (2. 162–8), so that they emerge as more clearly the heirs of the Old Testament that he was. The final riposte comes in a comment on the Book of Revelation, since the writers of the Bible 'are prone to make woman the standard for all kinds of abominations; and even motherhood, which should be held most sacred, is used to illustrate the most revolting crimes' (2. 184).

MRS STANTON'S LEGACY

At her death in 1902 Mrs Stanton was still remembered as having regarded *The Woman's Bible* as her greatest achievement, though at her actual funeral service in her own home, shared with some of her family, the table on which the 'Declaration of Sentiments' from Seneca Falls had been written was at the head of the casket, which bore the *History of Women Suffrage* (Griffith 1984: 218). William Lloyd Garrison himself turned up for a memorial meeting and made essentially the same point for 'catholicity' which had been made by Susan B. Anthony:

Avoid the narrowness that often attaches to special reforms, and prevents the appreciation of cognate movements for humanity. Far greater than to be the partisan of any one single cause, however noble, is it to maintain a vital interest in every effort for human freedom. It was the breadth of vision and inclusive sympathy which was the highest distinction of Mrs Stanton. (*New York Times*, 20 November 1902)

And one contributor to *The Woman's Bible* made a plea that was arguably important for the future, since she declared that readers 'must not avoid the whirlpool of a masculine Bible only to split upon the rock of a feminine Bible alone', taking the Pentateuch as part of an organic whole, and believing that the book remained 'the soul's guide in the fulfilling of its destiny' (1. 147).

Over the next few generations women's access to the relevant skills for biblical criticism was to develop, but particularly in the period after World War II, when, for instance, women were at last admitted to Harvard Divinity School and accepted in a wider range of churches. The Second Vatican Council was also a major stimulus to reflection in both biblical studies and Christian doctrine. There were glimpses even in *The Woman's Bible* that a major reappraisal of central Christian doctrines would indeed be required, not least since it was a doctrinal framework which underlay the interpretation which had served women so ill. Mrs Stanton's book was reprinted yet again some years after its initial success on republication in the 1970s, when the Seattle-based Coalition Task Force on Women and Religion brought out its own edition with a collection of accompanying essays (Kern 2001: 7). Mrs Stanton's perspective and prejudices have come in for much criticism, in effect for being a woman of her own place and time, but she can be warmly appreciated as a most important catalyst not only in reform of social, civic, and political life, but for what has become 'feminist' biblical theology and criticism, dislodging exclusively male-centred perspectives. She is still provocative to read in her concern for relationships between the sexes, and, crucially, on the matter of how human beings understand and respond to God. Her wide sympathies would surely embrace not only greater knowledge of Judaism and Islam at the very least, but women's perceptions of God from across the globe and an extraordinary range of traditions. She would certainly expect women to be engaged in civic and political life, though she might be somewhat disappointed in women's continued commitment to their religious traditions. Feminist theology as a whole is much more complex than Mrs Stanton and her collaborators could ever have envisaged, but she remains exemplary in her intelligence and courage for the production of *The Woman's Bible*.

WORKS CITED

ELSHTAIN, J. B. (1981), *Public Man, Private Woman: Women in Social and Political Thought*. Oxford: Robertson.

GRIFFITH, E. (1982), *In Her Own Right: The Life of Elizabeth Cady Stanton*. New York: Oxford University Press.

KERN, K. (2001), *Mrs. Stanton's Bible*. Ithaca and London: Cornell University Press.

NEWSOM, C. A. and RINGE, S. H. (eds.) (1992), *The Women's Bible Commentary*. London: SPCK.

STANTON, E. C. (1985), *The Woman's Bible*. Edinburgh: Polygon (originally pub. 1895, 1898).

STEVENSON-MOESSNER, J. (1994), 'Elizabeth Cady Stanton, Reformer to Revolutionary: A Theological Trajectory', *Journal of the American Academy of Religion*, 62/3: 673–89 (includes the text of *The Slave's Appeal*).

FURTHER READING

DUBOIS, E. C. (ed.) (1992), *The Elizabeth Cady Stanton–Susan B. Anthony Reader: Correspondence, Writings, Speeches*. Boston: Northeastern University Press.

ELSHTAIN, J. B. (1982), *The Family in Political Thought*. Brighton: Harvester.

FIORENZA, E. S. (ed.) (1993/4), *Searching the Scriptures*: Vol. 1, *A Feminist Introduction*; Vol. 2, *A Feminist Commentary*. New York: Crossroad.

MARTIN, F. (1994), *The Feminist Question: Feminist Theology in the Light of Christian Tradition*. Edinburgh: T. & T. Clark.

MAYER, H. (1998), *All on Fire: William Lloyd Garrison and the Abolition of Slavery*. New York: St Martin's.

STANTON, F. C. (1993), *Eighty Years and More: Reminiscences 1815–1897*. Boston: Northeastern University Press (originally pub. 1898).

CHAPTER 22

UCHIMURA AND THE BIBLE IN JAPAN

ATSUHIRO ASANO

For twenty centuries God has been perfecting *Bushido* [the way of *samurai*] with this very moment in view. Christianity grafted upon *Bushido* will yet save the world.

(Uchimura 1916: 22. 161–2)

INTRODUCTION

The 'very moment' came, and Christianity, with its scripture, was reintroduced to the islands of the East. It was for the Japanese the encounter with the West that the nation had been resisting for no less than two centuries. Regardless of its origin, the Christian religion appeared to the recipients as the 'soul' behind all the eye-opening technologies, both constructive and destructive, which flooded the archipelago. The story of the reception of the Bible, therefore, is indivisible from that of the reception of Western civilization as a whole. So great was the impact of the encounter that Japanese identity would be irrevocably disturbed (Shively 1971: 79). Even greater was the identity crisis of those Japanese who accepted the message of the Bible, which was believed to be the 'soul book' of a foreign civilization. Since then, Japanese believers have constantly faced a critical question: how can one be a believer and yet remain Japanese? For the sake of mere survival of the fledgling religious communities, the story of the reception of the Bible, therefore, inevitably involved evaluation and redefinition of the world around them, which included both Christianity and their own traditions. Amalgamation of two traditions was necessary in order for the believers of the new religion to find their place in the world. This need led Kanzo Uchimura (1861–1930), the founder of a Christian community called *Mukyokai*, to the concept of indigenization expressed as 'Christianity grafted upon *Bushido*'. It helped him to gain confidence in the amalgamated identity of the 'Japanese Christian'. While all Japanese Christian communities at this period of emergence faced the challenge of securing their identity one way or another, Uchimura and his *Mukyokai*, in their peculiar social position, reflect the struggle more clearly than others.

In this chapter on 'Uchimura and the Bible in Japan' I will first clarify the motive behind his reception of the Bible in the brief historical description of Japan's encounter with Christianity and the emergence of Uchimura's community of *Mukyokai* (cf. Asano 2005: ch. 2; Caldarola 1979: ch. 2). Based upon the identified motivation, I will then survey Uchimura's writings with three applicational foci in mind, which stand out in his reading of the Bible; that is, the authentication of the marginal, reconsideration of patriotism, and redefinition of Christianity. Books, journal articles and diary entries that he left behind are all contained in the forty-one volumes of *Uchimura Kanzo Zenshu* ('The Complete Works of Kanzo Uchimura'—Uchimura 1980–2001). Among these, particular focus will be given to the series of expository essays on Paul's Letter to the Galatians, and other essays regarding major prophets, as Uchimura often compares them with the apostle Paul. Interest in these essays is due to the special affinity that Uchimura held toward the Galatians letter, to which his own life experience of community-building corresponds closely as an analogical narrative.

HISTORY: THE INTRODUCTION OF CHRISTIANITY AND EMERGENCE OF THE *MUKYOKAI*

Japan's Encounter with Christianity

The initial introduction of Christianity to Japan precedes the time of Uchimura by about 300 years. Francisco Xavier, from the Jesuits' mission, reached the southern island of Kyushu in 1549. The mission attracted more than a few warlords in the southern part of Japan, many of whom were no doubt motivated by the economic benefit that trade with Portugal would bring. Yet within less than a century of the arrival of Catholic missions the number of believers grew to about 300,000 (Boxer 1967: 321, 360). However, when Tokugawa Shogunate established its supreme power over the islands, the third Shogun Iemitsu began a systematic and wholesale persecution of the churches. This was considered necessary for the purpose of ensuring the purity of traditional religions, securing moral order, and protecting the nation from Western expansionism. The effort of extermination being complete, those who did not recant their faith were either executed (there were 40,000 martyrs) or went underground to preserve both their faith and their lives (cf. Harrington 1993; Whelan 1996). Fear and prejudice were planted in the hearts of the Japanese against the religion that the Westerners had brought (Ellison 1973: 178–9; Endo 1996). A seclusion policy was enacted by Iemitsu in 1639 as an extension of previous anti-Christian measures, and it practically locked up the country from the West for the next two hundred years. In this period of *Pax Tokugawa*, the Shogunate maintained a method of registering its subjects in order to search for secret believers and perpetuate fear of the 'evil' religion.

Pax Tokugawa came to an abrupt end when US commodore Perry visited Japan in 1853, an act which represented Western pressure to relinquish national seclusion and reopen the medieval gate to the land of the samurai. Japan faced a choice of either resisting the Western powers, in the end becoming their colonies, or Westernizing the country to gain power over and above her Asian neighbours, in order to be recognized as equal in power with the Western nations. Coinciding with this was the successful *coup d'état* led by dissatisfied warlords, which returned the rule of the country to the royal house in 1867, and the constitutional monarchy of Meiji inaugurated the modern era of Japan through Westernizing the nation (cf. Waswo 1996). Western technology was a necessary ingredient in modernizing Japan, and it was enthusiastically imported. Along with that, the much-feared and long-resisted religion of Christianity was finally allowed its re-entry, yet the majority of the people continued their prejudice against it (Shiono 2007; Morioka 1970: 215–16). Although initially the Meiji government supported an open and uncritical Westernizing policy, it quickly faced resistance, and the pendulum swung toward a strong nationalism. The Western powers forced the new government to discontinue all anti-Christian measures in 1873, but the government also enacted the Imperial Constitution (1889) and the Rescript of Education (1890), both of which confirmed the headship of the Emperor of Japan and its cult of National Shinto. Therefore, the tolerance of Christianity was conditioned by the Article 28 of the constitution, which states that 'any subject of imperial Japan, so long as he does not violate peace and order, or fail the duties of a subject, is allowed a freedom of religion', presuming the possible danger of the Christian religion. In the increasing fervour of imperial nationalism, Christians found themselves caught between two masters, the Emperor of the line of ages eternal (*Banse-Ikkei*) and the Lord of the ages to come.

Emergence of Uchimura's *Mukyokai*

The bewilderment caused by the identity crisis that the nation as a whole experienced in its encounter with the West was described by Shunsuke Kamei, one of Uchimura's disciples; 'The spirit of the Meiji era as a whole continued swinging between Japan and the West'; and he continues: 'in which Uchimura was shaken more violently than any other' (Kamei 1977: 222). How was Uchimura affected so greatly by the encounter, besides the fact that his strong personality tended to face conflicts directly?

Like many sons of the last samurai, who were disbanded and lost social status on the occasion of social restructurization at the dawn of the Meiji era, Kanzo Uchimura was eager to receive a Western education in the hope of promotion within the new society. Along with a few others of his class, Uchimura accepted Christianity and its scripture in 1877 as the new spiritual guide in his life journey through the missionary work of William Clark, who presided at the college where Uchimura studied ichthyology (Uchimura 1895: 3. 14–15). His conversion was at least partly motivated by his initial fascination with Western civilization. However, disgusted by the moral depravity of what he naively idealized as 'the Christian nation of America' during his time in the United States (1885–8), together with his previous conflict with denominational missionaries who were critical of his effort to form a non-denominational gathering of students for crossing denominational boundaries, Uchimura began to consider how he might express his Christian faith without the Western elements in it. When he returned to his country, Uchimura found Japan in the developing fervour of imperialistic nationalism, with the issuing of both the constitution and the educational rescript mentioned above. It was at the public ceremony of enactment of that rescript in 1890 that Uchimura failed to bow and pay respect to the imperial signature on the rescript copy. The media immediately publicized the incident as an unpardonable act of *lse majesté*, and caricaturized him as a national traitor and outlaw (Uchimura 1891: 36. 331–2). Considering himself a patriot, this unexpected result of the incident was the occasion for Uchimura to begin seeking the true meaning of patriotism (Uchimura 1898: 6. 64).

Humiliated and marginalized by the incident, Uchimura sought refuge among the churches, but he was denied it. This is because he had been highly critical of the denominational churches' tendency toward sectarianism, which they had adopted from foreign missionaries. Furthermore, churches distanced themselves from him because they feared the implication of sharing in the alleged act of high treason (Uchimura 1891: 36. 33). He records in one of his books the deep sorrow and frustration he felt over the experience of deracination: 'I have become *mukyokai* (belonging to no church) . . . I am denied the sanctuary where I worship and come near to God' (Uchimura 1893: 2. 26). Uchimura directly faced the divisiveness of Western Christianity, the media's labelling of him as an 'unpatriotic scandal', and denial from the churches. His response to these painful experiences was the formation of his own Christian community called '*Mukyokai*', which was founded in the year 1900. Since then, the *Mukyokai* has been known as a unique Christian gathering with strong emphases on anti-institutionalism (anti-denominational-ism), anti-ritualism, and pursuit of an indigenous expression of faith (Caldarola 1979: 67–8), claiming to adhere closely to the original biblical pattern of *Ecclesia* s (Brunner 1951: ch. 10; 1959: 147–55).

We must conclude this historical description with a remark on the motive behind Uchimura's reception of the Bible. Besides his conviction that the Bible, as the sacred scripture of his new-found religion, reveals the will of the living God to guide him, his community, and even his country, Uchimura was motivated to read the Bible because he found it to be a significant source of analogies closely related to his own life experience, and to those of the *Mukyokai*. The Bible became an important and useful literary source for the purpose of securing and establish-ing the *raison d'être* of his fledgling and marginalized community. As Uchimura sought to attain the original *Ecclesia* in his *Mukyokai*, the authenticity of the community hinged upon what the Bible taught about the world around them and about their very existence, which faced a great deal of adversity. In the next section we will observe how Uchimura would read the Bible and draw biblical analogies to the life experience of his community. Even though the *Mukyokai* and the denominational churches stood apart from each other, the churches shared similar experiences of marginalization in a country disdainful of Christianity. Therefore, what we find in Uchimura's reading of the Bible reflects how Japan encountered the religion as a whole.

TEXT: UCHIMURA AND THE BIBLE

Special Focus on Galatians

It is a peculiar tendency of the *Mukyokai* to preserve and compile the documents of their leaders for posterity, and consequently multi-volumes of their writings are available to us. While it is partly due to the fact that many of the leaders and community members were highly intellectual (Brunner 1951: 154), I have elsewhere argued that the uniqueness of the community, which was without the usual denominational or institutional identity markers, built a sense of camaraderie through owning the very text of their respectful leaders as a sort of artefact (Asano 2005: 209–11). In this way, Uchimura's writings are preserved as a spiritual heritage for *Mukyokai* members, and consequently for the rest of Japanese Christians as well. From his collected writings, I am especially interested in surveying Uchimura's expository essays on the Letter to the Galatians. I will also refer to his study on the two prophetic figures of Isaiah and Jeremiah.

In the preface to his series of exposition on Galatians, Uchimura speaks of his special affinity for the letter, saying; 'Luther calls the Galatian letter "my book", and likewise so can I. However, I owe to the letter more than Luther' (Uchimura 1926: 29. 458). Uchimura explains that while Luther failed to practice what the letter teaches, by becoming a pope of his own denomination, Uchimura perfected what the letter teaches and maintained the spirit of the *Mukyokai*, the original *Ecclesia*. He continues: 'if I am asked; "what is the biblical foundation for your *Mukyokai*?", then I will answer; "It is Paul's letter to the Galatians" . . . As long as Galatians remains in the Bible, the spirit of the *Mukyokai* will never perish' (ibid.). Therefore, for Uchimura, the Letter to the Galatians is the biblical foundation for his Christian existence, and it defends the *raison d'tre* of the faith community that he formed.

One of the notable features of Uchimura's exposition of Galatians is that he often compares Paul's life to that of the prophets Isaiah and Jeremiah (Uchimura 1928: 31.17–18). The image of lone prophets devoted to spiritual reform despite great opposition overlapped with Paul's biographical narrative in Galatians, and together aided the justification of what Uchimura felt called to accomplish (Ebisawa and Ouchi 1970: 282–3). In fact, Uchimura gives to the Book of Jeremiah the same evaluation as Galatians. He says: 'As long as the book of Jeremiah remains in the Bible, the spirit of the *Mukyokai* will never perish among Christian believers' (Uchimura 1926: 29. 354). While Uchimura acknowledges the theologically important role of Paul's letter to the Romans within the entire Bible (Uchimura 1928: 31. 7), the book he treasures most both for himself and for his community is the Letter to the Galatians. Therefore, we now turn to Uchimura's exposition of the letter.

Uchimura's Exposition

Authenticity of a Lone Prophet

As Uchimura begins his exposition of Galatians, he dwells extensively on the first verse of the letter, which claims the authenticity of Paul's autonomous apostleship. Uchimura calls this verse a 'stronghold of faith', and considers it Paul's invitation to become a lone prophetic voice. In the exposition of this verse, Uchimura compares Paul's painful experience with the 'circumcisers' to his own experience with denominational churches and missionaries, who denied his orthodoxy and doubted the genuineness of his faith (Uchimura 1926: 29. 18; Masaike 1970: 160–1). Uchimura understands his adverse experiences as symptoms of 'the present evil age' (Gal. 1: 4), and remarks that the presence of the evil age is why his commitment to God is criticized as unorthodox and abnormal (Uchimura 1926: 29. 24). Elsewhere comparing his experiences to those of Jesus, Paul, and Luther, who were also labelled as heretics by the ruling powers, Uchimura defines 'heresy' as follows: 'When truth stands alone without the approval of people, the world calls it heresy. When the emperor gives support to it, the world calls it orthodoxy. In the world of heterodoxy, the names are reversed. Blessed is he who is hated by "orthodoxy" because of his being a "heretic"' (Uchimura 1908: 16. 73, 82).

In his study of the prophet Isaiah, a reference is made back to Galatians 1:1. There, Uchimura emphasizes that the divine initiative of a prophetic call often meets human opposition. Then, still within the theme of a divinely initiated prophetic call, Uchimura stigmatizes denominational ministers by saying that they are called by missionaries or denominational meetings, not by God. The lack of an authorizing body to recognize the validity of his work is not a problem for Uchimura, because in Isaiah 63:1–6 God is seen to accomplish his work alone. Jesus went to the cross alone, and likewise alone did Paul embark on the Gentile mission (Uchimura 1928: 31. 58–60). They experienced loneliness in practising what they thought was God's will, the kind of solitary experience that Isaiah mentions: 'I looked, but there was no helper; I stared, but there was no one to sustain me' (Isa. 63:5) (Uchimura 1928: 31. 104–5). Again, with Galatians 1:1 in view and commenting on Jeremiah's call to be God's prophet against kings, nobles, priests, politicians, and the entire nation (cf. Jer. 1:15–2:13), Uchimura explains that Jeremiah was still young and 'had *no church* to depend upon' (Uchimura 1926: 29. 370–1). Here, Uchimura certainly projects his experience of lonely resolution onto the prophetic call of Jeremiah, because the state of this prophet resembles the early description of his state of *mukyokai* (non-church), that is: 'I have become *mukyokai*. No church have I that man made, no hymn do I hear that consoles my soul, nor a minister do I know who prays for me a blessing' (Uchimura 1893: 2. 36). Thus, comparing himself with Paul, Isaiah, and Jeremiah, Uchimura justifies his experience of marginalization as a sign of his authentic call from God.

Staying on the theme of prophetic call, Uchimura points out the important role that a wilderness experience plays in the life of a prophet (Gal. 1:15–17). He explains that in the wilderness such prophets as Moses, Elijah, John the Baptist, Jesus, and Paul either received divine revelation or had it deeply internalized. For Paul, the strength required for him to resist opposing pressure to circumcise Titus for the truth of the gospel (Gal. 2:1–10) is drawn from his learning and growing experience in the wilderness. Uchimura then reflects on his own experience, asking himself what this wilderness experience might hold. He says: '[it is] the wilderness of mercilessness. Today's cruel society and the churches are nothing but the wilderness in Japan. When ruthless criticism casts us out to the wilderness, there we hear the voice of God' (Uchimura 1926: 29. 30–5). For Uchimura, it is in this wilderness experience of an anti-Christian social ethos and painful denial from the churches that he is convinced of the truthfulness of his gospel.

In Galatians 3:1–5, Paul sends an accusation to his beloved believers in Galatia based upon a strong conviction in the truthfulness of his gospel. Uchimura finds a parallel of this rebuke in Jeremiah's prophetic accusation of spiritual depravity against his people (Jer. 2:11–13) (Uchimura 1926: 29. 48). It should be pointed out, however, that when Uchimura stresses the importance of Paul's prophetic role in Galatians, he is not only referring to Uchimura's own role as a prophet, but also inviting the *Mukyokai* believers to embrace their prophetic role. His exhortation for the believers to be a prophetic voice in their society is expressed in his study of Jeremiah 5. He says: 'At least Judah had Jeremiah. In our country, we do not find him. Having Jeremiah, who rebukes his people with the wrath of YHWH saying that there is no one righteous, Judah was far better than our country' (Uchimura 1926: 29. 391). Uchimura explains that Judah, in her spiritual depravity, still had a prophet to seek justice and raise an alerting voice, while modern Japan lacks that voice to steer its path, pointing the reader to their need of a prophet.

Paul's conflict with the Jerusalem church and its Jewish style of mission warns the modern interpreter of Paul to exercise caution not to overlook an inherent complexity in the process of the formation of Christian communities at their earliest stage, rather than simply assuming a monolithic view of Christian identity. For Uchimura and his community members, however, one aspect of community identity construction stood out from the rest. In it, Paul is praised for being faithful to his conviction and not hesitating to oppose even the Jerusalem leaders (Uchimura 1926: 29. 15–16). Thus, the image of the solitary prophet, convinced of divine revelation and the truthfulness of his gospel in the midst of opposing pressure, gives them confidence that opposition from both church and state is actually the mark of authenticity. Indeed, Uchimura understands the 'marks of Jesus' that Paul carries (Gal. 6:17) to be the scars from various forms of persecution reported in 2 Corinthians 11:23–5, and considers his painful and lasting memories of persecution and marginalization as his own marks of Jesus (Uchimura 1926: 29. 17, 19). Thus, the Galatian letter is a significant source of reference for the marginalized and lonely community in understanding the precedence of a reversal of authentic status.

Patriot's Wailing

As mentioned above, Uchimura's struggle between his national identity and Christian conscience caused him to redefine the idea of patriotism. Two incidents especially impressed upon him the urgency of resolving the 'necessary' yet uncomfortable idea of patriotism. First is the experience of extreme humiliation Uchimura endured during the incident of alleged high treason. Second is the result of the Sino-Japanese War (1894–5), which convinced him that an uncritical form of patriotism only betrays his love of nation. Uchimura initially considered the war as a righteous one and supported it as a means of securing justice in Asia (Uchimura 1894: 3. 39). However, in learning of the ruthless expansionism that resulted, he recanted his previous opinion and became highly critical of Japan's militarism, and of the churches that continued to support such rampant expansionism (Matuzawa 1971: 49–50; Uchimura 1895: 11. 296–7). As part of the process of resolving this problem, Uchimura looked again to the biblical prophets, and found in them the true image of a patriot.

Uchimura speaks on patriotism in an essay written just prior to the series of studies on Jeremiah in the same volume of *Seisho no Kenkyu*, almost as a preface to the study. He says:

I have two Js that I love; one is J for Jesus and the other J is for Japan. I cannot tell which I love more. If one is taken away, I do not have the reason to remain alive. . . . though Japan never treated me as Jesus loved me, I cannot help but love Japan. . . . (however), my patriotism does not express itself through militarism. I seek to make Japan known in the world for its commitment to justice. . . . and my work for the gospel is a patriot's action. (Uchimura 1926: 29. 351–2)

In Uchimura's understanding, God's prophetic call is often a call to be a patriot, one who says 'no' to the injustices of his nation, even at the cost of his own life. Prophetic action and patriotic action are closely connected for Uchimura, who constantly faced the problem of reconciling his religious identity with a national (ethnic) identity. While there is no extended reference to patriotism in his study of Galatians, Uchimura considers Paul's confession to be a portrayal of an exemplary patriotic attitude, which says: 'I have great sorrow and unceasing anguish in my heart' for his own people (Rom. 9:3–4) (Uchimura 1921: 26. 333–5). Commenting on Jeremiah 9:1, which says: 'O that my head were a spring of water, and my eyes a fountain of tears, so that I might weep day and night for the slain of my poor people', Uchimura asks the reader, 'where would you find anyone who cries so bitterly for his own nation as the great prophet Jeremiah? This is patriot's wailing' (Uchimura 1926: 29. 397). Uchimura associates his desperate cry against the injustice of his nation with Jeremiah's patriotic wailing. His sharply critical rhetoric is also likened to that of Jeremiah, in that it reflects his patriotic commitment (cf. Jer. 9:4–9) (Uchimura 1926: 29. 399).

Uchimura's re-evaluation of patriotism, however, owes most to the Book of Isaiah. He admits that before reading the prophets in the Hebrew Bible he never knew what it was to love his own country, and urges the reader to read the prophets in order to learn about true patriotism. Uchimura certainly read the prophets, especially Isaiah, and came to realize that '[patriotism] is the sentiment that I ought to cherish as a servant of Christ, and it is the path that I shall tread' (Uchimura 1928: 31. 44–5). He learns from Isaiah 2:1–4 a common feature of all patriotic prophets, which is to hold an ideal and divine vision for the nation and endeavour to accomplish that vision for God. The vision that Isaiah spoke of for Judah and Jerusalem is that all nations would gather and hear the Lord's instruction for peace through his people. Uchimura contrasts this vision of Isaiah with the Japanese imperialistic patriots, who import arms from the Western nations in order to fortify and build a powerfully violent nation, and deplores the superficiality and immaturity of their form of patriotism.

Ridding patriotism of militarism and finding patriotic models in the Bible, Uchimura held an ideal vision for his nation as Isaiah did for his, that Japanese Christianity would serve the cause of salvation across the world. In reconciling Japanese identity and Christian identity, the redefinition of patriotism was a necessary process for Uchimura. However, there was one other process he found necessary; that is, the redefinition of Japanese Christianity by freeing it from its Western elements. Therefore, he says in his essay entitled 'The Japanese and Christianity':

When Christ visited Japan, it was not a foreign invasion. Just as it says, 'He came to what was his own, and his own people did not accept him', Christ came to his own people. The Japanese are given the qualification to understand and serve him better than the Westerners . . . I think that Christianity will reach perfection when the Japanese look to Christ as their saviour. (Uchimura 1925: 29. 277)

This statement introduces the reader to Uchimura's peculiar directions in the redefinition of Christianity, that is, negatively disinheriting the West from Christianity and positively indigenizing it. This twofold direction is the final point to be made on Uchimura's reading of the Bible.

Disinheriting the West and Indigenizing Christianity

As long as Christianity is considered an ideology of Western civilization, it conflicts with the identity of the Japanese Christian, who inhabits a society with a long history of resisting and fearing the religion. Struggling with this problem, therefore, the Western forms of Christianity are differentiated from the true form of Christianity throughout Uchimura's writings, even those outside his exposition on Galatians. For example, Uchimura shares a rather provocative criticism of the Western Reformation traditions, not to mention the hierarchical institution of Catholicism: 'I detest Protestant Churches because they are not Protestant enough' (Uchimura 1928: 31. 134–5). However, Uchimura reflects, in his exposition on the third chapter of Galatians, a typical Lutheran approach to the relationship between faith and the Torah. In it, Uchimura emphasizes the discontinuity of Judaism and Christianity, and indeed comes very close to Luther's own expression—denoting the Torah as 'a hammer of death' for the unregenerate (Oswald 1963: 39)—by saying: 'The Law is like a whip that chases us toward the gospel' (Uchimura 1926: 29. 53). Even though Uchimura criticizes Luther for failing to accomplish what he taught, the Lutheran teaching itself corresponds with that of Uchimura. Thus, Uchimura thinks that he—not Luther or others in the Western traditions—is the one who perfects Paul's Protestant vision in the Letter to the Galatians (Uchimura 1926: 29. 458). For him, Western Protestantism was not able to do enough to accomplish the original vision of *Ecclesia*, void of human aspects of institutionalism (denominationalism) and of persistence in particular modes of rituals (ritualism).

Behind this sort of general criticism against institutionalism and ritualism were Uchimura's personal experiences as previously mentioned: disappointment with the 'sectionalism' of foreign missionaries and with the 'moral depravity' of the United States. However, there is a wider historical context. When Protestant missions started in the early Meiji era, some of the original missionaries and Japanese Christians gathered to discuss the vision of *Kirisuto Kokai* ('United Assembly of Christ'), in which Japanese churches were not to follow the divisive Western denominational polities, but seek to create a united assembly. This ecclesial direction was motivated in part by the fact that the original missionary endeavour was so small and weak that denominational missionaries had no choice but to cooperate with one another. However, this naive vision of *Kirisuto Kokai*, indifferent to a long tradition of denominationalism within Western Christianity, was said to be shattered by lack of agreement, mainly between the Presbyterian and Congregational approaches (Ebisawa and Ouchi 1970: 172).

The Letter to the Galatians is for Uchimura a primary source from which to draw anti-Western rhetoric for the purpose of disinheriting the West. It is rather curious that in his short introduction to the study of Galatians Uchimura spends half the space explaining how the subsequent study is designed to help the reader resist the influence of American Christianity. Commenting on the expansionism of the United States, he says, 'it is said that Americanism would destroy the world, but what triumphs over the great force of Americanism is Paul's gospel found in the Letter to the Galatians' (Uchimura 1926: 29. 458–9). Uchimura elsewhere defines 'American Christianity' as a materialistic, divisive religion of triumphalism (Uchimura 1927: 30. 368; 1916: 22. 368–9). Two years prior to writing his preface, the Exclusion Bill (or Johnson Act) was passed by the US Congress in 1924, which resulted in the regulation of Japanese immigrants to the United States. Uchimura, who had been very critical about the passing of the bill, may have at this occasion sharpened his rhetoric, particularly against America (Uchimura 1924: 28. 231–2). However, what may even seem to be a pathological degree of negative rhetoric against the United States probably reflects the depth of Uchimura's earlier disappointment with what he had imagined as the ideal Christian nation (Ota 1977: 158–9). In the body of his exposition, the opponents of Paul in Galatians who preach 'a different gospel' (Gal. 1:6–7) find their modern parallel in American missionaries, who preach divisive and exclusive denominationalism and ritualism. He draws the same conclusion in the interpretation of the false brothers in Jerusalem, who pressure to have Titus circumcised (Gal. 2:1–10). Here, Paul's resistance to the circumcision of gentiles becomes Uchimura's theological basis against the modern churches' insistence on baptism for denominational membership (Uchimura 1926: 29. 28–9). It should be noted that the need for redefining Christianity was keenly felt even among the Japanese denominational churches. Ebisawa and Ouchi, the authorities on Japanese ecclesial history, explain that the churches at that time generally understood that 'to enter into Christianity is not, as society generally, maliciously misunderstands, to disregard the benefit of the nation and accept the domination of Westerners by believing the Western religion. Rather, it is to firmly support the independence of the nation and to accomplish the renewal of its people' (Ebisawa and Ouchi 1970: 172). However, Uchimura thought that their criticism of the West was not thorough enough, and he directs Paul's strong rebuke against the caprices of the Galatians in accepting a different gospel (Gal. 3:1–5) to the Japanese churches. He says 'It is today's Japanese churches that are eager to follow the American churches. Believers are deceived into looking away from Jesus Christ crucified and depending on their own works of hand. Thus, the depravity of their faith is inevitable' (Uchimura 1926: 29. 49).

For Uchimura, Paul's treatment of the resistance he encountered in an effort to attain the divine vision of *Ecclesia* depicted in the letter to the Galatians was the primary source from which to the draw basis of justification for his sharp criticism of the Western form of Christianity and the Japanese churches that followed suit. Together with this process of disinheriting the Western elements, Uchimura was engaged in another process of adding a new dimension to understanding Christianity, that is, the indigenization of Christian faith. This took on a unique form of rhetoric. In his essay on '*Bushido* and Christianity', a direct connection between Christianity and *Bushido* is made:

Bushido is the finest product of Japan. But *Bushido* by itself cannot save Japan. Christianity grafted upon *Bushido* will be the finest product of the world. It will save, not only Japan, but the whole world. Now that Christianity is dying in Europe, America by its materialism cannot revive it. God is calling upon Japan to contribute its best to His service. There was meaning in the history of Japan. For twenty centuries God has been perfecting *Bushido* with this very moment in view. Christianity grafted upon *Bushido* will yet save the world. (Uchimura 1916: 22. 161–2)

Doing justice to the evaluation of domestic tradition is a difficult task, especially when one tries to critically redefine it on one hand, in the case of patriotism, and positively present it on the other hand, in the case of grafting Christianity upon it. For example, there is much debate on the origin and definition of *Bushido*, the way of samurai, but it has been popularized worldwide by Uchimura's college friend Inazo Nitobe, in his book *Bushido, the Soul of Japan*. Both Uchimura and Nitobe, being the sons of disbanded samurai and lacking in knowledge of Chinese and Japanese antiquity due to their earlier education being primarily in English, authored works that reflect a highly idealized and uncritical view of the past ruling class (Nitobe 1901; Powles 1995: 115; Ota 1977: 23; Maruyama 1963: p. xii). The nationalistic rhetoric of the period, with its emphasis on imperialistic expansion-ism, from which Uchimura distanced himself, found the idealized image of *Bushido* useful for its own promotion as well. On this point, Uchimura was inevitably conditioned culturally and historically in his pursuit of authentic identity. He accepted rather uncritically the Confucian ethics upon which *Bushido*'s moral system is based. Therefore he says: 'In the fundamental level of ideology, Confucianism and Christianity [grafted upon *Bushido*] are one and the same' (Uchimura 1928: 31. 25). For Uchimura, the close correspondence between Confucian and Christian moral teachings is the basis for his view, introduced earlier, that the Japanese are better able to understand and serve Christ than their Western counterparts. Incidentally, confined within the Confucian value system, Uchimura was not able to give a sustained evaluation of the popular view on the role of women in society (cf. Natsume 1951; 1977). His restrictive view on the role of women is not only reflected in the exposition of Galatians, but also in the studies of Isaiah and Jeremiah. Commenting on the baptismal liturgical saying in Galatians 3:28, Uchimura suddenly complains about the Western tendency to read egalitarianism into the text, which he labels as 'abnormal' (Uchimura 1926: 29. 381). Then he quickly points the reader to the *Haustafeln* teaching in Ephesians 5:22–4, and emphasizes that it corresponds closely with Confucian ideology (ibid. 55–8).

However, the very image of grafting Christianity upon *Bushido* certainly accomplished its purpose of helping his readers to gain confidence in their ambivalent identity. This confidence regarding the role of Japanese Christianity in the world reflects Uchimura's redefined patriotism, in that a patriot is to hold an ideal vision for his nation. In this process of indigenization, Paul himself becomes the samurai of all samurai. Closely connecting the Japanese and Hebrew cultures, and therefore bypassing the West, Uchimura comments:

Paul, a Jew and a disciple of Jesus the Christ, was a true samurai, the very embodiment of the spirit of *Bushido*. Said he: 'It were good for me rather to die, than that any man should make my glorying void' (1 Cor. 9:15). He preferred death to dishonour, to dependency, to begging for whatever cause. . . . then, none was more loyal to his master than Paul was to his . . . Independent, money-hating, loyal—Paul was a type of the old samurai, not to be found among modern Christians, both in America and Europe, and alas also in the samurai's Japan. (Uchimura 1920: 25. 362–3)

Here, Paul is read in the honour-and-shame matrix of *Bushido* which beautifies even death. Therefore, while Uchimura elsewhere gives a rather nuanced interpretation of Paul's balance between submission to and resistance against government pressure (Rom. 13:1-7) (Uchimura 1921: 26. 406), in this instance he makes Paul imply that martyr's death at the hand of the government authority is even honourable. In this process, what was once believed to be the soul-book of Western civilization is turned into the scripture of Japanese Christianity. With the heart of the samurai, Paul can now speak more convincingly than ever to the hearts of

Japanese believers, and consequently, as Uchimura confidently says in the article 'The Japanese and Christianity', they could not only appreciate the Bible as much as Western Christians, but could understand and obey it even better (Uchimura 1925: 29. 277).

CONCLUSION

Uchimura's approach to reading the Bible has been observed within the historical context of the social restructurization during the Meiji era, and the emergence of Christian communities, particularly his *Mukyokai*. Uchimura's evaluations of the world around him, at times even pathologically harsh and at other times surprisingly idealized, are features of his rhetoric of survival and justification of the new and uncomfortable identity that came into existence at the society's re-encounter with Christianity. Uchimura approached the Bible, the foundation of the new religion, in search of a reason for and significance of his existence and that of his *Mukyokai*. In his search, Uchimura was particularly attracted to those who also sit uncomfortably in the biblical scenes due to the prophetic roles given them in their experience of the divine call, such as Isaiah, Jeremiah, and particularly Paul, as reflected in his Letter to the Galatians.

Even when understood as reactionary rhetoric, one may be disturbed by the degree of polemic Uchimura expresses against the West, fearing the implication of violence caused by so sharp a criticism. Therefore, I conclude with an attempt to see him in perspective. Through the sharp criticism of Uchimura in his reaction to the encounter with Christianity, we may realize the unavoidable possibility of violence he felt can be caused even by well-meaning missionary endeavours reaching across nations and cultures. It implies a need for deep contemplation on modern Christian engagements of benevolence, and a careful interpretation of biblical texts regarding the effects of preaching the Christian gospel upon the intended recipients.

The Japanese churches contemporary with Uchimura had some degree of sympathy towards his intense responses to the encounter with Christianity because they struggled with a similar experience of marginalization. However, they generally distanced themselves from him because of the unattainable ideology of 'church that is not church' (Ebisawa and Ouchi 1970: 372–7). Because of this ideological peculiarity, the *Mukyokai* found itself in a unique place, set apart from society, even from the denominational churches. Even now, the *Mukyokai* continues to play a special prophetic role (cf. Turner 1969), reminding churches of the uncomfortable but significant beginning period of identity struggle for Japanese Christianity, in which what Uchimura understands the 'marks of Jesus' to be—scars of persecution and marginalization—were chiselled into the Japanese body of Christ as a whole.

One may be curious as to how Uchimura, with his sharply critical treatments of the United States and of Japan's militarism, would have reacted to the direct confrontation between the countries in the Pacific War. Although he did not live to see the beginning of it, his legacy is clearly seen in the lives of his disciples. It only suffices to mention Tadao Yanaihara of the Yanaihara Incident, which symbolizes the resistance against the thought control of the national government. The 'incident' refers to the ousting of Yanaihara from his celebrated post of professorship at the Imperial University of Tokyo in 1937 and the banning of his writings because of the anti-war stance clearly stated therein. In his *Kokka no Riso* ('Ideals of the Nation'), he reflects Uchimura's view on true patriotism, saying that if the nation fails to administer justice, which is primarily the protection of the weak from the intrusion on their human rights by the powerful, criticism should arise among the citizens (the text recorded and commented in Ienaga *et al.* 1993; Okawara 1987). Within the same year, human rights were brutally violated in the infamous atrocity at Nanjing. Meanwhile, the mainline denominational churches saw their old vision of unified assembly (*Kirisuto Kokai*) materialize in the most deformed and detestable way, as they yielded to pressure from the imperial government to support its expansionist vision and organize a unified religious institution under its direct and strict civilian control (Iegana *et al.* 1994).

Therefore, Japanese ecclesial history demonstrates at least two reminders for present churches. One is what Uchimura calls the 'marks of Jesus', that is, memories of the experience of being persecuted and marginalized for the newly held religion and its scripture. The other is what may be understood as a 'thorn in the flesh' (2 Cor. 12:7), the disturbing yet incurable memory of the experience of being a part, even though reluctantly, of the marginalizing power that threatened Japan's Asian neighbours. With both the marks of Jesus clearly chiselled and the thorn in the flesh deeply pierced, with tender compassion and repentant humility, the churches of Japan are to continue approaching the Bible for a meaningful reading of it for themselves and perhaps, as Uchimura envisioned, for the world.

BIBLIOGRAPHY

All the works of Kanzo Uchimura, from as early as 1877 till 1930, are contained (in Japanese) in Uchimura, Kanzo (1980–2001), *Uchimura Kanzo Zenshu* ['The Complete Works of Kanzo Uchimura'], 41 vols. Tokyo: Iwanami Shoten. References in the text give the original date of publication, followed by the volume and page numbers of this edition.

ASANO, ATSUHIRO (2005), *Community-Identity Construction in Galatians*. JSNTS 285; London and New York: T. & T. Clark Continuum.

BÄLTZ, ERWIN (1931), *Das Leben eines deutschen Arztes im erwachenden Japan. Tagebücher, Briefe, Berichte* herausgegeben von Toku Bältz. Stuttgart: J. Engelhorns Nachf.

BOXER, C. R. (1967), *The Christian Century in Japan, 1549–1650*. Berkeley and Los Angeles: University of California Press.

BRUNNER, EMIL (1951), *Das Misverständnis der Kirche*. Zürich: Zwingli-Verlag.

——(1959), 'Die christliche Nicht-Kirche-Bewegung in Japan: Gottlob Schrenk, dem Mann der Mission zum 80 Geburtstag', *Evangelische Theologie*, 4.

CALDAROLA, CARLO (1979), *Christianity: The Japanese Way*. Leiden: E. J. Brill.

EBISAWA, ARIMICHI and SABURO OUCHI (1970), *Nihon Kirisutokyo-shi* [The Church History of Japan]. Tokyo: Nihon Kirisutokyo Shuppan.

ELLISON, GEORGE (1973), *Deus Destroyed: The Image of Christianity in Early Modern Japan*. Cambridge: Harvard University Press.

GESSEL, VAN C. (1993), *Three Modern Novelists: Soseki, Tanizaki, Kawabata*. Tokyo: Kondansha International.

HARRINGTON, ANN H. (1993), *Japan's Hidden Christians*. Chicago: Loyola University Press.

IENAGA, SABURO *et al.* (eds.) (1993), *Nihon Heiwa-ron Taikei* [Compendia of Japanese Peace Studies]. Vol. 10 of 20 vols. Tokyo: Nihon Tosho Centre.

KAMEI, SHUNSUKE (1977), *Uchimura Kanzo: Meiji Seishin no Dohyo* [Kanzo Uchimura: A Milestone of the Spirit of the Meiji Era]. Tokyo: Chuokoron-sha.

MARUYAMA, MASAO (1963), *Thought and Behaviour in Modern Japanese Politics*. Oxford: Oxford University Press.

MASAIKE, HITOSHI (1970), *Uchimura Kanzo Den* [A Biography of Kanzo Uchimura]. Tokyo: Kyobunkwan.

MATUZAWA, HIROAKI (ed.) (1971), *Uchimura Kanzo*. Tokyo: Chuo Koron.

MORITOKA, KIYOMI (1970), *Nihon no Kindai-shakai to Kirishutokyo* [Japan's Early Modern Era and Christianity]. Tokyo: Hyoron-sha.

NATSUME, SOSEKI (1951), *Gubijinso* [A Red Poppy]. Tokyo: Shincho Bunko.

——(1957), *Sanshiro*, trans. Jay Rubin. Washington, DC: University of Washington Press.

NITOBE, INAZO (1901), *Bushido, The Soul of Japan: An Exposition of Japanese Thought*. Tokyo: Shokwabo.

OKAWARA, REIZO (ed.) (1987), *Yahaihara Jiken 50-nen* [50 Years Since the Yanaihara Incident]. Tokyo: Mokutan-sha.

OSWALD, HILTON C. (1963), *Luther's Works*, vol. 26, trans. Jaroslav Pelikan. St Louis: Concordia.

OTA, YUZO (1977), *Uchimura Kanzo: Sono Sekai-shugi to Nihon-shugi* [Kanzo Uchimura: On His Globalism and Nationalism]. Tokyo: Kenkyusha.

POWLES, CYRIL H. (1995), 'Bushido: Its Admirers and Critics', in John F. Howes (ed.), *Nitobe Inazo: Japan's Bridge Across the Pacific*. Oxford: Westview Press.

SHIONO, KAZUO (2007), *Kinkyo-koku Nippon no Hodo* [Media Reports on Japan as an Anti-Christian Nation]. *The Missionary Herald* (1825–73). Tokyo: Yusho-do Shuppan.

SHIVELY, DONALD H. (1971), 'The Japanization of the Middle Meiji', in D. H. Shively (ed.), *Tradition and Modernization in Japanese Culture*. Princeton: Princeton University Press.

TURNER, VICTOR (1969), *The Ritual Process: Structure and Anti-Structure*. New York: Aldine de Gruyter.

WASWO, ANN (1996), *Modern Japanese Society.* Oxford: Oxford University Press.
WHELAN, CHRISTAL (1996), *The Beginning of Heaven and Earth: The Sacred Book of Japan's Hidden Christians.* Honolulu: University of Hawai'i Press.

FURTHER READING

The following are works on Kanzo Uchimura and on the history of Meiji Japan which are available in English. The best historical account of Uchimura from his conversion to the early writing career is found in his autobiography: *How I Became a Christian: Out of My Diary* (Tokyo: Keiseisha, 1895). This work is now readily available in the third volume of *The Complete Works of Kanzo Uchimura* (1982). Caldarola 1979 offers a good sociological analysis of Uchimura and his *Mukyokai*. For the general history of Meiji Japan, see Waswo 1996. One can read about the background of the anti-Christian ethos of the period in the well-known novel by Shusaku Endo, *Silence*, trans. William Johnston (London: Peter Owen, 1996).

....

CHAPTER 23

ONE BIBLE, TWO PREACHERS: PATCHWORK SERMONS AND SACRED ART IN THE AMERICAN SOUTH

....

CAROL CROWN

WHEN former slave Harriet Powers (1837–1910), who could neither read nor write, finally decided in 1891 to sell her appliqué Bible quilt, she reluctantly settled for the sum of $5.00. In the process the Georgia native won lasting fame. Today one of her quilts is housed in the National Museum of American History, Smithsonian Institution, and another in the Museum of Fine Arts, Boston, where they are celebrated as masterpieces of African American folk art (Lyons 1997; Perry 1994; Fry 1990; Vlach 1990; Adams 1982: 67–76). Although appliqué, a technique in which pieces of fabric are sewn onto a background to form designs, is well known in both European and African traditions, Powers's quilts show a close association with the appliquéd cotton cloths made by the Fon people of Benin, West Africa (Vlach 1990:

44–54). Their large wall-hangings, which were created in honour of their kings, feature two kinds of appliquéd images. There are animals, such as lions, buffalo, birds, and sharks, which symbolize the king's identity, and pictorial scenes, representing events in a ruler's life. Powers's quilts contain similar images: animals— elephants, whales, pigs, and birds—and scenes illustrating specific events. Such parallels suggest that her quilts owe a strong debt to African traditions. The subject-matter of Powers's appliquéd scenes, on the other hand, which depicts Bible stories, astronomical events, and local legends, clearly reveal the influence of the West. Mediated most probably via oral traditions propagated by sermons and spirituals, the images Powers stitched testify to the artist's religious beliefs and love of Scripture. The quilts represent an extraordinary fusion of traditions from Africa and America and exemplify a rich tradition of vernacular art that still flourishes in the South.

Powers's quilts stand at a crossroads in the history of Southern folk art—caught at the intersection of what is typically described as traditional folk art and a new form of artistry called 'contemporary folk art'. By its nature, the quilt belongs to the realm of traditional folk art—that is, art fashioned by non-professional artists, fundamentally communal in nature, utilitarian in function, and traditional in outlook. This kind of art is associated with the European definition of the term 'folk art', which originated in the late nineteenth century when scholars began to study the artistic traditions of the European peasant class. This art—the art of the folk (*Volkunst*)—is rural in origin, communally based, and its techniques, subject-matter, and styles are handed down from one generation to another. Accordingly, in the United States the term designates the everyday art of such ethnic, social, and religious groups, as the Pennsylvania Dutch, certain Hispanic communities of New Mexico, or the Shakers, who have preserved their artistic traditions It is also applied, however, to the indigenous arts of America from colonial times to the twentieth century. Found in both rural and urban settings, American folk art of this kind, which was made by both skilled artisans and gifted amateurs, includes not only objects of daily use, such as furniture, samplers, quilts, and tavern signs, but also works of sculpture and painting more commonly associated with the fine arts.

Traditional folk art began to disappear in the United States during the late nineteenth century, just at the time when Powers was creating her two master-pieces. Machine-made goods slowly displaced the need for hand-made ones. In the Deep South, moreover, where the scholarship on folk art, and especially women's needlework, has been hampered by a variety of factors, including the devastation brought about by the American Civil War and the destruction caused by the South's high humidity and heat (Palmer 1988), Powers's quilts stand out as highly distinctive art works. Traditional southern folk art that features biblical imagery— samplers, silk embroidery, quilts, coverlets, and gravestones—is not only difficult to locate (Patterson 1983: 194–7) but also demonstrates the strong imprint of Western European artistic tradition and the use of age-old motifs (Wertkin 2004: 338, 449, 367, 329).

Powers's quilts have been related to a new usage of the term 'folk art' that emerged during the course of the twentieth century, when the work of an increasing number of unschooled artists gained recognition. Still used to designate the 'traditional' arts of the past, 'folk art' now came to identify the contemporary work of self-taught artists, individuals who had received no or little formal training in the arts and worked outside the artistic mainstream. Thus the term 'folk art' and also the phrase 'contemporary folk art' are both often applied to the works of such artists as William Edmondson, Howard Finster, Morris Hirschfield, John Kane, Grandma Moses, and Bill Traylor, whose mostly non-utilitarian creations are almost always highly individualistic in expression.

Powers's quilts, which are rife with biblical imagery and unchecked in creative energy, stand at the nexus of traditional and contemporary folk art and point to the future. This new direction can be seen above all in the way Powers imagines the events she represents. Her rendition of Adam and Eve in the Boston quilt represents the couple and the serpent, both typical motifs found in traditional folk art, although giving the snake two legs is unusual. New motifs are Adam's rib, the sun, moon, and, as Powers herself said, 'God's all seeing eye' and 'God's merciful hand' (Perry 1994: 5). This imagery is unique and imaginative. Powers's quilts may belong to a tradition—they do indeed represent the very best of an African-American vernacular tradition of pictorial quilts (Wahlman 1993: 60–7). However, the artist's inventive use of biblical imagery points not to the past—not to European nor African traditions—but to the future and the idiosyncratic creations of numerous twentieth-century, self-taught Southern artists, black or white. Often identified as contemporary folk artists, many of these twentieth-century artists also share with Powers a common interest in the Bible and a common religious heritage.

Evangelical Protestantism has dominated the South ever since the Second Great Awakening (1790s–1840s) brought Methodist circuit riders and Baptists, 'through a process akin to spontaneous generation', into the region (Wimbush 2000: 194). Although little is known of Powers's upbringing, she surely learned religion within the context of this tradition; she may have attended New Grove Baptist Church near her home in Athens, Georgia (Perry 1994). So pervasive is evangelical Christianity in the South today that many unschooled artists—even those not particularly religious—take the Bible as their subject-matter (Crown 2004). Making art primarily to satisfy individual needs, these artists are rarely commissioned by religious institutions. Most often, they understand the Bible through the lens of evangelical Christianity, still the preponderant religion in the South (Hill 2006: 59–62). This tradition insists on the Bible as the sole authority in belief, while teaching that each individual has 'direct and dynamic access to the Lord' (Wilson and Ferris 1989: 1269). Personal experience is the essence of this faith, and like Powers, contemporary folk artists often approach the Bible from distinctive points of view.

How two Southern vernacular artists, one working in the late nineteenth century and the other at the end of the twentieth, responded to the Bible, what they took from it, and how they made sense of what they learned, is the subject of this chapter. Within the century that separates Powers, the former slave, and the Revd Howard Finster (*c*.1915–2001), space-age illustrator and folk-art icon, religious imagery dominates the creations of contemporary folk artists in the South. Moreover, untold numbers of both black and white artists found inspiration in the Bible. Making art intended for a variety of purposes—devotional, didactic, proselytic, and also as social commentary—these untutored artists searched the Bible to find meaning for themselves. Looking at the art of Harriet Powers, a black woman and former slave, living a century ago, and the creations of a feisty Baptist preacher who died in the twenty-first century, underscores not only the many differences they share but also a startling number of similarities.

Powers's quilts are an especially good place to begin looking at the Bible's influence on the folk art of the American South. Her pictures appear like Athena out of the brow of Zeus, fully formed and masterfully created. They demonstrate how an unlettered seamstress who knew the Bible only through oral tradition constructed a sophisticated framework of faith that promised hope for the future and courage for today. Looking at the imagery of her quilts sheds light, moreover, on the tenacity of certain themes in the South. The Smithsonian quilt, dating from *c*.1886, and the one in Boston, *c*.1895, are rich in biblical scenes, which Powers identified in recorded descriptions (Perry 1994). Reading left to right, top to bottom, both quilts carry Bible scenes. The earlier one depicts eleven Bible scenes: 'Adam and Eve in the Garden of Eden', 'Eve has Born a Son', 'Satan Amidst the Seven Stars', 'Cain is Killing his Brother Abel,' 'Cain Goes into the Land of Nod', 'Jacob's Dream,' the 'Baptism of Christ', the 'Crucifixion', 'Judas Iscariot and the Thirty Pieces of Silver', the 'Last Supper', and the 'Holy Family: Joseph, the Virgin and the Infant Jesus'.[1] The Boston quilt is decorated with fifteen scenes: most biblically inspired, some duplicating scenes on the Smithsonian but also portraying 'Job Praying for his Enemies' and two others, one depicting Moses and the other Noah.[2] In each quilt Powers represented key Bible events, choosing those that highlight the story of humankind's fall from grace and its salvation in Christ, recognize the saintliness of Old Testament patriarchs, and give place to church rituals, such as Baptism and the Last Supper. The quilts display basic tenets of the Christian faith.

---

[1] Throughout this essay, the term 'sic.' is not employed; instead, every effort has been made to correctly transcribe the titles and descriptions that Powers and Finster gave their artworks, including Finster's handwritten messages that appear on many of his pictures.

[2] Top Row: 'Job Praying for his Enemies, Job's Crosses, Job's Coffin', 'The Dark Day of May 19, 1780', 'The Serpent Lifted Up by Moses', 'Adam and Eve in the Garden', 'John Baptizing Jesus'. Middle Row: 'Jonah Cast Overboard of the Ship', 'God Created Two of Every Kind,' 'The Falling of the Stars on November 13, 1833', 'Two of Every Kind of Animals' (continued), 'The Angels of Wrath and the Seven Vials'. Bottom Row: 'Cold Thursday, 10 of Feb. 1895', 'The Red Light Night of 1846', 'Rich People Who Were Taught Nothing of God', 'The Creation of the Animals' (continued), and the 'Crucifixion of Christ Between the Two Thieves'.

Into this fabric of Old and New Testament images Powers added several non-biblical motifs and contemporary scenes—depictions inspired by the secular realm yet still related to the theme of salvation. These are pictures of celestial phenomena and references to local legend, which deal with unusual astronomical and climatic events. They augment the salvific theme of each quilt, and broaden Powers's visual story. The scene of Judas on the Smithsonian quilt pictures him with a large disc that Powers identified as a 'star that appeared in 1886 for the first time in three hundred years', an event which she herself may have seen. References to such celestial phenomena occur most often in the Boston quilt, where entire scenes are given over to 'The Dark Day of May 19, 1780', 'The Falling of the Stars of November 13, 1833', and 'The Red Night Light of 1846'.

Referring to the falling stars of 1833, Powers explained: 'The people were frighten and thought the end of time had come. God's hand staid the stars. The varmints rushed out of their bed' (Perry 1994). Powers's account refers to a verifiable astronomical event, the famous Leonid meteor shower of 1833, which was similarly believed by those who actually saw it to signify the imminence of the Second Coming: One eyewitness exclaimed: 'See! The whole heavens are on fire! All the stars are falling!' Many thought the Day of Judgment was at hand and sought to prove it was a sign from Scripture that Christ would soon return to earth (Rogers 1833). The coming of the end-time is the real subject of Powers's astronomical scenes. It is also exemplified by the depiction of 'Cold Thursday, 10 of Feb. 1895', referring to a real and unnaturally heavy snowfall accompanied by sub-zero temperatures around Atlanta in 1895. Powers described the scene as 'A woman frozen while at prayer. A woman frozen at a gateway. A man with a sack of meal frozen. Isicles formed from the breath of a mule. All blue birds killed. A man frozen at his jug of liquor' (Perry 1994). Just like many people today, Powers saw in the unusual astronomical and climatic events of her time signs that the world had entered its last days.

Like many Christians of the mid-to-late nineteenth century, Powers was affected by widely circulating stories that the end of time was imminent. Preached by the Baptist laymen William Miller in the 1840s, the idea that the Bible's prophecies were about to be fulfilled had not diminished by the late 1890s. Rather, such beliefs continued to flourish, encouraging the establishment of the Jehovah's Witnesses, the Seventh-Day Adventist Church, and the Christian Advent Church (Boyer 1992; Crown 2004: 24–32). Two nineteenth-century black theologians, Theophilus Gould Steward and James Theodore Holly, posited that the black race would play a pivotal role in the unfolding of the end-time (Raboteau 1995: 54–5). In the South, where belief in Bible prophecy was propounded by evangelists and embraced by funda-mentalists, end-time beliefs infiltrated the secular world, where even today they are prominent.

Besides detailing the theological framework of Powers's faith, including her belief in Bible prophecy, the quilts also suggest how the former slave may have sought refuge in the Bible as a means to bolster her own bravery. In the aftermath of the Civil War and the establishment of the Ku Klux Klan, Georgia became one of the leading Southern states in terms of lynchings, a means used to maintain white supremacy. Among the figures represented on Powers's quilts are the Old Testament patriarchs and prophets Moses, Jacob, Noah, Jonah, and Job. They have been interpreted throughout the history of Christianity as precursors of Christ and as biblical heroes who overcame catastrophic odds through faith in God. They testify to Powers's personal resolve as well as to the influence of the black church, where such Old Testament figures continued to be important models of perseverance (Raboteau 1995: 17–36).

Perhaps the most puzzling image on Powers's quilt in Boston is the depiction of its sole secular subject, 'Rich People Who Were Taught Nothing of God'. In this depiction Powers portrayed a man and woman standing on either side of a clock, an object often found on African-American graves. Below them is a gigantically sized pig, the largest figure in the entire quilt. Powers explained that the scene portrays 'Bob Johnson and Kate Bell of Virginia. They told their parents to stop the clock at one and tomorrow it would strike one and so it did. This was the signal that they entered everlasting punishment. The independent hog which ran 500 miles from Ga. to Va. her name was Betts' (Perry 1994).

Without knowing the identities of Bob Johnson and Kate Bell (were they Powers's former owners?) and more about the story of the big sow Betts, it seems unlikely that anyone can offer a completely satisfying interpretation of this scene. From Powers's description, we learn that Bob Johnson and Kate Bell were both rich and unrighteous, sent to hell at the tolling of the clock, and damned for eternity. Powers's comments also suggest that the big sow Betts was probably inspired by local legend. The biblical designation of pigs as unclean beings, Betts's large, unwieldy body, and her central placement beneath the couple's feet heighten the scene's secular tone. Moreover, the picture's placement in the middle of the quilt's lowest register, framed by biblical scenes and prophetic, celestial events, forcefully asserts its theme of wickedness.

The depiction of Bob Johnson and Kate Bell is bound up with Powers's understanding of the world in which she lived. Evil exists—but in Powers's view, righteousness will triumph, a theme the artist introduced in the quilt's very first scene, at the upper left. This image returns us to the Bible and its Old Testament heroes as it takes up the story of Job, the epitome of suffering—and the very antithesis of the sinful couple and the legendary Betts. Identified by Powers as 'Job praying for his enemies, Job's crosses, Job's coffin', the scene, though grounded in the Bible, has no specific biblical source. Like the Book of Job, however, which is filled with striking descriptions of the universe, Powers's depiction is replete with celestial imagery. The picture features in its lower half a centrally placed, star-studded motif, often used by Powers to signify shooting stars. Above, two crosses frame a diamond that carries at each corner a sparkling star, emphasizing again

Powers fascination with the heavens. The diamond, which has been compared to the Congo cosmogram that symbolizes continuity in life (Diaz-Diocaretz 1985: 115; Wahlman 1993: 96), looks very much like something Powers could also have seen in the clear skies of the southern hemisphere: the asterism or subset of stars in the constellation Delphinus, known as 'Job's Coffin' (Sherrod 2001). Just below the quilt's diamond there are also two diagonally posed human forms and two similarly posed standing figures. All are unidentified, but presumably the two standing figures represent Job, the one on the right having hurled an object upwards. Perhaps the chorus of 'Job's Coffin', the old-time gospel favourite, which reads: 'Oh the hammer keeps a ringin' on Job's coffin Way over yonder in the buryin' ground', explains the implement being thrown (Mainer 1971).

Powers's depiction of Job praying for his enemies is layered in meaning. The afflictions Job suffered made him, even in the New Testament, an Old Testament type of Christ (Jas. 5:11). Job's crosses prefigure Jesus' cross—and tie the first scene of the quilt to the very last one at bottom right, the 'Crucifixion'. Like Jesus, Powers insists, Job suffered physical and mental pain and was vindicated. Moreover, as the artist's choice of title denotes, Job was, even in the midst of his tribulation, a pious and praiseworthy man: he prays for his enemies. In fact, the former slave may have readily identified with Job. As the emblem of suffering, Job often appears in African-American religious literature, song, and sermon (Solomon and Solomon 2002: 74).

Powers was apparently commissioned to make the Boston quilt by the faculty wives of Atlanta University as a gift for the retiring chairman of the university's board of trustees. If so, her decision to display as its introductory scene a symbol of the black condition—its suffering, endurance, piety, *and its rectitude*—is astonishing. Perhaps Powers, who told her story through the lens of a *black* evangelical Christian, could count on the naivety of the quilt's white audience. The emphasis placed on Job, along with the inclusion of other biblical patriarchs, would not, however, have gone unnoticed by her peers. Black Christians identified with the Jews of Exodus, whom God brought out of the land of Egypt and rescued from slavery. They were the American Israelites, and Job, like Moses, Noah, Jacob, and Jonah, was a symbol of not only the suffering God's people endured but also their victorious destiny. As black Americans, they were filled with hope for the future—the hope to imagine a radically different world than what they were experiencing in the present.

Powers once referred to the Smithsonian quilt as a 'Sermon in Patchwork' and announced her desire to use it to preach the gospel (Finch 1914: 493). Neither quilt is the right size for use as a bed cover—the Smithsonian's is too small, Boston's too big. Perhaps, as Reginia Perry suggests, Smith intended her handwork to be hung up and used as a teaching device (Perry 1994). In fashioning her Boston quilt, Powers created a Bible sermon that is the visual equivalent to the archetypal Creation sermon crafted by black preachers and described by James Weldon

Johnson in *God's Trombones*. The sermon, Johnson explained, 'began with the Creation, went on to the fall of man, rambled through the trials and tribulations of the Hebrew Children, came down to the redemption by Christ, and ended with the Judgment Day and a warning and an exhortation to sinners' (Johnson 1927). In her choice of subjects, Powers's quilts are equally expansive. Moreover, they show that Powers found in the Bible the means to nurture both her personal faith and communal resolve. The Bible explains creation, the existence of evil, and God's plan for his universe. It offers heroes to emulate, strength for the present, and faith for tomorrow. In the tradition of evangelical Protestantism, however, it is equally important to share the gospel's good news. For Powers, that meant preaching the gospel in patchwork.

Sixteen years after Powers died, Howard Finster was born in the mountains of southern Appalachia, where he spent most of his life as a backwoods country preacher. By 2001, when he died, Finster was a nationally recognized artist and—in a turn of events that Harriet Powers could hardly have imagined—his creations, hers, and others like theirs were among the holdings of major museums throughout the country (Turner 1989; Finster 1989). Perhaps best known for his spectacular, several-acre, outdoor garden/Bible park 'Paradise Gardens' and the World's Folk Art Church he built in Pennville, Georgia, Finster was a showman who dazzled the eyes and hearts of the nation. He began construction of Paradise Gardens around 1960, using cast-off objects—worn-out tires, Coca-cola bottles, chicken fence, old bicycles, lawnmowers, parts of television sets, garden statues, a Cadillac, bits of jewellery, mirror pieces, marbles, and old coins—concrete, and handwritten Bible signs. The World's Folk Art Church, the wedding-cake structure he built nearby, was not begun until the early 1980s. By then Finster was already becoming widely known as an ingenious artist.

Finster's painting career began on a winter's day in 1976, as he was refinishing a bicycle: a tiny face appeared in a smear of paint on the ball of his finger and a warm feeling came over him. It was his 'Holy-Ghost' feeling, and it told him God had 'called' him to make 'sacred art'. Doubting his ability, Finster pulled a dollar bill from his pocket, tacked it to a piece of plywood, and copied George Washington's portrait. He judged it a success. By his death, Finster had made 46,000 pieces of art (he numbered most of them), forming a highly creative body of work, most sprinkled liberally with Bible verses and folksy comments. By 1980 his work was featured in *Life Magazine*. In 1983 he mesmerized Johnny Carson when he appeared on the NBC *Tonight Show*, and in 1984 he was invited to participate in the Venice Biennale. In the following year *Rolling Stone* magazine chose Finster's design for the musical group Talking Heads' *Little Creatures* album as cover of the year (Finster 1989: 188). Featured in countless private and public collections, Finster's works are now included in the holdings of such prestigious institutions as the Library of Congress, the American Folk Art Museum, Atlanta's High Museum of Art, the Milwaukee Art Museum, and the Smithsonian American Art Museum.

'Born again' at age 13, Finster, who made it only through the sixth grade, began preaching as a teenager in 1932. In 1935 he married Pauline Freeman, with whom he had five children. From the family's home in north Georgia, Finster often served several churches simultaneously, ran tent revivals during the week (sometimes nearby, but also as far away as Florida), and worked as a handyman to support his family. Sometimes, Finster taught Sunday School, where he used chalk to diagram his lectures, and he advertised the use of Bible pictures when he led tent revivals, but most of the time he simply preached the Bible. His wife Pauline commented: 'After he got his own tent, he would be gone for a week at a time. He'd preach two or three revivals a summer and be gone all summer . . . He really studied the Bible as best he could. He studied every night. He would mark the pages for his sermons. A sermon would come out of anything that would cross his mind' (Turner 1989: 32).

Even after he formally retired from the church in 1965, Finster never stopped preaching. Saying that God had inspired him to build Paradise Gardens and to make 'sacred art', he threw himself into creating artworks, crafting them much like his sermons. Several of his handwritten sermons and sermon notes, on file in the Smithsonian's Archives of American Art, demonstrate that he often took a Bible verse to establish the theme of his sermon. One of his short sermons begins: 'Coming to you from St. Matthew 2–11, "And when they were come into the house they saw the young child with Mary". The subject is mothers of the Bible.' Finster also cites 1 Samuel 1–20, which tells the story of Hannah praying for a son, and Proverbs 31–26, describing a virtuous woman (Finster 1932–87: 4033). Finster interweaves the verses with his own comments to create an ode to motherhood. Likewise, a painting dated 1976 cites Bible verses, as Finster takes up the subject of humility. The painting displays a sign that reads: 'JOHN 13–5 HE POURETH WATER INTO A BASON AND BEGAN TO WASH THE DISCIPLES FEET.' It pictures a bright landscape with golden clouds above a flowery meadow where twelve barefooted figures are seated on a long bench, as the kneeling figure of Jesus pours water into a basin. A second Bible inscription reads:

DO UNTIL OTHERS AS I HAVE DONE UNTO YOU. WASH ONE ANOTHERS FEET FOR I HAVE GIVEN YOU AN EXAMPLE IF I YOUR LORD AND MASTER HAVE WASHED YOUR FEET YE ALSO AUGHT TO.

Whether sermonizing at the pulpit or in his artworks, Finster built his theology on the Bible. 'We believe in the Bible down to the last word', he once insisted (Finster 1932–87: 4034), and a small 1987 cut-out figure portrays him holding a Bible that boldly proclaims, 'I Preach the Bible'. Sometimes Finster limited his artistry to the text of the Bible itself. A striking painting now in the Smithsonian American Art Museum reads, 'ST. LUKE 5–20 AND WHEN HE SAW THEIR FAITH. HE SAID UNTO HIM. MAN THY SINS ARE FORGIVEN THEE.' Painted in bold red letters emblazoned with splashes of gold, the text is framed by two, elegant, lacelike branches, adorned with colourful blossoms.

As a Baptist preacher, Finster took the Bible at face-value, preferring a common-sense approach that emphasized its literal interpretation. He dismissed the concept of evolution out of hand. How could a monkey, he asked, become 'a human that could conquer space go to the moon split the adam and take Gods place in the world man that's just plain belona and bull earm any body that can believe that dont have a chance' (Finster 1932–87: 4033). In *7 Days of Creation*, of *c.*1976, Finster pronounces his belief in creationism. The painting displays the days of creation in seven compartments, each labelled Monday through Sunday and each displaying an abbreviated verse from Genesis. Saturday, the sixth day, is clearly labelled: 'GOD MADE THE BEAST OF THE EARTH AND CATTLE AFTER THEIR KIND GOD SAID LET US MAKE MAN IN OUR IMAGE.'

Time and again, Finster maintained that God has a plan for creation, 'God has blueprinted and strictly made this earth, engineered it that all different races of people and all different areas of this world would make our economy . . .'. He believed, moreover, that 'every living thing on earth is part of God. There is no life on planet earth without God. God is in the life of the smallest blade of grass that grows in the meadows . . . God is in the living grass and trees and animals . . . God is in every human being' (Finster 1932–87: 4034). Perhaps that is why it meant so much to Finster to recycle the lost and rejected bits of 'earth's planet' into his art. One of his most poignant works, which once hung in Paradise Gardens, pictures Finster wearing jacket, gloves, and cap. Rendered in paint on military cloth—a material that heightens the starkness of the scene, Finster carries a cross and stares sombrely at the viewer. 'I BUILT THIS PARK OF BROKEN PIECES TO TRY TO MEND A BROKEN WORLD OF PEOPLE WHO ARE TRAVELING THEIR LAST ROAD.'

Like Harriet Powers, Finster preached the great heroes of the Bible and its prophecies of the end-times. An early 1976 figurative image, 'Noah Being Warned', blends scripture and image into a warning. The scene represents a blue ocean filled with swimmers struggling to reach the ark, situated at the painting's centre. At the top appears: 'HEB 11: BY FAITH NOAH BEING WARNED OF GOD OF THINGS NOT SEEN AS YET MOVED WITH FEAR, PREPARED AN ARK TO THE SAVING OF HIS HOUSE.' At the bottom, quoting Matthew 24:37, a second citation reads: 'AS IN THE DAYS OF NOAH SO SHALL IT BE AS IN THE DAYS OF THE COMING OF THE SON OF MAN.' Finster adds: 'ONLY JESUS CAN SAVE IN THESE LAST DAYS.' Using the illustration of Noah's Ark and citations from the New Testament, Finster reminds the viewer of the Old Testament story and its Gospel corollaries, but adds his own words to emphasize the present.

Finster recognized the existence of sin and battled against it, just as Powers did. He combatted social ills such as the use of drugs, abortion, and alcoholism, and ranted about hijackings, warfare, and natural disasters as well as the world's ecological problems. The 'Devils Vice' of 1984 pictures a woman caught in its bright red grip. 'TOO LATE NOW,' she screams: 'THE DEVILS VICE WARNING DON'T GET TRAPPED IN THIS DEVICE . . . HOWARD FINSTER FROM GOD WARN-ING THE WORLD LAY OFF COCAINE.' In a later version, Finster rhymes, 'KEEP YOU SKY BLUE KEEP YOUR GRASS GREEN LAY OFF COCAIN'. He also saw in the mudslides, earthquakes, floods, and forest fires of the late twentieth century signs of the earth's coming demise. His 1976 painting, *THERE SHALL BE EARTH-qUAKES* pictures Jesus overlooking the desolate ground of an uprooted world. Another painting, *THE WORLD IS NOW LIVING BETWEEN TWO GREAT SUPER POWERS*, provides a checklist of the sins marring contemporary society. Finster exclaims:

IF YOU DON'T BELIEVE IN THE PROPHET TAKE ANOTHER LOOK AT WHAT THEY SAID WHICH IS NOW HAPPENING BEFORE YOUR EYES IN YOUR OWN TIME 1985 . . . THE WHOLE WORLD IS NOW LIVING BETWEEN TWO GREAT SUPER POWERS A BIT OF FEAR IS ON ALL PEOPLE.

Although Finster employed Bible imagery, portraying Jesus, angels, demons, heaven, and hell, he also chose to represent famous people, such as William Shakespeare, former US presidents Washington, Lincoln, Kennedy, and Carter, American inventors Eli Whitney and Henry Ford, and Southern music icons Hank Williams and Elvis Presley. Finster wanted to give his viewers 'a real message. Leonardo da Vinci and Apollo and Mona Lisa and all of them, people know them from the 1800s, from storybooks, they were familiar with. So I draw them and the little I know about them, so to attracts peoples' attention, so then they look at my message' (Finster 1932–87: 4034). To grab the viewer's eye, Finster also depicted subjects drawn from nature, such as cheetahs, wolves, rabbits, even termites, and especially dinosaurs. He employed witty titles (*AMERICAN DEVILS ARE MIGHTLY FRIENDLY*) and sometimes referenced sex. He also made numerous self-portraits, which he used as a means to confront disbelievers face to face. In a bust self-portrait dating 1987, Finster completely covered its surface in typical *horror vacui* style. Drawings of tiny houses and multi-levelled towers along with handwritten messages coat every available inch of the figure. The writing on its forehead says:

I AM NOT HERE TO JUDGE OR TO CONDEM. I AM HERE WITH FACTS OF THE TRUTH . . . WITHOUT A VISION THE PEOPLE PERISH . . . EVER HUMAN SHOULD KNOW THERE IS A BETTER WORLD . . . I HAVE VISIONS OF OTHER WORLDS. I BEEN OUT THERE.

The writing continues down the cheeks, nose, and below the lips, where Finster proclaims: 'I AM HERE AS A SECOND NOAH TO POINT THE PEOPLE TO THE WORLD BEYOND.' On the figure's left shoulder appears: 'BY HOWARD FINSTER FROM GOD MAN OF VISIONS ESTABLISHED AND RESOLVED FOR SURE.'

The titles Finster gave himself in such paintings—'A Second Noah', 'God's Last Red Light', and 'Man of Visions'—refer to the various roles he believed God had assigned him. Of these, 'Man of Visions' was undoubtedly most integral to his self-conception. Finster maintained that he had experienced his first vision as a child, when his dead sister Abbie Rose appeared to him as though she were on a staircase descending from heaven. She said, 'You are going to be a man of visions' (Finster 1932–87: 4034). Much later, after years of Bible study and a lifetime of visions, Finster understood what his sister meant. He knew the Bible, and he drew the obvious conclusions. On a scrap of paper, he jotted down, 'Hosea 12:10. I have multiplied visions and used similitudes by the ministry of the prophets. This is me in the Bible' (ibid. 4033). Elsewhere, he added: 'I am here to do a job. I'm not here just through accident or here because God wanted another person here. I was sent here to do this work, and I will get it done.' According to Finster's understanding of the Bible, moreover, he had actually come from another world to fulfill God's mission. 'It's all in the Bible. It tells there where I'm standing, that I came down from God to you. It took me sixty years to get to you. And now I'm fixing to go on my way back' (ibid. 4034).

Finster preached 'other worlds', and while his wife was genuinely chagrined, he believed that the references he found in the Bible to other worlds were actual planets with people living on them. Taking earth and heaven as a beginning point, he explained:

See when Jesus was here, he plainly said he come from a planet. He come from his Father. Well, his Father don't live around here—where he come from was a world with life on it. And He talked about He was on a planet with life on it. That's two planets . . . And Jesus said, 'If I go away, I will prepare a place for you.' Well, opposite to where God is, Jesus is making another planet, for his bride—his church—his people . . .

All right, that's the third world that will have life on it, and anybody can't see that is stupid. (Ibid. 4034)

Finster had seen those worlds in his visions. 'I got to realizin' there was other worlds. And I got to seein' 'em in my visions and goin' to 'em—visiting other worlds, seein' the people and what they done (Finster 1989: 180–1). He made those planets the subject of his art, creating thousands of artworks about his visions and even a whole book, entitled *Howard Finster's Vision of 1982: Vision of 200 Light Years Away Space Born of Three Generations from Earth to the Heaven of Heavens*, which teems with illustrations of spaceships, suns, stars, moons, and planets (Finster 1982). It celebrates the 200-year journey and final arrival of a space crew in heaven, where Jesus welcomes them. The book is charming in concept, hilarious in execution, wildly imaginative, yet reverent and sincere. 'It was a great meeting,' a crew-member writes, 'we looked out over the first heaven and said, oh grave where is thy victory and death where is thy sting. For it was our first time to be out from under wars and laws and death and sickness and fear' (ibid. 74).

Finster knew his Bible, but he also knew his heart. He often spoke of his Holy-Ghost feeling, which he first experienced as a child when he was born again. 'THE NIGHT I GOT THE HOLY GHOST IT WAS THE NIGHT I LOVED THE MOST', he wrote on a 1987 cut-out entitled, *MY WORK IS GOING OUT FROM THE GARDEN*. He received the Breath of God, he said, and he knew that feeling from any other feeling he'd ever experienced. It was a new feeling, the feeling he got when he was called to preach, when he was told to make 'sacred art', and when he had visions of other realms. That feeling was a guidepost that enabled him to balance the literal interpretation of the Bible with his personal experience of the divine: 'I am based on the King James Version of the New Testament of the Bible and the Old Bible and the prophets, and grace, truth, and justice for all, and my unexpected and plain visions from a real supreme being' (Hankla 1984: 12). For Finster, the Bible and the Holy Spirit intertwined, enabling him to create artworks that were based on religious beliefs yet ingenious in execution and effect. A dyed-in-the-wool evangelical, Finster believed that religious experience is the essence of faith. Filled with insight and originality, sometimes poignant, sometimes witty, but always creatively mesmerizing and sincere, Finster's art blurs the lines between highbrow and lowbrow, making him one of America's great artists.

Finster was the paradigm Southern evangelist, presenting the plan of salvation, preaching hellfire and damnation, and calling for conversion. Although preceding him by a century, Harriet Powers, an equally compelling artist, also preached Scripture. Both crafted their sermons visually, picturing the Bible's story of creation, retelling the feats of its Old Testament heroes, affirming the Bible's prophecies, and condemning humanity's vices. Intriguingly, the eyes of both were attracted upwards to heaven, where in the sky's firmament they felt God's majesty in the universe. Although so different in terms of gender, race, and time, both Southerners found in the Bible a way to explain the human condition, the means to live in the present, the confidence needed for tomorrow, and the inspiration to preach the Gospel.

Works Cited

Adams, Marie Jeanne (1982), 'The Harriet Powers Pictorial Quilts', in William Ferris, (ed.) *Afro-American Folk Art and Crafts*, 67–76. Jackson, Miss.: University Press of Mississippi.

Crown, Carol (ed.) (2004), *Coming Home! Self-taught Artists, the Bible and the American South*. Memphis, Tenn. and Jackson, Miss.: Art Museum of the University of Memphis and the University Press of Mississippi.

Diaz-Diocaretz, Myriam (1985), *Women, Feminist Identity, and Society in the 1980s: Selected Papers*. Amsterdam and Philadelphia: Benjamins.

Finch, Lucine (1914), 'A Sermon in Patchwork', *The Outlook*, 108/9 (28 Oct.): 493–5.

FINSTER, HOWARD (1932–87), 'Howard Finster Papers, 1932–1987', Archives of American Art, Smithsonian Institution. Microfilm reels 4033 and 4034.

——(1982), *Howard Finster's Vision of 1982: Vision of 200 Light Years Away, Space Born of Three Generations from Earth to the Heaven of Heavens*. Summerville, Ga.: Howard Finster.

——(1989), as told to Tom Patterson, *Howard Finster Stranger from Another World, Man of Visions, Now on This Earth*. New York, London, and Paris: Abbeville Press.

FRY, GLADYS-MARIE (1990), 'Harriet Powers: Portrait of an African-American Quilter', in *Stitched from the Soul: Slave Quilts from the Ante-Bellum South*, 84–91. New York: Dutton.

HANKLA, SUSAN (1984), 'Howard Finster is in My Dreams', in Ann F. Oppenhimer and Susan Hankla (eds.), *Sermons in Paint: A Howard Finster Folk Art Festival*, 11–12. Richmond, Va.: University of Richmond.

HILL, SAMUEL S. (ed.) (2006), *Religion, The New Encyclopedia of Southern Culture*, vol. 1. Chapel Hill, NC: Center for the Study of Southern Culture and the University of North Carolina Press.

JOHNSON, JAMES WELDON (1927), *Gods Trombones: Seven Negro Sermons in Verse*, 5th printing. New York: Viking Press. Electronic Edition, 'Documenting the American South', http://docsouth.unc.edu/southlit/johnson/johnson.htmll (accessed 7/24/08).

LYONS, MARY E. (1997), *Stitching Stars: The Story Quilts of Harriet Powers*. New York: Aladdin Paperbacks (first pub. 1993).

MAINER, J. E. (1971), *18 Gospel Favorites*, by J. E. Mainer and the Mountaineers. Recorded by Rural Rhythm, Arcadia, California.

New Georgia Encyclopedia. 'Lynching', http://www.georgiaencyclopedia.org (accessed 8/9/08).

PALMER, HEATHER (1988), 'Where Is Nineteenth-Century Southern Decorative Needlework?', *Southern Quarterly*, 27/1: 57–71.

PATTERSON, DANIEL W. (1983), 'The Bible and American Folk Arts', in *The Bible and American Arts and Letters*, Society of Biblical Literature Centennial Publications, 187–217. Philadelphis: Fortress Press, and Chico, Calif.: Scholars Press.

PERRY, REGENIA (1994), *Harriet Powers's Bible Quilts*, Rizzoli Art Series New York: Rizzoli International, distributed by St Martin's Press.

RABOTEAU, ALBERT. J. (1995), *Fire in the Bones: Reflections on African-American Religious History*. Boston: Beacon Press.

ROGERS, ELDER SAMUEL (1833), 'First-hand Account of 1833 Meteor Shower', http://science.nasa.gov/newhome/headlines/ast22jun99_2.htm (accessed 8/5//8).

SHERROD, P. C. (2001), 'Stars of Dephinus: Job's Coffin', http://www.weasner.com/etx/ref_guides/images/sherrod-jobscoffin.jpg (accessed 8/18/08).

SOLOMON, OLIVIA and SOLOMON, JACK (eds.) (2002), *Honey in the Rock: The Ruby Pickens Tart Collection of Religious Folk Songs from Sumter County, Alabama*. Macon, Ga.: Mercer University Press.

TURNER, JOHN F. (1989), *Howard Finster: Man of Visions*. New York: Alfred A. Knopf.

VLACH, JOHN MICHAEL (1990), *The Afro-American Tradition in Decorative Arts*. Athens, Ga.: University of Georgia Press.

WAHLMAN, MAUDE SOUTHWELL (1993), *Signs and Symbols: African Images in African-American Quilts*. New York: Studio Books in association with the Museum of American Folk Art.

WERTKIN, GERALD C. (ed.) (2004), *Encyclopedia of America Folk Art*. New York and London: Routledge.

WILSON, CHARLES REAGAN and FERRIS, WILLIAM (eds.) (1989), *Encyclopedia of Southern Culture*. Chapel Hill, NC: Center for the Study of Southern Culture at the University of Mississippi and the University of North Carolina Press.

WIMBUSH, VINCENT L. (ed.) (2000), *African Americans and the Bible: Sacred Texts and Social Textures*. New York and London: Continuum.

FURTHER READING

C. Kurt Dewhurst, Betty MacDowell, and Marshall MacDowell, *Religious Folk Art in America: Reflections of Faith* (New York: E. P. Dutton, 1983), treat the full range of religious folk art from a national perspective, while Crown 2004 and Crown and Russell (eds.), *Sacred and Profane: Voice and Vision in Southern Self-Taught Art* (Jackson, Miss.: University of Mississippi, 2007), examine contemporary folk art and religion in the South. Perry 1994 presents Powers's quilts in colour and includes her recorded description of both quilts. Another excellent source is Mary Lyons 1997. Maude Wahlman 1993 provides an overview of African-American quits. Also extremely valuable for the religious context are Boyer's *Prophecy Belief in Modern America Culture* (Cambridge, Mass.: Belknap Press of Harvard University Press, 1992), Hill 2006, Raboteau 1995, and Wimbush 2006.

For a good online illustration of Harriet Powers's quilt in the National Museum of American History, Smithsonian Institution, go to *The New Georgia Encyclopedia* at www. georgiaencyclopedia.org and search for the entry on 'Bible Quilt'. Images of Powers's second quilt can be found on the webpage of the Museum of Fine Arts, Boston. Go to www.mfa. org/collections/ and conduct a search for 'Harriet Powers'. A 'click to zoom' feature provides details. The two 1989 monographs on Finster, one by John Turner and the other by Finster and Patterson, are indispensible for their text and colour illustrations. A good online essay on Finster with colour photographs, 'Howard Finster: Man of Visions', is written by John Blackburn and can be found at http://xroads.virginia.edu/CAP/Finster/finster2.html. For both artists, also try Google Image Search.

CHAPTER 24

BOB DYLAN'S BIBLE

MICHAEL J. GILMOUR

Bob Dylan stands out among his peers. Few contemporary artists have endured so long, reinvented themselves so frequently and successfully (folk, rock, country, gospel music), and contributed in such diverse media (music, film, poetry, prose, sketches). What is more, there may be no other artist of the twentieth and twenty-first centuries with such an unusual list of significant honours: Grammy Awards; an Academy Award (2000); a Polar Music Prize (2000); a Kennedy Center Honour (1997); honorary doctorates (Princeton University; St Andrew's University); nominations for the Nobel Prize for Literature (about which see Ball 2007); and a Pulitzer Prize Special Citation (2008), among them. In addition to this impressive list, Bob Dylan's music and writing is often the subject of serious academic analysis from a variety of disciplinary perspectives, including literary, cultural, religious, and music studies.

The use of the Bible in the songs and other art forms that comprise the Bob Dylan canon defies simplistic systematization and containment within categories, and this is the principal point made in this short chapter. Dylan's art is idiosyncratic, involves constant blending and bending of his sources, and is often inconsistent; a biblical image or phrase used one way in one time and place may appear quite different in another.

Dylan's use of the Bible in his writing is well described by the term adaptation, defined by literary theorist Linda Hutcheon as 'a form of repetition without replication' (2006: p. xvi, cf. 4, 7, 149, 173, 176); a 'derivation that is not derivative—a work that is second without being secondary' (ibid. 9). As Dylan places biblical characters, themes, terms, and phrases into new settings there is inevitable change, but most readers and listeners will recognize the canonical origins just the same. This is significant because, as Hutcheon defines the term, adaptations usually announce the relationship with prior texts (ibid., pp. xiv, 3, 8). Dylan does this by typically invoking iconic stories and characters from the Bible familiar to most (the flood, the crucifixion; Abraham, Jesus, Judas, etc.). On other occasions, he explicitly identifies the Bible in songs: he mentions Leviticus and Deuteronomy in 'Jokerman' (*Infidels*, 1983; 2004*b*: 463); the Sermon on the Mount in 'Up To Me' (*Biograph*, 1985; 2004*b*: 348). Someone quotes 'the Bible' in 'Man in the Long Black Coat' (*Oh Mercy*, 1989; 2004*b*: 530); another reads it in 'Quit Your Lowdown Ways' (*Bootleg Series, Vol. 1–3*, 1991; 2004*b*: 35).

Hutcheon also distinguishes works that include only brief echoes of source material, 'short intertextual allusions', from those that involve 'extended engagements' (2006: 170, 9). Here too, her definition of adaptation is appropriate for Dylan's writing if we approach his works as a whole. The Dylan canon—consider, for instance, his selective, 600-page book *Lyrics: 1962–2001*—presents us with a persistent engagement with the Bible over a forty-year period (illustrated in Gilmour 2004: 105–41, which lists parallels between the songs and biblical passages chronologically according to release dates). If we add to this other projects, such as his films *Renaldo and Clara* (1978) and *Masked and Anonymous* (2003), published poetry (*Tarantula: Poems*, 1971), album liner-notes, and his prose autobiographical writing *Chronicles: Volume One* (2004), each of which dialogues with the Bible in one way or another, we clearly have an extended engagement with the Scriptures.

THE IMPORTANCE OF RECEIVED TRADITION IN BOB DYLAN'S ART

'A folk song', Bob Dylan writes, 'has over a thousand faces and you must meet them all if you want to play this stuff. A folk song might vary in meaning and it might not appear the same from one moment to the next. It depends on who's playing and who's listening' (2004*a*: 71). This freedom to adapt and rewrite, while remaining tethered to a 'textual' tradition, characterizes his use of the Bible. He returns to it constantly yet never uses it the same way twice. As texts, images, and ideas pass from one setting and medium to another, their meanings evolve in the process. It follows, then, that as Dylan brings biblical content into the world of his songs, something original emerges. Adaptation always involves change (Hutcheon 2006: pp. xvi, 16).

Bob Dylan constantly looks backwards as he writes, finding in stories from long ago a storehouse of imagery and wisdom that informs his own work in the present.

This fascination with received tradition extends to material from both recent memory and the distant past, the disparate literature of the Bible included. Dylan refers to himself as a 'thief of thoughts' in one poem ('11 Outlined Epitaphs'; 2000: 112), and is reluctant to name his influences in another because there are too many to count, and he would not want to miss any ('Joan Baez in Concert, Part 2'; 2000: 72). When Dylan comments on the subjects and sources that inspire his artistry, we observe a persistent sense of nostalgia in his reflections and hints of regret at the passing of time. He looks to stories from the past to bring meaning to the present moment because the 'modern world' holds little interest for him. As a young songwriter, he recalls, 'What was swinging, topical and up to date for me was stuff like the *Titanic* sinking, the Galveston flood, John Henry driving steel, John Hardy shooting a man on the West Virginia line. All this was current, played out and in the open. This was the news that I considered, followed and kept tabs on' (2004a: 20). In the liner-notes to his 1993 album *World Gone Wrong*, a collection of traditional songs, Dylan celebrates days gone by and describes 'these modern times' as 'the New Dark Ages'. He may regret these 'modern times' in the notes to *World Gone Wrong*, but he returns to these words, with a knowing wink, one suspects, for the title of a 2006 album. The phrase itself might originate with the 1936 Charlie Chaplin film of that name. If so, Dylan is once again celebrating voices from the past, finding them to be swinging and topical.

As Michael Gray puts it, Dylan 'insists on the continued relevance of these voices from the past, and takes us so deeply among them that he frees us from the tyranny of the present' (Gray 2000: 15). Dylan's interpreters frequently note this fascination with received tradition, especially American roots music (see e.g. Gray 2000: 17–44; Marcus 1997; Wilentz 2003). The title of Dylan's 2001 album *"Love and Theft"* speaks 'directly to his love for all forms of American music, as well as to his tendency to express that love by direct quotation, borrowing, or "theft"' (Scobie 2003: 305). That album, along with its predecessor *Time Out of Mind* (1997), 'is saturated with quotations, both musical and verbal' and its 'musical styles range over the whole history of twentieth-century American music' (Scobie 2003: 306).

The Bible is clearly one of the important sources for Dylan's writing, and while some exaggerate its significance for his work, others are guilty of underestimating the ways it informs and gives atmosphere to the songs. It is interesting to observe where and how he introduces the Bible in his lyrics and poems, but there is much more to this subject than mere identification of allusions and quotations. Christopher Ricks observes that 'Dylan not only opens his Bible, he opens up its radiations and its revelations' (Ricks 2003: 210–11). This is high praise, an acknowledgement that this musician's incorporation of biblical literature is often insightful, involving reflection, and frequent and deliberate irony. Before commenting further on Dylan's use of the Bible, however, some preliminary remarks about methodological questions are in order.

THE BIBLE AND BOB DYLAN'S BIOGRAPHY

When the late Ed Bradley interviewed Bob Dylan for an episode of the CBS program *60 Minutes* that originally aired on 5 December 2004, he asked the musician about his fans' tendency to use hyperbolic labels like 'prophet': 'I never wanted to be a prophet or a saviour,' he replied. 'Elvis maybe. I could see myself becoming him. But prophet? No' (author's transcription). Inevitably, the curious scrutinize the lives of celebrities, and this is certainly true in his case. There are many biographies and an intense interest in his private life. His reclusive nature and reluctance to give interviews feeds this curiosity—according to Ed Bradley in his *60 Minutes* segment, this was the first television interview with the singer in nearly twenty years. Even when he does speak publicly, he tends to be cryptic, often obfuscating more than illuminating his interviewers and audiences. Indeed, Dylan began his illustrious career by famously fabricating stories about his past after first arriving in New York City, telling tales he describes now as 'pure hokum-hophead talk' (Dylan 2004a: 8).

Because Dylan does not satisfy this craving for personal details, there is a tendency to scour lyrics for clues about his private life. The most famous interpreter engaged in this practice is A. J. Weberman who, finding evidence in song lyrics, argued Dylan was a heroin user (for details, see e.g. Sounes 2001: 262–5). A similar habit of over-interpretation emerges among those interested in religious dimensions of his life, with commentators mining the lyrics for biblical allusions and citations that might reveal clues about the singer's personal beliefs. This approach is highly problematic. Creative writers incorporate language or imagery—whether biblical or otherwise—for a wide number of reasons, that may have nothing to do with their personal spirituality. For instance, many biblical stories and themes are widely familiar to audiences and they evoke predictable assumptions and emotions. Knowing this, Dylan can anticipate how audiences will respond to particular expressions, which allows him to introduce variations to his sources for rhetorical and artistic effect. The shocking and ironic declaration that even Jesus would not forgive the masters of war (in the song of that name on *The Freewheelin' Bob Dylan*, 1963; 2004b: 56) assumes that audiences know the biblical backdrop (i.e. that Jesus is someone who forgives sins). Indeed, this jeremiad against militarism is only effective to the degree that audiences recognize the source and the irony at play in the lyrics.

On other occasions biblical terms and phrases may derive from non-biblical sources, coming to Dylan's songs only indirectly. For instance, the Bible's influence on the English language and literature is immeasurable and we cannot always determine if the songwriter is deliberately echoing a biblical passage or merely using a familiar turn of phrase with a biblical etymology. There are many examples of this kind of ambiguity in Dylan's lyrical imagery: a person said to be as innocent as a lamb ('Ballad in Plain D', *Another Side of Bob Dylan*, 1964; 2004*b*: 129; cf. Exod. 12:5; Lev. 23:12; 1 Pet. 1:19); conclusions written on a wall ('Love Minus Zero/No Limit', *Bringing It All Back Home*, 1965; 2004*b*: 145; cf. Dan. 5:1–30); a willingness to sacrifice the world for another ('Wedding Song', *Planet Waves*, 1974; 2004*b*: 326; cf. e.g. Matt. 19:27–9; Mark 10:28–30; Luke 18:28, 29b–30); 'forbidden fruit' ('Where Are You Tonight? [Journey Through Dark Heat]', *Street Legal*, 1978; 2004*b*: 395; also 'T.V. Talkin' Song', *Under the Red Sky*, 1990; 2004*b*: 549; cf. Gen. 3:1–6); someone crying out in the wilderness ('Tight Connection to My Heart [Has Anybody Seen My Love]', *Empire Burlesque*, 1985; 2004*b*: 490; cf. Matt. 3:1–6; 11:7–11; Mark 1:2–6; Luke 3:2–4; 7:24–8; John 1:23). In cases like this, one suspects the songwriter is not so much attempting to evoke the biblical sources behind the terms as simply using well-known idioms. On still other occasions, biblical material may provide nothing more than striking metaphors or, less profoundly still, language fitting a rhyming scheme, for example: first now, last later ('The Times They Are A-Changin'', *The Times They Are A-Changin'*, 1964; 2004*b*: 81; cf. Matt. 19:30; Mark 10:31; Luke 13:30); darkness at noon ('It's Alright, Ma (I'm Only Bleeding)', *Bringing It All Back Home*, 1965; 2004*b*: 156; cf. Matt. 27:45; Mark 15:33; Luke 23:44); a growling wildcat ('All Along the Watchtower', *John Wesley Harding*, 1967; 2004*b*: 224; cf. 1 Pet. 5:8).

The point here is that trying to reconstruct Dylan's religious views from his lyrics is fraught with pitfalls. Unless he explicitly tells us that a song reveals something about his religious convictions, such an exercise remains hopelessly subjective. Even if he were to provide such clues, interpreters should remain cautious just the same. Can we trust an artist who explains the work in question? He warns us about believing what he says on at least one occasion ('Trust Yourself'; *Empire Burlesque*, 1985; 2004*b*: 497).

There is wisdom in leaving speculations about Dylan's religious beliefs to the side when examining his use of the Bible. The three albums released during the so-called gospel period (*Slow Train Coming*, 1979; *Saved*, 1980; and *Shot of Love*, 1981) are provocative to be sure, and generate a great deal of discussion about his interest in fundamentalist Christianity (see esp. Webb 2006 for a thorough treatment of this period). However, to place interpretive emphasis on biographical considerations can obscure the fact that his use of the Bible is ubiquitous throughout all of his works, both before and after this gospel phase. Attempts to isolate Dylan's views on religion inevitably involve speculation, exaggeration, selectivity, and distortion. A better way to treat these albums is to consider this a period of time when Dylan's music underwent a genre shift. This is not to deny there was a genuine turn in his views on religion as well, but placing emphasis on the music, not biography, acknowledges the limitations of linking art with the artist. In this case, the songs of 1979–81 represent a recognizable musical style (contemporary Christian music), analogous in some ways to that used by other artists of the day like Larry Norman or Keith Green, for instance. He even contributes a harmonica solo to Keith Green's 'I Pledge My Head To Heaven' (on his album *So You Wanna Go Back To Egypt*,

1980) illustrating Dylan's willingness to participate in this musical form, and there is a clear attempt to write songs during this period suitable for this musical subculture. According to Keith Green's wife, Dylan even consulted her and her husband about the lyrics to *Slow Train Coming*, something supporting the idea that he was writing according to the conventions of this particular style (see Green and Hazard 2000: 290–2). And he was successful. The Gospel Music Association gave Dylan a Dove Award for *Slow Train Coming*. The album also earned his first Grammy Award.

Dylan's gospel period resembles other shifts in musical genre occurring throughout his career, from folk to rock, from rock to country, and so on. Every exploration of a new musical style involves a shift in vocabulary and idioms, and commentators should treat the gospel albums of 1979–81 as another stage in the ongoing evolution of Dylan's oeuvre. Approaching the gospel songs as part of a gradual shift in his writing also helps avoid the tendency toward an overly fixed periodization of his work. Certain themes appearing in the pre-gospel *Street Legal* (1978), for instance, appear to anticipate ideas found in the gospel album *Slow Train Coming* (1979). Similarly, the post-gospel *Infidels* (1983) is as rich in biblical allusions as the preceding gospel album *Shot of Love* (1981). The boundaries between his pre-gospel, gospel, and post-gospel writing are porous and fluid, not rigid.

Bob Dylan's Reception of the Bible: General Considerations

Bob Dylan's Bible often recalls the language of the King James (Authorized) Version, as in his use of the archaic 'unto others' in lyrics recalling the Sermon on the Mount ('Ain't Talkin''; *Modern Times*, 2006 [for lyrics to this album, see bobdylan.com]; cf. Matt. 5:43–4). Of course, he may read a variety of translations, and/or receive biblical imagery and phrases from any number of other sources. In the same song, his description of wheels flying in the heavens illustrates the most significant challenge for determining exactly what translation he uses. Here the obvious allusion to Ezekiel's vision (1:15–21) is a paraphrase and not dependent on any particular translation precursor. Bob Dylan's Bible is most often a unique rendition of Scripture because he shapes language for his own purposes, whether this means accommodating a rhyming pattern, introducing irony, or weaving images together. There are many examples of his unique rendering of biblical material. For instance, the titular phrase 'Spirit On the Water' (*Modern Times*, 2006) alludes to Genesis 1:2, but without exact dependence on any particular translation (cf. e.g. 'a wind from God swept over the face of the waters' (NRSV); 'the Spirit of God moved upon the face of the waters' (AV)).

There is a diverse bibliography commenting on Bob Dylan's use of the Bible and/ or religious dimensions in his work. Bert Cartwright's seminal analysis of this topic deserves particular notice. He approaches this subject by connecting biblical themes to various phases of the songwriter's career, and—the cautions about periodization noted above notwithstanding—this study remains the most important work on the subject (though unfortunately not widely available).

According to Cartwright, the first phase begins with Dylan's arrival in New York in 1961 and continues through to his motorcycle accident in 1966. During this time, Cartwright suggests, 'Dylan saw the Bible as part of the poor white and black cultures of America with which he sought to identify'. From 1966 through to 1973, a time of recovery from the accident and semi-retirement with his young family, Dylan's writing 'reveal[s] a more calculated use of the Bible', occasionally assuming a biblical perspective, though it is not 'personally claimed'. In Dylan's work in the third phase (1974–8) we see a writer using the Bible as 'a sophisticated artist who had learned consciously to work simultaneously on several levels of meaning', whereas the fourth period (1979–81) reveals Dylan's embrace of fundamentalist Christianity. The gospel songs during these years show Dylan's 'desire to express in life and song what his fresh study of the Bible as a believer was telling him'. Finally, Cartwright describes the fifth phase (1983 through to the publication of the book) as a time when Dylan's 'biblical faith had been internalized sufficiently for it to serve subtly as [his] worldview' (1992: 15).

If pressed to follow Cartwright's approach and characterize Dylan's use of the Bible after 1992, I would highlight two tendencies. One is the recurring introduction of apocalyptic overtones, as in his Academy Award-winning 'Things Have Changed', which announces that if indeed the Bible is right, 'the world will explode' (*The Essential Bob Dylan*, 2000; 2004b: 574; cf. 2 Pet. 3:7). We find another example in 'Cross the Green Mountain', from the Civil War film *Gods and Generals* (2002; the song appears on *Tell Tale Signs*, The Bootleg Series, Vol. 8, 2008), which includes an allusion to Revelation 13:1. The narrator recalls dreaming about a monster rising out of the sea and sweeping through the land. He adds the sombre warning that 'all must yield to the avenging God' (author's transcription). A second tendency, and an unlikely companion to the first, is the blending of humour with biblical and religious content, as in the witty description of a 'Po' Boy' (*"Love and Theft"*, 2001) who ends up feeding swine (2004b: 595; cf. Luke 15:15).

Humour also emerges when we consider the previously mentioned public fascination with Dylan's spirituality and his reluctance to speak directly to this subject. Whereas some of Dylan's contemporaries with strong religious convictions are unambiguous about their views (e.g. the Hindu George Harrison, as on the album *All Things Must Pass*, 1970; the Muslim Cat Stevens/Yusuf Islam, as on the albums *An Other Cup*, 2006 and *Roadsinger*, 2009; and the Christian Alice Cooper, as on the album *The Last Temptation*, 1994), Dylan's post-gospel lyrics and comments about religion remain cryptic. The very fact that *The Simpsons* can spoof Dylan's mysterious spirituality makes it clear that the mass-market American audience is at least generally familiar with his story—a Jew with interests in Christianity—otherwise the show's parody would not work. In the scene in question (episode 339), the family is watching television as an interviewer asks, 'So Bob, what religion are you converting to now?', to which Dylan responds, 'Well I'll tell ya one thing [incomprehensible mumbling] no more. Shalom' (author's transcription). One suspects Dylan plays into this persistent curiosity about his relationship to Judaism and Christianity when he sings tantalizingly about hiding his faith ('Dreamin' of You', *Tell Tale Signs*, The Bootleg Series, Vol. 8, 2008) or practising one that was long-abandoned ('Ain't Talkin'', *Modern Times*, 2006). For someone who insists on reading the latter biographically, it begs the question, which faith is he referring to? There may be a joke at play here; the title suggests the songwriter is not revealing anything to anyone.

Organizational strategies that categorize artistic works along perceived trajectories of development (like Cartwright's) are helpful to a degree, though attempts to compartmentalize artistic works rarely do justice to the entire canon in question. There are always exceptions to most boundaries analysts devise, and there is always the risk of oversimplification. Other models exist for approaching biblical and religious dimensions in Dylan's work. Christopher Ricks organizes his literary analysis of some of Dylan's songs (2003) around the traditional seven deadly sins (envy, covetousness, greed, sloth, lust, anger, pride), four cardinal virtues (justice, prudence, temperance, fortitude), and three heavenly graces (faith, hope, charity). Gilmour (2004) focuses on biblical themes in Dylan's writing, specifically the prophetic tradition, the Sermon on the Mount, apocalyptic thought, and redemption. There are also several books and articles commenting on Dylan's personal religious belief, usually from an explicitly Christian vantage-point or with a focus on the gospel phase (see e.g. Jacobs 2001: 97–108; Marshall and Ford 2002; Powell 2002: 277–86; Webb 2006; Williams 1996: 63–151). Others approach Dylan's spirituality from a Jewish perspective, among them Daniel Maoz, who proposes that the 'interpretive principles and methods of major kabbalistic interpreters have inspired Dylan, either directly or indirectly', a point he illustrates in a reading of Dylan's 1983 album *Infidels*. This album, according to Maoz, 'holds the key to understanding what is the *crux interpretum* for Dylan's unique manner of expression and perception of life and [the] afterlife' (2005: 4).

A SAMPLE PATTERN IN BOB DYLAN'S RECEPTION OF THE BIBLE

....

For the purpose of this short overview, I want to call attention to one recurring pattern in Dylan's use of the Bible, namely his appropriation of its stories in 'autobiographical' songs. What I mean by this are first-person narratives in which the storyteller applies to himself descriptions originating with biblical characters. This is a literary device, we should be clear, not a form of disclosure from Dylan himself about his religious faith, or worse, evidence of megalomania.

Whenever Bob Dylan adapts the Bible, he usually goes beyond mere repetition of earlier texts and introduces poetic innovation to his source material. For instance, the song 'You Changed My Life' (*Bootleg Series, Volumes 1–3*, 1991) refers to Jesus (presumably), with eyes of fire and feet of brass, and orphans waving palm branches as he passes, even though he remains an outcast in the very world he created (Dylan 2004*b*: 458). The beautiful lyrics of this song bring together a cluster of biblical allusions (among them Matt. 21:8; Rev. 1:14; 2:18; John 1:10–11) without disrupting the original sense of the individual passages (i.e. each refers to Jesus, likely the 'you' addressed by the singer). In this gospel-period song, Jesus is the object of a supplicant's poetic prayer.

There are other songs, however, when Dylan uses the first-person singular in adaptations of biblical stories and places himself within those narratives, thus removing the sacred Other altogether. Not infrequently, such appropriations of the Bible integrate stories about the passion and resurrection of Christ, and so it is that a woman removes a 'crown of thorns' from the singer's head in 'Shelter From the Storm', while others gamble for his clothes (*Blood On the Tracks*, 1975; 2004*b*: 345–6; cf. Matt. 27:29 and 35). In 'Spirit on the Water' (*Modern Times*, 2006), the narrator sweats blood while praying to the powers above, words alluding to Luke 22:44: 'being in an agony [Jesus] prayed more earnestly: and his sweat was as it were great drops of blood falling down to the ground' (AV). It is also clear that the subject-matter of the song has nothing to do with Jesus in the Garden of Gethsemane. The song opens with the narrator thinking about 'you baby'; the image of Jesus' earnest prayer and garden solitude in the Gospel story illustrates the intensity of the singer's longing for an absent love.

Another example of this adoption of terms recalling Jesus' story occurs in 'Ain't Talkin'' (*Modern Times*, 2006). While in the mystic garden the singer tells a woman that no one is around and the gardener has gone, words recalling the post-resurrection encounter between Mary Magdalene and Jesus (John 20:15–16). In the Gospel story, Jesus brings clarity to the situation after Mary confuses him with the gardener; Dylan's narrator does a similar thing. He also refers to his ability to call for heavenly aid; something Jesus could also do (Matt. 26:53). There is a much earlier example in the humorous 'Bob Dylan's 115th Dream'. Here the narrator asserts a parallel with Christ, though another contradicts his claim: 'I said, "You know they refused Jesus, too" I He said, "You're not Him"' (*Bringing It All Back Home*, 1965; Dylan 2004*b*: 149).

In addition to the Gospel stories, there are various allusions to the biblical prophets. Dylan cites Amos 7:14 in 'Long Time Gone' (2004*b*: 28–9), asserting that he is not a prophet, nor a prophet's son. Here the singer-songwriter, whom others often call a prophet (cf. the *60 Minutes* interview mentioned above), refers to the words of a real prophet who denies being one! Elsewhere, another Dylan narrator embraces the title prophet, in effect, by going into a valley full of dry bones ('Dignity', *Greatest Hits: Vol. 3*, 1994; 2004*b*: 541), an unambiguous reference to Ezekiel's vision (37:1–6). Perhaps the best-known example of Dylan's self-referential use of biblical language does not draw on either the prophetic or the Gospel traditions. He alludes to the Akedah (Gen. 22:1–19) in 'Highway 61 Revisited' (*Highway 61 Revisited*, 1965; 2004*b*: 178) in the line about God telling Abraham to kill his son on Highway 61. Dylan does not use the first-person singular, but the lyrics suggest this is another example self-referential writing because Abraham is the name of Bob's father, and Highway 61 runs through Duluth, Minnesota, where Bob was born.

We find Dylan appropriating religiously significant characterizations on film as well. There is a wonderful scene in his film *Renaldo and Clara*—by all appearances unscripted—when Dylan, playing a character named Renaldo, walks off a bus just as a sidewalk preacher is speaking about Jesus coming soon. Dylan is co-screenwriter for another film, *Masked and Anonymous* (2003), in which he plays a character with christological overtones that are hard to miss. His dead mother's name is Mary. The film begins with him rising out of a tomb (a jail). There are intriguing references to his 'return', a second coming. A man named Prospero (Cheech Morin) asks him if he is 'coming back', to which Fate (Dylan's character) replies: 'I did come back.' Later, when checking into the hotel, Fate observes 'I've been here before', and later still his mistress says, 'I wondered when you would return'. Nina Veronica (Jessica Lange) questions the currency of Fate's celebrity, after which Uncle Sweetheart (John Goodman) retorts: 'did Jesus have to walk on water twice to make his point?' Sweetheart later observes that Fate's musical comeback has the potential to 'save the world'. This is a difficult task, Fate admits, because 'it ain't easy being human' (author's transcription). Such moments in song and film are not self-aggrandizement, but rather Dylan at his humorous best. *Masked and Anonymous* makes this abundantly clear because it includes self-deprecating humour throughout, with jokes about an artist who is long past his prime (cf. his performance as aging rock star Billy Parker in the 1987 film *Hearts of Fire*). These self-referential uses of the Bible are tongue-in-cheek, involving perhaps a playful response to his fans' exaggerated claims.

As Dylan takes on these biblical roles, he also brings the Scriptures into dialogue with other stories. The song 'Sugar Baby', which closes the 2001 album *"Love and Theft"*, and 'Thunder On the Mountain', which opens the 2006 album *Modern Times*, illustrate this phenomena. I am assuming in what follows that Dylan deliberately plays one album off another and one song off another, but even if not, these songs illustrate not only Dylan's habit of participating in biblical stories but also his ability to weave those stories into other narratives. We also observe in a comparison of 'Sugar Baby' with 'Thunder On the Mountain' how the sense of a single biblical image (in this case the angel Gabriel) can shift during migration (Hutcheon's term, 2006: p. xvi) from one song and album to another. Bob Dylan's Bible, it follows, is not a stable, fixed point of reference but rather a storehouse of images that can morph into whatever he wants them to be in any given context.

The two songs in question follow one another in terms of album release-dates (one closing an album, the other opening the next). The closing verse of *"Love and Theft"* warns a woman to seek her maker before the angel Gabriel sounds his horn ('Sugar Baby'; Dylan, 2004*b*: 598). These words allude to a cluster of biblical images (see e.g. Eccl. 12:1; Isa. 51:13; Job 35:10; 1 Thess. 4:16; Rev. 8:6). The first song of his next full-length studio album, *Modern Times*, also incorporates biblical themes, including the sound of thunder on a mountain, and the sight of fire on the moon. The singer announces, 'Today's the day, gonna grab my trombone and blow' ('Thunder On the Mountain'). The title phrase of this song recalls the divine presence at Mount Sinai (Exod. 19:16, 19), where the sound of thunder and trumpets causes the people to tremble. The moon is also a recurring image in Scripture, as in Ecclesiastes 12:2 (see also Isa. 13:10; Ezek. 32:7; Joel 2:10; Matt. 24:29; Mark 13:24; Luke 21:25; Rev. 8:12; whereas Dylan mentions (red) fire on the moon, biblical writers describe the moon turning to (red) blood, e.g. Acts 2:20; Rev. 6:12).

The sequence of 'Sugar Baby' and 'Thunder On the Mountain'—as noted, one follows the other with respect to album release-dates—may involve a deliberately humorous segue. In the first song the anticipated angelic figure Gabriel is coming to blow his horn (cf. 1 Thess. 4:16). In the second, the singer assumes Gabriel's role himself, picking up his own horn (trombone). When Dylan uses the phrase 'Today's the *day*' to indicate the time he will sound his horn, he may have in mind the biblical phrase '*day* of the Lord'. Like Dylan, Joel links a horn-blast, a mountain, and celestial phenomena, including the moon, in his prophecy about the *day* of the Lord: 'Blow ye the trumpet in Zion, and sound an alarm in my holy mountain: let all the inhabitants of the land tremble: for the day of the LORD is cometh, for it is nigh at hand . . . the sun and moon shall be dark, and the stars shall withdraw their shining' (Joel 2:1, 10). All these elements—horn, day, mountain, moon—appear also in the 'Sugar Baby'–'Thunder On the Mountain' dyad.

In both songs, biblical imagery contributes to the singer's commentary about the women in question. In 'Sugar Baby' the singer speaks to a brainless woman who has abandoned the singer. He is a spurned lover, understandably angry with one whose 'charms' have broken many hearts. We could plausibly read his warning to watch out for the avenging angel Gabriel as the hyperbolic vitriol of the singer whose own heart was broken. By contrast, the narrator of 'Thunder On the Mountain' tells a very different story. He is actively pursuing this female—the American R&B artist Alicia Keys—and deeply sympathetic about *her* plight (not his own as in the earlier song), even shedding sympathetic tears on her behalf. When asked about this reference to Alicia Keys in an interview, Dylan said, 'I remember seeing her on the Grammys. I think I was on the show with her, I didn't meet her or anything. But I said to myself, "There's *nothing* about that girl I don't like"' (taken from Lethem 2006: 76). She clearly stands apart from the brainless heartbreaker of 'Sugar Baby'. In one song the horn-blowing Gabriel is an image expressing the singer's anger and heartbreak, and in the other the singer himself is a horn-blowing angel, one seeking to rescue a damsel in distress. Both songs draw inspiration from a biblical precursor.

However, the Bible is not the only inspiration here. Dylan opens *Modern Times* with a search for Alicia Keys, who was born, he tells us, in hell's kitchen (an area of New York City). Does this image allude to the Orpheus myth? If so, Dylan's musical, trombone-blowing narrator searches for the hell-bound Alicia Keys in the same way Orpheus searches for Eurydice in the underworld (there is even a remote resemblance between the names Alicia and Eurydice, with their soft 'c' sounds). In the Orpheus myth, the poet and musician journeys to the underworld in an effort to convince Hades and Persephone to let Eurydice return to the living. They allow her to return with him on the condition that he walk in front of her and not look back until they both reached the world of the living. Orpheus looks back, however, and consequently Eurydice disappears to the realm of the dead, this time forever. Here we see another dimension of Dylan's use of biblical material. He weaves Scripture into songs alongside other sources that inform the stories he tells.

Concluding Remarks

'Greed and lust I can understand,' Bob Dylan once said, 'but I can't understand the values of definition and confinement. Definition destroys' (taken from Cott 2006: p. xii). Adding commentary to this, Jonathan Cott describes Dylan as 'Elusive, oblique, mercurial, and always in motion,' adding, 'he has resisted in both his life and his work being categorized, encapsulated, finalized, conventionalized, canon-ized, and deified' (ibid., p. xii). His unwillingness to allow others to restrain and define him and his art is a well-known feature of Bob Dylan's mystique. We also find this refusal of confinement in his use of the Bible. At best, we may recognize broad tendencies and patterns in his use of this source that characterize periods of his career (Cartwright 1992), but beyond this rigid definitions do not help. Readers with even a passing knowledge of the Bible will recognize in Bob Dylan a songwriter who adapts the biblical writings with endless creativity and wit, or, to return to Hutcheon's phrase, one who repeats those stories without replicating them (2006: pp. xvi, 4, 7, 149, 173, 176).

WORKS CITED

BALL, G. (2007), 'Dylan and the Nobel', *Oral Tradition*, 22/1: 14–29.

CARTWRIGHT, B. (1992), *The Bible in the Lyrics of Bob Dylan*, 2nd edn. Wanted Man Study Series, no. 4. Bury: Wanted Man.

COTT, J. (ed.) (2006), *Bob Dylan: The Essential Interviews*. New York: Wenner Books.

DYLAN, B. (2000), *Lyrics: 1962–1985*. New York: Alfred A. Knopf.

——(2004a), *Chronicles: Volume I*. New York: Simon & Schuster.

——(2004b), *Lyrics: 1962–2001*. New York: Simon & Schuster.

GILMOUR, M. J. (2004), *Tangled Up in the Bible: Bob Dylan and Scripture*. New York and London: Continuum.

GRAY, M. (2000), *Song and Dance Man III: The Art of Bob Dylan*. New York and London: Continuum.

GREEN, M. and D. HAZARD (2000), *No Compromise: The Life Story of Keith Green*, rev. and expanded edn. Eugene: Harvest House Publishers.

HUTCHEON, L. (2006), *A Theory of Adaptation*. New York and London: Routledge.

JACOBS, A. (2001), *A Visit to Vanity Fair: Moral Essays on the Present Age*. Grand Rapids, Mich.: Brazos Press.

LETHEM, J. (2006), 'The Genius of Bob Dylan', *Rolling Stone*, 1008: 74–6, 78, 80, 128.

MAOZ, D. (2005), 'Shekhinah as Woman: Kabbalistic References in Dylan's *Infidels*', in M. J. Gilmour (ed.), *Call Me the Seeker: Listening to Religion in Popular Music*, 3–16. New York and London: Continuum.

MARCUS, G. (1997), *The Old, Weird America: The World of Bob Dylan's Basement Tapes*. New York: Picador USA.

MARSHALL, S. with M. FORD (2002), *Restless Pilgrim: The Spiritual Journey of Bob Dylan*. Lake Mary: Relevant Books.

POWELL, M. A. (2002), *Encyclopedia of Contemporary Christian Music*. Peabody: Hendrickson.

RICKS, C. (2003), *Dylan's Visions of Sin*. London: Penguin.

SCOBIE, S. (2003), *Alias Bob Dylan Revisited*. Calgary: Red Deer Press.

SOUNES, H. (2001), *Down the Highway: The Life of Bob Dylan*. New York: Grove Press.

WEBB, S. H. (2006), *Dylan Redeemed: From* Highway 61 *to* Saved. New York and London: Continuum.

WILENTZ, S. (2003), 'American Recordings: on *"Love and Theft"* and the Minstrel Boy', in N. CORCORAN (ed.), *'Do you, Mr Jones?': Bob Dylan with the Poets and Professors*, 295–305. London: Pimlico.

WILLIAMS, P. (1996), *Bob Dylan: Watching the River Flow, Observations on his Art-in-Progress 1966–1995*. London: Omnibus Press.

FURTHER READING

DETTMAR, K. J. H. (ed.) (2009), *The Cambridge Companion to Bob Dylan*. Cambridge Companions to American Studies. Cambridge: Cambridge University Press.

GRAY, M. (2006), *The Bob Dylan Encyclopedia*. New York and London: Continuum.

HEYLIN, C. (2001), *Bob Dylan: Behind the Shades, Take Two*. London: Penguin.

THOMSON, E. and D. GUTMAN (eds.) (2001), *The Dylan Companion*, updated and expanded edn. Cambridge, Mass.: Da Capo Press.

VARESI, A. (2002), *The Bob Dylan Albums: A Critical Study*. Toronto: Guernica.

....

CHAPTER 25

FROM JOHN'S GOSPEL TO DAN BROWN: THE MAGDALENE CODE

....

ROBIN GRIFFITH-JONES

I

....

Readers of Dan Brown's *The Da Vinci Code* will remember the exposition given to Sophie by Robert Langdon and Leigh Teabing halfway through the book.[1]

'The marriage of Jesus and Mary Magdalene is part of the historical record. Moreover, Jesus as a married man makes infinitely more sense than our standard biblical view of Jesus as a bachelor...If Jesus were not married, at least one of the Bible's gospels would have mentioned it, and offered some explanation for his unnatural state of bachelorhood.' (Sir Leigh Teabing (British Royal Historian) and Robert Langdon (Harvard symbologist), in Brown 2004: 329–30)

'The power of the female and her ability to produce life was once very sacred, but it posed a threat to the rise of the predominantly male Church, and so the sacred feminine was demonized and called unclean. It was *man*, not God, who created the concept of "original

---

[1] I draw extensively in this paper on my earlier publications that cover similar ground in more detail: Griffith-Jones: 2006, 2008*a*, and *b*.

sin", whereby Eve tasted of the apple and caused the downfall of the human race.' (Robert Langdon, in ibid. 322)

Dan Brown has mixed a potent cocktail: Jesus, Mary Magdalene, and sex; the Roman Catholic Church and age-old, international conspiracies. How, then, should scholars respond? It is easy to be dismissive: *The Da Vinci Code* is, after all, a *novel*; its characters' claims could tempt—let alone convince—only the most ignorant and credulous readers. Church leaders may be angry; Cardinal Bertone of Genoa urged Roman Catholic bookshops not to sell this book and Catholic readers not to read it. (This was arguably a self-defeating tactic: it *sounded* like the Roman Church trying to suppress a book which reveals how ruthlessly the Roman Church suppresses books.)[2] Various authors in 'popular' books have rebutted the novel's many and egregious errors of fact; I am among them (Griffith-Jones 2006). But scholars have no need to devote time—indeed, no warrant to waste time— attending to the book or its readers at all.

Brown himself, after all, may have taken his story less seriously than his critics do. The criminal mastermind in the novel is Leigh Teabing; his name combines the surnames of Richard Leigh and (in anagram) Michael Baigent, two of the authors of *The Holy Blood and the Holy Grail* (Baigent, Leigh, and Lincoln 1996; hereafter *Holy Blood*). Sophie's grandfather is Jacques Saunière; Fr Bérenger Saunière was in the 1890s the curé at Rennes-le-Château, central to the theories expounded in *Holy Blood*. And Bishop Aringarosa seems for most of the novel to be the hub from which radiate all the Church's conspiracies, but turns out to have been Teabing's dupe; his name is nearly the Italian for 'red herring'.

It remains oddly narrow, nonetheless, simply to patronize and dismiss Brown's book. First, the *Code*'s success is a symptom of currents and conditions in Western culture; the novel—in particular its characters' view of Jesus and the Bible—has grown from, mirrored, and influenced these currents. Among them is, I suggest, the following: Jesus is widely respected, far beyond the boundaries of the churches, as an ideal human being to whose standards we and our children do well to aspire; why (it is asked) should such an ideal human not have made and honoured the greatest commitment that one person can make to another—why should he not have been married? Whatever the answers may be, the question can be honestly asked. To suggest that Jesus was married is arguably to ascribe to marriage and to sex within marriage the ultimate excellence which the Roman Catholic Church, at the Second Vatican Council, still gave only to consecrated celibacy (Vatican II, 53. II.13). It is poignant and probably significant that a married Jesus is becoming more widely credited and valued while marriage itself, in the secularized West, becomes less popular and less binding.

---

[2] *Il Giornale*, March 2005, reported at www.theage.com.au/articles/2005/03/16/1110913654115.html? oneclick=true.

Secondly, the novel is prefaced by a page, entitled 'Fact', about the Priory of Sion and Opus Dei. This ends: 'All descriptions of artwork, architecture, documents and secret rituals in this novel are accurate.' Much of this page is, at best, seriously misleading; but those readers were not unduly naive who heard in it, before they entered the frame of the fiction itself, an honest authorial voice. The novel itself encourages that trust. Brown's characters speak fluently of mathematics, art history, the Templars, Constantine, the Bible, the Gnostic gospels, Jesus, and Mary Magdalene. This is a dazzling—even if spurious—range of intellectual reference. Some of the claims are surely reliable; Brown would not, after all, lie about mathematics. (He doesn't.) What, then, of the clearly contentious claims? A reader may well think back to the scandal (publicized in the film *Erin Brockovich*) of chemical dumping, or to Big Tobacco's conspiracy (publicized in *The Insider*) to suppress all evidence that nicotine is addictive. The reader is prepared to believe that powerful corporations become murderous under threat and that the truth will be exposed in a popular novel or star-studded film.

Novels with an historical back-story are, after all, widely read: readers of Robert Harris's *Pompeii*, a mere novel, will have believed (rightly) that they were learning accurately and in detail about volcanoes and provincial Roman society. At least one professional classicist (Jones 2004) praised Harris's books for the accuracy of their back-stories. (Novels are not, it seems, *qua* novels, unworthy of scholars' regard.) Most readers would not claim to know and would not greatly care exactly where the facts stopped and fiction started. Those who read historical novels and watch 'faction' films are quite comfortable with the clear principle and fuzzy edges of the distinction between the foreground drama and the back-story.

And thirdly, Dan Brown exploits and fortifies an already widespread suspicion: that the Church has consistently mistreated women. Historians and leaders of the Church may choose to dispute the charge; but it would be wilfully purblind to deny that there is prima facie a charge to be answered.

There is perhaps some intellectual snobbery behind the swift dismissal of the novel. The speculation that Jesus and Mary Magdalene were married was recently aired again by the distinguished playwright Howard Brenton in *Paul*, a play staged in 2005 at London's National Theatre. The apostle Paul meets Mary Magdalene and discovers she had been Jesus' wife (Brenton 2005: 37–8). She tells him:

Know why he married me? To spite his mother and father. They're rich, you know... They're stuck up too: aristocratic blood... They saw Yeshua as High Priest one day... Bright little kid he was too, they say. Knew the Torah off by heart. So when Yeshua took to the road with no shoes and a begging bowl, they weren't well pleased. Nothing compared though, to when he married me. They didn't like that, not one bit. But he was over thirty so he could insist. His mother was in charge of the wedding party of course, so you know what she did? Served water. Yeshua had wine brought in. No, they didn't like it one bit, having a daughter-in-law who was a whore.

Dan Brown's 'airport novel' was greeted by the churches' anger or scorn; Brenton's play, staged in London's most prestigious cultural complex, was treated as serious work of art. Both were following in a long tradition. In the response likely to be stirred by transgressive claims, context is all. (On the evening of my own visit to Brenton's play there were at least one bishop and two priests in the audience; others may have chosen not to wear clerical collars for such an outing. For an account of poems, novels, plays, operas, films and works of art which since the mid-nineteenth century have played on a sexual frisson between Jesus and Mary Magdalene, see Haskins 1993: 347–69.)

The question will not go away, whether Jesus and Mary Magdalene were married. But there is a more interesting question: why does it matter to so many people that they were or might have been? At issue, I suggest, is the question, was Jesus really human? The churches' Jesus is both wholly human and wholly God. As human, he is perfectly human in perfect conformity to God's will; and it is no longer self-evident (as intrinsic to humanity's highest calling) that this conformity entails Jesus' celibacy. Jesus' continence was central to Augustine's account of the Fall and our restoration in and by Christ. But a great many people (even inside the churches) do not recognize themselves as Augustinians now; and when the theo-logical rationale is dissolved which made sense of and reinforced the assumption that Jesus was celibate, it would be naively credulous not to re-examine the assumption itself. (None of this lessens the irony that Brown sets the human Jesus of the Gnostic gospels against the Jesus of the biblical gospels who—Brown's characters claim—is no less and no more than a god. This is untrue both to the biblical and to the Gnostic gospels—Griffith-Jones 2006, 2008a.)

We might still wonder whether many of the *Code*'s readers actually *believed* the claims made by its characters. There were, I suggest, a great many readers who did not know why *not* to believe the whole vast construction, and were prepared to acknowledge that 'there may be something in it'. This need reveal no more than an informal and uncommitted acquiescence which makes little difference to the believer's behaviour, attitudes, or relationships. It should not surprise us, however, if some readers have invested more heavily than this in claims which have articu-lated and strengthened vague, long-harboured doubts about the Jesus whom the churches proclaim and about those churches themselves. Here I admit to reliance on unsystematic personal encounters. I serve as Master of the Temple at the Temple Church in London, the setting for a scene in *The Da Vinci Code*. The Temple has been visited by many thousands of visitors who have been following the novel's trail. For over a year I gave a weekly talk here on the novel, and heard—at these talks and almost every day—responses to it from a small proportion but wide range of its readers. The informal tutorial given to Sophie by Robert and by Teabing had affected a good many of those whom I met. Its *honesty* was consis-tently praised: 'Christian philosophy decided to embezzle the female's creative power by ignoring biological truth and making *man* the creator. Genesis tells us that Eve was created from Adam's rib. Woman became an offshoot of man. And a sinful one at that. Genesis is the beginning of the end for the goddess' (Brown 2004: 322). Here, in direct opposition to the Church's narrative, is a counter-narrative casting the Church itself (rightly or wrongly) as autocratic, androcentric, and misogynist.

Mary Magdalene plays widely divergent roles in these competing narratives. The Western Church amalgamated her with the sinful woman (envisioned as a prostitute) who anointed Jesus (Luke 7:36–50) and with the Mary of Bethany who also anointed him (John 12:1–8). (I give a fuller account of this story in Griffith-Jones 2008*a*: 177–82, 207, 235–9.) So she was for centuries defined as a symbol of two forms of love, which—in this life that men imagined for her—she lived out one after the other: the first rampantly sexual, self-indulgent, dangerous to men and catastrophic for herself; the second spiritual, selfless, obedient.

She has in the past century evolved, to play a political role. She has been an icon of women-as-victims. But she is changing: she now represents the women who are escaping from victimhood in the twenty-first century as Mary herself has escaped from calumny; she is no longer the prostitute (used by men), but the woman falsely charged (by men) with prostitution. So she is becoming an example and an inspiration, a symbol of women's growing self-affirmation.

Beyond the churches, Mary's roles are growing. She has been reinvented as the mother of Jesus' child Sarah. She is being made to carry a lot of freight, in good measure because the New Testament offers so few and such limited models for women (let alone, for family life). Jesus is, in the imagination of our age, evolving too: he is becoming a husband and a father. So Mary Magdalene is now invoked not just in a confrontation of the sexes but in a search for harmony between them. And their (imagined) descendants give present reality to a Jesus who has otherwise faded into a shadow from the distant past.

Jesus himself, then, is being re-moulded in our generation as he has been re-moulded in the past, to exemplify the highest ideals of an age. 'The historical investigation of the life of Jesus', wrote Albert Schweitzer, in his classic survey of nineteenth-century studies of Jesus, 'did not take its rise from a purely historical interest; it turned to the Jesus of history as an ally in the struggle against the tyranny of dogma . . . Each successive epoch of theology found its own thoughts in Jesus; that was, indeed, the only way in which they could make him live' (Schweitzer 1910: 4–5).

At the end of the novel, Sophie accepts Robert's invitation to go with him to Florence; the hero and heroine will fall into each other's arms at last. It is a fitting end to the story. The film, however, ends without this assignation. At Rosslyn Sophie teasingly checks whether, as Jesus' descendant, she can walk on water. (She cannot.) Then she and Robert—with no spark of attraction between them—simply part. A story about modern freedom from the Church's fear of women and of sex ends with the hero and heroine saying a dull, sexless goodbye.

II

Several of the novel's themes were adopted from *The Holy Blood and the Holy Grail*. When co-author Henry Lincoln was asked if his book's claims were not incredible, he asked in reply: 'Is it more plausible that a man should be married and have children, or that he should be born of a virgin, attended by choirs of angels, walk on water and rise from the grave?'[3] Whatever—in Jesus' case—the answer may be, it is a sensible question.

To attend exclusively to the question of Jesus' marriage, however, is to evade the general charge laid by the novel's characters at the Church's door: that the Church has consistently marginalized and belittled women. Was Jesus (ever) married? There is no unambiguous evidence, either way, to enable us to decide, and not much ambiguous evidence either; the debate can be refined and subtle and, forever unresolved, can leave disputants as confident as ever of the view they have always maintained or presumed. Far more unsettling is the impassioned argument over the Church's treatment of women; and it may become clear in retrospect that Christian responses to the novel have shone the spotlight so brightly and narrowly on Jesus' supposed marriage that the charge of systemic misogyny has been (conveniently) forgotten in the surrounding darkness.

Have the churches, then, been blind to the roles of women to which the New Testament itself bears witness? Let us turn the light's beam onto a single passage in the New Testament: John's Easter story of Jesus and Mary Magdalene (John 20:1, 11–18). This is the one story to reveal an unquestionable (although ambiguous) intimacy between Jesus and Mary; ironically, the story is never mentioned in the *Code*. It can be understood only in relation to Old Testament typologies and to other passages within John's story, almost all of which are heavily gendered. And our current deafness to such contextual, typological understanding is a symptom of our deafness to the music of the gospels overall. Our acuity can spot but our imaginations cannot easily inhabit a typological world; and so the music which the gospels once played is generally just a score on which we can see patterns of notes which we will never hear. It is time to ask how accurately and how effectively—and simply *how*—can scholars bring this music off the page and back to life.

Creation began on Day One; God declared: 'Let there be light.' God would place Adam in the Garden of Eden, make him its gardener and bring all the creatures to him to be named (Gen. 2:19–20); so their creation was complete. And now on Day One, as the light rises, Jesus and Mary Magdalene meet in a garden. Adam and Eve are together again. There is in their Paradise no Judas, and so no serpent now. Mary mistakes Jesus for the gardener, he names her, and her new creation is complete.

---

[3] Quoted by L. Knight-Jadczyk (from a writing of 1982) in an article posted at www.cassiopaea. org/cass/grail_5g.htm.

The garden of death has become the garden of love where Solomon's lover has been searching for her beloved: 'And when I find him I will cling to him and will not let him go' (S. of S. 3: 4). But Jesus forbids Mary Magdalene, the lover who has found her beloved, to go on touching him: 'for I have not yet ascended.' Eden has been restored and all creation is made new.

This is beautifully sensuous; but what do its tone and details signify? For an answer we must explore two unfamiliar avenues: a similar frisson evoked elsewhere in the Gospel; and the further typologies of John's Easter story itself.

First, then, we look afresh at the Gospel. Characters step forward into the spotlight, have their scene with Jesus, and disappear. (Nicodemus, with three poignant scenes, is an exception.) Four scenes, nonetheless—one near the Gospel's start, two right at its centre, and one at its end—are linked with each other by their various protagonists: for Jesus meets, in each of these scenes, one or more women. First the Samaritan woman at the well; then Martha and Mary in Bethany; then Mary again, with the ointment; and finally Mary Magdalene.

The Samaritan woman has had a bad press from (male) scholars: in her guilt, we are told, she typifies the aberrant life of those who reel from desire to pleasure. This is not justified by the story John tells. The woman has been married five times and is now with a sixth man, but neither John nor his Jesus says she was immoral. (Sarah was married seven times and lost each husband to the demon Asmodeus, Tobit 3:7; the woman in the Sadducees' fable had seven husbands, Mark 12:18–23.) Perhaps scholars have sensed an air of intimacy between Jesus and the woman, and do not like it. (They cannot have a woman flirt with Jesus; still less, Jesus flirt with a woman.) So they ignore the story's palpably evocative setting: Jesus and the woman meet at a well; and such meetings in the Old Testament portend marriage (Gen. 24:1–21; 29:1–14, Exod. 2:16). 'A garden locked is my sister, my bride,' sings the bridegroom in the Song of Songs, 'a fountain sealed; an orchard with trees of myrrh and aloes; a well of living water' (S. of S. 4:12–15).

Is John suggesting that the woman and Jesus had an affair? Of course not. So why does John value this setting and its associations? Because the woman is more receptive than Jesus' own disciples (as the Gnostic commentator Heracleon saw: Pagels 1989); and there is something (however elusive) in the spark between Jesus and herself which enables her to be so. What are the readers to learn from this woman? To relate to Jesus with a frisson of attraction and intimacy. The readers shall be encouraged to allow themselves such a sensation again. Martha and Mary at Bethany are the central characters in the climactic story of Jesus' ministry, the mid-point point of the Gospel as a whole; Martha makes a ringing confession of Jesus' identity; Mary is the first person in the Gospel to touch him. (Jesus touches the blind man in 9:6, taking the initiative himself. Mary of Bethany does with her oil little less for Jesus than the anonymous sinner of Luke 7:38–50 did with her tears. It is easy to admit that the sinner's action is sexually charged; we should admit the same of Mary's.)

Mary Magdalene is the final figure in this series of women whose encounters with Jesus are strikingly intimate and sensuous. This atmosphere has long been noticed in passing: 'Christ', said Martin Luther in an informal conversation, 'was an adulterer for the first time with the woman at the well, for it was said, "Nobody knows what he is doing with her"' (John 4:27). Again with Magdalene, and still again with the adulterous woman (John 8:1–11), whom he let off so easily (Luther 1967, no. 1472, from 1532). Luther was certainly not claiming that Jesus was a serial lover; but he sensed the character of the stories. The exact significance of this sequence may be unclear, but the sequence is most unlikely to be of no significance at all.

And so to the further typologies underlying the Easter story itself. In the Temple of Solomon the inner area—the great Hall and beyond it, behind a veil, the most sacred Holy of Holies—was decorated with carvings of trees; so it recalled the first garden of creation and, both within and beyond it, the home of God himself.[4] As the Temple was Edenic and the high priest bore the beauty of Adam (Sirach 49:16–50:1 Hebr.), so Eden had been a sanctuary and Adam its high priest (Barker 1991: 69–70; 2003: 132). Mary Magdalene sees angels at the head and foot of the place where Jesus had been laid, with an empty space between (John 20:12), just as angels had flanked God's throne in the Holy of Holies. Throughout the Gospel, Jesus has been replacing in his own person the Jerusalem Temple, its roles and rituals (John 2:21; chs. 7–9). When Mary sees Jesus in this newly created Paradise, she sees him in the Temple which he himself is. Paradise is the dwelling of God and the place of visionary disclosure (cf. 2 Cor. 12:4); but Jesus insists that he is not yet ascended; this Eden is still *earthly*. The tomb, place of death, has become the Holy of Holies, the ultimate place of life; Mary Magdalene is in the garden outside, representing the Hall in Solomon's Temple which in turn represented the created world.

Rabbinic tradition suspected there had been burials under the Temple's altar (Mishnah Parah 3:2); in Talmudic tradition, the skull of Araunah the Jebusite was found there (P. Sotah 20a, Nedarim 39b, Pesahim 36b); and the archaeologist Rivka Gonen has interpreted the cave under the rock in the Dome of the Rock as having been in origin a Bronze Age shaft tomb (Gonen 1985). Some Jewish traditions claimed that Adam and Eve were buried on the site of the Temple (Ginzberg 1998: 5. 125–7, n. 137), from where—according to other traditions—the dust ('*adāmāh*) had been taken from which Adam was made (ibid. 73, n. 16).

Jesus clearly belongs in the Temple which he is. Mary seems—no less clearly—to be a privileged visitor. But this does not yet do justice to the Temple's decoration.

---

[4] 1 Kgs 6:18 (Hall), 29 (Holy of Holies; the exact sense is obscure, 6:29–30 are an ancient addition); 2 Chron. 3:5–6 (Hall), 3:16 (Holy of Holies). For emphasis upon the Hall as Eden/creation, the Holy of Holies as God's heaven beyond, see the account ascribed to R. Pinhas ben Ya'ir (2nd cent. CE), in Patai 1967: 108, explored further in Barker 1991: 57–103. For emphasis upon the edenic Holy of Holies, see Elior 2004: 244–50.

'God created the *'ādām* (human) in his own image, in the image of God he created him; male and female he created them' (Gen. 1:27). It was the two together, male and female, that constituted the created 'image'. It is no surprise, then, that when Ezekiel saw a vision, at the River Chebar, of the divine chariot-throne he saw both male and female figures. Strange grammatical switches abound in Ezekiel's description: between singular and plural nouns, and between masculine and feminine. This much, however, is clear: that the multiform figure beneath the firmament was properly denoted in the feminine:

> 1:5 Out of the midst [of the fire-flashing cloud] came four Living Ones (*hayyôt*) [fem. pl.], and their appearance was the likeness of a human ('*ādām*).

The description of the four *hayyôt* continues through Ezekiel 1:6-14. Each, it seems, was attended by a four-faced wheel:

> 1:15 Now as I beheld the Living Ones [fem. pl.], behold one wheel [masc.] upon the earth by the Living Ones [fem. pl.] with his [masc. singular] four faces.
>
> 1:19–20 And then the Living Ones [fem. pl.] went, the wheels went by them. And when the Living Ones [fem. pl.] were lifted up, the wheels were lifted up. The spirit (*rūah*) [fem.] of the Living One (*hayyāh*) [fem. sing.] was in the wheels.

That (single, grammatically singular) Living One recurs, now with multiple heads:

> 1:22 The likeness of the firmament upon the heads of the Living One (*hayyāh*) [fem. sing.] was like the gleam of terrible ice stretched out over their heads above.

Ezekiel will see another vision, which he links emphatically with the vision at the River Chebar:

> 10:20 This was the Living One [fem. sing.] that I saw beneath the God of Israel at the River Chebar.

Margaret Barker sums up the visions (Barker 2003: 170):

What Ezekiel described must have been 'his' holy of holies, appearing to him in exile. There are two parts to this vision; the figure on the throne, described as the likeness of the glory of the Lord enthroned above the firmament, and then whatever was beneath the firmament.

This seems to have been a fourfold Living One, a female figure, known as the Spirit of life, or perhaps it was the Spirit of Life within a fourfold group of Living Ones.

As there was a pairing above and below, so there was too from one side to the other. The cherubim who flanked the throne were readily identified as male and female. It was possible, 300 years after the Temple's destruction, to imagine them vividly: 'When Israel used to make the pilgrimage, they [the priests] would roll up the veil separating the Holy [the Hall] from the Holy of Holies, and show them the cherubim which were intertwined with one another, and say to them, "Behold, your love before God is like the love of male and female"' (B. Yoma 54a). (The kabbalists of later centuries would catch every nuance of male and female in the character of God and in the conditions that make possible the knowledge of God; Wolfson 2005.) We can hardly conceive now the sanctuary that John envisioned in his Easter story: the garden in which the new Solomon met his bride; the garden of Eden where Adam and Eve were told to be fruitful and multiply; the home of God's twofold image, the Adamic high priest and his consort Wisdom (Wisdom 7:26). Jesus, at once the new Temple and the high priest within it, has emerged from the tomb which became through his own presence the Holy of Holies. Mary Magdalene, unequivocally part of the created order, does not *intrude* upon the earthly but paradisiac 'Temple' where she meets Jesus; she represents the female Living One beneath the firmament of Ezekiel 1 who makes the ensemble complete. She is part of what she sees.

Yet again it is a woman who has the vital part to play opposite Jesus. It is arguable that John's Easter story is the one (and only) first-century source which the Gnostics had to hand as they assessed and deepened the significance of Mary Magdalene for their own spiritual self-understanding and instruction. The Gnostics were addressing, in their treatment of Jesus and Mary Magdalene, profound questions about the conditions of the possibility of the knowledge of God. We will challenge the Gnostics' answers, but should still be asking their questions: why are the women in John's Gospel so perceptive and so privileged?

Dan Brown's characters misread the Gnostic texts in which Mary Magdalene appears. (For most of these texts, the standard text will now be Meyer 2007. For discussion in detail, see Griffith-Jones 2008a.) In every such text, it certainly *matters* (not least to the male characters in the story) that she is a woman; but with a far more diverse significance than we are likely to see now. The *Gospel of Thomas* is in direct dispute with John (De Conick 2001): what John ascribed to Mary Magdalene, Thomas denied to her and to all women who did not become men. For the Valentinians of the *Gospel of Philip*, Mary was the Saviour's consort on earth as the Spirit was his consort in the Fullness and Wisdom was in heaven; since every spiritual individual (whether man or woman) was imagined as a woman on her way to union with her angel bridegroom, Mary Magdalene herself could be the model Gnostic, ascending towards the final bridal bedroom, the ultimate Holy of

Holies. In the *Gospel of Mary* she takes the role of the Beloved Disciple and of Jesus himself. In *Pistis Sophia* ('Faith Wisdom') she is the earthly embodiment of Faith-Wisdom herself as Faith-Wisdom should always have been, and so she is both guide and model for the individual Gnostic.

In the *Gospel of Mary, Gospel of Philip*, and *Pistis Sophia* Mary Magdalene is confronted antagonistically by Simon Peter; and we are likely to ask (and to be frustrated by our inability to answer confidently) questions about women's access to positions of authority within any communities whose leaders commissioned, authorized and/or used these texts.

In most of these portrayals, the Gnostics' Mary represents the human being who rises to the threshold of divinity; in the same stories Jesus represents divinity descending to the threshold of the human. Within the ancient androcentric world, Mary Magdalene and all the works of womankind were generally doomed to shine with a provisional splendour and then to be absorbed into maleness or utterly dissolved; but en route she had *as herself* a vital role in the Gnostic understanding of the fulfilment which is both now and not yet.

Mary Magdalene could be more than simply the recipient of revelation; she could be part of the truth revealed. As Jesus' companion on earth, she could represent the creative Wisdom of heaven and the Spirit of the Fullness beyond heaven; so that the ultimate revelation accessible on earth was of a still-irreducible *pair* of male and female, each with its own embodiment, each incomplete without the other.

Links, typologies, allusions: I hope with these paragraphs to have brought back to life not just the network of connections but their *centrality* to any understanding of John's Gospel. Let us clear more of the long-hidden paths to whose existence these enquiries have alerted us.

Pilate had brought Jesus out in a purple robe and crown of thorns: 'Behold, the man' (John 19:5). John evokes in chs. 18–19 the story of creation, cruelly distorted. The devil enters the garden; Jesus the new Adam, 'the Man', is displayed in mockery; and at his death, as the sixth day ends, everything is finished (*tetelestai*, 19:30). Such completion has been attained once before: 'The heaven and the earth . . . were completed (*sunetelesthēsan*); and God completed (*sunetelesen*) his work' (Gen. 2:1–2). The parody at Jesus' passion is grotesque, but the achievement is real. Jesus hands over the spirit at his death, and so imparts life. He does so at Passover, linked at the time of Jesus to creation.

'The resurrection,' Raymond Brown concedes, 'does not fit easily into John's theology of the crucifixion' (Brown 1966–70: 1013). All has been completed at Jesus' death and there is, therefore, nothing left undone. Readers should not expect—and do not get—in the Easter story an account of any further change or achievement. What then is the function of John's Easter story itself? The life of the new aeon was (I suggest) the life of those listeners in John's communities who themselves had risen into Eden. John's neophytes saw the sanctuary, Jesus' body, in the sanctuary that was Paradise; and those listeners were represented here by Mary Magdalene in the presence of the Jesus who *was* the place of encounter with God. For John, the listeners could grasp what was being revealed in his Easter story only if they had themselves—during and through their reception of the Gospel itself—gone through the rebirth from death that Lazarus had gone through in the story, *before* they read of the events which made that new life possible. Such listeners knew that the new creation had been completed in Jesus' death; they were not looking for anything new to happen in this Easter story, not for any evidence to persuade them that a miracle occurred in that garden. The Easter story showed them—and invited them in their imagination to inhabit—the part they had in this new world. The imagination at issue was not that which transforms a story (as beautifully expounded in Brown 1999), but that which enables a story to transform its audience.

Present-day readers may well ask if John's whole story is dissolving into poetic fantasy before our eyes. The answer is: No. Let us imagine the evangelist himself, author of that allusive Easter story, being asked whether he believed that Jesus had in fact been raised from his grave. He would have answered, I suspect, as follows: Yes, of course; but only those who have been born again from above can have any idea what claim is really being made by this statement.

Some startling challenges now lie before New Testament scholarship. What *difference* did John expect the rebirth to make in the neophyte's knowledge, trust, or the assurance of being beloved? (This will need to be studied with due recognition not just of the Gospel's reception but of the new social and ritual commitments made in preparation for, during, and after any formal admission to John's communities.) Was John claiming more than was justified, to give his Gospel and its catechists an unwarranted grandeur and power? And what distinguished such a vision of Edenic life—so far from our own experience of this world—from mere delusion?

John himself has left us some startling clues. A prime model for proper understanding undoubtedly lies in the sensibilities of his story's *women*; and it is time for New Testament scholars to ask what John is signifying by this specificity. (We are most unlikely to accept the Gnostics' answer to this question; but then we must find our own.) Secondly, such understanding is dependent on the full appropriation of the Gospel's typologies, the load-bearing girders which beneath the Gospel's façade shape and sustain its whole story. It would be perverse not to ask if John sees in women's sensibilities an aptitude for such—unifying, holistic, open-ended—typological imagination. (This is not to prejudge in favour of such a link; it is not obvious, after all, that John portrays the women within the story itself as thinking typologically.)

John Ashton has shown that John's whole Gospel is 'an apocalypse upside down, inside out' (Ashton 2007: 329). At issue throughout the Gospel is knowledge; but this knowledge is, for John, accessible only in and as rebirth from above, not through the regular apprehension of a regular story. (Among the eighteen distinguished scholars writing in Thatcher 2007, only Ashton—by discussing apocalypse—questions the character of the knowing demanded and offered by John.) It is a pressing task for New Testament scholars (and for Christian apologists) to analyse the epistemological and social conditions, the character and the content of a knowledge supposedly accessible in John's day (and perhaps now) only to those who could then (or who can now) be helpfully described as reborn from above.

This agenda is not likely to be widely adopted by New Testament scholars until ways can be found to make such poetic, typological readings fruitful and heartening to congregations. (A large proportion of such scholars are directly or indirectly working in the service of the Church.) It may have been possible, in the great days of allegorical exegesis in third-century Alexandria, for scholars such as Origen and their readers to trust in the truth of both the literal and the allegorical senses of scripture; in our day, the allegorical seems to be a slippery evasion of the literal. It is ironic that Dan Brown, whose characters get so much wrong in detail, got something far deeper nearly right: there is an esoteric layer (not in the churches' conspiratorial deceptions but) in the New Testament's own proclamation.

We can hardly be confident that the careful, exploratory work we need to undertake on the imagination will be given a quiet space in which the Gospel's music can be heard. But there is hope yet. *The Da Vinci Code* has represented and fortified a cultural ambience within which scholars, way beyond the novel's own readership, may find their ears attuned at last to John's rich, poetic story whose first hearers played the part of Mary Magdalene at one with Jesus in a new-born world.

Works Cited

ASHTON, J. (2007), *Understanding the Fourth Gospel.* Oxford: Oxford University Press.

BAIGENT, M., LEIGH, R., and LINCOLN, H. (1996), *The Holy Blood and the Holy Grail.* London: Arrow.

BARKER, M. (1991), *The Gate of Heaven.* London: SPCK.

——(2003), *The Great High Priest.* London and New York: T. & T. Clark.

BRENTON, H. (2005), *Paul.* London: Nick Hern.

BROWN, DAN (2004), *The Da Vinci Code.* London: Corgi.

BROWN, DAVID (1999), *Tradition and Imagination: Revelation and Change.* Oxford: Oxford University Press.

BROWN, R. E. (1966–70), *The Gospel According to John,* 2 vols. Garden City, NY: Doubleday.

DECONICK, A. D. (2001), *Voices of the Mystics: Early Christian Discourse in the Gospels of John and Thomas and other Ancient Christian Literature,* JSNT Supp. 157. Sheffield: Sheffield Academic Press.

ELIOR, R. (2004), *The Three Temples.* Oxford and Portland: Littman.

GINZBERG, L. (1998), *The Legends of the Jews*. Baltimore and London: Johns Hopkins University Press.

GONEN, R. (1985), 'Was the Site of the Jerusalem Temple Originally a Cemetery?', *BAR* (May–June), 44–55.

GRIFFITH-JONES, R. (2006), *The Da Vinci Code and the Secrets of the Temple*. London: SCM-Canterbury and Grand Rapids: Eerdmans.

——(2008*a*), *Mary Magdalene*. London: SCM-Canterbury; published in the USA as *Beloved Disciple*. San Francisco: HarperOne.

——(2008*b*), 'Transformation by a Text: The Gospel of John', in F. Flannery and R. Werline (eds.), *Experientia*, vol. 1. Atlanta, Ga.: SBL.

HASKINS, S. (1993), *Mary Magdalen: Myth and Metaphor*. New York: Riverhead.

JONES, P. (2004), Review of R. Harris, *Imperium*, in *Sunday Telegraph*, 10 Oct.

LUTHER, M. (1967), *Table Talk*, in *Luther's Works*, vol. 54. Philadelphia: Fortress.

MEYER, M. (ed.) (2007), *The Nag Hammadi Scriptures*. San Francisco: HarperOne.

PAGELS, E. H. (1989), *The Johannine Gospel in Gnostic Exegesis*, SBLMS, 17. Atlanta, Ga.: Scholars Press.

PATAI, R. (1967), *Man and Temple in Ancient Jewish Myth and Ritual*. New York: Ktav.

SCHWEITZER, A. (1910), *The Quest of the Historical Jesus*, trans. W. Montgomery. London: Black.

THATCHER, T. (2007), *What We Have Heard from the Beginning: The Past, Present and Future of Johannine Studies*. Waco, Tex.: Baylor University Press.

WOLFSON, E. R. (2005), *Language, Eros, Being: Kabbalistic Hermeneutics and Poetic Imagination*. New York: Fordham University Press.

FURTHER READING

On Mary Magdalene, Haskins 1993 is encyclopedic and indispensable. For a focus on the New Testament and Gnostics, J. Schaberg, *The Resurrection of Mary Magdalene* (New York and London: Continuum, 2002). On the Gnostics, H. Jonas, *The Gnostic Religion* (Boston: Beacon, 1958) is old but a classic; E. H. Pagels, *The Gnostic Gospels* (New York, Random House, 1979) has brought the texts to a wide audience. The definitive edition of the texts themselves will now be M. Meyer, ed., *The Nag Hammadi Scriptures* (San Francisco: HarperOne, 2007). On *The Da Vinci Code* itself, Griffith-Jones 2006 and (with emphasis on the New Testament and early church) B. D. Ehrman, *Truth and Fiction in 'The Da Vinci Code'* (Oxford: Oxford University Press, 2004). In R. Griffith-Jones, *The Four Witnesses* (San Francisco: Harper, 2000) I have tried to foster the imaginative, typological reading of the Gospels encouraged in this paper. Barker 1991 and 2003 and M. Barker, *Temple Themes in Christian Worship* (London and New York: Continuum, 2007) describe the spaces and liturgies which our imagination needs once more to inhabit.

CHAPTER 26

GNOSTIC INTERPRETATIONS OF GENESIS[1]

ISMO DUNDERBERG

INTRODUCTION

One noteworthy development in second-century Christianity was the emergence of teachers and groups claiming that the God described in the Hebrew Bible is not the supreme deity but only an inferior creator-God (demiurge). The Jewish God was demoted by a considerable number of early Christians, including Marcion; Basilides and Valentinus (both early Christian teachers from Egypt) and their followers; 'Sethians' (who regarded Seth, the third son of Adam and Eve, as their spiritual ancestor); Justin 'the Gnostic'; and several less well-known groups described in the works of Irenaeus of Lyons, Hippolytus of Rome, Tertullian of Carthage, and Epiphanius of Salamis.

The distinction between the perfect, unknown God and the inferior creator-God, who was identified with the God described in the Hebrew Bible, is usually regarded as one of the main tenets of 'Gnosticism' (cf. Marjanen 2008: 203–11). This term, however, may create a misleading impression of a unified 'heretical' front as

---

[1] I wish to thank Antti Marjanen and Tuomas Rasimus for their useful comments on the first draft of this article, which made me rethink and reformulate a number of issues, and saved me from some embarrassing errors; I am of course responsible for those remaining.

opposed to 'the early church' (King 2003). Not only did those Christians, who questioned the Jewish belief in one God, not form a single social body, but there is also a great variety in the exegetical methods they used and in their precise assessments of the creator-God.

For example, in his work known as *Antitheses*, Marcion simply listed items where Jesus' teaching about God and the way God is described in the Hebrew Bible seemed to be in an irreconcilable tension with each other. In this way, Marcion wanted to show that the perfect God Jesus proclaimed cannot be identical with the Jewish God, who is described in scripture as prone to anger, injustice, vengeance, and error (cf. Räisänen 2005: 107–9; for similar views of Apelles, Marcion's follower, see Benjamins 1999: 160–2). While Marcion's method was 'literalist', Sethians, Valentinians, and others interpreted the Book of Genesis allegorically and created new mythic tales based upon this text. Their interpretations were also more heavily indebted to Platonic philosophy than Marcion's: they thought that the visible world was created as an image of the truly divine realm, and they described the creator-God's actions in terms borrowed from, or alluding to, Plato's *Timaeus*.

These early Christian mythmakers agreed with each other that humans—either all or some of them—are relatives of the supreme God and for this reason superior to the creator-God, but they differed from each other in their precise assessments of the Jewish God. While the Valentinians usually considered this God ignorant but benevolent towards humankind, and towards Christians in particular, in Sethian and related myths the Jewish God becomes a satanic being whose main features are deceit, rampant sexual lust, and relentless hostility towards the divine essence deposited in humankind.

The conflicting views about the creator-God among the early Christian mythmakers go hand in hand with their equally divergent theories about the Hebrew Bible. There are some clear instances of 'protest exegesis': in some texts, the Jewish God and other protagonists of the Hebrew Bible are condemned or the roles attributed to them and their adversaries are radically reversed. Although protest exegesis is often considered to be part and parcel of the 'Gnostic' attitude towards the Hebrew Bible (e.g. Pearson 1990: 37–40), this view fails to do justice to the available evidence in its entirety. It has become abundantly clear that 'there is no single "gnostic exegesis"' (Williams 1996: 78). The relevant sources bear witness to a bewildering spectrum of interpretive strategies applied to the Book of Genesis, including not only rejection, but also (partial) acceptance, allegorical commentary, paraphrase, abbreviation, expansion, variation, creation of new tales and characters, parody, and mockery, to list just a few (cf. Nagel 1980).

This variety may be more readily understood in light of modern theories of intertextuality that draw attention to 'the ways in which the new texts *appropriate* previous material, establishing a complex system of relationships of opposition, agreement, partial agreement and reformulation' (Tull 1999: 169). An intertextual approach may also help us see with greater clarity why authors want to discuss texts with which they partially or completely disagree: 'In order to achieve credibility, a new text must show that the pertinent issues are being considered . . . even rejected ideas may be acknowledged and disputed rather than ignored' (Tull 1999: 170). In other words, Valentinians, Sethians, and other early Christian 'demiurgists' (for this term, see Williams 1996: 51–2) were part of a cultural context, where it was important enough to disagree with the Book of Genesis!

It is debated whether the groups critical of the Hebrew Bible originally emerged from heterodox Judaism (e.g. Pearson 1990; Rudolph 1997: 144–69; the suggested alternatives include the 'extreme' Jewish allegorizers, politically disappointed Jews, and disillusioned Jewish messianists), or whether their teaching presupposes Christian teaching (thus, e.g., Luttikhuizen 2006), in which Mosaic law was downgraded in different ways (e.g. as the opposite of grace, John 1:17). The debate may remain unresolved, but it has made two facts clear: (1) These groups knew, and were conversant with, various strands of Jewish traditions of interpreting Genesis (Pearson 1990); (2) most of the evidence for the views of these groups comes from sources that, as they now stand, presuppose a Christian self-understanding.

The Genesis exegesis of these groups often sought to resolve intellectual dilemmas posed by suspect aspects of God (especially anthropomorphisms and emotions) in the Hebrew Bible (Williams 1996: 54–79). However, critical reflection on the Book of Genesis was not only an intellectual enterprise. Instead, new social identities were created through exegesis. This was one way of drawing a boundary between these groups and the Jews, and also other Christians of lesser understanding, who subscribed to the Jewish belief in one God.

VALENTINIAN INTERPRETATIONS

In the second century the school of Valentinus was one of the most important new groups offering the mental freedom needed for a critical approach to the Hebrew Bible to develop.[2] Valentinus came from Egypt to Rome around 130 and attracted a significant number of followers there. His writings have not survived, except for less than a dozen brief quotations preserved in the works of his adversaries. The fragments, however, suffice to show Valentinus' keen interest in Genesis. Some of his allegorical explanations were quite conventional, such as the view that the 'leathern garments' mentioned in Genesis 3:21 denote human flesh (Valentinus,

---

[2] The school of Valentinus was not necessarily exclusivistic in its relationship to other Christians. Many Valentinians—perhaps the majority of them—also retained their membership in the broader Christian community and took part in its ritual life together with Christians of other persuasions.

Frag. 11 = Hippolytus, *Ref.* 10.13.4). The same idea can be found in Philo, Origen, and rabbinic texts (Markschies 1992: 286–7; Dunderberg 2008: 229, n. 62; for other Valentinian sources, see Irenaeus, *Her.* 1.5.5; Clement, *Exc. Theod.* 55).

A brief excerpt from Valentinus' teaching of immortality illustrates the way he used allusions to Genesis in his sermons (cf. Dunderberg 2008: 37–9): 'You are immortal from the beginning, and you are the children of eternal life. You wanted that death will be bestowed upon you in order that you use it up and waste it, so that death would die in you and through you. For when you, on the one hand, nullify the world, but, on the other, will not be dissolved, you rule over creation and the entire corruption' (Valentinus, Frag. 4 = Clement of Alexandria, *Strom.* 4.89.2–3.) Valentinus' way of addressing his audience as those who 'are immortal from the beginning' recalls the original state of the first human beings in paradise. The subsequent references to death in the next sentence allude to their loss of immortality (Gen. 3:19, 22–4), whereas the final part recalls Adam and Eve's birthright to rule over the world created by God (Gen. 1:28; cf. 2:19–20).

By Valentinus' time, both Jewish and Christian interpreters usually thought that Adam and Eve were immortal before the Fall. It was also commonplace to believe that *all* humans were immortal to begin with, but have chosen death in the same manner as Adam and Eve. Valentinus, however, disagrees with the latter conclusion. His usage of the present tense ('you *are* immortal . . . you *are* the children of eternal life') shows that he conceives of his addressees as having not lost their immortality (unlike Adam and Eve).

Moreover, unlike most of his Jewish and Christian contemporaries, Valentinus did not regard death as a punishment but explained it as serving a pedagogic purpose: his addressees must face death in order to learn how to destroy it. Valentinus probably understood 'death' and 'immortality' in terms of lifestyle rather than in terms of physical death or the lack thereof. For Hellenistic Jewish writers, such as Philo and the author of the Book of Wisdom, immortality meant first and foremost that one should hold to the correct way of life in obedience to the Torah. Likewise, death was a moral category rather than a physical fact: a person who has adopted the wrong lifestyle is, though physically alive, already spiritually dead. There is also a moral side to Valentinus' teaching: he promises that his addressees will become rulers over creation when they learn to 'nullify' the world. 'Ruling' is not meant here in the political or in the eschatological sense, but in an ethical one. Valentinus' teaching probably reflects a long philosophical tradition, in which the language of ruling was used to denote a person's perfect command of his or her inner self, especially one's ability not to give in to any irrational urges arising from the soul.

Another fragment of Valentinus shows a more critical stance towards Genesis. This fragment describes a primeval clash between Adam and the creator angels. There is a divine essence secretly deposited in Adam, which expresses itself in his frank speech. As soon as the angels recognize the 'pre-existent human being' in

Adam, they panic and try to destroy him (Valentinus, Frag. 1 = Clement, *Strom.* 2.36.2–4). This interpretation is based upon traditions similar to those in the Sethian *Secret Book of John* (see below). A new element in Valentinus' teaching is that the angels' fear was triggered by Adam's frank speech (*parrhēsia*). This addition creates a link to the philosophical tradition, where uncensored freedom of speech was one of the most important values. Frank speech was considered to be the philosopher's right and task in society. This context lends a new twist to Valentinus' interpretation: Adam shows towards his creators the same attitude of candour as philosophers did towards the tyrants in popular imagination, and the angels wanted to strike Adam dumb in the same manner as the tyrants sought to silence their critics (cf. Dunderberg 2008: 52–5). The intertextual fabric becomes, thus, especially thick here: first, Valentinus' interpretation is based not upon the story of Adam's creation as it stands in Genesis, but upon a Sethian recasting of this story; and second, the result of his modification of the Sethian tradition is a new story that takes on new meanings in the historical and cultural context of his audience.

Other teachers associated with the school of Valentinus were also active in interpreting Genesis. Valentinians were known for their division of humankind into three distinct classes, and they supported this view with an expanded version of Adam's creation. Irenaeus relates that, according to Valentinians, the creator-God formed the first human from 'diffused and unsettled matter (*hulē*)' and breathed (cf. Gen. 2:7) his own soul-essence into this being. At the same time, the divine Wisdom secretly supplied the first human with a spiritual essence, which should grow in humans like a foetus and finally enable 'the reception of what is perfect' (Irenaeus, *Against Heresies* 1.5.5–6). The first human, thus, consisted of three different essences: matter, soul, and spirit. This division was also the lens through which Valentinians looked at the world: in their classification, pagans were of the material essence doomed to perdition, whereas most Christians, and sometimes Jews, belonged to the 'soul-group' in the middle, and only some Christians could reach the most advanced, spiritual level. The division was also essential for the Valentinian theology of revelation. Valentinians maintained that there have always existed spiritual persons. Although the creator-God was ignorant of their essence, he showed special affection towards them and appointed them 'prophets, priests and kings' (Irenaeus, *Her.* 1.7.3). For this reason, the voice of the spiritual race can still be heard in the Hebrew Bible. However, the Bible also contains teaching stemming from the creator-God and humans. Therefore, while Valentinians did not abandon the Hebrew Bible altogether, they thought that critical analysis was needed to identify the different voices speaking in it.[3]

---

[3] A compact masterpiece of such an analysis is Ptolemaeus' *Letter to Flora* (quoted in Epiphanius, *Panarion* 33.3.1–7.10), in which the biblical law is divided into the creator-God's own legislation and human additions stemming from Moses and the elders. For a similar explanation applied to the prophets of the Hebrew Bible, see *Tri. Trac.* 113.

Excerpts from Theodotus, Clement of Alexandria's collection of Valentinian teachings, bears witness to more detailed interpretations of the story of Adam, Eve, and paradise. Theodotus explained the sentence 'male and female he created them' (Gen. 1:27) as denoting the angelic order ('male') and the human one ('female'). Just as Eve was separated from Adam, the two orders live now in separation, but the church (*ekklēsia*) of humans will finally be reunited with the angels (*Exc. Theod.* 21). This interpretation is based upon the idea that the original first human was neither male nor female but androgynous, and expresses the hope of salvation in terms of one's return to this original state; the same idea is also reflected in the *Gospel of Thomas* (22, 114), and possibly by Paul in Galatians 3:27–8 (cf. Meeks 1974).

Adam's sleep is interpreted in the *Excerpts*, just like in the Sethian texts to be discussed below, as an allegory for the soul's forgetting. Yet, this text also offers a positive allegorical interpretation of Adam's sleep: this story denotes how the divine word sowed 'the male seed' into a sleeping soul. This seed enables the soul's awakening by the Saviour (*Exc. Theod.* 2–3). Concerning Adam's words, 'this is bone of my bones and flesh of my flesh' (Gen. 2:23), the 'bone' refers to the divine soul which is the hard essence hidden in the flesh, whereas the 'flesh' refers to the material soul waging war against the divine one. Moral exhortation follows: instead of strengthening the material soul with sins, one should struggle with it and see to the dissolution of this soul (*Exc. Theod.* 51–3).

Adam's three sons stand for the three natures of humankind: the irrational (Cain), the rational and righteous (Abel), and the spiritual (Seth). One sign of Seth's special status is that he 'neither tends flocks nor tills the soil but produces a child' (*Exc. Theod.* 54, trans. Casey). It cannot be inferred from this interpretation that Valentinians despised physical work, but instead it reflects the ancient notion of a perfect human who does the right thing intuitively, without effort or having to be taught, instructed, or commanded.

Yet another reference to the spiritual race was seen in the biblical figure of Jacob-Israel, since 'Israel is an allegory for the spiritual person who will see God' (*Exc. Theod.* 56). The allegory is based upon a (mistaken) understanding of the word 'Israel' as meaning 'a man who sees God', which we also encounter in the works of Philo of Alexandria; this is one of the clearest indications that Valentinians were familiar with, and inspired by, Hellenistic Jewish exegesis of the Book of Genesis.

Interpretations of the first chapters of Genesis also loom large in another collection of Valentinian teachings, the *Gospel of Philip* (NHC II, 3). The gospel probably recalls Valentinus' own teaching in describing how Adam irritated the cosmic powers with his speech (70 [§ 80]). On the other hand, the gospel portrays Adam as the antitype of Christ (cf. Rom. 5:12–21; 1 Cor. 15:45–8). It describes Adam as being born of 'two virgins, from the spirit and the virgin earth'. It must be assumed that Adam, probably due to the earthly part in him, was subject to fall since the author continues that Christ had to be born of a virgin 'to mend the fall that took place in the beginning' (71 [§ 83]).

As in the *Excerpts of Theodotus*, Eve's creation is interpreted as an act of separation in the *Gospel of Philip*. The consequence of separation is death, but one's return to his or her original state obliterates death (68 [§ 71]). Christ's role is defined accordingly: his task is 'to repair the primeval separation, reunite the two, to give life to those who died as a result of the separation, and to unite them'. The reunion takes place in a 'bridal chamber' (70 [§ 78]); scholars debate whether this term refers to a distinct Valentinian ritual, or whether it should be rather understood less literally, for example, as denoting 'an implied aspect in the process of initiation' (thus Thomassen 2006: 100).

The paradise described in Genesis is portrayed in the *Gospel of Philip* as an entirely negative domain, characterized by commands and prohibitions ('[eat] this, do not eat'), while the tree of knowledge is located in another place where 'I can eat everything'. This tree is not identical with the tree of knowledge in the biblical paradise. The tree in paradise is identified with the Old Testament law, which supplied Adam with the knowledge of good and evil but could not save him from evil. The Old Testament law is, according to this passage, the cause of death for all those who ate from this tree of knowledge. In fact, death came into being not because of Adam's transgression but because, in paradise, God commanded to eat of some trees and not to eat of others (73–4 [§ 94]). This allegorical interpretation of paradise builds upon Paul's most negative comments about the law (as being ineffective, Gal. 3:21, and the indirect cause of death, Rom. 7:9–13).

Finally, the *Gospel of Philip* alludes to Cain, called 'the son of the serpent', and maintains that fratricide took place because he was born of adultery (60–1 [§ 41–2]; cf. John 8:44; 1 John 3:12, 15). The passage is based upon a Jewish tradition that Cain's father was not Adam but the devil, identified with the serpent in paradise (for references, see Rasimus 2009: 72–3, 92–3, 201). In the *Gospel of Philip* this tradition is used to warn against intercourse between those who are of unequal status; 'intercourse' should be probably understood metaphorically in this context rather than as 'sexual intercourse' (thus Meyer's translation in Meyer 2007: 168).

The *Tripartite Tractate* (NHC I, 5) draws a much gloomier picture of the creator-God than most other Valentinian sources. Accordingly, paradise is described in this text as a place of empty pleasure. The creator-God and his angels threaten Adam with death, and allow him to eat 'only the food of the bad trees', whereas they do not allow him to eat either from the tree of knowledge ('that tree which had the double character') or from the tree of life. The serpent is evaluated in two different ways: on the one hand it is itself an 'evil power', but on the other, the transgression it brought about and the subsequent expulsion of the first human beings from paradise were 'a work of providence', for in this manner humans learned how ephemeral the pleasures offered in paradise were when 'compared with the eternal existence of the place of rest' (*Tri. Trac.* 106–7; trans. Thomassen, in Meyer 2007).

Sethian and Related Texts

One of the groundbreaking contributions of Nag Hammadi scholarship has been Hans-Martin Schenke's identification of a large group of texts bearing witness to 'Sethian' theology (e.g. Schenke 1978; for Sethianism, see also Turner 2001; Williams 2005).[4] The term 'Sethian' was never used as a self-designation, but there were groups that designated themselves as the offspring of Seth, Adam's third son. While the Sethians probably did not form a unified social organization, they had a distinct set of beliefs and exegetical approaches in common (Williams 2005). One prominent mode of their literary activity was the creation of new etiological tales in critical dialogue with the Book of Genesis.

Sethian mythmakers envisaged the visible world as a reflection of the divine realm. Although defective, this reflection is clear enough to warrant continuity between the two worlds. What is more, the divine realm already hosts a 'human population', including Adamas, Seth, and the offspring of Seth. Adamas is the model that the lesser deities imitate in fashioning the earthly Adam, and the earthly Seth bears a resemblance to the heavenly Seth. Although humankind, which the inferior gods created, is imperfect, the fact that the first humans were modelled in the image of the pre-existing 'divine humans' means that the humans on earth have in themselves the potential for perfection and should strive for it (cf. Williams 2005: 39–40).

Sethians rewrote Genesis, on the one hand, to affirm that this potential exists in all human beings, and on the other, to describe impediments that may prevent one from reaching the goal. What gives a particular flavour to the Sethian Genesis exegesis is the claim that these impediments were brought about by the creator-God, called 'Yaldabaoth' in the Sethian and related traditions, and his lackeys. Yaldabaoth is identified with the Jewish God: just like the God of the Hebrew Bible (cf. Isa. 45:5; 46:9), Yaldabaoth claims to be the only god. In the Sethian and related traditions, however, this claim is considered to be empty boasting that needs to be corrected from above (e.g. *Secr. John* II, 11).

One of the most prominent Sethian texts is the *Secret Book of John*. The largest block of the Saviour's teaching in it comprises a radically rewritten version of Genesis. The text opens with a description of how the divine realm evolved and how the lesser deities, who created the world, came into being. This part of the story already contains numerous allusions to Genesis, such as the references to 'light', 'living water', 'image', all linked with the Father of All (II, 4), and the idea that 'everything was created by the word' (II, 7, trans. Meyer; cf. King 2006: 222–3;

---

[4] For a critical review and substantial modification of the Sethian hypothesis, see Rasimus, 2009; his suggestion is that 'we replace Schenke's category of Sethianism . . . with a wider one that includes texts that contain features of these. Barbeloite, Sethite, and Ophite materials [57].'

for a similar usage of Genesis traditions in the Sethian *Trimorphic Protennoia*, see Denzey 2001).

The subsequent part of *Secret John*, which is focused on the creation of human-kind, follows closely the narrative outline of Genesis 1–6:[5]

1. The first creation of Adam (*Secr. John* II, 15–20)
2. The second creation of Adam (II, 20–1)
3. Paradise (II, 21)
4. Adam's sleep (II, 22)
5. The creation of Eve (II, 22–3)
6. The births of Cain, Abel, and Seth (II, 24–5)
7. The flood (II, 28–9)
8. Angels and women (II, 29–30)

While the sequence of events in *Secret John* follows that in Genesis, each passage involves a substantial amount of creative mythmaking: new figures and events are introduced, and old ones are interpreted from a new perspective. One example of the new figures is the long list of the names of the angels responsible for different parts in Adam's 'soul-body' in the long version of *Secret John* (II, 15–19). Moreover, the crucial moments of the biblical creation story are retold from another perspective. *Secret John* follows Genesis in affirming that the creator-God breathed the divine spirit into Adam, but adds that Yaldabaoth simultaneously lost this spirit (II, 19). The text also describes how Adam's intelligence made him superior to his creators, and how they became envious and created him anew from 'fire, earth, water' and 'four fiery winds.' (II, 20–1). Paradise is described, as in the *Tripartite Tractate*, as a place of empty pleasures, by means of which the lesser deities try to lull Adam into ignorance. The Saviour, in turn, identifies himself as the one who instructed Adam and Eve to eat from the tree of knowledge (II, 22). Eve's creation is turned into a story of how the divine intellect wakes up humans (II, 22–3), while the subsequent story relates how Yaldabaoth 'defiled Eve' and conceived two sons, Elohim and Yahweh, a.k.a. Cain and Abel (23–4). The text follows Genesis in attributing the flood to the creator-God, who 'regretted everything that had happened through him', but it is added that it was due to the divine Forethought that Noah was rescued (II, 28; trans. Meyer).

While the biblical creation story was subject to considerable expansion also in ancient Jewish texts (e.g. 1 Enoch), the stance towards Genesis in *Secret John* is radically different from them. In this text, the Saviour expressly urges John *not* to believe what Moses 'said in his first book' (II, 22); similar comments on Moses

---

[5] The *Secret Book of John* is known in four different versions, which can be divided into long and short recensions. My references are to the version in Nag Hammadi Codex II, which is one of the two texts representing the long recension. Moreover, Irenaeus, *Against Heresies* 1.29 contains materials that are either derived from the *Secret Book of John* or traditions that are very similar to those in it. For the best synopsis of all four versions and the parallels in Irenaeus, see Waldstein and Wisse 1995.

abound in the text. This raises the question of how Genesis can be used at all, if such fundamental doubts are expressed concerning its alleged author. A closer look at the passages mentioning Moses in *Secret John* shows that he always stands for a *literal* interpretation of the Book of Genesis, as opposed to the allegorical reading promoted in *Secret John*. What is more, the literalistic 'Moses' interpretation is presented as the tradition known to the addressees of this text ('It is not as Moses wrote and *you heard*. . .', II, 22). The allegorical interpretation in *Secret John* is, thus, offered as a *new* revelation to them: the audience should abandon the literal 'Moses' interpretation and understand that the notion of God's spirit moving over the waters (Gen. 1:1) refers to Wisdom's agitation after she saw what Yaldabaoth, her son, did (II, 13); that Adam's sleep (Gen. 2:21) denotes ignorance (II, 22); that what was removed from Adam was the divine intellect residing in him, not his rib (Gen. 2:21; II, 22–3); and that Noah and other representatives of an 'immovable race' did not hide in the ark but found rescue 'in a bright cloud' (II, 29).

The Nature of the Rulers (NHC II, 4) offers a number of interpretations similar to those in *Secret John*. In this text the serpent is clearly a positive figure, instructing Adam and Eve that it was out of jealousy that Yaldabaoth, also called 'Samael' ('the blind god'), did not allow them to eat from the tree of knowledge (89–90). The text also introduces a new child of Adam and Eve, Norea. She is a powerful female figure who replaces Seth as the ancestor of the spiritual race (for Norea, see Pearson 1990: 84–94). Large sections of the *Nature of the Rulers* run parallel to a non-Sethian text called *On the Origin of the World* (NHC II, 5), which shows the popularity such mythmaking enjoyed among early Christians (cf. Rasimus 2009).

The *Revelation of Adam* offers yet another example of Sethian rewriting of the biblical narrative (NHC III, 2; IV, 2). The text presents itself as Adam's secret teaching to his son Seth (64, 67), who then transmitted it to his offspring (85). 'Adam' retells, in the first person, stories derived from Genesis, including Adam and Eve's creation; Adam's sleep; and stories related to Noah and his sons. This part ends with an allusion to the destruction of Sodom and Gomorrah (75), which is interpreted as the creator-God's attempt to destroy Seth's spiritual offspring (75; the same view is also attested in the Sethian *Holy Book of the Great Invisible Spirit*, NHC III, 56). Similar to Valentinian interpretations, the *Revelation of Adam* maintains that Adam and Eve formed a primordial unity before the angry creator-God divided them into two sexes. The result of their separation from each other was that the knowledge of the true God escaped them.

While Noah belonged to the immovable race in *Secret John*, in the *Revelation of Adam* he appears on the side of the inferior God, whom his sons are urged to 'serve . . . in fear and subservience' (72). A similar vacillation occurs in Sethian and related texts regarding the serpent's role: in some texts the serpent plays a positive role, in others a negative one (cf. Rasimus, 2009, 65–101). Such differences show that there was no normative form of Sethian Genesis exegesis (for a graphic illustration of this diversity, see the tables in Williams 1996: 61–2). Instead, myth-making in Sethian and related texts is innovative and constantly in flux; hence the great variation in details.

RADICAL REJECTION OF THE HEBREW BIBLE

Although there were already numerous instances of protest exegesis in Valentinian, Sethian, and related sources referred to above, the Book of Genesis still retains its value in them as a text that was relevant enough for allegorical interpretation and narrative expansion (cf. Rudolph 1997: 201). However radical the results thus achieved were, the umbilical cord to the Hebrew Bible is not completely cut in these sources.

In only a few Nag Hammadi texts is the Hebrew Bible condemned in its entirety. One example of the radical rejection is a text called *The Second Discourse of Great Seth* (NHC VII, 2). Its author rehashes a conventional Sethian tale of origin (52–3), but, unlike Sethians, does not see any continuity between the figures mentioned in the Hebrew Bible and the recipients of the true wisdom proclaimed by Jesus. While Sethians thought that the spiritual essence was deposited in Adam, the author of *Great Seth* mocks him as being merely 'a joke', and the same goes for Abraham, Isaac, Jacob, David, Solomon, the twelve prophets, Moses, and the creator-God. The author of *Great Seth* considers the gap between the old and the new covenant insurmountable. He insists that no one knew of Christ in advance, neither Moses nor anyone else: 'He did not know me, and none of those before him, from Adam to Moses and John the Baptizer, knew me or my siblings' (*Great Seth*, 63–4, trans. Meyer). The author's aggressive polemic is directed against the Jews, characterized by their observation of dietary laws and what the author calls 'bitter slavery'. And yet, although the author affirms that 'they never knew truth and they never will', he seems to entertain the hope that Jews may convert to Christianity: 'they can never find a mind of freedom to know, until they come know the Son of Humanity' (64, trans. Meyer).

Another text radically opposed to the Hebrew Bible is *The Testimony of Truth* (NHC IX, 3). Its author offers an abbreviated version of the story of Adam and Eve's Fall and expulsion from paradise, and then continues with sweeping criticism of the god who did not allow Adam to eat from the tree of knowledge nor knew where Adam was in paradise after the Fall. The conclusion: this god 'has certainly shown himself to be a malicious grudger'. Hence, 'those who read such things' are accused of great blindness (47, trans. Pearson). The paraphrase of Genesis builds upon Jewish haggadic traditions (Pearson 1990: 39–51), but the author's own attitude towards this story is similar to that of some other early Christians towards Greek myths. He clearly thinks that no benefits can be gleaned from reading the Hebrew Bible. The fact that, in the subsequent paragraph, the author needs to introduce the name of the Book of Exodus to his readers suggests that they were not very familiar with the Hebrew Bible. Whereas the author of *Great Seth* was opposed to the Jews, the *Testimony of Truth* bears witness to an inner-Christian conflict over 'who Christ really is' (32). In this conflict, the rebuttal of the Hebrew Bible is part of the boundary drawn against the 'ignorant' Christians who spoke in favour of martyrdom and physical resurrection (31–5).

Finally, mention should be made of Irenaeus' claim that some early Christians thought highly of the biblical anti-heroes, such as Cain, Esau, Core, the Sodomites—and Judas, the betrayer of Jesus. This would imply a deliberate reversal in assessing all the biblical traditions. One sign of this would be the *Gospel of Judas* which these Christians composed, according to Irenaeus (*Her.* 1.31.1). Doubts have been voiced as regards the existence of a distinct sect of 'Cainites' and a distinct 'Cainite' system of thought (e.g. Pearson 1990: 105; cf. Rasimus, 2009: 236–42). Be that as it may, Irenaeus' report cannot be only a figment of his imagination: two of the Nag Hammadi writings mentioned above (the *Revelation of Adam* and the *Holy Book of the Great Invisible Spirit*) provide first-hand evidence for a positive attitude towards the Sodomites (as Seth's offspring), and as we now know, an early Christian text called the *Gospel of Judas* really existed (*pace* Pearson 1990: 106, n. 43).

WORKS CITED

Primary Sources

CASEY, R. P. (ed.) (1934), *The Excerpta ex Theodoto of Clement of Alexandria*. London: Christophers.

MEYER, M. (ed.) (2007), *The Nag Hammadi Scriptures: The International Edition*. New York: HarperOne.

NHC Nag Hammadi Codices (for translations, see Layton 1987; Meyer 2007).

WALDSTEIN, M. and F. WISSE (1995), *The Apocryphon of John: Synopsis of Nag Hammadi Codices* II, 1; III,1; and IV,1 with BG 8502,2 (NHMS 33). Leiden: Brill.

Secondary Literature

BARR, J. (1993), *The Garden of Eden and the Hope of Immortality*. Minneapolis: Fortress.

BENJAMINS, H. S. (1999), 'Paradisiacal Life: The Story of Paradise in the Early Church', in G. P. Luttikhuizen (ed.), Paradise *Interpreted: Representations of Biblical Paradise in Judaism and Christianity*, 153–77. Themes in Biblical Narrative 2. Leiden: Brill.

DENZEY, N. (2001), 'Genesis Traditions in Conflict: The Use of Some Exegetical Tradtions in the Trimorphic Protennoia and the Johannine Prologue', *Vig.Chr.* 55: 20–44.

DUNDERBERG, I. (2008), *Beyond Gnosticism: Myth, Lifestyle, and Society in the School of Valentinus*. New York: Columbia University Press.

KING, K. L. (2003), *What is Gnosticism?* Cambridge, Mass.: The Belknap Press of Harvard University Press.

——(2006), *The Secret Revelation of John*. Cambridge, Mass: Harvard University Press.

LUTTIKHUIZEN, G. P. (2006), *Gnostic Revisions of Genesis Stories and Early Jesus Traditions*. NHMS 58. Leiden: Brill.

MARJANEN, A. (2008), 'Gnosticism', in S. Ashbrook Harvey and D. G. Hunter (eds.), *The Oxford Handbook of Early Christian Studies*, 203–20. Oxford: Oxford University Press.

MARKSCHIES, C. (1992), *Valentinus Gnosticus? Untersuchungen zur valentinianischen Gnosis; mit einem Kommentar zu den Fragmenten Valentins*. WUNT 65. Tübingen: Mohr Siebeck, 1992.

MEEKS, W. A. (1974), 'The Image of Androgyne: Some Uses of the Symbol in Earliest Christianity', *HR* 13: 165–208.

NAGEL, P. (1980), 'Die Auslegung der Paradieserzählung in der Gnosis', in Tröger 1980: 49–70.

PEARSON, B. A. (1990), *Gnosticism, Judaism, and Egyptian Christianity*. Minneapolis: Fortress.

RÄISÄNEN, H. (2005), 'Marcion', in Marjanen and Luomanen 2005: 100–24.

RASIMUS, T. (2009), *Paradise Reconsidered in Gnostic Mythmaking: Rethinking Sethianism in Light of the Ophite Myth and Ritual*. NHMS. Leiden: Brill.

RUDOLPH, K. (1997), *Gnosis und Spätantike Religionsgeschichte: Gesammelte Aufsätze*. NHMS 42. Leiden: Brill.

SCHENKE, H.-M. (1978), 'The Phenomenon and Significance of Gnostic Sethianism', in B. Layton (ed.), *The Rediscovery of Gnosticism*, 2. 588–616. SHR/Numen Supp. 41, 2 vols. Leiden: Brill.

THOMASSEN, E. (2006), *The Spiritual Seed: The Church of the 'Valentinians'*, NHMS 60. Leiden: Brill.

TULL, P. K. (1999), 'Rhetorical Criticism and Intertextuality', in S. L. McKenzie and S. R. Haynes (eds.), *To Each Its Own Meaning: An Introduction to Biblical Criticisms and their Application*. 2nd edn., 156–79. Louisville, Ky.: Westminster/John Knox.

TURNER, J. D. (2001), *Sethian Gnosticism and Platonic Tradition* (BCNH, Études 6), Quebec: Les Presses de L'Université Laval.

WILLIAMS, M. A. (1996), *Rethinking 'Gnosticism': An Argument for Dismantling a Dubious Category*. Princeton: Princeton University Press.

——(2005), 'Sethianism', in Marjanen and Luomanen 2005: 32–63.

FURTHER READING

DAWSON, D. (1992), *Allegorical Readers and Cultural Revision*. Berkeley: University of California Press.

LAYTON, B. (trans.) (1987), *The Gnostic Scriptures: A New Translation with Annotations and Introductions*. New York: Doubleday.

MARJANEN, A. and P. LUOMANEN (eds.) (2005), *A Companion to Second Century Christian 'Heretics'*, Vig.Chr. Supp. 76. Leiden: Brill.

TRÖGER, K.-W. (ed.) (1980), *Altes Testament—Frühjudentum—Gnosis: Neue Studien zu 'Gnosis und Bibel'*. Berlin: Evangelische Verlagsanstalt.

CHAPTER 27

SAMUEL WILBERFORCE, THOMAS HUXLEY, AND GENESIS

JOHN HEDLEY BROOKE

WHEN the British Association for the Advancement of Science met in Oxford in the summer of 1860, an event took place that subsequently acquired deep symbolic significance. Rumours had circulated during the meeting that the bishop of Oxford, Samuel Wilberforce, was to pronounce on the subject of Charles Darwin's theory of evolution, published a few months earlier in his *Origin of Species* (1859). Before an audience of several hundred at the recently completed Oxford Museum, the bishop seized his opportunity. As a rhetorical ploy he enquired of Thomas Henry Huxley, one of Darwin's staunch defenders, whether he would prefer to have an ape for an ancestor on his grandfather's or grandmother's side. According to legend, he quickly had his come-uppance. Huxley reportedly whispered to a neighbour: 'The Lord hath delivered him into mine hands', and promptly retaliated by declaring that he would rather have an ape for an ancestor than be connected with a man who used his great gifts to obscure the truth. Many years later, Isabel Sidgwick recalled that 'no one doubted [Huxley's] meaning, and the effect was tremendous. One lady fainted and had to be carried out; I, for one, jumped out of my seat' (Lucas 1979: 313–14).

Huxley's deflation of an overconfident bishop eventually came to symbolize the triumph of science over religious interference and duly passed into the mythology of scientific professionalism. Although it has proved impossible to reconstruct exactly what was said by either party, their encounter is invariably mentioned in connection with the reception of Darwin's theory. Fortunately, it is possible to go behind and beyond the anecdote, because the two antagonists each wrote long reviews of Darwin's *Origin* that accurately reveal their differences, Huxley seeing in the Darwinian theory the beginning of a new epoch in which the cultural issues raised were of such magnitude that, with prophetic accuracy, he judged them unlikely to be resolved in his generation (Huxley [1860] 1893: 24).

Reviewing Darwin

In Wilberforce's extensive review, published shortly after the Oxford meeting, the majority of space was devoted to what he regarded as the scientific and philosophical shortcomings of Darwin's theory (Wilberforce [1860] 1874). The fact that he believed these to be so demonstrable helps to explain the self-satisfied demeanour he displayed in public. Of the review, Darwin felt bound to say that it is 'uncommonly clever', that it 'picks out with skill all the most conjectural parts', and that it brings forward well all the difficulties: 'It quizzes me quite splendidly' (Darwin [1860] 1993: 293). However, as a prominent representative of the Anglican Church Wilberforce was unable to put theological questions into abeyance. He certainly did believe that a theory proposing continuity between humans and their animal progenitors threatened basic Christian doctrines. Reconciliation, in his view, would be impossible:

Man's derived supremacy over the earth; man's power of articulate speech; man's gift of reason; man's free-will and responsibility; man's fall and man's redemption; the incarnation of the Eternal Son; the indwelling of the Eternal Spirit,—all are equally and utterly irreconcilable with the degrading notion of the brute origin of him who was created in the image of God, and redeemed by the Eternal Son assuming to himself his nature. (Wilberforce [1860] 1874: 94)

Such exaltation of human uniqueness was, for Darwin, tantamount to arrogance and there was no such standing on dignity in Huxley's review. The idea that each species in the fossil record had been separately created by a deity who had 'thought fit to interfere with the natural course of events for the purpose of making a new ammonite' was aesthetically repulsive and was now shown to be unnecessary (Huxley [1860] 1893: 56). For Huxley, it was obvious that Darwin's view of the origin of living beings was 'utterly opposed to the Hebrew cosmogony' (ibid.).

And he, for his part, was unwilling to 'degrade Nature to the level of primitive Judaism' (ibid. 53). The respect accorded Genesis 'by nine-tenths of the civilised world' he regarded as anomalous, given the fate of other ancient cosmologies:

The myths of paganism are as dead as Osiris or Zeus, and the man who should revive them, in opposition to the knowledge of our time, would be justly laughed to scorn; but the coeval imaginations current among the rude inhabitants of Palestine, recorded by writers whose very name and age are admitted by every scholar to be unknown, have unfortunately not yet shared their fate. (Ibid. 51)

Deference to Genesis could only be injurious to a science of origins. By contrast, Darwin's science was the result of a rigorous methodology in which evidence had been patiently accumulated to authenticate the material derivation of new species from their precursors. Huxley made it clear in his review that he had doubts about the adequacy of natural selection as the mechanism of evolutionary change (ibid. 74). He would remain more willing than Darwin to give significance to sudden mutations in the evolutionary process (Bartholomew 1975). But his enthusiastic defence of Darwin's naturalistic approach was a delight to Darwin himself.

THE NATURE AND SCOPE OF BIBLICAL AUTHORITY

The timing of Darwin's publication coincided with a serious debate already taking place concerning how the creation narratives in Genesis should be read. During the 1850s F. D. Maurice had wrestled with the problem posed by the differences between the accounts in Genesis 1 and 2, differences that Huxley would later exploit to further impugn their authority (Huxley [1886] 1904: 199–200). Radical forms of biblical criticism from Germany were gradually penetrating theological discourse in Britain, and in 1860, the same year as the Wilberforce/Huxley debate, a collection of *Essays and Reviews* appeared with its message that the Bible should be read like any other book, its ancient authors reflecting the cultural presuppositions of their day. Revealingly, Wilberforce gave vent to a greater fury against Oxford's clerical contributors to this book than he showered on Darwin. The doctrines professed in *Essays and Reviews* he decried as 'altogether incompatible with the Bible and the Christian Faith as the Church of England has hitherto received it' (Wilberforce [1861] 1874: 106). That two Oxford professors should have contributed to such a book was a paradox 'rare' and 'startling'. A particular issue discussed in *Essays and Reviews* was the degree to which harmonization could be achieved between Genesis and geology. According to Charles Goodwin, who reflected on developments during the preceding fifty years, the harmonizers' cause was already lost (Goodwin 1860). It is significant that he could reach this judgement even before the impact of Darwin's science was felt.

HARMONIZING GENESIS WITH SCIENCE

Whereas Goodwin believed the harmonizers had harmed themselves as a consequence of the dissonance between their schemes, Huxley was even more adamant that they were trying to achieve the impossible (Huxley [1860] 1893: 52–5). Huxley, like Goodwin, appealed to geology, which with its gradual erosion of distinct, discrete epochs had now prevented any neat correlation between the stratigraphic column and the six 'days' of creation. In retrospect, an ironic pattern can be discerned in the fortunes of harmonizing projects. The more successful they were on one level, the more embarrassing they proved to be when the science moved on. Earlier in the nineteenth century the Oxford geologist William Buckland had argued that his science was not subversive of religion. On the contrary, it could actually support biblical authority. Buckland suggested that certain features of the Earth, such as smooth U-shaped valleys, would be inexplicable without the postulation of a relatively recent universal flood of the kind described in Genesis (Rudwick 2005: 610–13). This was to give a hostage to fortune, and it was not long before both he and his opposite number in Cambridge, Adam Sedgwick, had to concede they had overstated their case (Gillispie [1951] 1959: 142–3; Rupke 1983: 81). During the 1830s Charles Lyell, in his magisterial *Principles of Geology*, forced the retreat of a universal deluge and, a few years later, Louis Agassiz was appealing to glaciation rather than floodwater to explain the phenomena that had so impressed Buckland. Another harmonizing scheme associated with Buckland was to accommodate the immensity of geological time by postulating a gap between the events of 'In the beginning' and those of the first Genesis 'day'. This facilitated the view that biblical coverage did not stretch backwards beyond human history (Rupke 1983: 204–5). But where this became a device to protect a literal rendering of the days of creation, it had the effect of over-compressing the time during which distinctive flora and fauna had flourished in distinctively different epochs.

The most enduring and sophisticated scheme of conciliation relied on a metaphorical stretching of the Genesis days in such a way that the order of events in Genesis corresponded to the appearance of the main branches of life in the fossil record. Genesis was then deemed to provide a succinct, but not false, summary of knowledge that geology and palaeontology could amplify. One of the most elaborate schemes of this kind was produced by a prolific popularizer of geology, Hugh

Miller, who combined his geological interests with the editorship of *The Witness*, organ of the Free Church of Scotland, which had come into existence in 1843. Miller saw great significance in the fact that the architecture of fossil forms had presaged structures favoured by human architects—an indication of a shared aesthetic sensibility between man and his Maker. He also saw evidence both of progressive creation (emphatically not evolution) in the fossil record and of a degeneration, within each epoch, that resonated with his evangelical belief in a creation marred by the Fall. Crucially, Miller went to great lengths to show that the sequence of creation in the book of God's word matched that in the book of his works. Miller's *Testimony of the Rocks* was published posthumously in 1857. It, too, would prove vulnerable to scientific advance, notably to that of Darwin (Brooke 1996).

Harmonizing strategies had helped to marginalize the so-called 'Mosaic geologists'—those who presumed to *derive* their 'science' from Genesis and who, like the dean of York, William Cockburn, insisted on pitting the Bible against the British Association. But the constant readjusting of exegesis to accommodate geological innovation could have a cumulative effect, leading to a crisis in which the issues had to be seen differently. Darwin certainly exacerbated the problems by requiring a revision of what it meant to speak of the 'creation' of living forms. There was simply no need to posit innumerable *independent* acts of creation. At the time of writing the *Origin* Darwin favoured a Creator who created 'by laws' rather than by fiat (Brooke 2009). It was this that so appealed to Huxley.

THE DEPTH OF THE DARWINIAN CHALLENGE

Opposition to Darwin was not solely grounded in biblical authority. Wilberforce in his review objected to a 'dishonouring view of creation' (Wilberforce [1860] 1874: 97). Darwin's old Cambridge friend Adam Sedgwick reproached him for having deleted final causes from nature. Since natural selection was a perfecting mechanism, the appearance of design in living things could be deemed illusory. The less well-adapted had already perished during a long, tortuous process in which randomness and contingency had been inscribed in a fierce, competitive struggle for existence. To understand Darwin's vision, one had to see nature in a new way; one had to be 'staggered' (Darwin's word) by the extent of extinction. To experience the switch from the designed universe of William Paley to the seemingly undirected universe of Darwin was like a gestalt switch that could be similar to a conversion experience. As the naturalist Alfred Newton put it: 'all personal feeling apart, it came to me like the direct revelation of a higher power; and I awoke next morning with the consciousness that there was an end of all the mystery in the simple phrase, "Natural Selection"' (Cohen 1985: 593).

For Christians there were real concerns—particularly when the prospect of *human* evolution was brought into focus. In assessing the implications for the nature of the human soul and for the doctrine of the Fall (had we now risen, not fallen?), biblical considerations came to the fore. One of Darwin's friends among the clerical naturalists, Leonard Jenyns, immediately confronted him with the biblical account of the creation of woman, seeking guidance on the interpretation of Genesis 2:7, 21, and 22 (Darwin [1860] 1993: 14). The question whether Adam and Eve might not have been real people but rather symbolic of a first generation of humans emerging from pre-existing primates would remain a pressing issue, and one that changed the terms of an earlier debate about the existence of pre- and co-Adamites (Livingstone 2008: 154–68). In early Victorian society there was undoubtedly a strong psychological barrier to imagining the evolution of women in particular, and the question Wilberforce had put to Huxley on his preferred ancestral line, with its reference to Huxley's grandmother, may itself have contributed to perceptions of an ill-judged jibe.

WILBERFORCE, SCIENCE AND THE BIBLE

A striking feature of Wilberforce's long review of the *Origin* was its calculated avoidance of theological opprobrium. He left no doubt that he saw incompatibility between the new science and a Christian anthropology, but only in the closing pages of his critique did he dwell on theological issues. As noted above, by far the larger part of his review dwelled on scientific and philosophical problems associated with Darwin's thesis. These included difficulties identified by Darwin himself: for example, the paucity of intermediate forms in the fossil record. Wilberforce also berated Darwin for deserting the sanctified method of Baconian induction, and for replacing it with a rhetoric that commended a hypothesis, natural selection, that *could*, but perhaps (by Darwin's admission) only *might*, explain the full range of bio-geographical and fossil data. To add gravitas to his attack he invoked the authority of some of the most eminent *scientists* of his day, notably Charles Lyell and Richard Owen (Wilberforce [1860] 1874: 64, 70, 77).

Absent, therefore, from Wilberforce's review is a biblically based tirade against Darwin, in which proof-texts from Genesis are marshalled against competing biological claims. Indeed, Wilberforce prided himself on avoiding a trap into which many would fall: 'we have no sympathy with those who object to any facts or alleged facts in nature, or to any inference logically deduced from them, because they believe them to contradict what it appears to them is taught in Revelation' (ibid. 92). He even placed himself above the biblical exegetes who too readily appropriated the latest science to authenticate their texts: 'few things have more deeply injured the cause of religion than the busy fussy energy with which men, narrow and feeble alike in faith and in science, have bustled forth to reconcile all new discoveries in physics with the word of inspiration' (ibid. 93). He actually shared with one of the great physicists of the age, James Clerk Maxwell, the belief that because of the provisional character of scientific theories it was dangerous to tie the meaning of biblical verses to them. When that happened, Revelation was 'committed to declare an absolute agreement with what turns out after all to have been a misconception or an error' (ibid.). This does not mean, however, that Genesis 1 and 2 were irrelevant to Wilberforce's attack. On the contrary, the trouble with Darwin's theory was that it violated the whole tenor of Scripture, 'the whole scheme of God's dealings with man as recorded in His word' (ibid. 94). There were already Christian commentators who disagreed with him, and there have been many since; but Wilberforce correctly perceived that a thoroughly naturalistic account of human origins and development was bound to change perceptions of God's relation to the world. The bottom line was that Darwin, whom he was willing to describe as a Christian, had supplied an 'ingenious theory for diffusing through- out creation the working and so the personality of the Creator' (ibid. 95). This was a Creator deprived of the fullness of His glory.

WILBERFORCE AND HUXLEY IN CONTEXT

Wilberforce undoubtedly felt he was defending the Anglican Church at a time when it was under threat on many fronts—not simply from innovative science but from a rapid expansion of secular literature designed to appeal to an increasingly literate public. This was also a time when the established Church was facing competition from a strengthening nonconformity in religion and was also lament- ing the desertion of high-profile figures to the Church of Rome. Wilberforce witnessed that desertion within his own family, several of its members leaving the Anglican fold. The stand he took against Huxley at the British Association meeting must also have been motivated by a special sense of responsibility, given that, as bishop of Oxford, he was on home ground.

For a rising group of scientists seeking to turn science into a profession, Oxford had other connotations—as a university in which it had been notoriously difficult to instigate and institutionalize scientific study (Corsi 1988). When William Buck- land left Oxford to become dean of Westminster, he had declared that the struggle to bring a scientific culture and awareness to the university was a lost cause. Huxley was the most vigorous campaigner for professional opportunities and standards in the sciences, complaining early in his career that a reputation in science brought honour but no money. He was himself so impecunious that he had to postpone his marriage for many years. There were battles to fight and, with nonconformist spirit, he developed an aversion to the privileges bestowed by Oxford and Cambridge. In particular, he shared with the crypto-Unitarian Charles Lyell the belief that the conduct of scientific research should not be in the hands of clerical amateurs whose time and loyalties were necessarily divided. The tradition of the parson naturalist had been long established in England, generating a literature of natural theology in which arguments for design were conspicuous—exemplified most famously by Paley's *Natural Theology* (1802), a text that Darwin both absorbed and subverted (Brooke 1985; Brooke and Cantor 1998: 161–7). Among the attractions of Darwin's theory for Huxley was its embodiment of rigorous scientific standards, enabling it to be used to embarrass the biblically based worldview of those clerics who, like Wilberforce, had pretensions to scientific knowledge (Turner 1978). Whereas one of Wilberforce's grievances was that Darwin had deserted the hallowed Baconian method, Huxley rejoiced in the power of a hypothetico-deductive methodology that had already been vindicated in the physical sciences. When Wilberforce tried to embarrass him in their public encounter, Huxley must have felt that, metaphorically at least, he deserved a punching. With all these considerations in mind, it is not difficult to understand why the altercation took place—a debate that each thought he had won and which prompted a nicely judged report in the *Athenaeum* to the effect that the two antagonists 'have each found foemen worthy of their steel, and made their charges and counter charges very much to their own satisfaction and the delight of their respective friends' (Brooke 2001: 128).

HUXLEY ON SCIENCE AND RELIGION

That verdict in the *Athenaeum* rather disproves the common view that Huxley scored a victory over Wilberforce, a victory for science over religion. This popular view does not stand up to scholarly scrutiny (Brooke 2001; Gilley 1981; James 2005; Livingstone 2009; Lucas 1979), and is incorrect for several reasons. As Huxley's son Leonard conceded, given the time and place the majority of the audience would almost certainly have been on the bishop's side. Huxley showed courage in insulting a distinguished prelate, but it is not even clear how far his voice carried. The altercation between them undoubtedly caused a stir, the ripples visible in the correspondence of the Darwin circle in the days immediately following (Darwin [1860] 1993: 270–85). But far from being an event with consequences, it disappeared from public awareness for almost thirty years until, in the late 1880s and early 1890s, it was resurrected to enliven the *Life and Letters* of Darwin, of Joseph Hooker, and of Huxley himself (James 2005). Retrospectively, it could then become the foundation myth of a professional scientific culture. As one of Huxley's most sympathetic biographers has insisted, talk of a victory is ridiculous (Desmond 1994).

There is an additional reason why it is simplistic to portray Huxley as a victor for science over religion: he did not himself believe that, when properly understood, there was antagonism between them (Lightman 2001). As Owen Chadwick pointed out, members of an early Victorian public could be captivated by 'science versus religion' when they might not be especially interested in either science or religion (Chadwick 1975). The same could doubtless be said of many today. But whatever happened in the Oxford Museum, Huxley distanced himself from the common construction:

The antagonism between science and religion, about which we hear so much, appears to me to be purely factitious—fabricated, on the one hand, by short-sighted religious people who confound a certain branch of science, theology, with religion; and, on the other, by equally short-sighted scientific people who forget that science takes for its province only that which is susceptible of clear intellectual comprehension; and that, outside the boundaries of that province, they must be content with imagination, with hope, and with ignorance. (Huxley [1885] 1904: 160–1)

Deploying these distinctions, Huxley had no compunction in attacking theology and theologians, especially when their pretensions to knowledge smacked of bad science. Religion, as he understood it, was a quite different matter, rooted in the depths of human nature. Far from disowning a religious sensibility, Huxley admitted to Darwin's cousin, Francis Galton, in 1873 that he experienced a 'profound religious tendency capable of fanaticism, but tempered by no less profound theological scepticism' (Lightman 2001: 347). For Huxley, science and religion occupied two separate spheres, corresponding to different domains of human experience. He perceived himself to be fighting for a 'New Reformation' and, surprising though it may be to those who would enlist him in support of a materialistic atheism, he turned to the Old Testament for an ideal to which he could relate. This was to be found not in Genesis but in the prophetic insight of Micah: 'And what doth the Lord require of thee, but to do justly, and to love mercy, and to walk humbly with thy God.' Huxley was not alone among scientific purifiers of religion in seeking a simple ideal. Any addition or subtraction from 'this great saying of Micah' was a mutilation (Huxley [1885] 1904: 161–2). Of one thing he was sure: 'the antagonism of science is not to religion, but to the heathen survivals and the bad philosophy under which religion herself is often well-nigh crushed' (ibid. 162).

HUXLEY AND GENESIS

Because Huxley wished to assign scientific and religious discourse to separate spheres, he could be pugilistic when lay or clerical apologists invoked scientific knowledge to buttress their cause. The statesman William Gladstone, more than Samuel Wilberforce, was to experience the full bite of Huxley's terrier-like attacks. It is in Huxley's quarrel with Gladstone that we see most clearly his attitude to what he called the 'cosmogony of Genesis'. Surely, he surmised, 'the prophet's staff would have made swift acquaintance with the head of the scholar who had asked Micah whether, peradventure, the Lord further required of him an implicit belief in the accuracy of the cosmogony of Genesis' (Huxley [1885] 1904: 162). The problem was that, despite advances in palaeontology and evolutionary theory, Gladstone was among those insisting that what science had to say could still be harmonized with the sacred text.

Gladstone saw such a concordance between the sequence of creation in Genesis (from a water to an air to a land population) and the disclosures of natural science that he could affirm in the Pentateuch a knowledge that was divine, a 'revelation of truth'. Huxley demurred. The palaeontological evidence simply could not support the notion that birds had been created on the fifth day and creeping things on the sixth. Lizards had preceded birds and, playing biblical exegetes at their own game, Huxley gleefully displayed the lizards of Leviticus, which were there included among the creeping things (ibid. 170). Contrary to the impression Gladstone wished to give, Huxley could find no analogy between the nebular hypothesis of the physical astronomers and the Genesis reference to darkness 'upon the face of the deep' (ibid. 189). And worse still, it was simply 'not true that the species composing any one of the three populations originated during any one of three successive periods of time, and not at any other of these' (ibid. 156). To claim a privileged status for an ancient text on the ground that it contained or presaged conclusions later established by science was a losing strategy, and Huxley went to town in exposing its deficiencies. Genesis had neither more nor less scientific importance than the creation myths of the Egyptians and Babylonians.

Instead of affirming a direct concordance between Genesis and science, an older, alternative principle was sometimes invoked by Christian apologists to the effect that the language of Scripture had been specially accommodated to common human limitations and should not therefore be expected to be sophisticated in its scientific reference. Huxley was no more forgiving of this line of argument than of Gladstone's: 'It is sometimes said that, had the statements contained in the first chapter of Genesis been scientifically true, they would have been unintelligible to ignorant people; but how is the matter mended if, being scientifically untrue, they must needs be rejected by instructed people?' (ibid. 182). For Huxley, the creation narratives were precisely that: antiquated and obsolete science. With his lay sermons and zealous advocacy of scientific learning, he probably did more than anyone in the Victorian period to promote that view.

GENESIS IN THE POST-DARWINIAN DEBATES

The immediate effect of Darwin's science on the interpretation of the opening chapters of Genesis has been described as surprisingly minimal (Rogerson 2009). Why might this have been the case? It should not be overlooked that public debate concerning the transformation of species had been taking place in Britain for at least fifteen years before Darwin's *Origin* was published. This was occasioned by the anonymous publication in 1844 of Robert Chambers's *Vestiges of the Natural History of Creation*. In his presentation of a 'development hypothesis', Chambers made no exception of humans, with the consequence that many of the philosophical and theological issues later raised by the *Origin of Species* had already been in public circulation. For readers with religious scruples, Chambers had sweetened the pill with a coating of natural theology in which a 'law of development' presupposed a divine legislator—a move that pacified some but which only confirmed to others the emptiness of such a deistic formula (Brooke 1997: 68). *Vestiges* was vulnerable to the charge that it lacked scientific rigour. Indeed, it had been savaged by Huxley. But it attracted a large and diverse readership as speculation mounted concerning the identity of its audacious author (Secord 2000). Accordingly, Darwin's theory can scarcely be said to have hit the Victorian scene like a bolt from the blue. As we have already seen, critics of the harmonization programme were already exploiting geological discoveries before Darwin's work became well known. Conversely, Gladstone exemplifies the resilience of the post-Darwinian harmonizers, despite the polemics of Huxley and other biblical critics.

Not before about 1875 was a consensus in favour of Darwin's theory of 'descent with modification' sufficiently pronounced among scientists themselves to create real pressure for change (Roberts 1988). Even that consensus did not extend to a general adoption of Darwin's mechanism of natural selection (Bowler 1983). As noted earlier, Huxley himself gave prominence to sudden mutations that Darwin excluded from his theory of gradual change. Eminent scientists were also expressing doubts as to whether natural selection could explain such attributes of the human mind as an aesthetic sensibility, which it was difficult to believe had survival value. Charles Lyell, and even the co-founder of the theory of evolution by natural selection, Alfred Russel Wallace, were among them (Fichman 2001). This created space for claims that divine activity in some form had been instrumental in creating what was most distinctive in human consciousness and personhood—attributes such as reason, creativity, freedom, and conscience. Additionally, of course, the Darwinian impact would be negligible for those clerical figures who believed they already had all the answers. When a young teacher at Rugby School, Canon J. M. Wilson, gave his father a copy of Darwin's *Origin* for Christmas in 1859, the older cleric was not amused: 'I cannot conceive how a book can be written on the subject. We know all there is to be known about it. God created plants and animals and man out of the ground' (Simpson 1925: 177).

It is, then, possible to exaggerate the Darwinian impact. Nevertheless, new rounds of conflict certainly ensued, not least because Darwinian theory was an attractive resource for those with even more radical agendas to pursue than Huxley's. In the United States, the feminist leader Elizabeth Cady Stanton observed that 'the real difficulty in woman's case is that the whole foundation of the Christian religion rests on her temptation and man's fall'. If, however, 'we accept the Darwinian theory, that the race has been a gradual growth from the lower to a higher form of life, and the story of the fall is a myth, we can exonerate the snake, emancipate the woman, and reconstruct a more rational religion for the nineteenth century' (Stanton 1993: 214).

The reconstruction of a more rational religion was also in the hands of academic theologians who were often themselves the subject of controversy and abuse. A well-known example is that of F. D. Maurice, who was forced to resign from his chair at King's College London for questioning the doctrine of eternal damnation for the unregenerate. Maurice had earlier devised a way of integrating the two creation narratives in Genesis 1 and 2 without conceding that they had separate sources (Rogerson 2009). In Genesis 1 was an idealized account of creation, as it had been envisaged in the mind of God. In Genesis 2 was an account corresponding to the actual creation of humanity. Again, however, it would be wrong to exaggerate the influence of Darwin. In 1851, eight years before Darwin published, Maurice was admonishing those who tried to place restrictions on scientific research. In common with Huxley, albeit with a different purpose, he dismissed the efforts of harmonizers to make Genesis, however summarily, speak correct science. Whereas for Huxley this was a scientifically misguided enterprise, for Maurice and for other theologians both before and after, it was theologically misguided. There were deeper spiritual meanings in Genesis that were obscured by a preoccupation with scientific verisimilitude.

It is beyond the scope of this chapter to sample the great diversity of these deeper existential and spiritual meanings that have been located in the creation narratives. Maurice himself insisted that their purpose was not to encourage people to think that the world had been created in six days, or even in six epochs. It was rather to deliver humanity from idolatry by teaching that everything ultimately depended on a divine order at the heart of reality. Where that view was held, Darwin's theory did not have to be an overbearing obstacle to faith. Indeed, Maurice 'never tired of quoting the spirit of Mr. Darwin's investigations as a lesson and a model for churchmen' (Moore 1979: 89–90). There was also a churchman who, because of his courageous spirit (too radical for Maurice), was a model for Huxley and Darwin. This was the bishop of Natal, John Colenso, vilified by the church establishment for his analysis of the Pentateuch but adamant that the advances of modern science were all part of God's continuing revelation. What mattered to Colenso was not faith 'in the mere Book, but in that Living Word which speaks in the Book, and speaks also by the lips of apostles and prophets in all ages, of all good men and true, whose heart God's Spirit has quickened to be the bearers of His message of truth to their fellow men' (Rogerson 2009). For many later commentators, the primary message of truth contained in Genesis had little or nothing to do with the mechanics of creation. It had much more to do with the nature of a relationship between the Creator and an estranged humanity.

During the Oxford meeting of the British Association, at which Wilberforce and Huxley had their exchange, a sermon was preached by Frederick Temple on the relations between science and religion (Temple 1860). A future archbishop of Canterbury, Temple was tacitly receptive towards Darwin's science, welcoming the extension of the domain of natural laws and warning against the repeated mistake of erecting a religious apologia on what the sciences could not yet explain. The jurisdiction of such a god-of-the-gaps was bound to shrink. The fact that Temple had been one of Wilberforce's ordinands and that he was also the opening contributor to *Essays and Reviews* was particularly painful for the bishop, who publicly exhorted him to 'disclaim his agreement with the views with which he is here connected' (Wilberforce [1861] 1874: 109). The point is that Wilberforce must not be assumed to typify a monolithic Christian reaction to Darwin. It is the diversity of response that needs to be underlined. An early convert was the Christian socialist Charles Kingsley, who delighted Darwin with the news that he had 'gradually learnt to see that it is just as noble a conception of Deity, to believe that he created primal forms capable of self development into all forms needful pro tempore and pro loco, as to believe that He required a fresh act of intervention to supply the lacunas which he himself had made' (Darwin 1991: 379–80). Was not the former the 'loftier thought'?

Darwinism was clearly divisive within Christendom and has continued to be so. In his book *What is Darwinism?* (1874) the Princeton theologian Charles Hodge rejected the mechanism of natural selection on the ground that it evacuated the concept of design in living organisms. But, by contrast, Harvard's Professor of Botany, Asa Gray, also a Presbyterian, set a precedent for commending Darwin's theory not only for its scientific merits but also as the basis of a possible theodicy. In one respect, by highlighting perpetual warfare in nature, Darwin's theory intensified the problem of pain and suffering. Nevertheless, Gray argued, it was this same struggle for survival that had been the *sine qua non* of the very possibility of evolutionary progression, without which human beings themselves would never have come into existence (Gray [1876] 1963: 310–11).

This was a long way from ascribing the prevalence of pain to the consequences of the Fall. However, the Fall narrative was not completely denuded by Darwinism. In a new sense it could be said to express in mythical terms a biological reality as well as a sense of spiritual estrangement. A propensity to sinfulness and selfishness could now be interpreted as the legacy from an animal past. Herbert Spencer took this view, as did Huxley, who was never averse to a bit of secular theologizing. Of human self-centredness and self-assertion, Huxley wrote that it had been the condition of victory in the struggle for existence. But as an inheritance it was real enough, nothing less than 'the reality at the bottom of the doctrine of original sin' (Brooke 1991: 313). By the close of the nineteenth century Huxley's rendering had been assimilated by many representatives of theological liberalism. In his *The Theology of an Evolutionist* (1897), Lyman Abbott saw new meaning in the old adage that immoral acts were lapses into animality. That same animal ancestry was what had made Darwinian theory anathema to Wilberforce, while for Darwin himself it perfectly conformed to what an authentic humility required.

WORKS CITED

BARTHOLOMEW, M. J. (1975), 'Huxley's Defence of Darwin', *Annals of Science*, 32: 525–35.
BOWLER, P. J. (1983), *The Eclipse of Darwinism*. Baltimore: Johns Hopkins University Press.
BROOKE, J. H. (1985), 'The Relations between Darwin's Science and his Religion', in J. Durant (ed.), *Darwinism and Divinity*, 40–75. Oxford: Blackwell.
——(1991), *Science and Religion: Some Historical Perspectives*. Cambridge: Cambridge University Press.
——(1996), 'Like Minds: The God of Hugh Miller', in M. Shortland (ed.), *Hugh Miller and the Controversies of Victorian Science*, 171–86. Oxford: Oxford University Press.
——(1997), 'The Natural Theology of the Geologists: Some Theological Strata', in L. J. Jordanova and R. Porter (eds.), *Images of the Earth: Essays in the History of the Environmental Sciences*, 2nd edn., 53–74. Oxford: Alden Press.
——(2001), 'The Wilberforce-Huxley Debate: Why Did It Happen?' *Science and Christian Belief*, 13: 127–41.
——(2009), '"Laws Impressed on Matter by the Creator"?: The *Origin* and the Question of Religion', in R. Richards and M. Ruse (eds.), *The Cambridge Companion to the 'Origin of Species'*, 256–74. Cambridge and New York: Cambridge University Press.
——and CANTOR, G. N. (1998), *Reconstructing Nature: The Engagement of Science and Religion*. Edinburgh: T. & T. Clark.
CHADWICK, O. (1975), *The Secularization of the European Mind in the Nineteenth Century*. Cambridge: Cambridge University Press.

COHEN, I. B. (1985), 'Three Notes on the Reception of Darwin's Ideas on Natural Selection (Henry Baker Tristram, Alfred Newton, Samuel Wilberforce)', in D. Kohn (ed.), *The Darwinian Heritage*, 589–607. Princeton: Princeton University Press.

CORSI, P. (1988), *Science and Religion: Baden Powell and the Anglican Debate, 1800–1860*. Cambridge: Cambridge University Press.

DARWIN, C. (1991), *The Correspondence of Charles Darwin*, ed. F. Burkhardt, vol. 7. Cambridge: Cambridge University Press.

——(1993), *The Correspondence of Charles Darwin*, ed. F. Burkhardt, vol. 8. Cambridge: Cambridge University Press.

DESMOND, A. (1994), *Huxley: The Devil's Disciple*. London: Penguin.

FICHMAN, M. (2001), 'Science in Theistic Contexts: A Case Study of Alfred Russel Wallace on Human Evolution', *Osiris*, 16: 227–50.

GILLEY, S. (1981), 'The Huxley–Wilberforce Debate: A Reconstruction', in K. Robbins (ed.), *Religion and Humanism: Studies in Church History*, 17, 325–40. Oxford: Blackwell.

GILLISPIE, C. C. ([1951] 1959), *Genesis and Geology*. New York: Harper.

GOODWIN, C. W. (1860), 'On the Mosaic Cosmogony', in *Essays and Reviews*. London: Longman.

GRAY, A. ([1876] 1963), *Darwiniana*, ed. A. H. Dupree. Cambridge Mass.: Harvard University Press.

JAMES, F. A. J. L. (2005), 'An "Open Clash between Science and the Church"?: Wilberforce, Huxley and Hooker on Darwin at the British Association, Oxford, 1860', in D. M. Knight and M. D. Eddy (eds.), *Science and Beliefs: From Natural Philosophy to Natural Science, 1700–1900*, 171–93. Aldershot: Ashgate.

HUXLEY, T. H. ([1860] 1893), 'The Origin of Species', in T. H. Huxley, *Darwiniana: Essays*, 22–79. London: Macmillan.

——([1885] 1904), 'The Interpreters of Genesis and the Interpreters of Nature', in T. H. Huxley, *Science and Hebrew Tradition: Essays*, 139–63. London: Macmillan.

——([1886] 1904), 'Mr. Gladstone and Genesis', in T. H. Huxley, *Science and Hebrew Tradition: Essays*, 164–200. London: Macmillan.

LIGHTMAN, B. (2001), 'Victorian Sciences and Religions: Discordant Harmonies', *Osiris*, 16: 343–66.

LIVINGSTONE, D. N. (2008), *Adam's Ancestors: Race, Religion and the Politics of Human Origins*. Baltimore: Johns Hopkins University Press.

——(2009), 'The Mythology of the Wilberforce/Huxley Debate', in R. L. Numbers (ed.), *Galileo Goes to Jail and Other Myths in Science and Religion*, ch. 17. Cambridge Mass.: Harvard University Press.

LUCAS, J. R. (1979), 'Wilberforce and Huxley: A Legendary Encounter', *Historical Journal*, 22: 313–30.

MOORE, J. R. (1979), *The Post-Darwinian Controversies: A Study of the Protestant Struggle to Come to Terms with Darwin in Great Britain and America 1870–1900*. Cambridge: Cambridge University Press.

ROBERTS, J. H. (1988), *Darwinism and the Divine in America: Protestant Intellectuals and Organic Evolution 1859–1900*. Madison, Wisc.: University of Wisconsin Press.

ROGERSON, J. (2009), 'What Difference did Darwin Make? The Interpretation of Genesis in the Nineteenth century', in S. C. Barton and D. Wilkinson (eds.), *Reading Genesis after Darwin*, 75–91. New York: Oxford University Press.

RUDWICK, M. J. S. (2005), *Bursting the Limits of Time: The Reconstruction of Geohistory in the Age of Revolution*. Chicago: University of Chicago Press.

RUPKE, N. A. (1983), *The Great Chain of History: William Buckland and the English School of Geology 1814–1849*. Oxford: Oxford University Press.

SECORD, J. A. (2000), *Victorian Sensation: The Extraordinary Publication, Reception, and Secret Authorship of 'Vestiges of the Natural History of Creation'*. Chicago: University of Chicago Press.

SIMPSON, J. Y. (1925), *Landmarks in the Struggle between Science and Religion*. London: Hodder & Stoughton.

STANTON, E. C. (1993), *The Woman's Bible*, vol. 2, reprint. Boston: Northeastern University Press.

TEMPLE, F. (1860), *The Present Relations of Science to Religion*. Oxford: Parker.

TURNER, F. M. (1978), 'The Victorian Conflict between Science and Religion: A Professional Dimension', *Isis*, 69: 356–76.

WILBERFORCE, S. ([1860] 1874), 'Darwin's *Origin of Species*', in S. Wilberforce, *Essays Contributed to the Quarterly Review*, 1. 52–103. London: Murray.

——([1861] 1874), '*Essays and Reviews*', in S. Wilberforce, *Essays Contributed to the Quarterly Review*, 1. 104–83. London: Murray.

FURTHER READING

As well as Brooke 1991, 2001; Gilley 1981; James 2005; and Lucas 1979, see:

BARTON, S. C. and WILKINSON, D. (eds.) (2009), *Reading Genesis after Darwin*. New York: Oxford University Press.

NUMBERS, R. L., ed. (2009), *Galileo Goes to Jail and Other Myths in Science and Religion*. Cambridge Mass.: Harvard University Press.

TURNER, F. M. (1993), *Contesting Cultural Authority: Essays in Victorian Cultural Life*. Cambridge: Cambridge University Press.

CHAPTER 28

SODOMY AND GENDERED LOVE: READING GENESIS 19 IN THE ANGLICAN COMMUNION

JAY EMERSON JOHNSON

IN Matthew's Gospel Jesus sends out his disciples to proclaim good news and to do the work of ministry. He concludes their commissioning by evoking a story of divine retribution from Genesis 19. 'It will be more tolerable for the land of Sodom and Gomorrah on the day of judgment', he says, than for any town that does not receive these newly commissioned disciples (Matt. 10:15). This sudden evocation of Genesis seems rather arbitrary unless perhaps Matthew intended the act of sending disciples to signal the historical precedent he had in mind. Just as angelic messengers were sent to Sodom (Gen. 19:1) so also Jesus sends his own messengers to the towns and villages of Galilee. But Sodom refuses to receive these divine emissaries graciously; the whole city—'to the last man', we read—sought instead to do these guests violence (Gen. 19:4). Such inhospitality amounts to nothing less than that ancient city's rejection of God. By linking Jesus' disciples to the angels in Genesis,

Matthew portrays Jesus' own mission as divine and the fate of those who reject his disciples as even worse than the fate of Sodom's citizens.

This Matthean passage appears occasionally in the lectionaries used by Anglican Christians worldwide for Sunday worship. Whatever a given preacher may or may not say about that text, Jesus' warning will quickly evoke the sin of 'Sodomites' known as 'sodomy'. The parishioners listening to Matthew's Gospel will not need to consider any parallel between the sending of angels and the sending of disciples nor will they need to read the story in Genesis to understand the nature of the sin committed by the inhabitants of Sodom; they already know. Anglican Christians today (among many others) treat the meaning of sodomy as nearly self-evident, without any consideration of whether first-century assumptions match their own concerning what the texts from Matthew and Genesis mean.

As Dale Martin has noted, however: 'Texts don't mean. People mean with texts' (2006: 1). Martin's deceptively simple observation exposes both the bloated and reductionistic 'career' of the story from Genesis 19, or what Michael Carden describes as the 'post-text' in the history of its interpretation and reception (2004: 4). Whatever Matthew's Jesus might have intended by evoking the fate of Sodom and Gomorrah cannot now be easily disentangled from the medieval Latin invention of sodomy as a particular category of sexual sin nor from the rhetorical use of this classification in modern ecclesiastical debates concerning the moral status of 'homosexual' persons and the relation of those debates to Western jurisprudence and civil rights. Whatever people now mean by referring to the name of that ancient city in Genesis 19 carries with it the whole of that cultural, religious, and legal history without any need to reference the history itself. 'Sodomy' can stand alone as an effective shorthand marker in both speech and policy to describe a particular sexual act, most frequently, if not exclusively, an act committed by 'homosexual' men.[1]

As early as 1955 Derrick Sherwin Bailey attempted just such a biblical and cultural disentanglement, to snip the historical thread between Genesis 19 and the loving relationships formed between people of the same sex. In doing so, Bailey offered one of the earliest attempts to reread the Genesis text with a view toward what the 'wickedness' of Sodom and Gomorrah may have entailed, including a violation of ancient hospitality codes, gang rape, and even ethnic arrogance. Multiple scholarly interventions of this type since the mid-twentieth century have not, however, soothed the ferocity of the debates around 'homosexuality' in the Anglican Communion, which only intensified in the wake of the 2003 election in the Episcopal Church USA (ECUSA) of Gene Robinson—an openly gay and

---

[1] 'Homosexuality' will appear in quotation marks throughout this essay, not least because this medical neologism from the nineteenth century is rejected by most of those it is meant to describe. This is especially important when dealing with biblical texts, as there are no Hebrew, Greek, or Latin equivalents to the modern notion of a 'homosexual' orientation or identity.

partnered priest—as bishop of New Hampshire. This intensification, carrying with it the potential for schism in the Communion, bears witness to the insufficiency of modern biblical scholarship to mitigate the power of Sodom and Gomorrah in the religious imagination. Contextualizing and historicizing the fate of those ancient cities cannot by itself deconstruct the categorical meaning of sodomy and what this act implies concerning divine punishment.

The decision in 2002 by the Canadian diocese of New Westminster to bless liturgically same-sex unions, together with the 2003 election and ordination of Gene Robinson in the American church, marked a watershed moment for Anglican Christians worldwide. The significance of this moment lies not, as one might presume, primarily in the ecclesial fault-lines it seemed to draw between the churches of the North Atlantic and the so-called global South. This moment exposed a rhetorical shift in the debate itself, which had been percolating for some time but was made clear by the swift objections to the Canadian and American decisions. While those objections retained their reliance on biblical arguments, the rhetoric shifted away from the standard citations that had been typical of twentieth-century approaches. Absent from those citations, with the rare exception, was any mention of Genesis 19. This shift cannot be explained solely by the success of critical biblical scholarship to reframe what the biblical writer described as the 'wickedness' of Sodom and Gomorrah. The issue at hand in both New Westminster and New Hampshire turned not on the act of sodomy but on loving and committed relationships—the blessing of unions and the faithful partnership with another man in which Gene Robinson was engaged. The biblical rhetoric thus turned more explicitly to the doctrine of creation, especially to the notion of 'gender complementarity' as the divine intent in marriage. The significance of this rhetorical shift notwithstanding, sodomy has not lost its power to evoke the sinfulness of 'homosexuality'.[2]

As I intend to suggest in what follows, arguments for properly ordering human relations based on a strictly binary construction of gender rely on the very same assumptions that fuelled the construction of sodomy as that which warranted divine punishment on the citizens of Sodom. Historical and social constructions of this type at the intersection of religion, culture, and human sexuality illustrate particularly well the differences between modern biblical scholarship on the one hand, and the religious and cultural reception of biblical texts on the other. The controversy over 'homosexuality' in the Anglican Communion further illustrates the challenges in employing the insights of biblical scholarship in the midst of highly charged social and ecclesial debates. Those engaged in the historical-critical

---

[2] This was illustrated quite vividly during Gene Robinson's ordination as bishop of New Hampshire when one of the objectors to the ordination stood up during the liturgy and described, not the quality of the relationship in which Bishop Robinson was engaged, but what anal intercourse entails, in graphic physiological detail.

study of Scripture may aspire to 'objective' interpretations of the text, even if such objectivity remains elusive. Analysing the history of the text's reception, however, entangles the interpreter in the cultural and religious uses of a given text—uses which may or may not rely on the results of historical-critical investigation. Analysing such entanglements will necessarily foreground not only theology, spiritual practice, and ecclesial politics but also the subjective appropriation of a text by a variety of faith communities for rhetorical, if not polemical, ends (see Thompson, 2007).

The curious 'career' of Genesis 19 in the Anglican Communion offers in microcosm the broader complexities involved in analysing the cultural and religious reception of biblical texts. Here I will sketch those complexities in three steps, first with reference to the resilience of sodomy in the religious imagination and Western jurisprudence, a resilience that need not rely on the actual content of the biblical text. Second, I will place that resilience of sodomy's popular meaning more particularly in the context of shifting and unstable relations among the provinces of the worldwide Anglican Communion. Most news media reports notwithstanding, Gene Robinson's episcopate should be seen not as the cause but as a symptom of the Communion's instability as it struggles to come to terms with the legacy of Western colonialism; in that context, 'sodomy' functions mostly as a religious and cultural trope for delineating post- and neo-colonial fault-lines. Lastly, I want to suggest that these early twenty-first-century controversies in the Anglican Communion turn not on 'homosexuality' per se but on the gendered ordering of human relations. Highlighting the theological construction of gender in today's debates not only sheds light on the peculiar reception history of Genesis 19; it also suggests a renewed reading of that biblical text in which idolatry emerges as a better definition of that ancient city's sin known as sodomy.

SODOMY IN THE RELIGIOUS IMAGINATION AND WESTERN JURISPRUDENCE

Michael Carden recalls seeing as a teenager the depiction of Sodom and Gomorrah in John Huston's film *The Bible . . . In the Beginning*. As Carden notes, Huston chose to fill in many of the narrative and descriptive gaps in the Genesis text by portraying Sodom as a 'hothouse of homosexuality', something akin to a perpetual 'lesbian and gay Mardi Gras' replete with effeminate, predatory gay men (2004: 5). Nearly thirty years after the release of that film, I prepared to move from my suburban Chicago home to the San Francisco Bay Area. A colleague jokingly warned me about what I would find in that 'Sodom by the sea'. What I found, in part, was a good number of people, many of them non-churchgoing gay men, who knew exactly what 'sodomy' means without ever having picked up a Bible, let alone read the text from Genesis 19 (though perhaps like Carden they had seen Huston's film). Whereas Carden describes the medieval Latin construction of the Sodomite as a person who possesses a 'dual nationality'—at once a citizen of Sodom and a species of sexual transgressor (2004: 164)—Sodom itself has evolved into a city of dual identity, at once an ancient biblical city and any other locale where the sin of Sodomites appears to run rampant.

Despite decades of biblical scholarship refuting the link between that Genesis text and 'homosexuality', sodomy continues to inhabit both the cultural and religious imagination as referring to a particular sexual act, mostly if not always between men. This imaginative and persistent construction of sodomy cuts across both time and place, defying otherwise appropriate academic disclaimers concerning historical and social context. So while sodomy could refer to a variety of deplorable acts in the history of western Christian traditions (some of them quite vaguely and imprecisely defined), the trajectory of its evocative power eventually began to coalesce around sexuality and one kind of sexual act in particular that discloses the deeply gendered history of the reception of Genesis 19. The cross-cultural resilience of sodomy in the religious imagination resides precisely there, in its nearly unassailable bond with gender transgression, as Huston's film portrayal strongly implies.

The question of when and how Sodomites became explicitly associated with the sin widely known today as sodomy entails much more than scrutinizing Genesis 19 with the tools of modern historical-critical method; Huston presumably employed no such method for filling in the many lacunae in that text. Any investigation of sodomy's origins necessarily draws into its orbit a labyrinthine history of Christian theological construction, the evolution of institutional church power, and the cultural develop-ment of European sexual mores. As Mark Jordan reminds us, sexual vocabulary is particularly rich in metaphors and allusions, and geographical metaphors especially require historical sleuthing for their meaning (1997: 7). Or, as Huston's film illus-trates and as Avivah Gottlieb Zornberg describes it, biblical reading often involves as much creation as interpretation (quoted in Carden 2004: 4).

The reception history of Genesis 19 began of course with the ancient Israelites themselves. Remarkably, no other incident from Genesis is cited as often in both Jewish and Christian scriptures as the destruction of Sodom. The frequency of its citation, however, is not matched by any clarity concerning the reason for the city's destruction. A notable exception appears in the prophet Ezekiel. 'This was the guilt of your sister Sodom: she and her daughters had pride, excess of food and prosperous ease, but did not aid the poor and needy' (Ezek. 16:49).[3] Conspicuously

---

[3] Ezekiel's description represents the approach most often taken by writers in the Hebrew Bible, where the sin of Sodom is rarely if ever identified with sexual immorality but always in association with violence or injustice (see Boyarin, 2007 and Scroggs, 1983).

absent from Ezekiel's description is any mention of the sexual meaning sodomy achieved in the religious imagination over many centuries and across diverse cultures. For those more particular meanings one must trace an ecclesial arc from at least as early as Justin Martyr in the second century (for whom the story of Sodom served as both anti-Jewish polemic and evidence of the Holy Trinity in the Hebrew Scriptures), through Gregory the Great in the sixth century (who linked the means of Sodom's destruction by fire and sulphur to 'sins of the flesh') and on to Peter Damian, whose eleventh-century *Book of Gomorrah* marks the medieval invention of sodomy (*sodomia*) as referring explicitly to same-sex sexual acts while retaining the multitude of retributive horrors linked to the fate of Sodom and Gomorrah from previous centuries.

Peter Damian's reduction of Sodom's religious and cultural career, however, does not represent an entirely innovative treatment as much as a selective refinement of what had been gestating in the reception history of Genesis 19 for generations. The roots of this medieval refinement and the gendered overtones in its legacy appear early in Christian history, at first as a generalized warning to avoid the over-indulgence exemplified by Sodom's citizens (gluttony being linked, in slip-pery-slope fashion, to inordinate passions of the flesh), but rather quickly as a thoroughly sexualized discourse. Whereas Clement of Alexandria in the second century refers generally to the 'fornication' of Sodomites, the *Apostolic Constitutions* of the latter half of the fourth century clearly identifies the sin of Sodom as 'contrary to nature,' and for the first time links sodomy to Leviticus 18:22 and that text's prohibition against male–male intercourse (Carden 2004: 125).

The appeal to 'nature' and therefore to God's own intent in creation provides the indispensable lens through which to view the otherwise peculiar history of sod-omy's invention and its gendered legacy. One of those historical peculiarities appears in the scant attention given to the striking parallel to Genesis 19 found in Judges 19. In the latter text, a host is faced with the same dilemma as Lot was in the story from Genesis. In Judges, however, no angelic intervention prevents the sexual sacrifice of a woman to fulfil the requirements of a hospitable household. Despite the dramatic display of divine judgement on the cities in Genesis, what transpires in the story from Judges is in some ways more horrifying. The woman in that story, an anonymous concubine, is brutally raped by Benjamite men in Gibeah and is later ritually dismembered to prompt retributive military action by Israel (see Judg. 20:6–11).

One might suppose that this horrific story would fuel the religious and moral imagination at least as much as what happened to the inhabitants of Sodom and Gomorrah. But no Hollywood films were made depicting the fate of the concubine at the hands of the Benjamite tribe in Gibeah, nor of the swift, though 'merely' human retribution inflicted on the Benjamites by Israel. No European legal statute or medieval penitential category emerged to describe the rape and ritualistic dismemberment of that nameless concubine. As both Jordan and Carden note, there is no sin of the Benjamites referred to as 'Benjamy' or sinners as 'Gibeahthites' as there are 'sodomy' and 'Sodomites' in the reception history of these texts (Jordan 1997: 30; Carden 2004: 8).

What has so captured the religious imagination in Genesis 19 that the story of Sodom's fate stands in paradigmatic fashion for, as Edith Humphrey has described it, 'the primal rebellion against God' (2004: 36)? The endless fascination, if not the anxiety, produced by this text surely derives in part from the divine punishment levelled against Sodom and Gomorrah in contrast to the mere human retribution unleashed against Gibeah. While humans can turn to myriad historical and contemporary images for human military might, the sheer spectacle of divine wrath unleashed with shock and awe against Sodom and Gomorrah prompts an altogether different level of religious imagination. Yet this alone would not suffice to explain the near obsession with Sodom's fate in Christian traditions and ecclesial debates. Analysing this preoccupation with Genesis 19 involves the theological accretions layered over the text and its eventual refinement as a tool for both cultural and institutional power. Sodomy has proved singularly useful in that regard, as Mark Jordan has argued, not because of its precise biblical definition but because of its malleability and therefore utility to mask violent exercises of power. Sodomy has meant whatever was useful for the exercise of such power at the time and, as Jordan puts it, 'to justify a dozen differently motivated oppressions' (1997: 163).

The seemingly endless malleability of sodomy's meaning might well lead one to wonder whether the religious imagination could bear the possibility of divine judgement unfurled against a community of pride, inhospitality, and economic injustice, as the Genesis text might plausibly imply and as the passage from Ezekiel, among others, strongly suggests. After all, who then could stand? Who then is not condemned? The horrors of God's wrath suffered by the citizens of Sodom and Gomorrah must instead be reserved for those who in effect cannot repent, for those who are actually incapable of repentance. Sodomy must, in other words, instantiate the quintessence of human opposition to divine will and order as an enduring counter-example to the truly faithful, indeed as a foil for what it means to be human at all. This is Edith Humphrey's very point in identifying 'homoerotic activity' with humanity's 'primal rebellion against God', a view echoed in a 2003 statement by Peter Akinola, the Anglican archbishop of Nigeria. For Akinola, setting aside the 'divine arrangement' of marriage as between a man and a woman is an 'assault on the sovereignty of God'. In a rather startling rhetorical move, Akinola compares this assault to the human depletion of the ozone layer in so far as 'homosexuality' marks a 'terrible violation of the harmony of the eco-system of which mankind is a part' (quoted in Bates 2004: 39).

Linking the sin of sodomy to ecological degradation may seem startling, but it is not entirely without historical precedent. Christian antiquity gradually witnessed the rhetorical usefulness of Sodom's demise for a nascent, particularly Christian doctrine of creation. The notion that God's creative intent for humanity appears most vividly in gender differentiation provided a theological gloss for casting Sodomites as the paragon of divine rejection. Actually, given these Christian discourses on 'nature', one might notice the rhetorical trajectory running in the other direction: the horrors of divine wrath inflicted on Sodomites presented an opportunity to underwrite biblically a *gendered* discourse on nature. For such a supposition the history of sodomy in western jurisprudence provides ample evidence.

Among the many legacies of the union between European society and institutional Christianity, legal precedents and patterns of jurisprudence surely rank high on the list, including the role the Bible has played in shaping those precedents. How to characterize that history with respect to sexuality and especially sodomy remains contested on several fronts. John Boswell's pioneering research in the 1980s led him to conclude that the religious/civic condemnation of male 'homosexuality' derives primarily from eleventh- and twelfth-century developments. Philip Kennedy begs to differ with this assessment, by noting that as early as Tertullian in the late second to early third century Christian thinkers advocated the death penalty for same-sex relations. In the ninth century Benedict of Levita likewise argued that sodomy ought to be punishable by death, and attributed his text to Charlemagne, lending the weight of imperial decree to this religious injunction. And beginning in the eleventh century and stretching through the sixteenth, a succession of European city-states cited the Bible for their authority to execute 'homosexuals' (Kennedy 2005: 303).

Both Boswell and Mark Jordan, however, nuance this history with respect to what precisely constitutes 'sodomy'. On that question, Peter Damian's *Book of Gomorrah* still stands as the cultural and religious watershed, providing a retrospective and prospective lens through which to read the history of sodomy both backwards and forwards. By construing sodomy explicitly as sexual relations between men, Peter Damian's text settled any lingering doubts about sodomy's previous career and clarified the justification of dozens of 'burnings, beheadings, drownings, and hangings of homosexuals' in both Calvin's Geneva and Georgian England (Kennedy 2005: 304).

This long cultural history of sodomy, inflected and informed by religious and biblical rhetoric, stands behind several key twentieth-century judicial rulings and the reasoning that informed them. In a series of legal cases beginning in the 1980s and leading up to the landmark *Lawrence* v. *Texas* case in the US Supreme Court in 2003, the issue turned once again to defining exactly what 'sodomy' is and, significantly, the role played by gender in any such definition. Among the states that prohibited sodomy at that time, many of them defined it as 'non-procreative sex' of any kind, regardless of the gender of the parties involved. Some states, however, targeted 'gay sex' exclusively in their definitions. This distinction raised the Constitutional question of equal protection under the law and divided the Supreme Court among those who focused on 'homosexual sodomy', and thus not only a specific act but a gendered one, and those who relied on issues concerning the right of privacy in a relationship between consenting adults (Johnson 2006: 175–7).

This trajectory in western jurisprudence serves to highlight the modern reading and reception of Genesis 19 as relying not on the tools of critical biblical scholarship but instead, as US Supreme Court Chief Justice Warren Burger argued regarding state sodomy laws, on the 'long-standing Judaeo-Christian values on which Western Civilization was based' (Johnson 2006: 171). In effect, those 'values' do not reflect a rejection of that 'love which dare not speak its name' but of a particular sexual act that had for centuries been punishable by death. Thus, when the US Supreme Court decision in *Lawrence* v. *Texas* overturned state sodomy statutes (the same year in which Gene Robinson was elected bishop of New Hampshire) it was not for the most part heterosexual married couples but gay men who took to the streets in celebration. These celebrants were clearly not relishing their new-found legal permission to practice inhospitality to strangers, gang rape, or ethnic arrogance. The modern reception of Genesis 19, thoroughly imprinted by the text's ancient and medieval history, had condensed the practice of 'sodomites' (gay men) to 'sodomy' (anal intercourse), regardless of those few legal statutes that made no distinction between the gender of those engaging in the act.

The policies and postures of religious institutions do not usually, of course, follow the lead of civic judicial rulings. I do not mean only that religious institutions are not bound in their policy-making by the decisions of civil magistrates and judges. The US Supreme Court may have evacuated the state's power to regulate and monitor the sexual behaviour of adults with respect to a specific form of that behaviour, but the court did nothing to loosen the cultural and religious bond between that behaviour and the sin supposedly condemned by God of those inhabitants of an ancient city called Sodom. The Court's decision in effect legalized 'sodomy', which only reinforced the already long-established conviction that same-sex intercourse constitutes that particular 'sin'—constitutes, that is, 'Sodomites' as such. However one wishes to characterize the American scene, it is important to note that no similar easing of legal restrictions has transpired in those regions of the Anglican Communion where opposition to Gene Robinson's election has been the most pronounced; at the time of his election, same-sex relationships were illegal in twenty-nine African states, and in some of those states engaging in such relationships is still subject to the death penalty.

The objections to Bishop Robinson's election and eventually the threats of schism it would produce in the Anglican Communion led Rowan Williams, the archbishop of Canterbury, to establish a commission to study and address this growing sense of ecclesial crisis. Significantly, this commission's charter expressly excluded dealing with the theological and biblical issues concerning 'homosexuality' and limited its work to an analysis of the Anglican Communion's ecclesial relations and to discerning ways in which the Communion could remain intact.

The 2004 product of the commission, known as the Windsor Report, while making recommendations for securing the 'bonds of affection' among Anglican provinces and providing for 'instruments of unity', clearly placed the burden of such unity on justifying the acceptance of same-sex relationships. The Report notes, for example, that in the wake of Gene Robinson's election and the decision by the Canadian Diocese of New Westminster to bless same-sex unions, 'the overwhelming response from other Christians both inside and outside the Anglican family has been to regard these developments as departures from genuine, apostolic Christian faith' (2004: 18). The extent to which issues dealing with 'homosexuality' can be considered in any way inherent to 'apostolic Christian faith' demonstrates the tenacity of sodomy's historical career in the religious imagination. If Gene Robinson's 'homosexual' relationship departs from apostolic Christian faith it does so by betraying the gendered construal of the doctrine of creation that emerged in tandem with the portrayal of Sodom as a city defined by 'unnatural' acts—just as the fourth-century *Apostolic Constitutions* had declared.

PROVINCIAL POLITICS AND NEO-COLONIAL RELATIONS

The ecclesial politics of the Anglican Communion began visibly to shift during the 1988 Lambeth Conference of bishops. The number of African bishops in attendance had doubled since the previous conference just ten years earlier, and less than two-thirds of the participants were white. Ten years later in 1998, and for the first time in Anglican history, this once-a-decade gathering included more representatives from global South than from North Atlantic dioceses. Moreover, these global South bishops were no longer American or European ex-patriots or missionary bishops of the colonial era. Born in the dioceses they now represented at Lambeth, these bishops were certainly raised in the legacy of colonial Christianity, but they brought with them many different cultural perspectives and sensibilities, as the conversations and debates during both the 1988 and 1998 conferences clearly illustrated. Today, the vast majority of Anglicans do not speak English as their native language, and the second-largest province in the Communion is led by Nigerian Archbishop Peter Akinola.[4]

[4] Tracking church members has always resembled more an art than a science. Nonetheless, it is apparently the case that at the time of Gene Robinson's election, the Anglican province of Nigeria was at least as large as the Church of England. If one were to exclude merely nominal members of the latter, the former would be larger.

Clues to the significance of this geographical shift for human sexuality appear in one of the presenting causes of the first Lambeth Conference convened in 1867. The Anglican Church of Canada had, two years previously, urged the archbishop of Canterbury to establish a 'global forum' for adjudicating disputes among world-wide Anglicans, prompted in part by the crisis over the South African episcopate of John William Colenso (1814–83). Colenso, a priest of the Church of England, was appointed bishop of the newly formed diocese of Natal in southern Africa in 1853. Prior to this appointment, Colenso's missionary work had led him to reconsider a number of standard approaches to biblical interpretation regarding Christian theology and ethics. Among those issues was whether African converts to Christianity ought to give up the practice of polygamy for the sake of Christian faith; Bishop Colenso, while not a proponent of polygamous families, did not believe so. In his words: 'The price of conversion to Christianity should never be the dissolution of the family and perhaps the destitution of wives and children' (quoted in Sachs 1993: 142–3).

Colenso's innovative approach to biblical interpretation as well as questions concerning jurisdictional oversight contributed to the need for that first gathering of Anglican bishops at Lambeth Palace. None of the questions considered by that conference was resolved by that conference until Lambeth 1988, when the bishops agreed to respect cultural diversity regarding monogamy and polygamy.[5] This resolution highlights the twin issues with which the Anglican Communion has struggled from the beginning: biblical interpretation (and thus the authority of Scripture) and episcopal oversight in relation to Canterbury. The historical fragility of this global communion of churches—deriving in part from the ambiguity of what 'communion' itself actually entails—now bears the weight of new pressures on several fronts. Not least are the economic and cultural forces of global capitalism, frequently perceived and experienced in the global South as a European but especially an American moment of neo-colonialism. In the midst of globalization, the assertion of new-found ecclesial influence in the global South expresses religiously a broader cultural resistance to neo-colonial control: the archbishop of Canterbury, no less than the Presiding Bishop of ECUSA, must not impose Western cultural sensibilities on the rest of the Communion. Archbishop Akinola made this quite plain when he declared his intention in 2003 to 'defend orthodoxy' and to 'banish the erroneous teachings you [in the West] plan to impose on us' (quoted in Bates 2004: 192).

One might suppose that such resistance to neo-colonial power would find expression in inculturated forms of biblical interpretation and theological

---

[5] Resolutions from both the 1988 and 1998 Lambeth Conferences reflect carefully nuanced positions that permitted, under certain conditions, pastoral discretion concerning polygamy. David Gitari, who was then the archbishop of Kenya, argued that from a biblical perspective polygamy was probably more Christian than divorce (1984).

reflection. Philip Jenkins (2006), for example, has argued that for Christians in the global South the biblical world is much closer to their own than it is to the world of the North Atlantic. For Jenkins, this makes biblical texts more directly applicable to the social and economic realities of Anglicans in the southern hemisphere. Perhaps so, yet these efforts to contextualize and inculturate biblical theologies do not usually extend very far into the realms of gender and human sexuality. Following Jenkins's lead, we might expect a reading of Genesis 19 that stresses hospitality and economic justice to thrive in locations emerging from the legacy of colonial imposition; but this has not been the case. The definition of 'sodomy', whether in sub-Saharan Africa or churches in South-East Asia, still relies on Western European logic and rhetoric, exemplified by Peter Damian's medieval text.

Inculturated readings of biblical texts flourish when those readings pose relatively little threat to well-established interpretations or when those readings can serve to loosen the grip of Western imperialism. In both cases notions of biblical authority remain intact. Dismantling the post-text career of Genesis 19, however, fails to meet either of those tests. The definition of sodomy attached to that text is well established both culturally and religiously, and a reassessment of that definition would at least appear as acquiescence to Western liberalism—a weakening of biblical authority, in other words. As Rowan Williams observed in 2002, for most people, whether in the North Atlantic or the global South, the ordination of gay people is not primarily about sex, 'it is about what you think of the authority of the Bible' (quoted in Bates 2004: 153).

Even in North Atlantic contexts, historical-critical method left virtually untouched those biblical passages that appeared to condemn 'homosexuality' until broader cultural sensibilities began to shift. Critical reassessments of those key passages, including Genesis 19, rose in tandem with new American social movements traced from the early 'homophiles' in the 1950s to the Stonewall Rebellion in 1969 and 'second wave' feminism. With rare exceptions, no similar movements of liberation have transpired in non-western locales, to which the second-class status of women in many of those regions clearly bears witness. Even in parts of the United States many would lament the lack of progress on this issue. As Horace Griffin has observed, African-American Christians treat biblical texts unevenly, critiquing Pauline passages concerning slavery on the one hand while uncritically citing Pauline passages concerning sexuality on the other (2006: 73). The Bible itself, in other words, does not usually generate social values; it is instead more often employed and cited to support already established cultural sensibilities.

This important distinction between the reception of biblical texts and their historical-critical interpretation rarely appears in the analysis of inter-provincial relations in the Anglican Communion. Since the 1998 Lambeth Conference, which passed a resolution declaring 'homosexual practice' to be 'incompatible with Scripture', some commentators have been content to suppose that the bishops of the global South suffer from a lack of biblical sophistication of the kind that is simply assumed by the modern West. This supposition however, reminiscent of the paternalism that marked the colonial missionary enterprise of the nineteenth century, fails to account for the opposition to Gene Robinson's election by some Europeans and Americans as well as the support for that election among a growing number of clergy and laity in the global South. Indeed, dismantling the cultural and religious reception of Sodom's fate as the very same fate that awaits all 'homosexuals' describes a task still under way in many parts of the North Atlantic, let alone those regions of the Anglican Communion still uncertain about their (neo)colonial relationship to Canterbury.

For those reasons among others, focusing exclusively on the operation of neo-colonial 'control' and 'imposition' fails to address the complexities inherent to dealing with questions of human sexuality and gender. The ecclesial fault-lines in the Anglican Communion apparently drawn by 'homosexuality' do not cut neatly between North Atlantic cultures and the perspectives of African, Asian, and South American Anglicans. Instead, the emerging realignment of ecclesial power and politics among Anglicans more closely resembles the gerrymandering of legislative districts with which Americans are so familiar. The 2005 creation of CANA (the Convocation of Anglicans in North America) by Archbishop Akinola illustrates the fluidity of such affiliations, as CANA in effect represents an ideological rather than a geographical jurisdiction in the United States.

In both northern and southern hemispheres, better or 'more sophisticated' biblical interpretation of key passages will not suffice for addressing these inter-provincial complexities. To a large extent the biblical texts are irrelevant, given the cultural history of sodomy in the religious imagination and its entanglements with the socio-religious construction of gendered relations. The Colenso affair of the nineteenth century still proves illustrative here. One might suppose in that case that polygamy, though troubling and not ideal, could be tolerated within certain limits in light of the biblical precedent for such a practice in the Hebrew Scrip-tures; or, as was the case at both the 1988 and 1998 Lambeth Conferences, for the sake of the economic well-being of women. More likely, however, as the tenor of contemporary debates suggests, the (limited) tolerance of polygamy is directly proportional to the lack of any threat it poses to the gendered order of marital relations, more particularly to the patriarchal ordering of a household.[6] Sodomy, by contrast, achieves its conceptual force and effect precisely in its betrayal of male power and privilege. Rather than the historical-critical method of modern biblical scholarship, the gendered ordering of human relationships has gerrymandered the

---

[6] Equally illuminating on this point is no less an 'Anglican' figure than King Henry VIII. His desire for a male heir, which his wife Catherine of Aragon was apparently unable to provide, led some to appeal to the practice of polygamy among the patriarchs of ancient Israel as a solution to Henry's predicament rather than divorce. Among them was no less a Reformation figure than Martin Luther— who had been asked to advise Henry on this matter—and who opposed divorce and thus proposed bigamy instead (see Thompson 2007: 84).

Anglican Communion. If that is the case, then the American cultural arc traced from homophile to gay-liberation movements may well be less significant than second-wave feminism, including the ordination of women, for analysing the reception history of Genesis 19. Understanding that history as a thoroughly gendered history sheds considerable light on the ecclesial machinations of early twenty-first-century Anglican Christians. In that light, controversies over 'homosexuality' point to a broader horizon of concern for Anglicans and for Christianity more generally—the gendered order of God's creation.

Gendered Love, Idolatry, and the Future of Anglican Christianity

The 2004 Windsor Report belongs to a long history of attempts to articulate whether and how Anglican Christians worldwide constitute a single 'communion' of churches. Speculation in some quarters that the Report would prompt a significant 'realignment' of the Communion fails to appreciate how much the Communion had already realigned well before the Report's commission began its work. The decision in the 1970s and 1980s to ordain women to the priesthood and especially to the episcopate in a few provinces of the Communion—over the objections of many others—began to redraw Anglican relations in ways that foreshadowed the outcry over Gene Robinson's election in 2003. Indeed, these moments are closely linked. Yet the Windsor Report adopts a surprisingly sanguine posture toward the ordination of women, as if the gendered ordering of ecclesial relations remains distinct from the controversy over 'homosexuality', and even more that the question of women's ordination is in some way 'settled'. To the contrary, for many provinces in the Communion (including within the North Atlantic) the ordination of women continues to cause as much consternation as the ordination of gay and lesbian people and the liturgical blessing of their relationships.

The strong bond between these issues appeared clearly and quickly in the complaints levelled against the 2006 election of Katharine Jefferts Schori as the Presiding Bishop of ECUSA, the first woman to serve as an Anglican primate and who, not coincidentally, publicly supported Gene Robinson's election as bishop of New Hampshire. The very same front-page *New York Times* article that first reported her election also reported the objections to it, with critics citing her election as further evidence of ECUSA's 'drift from the shared beliefs of the Anglican Communion' (Banarjee 2006). Critics of Bishop Schori's primatial authority may object to her gender or to her support for Gene Robinson and same-sex couples more generally. In the end, however, both objections spring from the same theological conviction: Her position and her policies violate God's own gendered order of creation. How, or even whether, this fundamental theology of gender will be addressed, I would argue, will determine the future shape of the Anglican Communion.

Anglican Christianity and the worldwide communion it generated have undergone nearly constant revisions and rearticulations since the sixteenth century English Reformation. It now appears that twenty-first-century realignments will be shaped not so much by 'homosexuality' per se but by the construal of human love and intimacy as divinely gendered. Still more fundamental in this view, particular relationships ought to represent in iconic fashion the broader social and institutional relations of the Church as it bears witness to God's providential order of creation. Just as the resilience of sodomy in the religious imagination reflects a theological commitment to the gendered ordering of marriage, a properly ordered marriage reflects a well-ordered society, which in turn conforms to the Creator's own design. The reception history of Genesis 19 is, in other words, a thoroughly gendered history and with implications extending well beyond the question of including gay and lesbian people in Christian churches.

The tenacity of this broader theological paradigm sheds further light on why historical-critical method in biblical scholarship so often fails to gain any real traction in ecclesial debates around sexuality and marriage. Considering the reception history of texts like Genesis 19 is to consider how such texts are received into an already established set of religious convictions about and cultural commitments to a gendered construction of reality. So while Rowan Williams maintains that only the human relationship rather than a particular sexual act suffices as a proper location for theological reflection on sexual ethics (1996: 63), this claim ignores the extent to which human relationships are always already gendered, both for biblical writers and in contemporary societies. Richard Kirker reminds us that few, if any, commentators would deny that Jesus enjoyed intimate, loving relationships with other men; he just didn't commit sodomy with them (2005: 327). To do so would have violated the dignity and privilege of being a man in a gendered society, the horror of which is dramatically memorialized in the fate suffered by the citizens of Sodom. Or as William Stacy Johnson notes, frequently overlooked in the comparisons of Genesis 19 and Judges 19 is that the men in both stories simply assumed that raping a woman was more acceptable than raping a man (2006: 49).

Noting and analysing degrees of acceptability, however, risks missing the severity of the gender distinctions reflected in these ancient texts. Pairing Genesis 19 with the Levitical holiness code makes those distinctions clearer. There is ample historical precedent for reading Genesis 19 through a Levitical lens, stretching back to the fourth-century *Apostolic Constitutions*. While the standard reading of Leviticus 18:22 would prohibit anal intercourse between men, the 'abomination' identified in that text resides quite explicitly in treating a man as one would treat a woman.

The absence of any parallel prohibition against sex between women underscores the male privilege enshrined in this text (Boyarin 2007: 136). Thus, while the rape of the concubine in Judges 19 is clearly unfortunate and deserving of punishment (though mostly as one would be punished for stealing private property), Leviticus clarifies the underlying logic of both Genesis 19 and Judges 19: truly horrifying would be doing the same thing to a man.

The sanctity of these gender distinctions, and especially of male privilege, while clearly rooted in ancient texts and practices, thoroughly inflects the dynamics of modern western culture. As for biblical writers so also for the modern West, 'homosexuals' provoke such intense and passionate controversy not because of their loving or committed relationships but because their sexual acts are perceived as a transgression of a properly gendered order of reality. George Chauncey's research in World War I-era American society proves particularly illuminating in that regard, especially his analysis of the gendered construction of sexual behaviour in the American military. Chauncey investigated the fallout from a 1919 naval investigation of 'homosexuality' in Newport, Rhode Island, which quickly spread to the local ministerial association, as some of the sailors staying at the Newport YMCA accused a prominent Episcopal priest of making sexual advances in the course of his pastoral care. The ministerial association, including the Episcopal bishop of Rhode Island, vigorously defended the accused so as to prevent the accusations from spreading to other ministers. The concern here, however, had little if anything to do with a potential epidemic of sexual misconduct; instead, as Chauncey demonstrates, the association worried about the gender implications associated with the affectations of class and pastoral compassion. As upper-class clergy offered compassionate care to working-class sailors, the sailors perceived this care as effeminate and therefore a solicitation of sexual relations. The guilt or innocence of the accused priest mattered less to the ministerial association than defending the sexual propriety of their own gendered religious practice. Significantly, the defence they offered relied on arguing that masculinity is not compromised in acts of compassion (Chauncey 1989: 308). Put in another way, just because a man is religious doesn't make him effeminate. The fact that these ministers felt compelled to make such an argument is as striking as the argument itself.

Chauncey's research points more broadly to the explicitly gendered construal of what male 'homosexuality' implies for men and masculinity in American culture, which is precisely the issue lurking behind the history of sodomy's religious and cultural invention. As Chauncey's study implies, the culture wars with which American society has been living for decades, now roiling the worldwide Anglican Communion, are fuelled not so much by the spectre of sexual perversion among Christian clergy as by the threat same-sex relationships pose to the gendered ordering of both church and state, if not also the whole of God's creation.

Andrew Carey, son of the former archbishop of Canterbury George Carey, underscores the importance of this gender paradigm by declaring that Scripture's prohibition against 'homosexuality' derives not from a selective reading of a few passages (like Genesis 19 or Leviticus 18) but from 'an entire theology and anthropology arising from the creation narrative'. The relatively few passages dealing explicitly with 'homosexuality', he argues, 'only make sense in the light of the bias of scripture towards the complementarity of men and women as the ideal of God's created order' (quoted in Bates 2004: 39).

The notion of order itself predominates in this theological paradigm in so far as the proper ordering of gender relations conforms necessarily to divine order, the abandonment of which would signal an imminent collapse of human society on a broad scale. While an extreme, if not alarmist, position to some, this view informed the dissenting opinion of US Supreme Court Justice Antonin Scalia concerning *Lawrence* v. *Texas*. Society has a right to reject 'homosexuality', he argued, for to do otherwise would result in a 'massive disruption of the current social order' (quoted in Johnson 2007: 162). Edith Humphrey likewise maintains this broader, gendered horizon in her analysis, which for her cuts to the very heart of Christian faith and doctrine: 'The difference in gender of husband and wife, united in marriage points to the wonder of the Trinity, our ultimate pattern of "other-but-same in relationship." Homoerotic relations reject the gift of sexual otherness and cannot echo the nature of the Trinity' (2004: 36). In short, Gene Robinson's episcopate represents not just sexual immorality but heresy, an abandonment of historic Christian faith.

As with every previous generation, Anglican Christians of the twenty-first century face the question of not whether but how the Anglican Communion will 'realign' and what shape it will adopt for its inter-provincial relations. The Windsor Report provides one possible approach by creating and/or strengthening various 'instruments of unity'. While some have complained about the centralization of this approach, or its 'quasi-papal' model of authority (Countryman 2005: 5), others have objected to the Report's uncritical if not naive adoption of Scripture as the basis for Anglican unity. As Lisa Isherwood has suggested, the Report generally fails to distinguish between unity and uniformity regarding the interpretation of Scripture and how such interpretation ought to proceed. Even more telling, while the Report accepts that 'scripture may be open to regional reading . . . gendered reading is not even mentioned' (2005: 50).

As I have been proposing here, the reductionistic career of Genesis 19 in Christian history has served a double purpose simultaneously: to vilify both religiously and politically a whole segment of the human population (same-gender-loving people), and to maintain theologically the inferior status of another (women). The deeply gendered theological construction of love and of creation that this history has both generated and justified has also served to obscure a broader range of insights that Genesis 19 might otherwise have prompted. Fresh readings of Sodom's fate might suggest how the text itself contains the seeds of unmaking the peculiar history of its reception.

Any such fresh reading would begin not with the biblical text but with the history of (mis)reading Genesis 19 as a story about 'homosexuality', which illustrates the very posture of Sodom's citizens toward God that the story condemns. This reading would help to explain the virtual lack of sexual immorality in later biblical texts that catalogue Sodom's vices, as well as the otherwise strangely uneven treatment of Genesis 19 and Judges 19 among both biblical writers and later commentators. The story of Sodom's demise, in contrast to the fate of the concubine in Judges, turns not on 'unnatural' sexual acts nor even violent ones. It turns rather on the arrogant attempt of Sodom's citizens to seize the divine on their own terms—to *know* God when and how they choose. As Maggie Ross has noted, 'the Sodomites are sexually indiscriminate. Lot offers his daughters, knowing that they will do just as well as the "two men" who are the presenting and tangible aspects of the mercy of God. The men of Sodom wish to grasp and know these surrogates to give themselves the illusion of grasping God' (2007: p. xxiii).

Ross thus departs from the more typical mode of contextualizing Genesis 19 with reference to ancient sexual practices and opens a much broader horizon of engagement with the text and the history of its reception. Echoing the oldest Christian commentaries on this text, Ross draws our attention to the metaphorical use of sexuality in the story of Sodom; the story is not about sex but about God, and more particularly idolatry, as Edith Humphrey has also argued, but for different reasons. To read Genesis 19 as a story about sexual misconduct, Ross insists, is to miss the point. 'The story of Sodom', she writes, 'is a mordant satire on the idolatry of that great shopping mall at the end of the Dead Sea, a consumer culture that can inculturate religion only as a commodity by attempting to grasp an aspect of God' (2007: p. xxiii). I would argue that this reading of Genesis 19 and its curious career in Christian history—a reading that foregrounds the perennial human desire for certainty in our knowledge of God and on our own terms—this reading and its implications for Christian faith and practice will shape the future of the Anglican Communion's provincial relations.

Today's vast marketplace of religious commodities, no less than its ancient analogue in Sodom, presents a nearly irresistible temptation to choose swift gratification and the illusory security of idols. Those engaged in internecine religious debate seem always to face this temptation and to risk replicating the posture of the Sodomites in their attempt to seize God for themselves. The bitter conflict over human sexuality and gendered relations is no exception. As Elizabeth Stuart has suggested, the intractable ecclesial impasse marked by lesbian and gay relationships has led both sides in this stalemate to create an idol from the institution of marriage (2003: 3). So even as the text of Genesis 19 has retreated from centre-stage, sodomy continues to shape the drama of Anglican Christianity, not as the sin of 'homosexuality' but with its ancient meaning made new: idolatry. In that light, the allusion to Genesis 19 in Matthew's Gospel still stands as a cautionary tale for the Anglican Communion and for all Christians, regardless of gender or sexual orientation. For Matthew's Jesus, Sodom and Gomorrah's sin was the failure to extend hospitality—not to each other but to God. If subsequent Christian communities had followed this Matthean lead in defining 'sodomy', the reception history of Genesis 19 would surely look quite different; and indeed, so would the history of ecclesial conflict.

WORKS CITED

BAILEY, DERRICK SHERWIN (1955), *Homosexuality and the Western Christian Tradition*. London: Longmans, Green.

BANARJEE, NEELA (2006), 'Woman is Named Episcopal Leader', *New York Times*, 19 June.

BATES, STEPHEN (2004), *A Church at War: Anglicans and Homosexuality*. London and New York: I. B. Tauris.

BOSWELL, JOHN (1980), *Christianity, Social Tolerance, and Homosexuality: Gay People in Western Europe from the Beginning of the Christian Era to the Fourteenth Century*. Chicago and London: University of Chicago Press.

BOYARIN, DANIEL (2007), 'Against Rabbinic Sexuality: Textual Reasoning and the Jewish Theology of Sex', in Gerard Loughlin (ed.), *Queer Theology: Rethinking the Western Body*, 131–46. Oxford: Blackwell Publishing.

CARDEN, MICHAEL (2004), *Sodomy: A History of a Christian Biblical Myth*. London: Equinox.

CHAUNCEY, GEORGE (1989), 'Christian Brotherhood or Sexual Perversion? Homosexual Identities and the Construction of Sexual Boundaries in the World War I Era', in Martin Duberman (ed.), *Hidden from History: Reclaiming the Gay and Lesbian Past*, 294–317. New York: New American Library.

COUNTRYMAN, WILLIAM L. (2005), 'Politics, Polity, and the Bible as Hostage', in Andrew Linzey and Richard Kirker (eds.), *Gays and the Future of Anglicanism: Responses to the Windsor Report*, 2–16. Winchester and New York: O Books.

GITARI, DAVID (1984), 'The Church and Polygamy', *Transformation*, 1/1: 3.

GRIFFIN, HORACE L. (2006), *Their Own Receive Them Not: African American Lesbians and Gays in Black Churches*. Cleveland, Ohio: Pilgrim Press.

HUMPHREY, EDITH (2004), 'What God Hath Not Joined: Why Marriage was Designed for Male and Female', *Christianity Today*, 48/9: 36.

ISHERWOOD, LISA (2005), 'Scripture for Liberation', in Andrew Linzey and Richard Kirker (eds.), *Gays and the Future of Anglicanism: Responses to the Windsor Report*, 49–59. Winchester and New York: O Books.

JENKINS, PHILIP (2006), *The New Faces of Christianity: Believing the Bible in the Global South*. London: Oxford University Press.

JOHNSON, WILLIAM STACEY (2006), *A Time to Embrace: Same-Gender Relationships in Religion, Law, and Politics*. Grand Rapids, Mich.: Eerdmans.

——(2007), 'Empire and Order: The Gospel and Same-Gender Relationships', *Biblical Theology Bulletin*, 37/4: 161–73.

JORDAN, MARK (1997), *The Invention of Sodomy in Christian Theology*. Chicago and London: University of Chicago Press.

KENNEDY, PHILIP (2005), 'God's Good News for Gays', in Andrew Linzey and Richard Kirker (eds.), *Gays and the Future of Anglicanism: Responses to the Windsor Report*, 299–314. Winchester and New York: O Books.

KIRKER, RICHARD (2005), 'Afterword: Why Gays Refuse To Be Unchurched', in Andrew Linzey and Richard Kirker (eds.), *Gays and the Future of Anglicanism: Responses to the Windsor Report*, 326–34. Winchester and New York: O Books.

Lambeth Commission on Communion (2004), *The Windsor Report*. London: Anglican Communion Office.

MARTIN, DALE (2006), *Sex and the Single Savior: Gender and Sexuality in Biblical Interpretation*. Louisville, Ky.: Westminster/John Knox Press.

ROSS, MAGGIE (2007), *Pillars of Flame: Power, Priesthood, and Spiritual Maturity*. New York: Seabury Books.

SACHS, WILLIAM (1993), *The Transformation of Anglicanism: From State Church to Global Communion*. Cambridge: Cambridge University Press.

SCROGGS, ROBIN (1983), *The New Testament and Homosexuality: Contextual Background for a Contemporary Debate*. Philadelphia: Fortress Press.

STUART, ELIZABETH (2003), *Gay and Lesbian Theologies: Repetitions with Critical Difference*. Hampshire and Burlington: Ashgate Publishing.

THATCHER, ADRIAN (2005), '"Impaired" Communion: Some Questions', in Andrew Linzey and Richard Kirker (eds.), *Gays and the Future of Anglicanism: Responses to the Windsor Report*, 274–82. Winchester and New York: O Books.

THOMPSON, JOHN L. (2007), *Reading the Bible with the Dead: What You Can Learn from the History of Exegesis that You Can't Learn from Exegesis Alone*. Grand Rapids, Mich.: Eerdmans.

WILLIAMS, ROWAN (1996), 'The Body's Grace', in Charles Hefling (ed.), *Our Selves, Our Souls and Bodies: Sexuality and the Household of God*, 58–68. Cambridge: Cowley Publications.

FURTHER READING

GREENBERG, STEVEN (2004), *Wrestling with God and Men: Homosexuality in the Jewish Tradition*. Madison, Wisc.: University of Wisconsin Press.

HALPERIN, DAVID M. (2002), *How To Do the History of Homosexuality*. Chicago: University of Chicago Press.

JORDAN, MARK D. (2002), *The Ethics of Sex*. Oxford: Blackwell Publishers.

NISSINEN, MARTTI (1998), *Homoeroticism in the Biblical World: A Historical Perspective*. Minneapolis: Fortress Press.

O'DONOVAN, OLIVER (2008), *Church in Crisis: The Gay Controversy and the Anglican Communion*. Eugene, Oreg.: Cascade Books.

ROGERS, JACK (2006), *Jesus, the Bible, and Homosexuality: Explode the Myths, Heal the Church*. Louisville, Ky.: Westminster/John Knox Press.

CHAPTER 29

....

EXODUS IN EARLY TWENTIETH-CENTURY AMERICA: CHARLES REYNOLDS BROWN AND LAWRENCE LANGNER

....

SCOTT M. LANGSTON

THE questions scholars are raising in regard to the biblical text are changing. While this change is slow, it nonetheless is occurring. More and more scholars are expanding the range of questions from those related to the text's form, content, and 'original' settings to those concerned with the Bible's impact on various cultures and times. To see this development one only has to look at the addition within the last few years of the 'Use, Influence, and Impact of the Bible' section to the Society of Biblical Literature Annual Meeting, the increasing number of publications devoted to the Bible's reception history, such as *The Blackwell Bible Commentary* series and this handbook itself, as well as the establishment of Oxford's Centre for Reception History of the Bible. With increasing frequency biblical scholars are asking, 'What does the Bible do?', in recognition that the Bible's impact on individuals, societies, and cultures (and vice-versa) is an important part of understanding the Bible holistically. Unquestionably, understanding a text's inception and formation remains at the heart of biblical studies, but the move to study its wider impact promises to engage a larger number of fields and practitioners and broaden the horizons of biblical scholars.

As part of this holistic focus Exodus has proven especially fertile, particularly as a paradigm for critiquing, challenging, and/or overthrowing systems and groups deemed to be oppressive. Interacting with a variety of outside factors, the biblical text has proven flexible enough to accommodate a multitude of distinctions, visions, and solutions. Its narrative of a suffering people who with divine help overcome a more powerful oppressor has inspired individuals and groups since its inception. Using the narrative as an authoritative framework for understanding and reacting to their own plight, countless groups have found hope, even identifying in day-to-day life divine actions taken on their behalf. Furthermore, the clear distinctions made in the biblical exodus between good and evil have allowed subsequent readers to draw contemporary parallels and then articulate visions of a Promised Land that offer alternatives to their current conditions.

THE SOCIAL, ECONOMIC, AND INDUSTRIAL IN EXODUS

Moses' words to Pharaoh, 'Let my people go' (Exod. 5:1), have in one form or another served as a rallying-cry for oppressed groups throughout the centuries. Charles Reynolds Brown, a Congregational minister and later dean of Yale Divinity School from 1911 to 1928, affirmed this cry as 'God's word of searching rebuke to industrial conditions unjust and degrading; it was His appeal to the powerful and prosperous class which was responsible for those conditions to change them; and it was also the proclamation of His interest in and His purpose for each humble toiler' (1910: 89–90). Brown read and applied Exodus to the economic conditions of his day, but oppressed people living in different times and circumstances would have had little trouble making his words fit their situations. They too would readily identify themselves as the people on whose behalf God had taken up their cause against unjust abuses of power. Groups as diverse as African-Americans, Jews, American colonists, Confederates, Boer Voortrekkers, and black South Africans have all found Exodus useful in challenging their Egyptians (respectively, white Americans, Christians, the British, the United States, and white South Africans) (Langston 2006: 81–5, 138–53). Brown's application of Exodus illustrates some of its elements to which readers across the centuries have responded.

This future dean of Yale Divinity School read Exodus during a period of great social, economic, and industrial upheaval. In the latter part of the nineteenth and early twentieth centuries the United States experienced rapid industrialization, accompanied by the growth of large corporations and trusts that dominated particular industries (for overviews of the period, see Edwards 2006, Gould 2001, and Trachtenberg 2007). These developments created tremendous economic pressures, especially as the gulf between rich and poor widened considerably and wage-earners struggled to combat the virtually unchecked power of corporate owners. Both Americans and immigrants streamed into cities searching for work, all the while creating daunting problems for officials, among them adequate housing, jobs with livable wages, and sanitary living spaces. Many lived in wretched conditions, and working for wages came to be known as wage-slavery. With little government support for their cause, some workers attempted to form unions, although these were unpopular with most Americans. Corporate owners did not hesitate to use harsh tactics, and those who joined unions were typically characterized as being un-American or sympathetic to socialism. A national debate arose that, among other things, had Americans arguing over the federal government's role and responsibility to respond to such issues, society's duty to help individuals adversely affected by circumstances often beyond their control, and an individual's responsibility for their own fate. By the time Brown delivered the Lyman Beecher Lectures at Yale University in 1905–6, Progressivism, the Social Gospel, and Christian Socialism were among many responses advocating a more active part to be taken by society as a whole and government in particular for solving these problems, while others rose in support of the Gospel of Wealth, free market competition, and laissez-faire government as expressions of individual freedom and responsibility.

Brown entitled his lecture series 'The Social Message of the Modern Pulpit' (later published in 1910 under that same title), arguing that the 'supreme need of the hour' was 'making thorough application of the principles of the Gospel of Jesus Christ to the conditions of every-day life' (Brown 1910: 4–5). By this, he meant addressing economic and industrial developments and their concomitant social impact from a Christian perspective. To do so he turned to the Bible, emphasizing the social aspects of its message. He understood the origins of the 'Hebrew Church' and the Christian Church as having occurred in experiences of 'social readjustment', the former arising from early Christians holding their possessions in common (something Brown frankly admitted was 'voluntary communism') and the latter developing in the Israelite exodus from Egyptian slavery (ibid. 5–7). Thus the Bible seemed particularly well suited to address the day's social problems, which led Brown to assert: 'The labor question is always more than an economic question, a struggle as to hours and wages—it is preeminently a spiritual question wherein the souls of men made in the likeness and image of God are at stake' (ibid. 65). He understood labour and economics to be more than means for supplying physical wants and needs, although this was important. The economic order must, in his words, 'become a divinely appointed agency for making men', that is, it must build up 'human values' and produce 'high moral results'. In striving to construct a 'more equitable social order', he envisioned the Church fulfilling its role 'by shaming low ideals, by overcoming greed, by opposing that lack of consideration between man and man which lies at the root of the trouble', rather than 'devising economic schemes' or 'proposing schedules of wages'; the Church, after all, was not an 'economist' (ibid. 246, 248–9). This interpretive framework guided him in focusing on certain elements in Exodus, while looking past—perhaps unconsciously—others.

Brown contextualized Exodus socially, economically, and industrially, leading him to conclude that it was 'the story of an ancient labor movement' that addressed 'the relation of God to the industrial and political, to the social and religious well-being of a whole people'. He subordinated individual applications in favour of a group reading, in this case, 'the freeing and training, the humanizing and spiritualizing of a whole race of men'. He believed that anyone could 'instantly' see how useful Exodus would be 'for the whole movement toward social and industrial betterment in our own time' (ibid. 70–2). Of course, Exodus has a long tradition of being interpreted from the perspective of the individual; its many characters—Amram, Jocheved, Miriam, Moses, Aaron, Zipporah, Pharaoh, Pharoah's daughter, and others—have provided readers with ample opportunities to use it as a commentary and guide to individual experiences. What is more, texts like the Ten Commandments (Exod. 20:1–17) have commonly been applied as a standard of individual morality. These readings foreground individual feats and experiences rather than those of the Israelites as a whole (see, for instance, the numerous biographies and novels about Moses, ranging from ancient works such as Philo's *On the Life of Moses* and Gregory of Nyssa's *The Life of Moses*, to twentieth-century works like Louis Untermeyer's *Moses*, Sholem Asch's *Moses*, and Zora Neale Hurston's *Moses, Man of the Mountain*). For these readers the collective Israelites play a supporting role to that of the individual characters. The interplay of individuals and groups in Exodus, however, allows emphasis on either perspective. Brown chose the latter—finding it 'profoundly significant' that the book's main theme was not 'individual safety and culture', but 'the regeneration of an entire people through a radical modification of the industrial and political conditions under which they lived' (Brown 1910: 72)—and interpreted and applied the book accordingly.

Reading Exodus primarily as the story of the Israelites' deliverance causes Brown to de-emphasize the book as a chronicle of Moses' feats. Moses, then, acts as an 'industrial deliverer' and kills an Egyptian for abusing an Israelite (Exod. 2:11–14) as an expression of 'race loyalty and class feeling, instant sympathy with the oppressed, and that genuinely democratic spirit which ever characterized him'. Simply put, Moses was a 'warm-hearted champion of the rights of the people', someone who, like Abraham Lincoln, encountered social injustice early in life (in Lincoln's case, slavery) and vowed to do something about it (Brown 1910: 111–14). While interpreters since ancient times have typically used this event to extol Moses, casting it as an act indicative of his high character (Langston 2006: 35–7), Brown understands it as a necessary step in the development of the industrial deliverance movement—the emergence of 'worthy leaders', the lack of which Brown bemoaned in the modern counterpart. He concludes that if the modern movement for industrial freedom is to succeed, it needs leaders who, like Moses, 'come up from the ranks', rather than 'wise professors of economics from the university, or canny millionaires' (Brown 1910: 122–3). Thus, the story of Moses killing the Egyptian becomes more about the movement for freedom than about Moses himself, and demonstrates how the social, economic, and industrial concerns of Exodus converge with those of contemporary American society to make the text useful.

EXODUS AS A SOURCE OF CRITIQUE

In addition to being fertile ground for interpretations shaped by both individual and group concerns, Exodus has been especially useful for groups critiquing and challenging oppressive social institutions or peoples. By virtue of its place within Jewish and Christian scripture, it provides an authoritative framework, as well as a vocabulary and conceptual basis for building and carrying out these critiques. Oppressed groups can with canonical authority identify their opponents as Egyptians and themselves as Israelites, thereby clearly distinguishing hero and villain and helping them chip away at the dominant group's power and authority within that society. This is exactly what Brown did as he attempted to challenge the capitalistic and industrial status quo in America.

Brown connected several passages in Exodus with what he believed were evils in contemporary American economics. He turned to the very words of Exodus to illustrate the American workers' plight at the hands of capitalists and industrialists and legitimate their grievances. For instance, he contended that if the words 'Egypt' and 'Israel' were removed from Exodus 1 the chapter would read 'as an accurate description of many situations in the life of our own Republic' (Brown 1910: 77–8). He easily correlated the suffering of the Israelites at the hands of the Egyptians with that endured by American workers, both labouring long hours for low wages, living in deplorable conditions, and possessing little power to change their respective situations. Arduous labour resulting only in poverty for the masses seemed to Brown to be the modern manifestation of the ancient Israelites' plight, and led him to assert: 'Here in our own world of modern industry the prosperous and the fortunate have forced many of the children of America to serve with rigor, and have made their lives bitter with hard bondage.' In a series of rhetorical questions, he drove the point home:

Are there not wage-slaves among us—the main difference being that their virtual owners have now been freed from the responsibility of caring for them when they are sick or unemployed? ... Are there not hundreds of tired clerks and book-keepers, insufficiently paid, working often far into the night, in close, dark quarters, with abundance of bad air, sometimes in those hideous little 'upper berths' of offices put in against the ceiling like swallows' nests to save floor space and rent? ... Have not New York and Chicago and San Francisco something to say about lives made bitter with hard bondage, as well as Thebes and Karnak?

Having established the identity of modern-day Israelites, he made explicit that of their Pharaohs: 'Pharaohs are being bred to-day in modern counting rooms as they were in the palaces along the Nile ... ' Furthermore, he implicated the officers of the Standard Oil Company who, according to Brown, in 1902 raised the price of coal-oil—a fuel used especially by the poorer classes to cook and light and heat homes—just as winter approached and during a time of significant coal shortages (created by striking coal workers). The connection seemed clear: 'Indifference, inhumanity, cruelty to the helpless—alas, they are not ancient history, for the advance in the price of coal-oil was but a modern echo of Pharaoh's words, "Who is the Lord, that I should obey his voice and let these people go?"' (ibid. 77–9).

Brown acknowledged that wage-workers were not flawless, nor were all employers evil. He instead placed the ultimate blame on an economic system based on ruthless competition and driven by demand for cheaper and cheaper goods at all levels— from the manufacturer to the customer. The American worker in turn suffered as manufacturers and employers competed to provide these cheaper goods often by paying low wages. He concluded: 'We cannot become partners in Pharaoh's inhumanity and say: "Who are all these unknown workers, that we should care for them?"' (ibid. 94, 98–9, 103–4). Ancient Egypt, of course, was not built on capitalism, but Brown was not reading the text as a historical critic. Instead, he was operating as a social critic. The biblical text's identification of a power (Pharaoh) that abused a people (the Israelites) for its own gain made the differences in economic systems of little import. What mattered was the social injustice, and at that point there were plenty of similarities between the biblical Israelites and modern American workers. Thus, Brown could invoke the story's biblical authority on behalf of the labouring classes and draw clear lines between right and wrong in American industry.

Not only did texts from Exodus aid his ability to distinguish hero and villain in American society, but they also enabled him to critique the way economic gains were distributed throughout American society, or what Brown called 'the bread-and butter problem'. Turning to Exodus 16 and the distribution of manna among the Israelites, he pointed out how the manna was distributed democratically, 'each man according to his eating'. With this principle sounding 'the note of an equitably organized industrial system', no leisure class lived off the labour of others, nor did the strong unfairly monopolize resources. Brown made it clear that this principle applied to more than just manna: 'It is surely the divine intention that the land and the mines, the forests and the water-power, shall all be administered, not in the interest of the privileged few, but for the good of the producing many.' He, however, did not go so far as advocating socialism, but did affirm private owner-ship of land—at least when guided by this principle from Exodus. Individuals or corporations who 'created an unnatural and injurious monopoly of these common resources' destroyed any justification for private ownership of those particular resources. Nor did Brown call for absolute equality among all members of socie-ty—he recognized that differences in ability created inequality—but he did urge a distribution of resources that left no one in need, something at which the American system failed miserably (ibid. 185–92).

Since antiquity readers of Exodus 16 have found varying ideas within it, empha-sizing things such as the provision of God, the greatness of Moses, the truth of Christianity, different ways of expressing faith, and even divine justification for vegetarianism (Langston 2006: 171–82). Indeed, in each instance the interpreter's social setting helps bring these readings to light. Brown was no different. He had found what he believed was a solution to the ills produced by America's industrial system, and by highlighting the positive aspects of the biblical system he could critique its contemporary counterpart, pointing out how it fell short of the biblical ideal. Thus Exodus helped Brown in his critique by portraying a system in which no one did without (all the Israelites had plenty of manna), and thereby providing a foil against which he could easily expose the deficiencies of the American system. When confronted with the biblical ideal, he had only to discover its secret, which for him was the principle: 'each man according to his eating'. Brown combined this principle with another he found in Exodus 20:24: 'An altar shalt thou make, and offer thereon burnt offerings and peace offerings.' Simply put, this verse espoused the necessity of a sacrificial life. Brown recognized that the sacrificial system often seemed meaningless to modern readers, but he still saw symbolic value in it; that is, it 'aided in the development of that habit of mind which subordinates private interest to the larger good'. This applied to both capitalists and labour unions, and led him to decry increased personal extravagance manifested in such things as frequenting expensive hotels and owning palatial yachts while the poor struggled to survive and child labour continued (ibid. 219–27). Once again, Brown chose a social application over an individual one. Both were connected, but the social received prominence, while Exodus provided the vocabulary, concepts, and justification to carry out his critique.

EXODUS AS A SOURCE OF HOPE

Throughout its reception history Exodus has provided hope to oppressed groups. Its improbable story of the powerful Egyptian Pharaoh being overthrown by tortured and abused slaves who possessed few resources yet received divine aid has helped groups maintain hope in miserable circumstances. Those groups mentioned earlier in this chapter, as well as many more, have been inspired by the Exodus story in their struggles to survive and obtain better living conditions. Undoubtedly, the text's emphasis on material aspects such as labour conditions, violence, and the struggle between oppressor and oppressed have combined with its supernatural elements to help oppressed groups identify tangible evidence of the divine working on their behalf in contemporary events. This, in turn, inspires hope.

Charles Reynolds Brown's use of Exodus illustrates how the text has been a source of hope. Confronted with oppressive social conditions, the American poor had little reason to feel confident they could overcome powerful corporations and wealthy individuals in their struggle to survive. Brown, however, was convinced otherwise, finding in Exodus a guide for understanding modern events. Turning to the plagues sent by God to force Pharaoh to free the Israelites (Exod. 6–11), Brown asserted: 'it is forever true that selfish inhumanity in organized life will be overtaken by industrial darkness and storm; it will be stung and bitten by myriads of petty annoyances; it will be made sick and sore by the outbreak of social disease.' He, however, did not leave this as a general principle, but connected it to a specific modern event—'the white plague', or tuberculosis. Citing the vast numbers of Americans infected with this disease, especially those living and working in the cities' tenement houses and sweat-shops, he declared:

And what does all this frightful menace to the national health mean but a modern embodiment of the truth contained in that old Exodus narrative. God be praised for microbes and bacilli! . . . Out of those wretched tenements, with their pinched faces, narrow chests, and hollow coughs, the voice of God comes, and it says again as it said of old, 'Deliver my people from these inhuman conditions; if thou shalt refuse, I will smite all thy borders with the white plague.'

On the surface it might appear that tuberculosis was a plague inflicted largely upon the poor, but Brown made it clear that tuberculosis knew no class lines and could easily spread if not dealt with by all of American society. What is more, he believed it to be an outward symbol of 'an inner and spiritual peril', a 'moral tuberculosis' that threatened to consume the souls of those in power (Brown 1910: 159, 162–3). The Exodus story's identification of the plagues as the divine medium for liberating the oppressed gave Brown precedence to interpret contemporary events similarly and thus offer the poor some hope that their suffering was not merely the result of their powerlessness, but was indeed the tool of God to bring about their deliverance.

Brown likewise found a harbinger of hope for American workers in the Israelites' Red Sea experience (Exod. 14). Both groups confronted seemingly hopeless situations that threatened their very existence. For Americans, a Red Sea blocked their advance toward 'social amelioration', while at the same time, 'on the right hand there is the greed of many employers who want a lion's share of the general product' and 'on the left hand there is the greed of many misguided wage-earners who clamor for more than is consistent with a successful continuance of the business'. Behind them 'there are the horses and chariots of a bargain-hunting public, wishing to buy goods in abundance at prices lower than they can be produced for under wholesome and equitable conditions'. How could the American poor ever hope to overcome these powerful forces? Switching paradigms to the pillar and cloud that led the Israelites through the wilderness, Brown did not see deliverance coming in a single event, but over years, and reasoned that a people who could develop an industrial system like that of the United States could also develop one with a more equitable way of sharing its wealth. The situation was by no means hopeless. It could be remedied, but Americans must be willing to listen to the divine voice calling to them 'out of the darkness and the cloud, saying: "Speak to the children of America, that they go forward into a more justly administered, economic life"' (Brown 1910: 182–4).

The American poor could take heart even in their bleak situation. Just as the Israelites overcame seemingly insurmountable obstacles, so they too could have the same success if they would be willing to engage in the long struggle to obtain their Promised Land. The Exodus story presented this promise: 'There stands forever on the side of every better impulse in the human heart, every yearning after a truer life, every stirring of the sense of the obligation to others, this same constant, powerful, effective Ally! . . . When the returns are all in, the fact remains that there is One with us stronger than they [i.e. their opponents]' (ibid. 244). Defeat could only occur if the American Israelites failed to move forward in their quest for a more equitable society. While the struggle to obtain this modern Promised Land would be difficult and setbacks would occur, the ultimate outcome was not in doubt. The symptoms of divine deliverance first revealed in Exodus were indeed present in America.

THE FLEXIBILITY OF EXODUS: VISIONS OF THE PROMISED LAND

The ultimate culmination of the Exodus story in the Promised Land has allowed its readers to articulate visions in stark contrast from that of their Egyptians. The contrast between Egyptian slavery and the establishment of the Israelite nation in Canaan, with the intervening developments during the wilderness wanderings, provides groups with a framework for not only expressing discontent with their current circumstances, but also offering an alternative in its place. As has been seen, Charles Reynolds Brown portrayed a social vision quite different from that current in early twentieth-century America. The biblical story has proven flexible enough that, even when readers basically agree on the identity of their Egyptians, different visions of the Promised Land and ways of achieving it can be accommodated. Lawrence Langner, a British-born producer, writer, director, and founder of the Theatre Guild (1918) in New York City, and an internationally known patent attorney, concurs with Brown that the American industrial system had produced many evils, but he articulates a substantially different solution. They in essence agree on the Pharaoh, but disagree on the modern counterparts to Moses and the Promised Land.

Langner expressed his ideas in a 1924 play entitled *Moses: A Play, a Protest, and a Proposal.* He follows Reynolds in decrying the modern industrial system and the materialism it had spawned, but argues that only art can effectively combat the problems arising from materialism. Modern American society had tried to address these issues—albeit ineffectively—through the Mosaic tradition of preaching or legislating against them. Yet Moses, in Langner's eyes, had come to represent the legalism of an industrial age that dehumanized people, essentially turning them into nothing more than machines. He, therefore, calls for a re-evaluation of Moses, or more precisely, of his legacy, while advocating a society that values artistic creation at least as much as creating inventions and businesses (Langner 1924: p. xlv).

Although he does not contest Moses' greatness, Langner reinterprets him by questioning the positive impact of his deeds. He is troubled by western culture having transformed Moses from liberator to lawmaker and thus making him representative of a legalistic tyranny that modern industrialized nations had embraced. Noting how the United States had perverted its original democratic heritage largely under this influence, Langer comments: 'We are no longer the subjects of a Pharaoh or a King George, yet we are indifferent alike to the tyrannies of a Moses or of a cowardly Congress which sells its honor for votes to bullying minorities of fanatics who impose their prohibitions upon the rest of us.' This, no doubt, refers to a host of state and national laws enacted in the 1920s as part of the period's social and political conservatism, including the eighteenth amendment to the US Constitution, which outlawed 'the manufacture, sale, or transportation of intoxicating liquors', otherwise known as Prohibition. Langner also characterizes Moses as a 'nationalist of the first order' because he preached that the Israelites were God's chosen people, something which modern Americans mimicked when they enthusiastically referred to America as 'God's own country'. Believing that this kind of national pride typically creates a patriotism and racial separation that result in war, he criticizes the wave of patriotism that swept the country in the years after World War I and manifested itself in movements such as the Red Scare of 1919–20, declarations of 'one hundred percent Americanism', President Warren G. Harding's frequent repetition of 'America First', the Emergency Immigration Act of 1921 (which established quotas and helped reduce the flow of immigration), and the revival of the Ku Klux Klan with its embrace of pro-American and anti-Catholic, anti-Jewish, anti-immigrant, and anti-African-American sentiments. In a sense,

Moses' legalism and patriotism fed a pharaonic attitude in Americans (Langner 1924: pp. xxi, xxxiii, xxxvi–xxxvii).

More troubling for Langner, though, was how Moses the lawmaker had contributed to America's 'so-called Political Liberty' by inspiring legislation on 'any and all of the problems of humanity'. So pervasive was this 'formula of Moses' that it had 'run riot in the United States'. Controlled by modern materialism and saddled with a legislative mindset, Americans had forgotten people's need for beauty, especially that expressed in art and by craftsmanship that machines could never replicate. Convinced that most people possessed some desire to create, he argued that as the modern industrial system took away opportunities for creating works of beauty, people turned to producing possessions. In Langner's words: 'Men still build for the gods, but they more often build for six percent on the investment' (ibid., pp. xxxvli–xxxvlii, xl).

Langner continues his reappraisal of Moses and Exodus, subtly calling attention to the differences in the text's social context and that of modern America. Wanting to challenge America's materialism, legalism, blind patriotism, and neglect of the arts, he recasts the exodus by making Miriam, not Moses, the hero. Moses' actions no longer receive the benefit of the doubt, but instead are closely scrutinized and ultimately rejected as models for social behaviour. With Miriam representing the artist, and Moses the lawmaker, they argue the merits of their respective traditions throughout Langner's play, and in doing so articulate different visions of the Promised Land. Miriam constantly chides her brother for his legalism and for wanting to lead the Israelites out of Egypt so they can become 'shepherds and cattle raisers, instead of brickmakers and builders'. She implores him to take with them 'all the beauty we have felt in Egypt . . . to teach our people sculpture and all the other crafts'. She realizes, however, that this will never happen, because Moses loves law and produces nothing but temples of justice and invisible images found only in the mind. When Moses expresses disdain for the Israelites' greed, Miriam exhorts him to not be so intolerant and suggests that the people need to be taught to dream of God rather than money. 'People without imagination have never dreamed of Him [i.e. God], for they cannot love a god they cannot see, so they love the wealth which they can see.' When Miriam suggests that making an image of God would teach the people to love him, Moses denounces this as idolatry. Miriam retorts that an image is merely a symbol of God, not an object of worship, but Moses will have nothing of it, exclaiming that God does not need images because 'He manifests Himself by His changeless laws' (ibid. 41–2, 66–9). The biblical text clearly condemns image-making, but Langner rejects its applicability to modern times, showing how a legalism not balanced by the arts actually produces idolatry. While he embraces the text's condemnation of idolatry, he disagrees with its identification of the cause—image-making—and its cure—legalism. He attempts to demonstrate that blindly applying the text's cure for idolatry in ancient times actually creates idolatry in modern times. Modern industrialized societies have essentially used the Bible—undoubtedly unintentionally—to help create an idola-trous society.

Langner continues to press the point as the play moves quickly past the plagues and the exodus, focusing instead on Moses' lawmaking at Sinai. Upon hearing that Moses has forbidden graven images, Miriam thinks Moses is out of control and resolves that his lawmaking must stop. Caleb tells her that Moses had even embarked on a project to supplement Exodus with a book called Deuteronomy: 'in it is to be written every possible law to meet every possible situation.' Undoubt-edly, according to Miriam, Moses will also write all the impossible laws for all the impossible situations. She remembers that even as a child he had 'a mania for rules and regulations. His dogs were the best trained animals in the Palace.' When Jethro—described as 'a sour-looking old man, stern and weather-beaten'—comes looking for Moses, Miriam comments that he is partaking in his favourite pastime since having left Egypt—sitting in judgement (ibid. 107, 109).

Soon Moses and Miriam are debating again. When Moses complains that the people murmur against him, Jethro attributes this to the Israelites not fearing Moses enough, and suggests he should appoint more judges over the people. Miriam, however, disagrees, asserting that if people were taught to love each other they would not need so many laws. Moses finds nothing wrong with love, but contends that it ultimately is not sufficient for maintaining society. 'Men must be ruled by Justice, by rewarding those that do good and punishing them that do evil.' If people fear the law's punishment, they will deal justly with their neighbour. The law gives freedom 'by prohibiting them from doing as they please' and adversely affecting their neighbour. Moses adds later that permitting images will cause Israel to abandon God and make idols. Miriam, however, charges that without artists they will become a nation of traders, moneychangers, and usurers, worshipping their cattle, land, goods, and gold, and coveting their neighbours' property. Moses replies that he has a law forbidding coveting and firmly pro-nounces: 'The law *shall* be obeyed.' Miriam remains equally adamant, telling Moses that the law banning images is the worst he has made because it turns a God-given desire into a sin, and when enacted in the name of God it makes people hate all laws. Undaunted, Moses resolves to ascend Sinai and chisel the law in stone; Miriam charges that he has become a fanatic. The rift between the two continues to widen, with Moses essentially banishing Miriam after the golden calf incident. Years pass, and Miriam dies. With the Israelites on the brink of the Promised Land, Moses listens to them quarrel over who will get the best land and concludes that Miriam had been right after all—his legalism had caused the people to be even more materialistic. He, 'a lonely, broken old man', watches the Israelites enter the Promised Land, each giving 'a barbaric war-cry, brandishing his weapons, his eyes gleaming at the promise of rich plunder'. Langner's point is clear—materialism cannot be solved merely by making laws; such an obsession leads only to increased materialism, which in turn leads to war. The parallel with modern society, fresh from its first world war, could not be clearer (ibid. 109–14, 118–23, 129, 184–7).

Langner's play immediately raises a question: will the biblical text support such a reading? Simply put, the answer is yes; but certainly not in the manner it has traditionally been framed. Langner adopts the biblical exodus' framework of good struggling against evil, but has complicated it by poking holes in a simplistic portrayal that draws clear lines between good and evil, Israelite and Egyptian, Moses and Pharaoh. Instead, he perceives evil to be more dynamic and insidious, casting Moses as both liberator and oppressor. Furthermore, he uses the text itself to challenge traditional readings, finding the real nuggets of insight in passages and personalities that have been underplayed. He also uses the failures of modern industrialism to uncover an interpretive vein hidden in the text by centuries of interpretation that made the legal tradition the antidote to social evils. He, therefore, is able to propose artistic expression, represented in the figure of Miriam, as the oppressed tradition in need of liberation from its Mosaic counterpart.

There is actually another vision of the Promised Land at work in Langner's play: that represented by Moses and based on material abundance and law. Charles Reynolds Brown conceived yet another, based on social justice and equity. All three, like so many others, are firmly rooted in Exodus, which has proven a suitable environment to nourish each vision. Social conditions and other factors outside the text, however, have combined to make some a reality and others not.

CONCLUSION

Understanding Exodus holistically demonstrates how it has reached beyond its original community and interacted with numerous variables to produce a variety of impacts. Individuals and groups throughout the centuries have activated its passages, personalities, images, and events to meet the conditions they confronted. Yet Exodus is not a text that sits passively, obediently being moulded and shaped by the reader. Instead, it also stimulates and shapes readers' thoughts and actions, providing vocabulary for challenging powerful groups and inspiring hope and alternative social visions. Its social, economic, and industrial conditions have provided conduits through which later readers have unearthed its contents, combining them with contemporary circumstances in order to engage and impact on their own societies. This influence, in turn, highlights the need to better understand the reception history of Exodus not merely as a scholarly endeavour, but as one that enlightens diverse human experiences. Much work remains to be done.

Works Cited

Asch, Sholem (1951), *Moses*, trans. Maurice Samuel. New York: G. P. Putnam's Sons.

Brown, Charles Reynolds (1910), *The Social Message of the Pulpit*. New York: Charles Scribner's Sons.

Edwards, Rebecca (2006), *New Spirits: Americans in the Gilded Age, 1865–1905*. Oxford: Oxford University Press.

Gould, Louis L. (2001), *America in the Progressive Era, 1890–1914*. Harlow: Longman.

Gregory of Nyssa (1978), *The Life of Moses*, trans. Abraham J. Malherbe and Everett Ferguson. New York: Paulist Press.

Hurston, Zora Neale (1991), *Moses: Man of the Mountain*. New York: Harper Perennial.

Langner, Lawrence (1924), *Moses: A Play, A Protest, and A Proposal*. New York: Boni & Liveright.

Langston, Scott M. (2006), *Exodus Through the Centuries*. Blackwell Bible Commentary. Oxford: Blackwell Publishing.

Philo (1935), *On the Life of Moses*, trans. F. H. Colson. In *Philo*, vol. 6. Loeb Classical Library. Cambridge, Mass.: Harvard University Press.

Trachtenberg, Alan (2007), *The Incorporation of America: Culture and Society in the Gilded Age*, 25th Anniversary Edition. New York: Hill & Wang.

Untermeyer, Louis (1928), *Moses: A Novel*. New York: Harcourt, Brace & Co.

Further Reading

There are many works that deal with uses of specific passages and people in Exodus or with specific groups or periods that used Exodus. For example, *Exodus, Leviticus, Numbers, Deuteronomy*, in the Ancient Christian Commentary on Scripture, ed. Joseph T. Lienhard (Downer's Grove, Ill.: InterVarsity Press, 2001) is a good source for the use of Exodus in the early church. Eddie Glaude's, *Exodus! Religion, Race, and Nation in Early-Nineteenth Century Black America* (Chicago: University of Chicago Press, 2000) treats in detail the political uses of Exodus in the African American community, while the *Encyclopedia Judaica*, ed. Geoffrey Wigoder (Jerusalem: Keter Publishing House, 1971), s.v. 'Moses', offers a helpful essay on Moses. For an extensive survey and bibliography of the reception history of Exodus as a whole see Langston 2006. A good, brief overview can be found in the *Dictionary of Biblical Interpretation*'s entry, 'Exodus, Book of' (ed. John H. Hayes, Nashville, Tenn.: Abingdon, 1999).

....

CHAPTER 30

EXODUS IN LATIN AMERICA

....

PAULO NOGUEIRA

THE reception of religious symbols and texts occurs by means of choices—not always conscious ones—that give the first keynote of the interpretation. Popular culture in particular has a preference for the fragmentary. The fragment can be transformed into a central symbol that generates other powerful symbols and narratives. In biblical interpretation the role of the chosen fragment is what determines the constitution of new readings. Of what are those fragments made? They could be a character, a scene, a speech, a semantic displacement. Everything can become central in the new reading. The popular reading does not compromise with encyclopedic knowledge, with didactics that seek to achieve a balance among the constituent parts of a narrative. Instead, from the fragment can emerge a new complex full of new meanings.

This seems to be the case with the Latin American reception of what I call the 'exodus complex', even with the paradigmatic interpretation of the exodus associated with the Theology of Liberation. In its popular reception—and here I am not talking about the Book of Exodus, but about the imagery of exodus in general—the choices are more subtle. Here the exodus is changed into a transfigured symbol through which human existence can be interpreted.

I will present my discussion in two parts. First I will focus on the exodus in the Latin American Bible movement (Movimento Bíblico Latino-Americano) related to the Theology of Liberation. After that I will look at the symbol of the exodus in popular culture, as it is expressed outside of the norms of theological language. My hypothesis is that there is a tension between both traditions. The popular tradition seems never to have addressed the whole of the exodus narrative, instead making choices that have transformed this key liberation symbol into something very different. Popular culture stresses different topics from those which are important for a theological reading. While not undertaking a review the most important Latin American authors on the Book of the Exodus (the bibliography that follows will enable the reader to find some of these), my more modest aim is to point out the key options which both kinds of approach to the exodus offer, and to show how they contradict each other. It may also be possible to highlight their different hermeneutics. So the interest here is centred on the interpretative processes, and the choices, classifications, and new discourses that arise from these.

The Exodus as Liberation Paradigm

At the outset it is necessary to make a distinction: although closely connected with the Theology of Liberation and often understood as being part of it, the Latin American Bible reading movement has to be seen as something quite different where interpretation of the exodus is concerned. The two run in parallel, but their paths are independent. If the Theology of Liberation established a dialogue with concilliar documents and with the broader theological tradition of the western world in establishing its presuppositions and methods, the Latin American Bible reading's approach to biblical interpretation was developed through work among poor communities and Bible-reading groups, and above all among the 'base' communities (*comunidades eclesiais de base*). This kind of insertion into the life of Catholic and Protestant-ecumenical communities has put Latin American biblical interpretation at the heart of the liberation movement. It is not only a question of a new theological formulation of dogma, but of a *new way in which people read the Bible in in community*, having regard to the social problems facing them, making a fluid transition between past and present, as well as illuminating the present by considering the manifestations of God in the past.

In order to understand the special contribution made by the reading of Exodus in Latin America, it is necessary to know the hermeneutic dynamic by which it is understood. It is possible to summarize the hermeneutic outlook of Latin American readings in a very simple—though definite—way:

(a) in the Bible, present and past penetrate each other;
(b) the social issues facing the poor are what most decisively determine the way the text is to be approached;
(c) the liberating axis of the exodus is reinterpreted constantly, both inside scripture (linking the Old and New Testaments) and in people's lives.

This kind of hermeneutics triggered a revolution in the way that communities read the Bible. A first systematization of that process has been made by Fr. Carlos Mesters in his seminal *Por trás das palavras*.[1] This handbook of liberation hermeneutics of the Bible has its origin in the praxis of reading the text with the poor in the communities where Mesters worked. To summarize its main principle: Mesters begins by reflecting on the silence of the common people in response to the standard clerical reading of the Bible. He was one of the first to wake us up to the fact that the churches' reading of the Bible seemed concerned with questions that the poor never asked, with perspectives from a past that was irrelevant to them and in dialogue with interpreters from continents other than their own. The people's silence before the Bible stemmed from this wrong approach. The Bible can be considered word of God only when it is rooted in the life of the people and can be seen to answer their questions. That is why the Bible produces an infinite number of readings, because there are so many different readers engendering new questions and new answers. In the case of Latin America, the main subject of its reading is the plight of the poor, and the context of their reading is the historical one of capitalist oppression. But the principle that there are as many readings as readers goes back to scripture itself. The history of salvation that is recounted in the Bible reinterprets again and again God's liberating acts in favour of his people.

This hermeneutics of interaction between text and the reader's world has also been developed by Jos Severino Croatto.[2] He sees biblical interpretation as a process of constant 'production of meaning' (*produccin de sentido*). The Bible is the proper site for receiving inspiration from the liberating acts of God in the past and for the production of new praxis in the present. This happens when there is a fusion of the world of the text with the world of the reader. It has not only to do with an actualization of the message but with a process of re-creation of that message. It was through this kind of reading process that the exodus was interpreted in the Latin American communities. Those involved in this process of popular interpretation played a key role in discovering the reserves of meaning embedded in the text.[3]

In this sense the exodus is more than an exemplary happening in the past, a part of the history of salvation or just a theological reference. The exodus becomes an event re-created in the people's world, full of new meanings. Just as the history of the exodus has emerged at different moments in the past and has been read in ways appropriate to these, as we see from its record in the Bible (in the Exile, in the message of the prophets, in Jesus of Nazareth, in the Apocalypse, among others), so

---

[1] *Por trás das palavras*, vol. 1: *Um estudo sobre a porta de entrada no mundo da Bíblia* (Petrópolis: Vozes, 1980).

[2] *Hermenêutica bíblica. Por uma teoria de la lectura como producción de sentido* (Buenos Aires: Ediciones La Aurora, 1984).

[3] See J. S. Croatto, *Êxodo. Uma hermenêutica da liberdade* (São Paulo: Paulinas, 1981), 33.

it can also become reality in the actual life of the people today and can originate a new praxis. But it is not a new exodus; it is the same liberation experience that extends itself in history in the process of reinterpretation. In the words of Croatto: 'the exodus is a happening (*acontecimiento*) full of meaning . . . and it still has not been concluded. It is our task to continue the exodus, because it was not a happening for the Hebrews alone but a manifestation of a liberating plan of God for all nations. Hermeneutically it is viable to understand ourselves through the exodus and, above all, to understand the exodus through our situation of "enslaved" people, economically, politically, socially, and culturally.'[4]

The centrality of the exodus in Latin American biblical interpretation has been stressed by Milton Schwantes in an article from 1988: 'The exodus is a paradigm . . . is like a lamp that lights all biblical history.' And he goes on to say: 'the communities of the poor people are fed by it.'[5] In fact the employment of the exodus as a symbol against oppression is older than Liberation Theology. At the beginning of the colonization of Latin America many voices, such as Jeronimo de Mendieta (1524–1604), Torbio Benadete or Motolinia (16th cent.), Diego Humanzono (1660–76), and Bartolom de las Casas (1474?–1566), protested against the violence to which the native population had been subjected.[6] But the transformation of the exodus into a living symbol of God's liberating presence and work in the world, not in the past but in our immediate present, has occurred only now through the biblical interpretation developed in the base communities and their bible groups.

This dynamic interpretation of the exodus not only had consequences for the present age, in its renewal of the exodus as symbol, but was read back also from the present liberating context into the biblical text itself. The Bible history has been rewritten using the vocabulary and hermeneutical keys of the present.

The role of Latin American hermeneutics of the exodus can be seen in the structure of the seminal work of Jorge Pixley, *Éxodo, una lectura evangélica y popular*,[7] where the biblical account is examined under the following headings:

I. the oppression: project of death (1:1–2:22);
II. the liberation: project of life (2:23–13:16);
III. the dangers of the journey to the land flowing with milk and honey, and the first counter-revolutionary problems (13:17–18:27);
IV. the bases for the new society (19:1–40:38).

---

[4] J. S. Croatto, *Éxodo* 40–1. See also 'A relevância sócio-histórica e hermenêutica do êxodo', *Concilium*, 209 (1987/1), 135.

[5] 'O êxodo como evento exemplar', *Estudos Bíblicos*, 16 (1988), 9.

[6] Valmor da Silva, 'Clamor e Escuta: O grito a Deus em situações extremas'. Tese doutoral. São Bernardo do Campo: Universidade Metodista de São Paulo (1996), 58–9.

[7] México, DF: Casa Unida de Publicaciones, 1983. For the English translation see 'Further Reading' below.

A second example is the *Bíblia Edição Pastoral*, edited by Euclides Balancin, Ivo Storniolo, and Jos Bortolini.[8] This edition of the Bible, produced for the popular reader, is structured around the key issue of liberation. The biblical account of the exodus is seen to be permeated with the questions raised by the Latin American approach. In the introduction to the Book of Exodus we find a statement about the paradigmatic function of this book in the Bible:

Whoever ignores the message of Exodus will never understand the meaning of the whole Bible . . . The fundamental question of the Exodus is: 'who is the real God?' The answer that we find here is the same that appears in the whole Bible and, above all, in the preaching, mission, and person of Jesus. That is why the Book of Exodus is of great importance for understanding the meaning of Jesus as the son of God and for understanding the kingdom of God. Without the exodus the Bible would lose its departure point that leads us to Jesus Christ for the construction of his kingdom with him. (68)

It is interesting to note how the reader of the Book of Exodus is guided through the titles given to each paragraph. I reproduce here all those from chapters 1 to 13, then the headings of the main sections only from chapter 13. These make it clear what kind of reading is suggested:

I. The oppression: the project of death
    The emergence of a people (1:1–7)
  Struggle between death and life
      Oppression paralyzes the people (1:8–14)
      The oppressor is unable to eliminate life (1:15–22)
      Life inside the oppressor's house (2:1–10)
      Solidarity with the oppressed (2:11–22)

II. The liberation: the project of life
 1. God hears the cry of the oppressed (2:23–5)

 2. God answers the cry of his people
      Experience provokes decision (3:1–10)
      The name of God (3:11–15)
      Project of liberation (3:16–22)
      Moses demystifies the oppressor's ideology (4:1–9)
      The call of Moses (4:10–17)
      Moses departs to Egypt (4:18–23)
      The circumcision of Moses' son (4:24–31)

 3. The failing of the legal way
      The God of the marginalized (5:1–5)
      The oppressor's counter-attack (5:6–14)

---

[8] São Paulo: Edições Paulinas, 1990.

Did the project fail? (5:15–21)
The project will carry on by force (5:23–6:13)
Moses and Aaron are brothers and Levites (6:14–27)
God takes the initiative (6:28–7:7)

4. The struggle for liberation
The future begins (7:8–13)
From water of life to blood of death (7:14–24)
A fraudulent negotiation (7:25–8:11)
The oppressor's ideology is demystified (8:12–15)
The oppressor recognizes the power of Yahweh (8:16–28)
Yahweh is with his people (9:1–7)
The ideology of the oppressor is defeated (9:8–12)
Interests divide the dominant class (9:13–35)
Don't surrender in anything (10:1–20)
The oppressor appealed for violence (10:21–9)
Just one step for victory (11:1–10)
Passover: memorial of liberation (12:1–14)
Building a new society (12:15–20)
Conservation of the memory of liberation (12:21–8)
Final victory (12:29–36)
The vigil of liberation (12:17–42)
Ritual and commitment (12:43–51)
Yahweh is the Lord of his people (13:1–10)
Yahweh, God of life (13:11–16)

III. The march for liberty: difficulties and dangers
(13:17–18:27)

IV. The bases for a new society
(19:1–40:38)

This translation of the Bible guides readers, through these titles and through semantic orientation, towards a political understanding of the text. The oppositions are clearly marked: a project of death against a project of life, oppression against liberation. The plot of the narrative is reduced to political oppositions, the discourses to ideologies, and the characters to liberator and oppressor. The role of the people is to resist and struggle with Moses. The engagement takes the shape of revolutionary liberation. Meanings that go beyond this do not play any role in this kind of guided reading. The Theology of Liberation seems to have assumed the role of an exclusive exodus theology.

THE RE-CREATION OF THE EXODUS
IN POPULAR CULTURE

I began my exposition of the reception of the exodus in Latin America with the Bible reading associated with the Theology of Liberation and with engaged communities because I believe this to be the first conscious and programmatic reading of the exodus as a central axis of the Bible and of church and community praxis. But by that I am not claiming that this is the primary reading of the exodus in Latin America or even that it is the most important. I will now examine a symbolic way of reading the exodus imagery that is both more probing and more fragmentary than that found in engaged exegesis. It is important to stress that in that biblical *reading* themes and imagery are more important than texts. Let me clarify some of these fundamental points.

I refer here to themes and imagery instead of texts because I recognize that in the Catholic and hybrid Latin American cultures the Bible has not been the subject of direct interpretation (in the explicit relationship of text to reader) due to a variety of historical reasons, such as illiteracy, unavailability of the biblical text, and the absence of the church's teaching methods developed in Europe. But this has not only to do with objective restrictions imposed on the popular reader, but also with his creative way of accessing and transforming the religious traditions that shows a preference for memory, orality, symbiotic transformation of high culture through distorted *lendaria* (legends), and grotesque and ironic adaptations of it. The popular interpreter's procedure in reading is characterized by two main features: a probing ingenuity, and an approach that conceives of the text in question as a mosaic of discrete fragments.

His interpretations can be ingenious because he is not reliant on the support of the text and has no commitment to the church or to clerically approved readings of the Bible. It is fragmentary because common people read from a vital perspective—the questions of everyday life are decisive in directing the choice of elements they will focus on. From what is just a part of the original text a whole new account can emerge. The fragments are selected and newly arranged according the syncretistic cultural horizons and the everyday questions that challenge people. Everything that is not related to the vital field of everyday life is discarded.

When speaking of the popular reception of the exodus complex in Latin America—and in this section from Brazil as well—we have to be aware of the limitations described above. The exodus has been transformed into other narratives that express an archetypical theme in Brazilian culture: the *peregrination*. People journey in search of better conditions of life, but this also symbolizes a wider journey, as they walk to encounter the sacred. This relationship with people's symbolic wanderings has been pointed out by Valmor da Silva when he identified analogies with the exodus in the Guarani wanderings in search of the *terra sem males* ('land without sickness'), or with the Quilombolas who fled to the country in order to escape slavery and to organize free and alternative communities.[9] The biblical motives are present in a subtle way in pilgrimages to traditional holy places of worship such as Aparecida do Norte, Juazeiro, Bom Jesus da Lapa, and others. Pilgrimage becomes a new exodus also when the people follow new messiahs in the *sertão*, the arid and remote interior of northern Brazil. They are wanderings towards liberation, to a new and Promised Land. Wandering is a profound expression of this deep dream of liberation. It is a biblical reading made with bodies and their movements and gestures.

I would like to illustrate this kind of exodus representation by looking at a specific poem that, although written by one of the most important poets of twentieth-century Brazil, reflects popular traditions and language. *Morte e Vida Severina* ('Death and Life Severina'), by João Cabral de Melo Neto, was written in the 1950s.[10] This poem has had a great impact in the Brazilian literary world, expressing as it does the life of the north-eastern migrant who leaves his arid and unfairly divided motherland and wanders towards the cities on the coast or to the country's main cities, Rio de Janeiro and São Paulo, in the south-east of Brazil. In this respect the poem anticipates the great migration of people from the north-east to the south that took place in the 1960s and 1970s. It is a foundational text of north-eastern Brazilian culture. In my understanding it is also an important translation of the exodus in terms of Brazilian popular culture. The reading of the exodus in *Morte e Vida Severina* is oblique but undeniable. In what follows I will examine the structure of the poem and identify some of the exodus theme's appearances in its key moments.

1. Severino, the main character presents himself. His identity is not well defined (Severino is a common name in the north-east of Brazil). He plays with his name, showing that he is not a man of importance, like other Severinos. The only thing that defines their identity is their early death:

> Iguais em tudo na vida,
> morremos de morte igual,
> mesma morte severina:
> que é a morte que se morre
> de velhice antes dos trinta,
> de emboscada antes dos vinte,
> de fome um pouco por dia...
>
> Equal in everything in life,
> we die of an equal death,

---

[9] *Deus ouve o clamor do povo. Teologia do Êxodo* (São Paulo: Paulinas, 2004), 100.
[10] Rio de Janeiro: Nova Fronteira, 2000.

> the same severina death:
> that is dying from the death
> of old age before thirty,
> of ambush before twenty,
> of hunger a little every day . . .

Besides death, the only mark of his identity is the fact that he is 'the Severino that before your presence *migrates*'. Exodus as an escape from death constitutes his identity.

2. Severino meets two men carrying a corpse in a net. He compares his own journey with that of the dead man. But he believes that the dead man is luckier than him, because he does not have to come back. His journey is finished. Severino's, in contrast, is too long and full of suffering.

3. Severino continues his journey in the direction of the sea, walking along the Capibaribe river. The city of Recife, close to the sea, is his destiny and gives him the hope of confounding death. But the river that gives him his orientation (crossing the *sertão* towards the sea) is dry and abandons him.

We can observe here the inversion and adaptation of some exodus elements: the end of Severino's journey is the sea. And a river (a dry river, indeed) is his guide. His exodus is crossing the desert of a dry river.

4. After many meetings with death, Severino is tempted to give up his journey and live in one of the towns on the way. His wish to settle in the desert is the equivalent of the murmuring of the Israelites and their wish to return to Egypt.

5. When Severino arrives in the Zona da Mata he sees a false Promised Land:

> Bem me diziam que a terra
> se faz mais branda e macia
> quanto mais do litoral
> a viagem se aproxima.
> Agora afinal cheguei
> nessa terra que diziam.
> Como ela é uma terra doce
> para os pés e para a vista.
> Os rios que correm aqui
> têm a água vitalícia.

> People told me that the soil
> is more gentle and tender
> as close to the shore
> the journey approaches.
> Now finally I arrive
> in that land I heard of.
> How sweet is this land
> for the eyes and to the feet.
> And the river that flow here
> are the waters of life.

The poem contains many elements like these that evoke the Promised Land and paradise. But precisely here lies the cruelty of the text: the gentle and tender soil is the reason for death, the death from which Severino is escaping. Ownership of the land is concentrated in the hands of a few powerful men, and is reserved for the worker in only one form: as a grave. Friends of a dead worker sing:

> Essa cova em que estás
> […]
> é a parte que lhe cabe
> deste latifúndio.
> […]
> é a terra que querias
> ver dividida.

> This grave where you rest
> […]
> is the portion you receive
> from this large estate
> […]
> is the land you wished
> to see divided.

The grave is his possession, where he will finally plant not seed, but his own body.

6. Realizing that this is a false Promised Land, Severino continues his journey/ exodus to Recife.

7. When Severino arrives in Recife he hears the conversation of two gravediggers who ask themselves why the people migrate from the *sertão* to their city. They consider the journey of these people to be meaningless. Their exodus is an illusion:

> 'Éa gente retirante
> que vem do Sertão de longe.
> […]
> E que então, ao chegar,
> não tem mais o que esperar.
> Não podem continuar
> pois tem pela frente o mar.
> […]
> Jamais entenderei:
> essa gente do Sertão
> que desce para o litoral, sem razão.

> Seu Êxodo é um retorno para a morte.
> […]
> aí está o seu erro:
> vêm seguindo seu próprio enterro.'

> 'They are people that migrate
> who come from the *sertão* far away.

> [. . .]
> And then, when they arrive
> have nothing to hope for.
> They cannot go further,
> they have the sea in front.
> [. . .]
> I'll never understand
> the people from the *sertão*
> coming down to the coast, without reason.
>
> Their exodus is a return to death
> [. . .]
> That is their mistake:
> they follow their own burial.'

8. Severino loses hope and considers jumping to his death. A wharf-dweller plays with the metaphor of the sea and makes Severino give up his intention. This man is Jos, *mestre carpina*, a carpenter. Their conversation is interrupted when a woman announces: 'Don't you know that your son has come? Don't you know that your son has jumped into life?'

9. The carpenter's child is visited by the poor people of the wharf. They give him gifts that are symbols of their poverty. The account transforms itself into a Christmas history. Exodus is alive again in the Christmas story that surprises Severino. But other images from the exodus appear here and there, like the gypsies from Egypt that visit the boy.

10. Hope is renewed with the birth of this young Jesus/Moses from the swamp. His beauty is marked by smallness, paleness, and fragility. But it doesn't matter: the beauty of the boy comes from the fact that he is a new life, that he comes from the poor people, because life finds its way, because life explodes again, even when this explosion is so weak, a 'severina' explosion.

This exodus represented by the famous poem of João Cabral de Melo Neto has nothing to do with possessing the land or with liberation in the grand style. It ends with a delicate suggestion of hope. The poem is silent about Severino's fate. A small and poor swamp child is presented as the rebirth of the exodus hope. What is the meaning of crossing the desert (*sertão*)? Crossing the desert is an endless metaphor for the whole life. Severino arrives in Recife, by the sea, where he encounters poverty and suffering. Is the poem a kind of anti-exodus? Or is this presentation of the life of the suffering people as an endless journey, as a constant running from death, a new account of the exodus? That kind of minimalist conception of the exodus that we find in other works, like the novel *Vidas Secas* by Graciliano Ramos, the song 'Romaria' by Renato Teixeira, and the movie *Deus e o Diabo na Terra do Sol* (*Black God, White Devil*) by Glauber Rocha, expresses, in my view, some of the evocations of the exodus of Brazilian (and maybe Latin American) popular culture in which hope and resignation seems to make a covenant.

I would like to conclude this open-ended presentation of the rich field of symbols and accounts developed around the exodus with a paradigmatic image of migrants as found in the work of Cndido Portinari: *Os Retirantes*, painted in 1944, ten years before the poem of João Cabral de Melo Neto (fig. 30.1). It is not itself an intentional depiction of the exodus, but the image is full of the same consciousness of life as a wandering in the face of death, injustice, and oppression. As in *Morte e Vida Severina*, it seems that death has an advantage, that the desert is overwhelming. The people that migrate (*os retirantes*) walk together through the

Fig. 30.1. *Os Retirantes*, Cândido Portinari, 1944. Reproduced by permission of the São Paulo Museum of Art.

desert carrying their few belongings. The atmosphere is desolate. There is no vegetation. Everything is dry. Dry also are the faces and their expressions. On the earth bones are scattered as a sign of already present death. Imminent death is announced by the birds of prey in the sky. The scrawny bodies—of the children above all—show from whom it is expected. Gazing at this picture makes us aware that the experience of the exodus—or the challenge of the exodus—is a reality for millions of people, not only in Latin America but throughout the world today.

Further Reading

Bloch, Ernst, *Atheism in Christianity: The Religion of the Exodus and the Kingdom.* London: Verso, 2009.

Gutiérrez, Gustavo, *A Theology of Liberation: History, Politics, and Salvation.* London: SCM, 2001.

Mesters, Carlos, *Defenseless Flower: A New Reading of the Bible.* Maryknoll and London: Orbis Books; Catholic Institute for International Relations, 1989.

Moltmann, Jürgen, *Theology of Hope: On the Ground and the Implications for a Christian Eschatology.* London: SCM, 2002.

Pixley, Jorge V. *God's Kingdom.* London: SCM, 1981.

——*On Exodus: A Liberation Perspective.* Maryknoll, NY: Orbis Books, 1987.

Rowland, Christopher, *The Cambridge Companion to Liberation Theology,* 2nd edn. Cambridge: Cambridge University Press, 2007.

Walzer, Michael, *Exodus and Revolution.* New York: Basic Books, 1984.

CHAPTER 31

··

ELIHU'S SPIRITUAL SENSATION: WILLIAM BLAKE'S *ILLUSTRATIONS OF THE BOOK OF JOB*

··

EMMA MASON

'Why is the Bible more Entertaining & Instructive than any other Book?,' Blake wrote to John Trusler in 1799: 'Is it not because [it is] addressed to the Imagination, which is spiritual sensation . . . ?' (Erdman 1970: 677). Here Blake suggests that the Bible is engaging, not simply because of its content, but because of its impact on the reader's senses: in addressing the 'imagination' or 'spiritual sensation'—the creative part of us that feels—the Bible shapes the reader as an affective addressee who in turn might approach it in an emotional, rather than historical or literal, manner. For Blake, echoing the eighteenth-century literary critic Robert Lowth, the Bible is not a unified story or aesthetic experience, but rather a series of snapshots of different feelings and acts best processed through the imagination. This chapter explores Blake's reading of the Book of Job as a transformative text that shifts and changes meaning through its affective reception by readers. While the Enlightenment attempted to shame not only religious believers but those who approached their society through any form of intense feeling (rather than more polite forms of sensibility), Blake sought to re-emotionalize readers by teaching them how to read the Bible, and thus how to read their world.

Recent criticism has focused on this intense feeling by addressing discourses of enthusiasm, a field of scholarship led by critics such as Jon Mee, Clement Hawes, and Shaun Irlam. But many of Blake's texts are neither straightforwardly enthusiastic nor expressive of its rehabilitated set of meanings: instead, they produce a feeling of 'entertainment' and 'instruction' that stabilizes ways of being in fragmented and alienated communities, rather than forcing the reader transcendentally beyond or outside of them. These ways of being, as Blake's *Songs of Innocence and Experience* show, constitute an ability to live within dynamic contraries, a state he most clearly depicts, I think, in the *Illustrations of the Book of Job*, begun in 1785 but not produced as a full set of twenty-one engravings until 1825. Like the *Songs*, composed after Blake's earlier interest in Job, the *Illustrations* make little or no sense if read as a progressive narrative moving from a description of sin to one of redemption. Nor can they be read computationally, as if some symbols mean one thing and others mean another until a 'system' emerges which explains the text away. I suggest here that the *Illustrations* mean more when read for their spirit and sensation, rather than their letter or system. In other words, they make sense through our reception of their emotional content rather than their allegorical or material allusions.

This chapter is concerned to think about the way the *Illustrations* forward a reading methodology that enables an emotional connection with them that might form a template for interaction with texts and also with people. While I will suggest that this connection between reading and relating is implicit in Blake's work, I would like also to refer to Teresa Brennan's concept of discernment, or 'living attention', to theorize this emotional connection in a manner that might help open up Blake's own concept of 'spiritual discernment' (referred to on Plate I of the *Illustrations*). Brennan uses the word 'discernment' to signify a process of affective understanding that enables us to detect both the feelings of others and also the way in which affects move between us and other people. Affects, Brennan writes, are like affective radio waves (emotional 'pheromones') that move from our bodies into the atmosphere only to be absorbed by others through smell or touch. Once received, these pheromones infect our bodies and nervous systems and then physiologically change how we feel, and thus our reaction to and perception and reception of the world (Brennan 2004: 68–71).

With the influence of the Enlightenment's concept of a closed, bounded idea of the self anchored in the mind, however, reciprocal discernment is almost impossible, individuals being locked within a mind that refuses to let feelings in or out. Brennan argues that because of this we are not only cut off from our own feelings, but we are also unable to receive or react to those around us, sealed off from them emotionally and biologically. Driven by the mind, rather than bodily feelings, then, we privilege a path 'that makes no sense for the living organism, only for the ego', one which fatally allows us to make only ideologically acceptable, rather than personally or communally suitable, choices and decisions (ibid. 116). The ego, Brennan writes, is so 'focused on its own ends and judgemental structure' that it 'cannot attend' in a 'receptive way' to the body in which it lives. We consequently assess others through our own ideological binds, judging their feelings rather than discerning them, directing negative affect towards them and reading only their own ego-driven thoughts rather than sensing their feelings. Discernment does not plough through the ego to get to 'real' feeling, however, but instead is a way of reading emotions that is alert to that 'fear or anxiety or grief or other sense of loss' that the ego maintains in order that we constantly pay attention to it (ibid. 119). Forever under threat by the very rules it reinforces, the ego defends itself by forcing us to identify with it over our feelings. Brennan's 'discerner', however, is able to overrule these demands by picking up on the other's feelings by sensing them— touching, hearing, smelling, seeing, tasting—and then slowly deducing what he or she feels regardless of whatever the ego registers.

Blake's 'spiritual discernment' parallels Brennan's 'living attention', but regards the sensing process as imaginative. This does not mean he shifts perception back into the mind, but rather that he understands the imagination as an emotionally sensitive facility that shapes feelings within and without the self into a lens through which the individual perceives the world. As I argue here, Blake's exemplary discerner is the biblical figure Elihu, who, addressing Job and his ostensible friends, angrily insists that only God has licence to judge (Job 34:23). If mortals try to assume such a critical role, Elihu claims, they will themselves 'seize' up emotionally and be stripped of the ability to perceive with any clarity or vision (Job 36:31). Elihu is in control of his sharply tuned emotions and careful rational sense because he perceives through his felt responses to God and others, free of an ego which blocks full engagement with the world.

Emotions do not simply help us to register and record facts in a more sustained way, however. As Mark Wynn argues, emotions also spell out the content of religious experience in a manner theological explanation cannot, so granting us an affectively informed way of approaching interpersonal values between people, an idea at the centre of Blake's own christological understanding. Blake's Elihu shows the reader that religious experience is affective, but further implies that its cognitive significance has material effects: emotional perception informs the imagination while the imagination allows the individual to see the world as human. Feeling is then ultimately responsible for compassionate acts engendered by an affectively fuelled capacity for invention and vision. This aspect of Blake's poetry is sometimes buried by historical readings, I argue here, because they are more interested in the letter of Blake's work than in its spirit, regarding his texts and images as receptacles of ideas rather than guides to feeling. What follows is a consideration of Blake's own implicit resistance to historical decodings of his work: first, through a discussion of his understanding of 'opposites' and 'contraries'; and second, in a reading of the *Illustrations*, which argues that the imagination, or 'spiritual sensation', offers the reader a way into Brennan's 'living attention' as an artistic as well as ethical way of relating.

READING BLAKE: THE LETTER OF HISTORY

Recent criticism has tended to squeeze out the emotional or spiritual meaning of Blake's work by focusing on its historical or materialist implications. In doing so, many critics build their readings of the text on external discourses that might be connected with it, rather than working through Blake's sometimes dense style. Much textual analysis of Blake either focuses on the materiality of the physical artwork to the extent that the text itself becomes irrelevant, or leaves behind Blake's writing and images to favour related discussions of historical, philosophical, or social referents. I note discuss the dominance of historical criticism in eighteenth-century studies, not to assert a general critique of this methodology, but to point out its specific failure to engage with Blake's work, one that consequently discourages readers from reading him.

Attacking those Enlightenment values from which the discipline of history emerges, Blake creates a system of dynamic contraries that reveal to his readers that while we tend to understand the world through opposites, we must do so by creating a dialectical space between terms, rather than valuing one over the other. Constructed on the binary innocence and experience, for example, the *Songs* challenge two assumptions: first, that opposites cannot be concurrent; and second, that they stand in linear relationship to each other. We presuppose, for example, that we move from one state (innocence) to another (experience), from good to bad, ignorance to knowledge. Blake, however, suggests that contrary states are simultaneous and exist in parallel: the only way to shut down a contrary is to sever one half of it by privileging the other side of the pair. This splitting process is thus predicated on the negation of one side of the pair, which is then rendered inferior and consequently devalued. As Blake stresses in *Jerusalem: The Emanation of the Great Albion* (pl. 10):

> They take the Two Contraries which are calld Qualities, with which
> Every Substance is clothed, they name them Good & Evil
> From them they make an Abstract, which is a Negation
> Not only of the Substance from which it is derived
> A murderer of its own Body: but also a murderer
> Of every Divine Member: it is the Reasoning Power
> An Abstract objecting power, that Negatives every thing
> This is the Spectre of Man.

Negations are always destructive for Blake because they are founded on abstractions or generalized stories (ideologies) about one side of a pair; these stories come to make sense as 'reality' if they go unchallenged and begin to crush those who do not or cannot conform to them. As Jonathan Roberts argues, this kind of abstraction is always non-human for Blake (it is the 'Spectre of Man' rather than a living being that we see in the quotation above), human life residing instead in 'minute particulars', individual instances of specific people in actual situations (2007: 53). Simply behaving well or badly without thinking about it is meaningless for Blake, a mistake Job falls prey to in the opening plates of the *Illustrations* by upholding ideas of 'goodness' over the situation of particular human experiences.

All human experiences, however, do involve contraries, which differ from negations in that they keep both sides of a pair in an actively reciprocal relationship: 'Negations are not Contraries: Contraries mutually Exist: But Negations Exist Not' (*Jerusalem*, pl. 17). Blake shows that we urgently need to bring the two sides of any aspect of existence back into relationship by recognizing their respective qualities and differences without judging them or, as Roberts writes, without attaching 'moral labels to them' (2007: 45). Polarities are never neutralized in Blake's work, but are always kept in flux. Negations, on the other hand, prevent a diversity of meaning by associating one side with 'good' and the other side with 'evil': the political implications of such a process for reinforcing ideologically received hierarchies result in a series of prejudices concerning gender, sexuality, race, class, and so on. The abstract narratives which found these hierarchies may seem to superficially benefit some, but ultimately fail everyone because of the interdependency of all involved, gathered as we all are for Blake in a divine body. As St Paul states in a passage that resonates with Blake's understanding of the 'human' as an all-embracing, living divine body:

For as the body is one, and hath many members, and all the members of that one body, being many, are one body: so also is Christ ... there should be no schism in the body; but that the members should have the same care one for another. And whether one member suffer, all the members suffer with it; or one member be honoured, all the members rejoice with it. Now ye are the body of Christ, and members in particular. (1 Cor. 12:12, 25–7)

Individual humans, or 'members in particular', then, only suffer if positioned in non-particular, or abstract, situations, removed from specificity either by perception (as in the case of Job, whose 'sin' is to misconstrue his world) or by representation (God as a cruel and punitive judge as opposed to a compassionate, forgiving being). Blake has little interest in the Old Testament God unless it concerns stripping him down to the ideas he comprises—tyranny, judgement, war, rule, wrath—and then pointing out his similarity with what we have traditionally called 'the devil'. Instead, Blake understands God through the example of Jesus, a personification of love as an active principle, that is, some-thing we engage in with others, whoever they are, and the fuel behind interpreta-tion, whereby 'abstract responses to individuals are humanized in the light of compassion' (Roberts 2007: 62). While the religious authorities Jesus is pitted against in the Gospels continually demand rigid, literal applications of the law, Jesus is invested instead in understanding the law through love, that is, the human aspect of any given situation. Jesus is God in human form because he privileges love as a hermeneutical tool for understanding the specificity of human actions and feelings, and in doing so reminds us that the whole point of Old Testament law is to reinforce God's love. When one of the Pharisees pushes Jesus to name the greatest commandments, for example: 'Jesus said unto him, Thou shalt love the Lord thy God with all thy heart, and with all thy soul, and with all thy mind. This is the first and great commandment. And the second is like unto it, Thou shalt love thy neighbour as thyself. On these two commandments hang all the law and the prophets' (Matt. 22:37–40). Those who misread the law as an abstract system are, in Paul's famous contrary, guided by the letter rather than the spirit of the law (Rom. 7:6; 2 Cor. 3:6), the 'spirit' dovetailing with the 'spiritual sensation' of Blake's imaginative processing. The prevailing historical readings of Blake largely attend to the letter of criticism, offering literal analyses of his work through references to the printing-press, engraving techniques, religious sects, denominational affiliations, metropolitan life—that is, anything that abstracts his work into allusions outside of it that the critic can then concretize into a fact. We then lose the spirit of the text, one more difficult to capture on paper but nevertheless that which is integral to Blake's expectation of our imaginative engagement with it. Paul focuses on the intermediary relation-ship between letter and spirit in Romans and Corinthians, arguing in the former that one is only released from the 'oldness of the letter' by the 'newness of spirit' (Rom. 7:6). Unworkable in isolation, letter and spirit are interdependent: 'the law is spiritual' (7:14), he writes, just as the spirit is aimless without 'delight in the law' (7.22). Even Paul's declaration in 2 Corinthians, 'for the letter killeth, but the spirit giveth life' (3:6), is offset by his insistence that the law of the Old Testament is refuelled by the spirit of the new, the 'veil' (3:14) which hides the light of the law 'done away in Christ' (3:14), who represents 'Spirit' (3:17) and so love. The spirit, then, is an emotive force that one feels, which then guides one's perception of the world, shaping its laws to respect them while rendering them animate, flexible, and human. The intermediary between spirit and perception is the imagination, for Blake; 'Imagination, which is spiritual sensation', translates spirit-led emotions into observation, or vision.

IMAGINATION, OR SPIRITUAL SENSATION

The *Illustrations* offer us an example of how Blake directs his reader towards implementing his or her own spirit-led emotions when reading and so developing a personal perception of the text. That the *Illustrations* are about perception is a critical given, Joseph Wicksteed's influential early twentieth-century reading of the sequence offering a series of cracked codes to enable a certain way of viewing the plates. Thus Blake's images of scrolls represent spiritual texts or meanings (good), while his depiction of books convey worldly, temporal, or law-based meanings (bad); Gothic buildings are Christian (good), while Druidic or classical buildings are more suspect (bad). While Wicksteed's account is more sophisticated than this summary allows, it nevertheless produces a kind of oppositional reading of *Job* that seeps into even the most celebrated accounts of the *Illustrations* by critics like Andrew Wright, Bo Lindberg, and Kathleen Raine. As discussed above, oppositional reading is anathema for Blake, partly because it is unable to do justice to emotionally imaginative reading, outlined throughout the *Illustrations*. From the title-page, with its quill-bearing angels who indicate that this story of redemption is bound to creativity and the imagination, the emotions are central: each angel facially conveys a different feeling, and the fluffy cloud which roots the plate's frame offers a sense of lightness and comfort to a reader expectant of a more tragic biblical retelling.

Blake points to the real tragedy of Job immediately in Plate I ('Job and his Family'), not by the introduction of Satan's cruel pact with God, but instead through a depiction of Job and his family sitting around moribund under a tree. Their unquestioning obedience to God here, praying dutifully but without any apparent feeling or sense of why they pray, is indicated by their refusal to acknowledge or take pleasure in the musical instruments above them and their reliance on books which Job and his wife hold but do not look at. Job is even more in the dark than his wife, positioned on the night-time side of the image and unable to feel the warmth of the sun behind him, obscured as it is by a Gothic church. The church may be capable of transmitting this light, as it might potentially diffuse feeling among its members through its use of the law, but Blake warns the reader that such transmission must be emotionally led, placing the words 'The Letter Killeth | The Spirit giveth Life | It is Spiritually Discerned' (from 2 Cor. 3:6 and 1 Cor. 2:14) in the middle of the opening text from Job ('There was a Man in the Land of Uz . . . ').

If discernment is a way of reading emotion through the senses for Brennan, then spiritual discernment implies a compassionately driven mode of perception motivated by the imagination for Blake. Job cannot discern at this point in the narrative because he is unable to think or feel for himself and has no understanding of his relationship with God beyond that of what is institutionally demanded by religious law. By Plate II ('Satan before the Throne of God'), Blake has depicted this letter-ruled vision of God as an emanation deriving from Job's faulty reading of the scriptures (he ignores the scrolls the angels try to show him) and who sits in judgement above him. God's facial expression, however, is one of boredom and hopelessness, his fingers indifferently gesturing below in a kind of exhausted acknowledgement of the figure from whence he came.

Job's perception of God as a weary, austere, and exacting tyrant is held in place by Satan, a frantic but powerful intermediary who leaps dismissively over Job while contemptuously throwing his arms up to God. Yet Satan too is a product of Job's vision, as Blake underlines in Plate III ('The Destruction of Job's Sons'), no longer a bounding sprite here, but rather a vampiric demon casting down a furious judgement on Job's children who refuse to respect the moral law that so enslaves their father. They are dead to Job, perhaps not physically as in the scriptural narrative (Blake brings the same figures back in the final plate) but because of their willingness to at once interpret and feel God as creative sensation and consequent spiritual freedom. Job's inability to feel is strongly represented in Plate V ('Satan Going Forth from the Presence of the Lord'), wherein his lack of imagination is directly connected to his impotent compassion, dutifully, but miserably, depositing a block of bland-looking bread into the hand of an oncoming beggar. God turns away, achingly weary of the limited frame Job binds him in, and even Satan anxiously flails, fearful that Job's refusal to engage with emotion will bar him both from the acts of destruction shown in Plate III and the cruel tortures enacted in Plate VI ('Satan Smiting Job with Boils').

Without the capacity for anger, terror, and rage, Blake shows us, one cannot understand compassion, peace, or kindness: one may choose not to act on the more vicious of these feelings, but a sense of what their expressive content emotionally signifies is imperative to the achievement of discerning its presence in others. In the sorrowful Plate VII ('Job's Comforters'), for example, Job's complacent and ideologically subsumed friends respond to his newly fallen state with hysteria, their arms waving feverishly to form a fire-like outline that mirrors the ominous glow issuing from the space once filled with the sun. Such embellished feeling becomes a kind of parodic performance of the emotion voiced, the three friends hypnotically rehearsing circling arguments that come to nothing. The form of the scriptural depiction of their lecture is lengthy, dull, and supercilious while Blake's illustrations bring out the cowardly (Plate VIII, 'Job's Despair'), monotonous (Plate IX, 'The Vision of Eliphaz'), and lifeless (Plate X, 'Job Rebuked by his Friends') aspect of their beings. Their heavy-robed, beard-covered bodies headed by artificially robotic stares almost dehumanize them, the friends' transmission of a very toxic affect literalized by the accusatory flutter of their gesticulating arms and fingers in Plate X (see fig. 31.1).

That their own bad feeling is projected onto those they direct their negativity towards is clear from the twisted, almost skeletal face of Job's wife, huddled as she is into an affective position of incomprehension and despair. While Job's friends

Fig. 31.1. Job rebuked by his friends. Plate X, 'The Just Upright Man', William Blake, *Engraved Illustrations of the Book of Job*. Collection of Robert N. Essick. Copyright © 2009 the William Blake Archive. Used with permission.

judge, she discerns, assessing her husband's self-pity as consuming and destructive while her gentle but pleading gaze desperately begs him to resist the onslaught by which he is challenged. As Job's affective side, she embodies the emotion he might feel once freed from the letter into the spirit, but his anxious reaction to those he engages with here accelerates into terror within Plate XI ('Job's Evil Dreams'), his horrible nightmares overwhelming him with a vision of a scaly hybrid of good and evil shaped in the image of himself. That Job physically looks like what he nightmarishly conjures, however, literalizes his God–Satan confusion in a way that terrifies him into an emotional shock that reawakens his feelings. While Job longs to be free of the feverish night in which he seems locked, the experience of pain so vividly depicted in the plate opens him to the possibility of its opposite. The narrative has moved from his opening assumption of an unfelt guise of goodness, accompanied as it was by an inability to feel hurt, into a recognition that this previous state was not a real self at all, but a compulsive and insecure one held in place by the mind alone.

As this rational impostor is dismantled, Job physically assumes a look of withdrawal, shivering in Plate XII ('The Wrath of Elihu', fig. 31.2) as he grieves for his past self. Yet most important here is the figure of Elihu, a projection of what Job might become and whose towering beauty cows his friends but overjoys his wife, so grateful that she sits motionlessly praying, buried in her knees. Elihu is key for Blake primarily because he is able to think and feel for himself free of the letter, the law, convention, or ideology and so is ideally placed to perceive the world through imagination and feeling. The King James text immediately stresses Elihu's capacity for discernment, iterating through his words his patient, level, and attentive approach to others and ability to listen and observe where Job's three friends judge and accuse: 'Behold, I waited for your words; I gave ear to your reasons, whilst ye searched out what to say. Yea I attended unto you' (Job 32:11–12). Free from his own ego, Elihu carefully engages with others by granting them his attention developed through his affective, rather than dogmatic, relationship with God: 'My words shall be of the uprightness of my heart: and my lips shall utter knowledge clearly. The Spirit of God hath made me, and the breath of the Almighty hath given me life' (Job 33:3–4).

Working through the 'spirit' while the 'letter' traps Job's three friends, Elihu is able to directly tune into God's energy, which shines from the sky through twelve sparkling stars serving to illuminate Elihu's flawlessly formed body and intense gaze. A model of the divine human, the perfection of Elihu's body is a symbol of Blake's realization of the human as a potentially ideal 'mode of vision' (a way of seeing the world), and mode of existence (a way of living through compassion and feeling) (Mellor 1971: 596). He uses his vision or perception of the world to order the energy around him into imaginative forms, but is also able to see beyond them to reach outside of his own psychological boundaries and into the thoughts and feelings of others. In doing so, Elihu considers the world as an act of imaginative

Fig. 31.2. The wrath of Elihu. Plate XII, 'I am Young & ye are very Old', William Blake, *Engraved Illustrations of the Book of Job*. Collection of Robert N. Essick. Copyright © 2009 the William Blake Archive. Used with permission.

creation, declaring in the King James version of the narrative that God speaks in multiple voices, 'yet man perceiveth it not. In a dream, in a vision of the night, when deep sleep falleth upon men, in slumberings upon the bed; Then he openeth the ears of men, and sealeth their instruction, That he may withdraw man from his purpose' (Job 33:14–17). Everything Job demands from God, then, is already there for him, Elihu suggests, and Blake portrays a sleepy Job touching, but refusing to engage with, an unopened scroll, at the foot of the plate. Revelation or truth is always already there for those who choose to discern it in dreams, myths, and art for Blake, who decorates this magical plate in the series with much of chapter 33, along with related verses regarding vision and looking, to remind us of Elihu's imaginative role. Yet this role is primarily an emotional one, fuelled by his 'sense' and 'spirit', two words continually used in the biblical narrative, to sensitize humanity with the 'light of the living' (Job 33:30), or as Brennan puts it, with 'living attention'. Elihu's message is that Job and his friends must learn to register God directly in felt responses to him rather than through a series of laws that may or may not later engender a felt response. Feeling functions as a way of seeing God, lighting up what matters and then teaching us how to respond: feelings are vehicles for the revelation of what is truly valuable (they enable us to 'know among ourselves what is good', Job 34:4); free us from ideologically produced conceptualizations of ourselves and others (they release us from the hold of 'judgement and justice', Job 36:17); and they cast the mind forward so that it might sense how to resolve a human tension or anxiety (by allowing us to feel, if not comprehend, the 'marvellous' thundering of God's voice (Job 37:5).

   Job's friends fail to address any of the problems raised by the narrative because they are trapped by the letter of their own understanding; the friends' cognitive disability is heightened for Job, whose grasp of his own terrible state is not emotionally processed but remains on the level of melodrama. He cannot feel his own feelings because he is unable to respond emotionally to those of others, dehumanizing them in the process and so denying them access to the divine. When Elihu discloses this to Job, the impact is visibly one of shock, Job's hair standing up on end in Plate XIII ('The Lord Answering Job out of the Whirlwind'), even as his wife for the first time in the series looks animated and beautiful, able as she now is to emotionally discern the calm and tranquil God portrayed in the enchanting and joyful Plate XIV ('The Creation'). It is this shock, however, that jolts Job out of his complacency and triggers his emotional redemption in the remaining plates. This redemption begins when he confronts and dismisses his ideological hallucinations of God and Satan in Plate XVI ('The Fall of Satan'), an act that visibly comforts his wife but drives his judgemental friends into a position of deformed terror at the bottom right of the plate. Satan's complete incapacity for discernment or vision is accentuated here by his blind and bound falling body, unable to receive or transmit any feelings and cast into hell-fire by a disillusioned God who regretfully waves goodbye to the 'evil' which sustained his 'good'. For if

Job refuses to give energy to his vision of a dogmatic God, still sitting in judgement at the top of the plate, this God must make his exit. We see finally that this inflexible and now outdated model of God is thus replaced in Plate XVII ('The Vision of God') by a glorious, shining, and merciful figure who imbues Job, his wife, and the entire image with sensation and compassion: as readers we can almost feel the warmth issuing from the dominantly placed sun. The blazingly bright affect God touches Job and his wife with in Plate XVII, too much for the friends to even engage with, sparks Job's imagination so that where he once heard God's word but could not understand it, he now has learned to see using an emotionally reconfigured mode of perception: 'I have heard thee with the hearing of the Ear but now my Eye seeth thee' (Job 42:5).

By Plate XVIII ('Job's Sacrifice') we see a now emotionally open Job, his arms ready to embrace that which he believes in and feels, symbolized both by the heart-shaped fire he stands before and the now-overpowering heat of the sun. The stress on light here suggests to us that Job's imagination has been reawakened with the recognition that his own emotional truth must be created through love (he prays together with his wife and now-forgiven friends) and art (his paint-brushes are set up ready in the bottom frame of the plate together with his scrolls and now-opened books). Enabled to feel love and compassion, Job understands that his previous habit of projecting images of what he thought people and the world represented is overturned by his feelings, productive as they are of creation and energy: the fields in Plate XIX ('Job Accepting Charity') are filled with wheat, and Plate XX ('Job and his Daughters') is abundant with leafiness, music, and Job's love for his daughters. Blake's insertion of 'If I ascend up into heaven, thou art there: if I make my bed in hell, behold, thou art there' (Ps. 139.8) is suggestive not only of the fact that Job has finally found God, but that God's affection dynamically moves everywhere, transmitted across boundaries to offer all believers a connection.

The final plate ('Job and his Wife Restored to Prosperity', fig. 31.3) is a model of affective connectivity, the music Job and his family play an artistic embodiment of their beliefs but also an indication that feeling, like music, cannot be fixed or made permanent but must be constantly restarted and replayed. Amidst their imaginative creation everyone is awake and vibrant, the dead children resurrected, and even the sheep serenely listen on while the contented dog dozes with them. Certainly the close of the sequence is a bringing together of biblical references to the lamb of Revelation and the song of Moses, both texts intent on presenting Job to readers as a model of perceiving and reading.

There is also a darker and gentler side to Plate XXI that balances the bright light of the sun at the right of the frame and, filled with stars and a crisp crescent moon, recalls the starry shadows through which Elihu entered the narrative in Plate XII. Job and his family now resemble Elihu as he appeared in this earlier plate: upright, glowing, physically graceful, and looking longingly towards God while their imaginations process such feeling back into the music they make. The instruments so

Fig. 31.3. Job and his wife restored to prosperity. Plate XXI, 'So the Lord blessed the latter end of Job', William Blake, *Engraved Illustrations of the Book of Job*. Collection of Robert N. Essick. Copyright © 2009 the William Blake Archive. Used with permission.

cut off from Job and his family in Plate I are restored to them, and Job's most creative daughter, pictured crushed and unconscious in Plate III with her lyre, is moved to the centre of the plate in order to transmit the good feelings of the narrative. She is almost like an emotional fuse-breaker who trips available models of feeling that could potentially spill into enthusiam on the one hand or piousness on the other. Elihu and Job's daughter emit the same affect throughout the narrative, and it is from both of them that Job learns to marry the affective and cognitive content of his belief through an imagination which translates it into material action (both artistic and compassionate).

I want to argue that Blake invites us to read his work in this way, beginning with our felt response to it and finding the material implications from this approach, rather than beginning inside a historical frame that reproduces the text as a set of data. This latter methodology blocks discernment and encourages judgement, but the ideological drive behind such criticism often remains obscured by a claim to evidence and fact. Reading for feeling is not value-free, of course, and this chapter has been concerned to approach the *Illustrations* through their emotional content in order to meaningfully explore Blake's affective understanding of religion, art, and the imagination as a combined forum for elevating compassion. This, then, the creative and ethical message of the *Illustrations*, is why Blake found the Bible 'more Entertaining & Instructive than any other Book', a series of stories written to change how readers feel (rather than fulfil them historically or aesthetically) by allowing them to access the imagination through sensation.

Works Cited

BRENNAN, T. (2004), *The Transmission of Affect*. Ithaca, NY: Cornell University Press.

DAMON, S. F. (1966), *Blake's Job: William Blake's Illustrations of the Book of Job with an Introduction and Commentary*. Providence, RI: Brown University Press.

ERDMAN, D. V. (ed.) (1970), *The Poetry and Prose of William Blake*. New York: Doubleday.

HAWES, C. (1996), *Mania and Literary Style: The Rhetoric of Enthusiasm from the Ranters to Christopher Smart*. Cambridge: Cambridge University Press.

IRLAM, S. (1999), *Elations: The Poetics of Enthusiasm in Eighteenth-Century Britain*. Stanford: Stanford University Press.

LINDBERG, B. (1973), *William Blake's Illustrations to the Book of Job*. Åbo: Åbo akademi.

LOWTH, R. (1787), *Lectures on the Sacred Poetry of the Hebrews; De sacra poesi Hebraeorum*. London: J. Johnson.

MEE, J. (2003), *Romanticism, Enthusiasm, and Regulation: Poetics and the Policing of Culture in the Romantic Period*. Oxford: Oxford University Press.

MELLOR, A. K. (1971), 'The Human Form Divine and the Structure of Blake's *Jerusalem*', *Studies in English Literature 1500–1900*, 11/4: 595–620.

——(1974), *Blake's Human Form Divine*. Los Angeles: University of California Press.

RAINE, K. (1982), *The Human Face of God: William Blake and the Book of Job*. London: Thames & Hudson.

ROBERTS, J. (2007), *William Blake's Poetry*. London: Continuum.

ROBINSON, J. (2007), *Deeper than Reason: Emotion and its Role in Literature, Music and Art*. Oxford: Oxford University Press.

SHERMAN, N. (1989), *The Fabric of Character: Aristotle's Theory of Virtue*. Oxford: Clarendon Press.

VINE, S. (1993), *Blake's Poetry: Spectral Visions*. London: St Martin's Press.

WICKSTEED, J. (1910), *Blake's Vision of the Book of Job with Reproductions of the Illustrations: A Study*. New York: E. P. Dutton & Co.

WRIGHT, A. (1972), *Blake's Job: A Commentary*. Oxford: Clarendon Press.

WYNN, M. (2005), *Emotional Experience and Religious Understanding: Integrating Perception, Conception and Feeling*. Cambridge: Cambridge University Press.

CHAPTER 32

EZEKIEL 1 AND THE NATION OF ISLAM

MICHAEL LIEB

EZEKIEL 1

The first chapter of the Book of Ezekiel inaugurates one of the most profound events in Hebrew Scriptures. Extending well beyond the first chapter and reappearing later in the prophecy, this event represents Ezekiel's encounter with God in the form of an overwhelming vision. By means of this vision, the prophet is called upon to proclaim the divine message to his people in exile during the period of the Babylonian Captivity. Although the vision that the prophet experiences defies precise conceptualization, it is possible to provide an account of some of its primary features. As the vision unfolds, Ezekiel, in exile on the shores of the River Chebar in Babylon, beholds 'a stormy wind' approaching from the north, 'and a great cloud, with brightness round about it, and fire flashing forth continually, and in the midst of the fire, as it were gleaming bronze'. 'From the midst of it came the likeness of four living creatures', each with four faces (those of a man, a lion, an ox, and an eagle) and each with four wings (two of which stretched downward and two of which stretched upward). 'In the midst of the living creatures there was something that looked like burning coals of fire . . . and out of the fire went forth lightning.' Accompanying each of the living creatures there appeared four remarkable wheels, 'and the four had the same likeness, their construction being as it were a wheel within a wheel'. The rims of the wheels were 'full of eyes round about. And when the living creatures went, the wheels went beside them; and when the living creatures rose from the earth, the wheels rose. Wherever the spirit would go, they went, and the wheels rose along with them; for the spirit of the living creatures was in the wheels.' Over the heads of the living creatures there was the likeness of a crystal firmament, and above the firmament there was the likeness of a throne, upon which was 'a likeness as it were of a human form'. 'And upward from what had the appearance of his loins,' Ezekiel says, 'I saw as it were the appearance of fire, and there was brightness round about him.' 'Like the appearance of the bow that is in the cloud on the day of the rain, so was the appearance of the brightness round about.' This, concludes Ezekiel, 'was the appearance of the likeness of the glory of the Lord' (Ezek. 1:1–28).

As the basis of Jewish mysticism in the early centuries and beyond, this vision was customarily designated the Work of the Chariot. What the prophet beholds has come to be known, then, as the 'chariot' (or 'throne-chariot'). Because the word 'chariot' does not actually appear in the first chapter, this nomenclature might be considered a trope or at least a means of providing a local habitation and a name for that which defies naming. Although perhaps running contrary to the spirit of the vision as unknowable and ineffable, the act of naming arises in part as a result of what is already latent in the text itself, for this vision, after all, embodies its own act of 'construction'. In a sense, it is a vehicle with its own momentum, indeed, its own 'technology', manifested in the revolving wheels, among other chariot-like appurtenances. Thus, what is conceived figuratively might well be interpreted 'literally' as the thing in itself. For those inclined to read the text from this perspective, the vision represents the wellspring of the impulse to fashion a technology out of the ineffable, the inexpressible, the unknowable. This is particularly the way in which the vision has been interpreted in the modern world. As such, the vision of Ezekiel re-emerges as any one of several wonders of technology, ranging from locomotives to interplanetary space vehicles.

BLACK NATIONALISM

One of the most compelling of these enactments is an airborne vehicle that lies at the heart of the Nation of Islam, a fascinating, controversial, and politically charged movement that has assumed genuine significance in the cultural life of America. With its emphasis on apocalyptic matters and its enduring concern with the import of the visionary experience, the Nation of Islam represents a crucial moment in the struggle for identity in the cause of Black Nationalism. As much as the Nation identifies itself with the Qur'an as a source-text for all things Islamic, it is the Bible itself—and, in particular, the vision of Ezekiel—that has underscored much of the theology, as well as the ideology, of this movement from the time of its formation in the early twentieth century through the present. To understand the way in which the vision of Ezekiel is integrated into the life of the Nation, one must address the teachings and experiences of its two most important exponents: the Honorable Elijah Muhammad, known to the Nation as the Messenger of Allah, and the Honorable Minister Louis Farrakhan, the controversial student of the Messenger. Through them, the vision of Ezekiel assumes its own bearing as a vehicle that has ties at once with 'popular culture' and at the same time with the most profound of religious experiences. Designated the Mother Wheel, the Mother Plane, or the Mother Ship, as well as simply the Wheel, this vehicle is not only a marvel of technology but an emblem of the ultimate triumph of the black man over his white oppressor.

ELIJAH MUHAMMAD (1897–1975)

As the Messenger of Allah, Elijah Muhammad dedicated himself to the 'restoration of the most despised and brutalized segment of American Christianity back to a level of dignity and self-appreciation'. The slums of the black ghettos were his initial 'parish', his converts the 'slum-created outcasts of developing technocratic society'. His followers were those 'most battered by racism and stifled by convention' (Lincoln 1989: 346). The son of an itinerant Baptist preacher, Elijah Muhammad (whose original 'slave name' was Elijah Poole) was infused with the kind of teaching reflected in his given name 'Elijah', but it was not *that* prophet that Elijah Muhammad viewed most immediately as the source of so much of his inspiration. Rather, it was Ezekiel. (To be sure, both Elijah and Ezekiel may be said to embody the notion of the 'chariot' as sublime vehicle, and traditionally they are often conflated, but for the purposes of the discussion at hand it is Ezekiel who takes centre-stage.) In order to realize the nature of Ezekiel's presence in the thought of Elijah Muhammad, one must have a sense of the context through which the Mother Plane was originally disclosed.

In his pioneering book *Message to the Blackman in America*, Elijah Muhammad recounts how his life underwent a transformation as the result of his encounter with a mysterious fair-skinned man in the city of Detroit during the tumultuous period of the Depression. Known as Master Fard Muhammad, this man revealed himself to the young Elijah Poole as God, Allah himself. As a Mahdi or Messiah, he had come to liberate his long-suffering people and to educate them through a knowledge of 'self'. They were taught their noble lineage as a people descended from an ancient race called the Tribe of Shabbaz. They were, in fact, the 'original people' out of whom all races have since arisen. Having been reclaimed, the offspring of this people fittingly called themselves the 'Lost-Found Nation of Islam in the Wilderness of North America'. It was by means of Fard's teachings and an unwavering adherence to Fard's ways that Elijah Poole was deemed worthy to receive his calling as the Honorable Elijah Muhammad. After the departure of Master Fard Muhammad, Elijah Muhammad assumed the leadership of the Nation as the Messenger of Allah (Muhammad 1965: 17–18).

Fundamental to the teachings of Master Fard Muhammad was the Mother Plane. Once again, in his *Message to the Blackman in America* Elijah Muhammad recalls how he first came to know about the existence of the Mother Plane. At the appropriate juncture in Elijah Muhammad's training, Master Fard 'pointed out a destructive dreadful-looking plane' in the form of a wheel in the sky. A wonder of technology, this plane was constructed as 'a humanly built planet'. Those who seek the truth, Elijah Muhammad observes, can see the Mother Plane even today. It is up there now and is actually visible twice a week. Its presence is no secret. Although one might be astonished that such an object is visible so often, it has been hovering in that position since biblical times. In fact, this is the same object that the prophet Ezekiel saw 'a long time ago' (Muhammad 1965: 17–18). Such is the account that Elijah Muhammad provides of his first sighting of the Mother Plane. Particularly in the context of the vision that inaugurates the Book of Ezekiel, this account is remarkable in many respects, especially considering the terms in which it is cast. Unlike the overwhelming sense of awe and mystery surrounding Ezekiel's vision, Elijah Muhammad's account is essentially reportorial. Although the Mother Plane is certainly 'dreadful looking', the qualities of awe or mystery are not emphasized the way they are in Ezekiel. The truth of its existence is no secret to those who know. Nor is it a 'vision' in the biblical sense; it is, rather, the real thing, an immense machine that can be measured, half-a-mile by a half-a-mile square. As such, it is not only a real and verifiable entity among those who know it is 'there', but also an entity that, once known, can only be described as 'in your face'. It arises from a perspective that is downright apocalyptic. According to Elijah Muhammad, the Mother Plane was built for the purpose of destroying the present world. This is the world of the slave-master, the spawn of the 'big-head' scientist known as Yacub through whom the white race was genetically manufactured over the centuries. Thus conceived, the Mother Plane becomes the awesome vehicle of vengeance that will swoop down to destroy the oppressor and to reclaim the oppressed. Every follower of Elijah Muhammad knows that the 'promis'd end' is upon us. Members of the Nation await the destruction of civilization with bombs, poison gas, and finally with fire.

As apocalyptic vehicle, the Mother Plane, then, exhibits all the qualities of a 'machine', indeed the machine to end all machines. Although imbued with an aura of that which has been miraculously fashioned, the Mother Plane is still a 'man-ufactured' vehicle, a true testament to the triumph of research undertaken in the name of 'science'. Various accounts of the manufacture of the Mother Plane exist, including what might be called the 'Asian connection'. Constructed of the 'finest steel in Asia' on the island of Japan in 1929, the Plane benefited from the labours of 'Black, Brown, Red and Yellow Scientists'. The vehicle has a speed of up to 9,000 miles per hour. Within the Mother Plane are 1,500 small circular planes, each of which carries three bombs. Weighing 2 tons each, the bombs are designed to drill into the earth upon contact and to explode as a sign of the vengeance of Allah. From the perspective of the Asiatic connection, the unthinkable occurred on 7 December 1941. The War of Armageddon known to Elijah Muhammad since Bible school, the race war that he had anticipated as a young man, and the destructive power of the Mother Plane 'moved nightmarishly close to reality: the Japanese—"Allah's Asiatic army"—bombed Pearl Harbor, the U.S. base in Hawaii' (Evanzz 1999: 130–1).

Such, in short, is the story of the Mother Plane as both a phenomenon crucial to the theology of the Nation of Islam and as a product of the Nation's apocalyptic sensibility. To be sure, one might well feel inclined to view this phenomenon as suspect. In fact, it was so viewed by Elijah Muhammad's own son Wallace (Imam Warith Deen Mohammed 1938–2008), who assumed control of the Nation after his father's death in 1975. The new chief minister made clear his intentions of ridding his people of what he called 'all this spiritual spookiness' (Lieb 1998: 178–9). The Mother Plane was, of course, included in that ban. Should one be inclined to adopt such an outlook, it might be well to pause before dismissing the matter out of hand. If one is to take the Nation seriously, one must take its tenets seriously. But there is another reason not to be dismissive. Uncle Sam himself, the father of the Patriot Act in our own time, accorded the Mother Plane high priority. During the time of Elijah Muhammad, the Mother Plane, in fact, became a recurrent theme in the surveillance activities of the Federal Bureau of Investigation and of its offshoot, the Counter Intelligence Program (COINTELPRO).[1]

In a confidential file (105-24822), dated 8 July 1957, the FBI cites the work of its informants (with names deleted) to the effect that the United States government needs to pay close attention to the apocalyptic beliefs of the Nation, including the conviction that 'we are now living in the days of judgment'. Under the heading *Destruction of the World*, the file cites the statement: 'Allah [has] pointed out to us a dreadful looking plane that is made like a wheel in the sky today. . . . Ezekiel saw it a long time ago. It was built for the purpose of destroying the present world.' Similar kinds of information are accorded high priority elsewhere in the FBI files. For example, in a memorandum dated 1971, the Chicago office of the FBI warns J. Edgar

---

[1] The FBI files on Elijah Muhammad confirm this observation. Now available through the Internet, the various memos, letters, and reports that resulted from the surveillance of the Messenger make for fascinating reading, especially when it comes to the Mother Plane (http://foia.fbi.gov). (References in my text are to this site.)

Hoover that the Nation of Islam has been instrumental in fostering the belief that a time of judgement is upon us all and that the destruction of the world is at hand. Finally, in a confidential memorandum dated 8 November 1972, the FBI alerts the Department of Justice that 'Allah is ready to attack America out of his universe'. The memorandum then goes on to disclose the secret of the Mother Plane as set forth in Elijah Muhammad's speech to his congregants, dated 14 July 1972: 'In the book of Ezekiel, there is prophesized about a wheel in a wheel. It's up there now. The devil knows it's up there. . . . This plane represents the Mother plane. . . . Ezekiel said he'd come out and drop a bomb . . .' This statement is then followed by a long and detailed description of the Mother Plane, how it operates and what it plans to do. Thus, the FBI files on Elijah Muhammad are such that the Mother Plane becomes time and again the subject of close scrutiny. At the very least, this vehicle assumed for the United States government then the status of what one might now place under the heading of Weapons of Mass Destruction (the so-called WMDs). The products of our terror-filled era of post-9/11, these weapons, we are told, have been developed by rogue governments that must be countered with our own Weapons of Mass Destruction.[2]

LOUIS FARRAKHAN (1933–)

Although the entire set of beliefs concerning the Mother Plane was rendered untenable after the death of the Honorable Elijah Muhammad in 1975, allegiance to the principles of the Messenger (including the Mother Plane) enjoyed a new life with the Honorable Minister Louis Farrakhan's rise to power in 1978. Farrakhan's legitimation of the concept of the Mother Plane became a crucial aspect of his quest for identity, as well as his sense of vocation. Whereas the Mother Plane certainly represents a 'reality' for the Minister, he also internalizes his experience of it to the point that the 'actual' and the 'visionary' overlap. As Farrakhan conceived the Mother Plane from the very outset of his administration up to the present, this vehicle is not simply an object 'out there' to be beheld on set times. Rather, it is an object both visible to Farrakhan and active in his mental landscape. The extent to which such is the case is made evident in his various addresses, principally ranging from 1986 to 1995, all of them on videotape. Delivered at a press conference on 24 October 1989, at the J. W. Marriott Hotel, Washington, DC, an address called 'The

[2] It should be noted that Malcolm X is missing from the present account. In part, this lacuna is the result of Malcolm X's departure from the beliefs of the Nation, and the fact that his discourse did not move in the direction of the Mother Plane. See, however, Wayne Taylor (2005: 53–4).

Great Announcement: The Final Warning' represents Farrakhan's first public 'announcement' of his 'take' on the Mother Plane. The term 'announcement' is to be found as the title of the seventy-eighth chapter or *surah* in the Qur'an. There, the title 'The Announcement' ('An-Naba") alludes to the judgement upon those who will be resurrected and those who will be damned. As such, the title of the seventy-eighth *surah* suggests the potentially conflagratory nature of Farrakhan's own announcement, which describes for the first time at a public gathering both his experience on the Wheel and the significance of that experience. 'Experience' is the operative term here, because Farrakhan maintains that he did not simply 'see' the Mother Plane, as Elijah Muhammad had. Rather, he found himself transported to the Wheel both in body and in spirit, there to participate in his own psychic drama. As such, the event represents for him a primal scene in his religious calling as the student and follower of the Honorable Elijah Muhammad.

All of Farrakhan's speeches on the subject of the Mother Plane assume the form of 'performances', that is, the dramatization of visionary experience through the medium of taped video/audio delivery (Lieb 1998: 200–3). It is the performative dimension of Farrakhan's act of bearing witness that defines his message and its mode of delivery. Thus, in his press conference the vision is conceived as 'enactment' or high theatre: the public forum becomes the theatre of that event. Both in the *Final Call* and in the subsequently published pamphlet, *The Announcement*, Farrakhan appears in a photograph proclaiming his message. He is seen standing at the midpoint of a long table, flanked on either side by family, friends, and colleagues, including the Revd Al Sharpton, Kadijah Farrakhan (wife of Farrakhan), Tynnetta Muhammad, and others of importance to the Minister's administration. Marshalled in a row behind Farrakhan are members of the Fruit of Islam (the Nation's paramilitary defence force), and on a wall behind them hangs the Nation of Islam flag with its crescent and star. Before the table and facing Farrakhan are photographers and members of the press. In the videotape of the press conference the event is brought to life. The camera first pans the entire room to provide a sense of the size and scope of the affair. With the audience waiting in hushed expectation, the room becomes a receptacle for the drama of oratory that is about to unfold. All eyes are on the speaker, whose deportment, gestures, and vocal intonation reinforce the compelling nature of his message. After the speech is concluded, the speaker invites no comments or questions. The oracle has been issued, the speaker and his retinue depart, and the rest is silence.

The account of his experience makes for grand theatre. Having delivered an address before some 19,000 people at the Los Angeles Forum in September 1985, Farrakhan feels the need to retreat to a site he has visited before: Tepoztlan, an Aztec village ten-to-twelve miles north-east of Cuernavaca in central Mexico. There he finds the space needed to meditate and pray. His pilgrimage to Tepoztlan, he believes, will allow him to escape the accusations levelled by the press in Los Angeles that he is nothing but an anti-Semite, a bigot, a demagogue, and a hate-monger.

Because his attempts to rectify these charges are 'too little, too late', the retreat to Tepoztlan comes at precisely the right time for him. He is especially fond of climbing a mountain in Tepoztlan he has climbed several times before. On the evening of 17 September he begins the climb again, with a few selected companions. It is during his climb that he has his vision of a wheel-shaped transport vehicle that is one of the myriad of smaller vehicle stationed within the Wheel of Wheels, the Mother Plane. A voice from the vehicle calls on him to board, whereupon a thick and heavy beam of light transports him into the vehicle itself. The vehicle then returns to the Mother Plane. Disembarking from the transport vehicle, he is led through dark tunnels to a room within a room, a veritable *sanctum sanctorum*. At the centre of the ceiling of the enclosure he sees a speaker that emits a voice he immediately recognizes as that of Elijah Muhammad. As the voice speaks, in short, cryptic sentences, a scroll with writing rolls down before his eyes. Like the prophet of old on the shores of the Chebar, Farrakhan ingests the scroll with its message as a sign of his prophetic mission. It is his calling, after all. The message itself is as follows: 'President Reagan has met with the Joint Chiefs of Staff to plan a war. I [Elijah Muhammad] want you to hold a press conference in Washington, D.C. and announce their plan and say to the world that you got the information from me on the Wheel.' Once again, the vision of the Mother Plane is steeped in conspiracy. This time, however, the issue appears to be that of a government conspiracy that the seer of the vision is charged to make public (Lieb 1998: 212–13).

It would be an understatement to say that the public found Farrakhan's account of the Mother Plane of interest. From Thursday, 1 March until Saturday, 3 March 1990, the *Washington Post* carried stories and editorials concerning both the Mother Plane and the message that Farrakhan had delivered in *The Announcement*. At a 2½ -hour breakfast meeting with the editorial staff of the *Post*, Farrakhan alleges that one of the editors asked in scorn, 'What about this "Wheel" business?' Farrakhan responded not only by listing all the US presidents that had seen it but also by providing additional evidence of its existence, to which one of the editors in attendance whispered excitedly to a colleague seated with him: 'He knows, he knows, he knows!' (Lieb 1998: 298, n. 37). In the account that the *Post* offers, the element of scorn is essentially erased, but the questions remain, nonetheless. In any case, the '"Wheel" business' assumes front-and-centre-spread importance. After citing all the notables that have expressed interest in the subject for over fifty years, Farrakhan observes that for the US government, the subject has been 'above Top Secret, not just Top Secret, but above Top Secret'. He then traces the history of the Mother Plane to the Nation of Islam by recounting Elijah Muhammad's statements about it. Sensitive to nomenclature, he says with a certain pique: 'You call them Unidentified Flying Objects. They're not that to us. They're referred to in the writings of Ezekiel the Prophet as the wheel within a wheel.' This is what Farrakhan not only beheld but experienced first hand in Tepoztlan. Recounting the complex history of the Mother Plane as the very object that Ezekiel beheld in the sixth-century BCE, he pauses to reflect on the textual foundations of the vision. 'My mind', he says, 'goes to scripture because that's my orientation' (*Washington Post*, Thursday, 1 March 1990, A17–18). It is an orientation that has remained with him through his entire career.

From the perspective of that career, one is tempted to observe that the prophetic calling that Farrakhan received on the Wheel is part of his very being. He is haunted by wheels that follow him on his various journeys, whether domestic or international. In response to the presence of these wheels, he does not hesitate to proclaim: 'I am telling America that wherever I am the Wheel is!' He is connected to the Wheel; he receives his energy from it, his power from it, his authority from it, his 'juice' from it. Lying in bed, he hears far-off voices and beholds transcendent sights, all emanating from the Wheel. He is not a drunken man, he declares; he is not a crazy man. We all have had dreams, some foolish, others real. His dream is a vision, one that gives him purpose and shows him the way. During the years following the onset of his vision, he speaks before the representatives of eighty nations at the Second Mathaba Conference in Tripoli. There, he warns Mu'ammar Ghadafi of an impending attack by the United States and, at the same time, issues a warning to President Reagan and Secretary of State George Schultz not to bomb Libya. Refusing to heed the warning, the United States launches its attack shortly thereafter. During all of the confrontation on the Gulf of Sidra, it is reported in the press that a bright orange object has been sited over the Mediterranean. That orange object, of course, is the Mother Plane. Is this the event that should have prompted Farrakhan to hold a press conference? Apparently it is not, for it is not until four years after the original vision that he understands the full weight of his charge, which is to disclose a new conspiracy, one that involves not Reagan and Schultz but Bush and Powell. Thus, at the press conference recorded in *The Announcement* he says: 'I am here to announce today that President Bush has met with his Joint Chiefs of Staff under the direction of General Colin Powell, to plan a war against the black people of America, the Nation of Islam and Louis Farrakhan, with particular emphasis on our black youth, under the guise of a war against drug sellers, drug users, gangs and violence—all under the heading of extremely urgent national security.' The particular object of this denunciation is, of course, the Federal Bureau of Investigation (FBI), which has been attempting to destroy the Nation of Islam since 1940. With its so-called anti-terrorist task force, the FBI has sought the undoing not just of the Nation of Islam but of Farrakhan himself. It has launched a covert 'attack on Louis Farrakhan with the purpose of discrediting, embarrassing and ultimately causing the death of Louis Farrakhan' (Lieb 1998: 215). Underlying Farrakhan's press-conference message is a theme that runs throughout all his discourse. It is a theme that involves not just the conspira-torial dimensions already discussed but what might be called the persecutorial dimensions reflected in Farrakhan's outlook. Those dimensions embrace not simply the United States government and society at large but what Farrakhan calls 'the Jewish community', a community with which he has been struggling for years. That struggle frames his experience of the Mother Plane in a way that it never did for Elijah Muhammad. At the centre of this struggle is Louis Farrakhan's sense of self. It is a selfhood born of struggle, forged in controversy, and desperately attempting to find a peace that surpasses all understanding.

The best way of gaining insight into the struggle is to consult a speech that Farrakhan delivered at the Mosque Maryam on 26 April 1992. There is a tape that speaks directly to this aspect. Titled 'The Shock of the Hour', the speech derives its impetus from *surah* 22:2 of the Qur'an ('The great upheaval of the Hour will indeed be terrible'), There is no way of softening the message of this speech, the tone of which is strident and disturbing, as well as derisive. It is no doubt among the Minister's most 'apocalyptic' performances. Toward the end of the speech, even he is prompted to observe that he has 'never talked like this before'. At the centre of the speech is the Mother Plane, which will descend upon the white race at the end of time to destroy all in its path. Although this kind of thing is a staple of Elijah Muhammad's thinking, Farrakhan provides a new animus for his anger, focusing on the Jews. He fires off allegation after allegation in a series of salvos against the Jews who have been seeking to undermine him. Claiming that the Jews rule the currency and control the banks, he maintains that it is even possible to see the Star of David embedded as a secret sign in the depiction of the eagle on the dollar bill. Disclosing the 'conspiracy' between the United States and Israel, he declares that 'the real Israel is over here'. It is called 'the United States of America, run by Jews'. It was the Jews, he says, who fought against Nat Turner, who worked against Frederick Douglas, Marcus Garvey, Malcolm X, and Dr Martin Luther King. 'Jews in the government, in the Justice department, Jews that worked against the prophets of God', and Jews who are now seeking to undermine Louis Farrakhan. 'I have greater enemies against me in this movement', he alleges, 'than Moses had against him, than Jesus had against him, than Prophet Muhammad had against him. My enemies', he declares, 'are greater than all their enemies combined' (Lieb 1998: 216–19). It is against these enemies that he takes up arms, it is these that he calls upon the Mother Plane to eliminate. It is in the spirit of this kind of rhetoric that the Mother Plane assumes a bearing that is entirely apocalyptic and destructive. In dealing with the history of the Mother Plane, one must be aware of this dark and disturbing side of a personality constantly in a state of struggle. The question is whether the man who delivered the address called 'The Shock of the Hour' some fifteen years ago is of the same mind today.

In this connection, it is interesting to note developments that have occurred in the post-9/11 era. Given what is known about the Farrakhan's professed beliefs, the terrorist attack on the Twin Towers of the World Trade Center and on the Pentagon on 11 September 2001 is an event that would appear to have all the 'markings' of the Mother Plane. Here, surely, was the opportunity to draw upon the traditions of radical militancy embraced by the Nation from the very beginning and to declare in the spirit of Malcolm X that the 'pigeons have come home to roost'. Under the circumstances, the idea of viewing this tragedy in those terms would certainly not have been difficult. In fact, one might view such a reading as almost inevitable. Significantly, the transcript of an Osama bin Laden tape dated 13 December 2001 makes it clear that Bin Laden himself did not hesitate to associate the attack with visionary aircraft of one sort or another. Those in conversation with Bin Laden shortly after the attack speak of having had anticipatory visions of planes crashing into large buildings in New York and Washington, DC. These are all visions that for Bin Laden lend credence to the jihad that has been mounted against the devil.[3] Now, it is perfectly apparent that Louis Farrakhan could have taken his cue from this kind of thing, and, in looking upon the attacks as a sign of Allah's divine retribution, could have invoked the Mother Plane and its retributive bearing in order to lend credence to the terrorist attack. In fact, Farrakhan might well have undertaken an address in the spirit of 'The Shock of the Hour' to justify the barbarity that was thrust upon the world that fateful day. But he did no such thing.

Instead, he responded to the tragedy in a 'World Press Conference from Mosque Maryam' on Sunday, 16 September 2001. Making no references to mother planes of any sort, he issued the following statement: 'Words are inadequate to express the pain, the sadness, the anguish that has moved my spirit to come before you today to speak from my heart to your hearts, and beyond this room to the hearts of a nation grieved, angry, and in mourning. And beyond this nation to the nations of the world who have been and will be affected by this tragedy that has come to the United States of America.' On behalf of the Nation of Islam and of the Muslims here and abroad, he did not hesitate, as he says, to 'condemn this vicious and atrocious attack on the United States'. The statement goes on to declare that, 'though the pain that Black people have suffered in America has caused me to be angry with the country of my birth . . . in my maturation, I know that with all of America's problems, she's the greatest nation on this earth'. As a citizen of this nation, he declares, 'I do not wish to see harm come to her'. Set against the rhetoric that has distinguished the Nation of Islam since its founding, the diplomacy reflected in this response is quite remarkable. The only reference to planes is one that castigates not the United States but those 'perpetrators of this crime' who 'turned the symbol of the nation's aviation and technological brilliance' into 'missiles and messengers of death and destruction'.[4] Where is the Mother Plane in all this? For Minister Farrakhan, it is nowhere to be found—at least, not in his official statement for the press. Does that mean that the Mother Plane will no longer appear? That is hardly the case. The Minister fully anticipates returning there after all his work is completed.

---

[3] Transcript and annotations are prepared by George Michael and Kassem M. Wahba. The conversation itself was possibly recorded in mid-November in Qandahar, Afghanistan. The transcript can be found that following Internet address: http://www.salon.com.

[4] I use the text of the press conference from the following Internet site: http://www.noi.org.

Works Cited

Al-Qur'an (1993), trans. Ahmed Ali. Princeton: Princeton University Press.

Bin Laden, Osama Transcript (2001). http://www.salon.com.

Evanzz, Karl (1999), *The Messenger: The Rise and Fall of Elijah Muhammad.* New York: Pantheon Books.

Farrakhan, Louis (1989), *The Announcement: A Final Warning to the U.S. Government.* Chicago: Final Call.

——(1989), 'The Great Announcement: The Final Warning' (VHS Video of the Press Conference, J. W. Marriott Hotel, Washington, DC, 24 Oct. 1989).

——(1989), 'The Great Announcement: The Final Warning', *Final Call* (30 Nov.), 16–17, 29–30.

——(1992), 'The Shock of the Hour' (Audio Tape of the Message, Mosque Maryam, Chicago, Illinois, 26 Apr. 1992).

——(2001), World Press Conference, Mosque Maryam, 16 Sept. 2001; http://www.noi.org.

Federal Bureau of Investigation, Department of Justice (1973), File 105-24822; http://foia.fbi.gov.

Lieb, Michael (1998), *Children of Ezekiel: Aliens, UFOs, the Crisis of Race, and the Advent of End Time.* Durham, NC: Duke University Press.

Lincoln, C. Eric (1989), 'The Muslim Mission in the Context of American Social History', in Gayraud Wilmore (ed.), *African American Religious Studies: An Interdisciplinary Anthology.* Durham, NC: Duke University Press.

Muhammad, Elijah (1965), *Message to the Blackman in America.* Philadelphia: House of Knowledge Publications.

Taylor, Wayne (2005), 'Premillennium Tension: Malcolm X and the Eschatology of the Nation of Islam'. Souls, 7/1: 52–65.

Further Reading

In addition to the items listed above, there are several crucial sources on the subject that should not be overlooked. These include primary material that stems from the Nation of Islam itself and secondary material concerning the relationship between Ezekiel 1 and the Mother Plane. For Elijah Muhammad's meditations on the issue, see his book *The Fall of America* (Chicago: Muhammad's Temple of Islam No. 2, 1973), as well as a series of articles by Elijah Muhammad in his newspaper *Muhammad Speaks* (May–Sept. 1973). Also crucial to an understanding of Elijah Muhammad is the organization Coalition for the Remembrance of Elijah (with its Web site http://www.croe.org). For Louis Farrakhan one must consult the work of Jabril Muhammad, whose writings are essential to the topic. See, in particular, his articles in the *Final Call*, as well as his other writings. It is also important to consult the Internet, which has assumed a crucial role in the efforts of the Nation of Islam to trace its own history and to disseminate its beliefs. In recent years scholarly material on the Nation of Islam has proliferated. Still invaluable are C. Eric Lincoln's pioneering study *The Black Muslims in America* (1961; 3rd edn. Grand Rapids, Mich.: Eerdmans, 1994) and E. U. Essien-Udom, *Black Nationalism: A Search for Identity in America* (Chicago: University of Chicago Press, 1962). Also of major importance are Mattias Gardell, *In the Name of Elijah Muhammad: Louise Farrakhan and the Nation of Islam* (Durham, NC: Duke University Press, 1996) and Claude Andrew Clegg III, *An Original Man: The Life and Times of Elijah Muhammad* (New York: St Martin's, 1997).

CHAPTER 33

POST-HOLOCAUST JEWISH INTERPRETATIONS OF JOB

ISABEL WOLLASTON

THERE is a long-standing Jewish tradition, both religious and secular, of responding to catastrophe in the present by recalling, and recasting, models and archetypes from the past, particularly from the Bible. They may be recalled literally, as traditionally understood, or rewritten, even parodied (often violently), in order to challenge and/or subvert more traditional readings. Interrogating and/or deconstructing traditional responses and archetypes is present in scripture (the Book of Job is a prime example), and in midrashic readings that seek to tease out the tensions, gaps, and silences in the biblical text. If, as James Young suggests, a 'self-reflexive questioning of the available archetypes' is *the* typical Jewish response to catastrophe as writers and artists turn to 'the only system of myths, precedents, figures, and archetypes available to them' (1988: 95, 97; Roskies 1988), then it is hardly surprising that writing and rewriting biblical archetypes is a recurrent motif within Jewish literary, artistic, and theological responses to the Holocaust.

The first part of this chapter analyses different forms post-Holocaust biblical hermeneutics can take. The next section briefly explores the complexities and tensions within the biblical Book of Job. The final part then considers a range of post-Holocaust Jewish interpretations of Job and the relevance this biblical figure and text might have to the realities of the Holocaust and living in a post-Holocaust world.

POST-HOLOCAUST BIBLICAL HERMENEUTICS

In his essay 'The Man of Today and the Jewish Bible' (1936), Martin Buber states that 'each generation must struggle with the Bible in its turn and come to terms with it' (Biemann 2002: 51). His challenge prompts us to ask how those who lived through the Holocaust and in its aftermath have struggled and come to terms with the Bible. There is a substantial literature on Jewish–Christian relations, primarily focusing on the relationship between Christian anti-Judaism, racial antisemitism, and the Holocaust (e.g. Ruether 1974; Frederiksen and Reinhartz 2002), and a growing number of artistic, literary, and theological explorations of the use of biblical archetypes during and after the Holocaust. Yet, despite burgeoning interest in how Jews and Christians read the Bible, and other religious texts, both separately and together, there is relatively limited discussion of post-Holocaust biblical hermeneutics per se. Tod Linafelt of Georgetown University has played a key role in bringing about change, both offering his own vision of post-Holocaust biblical hermeneutics and providing a forum for others to do so in collections such as *Strange Fire: Reading the Bible after the Holocaust* (2000) and *A Shadow of Glory: Reading the New Testament after the Holocaust* (2002). The emergence of post-Holocaust biblical hermeneutics on the scholarly agenda is evident from the inclusion of an entry (by Linafelt) on 'Biblical Interpretation and the Holocaust' in the two-volume *Dictionary of Biblical Interpretation* (1999), whereas there was no such entry in the multi-volume *Anchor Bible Dictionary* (1992).

Linafelt was inspired, in part, by the work of Emil Fackenheim (1916–2003), David Blumenthal (b. 1938), and Elie Wiesel (b. 1928). Fackenheim's Sherman Lectures, delivered at the University of Manchester in November 1987 and later published as *The Jewish Bible after the Holocaust: A Re-reading* (1990), evaluate Buber's approach in the light of the Holocaust. Fackenheim comments briefly on specific biblical texts, but offers little sustained reflection on post-Holocaust biblical hermeneutics. Like Fackenheim's lectures, David Blumenthal's *Facing the Abusing God: A Theology of Protest* (1993) directly addresses the situation of Jews after the Holocaust, but differs in its very self-conscious articulation of a specifically *Jewish* approach to theology and, by implication, biblical hermeneutics. He believes that a distinctively *Jewish* theology must be rooted in an ongoing dialogue with the biblical text and Jewish tradition. Just as this text and tradition incorporate multiple, even contradictory, perspectives, so too must any Jewish theology or reflection upon them. 'Text-ing' (1993: 57–189), the central section of *Facing the Abusing God*, embodies Blumenthal's approach. It consists of four commentaries on four psalms, presented as a grouped textual field in the manner of a page of the Talmud. The four are Psalm 128 (described by Blumenthal as an expression of blessing and blessedness), Psalm 44 (a psalm of national anger), Psalm 109 (a psalm of personal anger), and Psalm 27 (a psalm of healing). The commentaries offer four very different approaches and perspectives: 'Words' consists of philological and exegetical insights; 'Sparks' draws on spiritual and mystical traditions within Judaism; 'Affections' gives voice to the externally directed rage of 'the abused person who has moved towards a righteous anger and moral outrage' (1993: 134); 'Con-verses' strives to capture the voice of 'the abused person who is walled in by silence' and directs their rage inward (ibid. 134).

As is evident in even this brief discussion 'post-Holocaust' is interpreted in many different ways. In straightforward chronological terms it refers to that which *comes after*, that is, post-dates, the Holocaust. However, for Linafelt, post-Holocaust biblical hermeneutics are explicit reflections on the nature and meaning of the biblical text *in the light of the Holocaust*, regardless of whether it is understood as historically or theologically unique. Other definitions are more restrictive, with 'post-Holocaust' confined to approaches premised on the belief that the Holocaust marks a radical break or rupture with what went before, such that 'each piece of tradition—text, principle, belief, image, model, or practice—must be reclaimed from this side of Auschwitz and from a vantage point in part darkened by these events' (Morgan 2001: 217). A reading of the biblical text can therefore be 'post-Holocaust', understood in these two senses, regardless of whether it is contemporaneous with events or comes *after*. Tania Oldenhage adds an additional element to this discussion in arguing that a distinctively *Christian* post-Holocaust biblical hermeneutics should also acknowledge and address the complexities of reading scriptural texts when they, and their history of interpretation, are 'tainted' by anti-Judaism (2002: 139–51).

Orthodox Jewish responses to the Holocaust, such as those of Joseph Solo-veitchik (1903–93) and Eliezer Berkovits (1908–92), are 'post-Holocaust' in Lina-felt's sense of the term: they explicitly address the question of faith after the Holocaust, but reject any suggestion that the Holocaust marks a radical break between past and present. Instead, they emphasize continuity and the ongoing relevance of traditional responses to catastrophe. By contrast, the work of Wiesel, Fackenheim, and Richard Rubenstein (b. 1924) is 'post-Holocaust' in both senses, because they focus on the discontinuities created by the Holocaust and decon-struct, rewrite, even reject, traditional responses to catastrophe and readings of the biblical text. For Rubenstein, 'the experience of our time has exploded our ancient categories of meaning' (Linafelt 2000: 246), whilst Fackenheim believes that 'an abyss has opened up between the Book, then and there, and this 'generation' here and now' (1990: 17). Blumenthal's work is 'post-Holocaust' in a different sense again, in that he seeks to synthesize more-traditional approaches with insights from Holocaust theology. He is acutely conscious of writing after Holocaust and of the need to confront what he believes are the distinctive challenges facing Jews living in a post-Holocaust world, but he combines this with an emphasis on continuity and respect for traditional methods of interpretation, embodied in his insistence on presenting the commentaries on his four chosen psalms as a grouped textual field.[1] Blumenthal juxtaposes the voices of those who still believe that the tradition contains resources for responding to catastrophe, even on the scale of the Holocaust, with those who question the relevance of the Bible and tradition in a post-Holocaust world, arguing that both approaches have validity and deserve to be heard. The tensions between the two are left largely unresolved.

Despite such marked differences in approach, a broad consensus is emerging that post-Holocaust biblical hermeneutics should incorporate, and be interrupted by, the testimony of victims and survivors. Attention to testimony and sensitivity to the realities of the lived experience of atrocity often results in a suspicion of readings of the biblical text that seek to explain away, rationalize, or justify innocent suffering. Such suspicion can take the form of protest over the injustice of the suffering of the innocent and/or a pronounced privileging of anti-theodicy over traditional justifications of suffering or theodicies (Braiterman 1998: 35–59, 161–78). Blumenthal is typical in maintaining that, after the Holocaust, 'protest is a religiously proper faith stance toward God' (1993: 253). Such privileging of protest and anti-theodicy in the face of innocent suffering accounts, at least in part, for the interest in, even preoccupation with, Job during and after the Holocaust.

The survivor-writer Elie Wiesel is particularly influential in this context. He prioritizes testimony and protest and has developed a distinctive personal post-Holocaust biblical hermeneutics. He prefers to present himself as a survivor-witness and 'teller of tales' rather than a 'scholar'. For Wiesel, the majority of scholars engage in a second-order discipline, commenting on, and presuming to understand, an event of which they have no 'true' knowledge because they were not 'there', that is, of which they have no first-hand experience. In relation to suffering in general and the Holocaust in particular, Wiesel argues, true knowledge belongs to the victims and survivors. He therefore prefers the work of scholars who acknowledge their dependency on the testimony of those who were 'there'.

Whilst primarily known as a speaker, writer, and advocate on issues related to the Holocaust and human rights (hence the award of the Nobel Peace Prize in 1986), Wiesel has also lectured widely and written on stories from the Bible, Talmud, midrash, and the Hasidic tradition. He describes his approach as a teller of tales as quintessentially Jewish, likening himself to a *maggid* (one who relates; an itinerant preacher). In his lectures and essays he explores a range of midrashic

---

[1] It should be noted that Blumenthal, like Berkovits, prefers to use the lower case for 'holocaust'.

interpretations of biblical, Talmudic, and Hasidic texts, together with his own retellings of these stories in the light of the Holocaust. Wiesel often presents this approach as an *alternative* to theology, but such claims are not to be taken at face-value given the long-standing Jewish tradition of storytelling as a vehicle *for* theology, so evident in the Bible, midrash, Aggadah, and the tales of the Hasidim: the very traditions Wiesel identifies himself with.

Wiesel suggests that telling such tales enables him to look away from the harsh realities of the Holocaust. However, this overlooks the central role these tales play in his strategy for talking about the Holocaust: retelling tales from the Bible, Talmud, and the Hasidic masters allows Wiesel to communicate what he believes is the untellable story of the Holocaust. By retelling such tales he pays tribute to, and reconnects with, his teachers and formative influences, as well as a disrupted, forever-lost, past (symbolized for Wiesel by his home town of Sighet). Yet retelling such tales serves as a constant reminder of the fate of the teachers who handed them down to him and reinforces what has been lost. For Wiesel, the gulf separating past and present, Sighet and Auschwitz, is such that 'the full range of implications' and 'deeper meanings' of the original biblical stories only becomes apparent when they are (re)read and retold in the light of the Holocaust (1976: pp. xiii–iv). He therefore rewrites the story of Cain and Abel as an account of the first genocide; Isaac becomes the first survivor, Jeremiah the first survivor-witness, and Job the 'contemporary' of Holocaust survivors. *Night*, Wiesel's memoir of the Holocaust, can be read as an extended rewriting of the *Akedah*, one in which the father is killed and the son survives, traumatized by his memories of that experience, but nevertheless compelled to tell the tale.

The insistence that any reading of the biblical text should be 'interrupted' by the testimony of victims and survivors of the Holocaust (there is disagreement over whether this should be extended to the testimony of victims and survivors of all instances of unjust suffering, abuse, or acts of genocide) results in increasing emphasis on the fractured, fragmented nature of post-Holocaust biblical hermeneutics. Testimony incorporates multiple perspectives, both complementary and contradictory. Post-Holocaust biblical hermeneutics attentive to such testimony is acutely conscious of the multivocal quality of individual texts (such as Job), as well as of scripture as a whole and the history of biblical interpretation. For Blumenthal, 'plurivocity and ambiguity, not univocity and consistency are the norm'. The best we can hope for, he suggests, is 'partial coherence' (1993: 14), and he makes a point of weaving multiple, contradictory, perspectives into the fabric of *Facing the Abusing God*. The four commentaries in 'Text-ing' are placed side by side with no attempt to resolve the contradictions between them. The next section, 'Re-sponse', includes Blumenthal's correspondence with two women openly critical of his views: Diane, an adult survivor of child abuse, and Wendy, a Christian systematic theologian (ibid. 195–225), and 'Beth's Psalm' (ibid. 227–32), a reflection on Psalm 27 by one of his students.

Post-Holocaust biblical hermeneutics emphasizes the fragile, ambiguous, contested character of biblical texts, and interrogates the text, as well as the reader or
interpreter, asking who is speaking and for what purpose. It is acutely conscious
both of the gulf that may separate the 'scholar' from the experience and testimony
of victims and survivors, and of the 'politics' of reading and interpretation: where is
the author, or the reader/interpreter, of that text located? Whose experience is
privileged, both in the biblical text and in the interpretation of that text? In the
process of reading, translation, and interpretation is any experience or voice
marginalized or silenced? Whose interests are served by particular readings, and
what are the practical consequences of adopting one interpretation rather than
another? Such questions should be borne in mind when considering the Book of
Job itself, its history of interpretation, and post-Holocaust Jewish interpretations
of Job.

THE BOOK OF JOB AS A CONTESTED TEXT
CONTAINING MULTIPLE PERSPECTIVES

Job is a complex, multifaceted text, consisting of a prose Prologue (chs. 1–2) and
Epilogue (42:7–17), separated by a series of poetic speeches. The text is polyphonic,
offering a range of voices and perspectives on the problem of suffering. In the
Prologue, set in the heavenly court, God describes Job as 'a blameless and upright
man, who fears God and turns away from evil' (1:8). This commendation prompts
Satan to ask 'does Job fear God for naught? Hast thou not put a hedge about him
and his house and all that he has, on every side?' (1:9). Satan counters by arguing
that Job does not complain because he has nothing to complain about, and might
well respond differently if he did. God agrees to Satan's request to test/torment/
torture Job to see whether a radical downturn in his fortunes will prompt him to
curse God (1:9–12, 2:1–6). In the Prologue Job makes no complaint (1:21): despite
the dramatic change in fortune, including the loss of his possessions and the
sudden deaths of his children (1:13–19), he 'did not sin or charge God with
wrong' (1:22), and rejects his wife's invitation to 'curse God, and die' (2:9).
However, in the poetic section Job abruptly changes tack and launches into an
'uncompromising defence of his innocence' (Blumenthal 1993: 15). A series of
exchanges (or rather monologues, given the limited interaction between the speakers) follow with his friends Eliphaz (chs. 4–5, 15, 22), Bildad (chs. 8, 18, 25), Zopar
(chs. 11, 20), and Elihu (chs. 32–7). The friends respond to Job's complaints by
arguing that God is indeed just because human suffering is invariably a consequence of human sin and therefore, in some sense at least, understandable. Finally,

Job receives a divine response from 'out of the whirlwind' (38–40:2, 40:6–41:34), a phrase Rabbi Albert Friedlander adopted as the title of his 1976 anthology of Holocaust literature. Yet, rather than providing 'an intellectually valid answer' (Berkovits 1973: 109), the divine response takes the form of rhetorical questions, none of which directly address Job's complaints, but instead focus on the majesty of creation. Finally, in the prose Epilogue God directly addresses Eliphaz: 'my wrath is kindled against your two friends; for you have not spoken of me what is right, as my servant Job has' (42: 7; there is no reference to Elihu who seems to have vanished from the text). We are then told that Job's fortunes were restored, 'twice as much as he had before' (42:10), with new children in place of those killed earlier (42:13–16). This Epilogue is particularly puzzling: first it seems to reintroduce the connection between faithfulness and good fortune, sin and suffering that both prompted Satan's initial challenge in the Prologue and underpins the friends' theology, even though we are told that what they said was not 'right'; second, it fails to refer to, and even seems oblivious of, the initial 'test' described in the Prologue and Satan's involvement.

How do these elements cohere, and what, if any, is the overall stance of the book's author(s)? Is there one Job or several different Jobs in the text; that is, how do we reconcile the faithful, patient Job of the Prologue (celebrated in Jas. 5:11); the impatient, protesting, even rebellious, Job of the dialogues (admired by Wiesel, Blumenthal, and others); and the reconciled but largely silent (or silenced) Job of the Epilogue? The difficulty in answering such questions, and reaching consensus as to what the text actually says, is particularly evident in the significantly different translations provided for that 'the most enigmatic of texts' (Blumenthal 1993: 254), verse 42:6, Job's response to the theophany 'out of the whirlwind'. Does he regret and/or retract his protest, abasing himself in the process? Is he satisfied simply to have provoked a divine response, that is, the personal encounter with God is in and of itself a sufficient 'answer' to his complaint? The King James Bible translates the verse as 'wherefore I abhor myself, and repent in dust and ashes', whereas the RSV reads 'therefore I despise myself, and repent in dust and ashes'. Berkovits uses the 1917 Jewish Publication Society translation, 'I abhor my words and repent, seeing I am dust and ashes' (1973: 69), while the 1985/8 JPS translation reads, 'therefore I recant and relent, being but dust and ashes'. Robert Gordis offers yet another variant, 'I abase myself and repent in dust and ashes' (1978: 491). Faced with such choice, Wiesel prefers his own loose paraphrase of Job's response: 'Yes, I am indeed small, insignificant; I had no right to speak, I am unworthy of Your words and thoughts. I didn't know, I didn't understand, I couldn't know. From now on I shall live with remorse, in dust and ashes' (1976: 231–2). Blumenthal also offers his own translation, but even then feels compelled to offer two alternatives: (a) 'therefore I am as nothing and I am remorseful, being [only] dust and ashes', and (b) 'therefore, I renounce and am comforted, being [only] dust and ashes', justifying this apparent indecision on the grounds that 'any twofold combination of the four verbs seems to me to be justified', noting pointedly, 'herein lies the difficulty' (1993: 254).

Commentators continue to argue over the relationship of the different components and the meaning of the book as a whole. Does Job advocate a traditional theodicy of suffering as punishment for sin, or reject this in favour of anti-theodicy and a theology of protest? Or does the book endorse both positions, leaving readers with an open question or conflict? Given the diversity of readings, down to the level of disputing the translation of particular verses, it is unsurprising that there are a similar range of post-Holocaust Jewish interpretations of Job.

POST-HOLOCAUST-JEWISH INTERPRETATIONS OF JOB

References to Job, during and after the Holocaust, are both generic (identifying victims and/or survivors of the Holocaust, children of survivors, or subsequent generations, with Job) and specific (utilizing particular verses or elements of Job's story).

In terms of specific textual references, Job's demand that his protest should be heard, 'O Earth, cover not my blood | And let my cry never cease' (16:18)—a demand which may or may not be met, depending on how one interprets the text—is thought particularly apposite; for example, Hilda Schiff chose it as the epigraph for her anthology of Holocaust poetry, and it is often cited in liturgies and speeches during commemorative ceremonies. It also features, in varying forms, on a number of Holocaust memorials, for example, at Bełżec; Bergen-Belsen; Bikernieki, near Riga; the Umschlagplatz, Warsaw; and the Chamber of the Holocaust, Mount Zion, Jerusalem. For Wiesel, the verse embodies an 'outcry which, from generation to generation, through pogroms and massacres, reverberates from one end of exile to the other' (1976: 229). Chaim Kaplan, writing in the Warsaw ghetto (he kept a diary up until his sudden deportation to Treblinka, where he is thought to have been killed in the summer of 1942), describes the execution of eight Jews for leaving the ghetto without permission, expressing his horror and outrage at this act via an abbreviated form of the verse: 'O earth, cover not thou my blood!' (19 November 1941, Katsh 1999: 280).

In more generic terms, the survivor and artist Samuel Bak describes Job as 'one of the Six Million' (Fewell, Phillips, and Sherwood 2008: 46). David Roskies cites the poet Yitzhak Katzenelson's *Job: A Biblical Tragedy in Three Acts* (Warsaw ghetto, June 1941; Katzenelson was killed in Auschwitz in 1944) as evidence that 'Job, the Bible's archetypal loner and victim of unwarranted suffering, was a natural choice for the Jews of Warsaw in the early months of the ghetto', but then adds that this was despite the fact that 'hardly anyone still believed in God's desperate self-defence from out of the whirlwind' (1984: 294). There is some evidence to support André Neher's claim that, 'at some time or another, every survivor of the Holocaust has felt himself to be Job' (1993: 63). Joseph Freeman called his memoir *Job: The Story of a Holocaust Survivor*, using quotations from the biblical text as epigraphs for its various sections (1996: 1, 13, 85), and Wiesel wrote a play, *The Trial of God (as it was held on February 25, 1649 in Shamgorod)* (1979), which Blumenthal describes as 'a modern re-reading' of Job (1993: 250). Wiesel admits that he was 'preoccupied with Job, especially in the early years after the war', and suggests that 'in those days he could be seen on every road of Europe.' (1976: 233–4; 1982: 97). He addresses the subject at length in the essay 'Job our Contemporary', in *Messengers of God*, and in *Job ou Dieu dans la tempête* (published in 1986 but yet to be translated into English). For Maurice Friedman, Wiesel himself is 'the Job of Auschwitz' (1987: 162, 169); whilst for Dan Mathewson, the survivor Samuel Bak embodies Friedman's description of the 'modern Job' (Fewell, Phillips, and Sherwood 2008: 159).

Whilst agreeing on Job's relevance to the Holocaust, others focus on the relationship between Job and non-survivors and/or later generations. Berkovits, who escaped from Nazi Germany in 1938, argues that non-survivors are in the position of 'Job's brother' (1973: 4–5, 69–70). Fackenheim, who fled Germany in 1939, believes post-Holocaust Jewry is in a position analogous to that of the children of Job referred to in the Epilogue (1990: 26, 94). For Alan Berger (1977), a non-survivor, it is the second generation, that is, children of survivors, who are 'Job's children'. Post-Holocaust, many Jewish commentators are particularly perturbed by the fate of Job's first children. They express concern that this is passed over without comment in the biblical text, as if such collateral damage is perfectly acceptable, and challenge any suggestion that the blessing of 'new' children in any way compensates for the death (or wilful, casual murder, sanctioned by God?) of their predecessors (Blumenthal 1993: 255; Fackenheim 2007: 262–3; Neher 1981: 43, 195; Rubenstein, in Linafelt 2000: 236; Zuckerman 1991: 32).

There are, however, also those who challenge Job's relevance to the situation of Jews during or after the Holocaust. In 1967 Buber famously referred to 'the survivors of Auschwitz, the Job of the gas chambers', questioning whether it was possible to ask them to follow the biblical Job and 'Give thanks unto the Lord, for He is good; for His Mercy endureth forever' (1995: 224, quoting Ps. 106:1). Rubenstein is more forthright. Whilst acknowledging that many 'Jewish theologians insist that the post-Auschwitz Jew is a contemporary exemplar of Job', he argues that it is 'a very serious mistake' to overlook the gulf separating the assumptions underpinning the biblical text (and the story of Job in particular) about the nature of the divine–human relationship, inter-human relationships, the human as created in the image of God, and the harsh realities of the Holocaust. He outlines his objections in typically bullish terms:

hideously afflicted, Job sat on his dung heap. No matter how terrible his condition became, he was at all times recognized as a person by both God and man. At Auschwitz, the Jew did not sit upon the dung heap. He became less than the dung heap...No 'Thou' was addressed to the Auschwitz Jew by either God or man. The Jew became a nonperson in the deepest sense. Neither his life nor his death mattered. There was no question because there was no Job. Job went up in smoke. His question went with him. (1968: pp. xviii–xix)

Yet Rubenstein also accepts that some Holocaust survivors, such as Wiesel, *do* regard Job's story as relevant to their own situation, but suggests this is only 'because he [Wiesel] survived and his sufferings were in truth a test for him' (Linafelt 2000: 242), the implication being that the story of Job is not relevant to those who did *not* survive. Steven Katz is also adamant that 'the Joban defence of tragedy, of suffering as the occasion for growth and overcoming, has little relevance to the Holocaust', arguing that, 'unlike Job of old, the Jews in the death camps were not protected from destruction' (2006: 34). Barry Levy, meanwhile, observes that the Book of Job is not included in the annual cycle of readings in synagogue, interpreting this as evidence that 'Judaism as a public religion is barely concerned with Job'. He concludes that the text's 'relevance to the Holocaust is moot' (Linafelt 2000: 53).

Even this small sample of responses prompts us to ask which Job is deemed (ir)relevant to the Holocaust. Is it the steadfast, patient Job; the more intemperate, protesting Job; or the reconciled Job, seemingly rewarded for his endurance and steadfastness in the face of tragedy? Orthodox Jewish readings of Job tend to emphasize the Job who is 'patient' or 'faithful' in the face of seemingly inexplicable suffering (as in Freeman's memoir). Berkovits insists that 'what happened to Job is wrong; it is terribly wrong' (1973: 68), but believes that this is precisely what makes Job's continuing faith remarkable. At the same time, he is careful to point out that there is a significant difference between the biblical Job and the 'Job of the gas chambers': for the latter there was no theophany; instead, 'God remained silent to the very end of the tragedy and the millions in the concentration camps were left alone to shift for themselves in the midst of infinite despair' (1973: 69). For Berkovits, there were two Jobs (or the 'Job of the gas chambers' responded in two very different ways): whilst one 'belatedly accepted the advice of Job's wife and turned his back on God', there is another who 'kept his faith to the end, who offered it at the very doors of the gas chambers, who was able to walk to his death defiantly singing his *Ani Mamin*—I Believe' (1973: 69). Whilst he acknowledges the existence and legitimacy of the first response, Berkovits indisputably privileges the second.

A very different Orthodox reading of Job in the context of the Holocaust is put forward by Joseph Soloveitchik, who questions whether the biblical Job was indeed patient or faithful, or even innocent. Rather, his suffering was justified and conveys an important lesson to both Job and the reader. In 'Kol Dodi Dofek: It is the Voice of My Beloved That Knocketh', originally delivered in 1956 at the Yeshiva University, New York, Soloveitchik argues that Job's complaints and claims of innocence demonstrate a preoccupation with his own suffering and an inability to see beyond his own concerns. However, as a result of his suffering, his discussions with his friends, and the divine response 'out of the whirlwind', Job comes to appreciate 'how strange and inappropriate his question was, how great was his ignorance'. True understanding comes only with the acceptance of his own sinfulness and acknowledgement that he was 'lacking in that great attribute of hesed, of loving kindness' (1993: 59). For Soloveitchik, Job's sufferings were not undeserved and his complaint is found to be unjustified. The Epilogue, therefore, provides a fitting conclusion to the story: 'the afflictions of Job found their true rectification when he extricated himself from his fenced-in confines, and the divine wrath was abated. 'And the Lord turned the captivity of Job, *when he prayed for his friends*' (Job 42:10)' (ibid. 62).

In contrast to such Orthodox readings, other survivors and Jewish commentators identify with the protesting, impatient Job of the dialogues. For Primo Levi, chemist, writer, and survivor of Auschwitz, Job was the embodiment of 'the just man oppressed by injustice' (2002: 11).[2] Wiesel and Blumenthal both emphasize the validity of Job's protest. According to Blumenthal, the Book of Job is 'the most forceful expression of a theology of protest' (1993: 250–1), whilst Wiesel identifies with the protesting Job who questions God's absolute justice (2006: 57; 1976: 229–30, 235) and is fiercely critical of both the friends (1976: 225–6) and the response 'out of the whirlwind', in which

God said nothing that Job could interpret as an answer or an explanation or a justification of his ordeals. God did not say: You sinned, you did wrong. Nor did he admit His own error. He dealt in generalities, offering nothing but vast simplifications. Job's individual experience, his personal misfortunes mattered little; what mattered was the context, the overall picture.   (ibid. 231)

Wiesel recalls that he was 'deeply troubled', 'offended', and 'insulted' by the reconciled Job's apparent 'surrender' in the Epilogue (ibid. 233–4): 'that biblical rebel should never have given in. At the last moment he should have reared up, shaken a fist, and with a resounding bellow defied the transcendent, inhuman Justice in which suffering has no weight in the battle' (1975: 52). Wiesel even speculates that 'the true ending was lost. That Job died without having repented, without having humiliated himself; that he succumbed to his grief an uncompromising and whole man' (1976: 233). Alternatively, he suggests, Job withdrew his complaint so quickly, without argument, so as to suggest to the discerning reader that 'he did not believe in his own confession' (ibid. 235). What other explanation (s) can there be, for 'Job knew, as we know, that he had committed no sin, he had nothing to reproach himself for, neither did God' (ibid. 218)? Wiesel questions the relevance of the reconciled Job to survivors of the Holocaust who were, at least in the immediate post-war period, 'wounded, robbed, mutilated. Certainly not happy. Nor resigned' (ibid. 234).

[2] It is notable that selected extracts from Job's protest (chs. 3, 7, 14) and the divine response (chs. 38; 40:15–24; 41) are the only biblical texts Primo Levi, a confirmed agnostic, includes in *The Search for Roots*, his personal selection of essential readings, and that they should come first.

In reflecting on the impact of the Holocaust on the visual arts, Ziva Amishai-Maisels observes that 'Job seemed to many artists to be the perfect symbol of the innocent Holocaust victims who have no control over the evils that befall them' (1993: 164). One striking artistic post-Holocaust Jewish interpretation of Job is by Nathan Rapoport (1911–87), whose 5-foot-high bronze sculpture *Job* (1967), figured as a concentration-camp inmate complete with a number (14527) on its left forearm, is located in the grounds of Yad Vashem, Israel's national Holocaust memorial and museum. (A second casting of the figure was in private ownership until 1986, when it was donated to the City of New York; it was installed in Forest Park in 1987). In many ways Rapoport's sculpture embodies the fragile, contested nature of post-Holocaust biblical hermeneutics, the biblical story of Job, and the diversity of post-Holocaust Jewish rewritings of it. Its meaning is ambiguous, as can be seen from this photograph taken by the author in April 2008 (fig. 33.1),

Fig. 33.1. Statue of Job in the ground of Yad Vashem. Photographer Isabel Wollaston.

allowing the viewer to respond as they wish. *Job's* head is thrown back, his lips slightly parted, eyes directed upward, and hands clasped. Is this a representation of the faithful Job, engaged in (silent) prayer? Rapoport's own comments support such a reading: 'he is praying. His body is covered with a ragged *tallit* [prayer shawl]. That is his armour, the symbol of his indestructible belief. He is ready to go to his death for *Kiddush Hashem*, the sanctification of God, with the eternal prayer of the Jewish people attesting to their faith in the one God, "Shma Yisrael"' (Amishai-Maisels 1993: 165). Yet the sculpture could also be taken to represent the protesting Job, wringing his hands in anguish, whose cry will never cease. Despite the sculptor's comments, it is unclear whether *Job* is an inmate of the camps (the presence of a tattoo suggests of Auschwitz) or a survivor, post-liberation. Unlike the replica of Rapoport's *Warsaw Ghetto Monument* (1948), which stands tall and proud, with the front and back of the original sculpture in Warsaw reproduced side by side to form the *Wall of Remembrance*, the dominant feature in Yad Vashem's Warsaw Ghetto Square (and the backdrop for the annual national commemoration on *Yom hashoah*), *Job* is smaller, less obviously heroic, and certainly less prominent: it is not even marked on the map in the *Visitor's Guide* currently on sale. Maybe the iconography of heroes and martyrs on the Warsaw Ghetto Monument is considered more accessible and reassuring, even more politically useful, as a Jewish representation of and response to the Holocaust, than the ambiguous, rather disturbing figure of *Job*—hence the decision to put one on prominent display, whilst the other is tucked away and virtually out of sight to the passing visitor.

Works Cited

AMISHAI-MAISELS, Z. (1993), *Depiction and Interpretation: The Influence of the Holocaust on the Visual Arts*. Oxford.

BERKOVITS, E. (1973), *Faith after the Holocaust*. New York.

BIEMANN, A. D. (ed.) (2002), *The Martin Buber Reader: Essential Writings*. Basingstoke.

BLUMENTHAL, D. (1993), *Facing the Abusing God: A Theology of Protest*. Louisville, Ky.

BRAITERMAN, Z. (1998), *(God) after Auschwitz: Tradition and Change in Post-Holocaust Jewish Thought*. Princeton.

BUBER, M. (1995), *On Judaism*, ed. N. Glazer. New York.

FACKENHEIM, E. (1990), *The Jewish Bible After the Holocaust: A Re-reading*. Manchester.

——(2007), *An Epitaph for German Judaism: From Halle to Jerusalem*. Madison, Wisc.

FEWELL, D. N., PHILLIPS, G. A., and SHERWOOD, Y. (eds.) (2008), *Representing the Irreparable: The Shoah, the Bible, and the Art of Samuel Bak*. Boston.

FREEMAN, J. (1996), *Job: The Story of a Holocaust Survivor*. St Paul.

FRIEDMAN, M. (1987), *Abraham Joshua Heschel and Elie Wiesel: You Are My Witnesses*. New York.

GORDIS, R. (1976), *The Book of Job: Commentary, New Translation and Special Studies*. New York.

KATSH, A. (ed.) (1999), *Scroll of Agony: The Warsaw Diary of Chaim A Kaplan*. Bloomington, Ind.

KATZ, S. (ed.) (2006), *The Impact of the Holocaust on Jewish Theology*. New York.

LEVI, P. (2002), *The Search for Roots: A Personal Anthology*. London.

LINAFELT, T. (ed.) (2000), *Strange Fire: Reading the Bible after the Holocaust*. Sheffield.

MORGAN, M. (2001), *Beyond Auschwitz: Post-Holocaust Jewish Thought in America*. Oxford.

NEHER, A. (1981), *The Exile of the Word: From the Silence of the Bible to the Silence of Auschwitz*. Philadelphia.

——(1993), The Book of Job and the Shoah, *Jewish Quarterly*, 40/2: 62–7.

OLDENHAGE, T. (2002), *Parables for our Time: Rereading New Testament Scholarship after the Holocaust*. Oxford.

ROSKIES, D. (1984), *Against the Apocalypse: Responses to Catastrophe in Modern Jewish Culture*. Cambridge.

——(ed.) (1988), *The Literature of Destruction: Jewish Responses to Catastrophe*. Philadelphia.

RUBENSTEIN, R. (1968), *The Religious Imagination: A Study in Psychoanalysis and Jewish Theology*. New York.

RUETHER, R. (1974), *Faith and Fratricide: Theological Roots of Anti-Semitism*. London.

SOLOVEITCHIK, J. (1993), 'Kol Dodi Dofek', in B. Rosenberg and F. Heuman (eds.), *Theological and Halakhic Reflections on the Holocaust*, 51–117. Hoboken.

WIESEL, E. (1975), *The Town Beyond the Wall*. London.

——(1976), *Messengers of God: Biblical Portraits and Legends*. New York.

——(1979), *The Trial of God*. New York.

——(2006), *Night*, new trans. London.

YOUNG, J. (1988), *Writing and Rewriting the Holocaust: Narrative and the Consequences of Interpretation*. Bloomington, Ind.

ZUCKERMAN, B. (1991), *Job the Silent: A Study in Historical Counterpoint*. New York.

FURTHER READING

BERGER, A. (1997), *Children of Job: American Second Generation Witnesses to the Holocaust*. Albany, NY.

FREDRIKSEN, P. and REINHARTZ, A. (eds.) (2002), *Jesus, Judaism and Christian Anti-Judaism*. Louisville, Ky.

KATZ, S., BIDERMAN, S., and GREENBERY, G. (eds.) (2007), *Wrestling with God: Jewish Theological Responses during and after the Holocaust*. Oxford.

LINAFELT, T. (1999), 'Biblical Interpretation and the Holocaust', in J. Hayes (ed.), *Dictionary of Biblical Interpretation, A–J*, 514–15. Nashville, Tenn.

——(ed.) (2002), *A Shadow of Glory: Reading the New Testament after the Holocaust*. London.

MORROW, W. (1986), 'Consolation, Rejection and Repentance in Job 42:6', *Journal of Biblical Literature*, 105/2: 211–25.

SWEENEY, M. (2008), *Reading the Hebrew Bible after the Shoah: Engaging Holocaust Theology*. Minneapolis.

TOLLERTON, D. C. (2007), 'Emancipation from the Whirlwind: Piety and Rebellion among Jewish-American Post-Holocaust and Christian Liberation Readings of Job', *Studies in Christian–Jewish Relations*, 2/2: 70–91.

....

CHAPTER 34

SEVENTH-DAY ADVENTISTS, DANIEL, AND REVELATION

....

KENNETH G. C. NEWPORT

INTRODUCTION

....

Already in this volume others have explored theories of interpretation and in particular have drawn attention to the extent to which the interpretation of the Bible is as much, if not more, a matter as who reads it as what is there read. That theoretical discussion is not repeated here. Rather, in this chapter a very specific example of how biblical texts and readers not only *might* but in fact *do* interact is presented. The case in point is the Seventh-day Adventist (SDA) church and their reading of number of biblical texts, most particularly the books of Daniel and Revelation.

The SDA church may be relatively unknown. It is, however, very significant. It currently reports over 15 million members. However, given that the church practices adult believers' baptism and counts as 'members' only those (adults) who have been baptized, the full number of those who belong to the community will be well above this. It is currently growing well, with something like 750,000 new members every year. The church is also asset-rich. For example, it operates what is quite possibly the largest Protestant educational system in the world, with numerous schools and nearly one hundred higher-educational institutions. The church runs about 650 hospitals, clinics, and other health institutions and is active in disaster relief and other humanitarian activities. The SDA church is hence a confident church. It is a church that has a loyal and rapidly growing membership.

The development of any church, its success or failure, is of course the result of numerous factors, historical, social, and cultural. It is important, however, that the members of any such body have a clear sense of divine favour and purpose. This is especially so where, as with the Seventh-day Adventists, its members are called upon to make significant financial and social sacrifices. One thing is certain: the SDA church certainly has just such a sense of divine favour and a clear view of its own importance in the wider plans of God, plans which are, according to the SDA church, nearing eschatological completion.

One of the ways in which the SDA church has been able to chart its own very precise co-ordinates on the ecclesiological map (and indeed to pinpoint its own place on the eschatological timetable) is through its interpretation of scripture. Among such groups the ability to find biblical proof for theological proposition is central. This statement is not quite a bland as it might first appear, for the Seventh-day Adventists are among a relatively small number of Christian communities who have claimed that among their number there has been exercised the ministry of a living prophetess who, through visions and other means, has been able to link the community directly with the divine. Despite having this extra-canonical access to truth, however, the SDA church has always been insistent that the prophetess, Ellen G. White (1827–1915), is (to use her own words) 'a lesser light to lead [others] to a greater light' (*Seventh-day Adventists Believe*, 228). That 'greater light' is the Bible, which, theoretically at least, is the ultimate source of authority for the community. One has to say 'theoretically', for some have argued that Seventh-day Adventist beliefs are based not so much on the Bible as on Ellen White's interpretation of the Bible (e.g. Hoekema 1963). That discussion can be left aside here, except to note just how strong and uncompromising the Adventist claim is, even in the context of having its own prophetess, that the Bible and the Bible alone is the source of authority. It is hence on the basis of the biblical text that the battle for self-definition must be waged and the quest for divine approval either won or lost. It is the Bible that is looked to to provide not only a sense of where the boundaries which separate the community from society at large lie, but also as the means by which internal division and theological disputes must be settled. In short, it is the Bible that is the mirror in which the community sees its own reflection. In this chapter, then, some of the highlights of that interpretative process are noted, with specific, though not exclusive, reference to the books of Daniel and Revelation.

The beginnings of Seventh-day Adventism can be traced to the aftermath of what has become known as 'the great disappointment', that is, the apparent non-events of 22 October 1844. Central here was the preaching of the New England farmer

William Miller (1782–1849) and his followers, preaching which was based upon the interpretation of a number of biblical passages, although it was the Book of Daniel that was very much the centre of attention. At its height the Millerite movement numbered something close to 50,000 members, all of whom looked expectantly to 22 October 1844 as the day on which Jesus would return physically and visibly to the earth.

The key passage in arriving at this date was Daniel 8:13–14. This passage was thought to contain within it a very important bit of information: the precise date of the return of Christ. It reads, in the KJV (which is the only translation relevant here, and hence the one used throughout):

Then I heard one saint speaking, and another saint said unto that certain saint which spake, How long shall be the vision concerning the daily sacrifice, and the transgression of desolation, to give both the sanctuary and the host to be trodden under foot? And he said unto me, Unto two thousand and three hundred days; then shall the sanctuary be cleansed.

William Miller was working within the context of Protestant, pre-millennial historicism, which is to say that he believed that Jesus would come *prior* to the onset of the one-thousand-year period depicted in Revelation 20, and that he viewed both Daniel and Revelation as being, at heart, a prophetic timetable which gave an account of the course of the history of God's people from Daniel's own time (accepted as being sixth century BCE) to the second coming of Christ. There were other interpretative paradigms operative in nineteenth-century America of course, and these included futurism (claiming that the biblical prophecies really only treat the last few years of history) and preterism (claiming that much of Daniel and Revelation was fulfilled prior to the fourth century CE), but Miller was distant from them. Coming at these texts, then, Miller was looking for evidence of the fulfilment of biblical prophecies throughout history and some indication of where, precisely, he and his community were on the chart of human and divine history. And, as is so common with such interpreters, Miller discovered that while the prophecies had been in the process of being fulfilled for centuries in the past, it was his world which would see the end of all things and the second coming of Christ (see further Newport 2000: 150–71; Rowe 2008).

Miller took the 'sanctuary' of Daniel 8:13–14 to be the earth, and the cleansing thereof to be the return of Christ, at which point sin would be banished. Through a complex scheme of interpretation of Daniel 8 (together with Dan. 9), Miller concluded that the period of 2,300 'days' (which he, like almost all Protestants of his time, took to mean literal years)[1] would end in 1843, a date which he later

---

[1] The view that a prophetic 'day' is to be interpreted as a literal year is one that is almost ubiquitous in Protestant literature from the mid sixteenth-century on. Among those who accepted it was Sir Isaac Newton, who once stated that 'in *Daniel's* Prophecies days are put for years' (Sir Isaac Newton *Observations on the Prophecies* (1733), 123). See further Newport 2000: 9–10.

adjusted to 1844 (his initial mistake was the failure to realize that there was no year 'o'). This date was arrived at by adding 2,300 years to 457 BCE (the presumed date when the events of Dan. 9.25 had commenced). First a number of his followers and finally Miller himself eventually fine-tuned this prediction to 22 October of that year. The precise day was determined by the date of the Day of Atonement in 1844 (the Millerites worked to the Karaite and not the rabbinic calendar). The argument was that, just as in the typical system the high priest came out of the most holy place to announce God's forgiveness to Israel, so Christ would come out of the antitypical sanctuary to redeem his people from the earth (see further Newport 2000: 164–5). Further biblical texts were brought in to support this reasoning so as to give an even more certain sense of the impending close of the age (Arasola 1990). Excitement mounted as the day drew near.

In the end, however, Christ did not return as predicted. Millerite Hiram Edson described the experience thus:

Our expectations were raised high, and thus we looked for our coming Lord until the clock tolled 12 at midnight. The day had then passed and our disappointment became a certainty. Our fondest hopes and expectations were blasted, and such a spirit of weeping came over us as I never experienced before. It seemed that the loss of all earthly friends could have been no comparison. We wept, and wept, till the day dawn [sic.]. (Numbers and Butler 1987: 215)

As scholars of failed prophecies know full well, however, such disappointment, while effecting a major crisis within a movement, will not of itself necessarily lead to its total extinction, and from the ashes of Millerism arose a number of other groups (perhaps as many as thirty-three). One of these was later to become the Seventh-day Adventist Church.

The transition from disappointed Millerite to confident Seventh-day Adventist is not particularly complicated, but it did require some imaginative theology. This is not the place to engage in a full discussion of that theology, except to note that whereas Miller had argued that the close of the 2,300 '[year-]days' of Daniel 8:14 would bring the return of Christ, those who were later to become Seventh-day Adventists argued that in fact the conclusion of that time period marked a different but equally significant point on the prophetic timetable. The scriptures were searched and soon the solution became plain.

The Epistle to the Hebrews talks extensively about a 'heavenly sanctuary' of which the earthly temple is but a shadow or a 'type'. Those later to become Seventh-day Adventists hence began to argue that although Miller had got the date right, he had got the event wrong. The 'cleansing of the sanctuary' was not, as Miller had argued, the return of Christ to the earth, but rather the celestial equivalent of what the earthly high priest did once a year, on the Day of Atonement, when he entered into the 'most holy place' to plead for the people of God, to sprinkle the blood of the slaughtered goat, and thereby to cleanse Israel of its collective and individual sin. These early Adventists (and we are still talking here about the 1840s) hence argued that on 22 October 1844 Christ had moved from the 'Holy Place', which he had entered upon his ascension, into the 'Most Holy Place' of the heavenly sanctuary. In the 'Holy Place' he had conducted a priestly ministry, just as on earth the regular services had gone on day-by-day in the earthly temple. However, on 22 October 1844, so it was argued, Christ, like his earthly antitype the high priest, had gone into the 'Holy of Holies' there to wind up those aspects of his ministry that were still to be accomplished prior to his return to earth to collect his own.

As was said, this is imaginative, but not, once the premises upon which it is built are accepted, without a clear basis in biblical exegesis. It may appear a bit strange to those outside of this community, but it is consistent. The early Adventist exegetical system was not without its own internal logic, nor lacking a coherent biblical narrative. More importantly, perhaps, it could not be proved wrong. After all, the claim 'Christ will come to earth on October 22, 1844' is clearly testable. Indeed, it had been tested and proven wrong. The statement 'Jesus moved from the heavenly antitypical Holy Place to the heavenly antitypical Most Holy Place on October 22, 1844' is not, however, one that can be open to disconfirmation. The biblical text is hence rescued from the (impossible) situation of being proven wrong. The community understands its mistake and hence its disappointment and the potential longer-term viability of the movement is therefore ensured. More work will need to be done to shore up the system of course, but at least the foundations of a system, foundations that following the catastrophic non-event of 22 October 1844 had been in danger of total subsidence and collapse, had now been underpinned.

It is important to note, however, that although the fledgling Adventist movement was wise enough not to gamble a second time on hitting the prophetic jackpot by fixing a new precise date for the second coming, it did in effect start the countdown. According to the theory, Christ was even now engaged in the closing stages of the process leading to the salvation of humankind, and there could be only a limited amount of time left before this final phase was complete. Perhaps it was for this reason that the movement at first shunned organizing itself formally. However, in 1863 it did just that, and took the name 'Seventh-day Adventist'. As its adoption of this name indicates, by this point the movement had taken some further crucial steps: it had, for example, begun to observe the seventh-day Sabbath and had also accepted the person of Ellen G. White as a latter-day prophetess. Health reform had also become a central concern—so central, in fact, that one of the early converts, John Harvey Kellogg, had invented a new breakfast cereal designed to promote health among the believers (see further Numbers 2008).

It is perhaps not surprising, given the level of disappointment or, to use the more specifically social-scientific terminology, the extent of the cognitive dissonance experienced, that some members of the group began to turn their attention to the question of their own possible prophetic role and identity. The immediate crisis had been overcome by rereading the relevant texts to discover the root of their mistake. The fulfilment of the prophecy had been moved, using Hebrews to support the argument, from the earthly to the celestial realm and thereby from the testable to the untestable. Once that task had been done, and done well, attention could be turned to longer-term issues. Typological interpretation had been central to Miller's scheme and central also to the reading strategy adopted by those who now saw that Hebrews must be read alongside the Book of Daniel if an accurate understanding of the plans of God were to be arrived at. And from these unpromising beginnings the early Seventh-day Adventists began to construct what was to become a highly complex interpretative scheme which both reassured the community of their privileged place in God's plans and also drove them hard in evangelism.[2] The eschatological drama was now in its first act, but it was destined to run to its cataclysmic conclusion; and by reading the scriptures the Seventh-day Adventists discovered that they were the key players.

In the process that followed, the Book of Revelation became absolutely central. For example, relatively early in the process attention was given to Revelation 10. Parts of this chapter read as follows

And I saw another mighty angel come down from heaven. And he had in his hand a little book open: and he set his right foot upon the sea, and his left foot on the earth, And cried with a loud voice. And the angel which I saw stand upon the sea and upon the earth lifted up his hand to heaven, And sware by him that liveth for ever and ever, who created heaven, and the things that therein are, and the earth, and the things that therein are, and the sea, and the things which are therein, that there should be time no longer . . . And the voice which I heard from heaven spake unto me again, and said, Go and take the little book which is open in the hand of the angel which standeth upon the sea and upon the earth. And I went unto the angel, and said unto him, Give me the little book. And he said unto me, Take it, and eat it up; and it shall make thy belly bitter, but it shall be in thy mouth sweet as honey. And I took the little book out of the angel's hand, and ate it up; and it was in my mouth sweet as honey: and as soon as I had eaten it, my belly was bitter. And he said unto me, Thou must prophesy again before many peoples, and nations, and tongues, and kings.

This passage was to become the cornerstone of the Seventh-day Adventist church's understanding of itself and of its mission in the world. The 'little book' which was eaten in Revelation 10:9–10, they discovered, was none other than the Book of Daniel, and the fact that it tasted sweet in the mouth but bitter in the stomach was a reference, so they argued, to the experience of excitement followed by disappointment that the preaching of the 2,300 days message had brought. It was noted, however, that following the bitter disappointment there came a divine imperative: 'he said unto me, "Thou must prophesy again before many peoples, and nations, and tongues, and kings" ' (Rev. 10:11). The group took this message to

---

[2] In the very early phase of development the 'Adventists' (not yet 'Seventh-day') actually shunned evangelism since, drawing on an interpretation of Matt. 25:10, they believed that on 22 October 1844 the 'door' to salvation had in effect been 'shut'. This view was not to last, however.

heart—they had been raised up and had had their faith tested by God. They had gone through the (sweet) experience of preaching the Millerite message and also through the (bitter) disappointment 22 October. Now they must now preach *again* to the world. This, then, was—and still is—a group with a message: undeterred by experience, it must prophesy about the imminent (and pre-millennial) second coming of Christ.

One can imagine just how comforting, indeed exciting, this discovery must have been, and how this understanding of Revelation 10, which is still operative in the SDA community, did give to a needy and confused people a clear sense of identity and purpose. The church has been allowed to go through 'the great disappoint-ment', but in the process of doing so has learnt to rely on God, to study the scriptures diligently, and to overcome, by faith informed by biblical proof, doubts, fears, depression, and the ridicule of the world. The ones born of this fire were the key players in the drama about to unfold. It is they who must 'testify again'—to give their witness to the world. Not only that, they were soon to have 'the Spirit of Prophecy' (cf. Rev. 19.10) in the person of Ellen G. White, which marked them out as the 'brethren' of the author of the Book of Revelation. They, like John, know who they are and know their place in God's plan. They know what they have to do. This is both a confirmation of divine approval and, importantly, an imperative for mission.

The very name that the Seventh-day Adventist Church was eventually to adopt is clearly indicative of the 'Adventist' aspect of the Church's theology. The church has always been, and still is, insistent upon its claim that it has been raised up by God in these last days to proclaim the nearness of the end and the warning given in Revelation 10:6 that 'time shall be no more'. Adventist interpreters take the 'time' here to mean not linear but prophetic time, and hence understand this verse as saying that there are no more specific prophetic time periods left to be fulfilled: 22 October 1844 is the very last date that is given in scripture. All the prophetic time periods have passed. According to Matthew 24:36, the precise date of that which is still yet to come, the actual appearance of the Son of Man, is unknown ('But about that day and hour no one knows, neither the angels of heaven, nor the Son, but only the Father'). It is therefore pointless trying to work out precisely when Jesus will come back; but it will be soon. That appearance was (and is) seen by the Seventh-day Adventists as being clearly predicted in many biblical passages; pas-sages such as Revelation 1:7, which members of the church see as a reference to the second coming of Christ, a time which will see a 'special' mini-resurrection of those who actually crucified him, that is, those who 'pierced him'. (In the Seventh-day Adventist system the rest of the wicked dead are not resurrected until the end of the literal one-thousand-year millennium of Rev. 20.) The coming will be literal, visible, cataclysmic, and final. Seventh-day Adventists have no place for 'the secret rapture' or for any non-visible or 'spiritual' coming of Christ.

A biblically saturated account of their own place on the map of world time was hence one of the ways in which the early Seventh-day Adventists defined their identity and came to terms with their 'great disappointment'. However, the church that emerged was not only 'Adventist' but also 'Seventh-day', and this other aspect of its theology is again reflected in its understanding of the scriptures and its own role as an end-time prophetic community. As has been shown, Adventists take the view that they must 'prophesy again'. But not only the divine imperative to preach but the very precise content of that preaching is something of which the SDA church quickly became aware. Again, the Book of Revelation was crucial as the community worked through its understanding of the task for which God had raised it up.

Central to the church's thinking on this issue are the 'three angels' messages' from Revelation 14:6–12. Indeed, this passage lies at the very heart of SDA self-identity, and thus the interpretation given to this passage by SDA commentators must be examined here in a little detail. Such a study gives a clear insight into the imaginative interaction that can sometimes result from the needs of the readers being coaxed into expression by the openness of the formal text. The passage reads:

And I saw another angel fly in the midst of heaven, having the everlasting gospel to preach unto them that dwell on the earth, and to every nation, and kindred, and tongue, and people, Saying with a loud voice, Fear God, and give glory to him; for the hour of his judgment is come: and worship him that made heaven, and earth, and the sea, and the fountains of waters. And there followed another angel, saying, Babylon is fallen, is fallen, that great city, because she made all nations drink of the wine of the wrath of her fornication. And the third angel followed them, saying with a loud voice, If any man worship the beast and his image, and receive his mark in his forehead, or in his hand, The same shall drink of the wine of the wrath of God, which is poured out without mixture into the cup of his indignation; and he shall be tormented with fire and brimstone in the presence of the holy angels, and in the presence of the Lamb: And the smoke of their torment ascendeth up for ever and ever: and they have no rest day nor night, who worship the beast and his image, and whosoever receiveth the mark of his name. Here is the patience of the saints: here are they that keep the commandments of God, and the faith of Jesus.

According to the Seventh-day Adventist reading of this passage, what we have here are the three central aspects of the message that the end-time community, the SDA church itself, is to proclaim, that is, the content of the message that the disappointed Millerites were called upon to 'prophesy again'. The first angel warns that the time of God's judgement has come. This links in clearly with the 'Adventist' understanding of things: Christ had begun the final stage of his ministry on 22 October 1844, and hence, to repeat the words of this text, 'the hour of his judgement [had] come'. However, according to the first angel, the one whom one is called to worship (i.e. the one whose hour of judgement [had] come) is the one 'that made heaven, and earth, and the sea, and the fountains of waters'. The exegetical reasoning is not hard to follow: eschatological expectation within the end-time community identity is linked with the worship of the creator. This is indeed the test. Those called to prophesy again must call others to worship the creator. But how, exactly, is this worship to be focused? How is the end-time community to worship the God 'that made heaven, and earth, and the sea, and the fountains of waters'?

The early Adventists noted that worship of the creator is specifically linked to the observance of the seventh-day Sabbath. This was on the basis of Exodus 20:8–11, which reads:

Remember the Sabbath day, to keep it holy. Six days shalt thou labour, and do all thy work: But the seventh day is the Sabbath of the Lord thy God: in it thou shalt not do any work, thou, nor thy son, nor thy daughter, thy manservant, nor thy maidservant, nor thy cattle, nor thy stranger that is within thy gates: For in six days the Lord made heaven and earth, the sea, and all that in them is, and rested the seventh day: wherefore the Lord blessed the Sabbath day, and hallowed it.

Seventh-day Adventist interpreters pick up on the obvious link here between the observance of the Sabbath and the worship of the creator, for, according to the Exodus passage, the Sabbath is in fact a memorial of the act of creation. 'Worship him that made heaven, and earth, and the sea, and the fountains of waters', from Revelation 14:7, is hence taken as a command to observe the Sabbath, for by observing the Sabbath, so the Exodus passage implies, we honour the creator.

Observance of the biblical seventh-day Sabbath from sunset on Friday to sundown on Saturday has significant implications and creates distinctiveness and disjunction between the community and the world in general. And the SDA church has confidently accepted the resultant friction with wider society that such a position entails. For example, the SDA will find it as this-worldly difficult as it is divinely required to secure employment that will be flexible enough to allow work to cease as early as mid-afternoon on a Friday. In perceived response to the call of the first angel, boundaries between the community and the wider world are drawn in a very particular way. The Adventist is significantly out of temporal step for those 'sacred hours' when he/she is worshipping 'him that made heaven, and earth, and the sea, and the fountains of waters'.

But if the Adventist has a clear sense of his/her own distinctiveness vis à vis the secular world, the same is equally true of the place of the same individual with regard to the rest of Christendom. Obviously, worshipping on a different day is part of that, but it goes deeper. And here the second angel's message is the key.

The second angel cries: 'Babylon is fallen, is fallen, that great city, because she made all nations drink of the wine of the wrath of her fornication.' Again, this is a central part of Seventh-day Adventist self-identity. 'Babylon' had long been understood as a symbol of confusion and apostasy and, in Protestant interpretation of this and other related passages, had been taken as a symbol of Roman Catholicism. Seventh-day Adventists took a similar line of interpretation, but went even further. 'Babylon', they argued (and many still argue today), is a symbol not just of Roman

Catholicism but of 'apostate Protestantism' as well (*SDABC* 7. 851–2). In other words, in these last days, so they argued, God had raised up a remnant people who were to proclaim the truth in the face of general error and apostasy. The SDA church was to announce this truth to the world in preparation for the eventual return of Christ. The rest of Christendom, 'Babylon', was apostate. Once again, one can see clearly enough how the biblical text is read in such a way as to underscore ecclesial self-identity. And once the community has accepted this agreed interpretation of the inspired text, it delivers a powerful sense of divine approval.

The third angel's message is the most terrifying of the three and is absolutely central to SDA mission. It announces: 'If any man worship the beast and his image, and receive his mark in his forehead, or in his hand, the same shall drink of the wine of the wrath of God, which is poured out without mixture into the cup of his indignation . . . and they have no rest day nor night, who worship the beast and his image, and whosoever receiveth the mark of his name.' The precise nature of this 'mark of the beast' has long exercised interpreters of this passage, and among those who are not wedded to a historical-critical reading of the text suggestions abound. (Indeed, even the shallowest of Internet trawls will quickly reveal just how extensive is the contemporary fascination with this subject). The Seventh-day Adventists took an interesting line on this, and again one which underscored their own sense of prophetic destiny. According to them, this 'mark of the beast' must be a symbol of some sort which identifies the one who has it as being one who follows the beast of Revelation 13:1–10, which is where the 'beast' whose mark this appears to be first emerges. So who is that beast of Revelation 13, he who has 'seven heads and ten horns' and 'the name of blasphemy upon his heads' and 'makes war with the saints'? Protestant interpreters from the sixteenth century on had generally identified this beast as the Roman Catholic church and/or the pope in particular (Brady 1983), and Seventh-day Adventists latched onto this understanding. The 'mark of the beast', then, must be something that identifies a person as being a follower of Rome, the great antichrist.

It will be recalled, however, that in Seventh-day Adventism there is also the concept of 'Babylon' more widely conceived, that is, of 'Apostate Protestantism', and this body too opposed God and his faithful remnant during the last days. The 'mark of the beast', therefore, while being identifiably Roman, must be something which those of 'Babylon' more generally also have. This 'mark of the beast' marks one out as being on the wrong side in the eschatological drama.

Seventh-day Adventists have long argued that the one factor which unites this disparate satanic conspiracy of Rome and apostate Protestantism is the setting up of a counterfeit Sabbath, namely Sunday, and such a view is widely seen even in contemporary or relatively recent Seventh-day Adventist literature. Thus, according to Seventh-day Adventist interpreters, the 'mark of the beast' is Sunday observance, since to observe Sunday is in effect to acknowledge the power and authority of the Roman Catholic church over God, since it was that church, so

Seventh-day Adventists argue, which changed the day of worship from Sabbath to Sunday. Of course, Seventh-day Adventists do not argue that going to church on Sunday means that one has the mark of the beast automatically; rather, they argue, the Sunday issue is the one concerning which those who live through the end-times will one day have to decide. The time will come, and may even be upon us already. God says 'keep the Sabbath', the church of Rome says 'observe the Sunday', and the one who, in full knowledge of the issue, chooses the latter over the former thereby receives the mark of the beast. This includes Sunday-keeping Protestants, since they too, unwittingly perhaps, are thereby paying homage to Rome, the antichrist. The Seventh-day Adventist church, however, the remnant church, obeys God rather than human decrees, and as a result the members of it are those of whom it can truly be said, again in the words of Revelation, 'they keep the commandments of God' (cf. Rev. 12:17; 14:12; 22:14).

The way in which the Seventh-day Adventist church interprets this passage from Revelation 14, then, clearly indicates that it sees itself as an end-time church, testifying prophetically to the pure biblical faith while awaiting the return of its Lord. In the final phase of the world's history it is that church, its members believe, that is the voice of the three angels of Revelation 14:6–12 calling people to 'worship the creator' (i.e. keep the Sabbath, a memorial thereof), recognize that 'Babylon' (false religion) has fallen and that those who continue to honour the Roman antichrist through the observance of Sunday and neglect of the Sabbath will receive the mark of the beast. The comments in *Seventh-day Adventists Believe* relating to these 'three angels' messages' are typical of the church's understanding of its role in general. The authors write: 'As John the Baptist prepared the way for Christ's first advent, so the Advent movement is preparing the way for His second advent— proclaiming the message of Rev 14.6–12, God's final call to get ready for the glorious return of the Saviour' (p. 342). This is a powerful interpretation of the text and one which gives great strength to the movement which adopts it. As Seventh-day Adventists gaze into the text of Revelation they see themselves and their mission clearly portrayed. They are a favoured people, a remnant, a 'called-out' people, the 'ek-klesia' of God. As such they take the words spoken with regard to Babylon in Revelation 18:4 very seriously: 'Come out of her, my people, that ye be not partakers of her sins, and that ye receive not of her plagues.'

It has been shown that in an effort to bring itself out in sharp relief against the general Christian background, the Seventh-day Adventist church has drawn substantially on the biblical text, especially the books of Daniel and Revelation, to argue for its own status as the true remnant church which has a divine commission both to exist and to preach its apocalyptic message to the world at large. The way in which the church has interpreted the text is an integral part of the story of how, from a very unpromising start among the ranks of the disappointed Millerites, the church has built itself up to be a highly motivated and highly successful movement, which seems now set for a period of rapid growth. Perhaps few outside of the community itself would wish to follow Seventh-day Adventist interpreters along what would appear to be the highly idiosyncratic exegetical pathways which they have explored. However, there can be no disputing that the Seventh-day Adventist interpretation of the text has been a powerful influence upon the lives of millions in the world today; and we would be wrong to dismiss as being of no consequence the kind of interpretation outlined above. Indeed, it could be argued that such interpretations (and of course there are countless other movements who have equally idiosyncratic schemes) are much more significant than are any number of those found in the pages of academic commentaries, at least when judged by the potential impact they may have on the lives of individuals and the nature of entire communities. As was noted above, the Seventh-day Adventist church is highly successful, and its huge institutional structures bear witness to the power of its own self-confidence and sense of identity. The exegesis may be strained—perhaps some might even be prepared to say it is 'wrong'—when judged by the kind of standards operative in the scholarly guild community. However, there can be no doubt that the exegesis has served the church well as its early ancestors struggled to survive in the hostile environment in which the disappointed Millerites first lived, and then, as the movement matured, in marking out clearly the conceptual boundaries of the community and helping it find its own space on what was in any case a very crowded ecclesial terrain. Whether the church will be forced to change its exegesis as it seeks to adapt to the huge demographic shifts in membership that are now on the horizon remains to be seen. But one thing does seem plain: in that kaleidoscopic wonderland that exists somewhere between the highly symbolic text and the motivated reader of it there are countless new identities yet to be found.

WORKS CITED

ARASOLA, KAI (1990), *The End of Historicism: Millerite Hermeneutic of Time Prophecies in the Old Testament*. Uppsala: University of Uppsala.

BRADY, DAVID (1983), *The Contribution of British Writers between 1560 and 1830 to the Interpretation of Revelation 13.16–18 (The Number of the Beast): A Study in the History of Exegesis*. Tübingen: J. C. B. Mohr [Paul Siebeck].

HOEKEMA, ANTHONY A. (1963), *The Four Major Cults: Christian Science, Jehovah's Witnesses, Mormonism, Seventh-Day Adventism*. Grand Rapids, Mich.: Eerdmans.

NEWPORT, KENNETH G. C. (2000), *Apocalypse and Millennium: Studies in Biblical Eisegesis*. Cambridge: Cambridge University Press.

NUMBERS, RONALD L. (2008), *Prophetess of Health: A Study of Ellen G. White*, 3rd edn. Grand Rapids, Mich.: Eerdmans.

——and BUTLER, JONATHAN M. (eds.) (1987), *The Disappointed: Millerism and Millenarianism in the Nineteenth Century*. Bloomington and Indianapolis: Indiana University Press.

Rowe, David L. (2008), *God's Strange Work: William Miller and the End of the World.* Grand Rapids, Mich.: Eerdmans.

Seventh-day Adventists Believe... A Biblical Exposition of 27 Fundamental Doctrines. Washington, DC: The Ministerial Association of the Seventh-day Adventist Church, 1988.

Further Reading

Bull, Malcolm and Lockhart, Keith (2007), *Seeking a Sanctuary: Seventh-day Adventism and the American Dream*, 2nd edn. Bloomington and Indianapolis: Indiana University Press.

Newport, Kenneth G. C. (2001), 'The Heavenly Millennium of Seventh-day Adventism', in Stephen Hunt (ed.), *Christian Millenarianism: From the Early Church to Waco.* London: Hurst & Co., 131–48.

Nichol, Francis D. (1944), *The Midnight Cry: A Defense of William Miller and the Millerites.* Washington, DC: Review and Herald Publishing Co.

O'Leary, Stephen (1998), *Arguing the Apocalypse: A Theory of Millennial Rhetoric.* New York: Oxford.

Seventh-day Adventist Bible Commentary (SDABC) (1957), 8 vols. Washington, DC: Review and Herald Publishing Association.

Stone, John R. (2000), *Expecting Armageddon: Essential Readings in Failed Prophecy.* New York: Routledge.

CHAPTER 35

ESTHER AND HITLER: A SECOND TRIUMPHANT PURIM

JO CARRUTHERS[1]

THE Book of Esther tells the tale of a prime minister, Haman, who, through various political machinations, attempts to annihilate the Jews of the ancient Persian empire (which, according to the story, then stretched from Ethiopia to India). Esther, queen of the empire and secretly a Jew, averts the disaster and, together with her uncle, Mordecai, is celebrated as the saviour of the Jews. The end of the book institutes Purim as a festival to celebrate 'rest from their enemies' and the turning of 'sorrow to gladness' and 'mourning into a good day'. As early as 1935 parallels were being drawn between this story and the politics of the Nazi party. In perhaps one of the earliest examples, the Christian writer Wilhemina Stitch, in her otherwise simpering portrayals of female heroines, *Women of the Bible*, comments on the Book of Esther: 'here is a man called Hitler whose temperament seems much akin to the villain of this piece' (1935: 250).

In Jewish tradition, associating an enemy of the Jews with Haman is an age-old custom, and it is the festival of Purim that provides a ritual enacting of the

[1] I am grateful to the Leverhulme Trust and the Research Councils UK for funding research time, and to the Leverhulme Trust and AHRC for travels funds, that have enabled the writing of this essay.

identification, and symbolic obliteration, of the current enemy of the Jews. The story of Esther is read in full at the festival, which accordingly provides the predominant frame for the reception of the story in Jewish tradition and places it in the context of the story of Israel and the Amalekites (as told in Exod. 17:8–6, Deut. 25:17–19, and 1 Sam. 15:1–34; for a more in-depth narrative of the relation between Amalek and Haman see Horowitz 2006: 1–4.). Celebrations are framed specifically by the reading of Deuteronomy 25:17–19 on the Sabbath before Purim, *Shabbat Zakhor* ('Sabbath of Remembrance'), which impels the congregation to 'Remember (*zakhor*) what Amalek did', namely, attacking the Jews whilst vulnerable on their exodus from Egypt (Exod. 17). Haman takes on the mantle of being this iconic enemy of the Jews because of the reference to him as an 'Agagite' in Esther 3:1, invoking the name of the king of the Amalekites, Agag. Historically, then, the term Amalekite was used in relation to various individuals and groups to mark them as enemies of the Jewish people (see the chapter 'Amalek' in Horowitz 2006). Although Hitler is only the last in a long line of Hamans, for many Hitler has become the unsurpassable fulfilment of the Haman–Amalekite typology.

The festival itself is geared around celebration of Haman's defeat, and despite the fact that the book carries Esther's name, it is Haman who is the anti-hero of the day. Celebrated in spring in the Jewish month of Adar, Purim is a festival of tragicomedy, and as such is characterized by contradictions, expressed in the leitmotif of the topsy-turvy. The festival mimics the contradictory impulses of horror and joy and of threat and release, as the terrors of immanent persecution are remembered only to be overwritten by an overwhelming sense of salvation. At the synagogue the most remarkable feature of the service is the reading of the *Megillah*, the scroll of Esther, accompanied by congregational uproar when the name Haman is read out. Obeying the injunction in 1 Samuel 25 to 'destroy the Amalekites', the name of Haman is obliterated from hearing as the participants shout, wave rattles, and stamp their feet so that his name is never actually heard throughout the retelling. Tradition tells of other practices of eradication: of putting Haman's name on the soles of shoes that would then be stamped, or on rocks that would be banged together (for more on the 'beating of Haman', see Goodman 1949: 324–5). Purim is in practice, then, very much about the celebration of Haman's defeat, marked overwhelmingly with the joy of survival.

During the period of the Third Reich there are numerous accounts of Jews drawing hope from the story of Esther as they saw its events replayed before their eyes. Miriam Chaikin outlines two notable examples of Purim celebrations during the war in her *Make Noise, Make Merry: The Story and Meaning of Purim* (a title which itself draws attention to the centrality of the 'smiting' of Haman to the festival). In *The Warsaw Diary of Chaim A. Kaplan*, found after World War II, the author writes of a Purim celebrated on 13 March 1941, in which the participants gather secretly. 'We came sad and left sad,' Kaplan writes, 'but we had some pleasant moments in between', gesturing towards the emotional relief from despair that many Jews found when they relived the story of Esther at Purim (Chaikin 1983: 72–3; see also Domnitch 2000: 72). Chaikin also cites Emmanuel Ringbaum who, writing from the Warsaw Ghetto, responded to corpses being carried through the streets to mass graves with: 'People hope for a new Purim to celebrate the down fall of the modern Haman, Hitler' (1983: 73). Towards the end of the war, the Jews of Casablanca instituted 'Purim Hitler' (a 'Little Purim' or *Purim Katan* in Jewish tradition, a local festival that imitates Purim in its celebration of a specific and local reprieve from threat or slaughter). Purim Hitler was celebrated on the second day of Kislev to commemorate the Allied forces landing on that date in Morocco in 1943, saving the Jewish community. They celebrate by reading *Megillat Hitler* (now held at the United States Holocaust Memorial Museum in Washington, DC), a scroll modelled on Esther that functions as a palimpsest, the biblical story overwritten with new historical significance as the story of threat and reprieve becomes specific to the Casablanca experience of celebration. Sometimes the relevance of Esther's story or a celebration of Purim isn't made explicit, the significance of the story being apparently all too obvious. There is evidence of Purim celebrations held at Terezin, a transit camp from 1941 to 1944. An inmate initiated an educational programme for children there, and amongst the recovered artworks now on display (hidden when the teacher was deported to Auschwitz) are pictures drawn by children for a celebration of Purim. There is also evidence of the performance of a folk-play *Esther* (directed by Nora Fryd, with music composed by Karel Reiner) at Terezin in 1943 (see Robit and Goldfarb 1999). Although there is nothing to indicate how the inmates at Terezin understood Purim in this context, testimonies from the same period suggest that, at the least, it was an opportunity to express a symbolic obliteration of Hitler–Haman if not even anticipation of Hitler's defeat. Rabbi Prinz, in his 'A Rabbi under the Hitler Regime', writes of wartime Purim services: 'Every time we read "Haman" the people heard Hitler, and the noise was deafening' (cited in Horowitz 2006: 86).

After Hitler's defeat, the festival of Purim provided an opportunity for the open celebration of Jewish salvation and, most poignantly, 'rest from their enemies', and the Purim–Hitler nexus becomes more apparent in writings after 1945. Joseph Greenstein's *Purim Portfolio*, published by the Zionist Organisation of America's National Education Department in 1946, gives an explicit rationale for Purim celebrations. Here Greenstein states that the festival symbolizes 'Jewish survival against the plotting and canards of Haman the prototype of Hitler', and goes on to explain that 'The observance of Purim this year will help us, for a few moments at least, to forget about the misery, the blood-shed, the torment and the agony of our people . . . will instil in us renewed courage and faith in mankind . . . the Jewish people will survive' (Greenstein 1946: 4). The function of Purim for Holocaust survivors is made explicit here: it provides a forum through which to celebrate Jewish survival, turning the focus from those lost to the remnant. Toby Blum-Dobkin describes a celebration of Purim at the Displaced Persons Centre in

Landsberg, Germany, in the same year. Having collected the testimonies of survivors, including her father Boris Blum (inmate 114520, Mojdanek), Blum-Dobkin explains that the inmates at the camp organized traditional celebrations: a reading of the *Megillah* (scroll of Esther), school performances, banquets, literary parodies, and a carnival. Her father explains that 'I saw in my imagination a Jewish carnival for the defeat of Hitler: the hanging of Hitler instead of Haman' (Blum-Dobkin 1979: 53). The camp is filled with images of hanging Hitlers and, in the tradition of dressing-up common to Purim, one inmate dressed as Hitler himself. Blum-Dobkin suggests that this masquerade provided psychological consolation: 'The masquerade dictates and controls the actions of the character he is playing; in performing the exaggerated Nazi salute, the Jew can mock the Nazi and emphasize the transfer of power' (ibid. 56). There are opposed drives evident in these two examples of Purim celebrations. Whilst Greenstein's reflections on his 1946 Purim demonstrates an inward impulse of celebration of Jewish salvation, Blum-Dobkin reveals here a concurrent outward impulse of celebrating the defeat of the enemy, even to the extent that those participating note a new sense of empowerment.

Although the Haman–Hitler connection offered relief to many, to others the association only iterates the senselessness of Jewish suffering. Elie Wiesel's *The Trial of God*, perhaps one of the best-known expressions of the theological despair 'after Auschwitz', is itself set at Purim and is even styled as a *Purimshpil* (a dramatic form specific to the festival); but it is not one that celebrates Haman's defeat. Instead, it dramatizes the theological anguish of the Holocaust for believers by putting God himself on trial for his apparent absence during the suffering. There are many detractors of the Haman–Hitler connection, including Jonathan Sacks, who considers links with the Book of Esther to underscore the disparities between Hitler's 'systematic programme of extinction' and earlier 'inquisitions and pogroms'. The essential difference is that 'redemption had always come, or if not redemption, refuge. In the Holocaust there was neither.' (1992: 28) Emil L. Fackenheim, in his *The Jewish Bible after the Holocaust*, proposes in the light of the Holocaust that Esther is a story of luck, not providence. Esther is 'a lesson in monumental good luck—a lesson supremely relevant, supremely painful, for a Jewish "generation" after a time of bad luck' (1990: 62). Henri Raczymow, continuing this theme of luck, cites the opinion of his Uncle Avrum, which illustrates further the problems involved in aligning the Nazis and Haman:

Some people in the ghetto still believe in their own luck, thinking that, like Haman in the Book of Esther, the Germans will flip coins—their life or their death. They forget that Haman was Oriental, and enjoyed gambling and irony. Not the Germans. The Germans are not gamblers. They don't consult the fates. They decide and they execute. And they have decided. Nothing will prevent them from acting, neither their victory, of course, nor their defeat. Because when Stalin, Roosevelt and Churchill defeat them—and they will defeat them—we will no longer exist, and from the ash of our corpses flowers will have grown. (1995: 81–2)

Celebration of victory at Purim is rendered meaningless in this account in which 'Nothing'—neither victory nor defeat—will hinder the inexorable will of Nazi destruction.

Nonetheless, many of those who lived through the Holocaust, both victims and survivors, meaningfully drew the connection. The association between the Nazis and Haman is made even more poignant for many Jewish writers by the fact that various Nazis themselves—Hitler included—made the association explicitly. In his excellent *A Book of Hiding*, Timothy Beal relates the story of Julius Streicher (itself cited from A. Roy Eckhart), who shouted 'Purimfest!' as he was being led to the gallows. 'Ironically,' Beal writes, 'with his exclamation, Streicher identified himself not only with Luther' (he defended himself at the Nuremburg trials by claiming that he was only 'putting Luther's recommendations into effect'), 'but also with Haman in the book of Esther, who is the architect of Jewish annihilation and who is ultimately sentenced to death on the very gallows he had built for the Jew Mordecai' (1997: 6). Beal expresses the appeal of Nazi self-reference to Hitler. He presumes Streicher's reference to Haman to be an afterthought, privileging his explicit self-association with Luther. That the reference is unintentional appears to make the irony only sweeter to Beal: the Nazi cites the story of Esther but is ignorant of its 'true' application: that those who oppose the Jews will inevitably fail.

There are various accounts that testify to Nazi awareness, and subversion of, Purim celebrations. Blum-Dobkin cites the account of Rabbi Shimon Huberband, who claimed that the Nazis hanged ten Jews on Purim in Zdunska Vola, Poland, in revenge for the hanging of the ten sons of Haman at the end of the Esther story (1979: 56). Domnitch alludes to the same episode, also explaining it 'as punishment for having hanged the ten sons of Haman' (2000: 73). The stories are cited here, it seems, as arrogant attempts by the Nazis to overwrite the Esther narrative and to underscore the new, Nazi narrative of Jewish defeat, not Jewish triumph. Again, the appeal is the irony of Nazi reference, even within the midst of their terrorizing, to a story that foretells their downfall.

Even more striking for many is Hitler's own apparent reference to himself as a second Haman. In fact, Hitler's reference to Purim, specifically that from his 1944 speech, has become the stuff of Jewish legend. Hitler addressed the Reichstag, as related by Philip Goodman in his seminal collection of Purim material, the *Purim Anthology*: 'In a speech by Hitler on January 30, 1944, he said that, if the Nazis went down to defeat, the Jews could celebrate "a second triumphant Purim"' (1949: 375). The account Goodman gives here is as bare and simple as I have cited above. Yet, under the title 'The Prophecy of Hitler', Goodman powerfully invokes a picture of Hitler fervid in his speechmaking, an image swiftly replaced by that of the instant of his failure, when his 'prophecy' was fulfilled. As such, Goodman dramatically resurrects the dramatic irony of Haman's fall in Hitler's defeat.

Hitler's reference appeals to many who have subsequently written on Purim and who repeat Goodman's reference and relish in Hitler's recognition of his own identity as a second Haman. Hitler's implicit self-identification seems to be so appealing for three reasons. First, there is the delicious sense of irony involved in Hitler's seemingly unwitting invocation of a story that foretells his own defeat, thwarting his over-inflated sense of destiny, similar to that evident in Beal's identification of irony in Streicher's 'Purimfest!' Hitler's speeches, like Purim, are replete with invocations of Providence, and yet ultimately it is Purim's narrative that is played out in history. In claiming divine support, both sides conflate history and morality, thereby constructing Hitler's defeat as an expression of divine displeasure. Second, it underlines the importance of the Esther account as a framing story for Jewish suffering: *even* Hitler—although probably unintentionally, or stupidly—recognized the Esther story as the most pertinent to his endeavours. Third, and most significantly, it appears that it is Hitler's self-designation as enemy of the Jews that makes his (already rather pernicious) position even more evil and makes his association with Haman more concretized. As self-assigned enemy, his is a purposeful attack. It is the *intent* to destroy, not merely destruction itself, that seems important and that fits him to the Amalekite model. Domnitch glosses the significance of the Amalekites and why they are so hated:

The purpose of Amalek's existence was to menace the Jews and challenge their existence. The Amalekites, who had the audacity to attack the Israelites as they headed toward Mount Sinai, despised the ideals, beliefs and values of the Jews to the point of obsession. For the Amalekites, there was no room in the world for coexistence between Amalek and the Jews, whose status as God's chosen people filled them with rage. Haman, as all Amalekites who preceded him, was fixated upon the destruction of Jewry. (2000: 202–3)

What is significant about Amalek for Domnitch is his identity as the aggressor, and importantly, an aggressor who even risks existence to achieve the eradication of the enemy. By associating Haman with Hitler, the centrality of his agenda to destroy Jewry is highlighted. Controversially, emphasis on Hitler's self-designated status as enemy makes the Holocaust more applicable to the story of Esther. As Fackenheim and others have pointed out, the lack of Jewish blood spilt in Esther is not echoed in the Holocaust. Yet, by focusing attention on Hitler's proclamation that he is a second Haman, his *intent* to annihilate Jewry is privileged. It is in his *intent* that he performatively resembles Haman, and it is his *intent* that is thwarted by Germany's defeat, despite the failure to prevent his annihilation of millions. In this specific sense, then, the Esther story better maps onto the Holocaust narrative. As such it substantiates 'Intentionist' historical readings of Hitler as someone, as David Engel explains, 'carefully calculated in advance to facilitate the ultimate goal of total murder', just like Haman, combating 'Functionalist' historical readings of the Holocaust in which mass murder evolved gradually 'in an administrative climate in which Hitler himself provided little concrete direction' (1999: 27). It is only within an Intentionist reading of Hitler that the Haman–Hitler connection makes any sense: it demands that Hitler acts from a 'motiveless malignancy' (as Coleridge characterized the actions of Iago), both evil and personally culpable.

Yet, it seems strange to liken yourself to the villain of a story that belongs to your enemies, and further to associate yourself with a villain who fails. Why would Hitler align himself with a failed persecutor of Jews, who exists in a book that overwhelmingly celebrates his defeat? Whilst Jewish legend records Hitler's reference to Purim, there has seemingly been no interest in his reasons for invoking the festival. Yet it is clear from his 1944 speech, as printed in the *New York Times* of 31 January, that he cites Purim in an oppositional way to that assumed. Hitler is not aligning himself with Haman or prophesying a second Purim for Jews in the light of his own downfall. Goodman's initial, very selective citation of Hitler's reference to Purim misrepresents its significance by removing its context, and the repeated use of Goodman as a source by succeeding writers has only worked to proliferate Hitler's 'Prophecy'. Even those, like Blum-Dobkin, who do cite the newspaper source more extensively continue to focus exclusively on its irony, an irony that is so breathtaking, it seems, that it has rendered investigation of Hitler's speech itself—readily available in translation in the *New York Times*—apparently superfluous. Yet it is a more profound analysis of Hitler's speech that reveals a striking resemblance to Haman. Hitler's citation of Purim is, in fact, to invoke common understandings of Purim as a triumphal, bloodthirsty carnival that signifies Jewish vindictiveness. As such, his reference to Purim posits Jews as aggressors—anticipating the 'destruction of Europe'—and as such he performs Haman's role in asserting himself as the protector of civilization. As I outline below, Hitler is not explicitly placing himself in a binary conflict with the Jews or proclaiming his animosity towards them. Instead, like Haman, he paints the Jews as enemies of the state, destructive and dangerous, and appeals to self-defence in order to justify attack.

Hitler gave his speech on 30 January 1944, over the radio, and, as Max Domarus notes, it was 'directed at his English opponents rather than at the German Volk' (2004: 2871). It is fitting, therefore, that the entire speech was printed in full the day after its delivery, in the *New York Times* (translated by the *United Press*) and was therefore readily available to Hitler's apparently intended English-speaking audience. It is this version of the speech that is primarily considered in what follows, because of its status as the contemporaneously received version. The *New York Times* relates in its commentary on the speech that 'It was wholly concerned with the alleged bolshevist threat to Europe and Germany's alleged part in standing it off single-handedly' ('Hitler Sees Peril of Russia to All', *New York Times*, 31 Jan. 1944). Or, as Domarus explains, Hitler tried to convince England that 'in the event of a German defeat, Europe and England would become Bolshevik' and that it would be 'in England's interest to let Germany win'. Yet, as many scholars have noted, Bolshevism and Jewry are conflated in Hitler's thinking, meaning that the speech was far from being 'wholly concerned' with Bolshevism. In *Mein Kampf*, as David Engel writes, Hitler sets up 'Marxism and Bolshevism as the Jews' main weapons in their perverted struggle for survival: by preaching international working-class solidarity across racial lines, these doctrines deflected people's loyalties from their own racial groups' (1999: 22–3). Engel claims that Hitler's association of Jewry and Bolshevism may have been 'especially credible to some because it was rooted in a comprehensive, seemingly scientific world-view' (ibid. 23); Marx was, after all, Jewish. To consider Hitler's speech to be 'wholly concerned' with the 'bolshevist threat to Europe' is to misunderstand his reference. Instead, it is very much concerned with his reiteration of the Jewish threat, as is made explicit at various points in the speech. Crucial to his representation of Russia's threat to European civilization is his construction of Bolshevism and Jewry as a deadly threat to Germany. It is in proving the danger of Jewry that the reference to Purim is made. Like Haman, Hitler presents the Jews as a threat to civilization, appealing to the empire's/allies' sense of self-protection, in order to create support for his assault.

The speech, unfortunately, contains a tortuous logic that requires lengthy commentary. Responding to the threat of Russian military success in Europe, Hitler claims that 'in this struggle there can be only one victor, and that will be either Germany or Soviet Russia. German victory means the preservation of Europe and a victory by Soviet Russia means its destruction.' He sets up the battle as one of irreconcilable difference that will result in the eradication of one side. Germany becomes a protector of European civilization against the uncivilized Russians, whom he paints as a threat to the ancient culture of Europe. He implicitly alludes to the cultural homogeneity widely associated with Bolshevik communism in explaining that Russian triumph would mean 'the oldest cultural Continent would have lost its essential traits of individuality'. Setting up Russia as a supreme threat, Hitler claims Germany as the only possible saviour of Europe.

Hitler then moves on to the use of biological imagery in the speech, a use of language that substantiates his claim that the Bolshevik and Jewish aim is annihilation of Germany. By drawing on ideas of disease, bacteria, and immunity, his allusions to the threat of Bolshevism and Jewry are set in a frame of reference that demands the extreme discourse of eradication. Hitler introduces medical metaphor as he insists that England (and those countries like her) has 'sold its soul to Judaism', and likens it to a diseased organism which must 'expel these bacteria by force from its body'. (It is remarkable, in the light of such comments, that the *New York Times* can claim that the speech is 'wholly concerned with the alleged bolshevist threat'.) Hitler extends his medical analogy to illustrate the danger to the political body: 'The opinion that it would be possible to live together peaceably and even to live in harmony with these ferments of decomposition is nothing but the belief that the body in time will reach a state in which it will assimilate cholera bacillus.'

Hitler's use of a metaphor of disease follows on from Luther's description of Jews as a 'plague' and the infamous anti-Semite Hermann Ahlwardt's reference to Jews as cholera, posing the possibility that he may be citing Ahlwardt here (on Luther and Ahlwardt see Hilberg 1996: 32–3). In a system in which disease and immunity cannot coexist, it becomes logical to insist that neither can Bolshevism/Jewry and Germany coexist. Russian intention against Germany—and, according to Hitler's logic, European civilization—must therefore be a desire for annihilation: 'the Kremlin would in case of victory decide on the complete extermination of the German people.' The pertinent question for Hitler becomes one of 'the salvation of Europe and the European states' by the strong-bodied Germany. He later claims: 'Thus alone Germany has become immune from all attempts to infect her with the Bolshevik virus.' Germany's very bodily presence, resistant to Russian infection, must, according to Hitler's logic, be eradicated by the Russians in order for them to be able to successfully infect Europe. It is this destruction of 'healthy' Germany by a Russia intent on infecting Europe that would lead to Jewish celebration. Throughout the speech Hitler is invoking a sense of Bolshevism and Jewry as being akin to bacteria, with Germany as the healthy body: Germany is both immune (having fought off Jewry) and under threat (from this new bacteria, Bolshevism). As such, Germany is somewhat paradoxically both strong and weak, victor and victim.

Hitler explicitly aligns this Russian annihilationist agenda with Jewish objectives: 'This aim is also the openly admitted intention of international Jewry.' He then goes on to warn that, 'Unless Germany is victorious', the 'bearer of this culture' will perish. Then comes his famous reference to Purim: 'Jewry could then celebrate the destruction of Europe by a second triumphant Purim festival.' Purim is therefore a celebration of destruction, and it is cited as proof of Jewish aggressive intention. It is notable that the editors of the *New York Times* include in parenthesis here, for those unfamiliar with Jewish tradition: '[The Purim festival marks the deliverance of the Jews from Haman.]' The fact that Hitler needed no such gloss demonstrates the currency of his reference to Purim: it was evidently one with which he presumed his listeners would be familiar.

It is worth briefly turning to the version of the speech printed in Max Domarus's four-volume collection of Hitler's speeches (which post-dated much of the critical work on Purim as it was available in English translation only in 2004 and in German in 1987). Domarus translates the line as: 'the devastating Jewish Ahasuerus [Xerxes] could celebrate the destruction of Europe in a second triumphant Purim festival' (2004: 2873), which includes the extra detail of the king of the Persian empire. In Hitler's allegorical framework, the king of the Persian empire could only represent the president of the United States, Franklin D. Roosevelt. Hitler calls the gentile Ahasuerus Jewish, intimating that his part in saving the Jewish people from the attack of Haman revealed a secret Jewish identity. Hitler is therefore not only conflating Bolshevism and Jewry, but the United States as well, ruled as it is by the 'Jewish Ahasuerus'; his message is that England, in guarding itself against Bolshevism, must also guard itself against Jews and the United States: all three wish for a Purim celebrating the destruction of Europe.

At the centre of Hitler's citation of Purim, then, is Jewry as the aggressor—he situates himself as a victim of Jewish violence, divinely preserved and engaged in military self-defence. (He lauds the German people for 'conducting this decisive life and death struggle', ascribing their preservation to 'the grace of God'.) He paints Nazi Germany in precisely these defensive terms: 'This unified state, based on a solid national and political organization, had to create forthwith armed forces which ... would be an adequate instrument to carry out the task of self defence.' This military defence is the secondary enacting of a more primary cultural self-defence, against Jews who are, for him, 'these bacteria'. Although his speech, like the racist logic it draws upon, is (necessarily) illogical, confused, and contradictory; his message is nonetheless clear. Indeed, it is the speech's paradoxes (that Germany is both strong and weak, for example) that make its intentions all the more compelling. He paints Jews as aggressors, and their potential celebration of Purim becomes a dance on the grave of a cultured Europe and civilization per se. It is this logic of repaying vengeful violence that makes sense of the alleged Nazi hanging of ten Polish Jews 'as punishment for having hanged the ten sons of Haman' (Domnitch 2000: 73; Blum-Dobkin calls it a 'sadistic reversal': 1979: 56). By presenting the hanging of the Jews as 'punishment', the Jews are represented as the perpetrators and the Nazi hangings become a response to aggression, in this case punishment and, as in Hitler's previous rhetoric, self-defence. It is such an appeal to self-defence that makes Haman's accusation of the Jews in Esther 3 succeed.

In invoking Purim to present Jewishness as inherently vengeful, Hitler was repeating what had become a common reading of the Book of Esther and would in all probability be familiar to those listening to the speech. It demonstrates that Hitler was cognizant of Christian anti-Semitic reception of Esther, if not with Jewish practice itself. It is an interpretation of Esther that can be traced back at least to the nineteenth century. In 1848 Edward Tottenham, in a sermon on the failure of the Gunpowder Plot of 1605, claims that there is 'much that is objectionable' in contemporary Purim celebrations. 'There is often great intemperance, and a spirit of revenge displayed, not merely in the record of Haman's cruelty ... but in the curses they pronounce on him' (Tottenham 1848: 13). Reading the Book of Esther to portray Jewishness as inherently violent and revengeful is what Elliot Horowitz calls a 'liberal-Anglican consensus' in the late nineteenth century (2006: 27). As late as 1954, *The Interpreter's Bible*, unreflectingly, states that 'There is in the book a spirit of revenge' (1954: 845–6). Horowitz cites various pre- and post-Holocaust examples of similar readings that demonstrate racist logic in their identification of the killings in Esther 9:2 as vengeful slaughter and, further, as representative of a Jewish 'character'. They interpret a group (the Jews) in light of one set of actions (Esther 9:2); but importantly, it is an interpretation of Esther 9:2 that is unsupported by textual evidence, the biblical text being typically laconic at this point. It must be remembered that the Jews are here still under threat from the *irreversible* edict ordering their slaughter; they are authorized only to defend themselves following a second edict that allows them 'to stand for their life, to destroy, and to slay, and to cause to perish, all the forces of the people and province that would assault them' (Esther 8:11; for further discussion see Carruthers, (2009)). In contrast to those who cite the passage as evidence of Jewish vengeance, many commentators note the detail of the Jews' refusal to take any plunder from those they slay as evidence that it was necessary self-defence (see Carruthers 2008: 256–65). Many of Horowitz's findings are breathtaking in the prejudice they reveal, perhaps because they are obviously so normative for the time. In one example he cites the Methodist scholar W. L. Northridge, who claims in 1937 that the book reveals 'Jewish vindictiveness at its worst', comparing the 'unworthy elements' in Judaism to a Christian 'spirit of love' (see Horowitz 2006: 37).

Hitler is drawing on a widely circulating Protestant reading of Esther that saw the slaughter at the end of the book as evidence of Jewish vengefulness per se. It is noteable that Horowitz, although providing the most extensive documentation of anti-Semitic reception of the Book of Esther to date, misses Hitler as one of its proponents. In the context of citing the Nazi's deliberate subversion of Jewish holidays, their 'perverse pleasure in suffusing Jewish holidays with suffering and slaughter', Horowitz cites Goodman's reference to Hitler's 1944 speech and his 'second triumphant Purim'. Horowitz's response, like Beal's, involves apparent irony as he goes on to note that Hitler was 'evidently' (2006: 91) unaware of the Casablanca local Purim that was already celebrating his (limited) defeat. Yet Hitler is not predicting Jewish response to his potential downfall but utilizing currently circulating prejudice against Jews to present Purim as evidence of Jewish aggression. Hitler is not reading the Book of Esther in his own unique way (although his mapping of Ahasuerus' 'Jewish sympathy' onto Roosevelt is novel). He takes a culturally resonant set of connections (Purim with aggression and social destruction) and maps it onto history to defend his own aggression. Hitler is merely escalating an existing sophistry: Jews equal Purim equals revenge.

It is striking that Jewish individuals and Hitler cite Purim for opposing purposes. We find here the reception of a biblical story functioning as a beacon of hope for one group and a firebrand of vilification for the other. Both are turning to the Book of Esther for what we might call historical narrative mapping: applying a narrative to historical events in order to make sense of those events by imposing an overarching logic or teleology. For Jews, Purim provides a narrative of divine providential protection; for Hitler, it provides an 'explanation' of Jewish character. In the case of Hitler's invocation of Purim, however, the Esther narrative is secondary and subservient to another narrative: that of the victim–victimizer dyad. Hitler's vilification of the Jews works according to the logic of this dyad in which victims are bestowed with an inherent innocence, and victimizers denied pity (on the Victim Triangle—Victim, Victimizer, and Rescuer—see Karpman 1968: 39–43). Michael Ovey explains the function of victim status, which signifies, amongst other things, 'moral innocence', 'unique authority', and 'non-accountability' (Ovey 2006). To identify one's enemies as victimizers, then, is to tap into a morally transcendent site of victimhood. Hitler's abuses in the name of 'victimhood' are not unique to him but, as David Keen outlines (in relation to 9/11 and the subsequent 'war on terror'), the invocation of victim status, through identification of an evil enemy, can be the pernicious beginnings of a spiral of violence that, far from alleviating feelings of threat or terror, exacerbates them to increase counter-aggression. The identification of an 'evil' enemy (and the implied self-status of victim) brings with it the *carte blanche* of violent behaviour against those which are deemed enemies. He warns: 'focusing exclusively on some demonised group—however vicious and violent it may be—creates space for abuses by diverse actors who claim to be opposing this group' (Keen 2006: 80). It justifies pre-emptive attacks on any who are deemed a threat and justifies violent annihilation of the enemy (see ibid. 19–23).

By merely alluding to Purim, Hitler invokes a set of apparently pervasive assumptions about Jews that need no rational construction or defence. As such, the sophistry of Hitler's position remains masked. Similarly overshadowed is the blatant lack of logic in his position: to defend slaughter through an accusation of slaughter. To engage more profoundly with the story of Esther itself is to risk its potential disruption of his logic. To interpret Esther as a book that 'proves' Jewish vengefulness overwhelmingly ignores that in the Book of Esther the plotting Haman is the aggressor. The persecution of the Jews is ignored and implicitly overwritten, unlike the threatening decree that, as irreversible, cannot be overwritten and still hangs over the Jews' heads. The invocation of Purim is a commitment to an inherently illogical stance as it vilifies an action (slaughter) whilst sanctifying it in the name of victimhood. There is, then, a gamut of stultifying identifications circulating at various levels in Hitler's speech: he constructs 'Jews' and 'victims' as non-historical, fixed identities oblivious to change or complexity. And indeed, the polarization of parties into evil–innocent and into victim–victimizer is a tempting move: especially when circumstances invite such an unambiguous response. Yet the invocation of singular, apparently self-evident identities, whilst reassuringly rigid, numbs critical engagement, as Jean-Paul Sartre warns: 'The more one is absorbed in fighting Evil, the less one is tempted to place the Good in question' (1948: 44). Sartre's warning compels a critical approach, so that any assignation of abstract and polarized characteristics, 'evil' or 'good', to a set of people or a person provokes suspicion.

Hitler's allusion to Purim in his speech fails to register long enough for critical engagement, and as such the story of Esther is not brought to bear on the arguments. Yet to keep the story of Esther in creative tension with its reception by Hitler intimates an even greater irony than that gestured towards by Beal or Horowitz. Hitler's reference to Purim demands that it be read in the light of Esther 3:8: Haman's strategy of misrepresenting the Jews to the king as a 'certain people' whose laws are 'diverse from those of every people' and counter to those of the empire. It is with reference to Purim, then, that Hitler not only inhabits the role of accuser, but does so by disquietingly replicating Haman's iconic role as enemy of the Jews.

WORKS CITED

BEAL, TIMOTHY (1997), *The Book of Hiding: Gender, Ethnicity, Annihilation and Esther*. London: Routledge.

BLUM-DOBKIN, TOBY (1979), 'The Landsburg Carnival: Purim in a Displaced Persons Center' in *Purim: The Face and the Mask: Essays and Catalogue at the Yeshiva University Museum February–June 1979*, 52–8. New York: Yeshiva University Museum.

CARRUTHERS, JO (2008), *Esther Through the Centuries*. Oxford: Blackwell.

——(2009), 'Writing, Interpretation and the Book of Esther: A Detour via Browning and Derrida', *Yearbook of English Studies*, 39/1–2: 58–71.

CHAIKIN, MIRIAM (1983), *Make Noise, Make Merry: The Story and Meaning of Purim*, illustrated by DEMI. New York: Clarion Books.

DOMARUS, MAX (2004), *Hitler: Speeches and Proclamations 1932–1945 and Commentary by a Contemporary*, vol. 4: *The Years 1941 to 1945*. Wauconda, Ill.: Balchazy-Carducci.

DOMNITCH, LARRY (2000), *The Jewish Holidays: A Journey Through History*. Northvale and Jerusalem: Jason Aronson Inc.

ENGEL, DAVID (1999), *The Holocaust: The Third Reich and the Jews*. Harlow: Longman.

FACKENHEIM, EMIL L. (1990), *The Jewish Bible after the Holocaust: A Re-reading*. Manchester: Manchester University Press.

GOODMAN, PHILIP ([1949] 1988), *The Purim Anthology*. Philadelphia, New York, and Jerusalem: Jewish Publication Society.

GREENSTEIN, JOSEPH (1946), *Purim Portfolio*. Zionist Organisation of America.

HILBERG, RAUL (1996), 'The Destruction of the European Jews: Precedents', in DAVID CESARANI (ed.), *The Final Solution: Origins and Implementation*, 21–42. London and New York: Routledge.

HITLER, ADOLF (31 Jan. 1944), text of Hitler Address Marking the 11th Anniversary of His National Socialist Regime, London, Jan. 30 (U.P.). The text of the speech by Adolf Hitler as broadcast by the German radio and recorded and translated by The United Press in the *New York Times*, pp. 4–5.

The Holy Scriptures (1917), Jewish Publication Society of America.

HOROWITZ, ELLIOT (2006), *Reckless Rites: Purim and the Legacy of Jewish Violence*. Princeton: Princeton University Press.

The Interpreter's Bible: The Holy Scriptures, vol. 3: *Esther* (1954). New York and Nashville: Abingdon Press.

KARPMAN, STEPHEN B. (1968), 'Fairy Tales and Script Drama Analysis'. in *Transactional Analysis Bulletin*, 7/26: 39–43.

KEEN, DAVID (2006), *Endless War?: Hidden Functions of the 'War on Terror'*. London, and Ann Arbor: Pluto Press.

OVEY, MICHAEL (2006), 'Victim Chic? The Rhetoric of Victimhood'. *Cambridge Papers*, 15/1 (March). www.jubilee-centre.org/online_documents/.

RACZYMOW, HENRI (1995), *Writing the Book of Esther*, trans. from the French by Dori Katz. London and New York: Holmes & Meier.

ROBIT, REBECCA and ALVIN GOLDFARB (eds.) (1999), *Theatrical Performance During the Holocaust: Texts/Documents/Memoirs*. Baltimore and London: Johns Hopkins University Press.

Sacks, Jonathan (1992), *Crisis and Covenant: Jewish Thought After the Holocaust*. Manchester and New York: Manchester University Press.

Sartre, Jean-Paul (1948), *Anti-Semite and Jew*, trans. George J. Becker. New York: Schocken Books.

Stitch, Wilhelmena (1935), *Women of the Bible*. London: Methuen & Co.

Tottenham, Edward (1848), *A Sermon Preached in Laura Chapel, Bath, on Sunday Evening, November 5th, 1848*. London: Hatchard & Sons & Simpkin, Marshall & Co.; Bath: M. A. Pocock, and Sims & Son.

Wiesel, Elie ([1979] 1995), *The Trial of God*, trans. Marion Wiesel. New York: Schocken.

Further Reading

As well as Beal 1997, Carruthers 2008, Engel 1999, Goodman 1988, and Horowitz 2006, see the collection *Purim: The Face and the Mask: Essays and Catalogue at the Yeshiva University Museum February–June 1979* (New York: Yeshiva University Museum).

CHAPTER 36

KIERKEGAARD ON THE LILIES AND THE BIRDS: MATTHEW 6

GEORGE PATTISON

'The upbuilding exposition thus strives in many ways to bring about the triumph of the eternal in human beings, but it by no means forgets the softness of a smile at the appropriate place, chiefly with the help of the lily and the bird. Oh, you who are in the midst of struggles, let yourself be softened. One can forget to laugh, but God preserve us all from ever forgetting to smile.'

After finishing the pseudonymous works that defined the first main period of his writing career (1843–6), after his bitter confrontation with the satirical newspaper *The Corsair* (1846), and as he moved towards the violent pamphleteering attack on the national church that dominated the last eighteen months of his life (1854–5), Kierkegaard's view of Christianity seems to have become progressively darker, more hostile to life in the world and to any compromise with the spirit of the age. During this time, Christian discipleship is described ever more one-sidedly in terms of renouncing the world in order to suffer with Christ. Yet there are many passages both in his published works and in his journals that demonstrate a far more complex and nuanced development. Prominent amongst these are the meditations ('discourses', as he mostly calls them) on the portrayal of the lilies of the field and the birds of the air in the Matthean Sermon on the Mount. But these 'teachers' do more than remind the struggling Christian to smile: they also serve to focus many of the themes of the entire authorship and to illustrate the freedom and imaginative power of Kierkegaard's use of Scripture. We shall take note of some of the echoes of the earlier writings later, but I begin with some general comments on Kierkegaard's relation to Scripture.

Kierkegaard was brought up in a pious Christian household. His family attended the Church of Our Lady, the main church in Copenhagen of the established Lutheran religion to which virtually all Danes then belonged, and the Kierkegaards were also involved with the Moravian meeting-house, a society within the State Church that offered a rather different—but, of course, no less biblical—experience of Christianity. Kierkegaard thus acquired an extensive and deep acquaintance with Scripture from his home, but when, in 1830, he began what would prove to be a ten-year study of theology at Copenhagen University, this would be transformed by exposure to the rigours of the academic study of the Bible. Although he seems to have spent much of his time as a student doing anything but studying theology, he was not entirely idle. One exercise, typical of the time, was to translate large sections of the New Testament into Latin, and Kierkegaard's translation of large parts of Acts and some sections of selected epistles survives (Cappelørn *et al.* 2007: 137–88). We also have his notes on Romans 9–16, that show a careful use of such contemporary aids as F. A. G. Tholuck's New Testament commentary and C. G. Bretschneider's lexicon (Cappelørn *et al.* 2008: 330–9). These notes show a high level of philological competence, as he dutifully checks Paul's language against both the Hebrew Bible and the Septuagint. Midway through Kierkegaard's student years, David Friedrich Strauss's *The Life of Jesus Critically Examined* was published, and although Kierkegaard's journals do not demonstrate that he actually read this, he certainly followed the ensuing debate very closely (ibid. 292–308).

His mature writings, however, show an approach to Scripture very different both from the scholarship of his university teachers and from the new criticism represented by Strauss. Whilst he came to see the latter as representing precisely the post- and even anti-Christian outcome of Hegelianism, he did not regard a relatively conservative scholarly approach as adequate to counter these forces. Such an approach can only ever yield an approximation to the meaning of the text, whereas Christianity requires an existentially decisive interpretation. Kierkegaard's own explicit views as to how this might be achieved can be focused in three characteristically vivid recommendations—two of them explicitly interpreting a key passage of Scripture—found in his work *For Self-Examination* (Kierkegaard 1962: 68 ff.).[1] The first is from the text that forms the basis for the first part of this

<hr/>

[1] *For Self-Examination* has not yet appeared in *Søren Kierkegaards Skrifter* [*SKS*] and the reference is therefore to the third edition of his collected works.

work (James 1:22–end), namely, that scripture is a 'mirror' reflecting back to us our true motivations and interests. Developing this idea, Kierkegaard's second recommendation draws an analogy with how we read a love-letter. He mocks the idea that we might read it in the way that scholars read Scripture. It would be a poor lover who read a letter from the beloved with scholarly detachment and objectivity: in this case, the subjective passion, the rush of blood to the head, and the haste to do what the letter-writer is asking are all the signs of a true reader—and, of course, the diametrical opposites of what is required for a scholarly approach. The third recommendation derives from Kierkegaard's reading of the story of Nathan and David, in which Nathan tells the king the story of a rich man with plentiful flocks who robbed his poor neighbour of the one little lamb he possessed; when David says that that man should die, Nathan rounds on him with the charge: 'thou art the man!', since the rich man's behaviour exactly mirrors that of David's adultery with Bathsheba. 'Thou art the man!' may, in this spirit, be a third, and decisive leitmotif of Kierkegaard's reading of Scripture. Importantly for the treatment of the lilies and the birds, this can be seen as applying both individually and socially (that is, as a message to the present age as a whole). In reading Scripture, we are not to focus on the mere surface of the text, and still less on its historical background, but on the truths about ourselves that it reflects back to us and on the self-transformations to which it calls us.

This approach gives Kierkegaard's approach to Scripture a certain sharpness, not to say severity. Yet—apart from not forgetting, when appropriate, to smile— we should also note the extraordinary freedom with which he treats Scripture. Although he sees 'obedience' as a key category in the relationship between the reader and the divine Word, Kierkegaard does not expound the biblical text in the manner of, for example, Neo-orthodox dogmatics. In Kierkegaard's practise as an interpreter of Scripture 'the Word', is not an external heteronomous power under which the reader is forced reluctantly to bow. As Jolita Pons put it, Scripture 'is not only a subject of discussion [for Kierkegaard], but also the structuring power behind [his] discourse' (Pons 2004: 52). In other words, Kierkegaard has internalized the language of Scripture into his own manner of speaking in such a way that he plays with it as freely as any proficient native speaker makes free with their mother-tongue. As Pons goes on to show, he is unashamed in inventing 'fictitious stories' on the basis of Scripture, deviating from the text by the use of free quotation, allusion, splicing of different texts, and surprising re-contextualizations—all of which are features of his discourses on the lilies and the birds.

Although Kierkegaard's interpretation of the story of the (near-) sacrifice of Isaac is his most widely known and far and away most extensively discussed interpretation of Scripture, it is by no means typical. Although it richly illustrates those stylistic features just listed, the message of 'fear and trembling' is only one side of what Kierkegaard finds in Scripture. As an early journal entry already stated: 'Fear and trembling is not the prime mover in faith, for that is love' (Cappelørn *et al.* 2008: 9). The lilies and the birds may provide a 'godly diversion' from the rigours of Christian living, (Kierkegaard 2004a: 282), but they are part of a larger group of texts used by Kierkegaard to draw out the dimension of love. Apart from the volume of discourses focusing exclusively on *Works of Love*, these texts include James 1:17 ('every good and perfect gift') and Luke 7 ('the woman who was a sinner'), which, like Matthew 6, are texts to which he returns on several occasions. Taken together with the meditations on the lilies and the birds, they demonstrate that Kierkegaard's vision of radical discipleship, even when stated in terms of hatred to the world, presupposes a theology of creation as a good and perfect gift, and on love as the freely chosen basis of the divine–human relationship. The full theological outworkings of this would take us far beyond the scope of this short study, but it is important to note it here, before we get into the detail of his work with the text.

Kierkegaard's treatment of Matthew 6 is found in writings of a kind he called 'discourses'.[2] He had published small sets of discourses throughout the period of his early pseudonymous writings, and, unlike those, these bore his name on the title-page. They also made explicit the religious intention of his authorship. For the most part the earlier discourses are referred to simply as 'upbuilding' (also translated 'edifying') discourses, suggesting a kind of religiousness that does not yet have a specific Christian focus. Their general form is akin to that of the contemporary sermon: they are mostly based on a Scripture text, and typically begin with a sometimes quite lengthy preamble that leads into a specification of the topic to be addressed. In keeping with this form, the reader is often addressed as 'My listener' or allusions are made to the church setting of the address. Kierkegaard himself insisted that they were not, however, sermons, since sermons presuppose the authority of ordination, and he, as a layman, could only speak 'without authority'. Nevertheless, the suggested ecclesiastical context is very striking in all of the Matthew 6 discourses. Each begins with a prayer, followed by the text, headed 'The Gospel for the 15TH Sunday after Trinity'. Indeed, Kierkegaard instructed his printer to use the same typeface as for the Danish Altar Book then in use (Kierkegaard 2004aK: 188–90)[3] and, in the case of the first set of these discourses, the rubric runs 'The Holy Gospel is written by the Evangelist Matthew, Chapter 6, verse 24 to the end', echoing the formula used in the spoken liturgy. The discourses in *Christian Discourses* are also prefaced by the heading 'Introit', further underlining this imagined liturgical context. Whilst marginal notes in Kierkegaard's own copy of the Altar Book indicate that this was indeed a primary resource in his early development of these discourses, the main point here is to be taken in the spirit of the mirror of the Word: that the reader is to read with the kind of seriousness and existential engagement appropriate to the solemnity of actual liturgy.

---

[2] For a full discussion of the discourses see Pattison 2002.

[3] 'K' refers to the volume of explanatory notes (Danish: *Kommentarer*) accompanying each volume of *SKS*.

The discourses dealing with Matthew 6 are found in three separately published works, and in a fourth that remained unpublished at Kierkegaard's death. I shall deal here primarily with the first three, which are also distinguished by their focus on the themes of the lilies and the birds, whilst the posthumously published discourse on 'Christ as Pattern' takes its cue from the opening line of the text 'No one can serve two masters'. However, this stern injunction is by no means absent from the 'godly diversion' provided by the lilies and the birds, as we shall see. The texts in question are the second (of three) parts of *Upbuilding Discourses in Various Spirits* (1847), entitled 'What we learn from the Lilies of the Field and the Birds of the Air'; the first (of four) parts of *Christian Discourses* (1848), entitled 'The Anxieties of the Pagans'; and a separately published collection of three discourses entitled *The Lily of the Field and the Bird of the Air: Three Godly Discourses* (1849)— in these titles, as throughout these discourses, Kierkegaard moves rather freely between plural and singular formulations of his subject. It will be noticed that the first group is subsumed under the earlier term '*upbuilding* discourses', whilst the second is specifically of 'Christian' discourses and the third is designated as comprising 'godly' discourses. In terms of Kierkegaard's own depiction of his trajectory as being from a non-specific religiousness to a radically Christian position, this suggests that these discourses occupy an interestingly ambiguous borderline position. If, as will become apparent, they show how Kierkegaard's theology of redemption and discipleship, despite some of its extreme formulations, is nevertheless dovetailed into a theology of creation, they might fairly be described as occupying a pivotal place in his authorship—and its interpretation. This assertion is strengthened by the observation that they belong to a two-year period that, biographically, marks just this transition and the emergence (by 1849) of Kierkegaard's new pseudonym, Anti-Climacus, representative of a powerfully anti-establishment version of Christianity that, Kierkegaard said, went beyond what even he himself was capable of. The year 1848 was also that of Denmark's bloodless revolution that led to a new constitution, including changing the basis of the church establishment from that of a State Church to the 'People's Church', that is, the church of the majority of the Danish people. These events too—and the broader tendencies they reflect—are mirrored in the writings on the lilies and the birds.

Each of these three sets of discourses is, as we have just seen, differently described ('upbuilding', 'Christian', 'godly'). Each of the first two sets also plays a specific role in the larger work to which it belongs, whilst the free-standing volume *The Lily of the Field and the Bird of the Air* needs to be seen in connection with the second edition of Kierkegaard's study of the confrontation between the aesthetic and ethical views of life, *Either/Or*, the best-selling of his pseudonymous works, that had raised cultural eyebrows by its apparent insider's view of post-Romantic nihilism. Each set therefore needs to be seen in its specific literary, biographical, and even philosophical and political context. Rather than go through the discourses one by one, however, I shall here seek merely to indicate some of the key themes common to them all, namely, the role of the aesthetic in relation to the religious; the critique of the age; inwardness and the *imago dei*; language and silence; temporality.

It has been noted that Kierkegaard himself represented his authorship as a movement from the aesthetic to the religious. In *Either/Or* the aesthetic point of view and way of life had been portrayed as presupposing an essentially nihilistic metaphysics, whilst the ethical point of view with which it was contrasted rested on the demand to choose one's life as a God-given task. Yet *Either/Or* itself implies that aesthetic nihilism is only possible because it builds on features that are integral to human life, including the joys and passions of the senses, not least of sensuous love. What the aesthetic Seducer does, however, is to tear these out of their proper contextualization in mutually responsible relationships and make them ends in themselves. In doing so he exemplifies the general tendency of the poetic to abstract from the complexity of real life and to fixate on one or other merely represented ideal. But such a violent disruption of the order of existence will finally lead the aesthete himself into a state of despair, since he has denied what alone could give real content or basis to his poetic desires and fantasies.

In different ways the drama of aesthetic self-destruction and of the confrontation between the aesthetic and the religious is repeated in each of the sets of discourses we are considering. In the first of the 1847 discourses Kierkegaard indulges in one of his most remarkable pieces of freely rewriting the Scriptural text (Pons's 'fictitious stories'), by introducing two 'tales' that are stylistically akin to those of H. C. Andersen, each beginning with the conventional 'Once upon a time...'. The first is about a lily that is happily living its flower-life until it is befriended by a chatty bird who gossips away about other places it has visited where the lilies are so 'splendid', 'joyful and cheerful', 'scented and colourful', as to be beyond description. Eventually the lily becomes discontented with its lot, and persuades the bird to pull it up and take it away to be with these other fabulous lilies. Of course, it withers and dies on the way (Kierkegaard 2004a: 266–8). This unhappy little tale effectively repeats the story told in *Either/Or*'s 'The Diary of a Seducer'—for, as Kierkegaard comments, we naturally imagine the flower as feminine, whilst the bird 'is the poet, the seducer, or what is poetic and seductive in human beings' (ibid. 269). Like the girl—and, of course, many readers—what destroys the lily is the arousal of purely imaginary needs and longings, fantasies that cannot be realized in the world as it is, yet in which, were it not to have been seduced by such empty possibilities, the flower might have lived happily ever after.

Christian Discourses too echoes *Either/Or*. The basic premise of these discourses is connected with Christ's words not to be 'like the gentiles' or pagans.[4]

---

[4] The Danish uses a term cognate with the English 'heathens', translated 'pagans' in newer translations of Kierkegaard's works.

But whereas Kierkegaard judges the pagans of pre-Christian times to have been relatively innocent, he takes the term as applying pre-eminently to those within Christendom who nevertheless live by pagan values. This corresponds closely to his analysis of sensuousness in the essay on Don Juan in the first part of *Either/Or*. Why? Because the viciousness of Don Juan's sensualism is precisely dependent on his refusing the possibilities of a higher, spiritual existence offered by Christianity. The 'pagans' of *Christian Discourses* are, for the most part, not exactly Don Juans, but fairly transparent ciphers for the bourgeois Christians of Kierkegaard's own time, preoccupied with success, status, and worldly goods—and constantly succumbing to the various forms of anxiety associated with their failure to secure these supposed goods. Essentially their error is like that of the victims of aesthetic seduction, namely, that they have been mesmerized by visions of imaginary aims and values, instead of being content with who they are. Like Don Juan in comparison with the innocent lovers of sensuousness in the pre-Christian era: 'the pagans who are found in Christendom have sunk the deepest; those of pagan times had not yet been raised to the level of Christianity, these have sunk lower than paganism; those belong to the fallen race, these, having been raised up, have fallen again, even deeper' (Kierkegaard 2004*b*: 24). Unsurprisingly, Kierkegaard's account of their predicament often resonates with the various forms of aesthetic despair found in the earlier work. This is especially striking in the sixth and seventh discourses, 'On the Anxiety of Self-torment', and 'On the Anxiety of Irresolution, Inconstancy, and Disconsolateness'. The description of the self-tormentor, whose anxiety about 'tomorrow' robs him both of his present and his past (as well as depriving him of a hopeful relation to 'tomorrow' itself), reprises the account of aesthetic despair figured in *Either/Or*'s essay on 'The Unhappiest Man'. Similarly, the 'disconsolate' pagan, who 'cares for nothing', who lives a living death, and is too world-weary even to despair (ibid. 97) reflects the aesthete of *Either/Or*'s 'Diapsalmata' who likewise 'cares for nothing' and is described by his ethical interlocutor in terms that are almost verbatim repeated here (Kierkegaard 2004*b*K: 138–9).

It is no surprise, then, when the first of the 1849 discourses opens by taking 'the poet' as exemplifying a relation to the lilies and the birds diametrically opposed to that of the gospel. The poet *wishes*, or *says* that he wishes, to be 'like' the lily and the bird, to go out and dwell in the midst of nature as a part of nature—alluding, of course, to the Romantic cult of nature and especially to the motif of the free spontaneity of birdsong as a model of the lyric poet's own vocation.[5] But what really occupies the poet is precisely his own saying of it. It is only as a fantasy, a dream, an ideal, that the poet *wishes* to go back to nature or to become 'as a child'. What is enticing about his wish is precisely its allusiveness, its mystery, and that it cannot be realized in the world as it is. Longing and fantasy take precedence over

---

[5] See Pattison 2007: 111–26.

reality. But it is quite otherwise in the case of the gospels. Here, as Kierkegaard says, 'the gospel dares to say to the poet that he *shall* be like the bird'—and, on this occasion, 'the gospel is so serious that not even the poet's most irresistible inventions can make it smile' (Kierkegaard 2006: 15).

Yet, as in *Either/Or* itself, the confrontation between the aesthetic and the religious is not crudely black-and-white. Kierkegaard had there critiqued the aesthetic in a work that had an essentially aesthetic form and that seemed to speak from within the aesthetic consciousness: so too in these discourses he allows himself 'godly' diversions, not only telling fairy-stories but, in *The Lily of the Field and the Bird of the Air*, rising to sparkling stylistic heights in his evocation of nature's essential silence, perhaps the final flourish of his virtuoso powers as a writer of extraordinarily lyrical prose poetry. This is not simple inconsistency, for what the lilies and the birds themselves teach is that there is an innocent aesthetic joy in the simple, creaturely reality of existing, including the varied forms and possibilities of human life. The error of 'the poet' and the aesthete is precisely their inability or refusal to stay with this, and their desire to 'go beyond' what is good in itself—thereby losing what is genuinely poetic and aesthetic: the glory of the lily, the free flight of the bird.

Why this matters to Kierkegaard is not because he has here and there noticed a stray aesthete who has lost his way in life. Rather, it is because he perceives an underlying aestheticism in the very spirit of the age. For the age is less and less capable of being contented with being human (the theme of the first of the 1847 Matthew 6 discourses), and more and more seeking a new way of life that, people imagine, will somehow be better than the way things are. The mechanism whereby this multiplication of what Kierkegaard believes to be impossible and insatiable desires occurs is *comparison*. The lily, he points out, is not compared to Solomon himself, merely to their respective raiment. 'Ah! But in human beings' constant social intercourse, in the many differences and in their different interactions, the inventiveness of a busy or anxious comparison makes one forget what it is to be a human being; one forgets it as a result of comparing one human being with another' (Kierkegaard 2004a: 265). That this is especially a problem for the present age is underlined in the second of the 1847 discourses:

One human being compares himself with others, one generation compares itself with another, and thus the accumulated mass of comparisons grows over humanity's head. As artifice and busyness increase, there will be more and more in each generation who slavishly work their whole lives away down in comparison's low, subterranean regions. Like miners who never see daylight, these unhappy ones will never come to see the light of that uplifting, simple, elementary thought as to how glorious it is to be human. (ibid. 286–7)

It is just these 'unhappy ones' whose situation is figured in the 'pagans' of the *Christian Discourses*. The evil of comparison is also, in Kierkegaard's view, decisive in fomenting the divisions between rich and poor, high and low. Far from sharing the hopes that liberal or revolutionary movements might reintegrate a fragmenting society, he asserted that only a religious acceptance of our common humanity could establish a secure basis for social flourishing—and it is just this that the lilies and the birds teach us.

That the conditions of the present age make learning from the lilies and the birds especially urgent is signalled in the prayer that prefaces the 1849 discourses, which begins by lamenting how hard it is to learn and how easy to forget what it is to be human in 'the human swarm'. The recurrent use in these discourses of the phrase 'out there', that is, out there with the lilies and the birds, enacts a gesture of separation from the life of the city with its swarming business, political, and cultural life (a gesture Kierkegaard himself enacted in this period by taking repeated carriage rides 'out there' to the Zealand countryside beyond the rapidly expanding boundaries of Copenhagen). That the sheer number of people crowded together in the modern city contributes to obscuring the basic realities of being human is also alluded to in the second 1849 discourse, when Kierkegaard speaks about 'the increasing indifference' that results from 'the intercourse with the many with whom one has intercourse in wide-ranging social relations without any essential inner content', and how 'the smaller the number' of social relations, the better placed we are to see their seriousness and to understand the either/or that obedience to God demands (Kierkegaard 2006: 27). Again, we can see this in terms of Kierkegaard restating a certain element in Romantic aestheticism, that is, the option for nature versus the city, at the same time as he also rejects the Romantic fantasy of returning human beings to a state of nature.[6] For the analogy of the lily and the bird, like all analogies, contains dissimilarity as well as similarity.

The dissimilarity that the analogy especially brings into view is the distinctiveness of human beings in creation: that they are capable of inwardness, of existing as 'Spirit', and are made in the image and likeness of God.[7] The lily and the bird are unconscious of their condition, but human beings are defined by consciousness—and even though consciousness exposes them to anxiety, it is privileged as 'the place where the eternal and the temporal constantly touch each other, where the eternal breaks into the temporal' (Kierkegaard 2004a: 292). Consciousness gives the possibility of—or rather requires—a self-consciously chosen God-relationship. There is an either/or that runs through human existence, an either/or that the gospel shows to be a choice to love or to hate God (Kierkegaard 2006: 26 ff.). Human beings not only can, they therefore 'shall' choose between God and Mammon (Kierkegaard 2004a: 302; 2006: 15), and 'seek first' God's kingdom 'within' (Kierkegaard 2004a: 304). This is not in the first instance a

---

[6] For the role of these discourses in the context of Kierkegaard's critique of the modern city see Pattison 1999: 127–30.

[7] Kierkegaard also discusses work as another positive feature of the distinctiveness of human existence. See Kierkegaard 2004a: 294–6.

matter of heroic discipleship but of simply accepting our dependence on God, which the lilies and birds practise spontaneously. Thus, the poor Christian despite his poverty, has the privilege (which the bird does not have) of praying and giving thanks for his daily bread (Kierkegaard 2004b: 33–4), whilst the rich Christian can learn to regard his wealth not as a possession but as a gift (ibid. 37 ff.).

The theological basis of the assertion that human consciousness is the point of intersection between time and the eternal is that we are made in the image and likeness of God, and the second of the Matthew 6 discourses in *Upbuilding Discourses in Various Spirits* contains Kierkegaard's most explicit statement of this, as well as of the concomitant difference between the lilies and the birds and human beings. 'In order to praise the lily, the gospel says that its glory exceeds that of Solomon: should it not be infinitely more glorious to be like God? The lily is not like God . . . it bears a mark that reminds us of God, it testifies [to God] since God has not left himself without witness in anything he has made . . . ' (Kierkegaard 2004a: 289). Nowhere in the visible creation can we find more than this, for no visible creature can bear the image of God, who 'is Spirit, is invisible, and the image of what is invisible is also invisible' (ibid. 289). Therefore, the glory of being human (of which the splendour of the lily is to remind us) is that we are Spirit. But how does this manifest itself? Not in human beings' lordship over creation, but in their capacity for worship. '[Human beings'] upright carriage is their distinction, but to cast oneself down in worship is still more glorious. All of nature is like the servant who reminds human beings, Lords of nature, to worship God' (ibid. 290). Human beings are like God by virtue of being Spirit, but since their spiritual relation to God is primarily to be one of worship (or, as in the second of the 1849 discourses, obedience), 'Human beings and God are not like one another in a direct way, but inversely: only when God has become the eternal and omnipresent object of worship in an infinite sense, and the human being is forever a worshipper, only then are they like one another' (ibid. 290).

This likeness is in the spiritual dimension of inwardness. Therefore, it eludes representation in anything external, even language. Once more the poet, as the virtuoso practitioner of language, poses a special danger, since he can so seductively substitute a merely represented world for the real world. Yet not just poetry but any act of speaking invites the listener to compare himself to and to understand himself in terms of his relation to something other than God (ibid. 260–1). The silence of the lilies and the birds is therefore especially suited to help us break through the possible deceits of language, something for which the person weighed down with anxiety must be particularly grateful (ibid. 260–1). To be able to talk is human beings' distinction over the animal kingdom, 'but in relation to God, it can easily be ruinous for human beings, to want to talk because they can. God is in heaven, human beings on earth—therefore they cannot easily talk together. God is all-knowing, but what human beings know is idle chatter' (Kierkegaard 2006: 17). The poet imagines that the voice of God speaks in the silence of nature, but Christians use nature's silence to become silent themselves, to wait upon God, and in silent waiting upon God to discover their kinship with God (ibid. 18). The silence of nature is not the voice of God, but nature's expression of reverence for God, nature's way of worshipping God (ibid. 22). By its silence it teaches us to become silent, and, in silence, to become able to pray that *God's* name should be hallowed, *God's* will be done (ibid. 24). That Kierkegaard should *tell* us all this, should *write* about it, sometimes rather poetically, might therefore seem self-defeating, and, as his extensive writings about communication show, this is a problem of which he was deeply aware. But it is also a partial explanation for why it is precisely in the discourse on learning silence from the lilies and the birds that he performs the extraordinarily lyrical evocation of nature's silence mentioned before. For this performance allows the musicality, the pure *sound* of language, to lead us beyond the purely representative or purely comparative functions of language.

The lilies and the birds teach us to become free of the modern world's self-created anxieties by offering a model of silent obedience, a model we are to replicate in our inward spiritual existence as creatures made in the image of God and who find fulfilment in worshipping Him. But one further feature of human beings' distinctive possibilities for a conscious relation to God must be mentioned: time. Kierkegaard's interpretation of time is one of his most distinctive contributions to the history of modern thought, and this interpretation plays an important role in each of these sets of discourses.

We have read how he defines consciousness as the meeting-point of time and the eternal, and this means that human beings 'have a dangerous enemy that the bird does not have' (Kierkegaard 2004a: 292), since they cannot avoid a conscious relation to time. The danger is especially apparent in relation to the warning offered by the text against 'taking thought for the morrow', for 'tomorrow', the future, is what can most tempt a human being into confusing fantasy and reality and substituting merely imagined needs and longings for the gifts given us in the actuality of existence. Kierkegaard illustrates this in the first of the 1847 discourses by supplementing the tale of the seduced lily with a similar tale about a wood-pigeon who has always found its daily bread, but is upset by an encounter with some tame doves who boast of how the farmer provides them with a secure food-supply. Eventually the wood-pigeon sneaks into the dovecote to share this supposed benefit—only to end up on the farmer's dinner table. The point of the story is that the root of the pigeon's fatal anxiety is not to be found in the moment when it begins comparing itself with the dove, but when it starts to compare one day with the next (ibid. 277–8). Kierkegaard expands on this idea in the sixth of the 1848 discourses, 'The Anxiety of Self-Torment', where, for example, he writes of 'the next day' as 'the boarding-plank by means of which anxiety's monstrous hordes get hold of "the individual's" little ship' (Kierkegaard 2004b: 81). Or, 'when a person is condemned to life imprisonment, the judgment states that he is condemned "for life", but the one who condemns himself to being anxious about the next day, [also] condemns himself "for life"' (ibid. 81). It is clearly self-defeating to want to overcome anxiety about the future by wondering what one is going to do about it. The only way forward is to ignore it, like the actor who looks out into a darkened auditorium, or a rower, whose back is turned to the direction in which he is rowing (ibid. 84–5). Human beings' relation to the eternal is not grounded in the future, the next day, but in 'this very day', a point that, Kierkegaard comments, rules out all apocalypticism (ibid. 83). Christ himself offers an example of what this might mean, since, conscious as he was of his impending crucifixion, he did not allow himself to be overwhelmed by anxiety but lived each day as sufficient to itself (ibid. 84–5). It is also the key to true joy: God's own blissfulness consists in the fact that 'he eternally says: Today; he who us eternally and infinitely present to himself in being "today"' (Kierkegaard 2006: 43). And if we would learn this joy, we have only (once more) to turn to the lily and the bird, since 'the lily and the bird are joy, because silently and obediently they are entirely present to themselves by being today' (ibid. 43).

In these and similar comments Kierkegaard commits himself to a view of truth as self-presence that has been the focus of considerable debate in recent Continental philosophy, following Derrida's critique of Heidegger for supposedly privileging a conception of truth as presence. The further discussion of how such a critique might apply to Kierkegaard and how the latter's view needs to be complemented by his treatment of gift, love, and redemption lies beyond the scope of this chapter. What has been shown here might be interpreted as demonstrating that Kierkegaard merely used Scripture as a platform for his own ideas by means of a set of rather free and unstructured associations of ideas. But this freedom could also be taken in a positive sense, as exemplifying a relation to Scripture in which the heteronomy of the divine Word has become fully integrated into the reader's own struggle for subjective truth. Kierkegaard's rejection of social, economic, and political factors in his analysis of and prescription for the maladies of the age may not suit our taste, but the lilies and birds undoubtedly helped him to articulate a distinctive response to modernity that would provide a striking alternative to both mainstream bourgeois and Marxist positions in the history of nineteenth- and twentieth-century ideas.

Works Cited

Cappelørn, N.-J. *et al.* (2007), *Kierkegaard's Journals and Notebooks*, vol. 1. Princeton: Princeton University Press.

——(2008), *Kierkegaard's Journals and Notebooks*, vol. 2. Princeton: Princeton University Press.

Kierkegaard, S. (1962), *Til Selvprøvelse, Samtiden anbefalet*, in *Samlede Vaerker*, vol. 17. Copenhagen: Gyldendal.

——(2004*a*), *Opbyggelige Taler i forskellig Aand*, in *Søren Kierkegaards Skrifter* [*SKS*], vol. 8. Copenhagen: Gad.

——(2004*b*), 'Christelige Taler', in *Søren Kierkegaards Skrifter*, vol. 10. Copenhagen: Gad.

——(2006), *Lilien paa Marken og Fuglen under Himlen*, in *Søren Kierkegaards Skrifter*, vol. 11. Copenhagen: Gad (pp. 7–48).

Pattison, G. (1999), *'Poor Paris!': Kierkegaard's Critique of the Spectacular City*. Berlin: de Gruyter.

——(2002), *Kierkegaard's Upbuilding Discourses: Philosophy, Literature and Theology*. London: Routledge.

——(2007), 'The Joy of Birdsong or Dialectical Lyrics', in Robert L. Perkins (ed.), *International Kierkegaard Commentary (18): Without Authority*. Macon, Ga.: Mercer University Press.

Pons, J. (2004), *Stealing a Gift: Kierkegaard's Pseudonyms and the Bible*. New York: Fordham University Press.

Further Reading

Hansen, P. G. (1924), *Søren Kierkegaard og Bibelen*. Copenhagen: Haase.

Pattison, G. (2005), *The Philosophy of Kierkegaard*. Chesham: Acumen.

Perkins, Robert L. (ed.) (2005), *International Kierkegaard Commentary (15): Upbuilding Discourses in Various Spirits*. Macon, Ga.: Mercer University Press.

——(ed.)(2007), *International Kierkegaard Commentary (18): Without Authority*. Macon, Ga.: Mercer University Press.

——(ed.) (2008), *International Kierkegaard Commentary (17): Christian Discourses*. Macon, Ga.: Mercer University Press.

Polk, T. H. (1997), *The Biblical Kierkegaard: Reading by the Rule of Faith*. Macon, Ga.: Mercer University Press.

···

GANDHI'S INTERPRETATION OF THE SERMON ON THE MOUNT

···

JEREMY HOLTOM

Just with a little love and understanding and goodwill and a refusal to
cooperate with an evil law he was able to break the backbone of the
British Empire. This, I think, is one of the most significant things that has
ever happened in the history of the world. More than 390 million people
achieved their freedom and they achieved it non-violently.

This homage to Mohandas K. Gandhi, and the ideals he embodied, came from
another great religious thinker, political tactician, and social reformer: Martin
Luther King Jr (Carson 2002: 129). King's conscious debt to Gandhi is arguably
just one example of the extent and depth of the Mahatma's influence. Even for
those who do not hold him in the same reverence, it is difficult to overestimate
Gandhi's historical importance as a key figure in the collapse of colonialism, a
promoter of the dialogue of world faiths, and a pioneer of practical, non-violent
protest. What follows is an attempt to explore the impact of one biblical text on
Gandhi's religious thought and actions. It is not an attempt to do justice to this
astonishing man's life, about which so much has already been written. We should
be mindful of Anthony Copley's warning that 'Gandhi's place in history is too

important to allow him to disappear behind a smokescreen of interpretations'
(Copley 1999: 103). It would be misguided and wrong to make any attempt to
understand Gandhi within a purely Christian context or to exaggerate his debt to
Christianity. Nonetheless, as will become apparent, a dialogue with Christianity
played an important part in the development of Gandhi's religious philosophy, and
the text of Matthew 5–7 was at its heart.

The Sermon on the Mount is one of the most commented upon and interpreted
biblical passages, yet in a real sense Gandhi's interpretation of it represents a unique
and significant point in the reception history of the Bible as a whole. Here we have a
Christian scripture being reverently received and dynamically applied by a man
who remained all his life a devoted adherent of the Hindu faith. Gandhi's particular
responses to the concepts contained in the Sermon on the Mount must therefore be
understood not only in the context of his dialogue with Christianity but in the
terms of his own Hindu faith as he understood and lived it. His uncompromising
belief in the inseparable nature of religion and politics is well known and clearly
stated in his autobiography: 'those who say that religion has nothing to do with
politics do not know what religion means' (Gandhi 1987: 453). It is natural,
therefore, that his interpretation of the Sermon on the Mount can only be properly
understood through analysis of how he applied it in his political campaigns in
South Africa and India. In this context it will be important to consider what the
text meant to Gandhi himself; what it meant to his, at least nominally Christian,
opponents; and how it impacted on the struggle and dialogue between them.

GANDHI AND CHRISTIANITY

So what did Christianity mean to Gandhi? This is not an easy question to answer,
and it is one with which he himself spent many years wrestling. There are senses in
which Gandhi both took inspiration from and reacted against his encounter with
the Christian religion. From his early formative years as a young law-student in
London and lawyer in South Africa, Gandhi had many earnest and positive
encounters with Christians, like his sincere and intimate Quaker friend Mr Coates,
who wanted to bring him into the fold of their faith. He was often moved by this,
but at times felt it oppressive. In a speech at the YMCA in Colombo in 1927 he
declared: 'There are some who will not even take my flat denial when I tell them
I am not a Christian' (Iyer 2005: 145). Much of the distance between Gandhi and
Christianity resulted from what he felt was the limitation of its compassionate ideal
to the human species, a limitation he did not see in the eastern religious traditions
of Hinduism and Buddhism. He once alienated himself from Christian friends by

declaring of the Buddha: 'Look at Gautama's compassion! It was not confined to mankind, it was extended to all living beings . . . One fails to notice this love for all living beings in the life of Jesus' (Gandhi 1987: 157). What most repelled Gandhi about Christianity, however, were the efforts of Christian missionaries to promulgate their faith and seek conversions by denigrating other faiths. In their zeal to spread Christianity in India, many missionaries were prone to railing against what they saw as the heathen idolatry they found there. The general view of Hinduism by many British Christians was epitomised in the saying of the famous evangelist William Wilberforce: 'Our religion is sublime, pure and beneficent. Theirs is mean, licentious and cruel' (James 1998: 224). As a young man growing up in Gujarat, Gandhi had profoundly negative experiences of the proselytizing activities of Christian missionaries who 'used to stand in a corner near the high school and hold forth, pouring their abuse upon Hindus and their gods. I could not endure this' (Gandhi 1987: 46). Reports of converts eating beef and drinking brandy did nothing to alter his negative impression.

Gandhi believed in the fundamental equality of all religions, and this belief made him mistrustful of anyone's wish to change the religion into which he was born. In his various journals he regularly questioned and challenged the desire of some Indians to adopt the Christian faith. He compared the practice of one's religion to marriage, arguing that just as a husband remains faithful to his wife, not because he believes that she is superior to all other women, but because he loves her, 'so does one remain irresistibly faithful to one's own religion and find full satisfaction in such adhesion' (Kumarappa 2002: 24). There was no question of Gandhi approving of any conversion as a change of religious faith, least of all of him abandoning the religion of his parents and homeland. He came to see value in Christianity, but nothing that he did not also see in Hinduism. For him, true conversion was not a change of faith but a change of heart and a deepened commitment to one's own religion.

Gandhi's Hinduism was not something he accepted blindly or without question. The title he gave his autobiography, 'The Story of My Experiments with Truth', is telling both of the absolute value he placed on *Sat*, or Truth, and of his approach to it. Truth was not something to be accepted from others but something to be discovered for oneself by trial and error. Where Gandhi found the beliefs and practices of Hinduism to be at odds with this truth he was its fiercest critic. He spoke against the sacrifice of animals to Kali (Gandhi 1987: 221), and his lifelong campaign in word and deed against untouchability is well known. There were, however, many fundamental principles of Hinduism to which Gandhi fully adhered. These he identified as belief in the scriptures, avatars, and the concept of rebirth; belief in what he felt was the true Vedic essence of *varnashrama dharma*, the caste system; belief in cow protection; acceptance of what westerners denounced as 'idol worship'; and belief in the principles of truth, non-violence, self-control, and in the oneness of God (Andrews 2003: 8). Hinduism is a diverse religion, arguably not only accepting but celebratory of its diversity, so it is difficult to speak of a 'typical Hindu'. Nonetheless, Anthony Copley has an important point to make when he says that 'Gandhi was in no way a typical Hindu, and in many ways his ideas were heretical in origin. He did not worship in temples. Prayer meetings owed more to Christian practice' (Copley 1999: 8). Gandhi had been brought up in a devout Hindu home by his Vaishnava parents, but from early life he was open to a breadth of religious influences. His parents took him to the Shiva temple as well as to their own temple, dedicated to Vishnu, and visitors to the house included family friends from the Muslim, Parsi, and Jain communities (Brown 1991: 16–18). All this doubtless contributed to Gandhi's fundamental conviction that no single religion has a monopoly on the truth and that true religion is something beyond the great faiths of the world. He stated: 'By religion I do not mean formal religion . . . but that religion which underlies all religions and leads us face to face with our maker' (Kumarappa 2002: 3). Gandhi's religion evolved over the course of his life. From birth to death he remained a Hindu, yet his conception of religion went beyond adherence to a particular faith.

It should by now be clear Gandhi was naturally highly open to drawing inspiration from the teachings of Jesus. He said: 'For many years I have regarded Jesus of Nazareth as one among the mighty teachers that the world has had' (Andrews 2003: 54). Nor was the high regard he felt towards the person of Jesus limited to his teachings, as the following comments from an article he wrote in 1941 illustrate: 'Jesus expressed as no other could the spirit and will of God. It is in this sense that I see him and recognise him as the Son of God. . . . I believe that he belongs not solely to Christianity but to the whole world' (Kumarappa 2002: 25). As a Hindu, it was easy for Gandhi to accept that God has many manifestations and to see Jesus as one such manifestation. There was no necessary contradiction between his devoted loyalty to and practice of his native faith and his acceptance of Jesus' words as compelling divine truth. Thus it was that Gandhi felt able, in a speech to Christian missionaries in Madras, to call himself 'a humble and impartial student of religion with great leanings towards Christianity' (Andrews 2003: 79). Gandhi had many close Christian friends and followers, and perhaps his greatest spiritual friend, confidant, and ally was the Christian pastor Charlie Andrews, whose own book on Gandhi's life and ideas gives much insight into the Mahatma's relationship with Christianity. Louis Fischer, one of Gandhi's biographers, describes their relationship thus: 'The Hindu saint had found no better saint than Andrews. The Christian Missionary had found no better Christian than Gandhi' (Fischer 1997: 308). It was, in part at least, through Andrews's influence that worship at Gandhi's ashrams made use of Christian hymns and Christian scriptures, of which unquestionably the most important was the Sermon on the Mount.

THE SPECIAL STATUS OF THE
SERMON ON THE MOUNT

Gandhi's attitude to religious scriptures in general deserves some clarification. From his early twenties onwards his spiritual search led him to read and reflect on a variety of texts from the world's great faiths, and he prescribed this to others. In a 1926 edition of the journal *Young India* he wrote: 'I hold that it is the duty of every cultured man or woman to read sympathetically the scriptures of the world' (Kumarappa 2002: 23). This belief he held to throughout his life, sometimes in the face of controversy. His public readings of the Qur'an at prayer meetings, designed to bring about Hindu–Muslim unity during the tense pre-Partition days of 1947, brought death-threats from Hindus accusing him of betrayal, and one letter calling him 'Mohamed Gandhi' (Fischer 1997: 578). Gandhi's approach to the scriptures of the world's great faiths was reverential and uncritical, yet not lacking in some discrimination. He wrote in 1936: 'Whilst I believe that the principle books are inspired . . . I cannot surrender my reason' (Kumarappa 2002: 22). His use of reason, as applied to scriptures, may perhaps best be described as a kind of moral intuition. What seemed to him to be true and good, wherever he found it, was accorded a special place in his heart.

For Gandhi no religious text had a greater personal value or spiritual and moral authority than the *Bhagavad Gita*. Ironically, he first encountered it, through English theosophist friends, in Sir Edwin Arnold's translation (Gandhi 1987: 76), yet it remained his constant solace throughout his life. In his own commentary on the text he exhorts his readers: 'We should honour and revere the Gita . . . it is a deity of the mind . . . we should read it daily as part of our prayer' (Gandhi 2005: 283). Yet the Sermon on the Mount was, for Gandhi, of almost equal importance. He wrote in 1927: 'Today, supposing I was deprived of the Gita and forgot all of its contents but had the Sermon [on the Mount] I should derive the same joy from it as I do from the Gita' (Kumarappa 2002: 25). Again, in a speech to missionaries in Madras, he said: 'The spirit of the Sermon on the Mount competes almost on equal terms with the Bhagavad Gita for the domination of my heart' (Andrews 2003: 78). Gandhi did not accept the Bible wholesale, but his own moral reason and intuition elevated these three chapters of Matthew's Gospel because he felt: 'The message of Jesus is contained in the Sermon on the Mount, unadulterated and taken as a whole . . . If I had to face only the Sermon on the Mount and my own interpretation of it I should not hesitate to say, "Oh yes I am a Christian"' (ibid. 54). It is clear that this passage of the Christian Bible represented for Gandhi a distillation of everything of value in the Christian religion. In order to understand why these three chapters of Matthew's Gospel had such a special significance for Gandhi we will need to look closely at the text itself and some of the reasons for the importance Gandhi ascribed to it.

Some Themes and Difficulties Involved in Interpreting the Text

In the Sermon on the Mount the author of Matthew presents the reader with a structured series of ethical pronouncements which are delivered directly from the mouth of Jesus. The text claims that its ethical precepts are not new in the sense of being a departure from, or replacement for, the commandments of the Torah revealed by God to Moses. Instead, they are a development to fruition of what was already revealed. Jesus states: 'Do not think I have come to abolish the Law or the prophets; I have come not to abolish them but to fulfil them' (Matt.5:17). The extent to which the Sermon upholds the Torah, as it claims, and the extent to which it is a radical departure from what has gone before is a thorny problem thrown up by the text, which has caused a good deal of consternation to Christian interpreters from the early Christian Fathers through to the present day. Harvey K. McArthur, in his excellent book on the Sermon, is forced to conclude that both interpretations are true, in that while the ethic of Jesus 'involved the abrogation of some aspects of the Mosaic tradition', it nonetheless 'represented a legitimate development' out of that tradition (McArthur 1960: 56). None of these theological concerns posed any problem to Gandhi, who felt no special urge to trace a thread of consistency through a religious tradition that was not his own. He simply disliked, and therefore disregarded, much of the Old Testament as a text that he struggled to read and of which he struggled to make any spiritual sense. He affirmed, however, that 'the New Testament produced a different impression, especially the Sermon on the Mount which went straight to my heart. I compared it with the Gita' (Gandhi 1987: 77). Thus Gandhi's reliance on personal, moral intuition in responding to scriptures permitted him to deal with any inconsistencies by simply ignoring the Old Testament and embracing parts of the New Testament. In this sense Gandhi is open to the charge that he has taken a 'pick-and-choose' approach to the Christian Bible, embracing what appealed to him and dismissing what did not. Nonetheless, there is textual evidence from the Sermon and other parts of the Bible in support of a special status and authority for these chapters which Gandhi revered.

The location of this teaching, delivered from a mountaintop, is significant in this respect. The majority of New Testament scholars argue that the Sermon on the Mount was not one continuous discourse delivered at one time and in one place by Jesus, but a collection of sayings compiled by the author of Matthew. The 'Mount' from which the Sermon is delivered is therefore symbolic of its relationship with the commandments received by Moses on Mount Sinai. As W. D. Davies puts it, 'when Jesus goes up the mountain to utter the Sermon on the Mount, he is speaking as the Mosaic Messiah and delivering Messianic Torah' (Davies and Allison 2004: 65). Essentially, the author of Matthew sets up these ethical pronouncements as having the very highest spiritual authority as the actual words of Jesus, speaking as the Messiah and the instigator of a new stage of divine revelation. In this sense the Sermon seems intended to supersede the former revelation of divine ethical ordinances revealed to Moses as their fulfilment and, indeed, replacement. This is made explicit in the text itself, when Jesus declares his pronouncements to be a higher ethic for those who would be salt and light, to improve and set an example for the world (Matt. 5:13). The follower of the principles the Sermon sets out is compared to someone who has built his house on the rock of spiritual certainty (Matt. 7:24). The special authority Gandhi ascribed to these chapters is therefore one they arguably claim for themselves. The Sermon claims nothing less for itself than to be the true standard of right conduct in the eyes of God.

The Sermon would not be the only religious text to make such a claim, and the reasons for its importance to Gandhi are more readily understood when we examine some of its themes and teachings. Opening with the Beatitudes, a list of statements about the nature of true blessedness and those to whom such a concept might be applied, it is immediately clear that the Sermon subverts worldly standards of human worth and value. The meek, the downtrodden, the persecuted, and those who struggle for purity in their own lives and justice in the wider community are those whom the Beatitudes exalt. The direct application of this passage to Gandhi's struggle on behalf of indentured labourers in South Africa or 'untouchables' in India is easy to observe. The Beatitudes almost read like a manifesto for the people whose cause Gandhi was to champion, as well as the manner in which he was to champion it.

Another key theme of the Sermon which accorded well with Gandhi's own perception of religion and ethics is that of inner purity and right intention. Jesus interprets the Torah in a new, radical, and authoritative way, replacing its commandments with more exacting injunctions, through a series of pronouncements which begin with 'You have heard it said' and proceed to 'But I tell you'. The prohibition on murder becomes an exhortation against anger, the ban on adultery becomes a rejection of all lustful desires, and so on. In many senses the ethics of the Sermon are an internalization of ethics, a move from the importance of specific actions to inner intentions, from the restriction of outward behaviour to cultivation of spiritual virtues. Prayer, fasting, and charity are rejected as acts of ethical value unless they are characterized by a purity of heart. All this had a natural appeal to Gandhi, whose strivings towards personal purity were characterized by his long struggle to adhere to his self-imposed vow of celibacy or *brahmacarya*, and who vigorously questioned his own motives even when fasting on behalf of others. The striving for perfection prescribed in the Sermon on the Mount was recognizable to Gandhi as the path of spiritual athleticism to which he had devoted himself.

The spiritual demands of the Sermon on the Mount, which Gandhi endorsed, involve an apparent inconsistency with other parts of the New Testament, in particular with the Pauline epistles. Paul is at pains to stress the fundamental importance of the Christian doctrine of salvation by the grace of God: 'For it is by grace that you have been saved, through faith—and this not from yourselves, it is the gift of God' (Eph. 2:8). The teaching of the Sermon on the Mount is seemingly at odds with this view, prescribing a path of personal holiness through effort. After a series of moral imperatives and injunctions, Jesus enjoins his followers to 'Be perfect...as your Father in heaven is perfect' (Matt.5:48). It is not the task of this chapter to explore the implications of this apparent conflict or how it was borne out between the followers of Paul and the followers of James, for example, in the early church. Nonetheless, the difficulty over whether the goal of religious perfection should be a reliance on divine grace or a striving for spiritual achievement is a fundamental religious dilemma, of relevance to the present discussion. The Sermon on the Mount seems to emphasize individual responsibility for moral action and self-improvement, and this appealed greatly to Gandhi. He reacted strongly against the assertion by a Plymouth Brother, whom he met in South Africa, that as all are sinners, any attempt at improvement or atonement is pointless. The Brother's argument ran that one must stop trying to change oneself for the better and instead rely on God's redeeming power alone, or face a life of restless, futile struggle. Gandhi's reply was unequivocal: 'If this be the Christianity acknowledged by all Christians I cannot accept it. I do not seek redemption from the consequences of my sin. I seek to be redeemed from sin itself rather from the very thought of sin. Until I have attained that end I shall be content to be restless' (Gandhi 1987: 125). Within the Christian faith, different Christians and Christian traditions have placed different emphasis on the role of grace and personal effort in the practice of religion. The difficulty of the Sermon on the Mount for some Christians is that it appears to emphasize the latter at the expense of the former, seeming—in the words of McArthur—to 'expound a religion of works, a religion of character, or, at least in some sense, a religion of human achievement' (McArthur 1960: 16). This difficulty did not exist for Gandhi, of whose religious faith and practice a better description could scarcely be given.

Perhaps the greatest problem posed by the Sermon on the Mount, however, is that of the great gulf between the moral ideal Jesus upholds and the moral standards actually practised by even the most devout of his followers. Throughout Christian history numerous attempts have been made by theologians and biblical interpreters to explain how or why Jesus in the Sermon on the Mount should make demands of his followers which are so exacting as to appear impossible. Among them are the view, held by many Roman Catholics, that the Sermon contains counsels for the clergy to achieve a higher spiritual standard than the precepts required of the laity; the suggestion by Martin Luther that the standards of the Sermon apply to the spiritual but not the temporal realm; the suggestion that the Sermon is not intended to provoke a response of obedience but one of repentance; the idea, popularized by Albert Schweitzer, that the Sermon was presented as an

Interimsethik, impractical for normal life but designed as an eschatological necessity (McArthur 1960: 106–27). These and other interpretations have attempted to soften the blow of this hard-hitting and troublesome text. Our concern is with Gandhi's interpretation, however, which takes the step, unthinkable to many, of taking the Sermon at face-value. Gandhi was not unmindful, either of his own and others' shortcomings in the face of such a religious ideal, or of the immense difficulties of meeting its standards. Nonetheless, he was uncompromising about the moral imperative of the Sermon. In an address delivered in Colombo he said: 'By all means drink deep of the fountains that are given to you in the Sermon on the Mount; but then you will have to put on sackcloth and ashes with regard to your failure to perform that which is taught in Christ's Sermon. For the teaching of the Sermon was meant for each and every one of us' (Andrews 2003: 58). From this speech, it could scarcely be clearer that Gandhi believed that the Sermon on the Mount, in spite of its exacting demands, presents us with a moral imperative which it is the duty of everyone to try wholeheartedly to follow.

TOLSTOY AND GANDHI

In taking such an absolutist view of the ethics of the Sermon, Gandhi was greatly influenced by the Russian novelist and radical religious thinker Count Leo Tolstoy, who had a profound impact on Gandhi's life and thought. Gandhi first encountered Tolstoy in his book *The Kingdom of God is Within You*, which takes the text of Matthew 5:39, 'Resist not evil by force', and uses it as a basis for a polemic against church and state and a call to return to Christ's teaching. Tolstoy asks: 'Did Christ really demand from his disciples that they should carry out what he taught them in the Sermon on the Mount?' (Tolstoy 2005: 34), and his answer throughout the book is a resounding: 'Yes.' Gandhi, as we have already seen, shared the view that 'the man who believes in salvation through faith in the redemption or the sacraments cannot devote all his powers to realising Christ's teaching in his life' (ibid. 70). The book's call for the need to strive towards inward perfection in terms of personal morality and outward perfection in terms of social justice (ibid. 52) struck a deep chord with Gandhi. Indeed, this dual striving is an apt description of his life's work. The impact of the book on him is clearly expressed in his own words: 'Tolstoy's "The Kingdom of God is Within You" overwhelmed me. It left an abiding impression on me' (Gandhi 1987: 136). That abiding impression expressed itself both in the relationship between the two men and in Gandhi's political actions.

Tolstoy's enormous literary success and considerable wealth did not bring him fulfilment, and a spiritual crisis in his fifties caused him to make radical changes in his life. He gave up luxuries and land, began to work alongside the peasants and to attract a community of like-minded people dedicated to the simple life and the pursuit of truth. This arguably provided part of the inspiration for Gandhi's ashrams in South Africa and then India, one of which was named 'Tolstoy farm'. Tolstoy wrote prolifically against the use of violence in war and punishment, against the injustices perpetrated by the state and the errors he perceived in the church, from which he was ultimately excommunicated. The admiration of Tolstoy and Gandhi became mutual as a correspondence developed between them. Tolstoy's last letter to Gandhi was received after the Russian writer's death. In it he wrote: 'The longer I live and especially now when I feel vividly the nearness of death, I want to tell others . . . what to my mind is of great importance, namely that which is called passive resistance but which in reality is nothing other than the teaching of love uncorrupted by false interpretations' (Fischer 1997: 129). Passive resistance, or *satyagraha*, had already become central to Gandhi's application of his beliefs to action and, like Tolstoy, he saw it as an essential expression of Jesus' teaching in the Sermon on the Mount. This teaching, for Gandhi, had a direct application to the political sphere. It meant taking action on behalf of the down-trodden and dispossessed, and it meant doing so without violence, taking literally, Jesus' injunction to offer another cheek to the person who strikes you.

THE SERMON ON THE MOUNT AND *SATYAGRAHA*

The term *satyagraha* was first suggested by Gandhi's relative and trusted supporter Maganlal Gandhi, in response to a competition Mohandas organized to find a suitable name for the new movement of civil disobedience that he had begun among the Indian community in South Africa. Gandhi was not satisfied with the term 'passive resistance' to describe what he was trying to do, on the grounds that it 'was too narrowly construed, that it was supposed to be a weapon of the weak, that it could be characterised by hatred and that it could finally manifest itself as violence' (Gandhi 1987: 291). The burning of houses by suffragettes, he reasoned, was called passive resistance, but such action was alien to his own concept of civil disobedience (Iyer 2005: 308). *Satyagraha*, from *sat*, 'truth', and *agraha*, 'firmness', was a more apt description of what was for Gandhi both a religious understanding of right conduct and the entire basis of his political method. This 'truth force' or 'soul force' is best described in its essence by Gandhi himself:

One who resorts to it does not have to break another's head; he may merely have his own head broken. He has to be prepared to die himself, suffering all the pain. In opposing the atrocious laws of the Government of South Africa, it was this method that we adopted . . . If you make laws to keep us suppressed in a wrongful manner . . . these laws will merely adorn the statute books. We will never obey them. (Iyer 2005: 305)

Satyagraha emerged, as a concept and as a political and religious discipline, out of Gandhi's opposition to a succession of such unjust laws in both South Africa and India. The key to its success lay in its ability to unite large groups of the populace in opposition to one particular piece of legislation, deemed unjust, and to ensure the moral high ground was kept through blamelessly non-violent methods of protest. While in Gandhi's long, active political life there were countless examples of *satyagraha* in action, for our present purposes one will suffice, perhaps Gandhi's greatest triumph: the salt march of 1930.

That salt, as a basic necessity in a climate such as that of the Indian subcontinent, should be taxed and controlled by an alien power is an injustice that is easy to comprehend. Gandhi chose this as his ground on which to oppose the Raj, and succeeded in turning it into a symbol of the illegitimacy of its rule. In a letter to Lord Irwin, before the commencement of this action, in which he challenged the legitimacy of the viceroy's salary at 5,000 times that of the average Indian, Gandhi stated that: 'Nothing but organised non-violence can check the organised violence of the British government' (Shirer 1980: 93). The protest that followed consisted of Gandhi and seventy-eight trusted *satyagrahis* walking the 240 miles from Gandhi's Sabarmati Ashram in Ahmedabad to the coast at Dandi, where they symbolically and illegally made salt. For Gandhi, as with all his *satyagraha* campaigns, this was both a political and a religious action. Judith Brown writes: 'a religious aura surrounded the whole enterprise. He and his followers kept quoting the gospels, presumably drawing comparisons between Gandhi and Christ, deliberately setting his face towards Jerusalem and confrontation with the authorities; the sale of Bibles among the Ahmedabad Hindus shot up' (Brown 1991: 237). The effect of this man's pilgrimage, smiling, striding, staff in hand, to make salt, was far-reaching. He had captured the imagination of ordinary people and was embarrassing and undermining the rule of the British administration. People were making and selling salt everywhere and, even after Gandhi's imprisonment a month later, the non-violent campaign continued. On 21 May 1930, 2,500 Congress volunteers marched on the government's Dharasana saltworks. They walked relentlessly forward, offering no resistance as the Indian police force, led by six British officers, clubbed them down with steel-tipped lathis. By midday there were at least 320 seriously wounded and two dead. The moral outrage felt across India, the world, and in England itself was arguably a major step towards Indian independence.

Part of the capacity of Gandhi's protest to provoke this response stemmed from its basis in the Sermon on the Mount. *Satyagraha* is not a Christian concept, although its parallels in the life and teaching of Jesus are widely recognizable. Its primary roots are in the Indian tradition of *ahimsa*, or non-violence, which for Gandhi was the highest of all sacred injunctions. In 1926 he wrote: 'God is none other than Truth. But Truth cannot be, never will be reached except through non-violence' (Iyer 2005: 240). *Ahimsa* is an important aspect of the Hindu tradition, but is even more central to Jainism. Gandhi had grown up in Gujarat, where the Jain community was influential, and Raychandbai, whom Gandhi cites as one of his most important religious influences (Gandhi 1987: 93), was a prominent Jain. That said, *ahimsa* for Gandhi was tied up in his understanding of the importance of the Sermon on the Mount, which also taught the radical non-violence of 'turning the other cheek' (Matt. 5:39). He wrote: 'Literally speaking ahimsa means "non-killing" but to me it has a world of meaning, and takes me into realms much higher, infinitely higher. It really means that you may not offend anybody; you may not harbour an uncharitable thought even in connection with one who may consider himself your enemy' (Andrews 2003: 63). It is not difficult to see Gandhi linking the Indian religious concept of *ahimsa* here with Jesus' injunction, in the Sermon on the Mount, to love one's enemies (Matt 5:44). Indeed, the comparison between *ahimsa* and the Christian concept of universal, unconditional love or *agapē* is so easy to make that Gandhi at times seems to use the terms interchangeably in support of *satyagraha*: 'If you express your love-ahimsa in such a manner that it impresses itself indelibly upon your so called enemy, he must return that love' (Andrews 2003: 64). While the Raj was generally very far from loving Gandhi, it nonetheless floundered to find an appropriate response to him, and was forced to seek out one that could meet the moral stature of his provocation.

THE RESPONSE OF THE RAJ TO GANDHI

On one level the British Government and the Raj justified its domination of the jewel in its empire as simply a defence of British interests. Winston Churchill, who famously referred to Gandhi as a seditious, half-naked fakir (James 1998: 533), made no bones about his desire to perpetuate the Raj as long as possible, declaring as late as 1940: 'We mean to hold our own. I have not become the King's first minister in order to preside over the liquidation of the British Empire' (ibid. 567). Nonetheless, even the most conservative defenders of the empire cherished a view that the Raj was beneficial to India and the Indian people, even if the latter failed to show much gratitude. Churchill himself said that British rule would be looked back upon as a 'Golden Age' and declared: 'We ought to be proud of the work we have done in India' (ibid. 582). It was widely argued that the Raj brought benefits to the Indian economy and infrastructure, that it brought peace, law and order, good government, and, perhaps most importantly, 'Christian civilization' where these could not otherwise exist.

This view is vividly expressed in R. J. Minney's 1929 book, *Shiva or The Future of India,* in which he argued that more forceful intervention was needed from the British to 'purge the Indian faiths of their iniquities' (Minney 1929: 6). He argued that without the benefits of the English language and the transport system introduced by the British, Indians would have neither the means nor sufficient unity to demand independence. He justifies British rule, not in terms of its benefits to Britain but of its absolute necessity for Indians:

One thing is certain: left to herself India can accomplish nothing. The three hundred million peoples have neither the wish nor the will to attain predominance or prosperity. They are content to jog along life's easiest path, sleeping, copulating, praying, over-indulging recklessly in each of these necessary functions, and, though they know it not, burdening the nation with the price of their folly. (ibid. 8)

Minney's book is a clear example of Britain's need to justify its position in terms of paternalistic concern, a position which became increasingly difficult to defend in the face of Gandhi's *satyagraha.* Even when *satyagraha* failed and widespread Indian violence erupted, as it did in the Punjab in 1919, incidents such as General Dyer's massacre of innocent unarmed civilians at Jallianwalla Bagh, Amritsar, served as reminders that the real basis of the Raj was ruthless military suppression.

Gandhi was something of a riddle to his opponents in the Raj. On the one hand he was a formidable and persistent problem to be dealt with, and on the other he represented a luminous and recognizable religious and moral authority. Lord Reading, who met Gandhi soon after becoming viceroy, in 1921 commented: 'His religious and moral views are admirable and indeed are on a remarkably high altitude, though I must confess my failure to understand his practice of them in politics' (Fischer 1997: 249). Nonetheless, the Raj did want to defend its own political position in India on moral grounds. Its justification of bringing Christian civilization to India could not be sustained while Indians were using tactics that were recognizable as the teachings of Jesus in action and the British were suppressing them with military force. The Sermon on the Mount was in this sense the religious, moral, and cultural interface between Gandhi's followers and the British rulers. The text was at the heart of dialogue that led to Indian Independence.

CONCLUSION

In the Sermon on the Mount the reader of the Bible is confronted with an ideal of holiness which claims for itself the highest importance and authority. Its radical nature and the difficulties of adhering to it make it natural to avoid face-value interpretations of the text. Gandhi's idealistic but practical application of the central tenets of the Sermon into action made the colonial rulers of the Raj to appear morally wanting by their own standards, and undermined any moral authority they could claim in India. Origen commented on the Sermon that: 'All the beatitudes that Jesus uttered in the Gospel he confirms by example' (Davies and Allison 2004: 69). Gandhi's interpretation of the text was that he should strive to implement it in his own life, leading others by his personal example. In the run-up to Indian Independence and Partition, when increasing antagonism and violence erupted between the Hindu and Muslim communities of East Bengal, Gandhi was to be found at Noakali, in the heart of the trouble. He lived among both communities, endeavouring to appoint in each village a Hindu and a Muslim who would be prepared to give their own lives to protect the safety of both communities. On this Fischer comments: '"But I say to you, love your enemies, bless those who curse you, do good to them that hate you and pray for them that despitefully use you and hate you . . ." Thus Jesus spoke. Thus Gandhi lived' (Fischer 1997: 560).

Of course, there were times when he got it wrong. Commenting on the 'Himalayan miscalculation' he made in overestimating his followers' commitment to non-violence in the 1919 *satyagraha* campaign, he stated: 'I have always held that only when one sees one's mistakes in a convex lens and does just the reverse in the case of others that one is able to arrive at a just estimate of the two' (Gandhi 1987: 423). The comparison to the text of Matthew 7:5, 'first take the log out of your own eye and then you will be able to see clearly to take the splinter out of your neighbour's eye', is easy to perceive. As a Hindu, Gandhi's religious interpretation of the Sermon on the Mount could be said to show it to Christians in a fresh light, though it is a light of familiar recognition. Gandhi's spiritual stature has been compared to Christ and to the Buddha. He was revered in his lifetime as a *Mahatma* by millions, and continues to be revered by Indians and others today. Whether he is worthy of these many accolades may be tested against the criteria for recognizing a true or false prophet according to the Sermon on the Mount: 'By their fruits you shall know them' (Matt. 7:20).

WORKS CITED

ANDREWS, C. F. (2003), *Mahatma Gandhi His Life and Ideas.* Woodstock, Vt.: Skylight Paths (first published 1930).

BROWN, J. (1991), *Gandhi, Prisoner of Hope.* London: Yale.

CARSON, C. (ed.) (2002), *The Autobiography of Martin Luther King Jr.* London: Abacus. (first published 1999).

COPLEY, A. (1999), *Gandhi Against the Tide.* Delhi: Oxford India Paperbacks (first published 1987).

DAVIES, W. D. and ALLISON, D. C. (2004), *Matthew: A Shorter Commentary*. London: T. & T. Clark.

FISCHER, L. (1997), *The Life of Mahatma Gandhi*. London: HarperCollins (first published 1951).

GANDHI, M. K. (1987), *An Autobiography, or The Story of my Experiments with Truth*. Harmondsworth: Penguin (first published 1929).

——(2005), *The Bhagavad Gita*. Delhi: Orient Paperbacks (first published 1980).

IYER, R. (ed.) (2005), *The Essential Writings of Mahatma Gandhi*. Delhi: Oxford India Paperbacks (first published 1991).

JAMES, L. (1998), *Raj: The Making and Unmaking of British India*. New York: St Martin's Press.

KUMARAPPA, B. (ed.) (2002), *My Religion—M. K. Gandhi*. Ahmedabad: Navajivan Trust (first published 1955).

MCARTHUR, H. K. (1960), *Understanding the Sermon on the Mount*. London: Epworth Press.

MINNEY, R. J. (1929), *Shiva, or The Future of India*. London: Keegan Paul, Trench, Trubner & Co.

SHIRER, W. L. (1980), *Gandhi: A Memoir*. New York: Touchstone.

TOLSTOY, L. (2005), *The Kingdom of God Is Within You*. Doylestown, Penn.: Wildside Press (published on request; first published 1894).

FURTHER READING

BROWN, J. (1994), *Modern India: The Origins of an Asian Democracy*. Oxford: Oxford University Press.

GANDHI, M. K. (ed. B. Kumarappa) (1961), *Non-Violent Resistance (Satyagraha)*. New York: Schocken Books (this volume first published 1951).

GANDHI, R. (2007), *Gandhi: The Man, his People and the Empire*. London: Haus Books.

KLOSTERMAIER, K. (1969), *Hindu and Christian in Vrindaban*. London: SCM Press.

——(1994), *A Survey of Hinduism*. New York: New York State University Press.

PATIL, V. T. (ed.) (1983), *Studies on Gandhi*. New Delhi: Sterling Publishers.

VORA, N. (ed.) (1999), *Gandhiji's Dialogue with Christianity*. New Delhi: Swaraj Peeth Trust.

CHAPTER 38

PREACHING, POLITICS, AND PAUL IN CONTEMPORARY AFRICAN-AMERICAN CHRISTIANITY

BRAD BRAXTON

INTRODUCTION

African-American Christian preachers have considered the Bible a sourcebook for preaching and politics, since African-American sermons have had to motivate a people on their long pilgrimage from social marginalization to social liberation. From the pulpit African-American preachers have inspired personal piety and political protest that have led to significant social revolutions, such as the abolition of slavery and the Civil Rights Movement. In African-American Christianity the interpretation of scripture has been the locus of both preaching and politics (Wimbush 2000: 1–43).

This chapter explores the homiletic and political nature of African-American biblical interpretation by investigating the use of the apostle Paul's letters in contemporary African-American sermons. In order to accomplish this, methodological insights from postcolonial studies will prove beneficial, and therefore, a synopsis of postcolonial studies and of its connections to African-American preaching is in order.

POSTCOLONIAL STUDIES AND
AFRICAN-AMERICAN PREACHING

Both postcolonial studies and African-American Christian preaching emphasize the impact of culture and the reality of social oppression (Segovia 2005: 23–78; LaRue 2000: 20–5). What, then, are the hermeneutical consequences of a critical dialogue between postcolonial studies and African-American preaching, especially as it pertains to the contemporary homiletic appropriation of Pauline texts? To pursue this question more fully, some frameworks must be established and some methodological issues addressed.

Postcolonial studies is a diverse and expanding set of interpretive practices and theories that place the colonialism and neo-colonialism of Europe and the United States at the centre of interpretive conversations. Broadly defined, it is a field that engages 'the overlapping issues of race, empire, diaspora, and ethnicity' (Sugirtharajah 1998: 15). More specifically, postcolonial studies is concerned with colonialism—'the organized deployment of racialized and gendered constructs for practices of acquiring and maintaining political control over other social groups, settling their lands with new residents, and/or exploiting that land and its peoples through military and administrative occupiers' (Taylor 2004: 42). Closely associated with colonialism is 'imperialism', which consists of a 'more coherent organizational form' by which colonizers present themselves as missionaries to the world (Deane 1995: 354). Postcolonial studies also examines the attempt of former colonizers to re-inscribe their colonial influence ('neo-colonialism' or 'neo-imperialism'), as well as the political and cultural possibilities that emerge when formerly colonized people resist and transcend colonialism's oppressive effects ('decolonization').

Thus, postcolonial studies invites interpreters to acknowledge more readily the current manifestations of imperialism that abound in many cultures. A keen interest in contemporary issues of liberation and oppression is also a hallmark of African-American biblical interpretation and preaching. When African-American preachers and parishioners come to the Bible, they 'are really interested in the question 'Does God save?' rather than the question 'Did God save long ago?' (Cannon 2002: 50). Many African Americans seek salvation not simply from their personal sins but also from the systematic sins of imperialism and racism that continue to bring destruction and death to African-American communities. Thus, in addition to calling for personal piety, African-American preaching has also ignited contemporary political resistance to imperial and racist onslaughts.

The enduring effects of imperialism and neo-imperialism are inescapable hermeneutical realities for politically engaged African-American interpreters of scripture (Segovia 2000). The European and North American empires of the fifteenth to the twenty-first centuries were founded upon (and became sinfully wealthy from) the colonial ravaging of Africa, the Caribbean, and the Americas that characterized the transatlantic slave trade (Higgins 1990; West 1999). Furthermore, while the outright physical brutality of the United States' 'slavocracy' abated in the mid-nineteenth century, the twentieth and twenty-first centuries unleashed political, economic, and ideological hostility—even brutality—against African Americans. The United States' slavery empire may have crumbled during the American Civil War in the 1860s, but the contemporary empire of white privilege has struck back with considerable force (Thandeka 1999; Dyson 2003; Harvey, Case, and Gorsline 2004).

While concern about contemporary imperialism is well within the scope of postcolonial studies, it is the coupling of that concern with strong homiletic interests that potentially can point postcolonial theological interpretation in some new and valuable directions. Postcolonial interpretation stresses the value of 'real' readers. Unfortunately, some postcolonial scholarship gives the impression that it is only concerned about 'real' readers who possess extensive university training.

After reading widely in recent postcolonial scholarship, two questions have occurred to me: (1) in what ways is this field still in colonial captivity to certain types of 'academic' language that reveal its close connections to socio-economic privilege? And (2) why are some postcolonial practitioners unwilling to produce scholarly resources that would be serviceable to 'non-academic' people caught up in actual struggle (Smith 1997: 130–1)? If it is to engage and empower 'real' readers, the language employed by postcolonial scholarship itself needs to be decolonized, so as to reflect a greater interest in the activities of astute 'imperial-resisters' who do not have extensive academic training.

R. S. Sugirtharajah has exhorted postcolonial practitioners to move beyond their 'high-caste moorings' to a greater concern for the 'vernacular' and folk idioms within various communities (Sugirtharajah 2004: 34–8). Indeed, it might be such investigation and use of folk practices and idioms among colonized people that will rescue postcolonial scholarship from the indictment of being just one more highfalutin academic enterprise that talks the liberation talk without walking the liberation walk.

In African-American culture, Christian preaching provides access entre to the vernacular of the people, especially as those people aspire to self-determination amid imperial oppression; and because of their shared emphasis on contemporary resistance to oppression, postcolonial studies and African-American Christian preaching can be stimulating conversation partners. The conversation ought to encourage more postcolonial practitioners to *really* empower *real* readers.

PREACHING AND PAUL

Having explained the reasons for my coupling of postcolonial studies and African-American Christian preaching, I now explore another interpretive tension: preaching and Paul. In a recent book I examined the centrality of preaching to Paul's ministry (Braxton 2004). Paul's letters (e.g. Rom 10:5–17 and 1 Cor 15:3–4) testify to the crucial role of preaching in his work, while scholars have argued that the orality of Paul's preaching reverberates throughout the letters themselves (Thompson 2001: 27; Webb 2004: 86–90). In this chapter, however, I want to trace the impact of Paul's letters upon contemporary preaching.

Biblical texts have overwhelmingly exerted their influence upon African-American Christian communities through the oral form of African-American preaching. Many Africans have always retained the traditional belief in the spoken and sung word as great repositories of truth and sacred wisdom; because of this cultural background the colonizers' systematic efforts to impose illiteracy upon African Americans did not prevent them from encoding their colonial resistance in a variety of *oral* forms, such as sermons, spirituals, work-songs, field-hollers, myths, folk-tales, and proverbs (Hurston 1981; Holmes 2002: 68–75). Given such a cultural and historical background, it should not be surprising that the most compelling African-American biblical interpretation is often more likely to be encountered in churches than read in scholarly commentaries. This statement is neither an endorsement of anti-intellectualism nor a devaluing of the remarkable scholarship produced by the small but growing guild of African-American biblical scholars (Blount 2007; Page 2010). Rather, it is an honest assessment of the enduring religious and political value of preaching in African-American Christian communities.

CONTEMPORARY AFRICAN-AMERICAN PREACHERS AND PAUL

African Americans have had a love–hate relationship with Paul. In the authentic letters (Romans, 1 and 2 Corinthians, Galatians, Philippians, 1 Thessalonians, and Philemon) Paul does not denounce Greco-Roman slavery, and offers ambiguous counsel about how enslaved Christians should act (Braxton 2000: 177–234). In the deutero-Pauline letters (i.e. those whose Pauline authorship is disputed by some authorities: Ephesians, Colossians, 2 Thessalonians, 1 and 2 Timothy, and Titus) he endorses conservative cultural norms which accept slaveholding as an indispensable pillar of Greco-Roman culture. At best, Paul's counsel in the deutero-Pauline letters inserts a modicum of 'Christian morality' into that slave culture but in no way overturns that culture in the name of radical social freedom.

Consequently, European and North American colonizers appealed generously to the Pauline legacy (and especially to the deutero-Pauline letters) to sanction their brutal treatment of millions of Africans (Martin 1991: 206–31; Venable-Ridley 1997: 212–33; Braxton 2000: 235–64). On the other hand, Allen Callahan has demonstrated that African Americans have found meaningful testimonies to emancipation in Paul's letters; according to Callahan, they have considered Paul an 'ambivalent witness to freedom' (Callahan 1998: 235–62).

In this chapter I begin where Callahan concludes his essay. Callahan succinctly reviews the complex history of African-American readings of Paul from the eighteenth century to 1997—the latest scholarship cited being his own 1997 commentary on Philemon (Callahan 1997). From the late 1990s to the present, how have African-American preachers been employing Paul's letters? Are they using them as tools of postcolonial struggle; as inducements to personal and communal piety; as unintentional instruments of neo-colonialism; or as some hybrid of these?

The African American Pulpit: The Historical Significance of a Journal

Callahan's synopsis of African-American engagements with Paul concludes essentially in 1997. The winter of that year also marked an important moment in African-American theological studies, as the first issue of *The African American Pulpit* (*TAAP*) was published. From its inception this journal has chronicled the genius of African-American preaching, and it is now 'the only African American-owned and operated, nondenominational homiletics [and ministry-focused] journal in North America (*TAAP* 2004, vol. 7, no. 2, p. 3).

As an agent of the African-American church and academy, *TAAP* records and enhances the African-American homiletic tradition by presenting sermons and essays by contemporary and historic African-American preachers and scholars. Gardner Taylor, a distinguished preacher in the United States, has summarized ably the significance of this theological journal: '*The African American Pulpit* provides the definitive, magisterial, historical record of that preaching which has grown out of the peculiar spiritual experience of fashioning a home for the soul in a strange land' (*TAAP* 2002, vol. 5, no. 2, back cover). African-American preaching is, in many regards, an imaginative biblical and theological response to the violent geographic and cultural exile created by historical and contemporary European and North American imperialism, and this journal chronicles the intonations and vibrations of (black) people trying to sing the Lord's song in a strange (white) land.

Contemporary Homiletic Appropriations of Paul: The Method

To assess how contemporary African-American preachers employ Paul's letters, I canvassed all the volumes of *TAAP* during its first ten years (Winter 1997–Fall 2007) to locate sermons preached on the authentic letters of Paul. Cumulatively, *TAAP* published over 500 sermons during those ten years. (This figure excludes submissions with alternative designations such as 'articles', 'vignettes', or 'lectures'). Of these, forty-two listed authentic Pauline passages as their primary or ancillary texts. I excluded sermons based on deutero-Pauline texts, which accounted for less than 5% of all the sermons published in *TAAP* during this ten-year span. Thus, less than 10 per cent of the sermons it published in this period were from authentic Pauline texts. Of these, thirty-four were preached by African-American men and eight by African-American women.

The reasons why preachers select some biblical texts for proclamation while neglecting others are complex and involve the concerns and biases of preachers and congregations, as well as the impact of current events. Thus, one cannot reduce that complexity to simple statistical analysis. Nevertheless, the statistics might indicate that on the whole African-American preachers are significantly less enamoured of Pauline texts than of other parts of the Christian canon. This is certainly the case with African-American women preachers, which is understandable given the role Paul's letters have played in the oppression of women (Williams 2004: 44–72).

It is intriguing to consider the distribution of the forty-two sermons across the seven Pauline letters. There were eleven sermons from Romans; four sermons from 1 Corinthians; thirteen sermons from 2 Corinthians; four sermons from Galatians; and ten sermons from Philippians. The apparent popularity of 2 Corinthians is understandable given its theological reflections on *weakness and suffering* (e.g. 2 Cor. 4–5, 12); *reconciliation* (2 Cor. 5); and *spiritual warfare* (2 Cor. 10)—themes that resonate deeply with African-American Christians. Of the eleven sermons from Romans, six sermons concentrate on Romans 8, where Paul speaks of *hope* and *divine providence*—again central theological motifs among African-American Christians. Paul's ambivalence on slavery can account for the absence of sermons on Philemon. However, the absence of sermons on 1 Thessalonians is surprising, since that letter emphasizes the sustaining power of relationships amid tribulation. The contemporary resonance with Pauline themes such as providence has deep historical roots. In his history of the earliest African-American churches, Henry Mitchell suggests that African slaves in the North American colonies would have easily appropriated certain aspects of Paul's theology, such as providence, since providence was a central motif in the African Traditional Religion they brought with them. Thus, while African slaves in the North American colonies might have rejected Paul's 'politics' concerning slavery, they found Paul to be a theological ally in other areas (Mitchell 2004: 16–19).

Contemporary Homiletic Appropriations of Paul: The Evidence

I will now examine three of these forty-two sermons to assess the postcolonial lessons they can teach or that need to be taught. While the classification of sermon types and goals is notoriously difficult, many of the sermons focused on one of three broad areas of concern: *pastoral* (encouraging and challenging listeners toward individual and communal spiritual maturity); *social justice* (commenting on or offering critiques of particular social dilemmas and inequities); and *prosperity* (exhorting *individuals* primarily to maximize their experiences and possessions, often with special emphasis on *financial well-being*). I have selected one sermon based on a Pauline text from each of these types.

For all three sermons, my investigations were based solely on the published manuscripts. A sermon *manuscript* is never a *sermon* but merely the written transcript of an embodied performance. African-American preachers and parishioners have known for centuries that the conveyance of deep truth is an emotive *and* cognitive enterprise involving *performance aspects*, such as gestures and tonality. My analyses of these sermons emphasize the *contextual* nature of the biblical interpretation in these sermons—the preacher's use of the contemporary cultural environment to engage scripture for theological purposes. Had space permitted, I also could have investigated more fully the *textual* nature of their interpretations— the preacher's attention to specific aspects of the biblical text in the shaping of the sermon's content. For each sermon, I offer a *description* summarizing its content, and an *analysis* which critically assesses how the sermon might contribute to or be strengthened by postcolonial approaches.

1. A Pastoral Sermon from a Pauline Text

Ella Pearson Mitchell: 'Rejoice Always' (Phil. 4:4–8)

The African American Pulpit, vol. 1, no. 2, pp. 25–31. At the time of this sermon's publication, the late Ella Pearson Mitchell was a visiting professor in the Doctor of Ministry program in homiletics at United Theological Seminary in Dayton, Ohio. She was a respected elder in African-American Christianity, having mentored several generations of clergy and scholars. For all the sermons discussed, the pagination in *TAAP* will be in parentheses.

Description

This sermon examines Paul's imperative to rejoice in the midst of the dispute between two female leaders in the Philippian church, Euodia and Syntyche. Just as Paul's theology of joy does not ignore the conflicts in that ancient community, so this sermon avoids a superficial contemporary treatment of joy. It emphasizes that Paul's imperative to rejoice comes immediately after a dispute involving women.

In the attempt to raise feminist concerns, Mitchell might have easily become sidetracked into a conventional critique of an authoritarian *male* apostle telling bickering *females* to settle down. Instead, through the creative use of folk wisdom and narrative, she artfully places female experience at the centre of the sermon, demonstrating the range of virtues and vices that women can display on their journey to a truly joyful existence. An example from the sermon's introduction is instructive. Rather than beginning by chronicling historical details about Paul and the Philippians, the sermon starts with a contemporary narrative from African-American female experience:

Not long ago, my sister shared with me a quaint saying. It went like this: 'Be sure to listen to people who sing while they work because mean people don't know no songs'. One could play it the other way and say that when people have no song or exhibit no sweetness as they work for the Lord and for the Kingdom, they tend to be mean, uptight, tense, and not easy to get along with. Maybe the same problem was part of the reason why Paul wrote the folks at Philippi, 'Rejoice in the Lord always: and again I say, Rejoice.' (p. 25)

With the fifth word of the sermon—'sister'—Mitchell begins a sophisticated contextual interpretation of Philippians' exhortation to ancient and contemporary 'sisters' whose power-struggles affect their communities. Women's experience is the rhetorical engine propelling this sermon. Mitchell uses folk wisdom from her sister (p. 25); the recounting of Euodia and Syntyche's dispute in Philippi (pp. 25–6); the story about a mean woman in a church who eventually had to smile (p. 27); and the story of her serving communion with her husband (p. 29). Finally, at the climax of the sermon, she valorizes indigenous heroes—her two grandmothers who were ex-slaves (pp. 29–30) and a mother who expresses uncontainable joy at the commencement ceremonies of a son who was the first in that family to graduate from college (pp. 30–1).

Additionally, the sermon's emphasis on the importance of tone in communal transformation is striking: 'But Paul is saying that we need to change the character of our communication if we want to have a better experience in Christ. We can't help people—male or female—change if by the very sound of our voices we have already declared ourselves to be their enemies' (p. 28).

Clearly, this pastoral sermon seeks to promote a more joyful, harmonious existence among the congregation. Yet it lacks many of the overt features associated with postcolonial analysis, such as a discussion of systematic oppression or imperial realities. The fingerprints of the Roman Empire are obviously on Philippians. Not only is Paul imprisoned by Roman authorities as he writes this letter (Phil 1: 12–18), but also he explicitly invokes the name of the emperor (Phil 4: 23). While Mitchell's sermon does not account overtly for such features of systematic oppression, her sermon still offers lessons to postcolonial practitioners.

Analysis

Two salient features of this sermon might facilitate postcolonial practice. First, it demonstrates the liberating potential of African-American *folk wisdom*. By folk wisdom I mean pragmatic knowledge emanating from 'the very blood and bones of an African American reality' that seeks personal and communal wholeness (Hopkins 1993: 2). This sermon begins with *folk wisdom* ('Be sure to listen to people who sing while they work because mean people don't know no songs', p. 25). Later, the sermon recasts the ancient fight between Euodia and Syntyche in contemporary *folk cadence* ('They done fell out over something, and now they ain't speaking to each other', p. 26).

In this pastoral sermon, Mitchell is aware of the hostility among many African-American women and between African-American women and men. While the sources of this hostility are legion, much of it is deeply rooted in European and North American slavery and imperialism. That imperialism—with its skin-colour caste system and sexual violence—*engendered* deep divisions in the African-American community. This previous racialized and sexualized violence of the imperialists is replicated, unfortunately, in many present African-American communities. Mitchell's sermon seeks to heal the lingering scourge of hostility by appealing to indigenous resources.

Some postcolonial practitioners have called for greater attention to be paid to indigenous resources. For instance, Mark Taylor affirms the 'anticolonialialist struggle' found in many 'spiritual communities'. He specifically cites 'the movements and resistance of African Americans and women in North America and elsewhere, who generated, respectively, black and feminist liberation theologies' (Taylor 2004: 48, 50). Many African-American churches are highly effective 'anticolonialist' spiritual communities. Thus, a fuller consideration of African-American churches as sites of postcolonial struggle will necessitate a more sympathetic and systematic investigation of African-American Christian preaching.

Second, this sermon's emphasis on the centrality of 'tone' in struggles for human transformation warrants serious consideration by postcolonial practitioners ('by the very sound of our voices we have already declared ourselves to be their enemies', p. 28). Often 'tone' in literature or 'tonality' in music involves a consideration of the mood or feeling created by the 'voice' or 'pitch' of the author or musician.

In the 'homiletical musicality' (Crawford 1995: 16) of African-American preaching, the tone of the written words of scripture and the 'tonality' of musical elements such as pitch and rhythm merge to address emotive and cognitive needs. In this regard, African-American preaching reflects its connection to various African cultures. Many African languages are 'tonal.' As such, words that are semantically identical assume different meanings based on the tone used in communicating. While the communication of tone or tonality is often considered an oral/aural matter, tone in preaching can be conveyed in a multiplicity of ways such as gestures, word-choice, and style of dress. Many African-American Christian congregations have a keen appreciation for 'tone' or 'tonality' in communication. Regardless of a preacher's scholarly attainments or lack thereof, some congregations will 'tune in' or 'tune out' preachers based on how preachers say what they say. In other words, a preacher's words might convey 'liberation' *conceptually* but 'colonial captivity' *tonally*.

Postcolonial practitioners—especially some in university contexts—might need to consider more fully how an improper tone can undermine declared objectives. The tone of some postcolonial scholarship is 'colonial.' Driven seemingly by imperial scholarly myths of 'discovering new territory' in an 'expansion of intellectual frontiers,' some postcolonial scholarship is riddled with obscure language and is apparently preoccupied with novelty for the sake of novelty. The assumption that scholars must constantly 'produce new knowledge' is a major pillar of the western academic enterprise (or empire).

Since many colonized people in the first and two-thirds worlds are connected to cultures where orality is highly valued, many of the world's oppressed citizens are 'tone savvy'. Therefore, when certain oppressed people regard scholars and their scholarship as irrelevant to emancipatory struggle, this dismissal might not be anti-intellectualism. Rather, it might be a savvy evaluation that the tone in scholars' work reflects *scholarship about* not *struggle with* those colonized people.

By paying more attention to the vernacular language of sermons, postcolonial practitioners can further cultivate their ability to communicate with persons whose everyday language involves what the homiletician Teresa Fry Brown calls 'sisterspeak'— 'informal, no-pretense, at-home, dangling-participles, double-negative, tell-it-like-it-is, intense-body-language speech' (Brown 1997: 81). Thus, postcolonial studies can avoid the troubling irony of presenting practical political aims in *impractical* language.

2. A SOCIAL JUSTICE SERMON
FROM A PAULINE TEXT

J. Alfred Smith, Sr.: 'An American Scandal: The Crisis of the Crucified' (1 Cor 2:1–2)

The African American Pulpit, vol. 1, no. 3, pp. 63–6. J. Alfred Smith, Sr. is the Senior Pastor Emeritus of the Allen Temple Baptist Church in Oakland, California. At the time of this sermon's publication, he was a *TAAP* Advisory Board Member. He, too, is a respected elder in African-American Christianity.

Description

This sermon explores the meaning of a theology of the cross in the context of a late twentieth-century African-American urban community. More specifically, Smith juxtaposes the cross and the US welfare reforms in the 1990s. The sermon begins with a striking poem:

> Three men fashioning a cross by which the fourth must die,
> and yet none asked of the other, and why and why,
> our living we must earn,
> what happens to the other man is none of our concern.

(p. 63)

The message implicit in this poem becomes explicit throughout the sermon: Regardless of their often confessed solidarity with poor people, who are the culture's crucified, many upper-middle-class Christians construct 'crosses' upon which the poor are executed. Smith elaborates further: 'Those times when a middle-class church dares preach about the cross are times of homiletical malfeasance and theological malpractice. This travesty occurs when poor people and powerless people are encouraged to carry their demeaning cross without resentment and rebellion but resignation, as did Jesus Christ: "And he never said a mumbling word"' (p. 63).

Two interpretive moves in the sermon's introduction deserve comment. First, by linking the cross to matters of socio-economic class ('our living we must earn'; 'a middle-class church'; 'poor people and powerless people'), the introduction shuns an apolitical atonement theology, where Jesus's blood cleanses the 'souls' of individuals, while the collective 'dirty laundry' of a comfortable elite remains unwashed. For Smith, as for Paul, 'to know *nothing* except Jesus Christ crucified' (1 Cor. 2:2) is to know and say *something* about political realities, such as domination based upon social class. When churches preach apolitically about the cross, they participate in further crucifixions. Smith distances himself from that harmful history of apolitical interpretations of Jesus's crucifixion (Terrell 1998).

Second, the introduction deftly uses an African-American folk resource—the words from a spiritual—to criticize upper-middle-class North American indifference about contemporary crucifixions of poor persons who depend on social welfare for survival. The spiritual 'He Never Said a Mumbling Word' narrates Jesus's heroism during the crucifixion. While this spiritual is aware of Jesus's words from the cross recorded in the Gospels, its declaration that Jesus 'never said a mumbling word' testifies to the willingness with which Jesus met his fate. Yet according to Smith, it is one thing for Jesus not to say a word during the crucifixion, but it is another thing when contemporary preaching enjoins further silence upon the poor who carry crosses and suffer economic executions. To the contrary, instead of commanding silence, churches should speak defiantly. Smith extends his indictment to include the theological academy:

The cross is sparsely preached as an expression of God's identification and solidarity with an oppressed underclass in need of redemption from the curse and stigma of welfare . . . Can courageous preachers of Calvary and the cream of the theological academy who speculate on the meaning of the atonement cooperate in putting human faces on that self-righteous cult of politicians and corporate leaders who enjoy tax loopholes, corporate welfare, and stock-market prosperity while insisting that the poor be grateful for workfare jobs that pay less than what is needed for safe housing, proper dental and medical care, as well as a few dollars for modest savings? Put a human face on welfare reform so that it does not become welfare deformation. (p. 64)

Clearly, the cross, for this African-American preacher, is not a legitimization of passive suffering. Rather, it is an exhortation for the church to 'be a caring and sensitive participant in responding to the cares of the crucified' (p. 65).

Analysis

This sermon demonstrates the importance of intra-communal critique—a crucial postcolonial practice needed in so many communities. It commends this practice in at least two ways.

First, the introductory poem identifies why crucifixions continue and how they might be stopped. Crucifixions continue, especially among the poor, because of a widespread unwillingness among economically comfortable 'cross-makers' to ask challenging questions about political policies and to stop participating in practices that keep these policies intact. The following lines in the poem note and criticize this unwillingness: 'and yet none asked of the other | and why and why | our living we must earn | what happens to the other man is none of our concern' (p. 63). Crucifixions might be stopped, or at least dramatically lessened, if upper-middle-class North American Christians would demonstrate greater solidarity with poor persons by asking questions that might expose hidden oppression and by fostering needed public dialogue.

As a relatively brief speech act, even a sophisticated sermon is limited in the degree to which it can examine a topic. Nevertheless, Smith employs a theology of the cross to question aspects of welfare reform, a pressing social issue at the time. While urgent debate about welfare reform has subsided in the United States, many other imperial practices and policies place poor persons in harm's way. By failing to ask critical questions about imperial practices and policies, churches are complicit with imperial 'cross-makers'. As the poem also intimates, when groups raise critical questions on behalf of marginalized communities, they can jeopardize their own security. Until such risks are taken, the imperial spirit will remain unchecked. Imperialism thrives by promoting hostility or apathy between different classes of people, thereby causing people to ignore the related experiences of oppression that could unite them in resistance.

Second, this sermon uses the indigenous resource of an African-American spiritual to engage in intra-communal critique. The unwillingness of African-American communities to provide robust critiques of their failings is another pernicious legacy of white privilege. Ideologically, white privilege has thrived on the oppressive dualism of 'superior–inferior', where the latter term describes African-American people and cultural practices. Thus, African Americans have expended considerable energy fending off this cultural colonization, with its caricatures of African-American life.

Yet in the legitimate struggles against external forces, many African-American communities have failed to direct similar energy toward internal critiques of their dilemmas and complicity with their oppressors. It was thought that for African-Americans to express publicly their failings or discontent about dysfunction within their own communities was to give the colonizers additional ammunition. Thus, the drive for healthy, intra-communal critique has been abandoned often in the name of 'closing the ranks' to promote racial solidarity. This sermon, however, demonstrates the effectiveness of an appeal to an indigenous African-American cultural resource (the spirituals) in order to provide a critique of that culture (the need for African-Americans to protest about the oppression of the poor).

3. A 'PROSPERITY' SERMON FROM A PAULINE TEXT

Jamal-Harrison Bryant, 'There's a Harvest Inside of Me' (2 Cor. 9:6–15)

The African American Pulpit, vol. 8, no. 3, pp. 63–8. Jamal-Harrison Bryant is the Pastor of Empowerment Temple African Methodist Episcopal Church in Baltimore, Maryland. He is a well known religious leader in the United States and is a frequent guest speaker on national broadcasts. His ministry epitomizes an intriguing trend toward prosperity preaching among some younger African-American clergy. While traditional themes of personal piety and social justice are not absent in their sermons, some younger African-American clergy accentuate the material and financial dimensions of God's 'blessings'. Prosperity preaching is not new in African-American religion, but younger clergy like Bryant have refined dimensions of it by combining charismatic preaching styles, technological savvy, and considerable intellectual training.

Description

Immediately, it is clear that this sermon will address financial matters. Its opening lines declare: 'I want to argue that how you treat your money is a reflection of how you treat yourself. This may sound a bit philosophical in nature, but your money is connected to your self-esteem' (p. 63). The sermon then moves from this 'philosophical' statement to a theological assertion that financial practices are an effective indicator of a believer's love—or lack thereof—for God. By establishing the connection between financial giving and God, the sermon's introduction prepares its listeners for an engagement with 2 Corinthians 9, where Paul underscores the theological implications of the financial collection for impoverished believers in Jerusalem.

The sermon, however, does not engage 2 Corinthians 9 in any great detail but instead presents a series of principles loosely based on the sowing-and-reaping metaphor in 2 Corinthians 9. The body of the sermon presents a *principle* based on verse 6 ('how you reap is how you sow', p. 65). It then recommends a *practice* based on verse 7 ('give cheerfully', p. 65). Finally, it examines the *produce* (the 'harvest', defined vaguely in financial, psychological, and theological terms, pp. 64–8).

Additionally, the sermon explores several other sub-principles: (1) 'You will always reap *more* than you sow' (p. 65, emphasis in the original); (2) 'You *always* reap what you sow' (p. 65, emphasis in the original); (3) 'The harvest is connected to the soil' (p. 65); (4) 'The climate has to be right . . . in order for a harvest to take place' (p. 66); (5) There is a 'principle of time'—the notion that with God's help believers can reap their harvest in the same season they sow (p. 67); (6) There is a 'principle of identity'—the notion that a seed undergoes transformation on the way to a harvest (p. 67); (7) There is a necessity to 'trust the 'gardener', who is God (p. 67).

The sermon's basic three-part structure (*principle, practice,* and *produce*) is clear and reflects the time-honoured homiletic use of alliteration. Yet the barrage of sub-principles proceeds at a fevered pace, with no sustained attention given to any of them. Thus, it was challenging to process the principles even after multiple readings of the sermon. While I wonder to what degree congregants were able to process this rapid-fire information, scholars studying trends in church and society have commented on the changing modes of perception among younger people who are progressively immersed in multimedia, electronic cultures (Sample 2005). Thus, Bryant's congregation, consisting of many young people, might have connected well with the sermon's sporadic logic.

In its original context this sermon's message of personal fulfillment might have been important for many people, despite its cursory engagement with 2 Corinthians 9. Nevertheless, a sermon coupling financial matters with rapid-fire, superficial argumentation might create, at least for certain people, issues concerning its tone and the character of the preacher as tone and character are mediated by the sermon. Such issues are similar to those confronted by Paul in 2 Corinthians. The Corinthians had raised concerns about Paul's character, especially as it pertained to his financial practices.

It is interesting to deliberate on some possible emotional responses to this sermon among people not theologically inclined toward prosperity themes, as this sermon defines those themes. Such persons might perceive a certain 'slickness' in the sermon's homiletic tone, likening features of the sermon to a finely rehearsed marketing presentation. For instance, the sermon uses the 'buzzwords' of prosperity preaching, such as 'season' and 'harvest', and creates an escalating mood of imminent expectation. It is filled with language and images declaring that *blessings* are on the horizon. This raises a question: is the rapid and repeated declaration of a soon-coming 'harvest', apart from a careful explanation of the nature of the harvest, theologically problematic, especially if the message is proclaimed to economically disadvantaged people?

Paul writes 2 Corinthians 8–9, and indeed the letter as a whole, to address charges of his insincerity and impure motives with regard to the Corinthians' finances. Paul attempts to dispel their doubts by patient argumentation and a continual reminder of the communal implications of their financial generosity (e.g. 2 Cor. 9:8, 12). In contrast, this sermon's hasty argumentation and underdeveloped communal orientation might potentially raise suspicions about its own motives. Thus, in spite of Bryant's considerable homiletic genius, the lack of a more solid exegetical and theological foundation exposes aspects of the sermon to criticism.

Analysis

This sermon could be strengthened by postcolonial considerations. It lacks any significant appreciation for systematic realities or social injustices that hinder the 'harvest' from coming to fruition in many individuals and communities. I offer three interrelated examples.

First, without accounting for the interlocking oppression created by forces such as racial, gender, or class discrimination, the sermon's depiction of God comes close to a divine sanctioning of the economic and spiritual lack in people lives. It declares: 'Any harvest that is God-ordained cannot be withheld . . . Look, if you don't have it, maybe God knew you couldn't hold it' (pp. 64–5). This part of the sermon raises such questions as: what about persons who have 'sowed' faithfully their time, talents, and meagre resources and still their 'harvests' have not come, because of systematic issues such as a lack of health insurance or a lifetime of working in minimum-wage jobs? Did not European and North American imperialists use a similar logic to deny many freedoms to African-American slaves ('Look, if you don't have *freedom*, maybe God knew you couldn't hold it)?

A greater awareness of postcolonial themes might sensitize African-American preachers to the role of 'sacralization' in the history of African-American oppression, that is, 'the transposing of an ideological concept into a tenet of religious faith (or a theological justification) in order to serve the vested interest of a particular . . . group' (Felder 1991: 128–9). European and North American imperialists used God to justify their oppression of Africans and African Americans; contemporary African-American preachers need to be careful, lest they use God to spiritualize systematic issues that foster poverty, thereby disempowering people already suffering under economic imperialism.

Second, postcolonial concerns might have led this sermon into a more careful examination of the moral and communal implications of certain theological terms. For instance, like much prosperity preaching it speaks often about the 'harvest', but fails to define the harvest clearly. The sermon declares: 'Tell yourself your harvest is coming. Everything you touch is about to blow up. (The term 'blow up' is a contemporary African-American, hip-hop idiom meaning 'to make it really big' or 'to become a social celebrity'). Everywhere my foot treads is already given to me. Everyone connected to me is about to walk in the harvest' (p. 66). Postcolonial considerations might prompt other poignant questions: does this kind of language convey the message of Jesus or a neo-colonial 'myth of Midas', luring people into a lust for possessions and a new servitude to economic consumption? Are some affluent African Americans reaping 'harvests' that might appear God-ordained, while in reality these harvests are simply the flowering of the seeds of greed and North American individualism (Andrews 2002: 50–88)? Have some African Americans succumbed to an economic materialism similar to the ideology supporting past and present European and North American imperialism?

Finally, Paul's exhortations in 2 Corinthians about money are rooted in a communitarian ethic. The Corinthians are urged to give so that persons in financial hardship in Jerusalem might be assisted. In many contemporary prosperity sermons, such as this one, benevolent giving is removed from a communitarian context and instead becomes a matter of securing an *individual's* destiny. Has benevolent religious giving among some African-American Christians morphed into a 'sanctified lottery', where people 'sow financial seeds'—the equivalent of 'buying a ticket'—with the hope of securing God's 'favor and financial blessings'— the equivalent of 'hitting the jackpot'? It would be unfortunate if contemporary prosperity sermons turned Paul's financial message to the Corinthians on its head.

Instead of exhorting people with economic means to give in order to assist the poor, such sermons might be inviting the poor to give generously—in church offerings and through the purchase of sermon DVDs and CDs at high-profile religious conferences—as the poor unintentionally widen the chasm between themselves and the affluent.

CONCLUSION

The interchange between postcolonial studies and African-American preaching holds significant promise. This dialogue can move postcolonial studies increasingly into the specifics of lived religion and away from scholarly abstractions, while it also can motivate African-American preachers and congregations to display more proudly the postcolonial techniques they have used for centuries in the quest for a liberated existence in the African diaspora. Finally, it can provide a vivid reminder that the parasitic spirit of empire can settle easily upon any culture or cultural practice for its host body.

WORKS CITED

The African American Pulpit (Winter 1997–Fall 2007), 1/1–10/4.

ANDREWS, D. (2002), *Practical Theology for Black Churches: Bridging Black Theology and African American Folk Religion*. Louisville, Ky.: Westminster/John Knox.

BLOUNT, B. (ed.) (2007), *True to Our Native Land: An African American New Testament Commentary*. Minneapolis: Fortress.

BRAXTON, B. (2000), *The Tyranny of Resolution: 1 Corinthians 7:17–24*. Atlanta, Ga.: Society of Biblical Literature.

——(2004), *Preaching Paul*. Nashville, Tenn.: Abingdon.

BROWN, T. (1997), 'Avoiding Asphyxiation: A Womanist Perspective on Intrapersonal and Interpersonal Transformation', in E. Townes (ed.), *Embracing the Spirit: Womanist Perspectives on Hope, Salvation, and Transformation*, 72–94. Maryknoll, NY: Orbis.

BRYANT, J.-H. (2005), 'There's a Harvest Inside of Me', *The African American Pulpit*, 8/3: 63–8.

CALLAHAN, A. (1997), *Embassy of Onesimus*. Valley Forge, Pa.: Trinity Press Int.

——(1998), '"Brother Saul": An Ambivalent Witness to Freedom', *Semeia*, 83–4: 235–62.

CANNON, K. (2002), *Teaching Preaching: Isaac Rufus Clark and Black Sacred Rhetoric*. New York: Continuum.

CRAWFORD, E. (1995), *The Hum: Call and Response in African American Preaching*. Nashville, Tenn.: Abingdon.

DEANE, S. (1995), 'Imperialism/Nationalism', in F. Lentricchia and T. McLaughlin (eds.), *Critical Terms for Literary Study*, 2nd edn., 354–68. Chicago: University of Chicago Press.

DYSON, M. (2003), *Open Mike: Reflections on Philosophy, Race, Sex, Culture, and Religion*. New York: Basic Civitas.

FELDER, C. (1991), 'Race, Racism, and the Biblical Narratives', in *Stony the Road We Trod: African American Biblical Interpretation*, 127–45. Minneapolis: Fortress.

HARVEY, J., K. CASE, and R. GORSLINE (eds.) (2004), *Disrupting White Supremacy from Within: White People on What We Need To Do*. Cleveland, Ohio: Pilgrim.

HIGGINS, N. (1990), *Black Odyssey: The African American Ordeal in Slavery*. New York: Vintage.

HOLMES, B. (2002), *Race and the Cosmos: An Invitation to View the World Differently*. Harrisburg, Pa.: Trinity Press Int.

HOPKINS, D. (1993), *Shoes that Fit Our Feet: Sources for a Constructive Black Theology*. Maryknoll, NY: Orbis.

HURSTON, Z. N. (1981), *The Sanctified Church: The Folklore Writings of Zora Neale Hurston*. Berkeley, Calif.: Turtle Island Foundation.

LaRUE, C. (2000), *The Heart of Black Preaching*. Louisville, Ky.: Westminster/John Knox.

MARTIN, C. (1991), 'The Haustafeln (Household Codes) in African American Biblical Interpretation: "Free Slaves" and "Subordinate Women"', in C. Felder (ed.), *Stony the Road We Trod: African American Biblical Interpretation*, 206–31. Minneapolis: Fortress.

MITCHELL, E. (1998), 'Rejoice Always', *The African American Pulpit*, 1/2: 25–31.

MITCHELL, H. (2004), *Black Church Beginnings: The Long-Hidden Realities of the First Years*. Grand Rapids, Mich: Eerdmans.

PAGE, H. (ed.) (2010), *The Africana Bible: Reading Israel's Scriptures from Africa and the African Diaspora*. Minneapolis: Fortress.

SAMPLE, T. (2005), *Powerful Persuasion: Multimedia Witness in Christian Worship*. Nashville, Tenn.: Abingdon.

SEGOVIA, F. (2000), *Decolonizing Biblical Studies: A View from the Margins*. Maryknoll, NY: Orbis.

——(2005), 'Mapping the Postcolonial Optic in Biblical Criticism: Meaning and Scope' in S. Moore and F. Segovia (eds.), *Postcolonial Biblical Criticism: Interdisciplinary Intersections*, 23–78. New York: Continuum.

SMITH, A. (1997), '"I Saw the Book Talk": A Cultural Studies Approach to the Ethics of an African American Biblical Hermeneutics', *Semeia*, 77: 115–38.

SMITH, J. A. SR. (1998), 'An American Scandal: The Crisis of the Crucified', *The African American Pulpit*, 1/3: 63–6.

SUGIRTHARAJAH, R. S. (1998), *Asian Biblical Hermeneutics and Postcolonialism: Contesting the Interpretations*. Maryknoll, NY: Orbis.

——(2004), 'Complacencies and Cul-de-sacs: Christian Theologies and Colonialism', in C. Keller, Michael Nausner, and M. Rivera (eds.), *Postcolonial Theologies: Divinity and Empire*, 22–38. St Louis: Chalice.

TAYLOR, M. (2004), 'Spirit and Liberation: Achieving Postcolonial Theology in the United States', in C. Keller, Michael Nausner, and M. Rivera (eds.), *Postcolonial Theologies: Divinity and Empire*, 39–55. St Louis: Chalice.

TERRELL, J. (1998), *Power in the Blood? The Cross in the African American Experience*. Maryknoll, NY: Orbis.

THANDEKA, (1999), *Learning to be White: Money, Race, and God in America.* New York: Continuum.

THOMPSON, J. (2001), *Preaching Like Paul: Homiletical Wisdom for Today.* Louisville, Ky.: Westminster/John Knox.

VENABLE-RIDLEY, C. (1997), 'Paul and the African American Community', in E. Townes (ed.), *Embracing the Spirit: Womanist Perspectives on Hope, Salvation, and Transformation,* 212–33. Maryknoll, NY: Orbis.

WEBB, S. (2004), *The Divine Voice: Christian Proclamation and the Theology of Sound.* Grand Rapids, Mich.: Brazos.

WEST, T. (1999), 'Spirit-Colonizing Violations: Racism, Sexual Violence and Black American Women', in N. Lewis and M. Fortune (eds.), *Remembering Conquest: Feminist/Womanist Perspectives on Religion, Colonization, and Sexual Violence,* 19–30. New York: Haworth.

WILLIAMS, D. (2004), *An End to This Strife: The Politics of Gender in African American Churches.* Minneapolis: Fortress.

WIMBUSH, V. (ed) (2000), *African Americans and the Bible: Sacred Texts and Social Textures.* New York: Continuum.

CHAPTER 39

RUSKIN, THE BIBLE, AND THE DEATH OF ROSE LA TOUCHE: A 'TORN MANUSCRIPT OF THE HUMAN SOUL'

ZOË BENNETT

INTRODUCTION

The illustration on page 577 is a page from an 11th or 12-century Greek Gospel Lectionary which belonged to John Ruskin, and which he annotated, in ink, at the foot of almost every page. There is reference to it in the Library Edition of Ruskin's work, where it is referred to as 10th century. (LE 34.702) It is currently in the British Library and does not appear to have been used or quoted in Ruskin scholarship, except those few quotations which have come down secondhand via W. G Collingwood's *Ruskin's Relics*. (Collingwood 1903; also found in LE 34. 703–5) Ruskin refers to this manuscript in *Fors* letter 49 (LE 28.244) as 'my best Greek MS'. To Rev F.A. Malleson in July 1875 he writes:

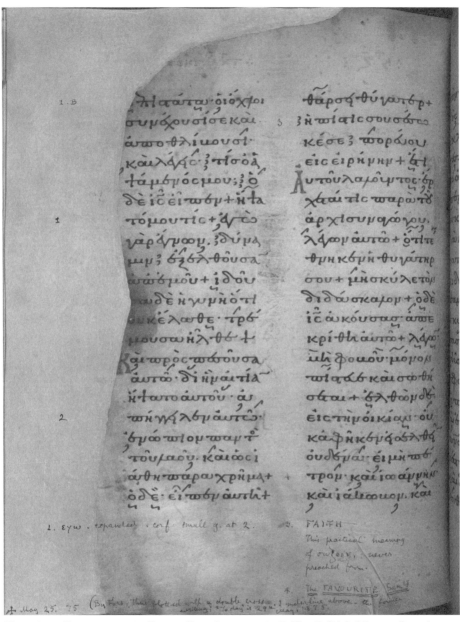

Fig. 39.1. Egerton 3046, Evangelistarium, p. 43 © The British Library Board.

For instance—one of my quite *bye* works in learning my business of a teacher—was to read the New Testament through in the earliest Greek MS. (eleventh century) which I could get hold of. I examined every syllable of it, and have more notes of various readings and on the real meanings of perverted passages than you would get through in a year's work.

(LE 37.172)

This page is dated both 25th May 1875, and subsequently 29th May 1875. The first is the date on which Rose La Touche died aged twenty seven, the second is the day after Ruskin heard of Rose's death, hence the first date on which he returned to reading this Lectionary after knowing she was dead.

> [W]hat would the intellect of Europe have become without Biblical literature? . . . The effect of Biblical poetry and legend on its intellect, must be traced farther, through decadent ages, and in unfenced fields;—producing 'Paradise Lost' for us, no less than the 'Divina Commedia';—Goethe's 'Faust,' and Byron's 'Cain,' no less than the 'Imitatio Christi.' Much more, must the scholar, who would compre-hend in any degree approaching to completeness, the influence of the Bible on mankind, be able to read the interpretations of it which rose into the great arts of Europe at their culmination . . .
>
> (LE 33. 112–13)[1]

Ruskin lays out here, with characteristic flair, the approach to the Bible which in contemporary biblical scholarship is known as *Wirkungsgeschichte* or Reception History. As an exercise in Reception History, this chapter will read Ruskin's personal appropriation of the gospel texts in the lectionary, within the context of his outlook as an intellectual and a public figure in Victorian Britain. Ruskin read and learned the Bible chapter by chapter as a child at his mother's knee; of which he said: 'this maternal installation in my mind of that property of chapters, I count very confidently the most precious, and, on the whole, the one *essential* part of all my education.' By this process his mother 'established my soul in life', and 'she gave me secure *ground* for all future life, practical or spiritual'(LE 35. 42–3). His writings, from all periods of his life, are peppered with biblical quotations (Gibbs 1898).

In his approach to the Bible Ruskin was to a certain extent a child of his age and context: in terms of what George Landow has identified as his typological understanding, (Landow 1980); and in terms of his context within Victorian debates on the inerrancy, infallibility, inspiration, and ethical and religious value of the Bible. He makes it clear that he used the Bible in his public writings because it was the currency of the religious and ethical understanding of his contemporaries (LE 17. 347–50) In Letter 8 of *Time and Tide* (March 1867), he writes that political economy is to be based on human honesty not on religion or policy, and that religion per se is worth nothing: 'a knave's religion is always the rottenest thing about him' (LE 17. 348). Ruskin claims to quote the Bible because the British public takes it seriously; that is to say, he uses it strategically in his writings. Of the four theories on the Bible he says are held by the British public— that it was dictated by God (inerrancy in our contemporary terms); that it can be trusted for all that is needed for human salvation (infallibility); that it is a true

---

[1] 'LE' references are to volume and page numbers of the 'Library Edition' of *The Works of John Ruskin* (for details see 'Works Cited' below).

record of God's dealings with the human race; and that it represents 'the best efforts which we hitherto know' and the 'best wisdom', but has no special authoritative claim beyond that of other religions—he appears to prefer the fourth, as he says: 'This has been, for the last half-century, the theory of the soundest scholars and thinkers of Europe' (LE 17. 350). He does add a fifth position—'incredulity . . . of any help given by any Divine power to the thoughts of men' (ibid.), but dismisses people in this position as 'insentient'.

It is significant that Ruskin did not lose his attachment to the Bible during the period of time after his 'unconversion' in 1858, when his religious journey took him from a Protestant and Evangelical faith, through his 'unconversion' and the espousal of what he calls 'the religion of Humanity', and then back to a more broad, catholic, and ecumenical Christian perspective (Burd 1979: 141, quoting from the *Fors* letter of March 1877). The famous 'Sunday letters', in which he instructs the girls at Winnington Hall in precise, detailed biblical exegesis, and would have them running around outdoors with lists of Bible verses in their pockets, snatching the occasional glance when they pause for breath, belong to the period immediately after his 'unconversion' (Burd 1969: 177).

'Ruskin went through many phases of faith, or, rather, through a long period of doubt, from which he came, in his late years, into a new and very simple acceptance of the Christian hope. *But at all times he took the Bible seriously*, and in many a passage he has made its thoughts and stories live for us with marvellous reality' (Collingwood 1903: 195, my italics). In reviewing Hilton's biography of Ruskin, George Landow asserts that this attitude to the Bible was normal at the time: 'The evidence Mr. Hilton adduces, that Ruskin "loved the Bible" and alludes to it with great "sensitivity," is simply beside the point in the Victorian period' (2001: 334).

Ruskin's annotations on the Gospel Lectionary manuscript described in the next section reveal the particular kind of 'love' which he had for the Bible, and the robust nature of his 'sensitivity' to it, in a way which helps illuminate his peculiar relationship to it throughout his period of, in many ways typically Victorian, doubt. It is possible to interpret Ruskin's attitude to and use of the Bible through a general understanding of the Victorians, or through Ruskin's public writings; this chapter will take a third route—the discussion of his hitherto unexplored private comments on a biblical text.

THE GOSPEL LECTIONARY TEXT

[H]e got into the habit of thinking with his pen . . . all the blank spaces are scribbled over with the thoughts that came as he read . . . I am very far from saying that this is a practice to be imitated; but anyone who wishes to follow Ruskin in his more intimate thoughts on the Bible, at the time of

crisis in 1875 when he was busy on this book, and when he was beginning
to turn from the agnostic attitude of his middle life to the old-fashioned
piety of his age—anyone who wants to get at his mind would find it here.

(Collingwood 1903: 198, 202)

W. G. Collingwood, Ruskin's secretary, identifies three biblical manuscripts that
Ruskin annotated in this way, which are described in the Library Edition as a tenth-
century Greek Gospels, an Old Testament in Greek, inscribed 'tenth century' but
dated by Ruskin's friend Dr Caspar Rene Gregory as 1463, and a Greek Psalter
(Collingwood 1903: 198–202; see also LE: 34. 701, 703). The Greek Psalter in the
Ruskin Museum at Coniston contains comments by Ruskin on the writing, gram-
mar, and translation; the Old Testament in Greek I have yet to examine; the Greek
Gospel Lectionary is the subject of this chapter.

A Gospel Lectionary is a collection of texts from any of the four Gospels which
are not set in the same order as in the Bible but in an order for public or private
reading according to the season of the church's year. Ruskin had a large collection
of both manuscript and printed Bibles and collections of Bible texts such as Psalters
and Lectionaries. He regularly—it seems daily, for most of his life—used such texts,
reading the Bible in Greek, including the Septuagint, the Greek translation of the
Old Testament.

The dates of most of Ruskin's annotations to this Gospel Lectionary run
sequentially from February to May 1875. They begin in February 1875 when Ruskin
paid his last visit to the sick and dying Rose La Touche. They end a week or so after
she died, three-and-a-half months later. Collingwood calls this period of Ruskin's
life 'a time of crisis'—a return to 'the old-fashioned piety of his age'. A more
complex and less conventional picture would need to take into account the
following interconnected factors: that Ruskin was about to enter into a new
phase of his religious understanding which was significantly shaped by the death,
at the age of 27, of Rose La Touche, the girl he had first met in 1858; that in 1878
he had his first major mental breakdown; and that the 'piety of Ruskin's age'
included spiritualist experiences, deep interest in both the communion of saints
and in pagan mythology, and a robustly critical attitude to much of conventional
Christian piety and church life.

The immediately striking thing about the pages of Ruskin's lectionary (fig. 39.1)
is the apparent sheer vandalism. He wrote on this page in ink. There are only two
places in a manuscript of 155 double-sided pages where he doesn't write on the
bottom of the page—the last twenty pages, and three pages in the middle where he
writes, 'I shall now leave the remainder pages clear, for their general look is spoiled
by my writing' (61v), 'I shall leave the pretty pages 61 and 62 unwritten on', but then
resumes his annotations, writing: 'This leaving blanks will not do—I do all
imperfectly' (63v). This sentiment accords well with Ruskin's relaxed attitude to
both the Bible and to his own belief and understanding throughout the marginalia.

It is a theme in Ruskin's self-understanding of importance to the interpretation of his annotations—'I find the Imperfect is the great tense of my life', he wrote in 1861 to his former tutor at Oxford, the Revd W. L. Brown (quoted in Birch 1988: 63).

The second striking thing is the privacy of it. It is like a diary, 'his more intimate thoughts on the Bible'. Burd records how Ruskin, 'Almost from the beginning... had kept one part of his diary "for intellect and the other for feeling". This second part was among those pages that he destroyed' (1969: 22). This dichotomy between intellect and feeling is evident in the diary-like notes on this Gospel text. It is intimate like a diary or a personal letter; these are Ruskin's comments to himself on his daily reading at a time of great turmoil. Yet the comments refer to issues of intellect rather than feeling, such as the scribe's formation of the letters, or the right translation of a Greek word. Ruskin's capacity, however, to turn the intellectual into more vivid words of feeling is quite amazing—even his comments on the formation of letters are peppered with personal reactions, empathy with the scribe, and anthropomorphisms about the letters which conjure feelings—'enthusiastic', 'curious', 'rich', 'feeble', 'small and mean'.

A third aspect of this text is how well it illustrates John Drury's point, in his delightful essay on Ruskin's 'bird-like' vision, that Ruskin's attention is fixed on particular details; Ruskin has an 'eye for idiosyncratic detail as sharp as' God's (Drury 2000: 170).

RUSKIN'S INTERPRETATION OF THE BIBLE

On the illustration below (fig. 39.2), dated 21 March 1875, are comments on a typical section of the Lectionary which includes John's Gospel chapter 14. This is part of a series of chapters known as the 'Farewell Discourses' material which is peculiar to the Gospel of John, though with some parallels to Luke 22, in which Jesus meditates with his disciples about his departure and return and the coming of the Spirit-Paraclete.

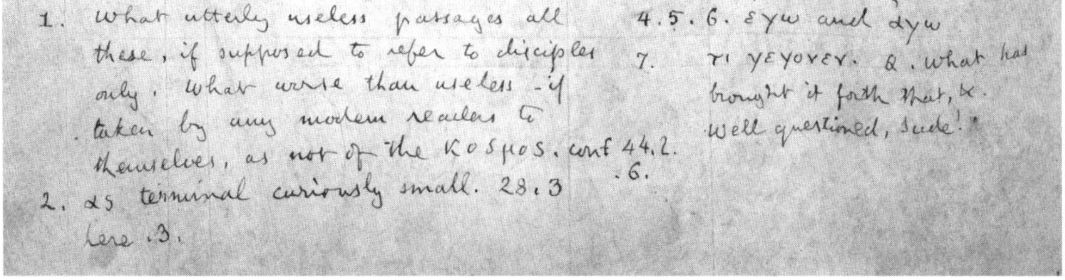

Fig. 39.2. Detail from Egerton 3046, Evangelistarium, p. 43 verso © The British Library Board.

In comment 1 Ruskin refers to John 14:17: 'Even the Spirit of truth; whom the world cannot receive, because it seeth him not, neither knoweth him: but ye know him; for he dwelleth with you, and shall be in you.' The English 'world' is the translation of the Greek word 'kosmos' to which Ruskin refers here. Here Jesus is telling his disciples, in riddles, in contrasts which at one point speak of abandonment and at another of divine presence, that they will have a special relationship with God through Jesus when the Holy Spirit comes and will be with them, and in them. The disciples are differentiated from the world.

Ruskin does not like this. All his comments in this part of the text are irritated and adversarial. 'What utterly useless passages all these, if supposed to refer to the disciples only. What worse than useless—if taken by any modern readers to themselves, as not of the kosmos.' Here we see, first, Ruskin's lack of interest in anything which has no contemporary relevance—the passages are useless if they only refer to a historical period and not to today. Second, Ruskin dislikes religious arrogance—they are even worse than useless if contemporary Christians start thinking they are better than other people because they are 'not of this world' and have some special revelation from and relationship to God. Then there is the importance of the kosmos—the world, this world—to Ruskin. Finally we see Ruskin's intense dislike of obscurity.

The comments at 2–6 show his attention to the formation of letters and to use of Greek words. These actually comprise the greater part of the annotations, but bear on the subject of this chapter only in so far as they exist in such profusion rather than in their details.

Comment 7 refers to verse 22, where Judas asks: 'Lord, how is it that thou wilt manifest thyself unto us, and not unto the world?' Ruskin's 'Well questioned, Jude!' not only illustrates again his abhorrence of splitting the religious and secular spheres but also beautifully encapsulates the way he enters into a kind of personal dialogue with the text, naturally and easily recording his reactions. 'How useless' and 'Well questioned' demonstrate something important about the ethos of Ruskin's relationship with the Bible which comes over in his annotations of this text. It is a kind of critical 'friendship', which is robust and consistently central to his life and thought. It indicates what he might mean by the sentiment from his biography *Praeterita* concerning his mother's gift in teaching him the Bible—'she gave me secure *ground*'.

The way Ruskin treated the text in this manuscript shows a man so utterly at home in the text of the Bible that he could afford to question it, even be contemptuous, without losing his relationship with it. This remark—from *Fors*, Letter 41, May 1874, quoted in Michael Wheeler's *Ruskin's God*—illustrates the point perfectly: 'My good wiseacre readers, I know as many flaws in the book of Genesis as the best of you, but I knew the book before I knew its flaws, while you know the flaws, and never have known the book, nor can know it' (Wheeler 1999: 23).

An Interrogative Approach

At the very beginning of the manuscript (2r) Ruskin remarks of Mark chapter 2 that there is 'a note of interrogation to the entire passage'. His comment on the persistent questioning of Jesus by the disciples could serve well as a description of his own interactions with the text. He is constantly asking questions. Why are these letters like this? Why is this word translated like this? Why on earth are we told the name of the servant of the high priest whose ear was cut off? Why does the centurion think Jesus' cry on the cross proves he is the Son of God? This puzzles him; that makes him curious; he expresses profound sympathy with the questions of Judas and the confusion of Thomas.

In one of his Sunday Winnington letters he says to the girls that they are to be 'quite clear in all your reading—& especially Bible reading, whether you really understand or not. Few people have the good sense to be vitally and thoroughly puzzled. They read all in a mist; and never come to a positive stop' (Burd 1969: 194). The capacity to be vitally and thoroughly puzzled is an important intellectual skill to Ruskin—and the courage to come to a positive stop an important trait of character. It is a kind of rigorous intellectual honesty. He expresses deep irritation at the lack of it in his correspondent the Revd Malleson: 'I *trust* in [my opinions] infinitely less than you do in those which you have formed simply by refusing to examine—or to think—or to know—what is doing in the world about you' (LE 37. 172). This incorrigibly interrogative streak in Ruskin is deeply related to his capacity to live with doubt and uncertainty and not to foreclose too early on a question.

A Partiality for Justice and Servanthood as the Heart of the Gospel

There is a passage in Luke's Gospel where Jesus declares, 'but he that is greatest among you, let him be as the younger; and he that is chief, as he that doth serve' (Luke 22). This, says Ruskin, is 'one of the most important in the New Testament' (136v) Such emphasis on the way of justice and the eschewing of status in favour of service is a repeated theme in these textual annotations. He even points in two of these passages to physical features of the text—golden lettering and enlargement of letters, as a sign of the importance of the content (8v and 136v).

In Matthew 25:36, the parable of the sheep and the goats, he translates *epeskepsasthe*, 'you took care of me or watched over me' as 'you became bishops to me' (he says 'It shall stand if ever I translate the chapter'). He notes critically both what should be the true function of 'overseers' or bishops, and the parallels with 'you served me' or 'became deacons to me' (28r–29r). Through the Greek words— *episkopein* and *diakonein*—for 'looking after' and 'serving' he has conflated the work of bishops (*episkopoi*) and deacons (*diakonoi*), drawing them both into the meaning of 'care' and 'service' rather than positions of authority and power. This is interesting in the light of other remarks he makes about bishops, for example in *Time and Tide* (LE 17. 378–80) and *Sesame and Lilies* (LE 18. 72–3), where he talks, at times quite vituperatively, of a bishop as being a person who should *see* and *account for* people, and who needs actually to know what is happening to his flock. The same themes of caring and service prevail.

A Dislike of Religious Exclusivity and Arrogance

Of Jesus' prayer that his disciples may be one as Jesus and God are one he comments, 'what frightful egotism and insolence a passage like this is like to put into weak heads' (50v). This is partly about dislike of arrogance, but also of sectarianism, and thus could be associated with the feelings he expresses at his 'unconversion' about the 'solitary and clerkless preacher, a somewhat stunted figure in a plain black coat', who held forth on 'the wickedness of the wide world' and 'the exclusive favour with God enjoyed by the between nineteen and twenty four elect members of his congregation' (LE 35. 495).

A Suspicion of the Obscure, Otherworldly, Eschatological, and 'Mystic'

Ruskin saves his most acerbic comments for things which are useless for life now in this world and this time. They are 'unintelligible', 'dreadful', 'useless nonsense', 'unimportant', 'dull', 'miserable'. The speculation about the woman who marries seven different brothers and which one she will be married to in heaven he regards as 'how useless—how prolonged!' (105r); the question of what you do with treasure (money) is important, but that people's treasure and thus hearts should be in heaven he regards as 'terribly misapplied' (103v); anything which has some unclear, unlikely, or impractical future fulfilment he dismisses as feeble, obscure, useless, vague, dreadful, hopeless, 'mystic' (33r, 43r, 106v, 131v).

'A Hermeneutic of Immediacy'

Ruskin takes a verse of the Bible and makes immediate links to a contemporary context. He is not doing this in order to make *prescriptive* deductions from biblical texts, in the manner of proof-texting; instead, he allows the resonances to evoke imaginative responses. So: 'I am innocent of the blood of this just person', says Pilate as he washes his hands, according to Matthew 27; 'How any popular electionist—or yielding governor can read the passages of Matthew—and not shrivel!' (58r), comments Ruskin. The chief priests say of the money Judas returns that it is not lawful to put blood-money into the treasury—'<u>Our</u> priests don't even warn our Chancellor of the Exchequer of such unlawfulnesss' (65r), says Ruskin. The mob who bay for the blood of Jesus are just acting as a mob—'in their way always, when with no answers' (66r). Pilate 'wishing to satisfy the crowd' provides 'a great sentence for the study of democracy' (136v, 131.4.6).

The Victorians, worked with a form of biblical interpretation centred round the type and the antitype (the sacrifice of Isaac was the type; the perfect sacrifice of Christ the antitype) and this typological thinking was extended into secular contexts. It became a way of thinking for Victorians (Landow 1980). It may be that some of this thinking lies behind what I have called Ruskin's 'hermeneutic of immediacy'—Pilate/a modern governor; priests/the Chancellor of the Exchequer—but there is not the movement one might expect between material and spiritual meanings, or lower and higher meanings. It is more like a hermeneutic, expounded by the liberation theologian Clodovis Boff as the 'correspondence of relationships' (1987: 146–50). By this he means that the correspondence is not between exact *terms* (priests today are exactly what priests were in the time of Jesus or the Old Testament) but between *relationships*—as the priests handled public money and should have been morally accountable, so does and should the Chancellor today.

Furthermore, Ruskin can be suspicious of 'types' just as he is suspicious of the mystic and the obscure. Birch, in *Ruskin's Myths*, points to a section in *Munera Pulveris* where Ruskin speaks of classic writers from Homer to Goethe hiding what is useful in their work 'under types which have rendered it quite useless to the multitude' (LE 17. 208, quoted in Birch 1988: 65). He advises his 'birds' at Winnington, in their Sunday letter, 'not to allow yourselves to be troubled with the talk going on at present respecting the typical or mythical meaning of portions of the Bible'; God will not blame them for 'taking His words too simply', but only for not attending or not obeying (Burd 1969: 187).

Ruskin is acutely aware of those texts which he considers unable to yield anything meaningful for the immediate and practical context. An example would be what we call 'apocalyptic' or 'eschatological' writings. Ruskin considers that these are texts which may have an original significance, but cannot be transposed into some later context and reference with any serious meaning. In commenting on the material in Mark 13, for example, in which Jesus, going up to Jerusalem to be crucified, speaks of the coming tribulations, Ruskin picks out the verse, 'But woe to them that are with child, and to them that give suck in those days!' and comments: 'It is this text which prevents any present or figurative use of all this page.' The human and highly contextual detail given here must refer to a specific historical time, and can only be taken in a literal historical sense. Thinking on these things is pointless (130r). Similarly, commenting on Jesus' statement to Caiaphas at his trial:

'Hereafter shall ye see the Son of man sitting on the right hand of power, and coming in the clouds of heaven' (Matt. 26:64), he writes: 'True or not, impossible now for Caiaphas to believe, in this form' (40v). Here Ruskin is in touch with the problematic which later led to Bultmann's demythologizing; such a statement, in the form it is made, is obscure, unbelievable, and hence of no use to the contemporary reader.

A Lifelong and Open Wrestling with Questions

This Lectionary text has been read and reread by Ruskin. The primary set of dates in his annotations is February–June 1875, but there are 1873 and 1877 dates as well. Indeed, the last page of the manuscript says confusingly, 'Finished. 11th May. 1875', and this is quoted in Deardon's catalogue, but Ruskin then continues, 'and reviewed for list of chapters, 9th June 1875' (Deardon 1966). The last dated entry is 8 June 1875. While there are thus marginal notes from various dates, leaving room in certain cases for some questions about when the note was written, the main marginal notes are clearly and sequentially dated in daily order from 24 February to 8 June 1875.

Ruskin shows in his notes that he is conscious of himself as a reader of the Bible whose understanding develops over a lifetime. His notes are full of 'I have never noticed before', 'I have never understood this'. He is constantly wrestling with the text—'what does this mean?', 'I must work this out'. Conscious of the iterative process of his understanding, he tolerates a high level of not understanding, of doubt and uncertainty, without running away from the text. This seems to me unusual in such a close reader of a sacred text; and it is refreshing. He works with the primary text, and is not a man who resorts to commentaries. Collingwood once asked Ruskin whether he had a concordance, and Ruskin answered, 'I'm ashamed to say that I have' (Collingwood 1903: 211). That lifetime dialogue with the 'plain old text' which Collingwood notes is beautifully encapsulated in Ruskin's comment on Luke 17:1–2, where Jesus says: 'It were better for him that a millstone were hanged about his neck, and he cast into the sea, than that he should offend [lit. 'put a *skandalon* in the way of'] one of these little ones.' Ruskin comments: 'After a life's thinking I have not the least idea what this passage means or what a skandalon is' (95r).

This attitude is well illustrated in one of his 'Winnington' letters to Margaret Bell:

my very first principle in Bible reading is neither to want to *bring* out anything—nor to be *afraid* of *finding* out anything; and only to make sure that whatever I read, I either *do*—or *don't* understand . . . all depends on taking [the words] precisely in their accurate and entire meaning: then, if we understand them on these terms, all is well; if, on those terms they appear inexplicable, mark the text as a short one—clearly—with the chalk—'That's a locked door'—Well, it would be odd if all doors were open at once—go on to another, and we shall perhaps find that one open when we come back. (Burd 1969: 156)

THE DEATH OF ROSE LA TOUCHE

For much of this chapter I have explored how Ruskin's private reading of the Bible illuminates his significant public use of it. In the final section I want to examine specifically the material which touches on the death of Rose La Touche. This is a rare example of the *explicit* intersection of his private life and his textual comments, and involves the creation of a new text, not only by marginal annotation, but by further annotation of the annotations. I refer to the page of text (fig. 39.3) written on 25 May and 29 May 1875.

At the period this manuscript was annotated Rose was dying. Ruskin began his annotated reading of this text on 24 February 1875. On 28 February Ruskin wrote of her to George MacDonald: 'Poor Rose is entirely broken,—like her lover, and what good there may be for either of us must be where heaven is—but I don't know that much of the Universe' (Hilton 2002: 584). Ruskin came from Brantwood in the Lake District to Herne Hill in London, 'very broken in will and thought' (diary entry, quoted in ibid. 583). He saw Rose in February. In March and April he travelled between Herne Hill and Oxford, knowing Rose's mind had gone.

To know this, and to see his notes on the raising of Lazarus written that February, in his delicate and clear handwriting, with comments on *highly notable* forms of Greek letters, *apposite studies of* ζ, gives a sense of a tidal wave of emotion held back by a filigree wire fence of immense inner determination, defiant and fragile at the same time. The possibility which suggests itself to me, that the interest and delight in the Greek—its translation, accents, and the formation of letters—is a consolation and solace to Ruskin, is borne out by frequent references to Greek from an earlier troubled period of his life. For example, he writes in a letter of 1861: 'I don't know what I'm going to do.—I'm a good deal stronger—by no means merrier—If I can go on reading Greek and going nowhere and feeling nothing it will be best for me' (quoted in Birch 1988: 63). Birch comments: 'The study of Greek seemed to represent a withdrawal from the troubles and perplexities of his situation' (ibid.).

A telling example is in relation to the raising of Lazarus. Ruskin's comment on verse John 11.21, 'my brother had not died' is as follows: '$ουκ$ $αν$ $ετεθνησκει$; *conf*

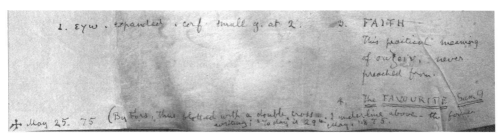

Fig. 39.3. Detail from Egerton 3046, Evangelistarium, p. 85 verso © The British Library Board.

Mary's ουκ αν απεθανε—*and in both,* ει ης—*strange rude Greek*' (10v). He is commenting on the tenses of the Greek, but he does not comment on the meaning. He knows Rose is dying while he is writing this.

The text which Ruskin was reading on the day Rose died, 25 May, was Luke 8:41–56. He returned to this page four days later, having now received news of her death, and made annotations to the annotations. (The details of his comments are shown in fig. 39.3.) The passage in question tells the story of how Jairus, a ruler of the synagogue, comes to Jesus begging him to heal his 12-year-old daughter who was dying. As Jesus is going to see the little girl, a woman with haemorrhaging which has persisted for twelve years touches Jesus' garment and he heals her. He then goes on to find the girl apparently dead but restores her to her parents and tells them to give her something to eat. The parallels with Rose La Touche are astounding. She was a girl of around 12 when Ruskin fell in love with her; some kind of anorexic condition is thought to be involved in her fatal illness—thus both eating and menstrual bleeding are significant; as with the woman who touched Jesus' garment, no physician had been able to heal her; her parents were complexly instrumental in the troubled nature of her relationship with Ruskin. She was dead; and Ruskin was full of grief.

He nowhere makes direct reference to this content. His attention is instead fixed on the physical features of the page he has annotated on the fateful day. The + on the verso is blotted and also has come out on the recto in a mirror image, presumably as Ruskin shut the book on 25 May:

+ *May 25.75 (By Fors, thus blotted with a double cross. I underline above the former writing;* 'today' is 29th *May. 1875*

Fors, fate, is an important word for Ruskin, signalling Force, Fortitude, and Fortune (Wheeler 1999: 207). What he has underlined is note 4: '*4 The FAVOUR-ITE saints*'. It is double underlined and refers to Jesus' taking no one except Peter, James, and John (v. 51). Presumably initially Ruskin made this comment to clarify the biblical narrative. The double underlining done when he returned to the text must have significance. Perhaps this points to Ruskin's identification of Rose with St Ursula and with his feeling for saints at around this time in his faith journey (Hilton 2002: 312–13). Possibly it is a reference to Rose's pet name for him, 'St Crumpet'. It might even be a reference to his own name, John, an insertion of himself into the narrative which bears his name and which tells of Jesus and the disciples going into the room to see the dead girl.

What we have on this page is something parallel to a diary and to personal letters, which thus supplements the letters and diary entries we have from this crucial time in Ruskin's life. In this case we have a personal response inscribed into his regular Bible reading and written as marginalia onto a biblical manuscript. This page becomes a dialogue with the written text. In its terse comments on the double blotting and its deliberate emphasis on the date, it becomes a carrier of intense emotion: intense but held in check. But it is striking that there is a deafening silence in respect of the central *content* of the text, a 12-year-old girl dying and being raised to life, and a woman being healed of a personal disorder.

The irony is that that on the Luke 8 passage Ruskin has created an obscure, enigmatic, riddling kind of text, in some ways resembling the John 14 text, which he abhorred. The fruits of his earlier comment have for him additional 'apocalyptic' import as the underlinings and the smudge become of deeper significance. Here is the moment which is beyond words when new signs signify, to those of us who are privileged to view it, a 'torn manuscript of the human soul'.

WORKS CITED

The Works of John Ruskin, Library Edition, ed. E. T. Cook, and A. Wedderburn, 39 vols. London: Allen; New York: Longmans, Green & Co., 1903–12. (indicated in text by LE, volume and page). Biblical quotations are from the King James Version, which was the English translation available to Ruskin.

BIRCH, D. (1988), *Ruskin's Myths*. Oxford: Clarendon Press.
BOFF, C. (1987), *Theology and Praxis: Epistemological Foundations*. Maryknoll, NY: Orbis.
BURD, V. A. (1969), *The Winnington Letters: John Ruskin's Correspondence with Margaret Alexis Bell and the Children at Winnington Hall*. Cambridge, Mass.: The Belknap Press of Harvard University Press.
——(1979), *John Ruskin and Rose La Touche: Her Unpublished Diaries of 1861 and 1867*. Oxford: Oxford University Press.
COLLINGWOOD, W. G. (1903), *Ruskin's Relics*. London: Isbister & Co.
DEARDEN, J. (1966), 'John Ruskin, the Collector: With a Catalogue of the Illuminated and Other Manuscripts formerly in his Collection', *Library*, 21/5: 124–54.
DRURY, J. (2000), 'Ruskin's Way: *tout a fait comme un oiseau*', in S. Collini, R. Whitmore, and B. Young (eds.), *British Intellectual History, 1750–1950*. 156–76. Cambridge: Cambridge University Press.
GIBBS, M. and E. (arranged by) (1898), *The Bible References in the Works of John Ruskin*. London: George Allen.
HILTON, T. (2002), *John Ruskin*. New Haven and London: Yale University Press.
LANDOW, G. P. (1980), *Victorian Types, Victorian Shadows*. Boston, London, and Henley: Routledge & Kegan Paul.
——(2001), Review of Tim Hilton's *John Ruskin: The Later Years*. *Albion* (Summer), 331–4.
WHEELER, M. (1999), *Ruskin's God*. Cambridge: Cambridge University Press.

FURTHER READING

As well as Hilton 2002, Landow 1980, and Wheeler 1999, see Z. Bennett, ' "To be taught to see is to gain word and thought at once": John Ruskin and Practical Theology', *Practical Theology* (2008), 1/1.

....

CHAPTER 40

KARL BARTH ON ROMANS

....

TIM GORRINGE

THE DIVINE ORGANISM: THE FIRST ROMANS

....

Round about 1909, Karl Barth observed in 1918, religion had become such a palpably powerful force that a special counter-blow against its 'history and presence' was urgently needed (Barth Romans, first edition [henceforth R1]: 400/1):

John Mott travelled from land to land with his word about 'the hour of decision', and we more or less believed him. Restless world committees were at work. In Basle the socialists were triumphant, in Edinburgh the Christians looked forward to the arrival of the kingdom of God. Signs and wonders did not fail to spring to the eye. But whether the concern of all this was really God's concern, whether God wanted all this—no one seriously asked that question!

These ironic remarks help explain the genesis of Barth's first Romans commentary, because it was the collapse of all these millennial dreams which sent him, with an armful of commentaries, to the apple tree in the garden at Safenwil to see whether there might not be in Paul any adequate response to the catastrophe of the First World War.

Barth wrestled with Romans all his life. Apart from the two great commentaries which I am considering here, there was also a Shorter Commentary, published in 1956; nearly a hundred pages of small print on Romans 9–11 in *Church Dogmatics* 2/2, the size of a small book; and an excursus on Romans 5 which was to have been included in *Church Dogmatics* 3/2 but which was published as a separate pamphlet. Responding to criticism of the first commentary by Wernle, Barth acknowledged that there were many passages which he still found difficult to understand: 'Strictly speaking, no single verse seems to me capable of a smooth interpretation' (Barth, *Romans*, second edition [henceforth R2]: 12).[1] It was part of Barth's genius as an exegete that he never allowed the text to become familiar.

Preparing the first commentary, Barth did his homework: he used the most recent historical critical commentaries by Zahn and Jülicher; he read Kutter's 'Romans as Catechism' and his book on Justification, which was an exposition of Romans 1–8; he read his father's lecture notes on Romans; he read older commentators like Bengel and Tholuck; but two commentaries clearly stood out— Luther's, and that of J. T. Beck, which provided him with the organic metaphor which was the main exegetical key to this edition. (Beintker 2005). Fortunately, Barth wrote in his preface, he was not forced to choose between the historical-critical method and the old doctrine of inspiration, but were he to do so he would unhesitatingly choose the latter. The task of the exegete is to see through the historical into the spirit of the Bible, which is the eternal Spirit, and to hear Paul, the 'prophet and apostle of the kingdom of God to all people in all ages' (R1: 3). In the latter sections of the book, especially, the exegete becomes the apostle and speaks urgently and directly to his contemporaries. Throughout Barth insisted that his one concern was exegesis. He had no intention of providing a free meditation on Paul's letter, but simply intended to expound it in his context, and in both commentaries he felt bound to the words of the text (R2: p. ix).[2]

Introducing the second commentary, Barth noted that: 'A wide reading of contemporary secular literature—especially newspapers!—is recommended to any one desirous of understanding the Epistle to the Romans', and this is more obvious in the first than in the second commentary (R2: 425). Barth wrote as someone who had internalized the great German literary tradition. Jülicher noted ironically in review that Schiller was quoted more often than was quite necessary, but Goethe was cited more than twice as often, and Barth had obviously been deeply struck by Spitteler's *Olympian Spring*, which won its author the Nobel Prize for literature in the year Barth's commentary appeared. The commentary is honeycombed with literary, historical, artistic, and political allusions.

---

[1] I have used Hoskyn's translation but sometimes added the German word to make the meaning clear.

[2] In 1932 he felt that it was written 'by another man to meet a situation belonging to another epoch': R2: p. vi.

THE THEOLOGICAL CENTRE

It is probably fair to say that prior to Barth, German-language reception of Romans was dominated either by Luther, and the question of 'justification by faith', for which the paradigm text might be Romans 4, or by pietism, with its emphasis on Christ's sacrifice for sin, for which the paradigm text would be Romans 3:25. Barth shifts the theological centre. He identifies the theme of the letter as 'our knowledge of God realised in Christ, in which God draws near not objectively but creatively and immediately, in which we not only see, but are seen, not only understand, but are understood, not only grasp, but are grasped' (R1: 19). Barth's christocentricity is already apparent: 'The power of God which breaks forth to realization in Christ comes to realization, the organic unity with God once more comes into play for both the world and human beings, the already executed turn "in the secrets of human hearts" is firmly planted in nature and history, where the faithfulness of God, opened up through him, meets human faith' (R1: 91).

Barth insists that the part be read by the whole and vice versa, and that there is no golden key (R2: p. viii). On the other hand, the letter is read through and through in the light of the resurrection, so that in a sense chapter 8 becomes the fulcrum. The theological focus of the commentary in the resurrection leads Barth to adopt the older Blumhardt's slogan, 'Christ is Victor'. 'In the death of Christ the struggle, and in his resurrection the victory, of divine reality over the powers of sin and death have been consummated' (R1: 98). The cross is not our salvation as suffering and struggle, but *through* the cross the glory of the Father, the resurrection, is inserted between us and our sin (R1: 215). The resurrection is 'a revelation of unmistakeable clarity' which reveals the meaning of the cross to us (R1: 98). The victory of God is accomplished 'in heaven' before it is realized on earth. This age is not the final one. There is 'not only a truth which is beyond this world (*jenseitige Wahrheit*) but there are also events beyond this world, a world history in heaven, an inner movement in God'. What we call 'history' and 'events' are but the confused reflection of turns that happen there. There is a distinction between 'so called' history, history 'in Adam', which human beings make for themselves, and 'actual' history, the history God makes, history 'in Christ' (R1: 66/7; 223–5). God's history breaks through into so-called history, and when this happens time is fulfilled by eternity in its deepest sense, in an 'eternal Now' (R1: 86/7). 'Breakthrough' moments are the moments when real history becomes visible, in which the kingdom (actual history) is established in the midst of so-called history. The breakthrough of God's power in Christ is not a 'historical' event, in the sense of an event which can be understood and assessed by the canons of Rankean historiography, but the 'uncovering of the never still, necessary reality in the cross section of time' (R1: 106).

RENEWING THE CURRENCY

Barth also saw that, despite the best efforts of men he admired, such as Kutter and Wilhelm Herrmann, specifically theological currency had become debased. He strove, therefore, to find a way once more to make the word 'God' strange: in a sense both commentaries are extensive attempts to insist that *Deus non est in genere.* Barth had read Nietzsche. In the first commentary he even uses 'the transvaluation of values' as the heading for one of his sections, but he did not need Nietzsche to alert him to the way the word 'God' functioned as an idolatrous projection. For Barth, it is a strategy of the powers to characterize God abstractly so that the idea of God becomes 'an ever more faded "religious" master concept for all sorts of inner worldly lordships and significant things' (R1: 36). Barth sought a middle way between the claims to experience of pietism and the scholarly distance of the Theological Guild to insist that we are confronted by the reality of the living God known in constantly renewed freshness and freedom: 'The depths of God, before which we stand as before an abyss, are his Godhead, his livingness' (R1: 460; Barth asserts here that God is not unfathomable, a claim he denies in the second commentary).

The eschatology of the commentary is part of this renewed coinage. In the exegesis of chapter 8 Barth insists that trust in God and eschatology and the solution to the puzzle of the world and eschatology cannot be separated (R1: 325, 332). 'God is a God of hope, a God who opens up perspectives for us, a God of coming things' (R1: 563).

CONFLICT WITH THE LORDLESS POWERS

The shift of theological centre does not mean that the question of justification is abandoned. On the contrary, it is raised by the question of Christian religiosity, which functions for Barth much as the indulgence controversy did for Luther. How could Germany's leading theologians, how could Herman Kutter, support the war effort! The fact that they did showed that there was a wound in theological thinking here which needed cauterizing. Throughout this commentary Barth speaks of a conflict with 'the lordless powers' and these were above all the powers of religion and morality, always especially strong supports of the dark powers (R1: 34, 290).[3] 'Lordless ideas are as deadly as all the lordless powers, no matter how pure and

---

[3] The theme was dropped in R2 and not taken up again until the final fragments of the Church Dogmatics.

elevated they may be!' (R1: 556). 'Evil has its deepest root in . . . the tactics of the kingdom of God, the lordless righteousness of human beings, in "Godlessness of the good" (Kutter)' (R1: 493). He was clear that what we are concerned with is not the sin of individuals but 'the great objective powers', the great idols of church, state, and social life (R1: 236, 244).

His reworking of the theme of justification meant that his critique was directed especially at the church, which turned the letter to the Romans into fragments of dead text and at the same time praised 'her' Paul, turned St Francis into the darling of all aesthetes, Luther into the patron of 'inwardness', 'Germanness', and 'evangelical freedom', and made the cross the symbol of highest humanity. In all these ways the church once again crucifies Christ (R1: 421/2). The Church is 'the grave of biblical truth' (R1: 361)'

In his exegesis of chapter 4 Barth attacked religious hero-worship as part of a false piety and religiosity which 'leads to nihilism' (R1: 33). Barth had been plagued by a pietist mission in the course of writing the commentary, and pietism attracts ferocious fire. 'The method of pietism is only possible, in its presuppositions and effects, under the wrath of God' (R1: 288). Faith cuts off the bypass through the spiritual constituted by pietism. 'It is direct and not indirect truth. It is unmediated' (R1: 160). This has nothing to do with religious 'experience': 'Psychologists should keep their hands off!' (R1: 320). Grace is not 'experience' but 'the divine presupposition, the new order under which we are placed, the altered world context to which we are led' (R1: 206/7). What we need is not a new religion but a new world (R1: 295). Pietism puts individual experience at the centre, but 'God cannot be honoured simply in a "personal" life. Truth is not for the individual' (R1: 272). In place of the individual is the organism of God's kingdom, in which we are rooted and need to grow (R1: 255). That God grasps us means that we share in the immediacy of the knowledge with which God knows Godself (R1: 158). Indeed, 'The concept of God is given us as immediately as our own Being' (R1: 28).

GROWTH IN THE ORGANISM OF THE LIVING GOD

Sin is bound up with the desire for autonomy, and therefore redemption is return to the Origin (*Ursprung*; Hoskyns translates 'Primal Origin'), which is what Christ accomplishes both for us and the whole cosmos (R1: 200). Through his obedience Christ fulfilled the true destiny of human life. His death was 'the fulfilment of a human life in the immediacy with God which had once again been found'. As such it introduced 'something new into world history, the fundamental overcoming of the old' (R1: 225). In him the Origin 'reappears' (R1: 53/65). Learning from Beck, Barth speaks of humanity being caught up in a process of organic growth. Through his reconciliation, 'the creative process of Life breaks forth which is our salvation' (R1: 175). Through the faith gifted us by the faithfulness of God we are 'organically implanted in the living growth of divine righteousness' (R1: 113). Christ's resurrection inserts us into the stream of organic life, so that: 'We simply stand within this process . . . we want to be nothing other than an organic particle of the creation, bound up with the whole, which is now reconciled with God' (R1: 171). We must live and grow in the organism which stems from Christ (R1: 227). The believer can only live ethically by living organically—homoeopathically, not allopathically! (R1: 544/5). Return to the Origin, through participation in the organism or movement, is what constitutes the 'process eschatology' of this commentary.[4] The statement that the living God is the answer to the questions of the present is immediately glossed with the remark: 'The movement itself is the constantly renewed answer' (R1: 153). There is a fundamental contrast: 'God's will versus my own, the knowledge of God in place of reflection, growth in place of artificiality, living as part of an organism as opposed to monadic living, faith as opposed to religion and church, justification rather than morality' (R1: 164).

Without endorsing liberal ideas of progress, Barth wishes to emphasize the sense of real movement and change in both human and cosmic history. The germ-cell of life has once again been planted in history and nature so that divine history grows within human world history (R1: 24). Both God and human beings are involved in a movement and follow a way. Adam-Christ marks 'the way of God in world history. A *way* of God. No stasis (*Zustand*) . . . no stable "reality". That you only find in hell. Where we are dealing with *God*, it goes forward, in the face of victorious decisions' (R1: 189). 'Spirit is growth and has its own authority in the law of growth' (R1: 316). We live and suffer not outside, but inside God's movement (R1: 155). God is with us not as an alien Stranger but as our nearest, most intimate acquaintance, his will not a 'strange rule which lies athwart our free feelings, but as the "pulse of our own organism" (Kutter), our own deepest, truest, freedom' (R1: 207). We live in a 'messianic present', inaugurated by the decisive turn in heaven, in which a life process is opened up on earth, in the psychological-historical side of our being. 'We are no longer the same. We are inserted in the process which carries forward from the beyond into the present' (R1: 166).

Barth contrasts organic growth with 'mechanical' change, change that is man-made: 'The divine grows organically, and so needs no more mechanical building up' (R1: 90).[5] This means in the first instance that, over against the insistence of the Christian socialists, we do not have to 'build' the kingdom. It does not come

---

[4] The term 'process eschatology' is Michael Beintker's (Beintker 1985: 24).

[5] 'The coming world comes not mechanically, but organically' (R1: 21). In *The Division of Labour in Society*, which was published in 1893, Émile Durkheim had distinguished between mechanical

through our efforts. 'There is life, which is grounded through the fullness, the outpouring, the breakthrough of the grace of God . . . and now organically unfolds itself'(R1: 195). In this 'unfolding' the true striving of idealism is finally honoured, so that Plato, Kant, and Fichte stand in a line with Moses as prophets of recovered immediacy. 'Where else than in Christ can idealism be *more* than idealism?' (R1: 104–5).

GRACE VERSUS ETHICS

Just as the reality of grace calls into question the individualism and human security of religion, so it challenges our understanding of morality. '"What shall I do?" Answer: Above all stop asking that question! Every word of it is ambiguous and confused' (R1: 263). This is because, when we are part of the organic life of the new community, every 'ought' flows 'organically' from our new being in the Spirit. In Christ there are no ethics. 'There is only the movement of God which demands each moment a quite specific knowledge of the situation and to which a necessary deed corresponds' (R1: 524). The answer to the moral question is not ethics but grace (R1: 203). Living in the kingdom of grace means serious, candid knowledge of unredeemed reality, clear consciousness of the responsibility of each individual, openness to the changing command of the hour, and readiness to take the next step which will bring the movement towards its goal (R1: 241). Our behaviour as Christians is shaped by mutual exhortation: 'Exhortation is not a law or an ideal, an establishing of how it ought to be but the reality of a life in which the ideal is engaged in fulfilment, step by step.' It is an expression of the whole community on the move (R1: 463).

Part of the attack on conventional ethics is an attack on religious socialism. 'Pacifism and social democracy do not represent the kingdom of God,' wrote Barth, 'but the old human kingdom in a new guise' (R1: 42). Those who develop critiques of the existing order can be prophets, but they can also be Pharisees. Instead of teaching about the goodness of God they place themselves in a partisan way over against most other people, more proud than the Godless (R1: 46). Although they stand theoretically on God's side, practically speaking they are God's 'worst hindrance' (R1: 47). They turn the gospel into a new law.

and organic solidarity, the former representing the taken-for-granted solidarity of pre industrial society, and the latter the solidarity industrial communities needed to work at and construct.

THE CHRISTIAN IN THE MIDST OF REVOLUTION

Barth reads the passage from Romans 12:16 to 13:10 under the heading of 'Superiority' (*Überlegenheit*): what he has in mind is what is at stake in *truly* overcoming the world. 'Your method is solidarity with the enemy. Not the feeble-spirited indifference, friendliness and tolerance over against his impossible way of doing things, not the false community of fire and water, but the mercy of God . . .' (R1: 498). Echoing Luther's understanding of freedom there is a dialectic of subordination and refusal to admit the legitimacy of the State. The State is characterized by naked power, the 'devilish art of the majority' (R1: 501–3). Christians can have nothing to do with this, because 'their State is in heaven'. Their stance over against the State is 'in principle revolutionary' in that they deny its fundamental principle of the use of power (R1: 503–5). Christians must be prepared to engage in political duties, but without absolute seriousness. On the contrary, their concern is with the 'absolute revolution of God' which 'revolutionises revolution' (R1: 234). Christianity 'does not agree with the State, it negates it—both its presupposition and its essence'. 'It is *more* than Leninism! As far as Christianity is concerned it is 'all or nothing' in the sense that the fulfilment it expects is not . . . the goal or result of a development or a gradual "ascent of man" but the discovery of a new creation or the substance of a new knowledge. *This* programme cannot be the object of any ethics' (R1: 505–7).

To be subject to the authorities, as Paul recommends, means not to take them seriously, to deny them ideological legitimation (to 'starve them religiously'). Barth takes it for granted that a Christian can have nothing to do with 'Monarchy, Capitalism, Militarism, Patriotism and Liberalism'. 'The divine may not be politicised nor the human theologised—not even for the benefit of democracy and social democracy.' We must not confuse divine renewal with human progress. Whatever is done against the present State can in no way represent the victory of God's kingdom (R1: 507–9). Revolt against the ruling powers leads to the region of God's wrath (R1: 509–10). If the worst comes to the worst we may, however, find ourselves in 'confused situations' in which evil cannot be overcome by good. We may then act with 'ethical determination', but this is outside the sphere of the Christian ethic: 'As regards the ethic of the confused situation, the New Testament has nothing to say' (R1: 495).

None of us can avoid complicity in the guilt of political realities. We need, therefore, to take part in State and Party life knowing that God will forgive 'even our political sins' (R1: 510). Even 'fundamentally dirty' political realities 'work together for good, with those who love God'. So long as the Christian remains true to her ways the mine is laid which will blow the idols sky-high (R1: 511–12). We must be careful, however, not to be untrue to God by marching into the political arena flying God's flag. It is certainly not God's spirit which drives a person to heroic political deeds. 'The Spirit does not knock at the hard shell of politics. It bursts it from inside!' (R1: 512–16). The important thing is to deny the State the

Pathos, seriousness, and importance, of the divine (R1: 516–17). In that we are all part of the fallen order of things we have no choice but to live ethically and politically, but 'we struggle against the State fundamentally and radically and—pay taxes . . . join the Party, fulfil the functions . . . which fall to us'. Respect to whom respect, Honour to whom honour—'but not one step further!'

Fulfil your duties without illusion, but no compromising of God! Payment of tax, but no incense to Caesar! Citizens' initiative and obedience but no combination of throne and altar, no Christian Patriotism, no democratic crusading. Strike and general strike, and street-fighting if needs be, but *no* religious justification and glorification of it! Military service as soldier or officer if needs be but under *no* circumstances army chaplain! Social-democratic but *not* religious socialist! The betrayal of the gospel is *not* part of your political duty.   (R1: 517–21)

'Only love builds the new world.' The State might not worry that we withhold only this final honour to it, but if it realized the danger of these revolutionary methods, then martyrdom might become a real possibility (R1: 522). The love of Christ remains faithful to 'the hope, the unquiet, the longing, the radical and permanent revolution' (R1: 353). At the present moment (1918!) Spirit can be nothing other than revolution—'precisely what we call revolution at the moment!' (R1: 316). Amidst the disappointments of contemporary socialism we look forward to the hour when the embers of Marxist dogma are newly kindled and 'the socialist Church will be resurrected in a socialist world' (R1: 444). In terms which anticipate liberation theology, he insists that the movement of the kingdom is 'fundamentally and one-sidedly a movement from below'. Whilst I can be a Jew to the Jews and a Greek to the Greeks I cannot be lord to the lords or an aesthete to the aesthetes. 'Over against everything which wants to be great I must take the standpoint of the small people, with whom God begins, not because they are virtuous but because *their* righteousness does not stand in the way, or at least, does less so' (R1: 490). The belief in God's revolution is quite clearly not meant to be the disarming of 'real' revolution (which is part of 'so called' history), but part of actual (that is, divine) history, which has concrete effects in the present.

THE DIVINE *KRISIS*: THE SECOND COMMENTARY ON ROMANS

One thousand copies of the first edition were printed. As they began to run out the publisher proposed a new edition. Barth demurred: instead he rewrote it. Positive and negative reviews, further study of Paul, the publication of posthumous writings by Overbeck, closer acquaintance with Plato and Kant, and the writings of Kierke-gaard and Dostoevsky all led to revision. Although there are many correspondences between the division of the material and the fundamental themes of the two commentaries, Barth is justified in speaking of it as a completely new commentary.[6] Out go all the literary quotations and allusions, out go the lordless powers, out goes, above all, the organic metaphor. In come the notorious mathematical metaphors which were to identify Barth for forty years in the English-speaking world, in comes Kierkegaard's 'infinite qualitative distinction', in come, as the dominant themes, KRISIS (Barth uses the Greek form in capitals) and 'the moment'.

As with the first commentary, the exegesis represents a response to events: 'The present situation in its complete concreteness is our starting point' (R2: 427). This included both the failure of the revolution in Germany and the brutal success of the Russian revolution. It was partly for this reason that Barth had to change the revolutionary tenor of his exegesis of the final chapters.

The hostile reaction of the New Testament Guild forced Barth to clarify his exegetical method. The question of the nature of interpretation, says Barth, is 'the supreme question' because the New Testament contains material which 'urgently and finally concerns the very marrow of human civilization' (R2: 9). He found in Scripture a revolutionary attack on the way the world was at present constituted. When he turned to the standard commentaries of Jülicher or Lietzmann, however, he found that they contained 'no more than a reconstruction of the text, a rendering of the Greek words and phrases by their precise equivalents, a number of additional notes in which archaeological and philological material is gathered together, and a more or less plausible arrangement of the subject matter' (R2: 6). They reduced the text to runes. The effect of this was to defuse its dangerous, subversive effect and to render it harmless. These commentaries, and this way of handling the text, were a sign of the subordination of the church to the bourgeois cultural norms expressed in the Prussian Academy. He contrasted them with the creative energy with which Luther or Calvin approached the task, so that 'Paul speaks, and the person of the sixteenth century hears'. What had to be done was to learn to measure words and phrases by 'that about which the documents are speaking'. 'The Word ought to be exposed in the words. Intelligent comment means that I am driven on till I stand with nothing before me but the enigma of the matter . . . till I know the author so well that I allow him to speak in my name and am even able to speak in his name myself' (R2: 8). The exegete must learn to 'attentively think after' (*nachdenken*) the concepts of the Apostle (R2: 11). As we do so, and the Word in the words becomes clear, this has practical, indeed explosive,

---

[6] Peter Winzeler argues that the first commentary is 'aufgehoben', taken up and subsumed, in the second (Winzeler 1982: 155).

consequences, which makes the practice of appending a homiletic commentary to the 'scientific, scholarly' one impossible.

REVELATION IN CHRIST

In the first commentary Barth had incautiously spoken of the immediate knowledge of God, but he had now learned from Kierkegaard that 'to be known directly is the characteristic mark of an idol'. The hidden God 'is not to be found in Romans, can neither be brought to speech nor written about, nor, indeed, "done", because God absolutely cannot be an object of human striving'. If God is known, it is the result only of a miracle (R2: 422). The name of this miracle is Jesus Christ. 'The content of the letter to the Romans is that the hidden God as such is the revealed God in Jesus Christ.' The letter's substance, theology, God's Word on human lips, is only possible on the grounds that this subject, the hidden God, has as its predicate the revealed God (R2: 422). That God is revealed does not, however, mean that we can count on such knowledge, make it our possession. On the contrary, precisely in Jesus 'God becomes truly secret, makes Godself known as the Unknown, speaks as the eternally Silent One. In Jesus God fends off all importunate intimacy, all religious impertinence' (R2: 98). God is 'unveiled' only as God is veiled. The revealed God remains the hidden God. The human historical Jesus bears witness to God, but is not himself revelation. The unveiling which remains a veiling is our knowledge of Christ in cross and resurrection. Christ's life, which can be understood solely in terms of passive obedience, is known only through the resurrection, this 'non historical historical event' (R2: 159, 204). The concept of resurrection emerges with the concept of death, that is, with the concept of the end of all historical things as such. The bodily resurrection of Christ stands ever and again over against his bodily crucifixion and nowhere else (R2: 205). It is the non-historical relating of the whole historical life of Jesus to its origin in God (R2: 195). As the Messiah, Jesus is the end of history. He can only be comprehended as Paradox (Kierkegaard), as Victor (Blumhardt), as Primal History (Overbeck). 'As Christ, Jesus is the plane which lies beyond our comprehension. The plane which is known to us, He intersects vertically from above . . . In the Resurrection the new world of the Holy Spirit touches the old world of the flesh, but touches it as a tangent touches a circle, that is, without touching it. And precisely because it does not touch it, it touches it as its frontier–as the new world' (R2: 29/30). These famous geometrical analogies are actually used very sparingly, though in the Anglo-Saxon world they were thought to constitute the heart of what Barth was saying.

THE WHOLLY OTHERNESS OF GOD

The geometrical and algebraic analogies—the minus sign outside the brackets of all human constructions—are used to insist on the Wholly Otherness of God. God can only be spoken of through paradox. If, in speaking of God's revelation in Christ, 'we have not trodden on the toes of every single human method of investigation and grievously annoyed it, we have spoken of something else' (R2: 278). 'That Other from which we have come and which is contrasted with all concrete, known, temporal, human existence can be in no manner wholly distinct unless it be in every manner wholly distinct' (R2: 115). As Kierkegaard had argued, a Christianity which had lost its ability to shock, and become a direct communication, becomes 'a tiny superficial thing, capable neither of inflicting deep wounds nor of healing them; by discovering an unreal and merely human compassion, it forgets the qualitative distinction between man and God' (R2: 29). Instead of organic connection we now have krisis—the judgement of God on all that we do, which stands over all history and all earthly existence (R2: 46 and often).

As in the first commentary, the qualitative distinction finds its expression in eschatology, no longer 'organic' but 'consistent'. 'A Christianity which is not absolutely and totally eschatology has absolutely and totally nothing to do with Christ' (R2: 314). This eschatology is the crisis which the death and resurrection of Christ faces us with, which makes any idea of 'progress' or normal movement impossible.

The critical, highly dialectical character of this knowledge of God is reflected in the faith which responds to it. If it aspires to be anything more than an empty space faith becomes—unbelief. Anything at all which might make faith the adoption of a point of view or method, whether it be paradox, brokenness, waiting on God—all this is nothing but works righteousness (R2: 56/7). Taking up the theme of the Bauhaus, Barth asserts that 'what is less—less positively certain and less surely guaranteed—is, in fact, more. "God" is the eternal, the last word, if we mean "faith only", if we mean the impossible possibility of the faithfulness of God' (R2: 113). The characteristic marks of Christianity are 'deprivation and hope' rather than having and being (R2: 36). The gospel is not there to give comfort but to witness to the power of God who raises the dead. 'It is the alarm cry, the fire bell, of a coming new world' (R2: 38). 'The gospel is not a truth amongst other truths. It places all truths in question' (R2: 35). This Word is so new, so unheard of, so unexpected, that it appears, is understood and taken on only as contradiction (R2: 38). Jesus comes 'not to change anything, not to improve the flesh through morality, to transfigure it through art, to rationalise it through science, to overcome it through the Fata Morgana of religion, but to proclaim the resurrection of the flesh, the new human being who recognizes herself in God, because she is made in God's image (*Ebenbild*), and in whom God recognises Godself since God is her pattern (*Urbild*)' (R2: 277). The response to this proclamation is faith. Faith is 'respect before the divine incognito, love of God which is conscious of the qualitative distinction between God and human beings, God and the world, affirmation of the resurrection as the turning point of the world, affirmation of the divine No! which brings us to a shuddering halt before God' (R2: 39). Faith itself is an 'impossible possibility', a phrase intended to contradict what liberal theology regarded as only too self-evident a human possibility (R2: 138). It is 'awe in the presence of the divine incognito; it is the love of God that is aware of the qualitative distinction between God and human beings and God and the world' (R2: 39). This is the faith which corresponds to the faithfulness of God and this is the theme of the letter (R2: 42). It is not a psychological occurrence. 'Rather, it is the advent of the "Moment" which is beyond all time, by which everything before and after is set in a new context' (R2: 125).

Faith runs together with hope. 'Whatever is not hope is stupid, a block, a chain, difficult and awkward, like the word "reality". It does not liberate us but takes us prisoner. It is not grace but judgement and ruin. It is not divine leading, but fate. It is not God but a mirror image of unredeemed human beings' (R2: 314).

THE DIALECTIC OF RELIGION

Where Paul spoke of *nomos* (law), Barth translated 'religion'. This means that religion has to be understood dialectically. Grace is the *krisis* from death to life. 'For this reason, nothing is so meaningless as the attempt to construct a religion out of the Gospel, and to set it as one human possibility amongst others' (R2: 225). Only when the 'criminal arrogance of religion' has been done away can we learn to think '*von Gott aus*', in other words, not from a starting-point in human subjectivity or religious experience (R2: 37). Why? Because religion functions as opiate, underwriting human illusions (R2: 236). In religion, human beings seek to master their world, and make themselves finally secure, but God cannot become the prisoner of any human programme. Religion is precisely where human beings bolt and bar themselves against God. Just where people believe they are raising themselves above common lusts and failings, precisely there, in religion, do they find themselves on 'the highest summit in the kingdom of sin' (R2: 242). 'Religion is not the Kingdom of God, even if it is the kingdom of God religion of Blumhardt's epigones, but human work' (R2: 366). It is no chance that 'the odour of death' hangs over these summits. Religion does not liberate us, 'indeed it imprisons us more surely than anything else' (R2: 276). It is the 'working capital' of sin. The boundary of religion is 'the line of death which cuts between what is possible with human beings and what is possible with God, between flesh and Spirit, time and eternity'. An irrepressible bourgeois reality, it refuses to die. 'Enough, it must die, and in God we are free of it' (R2: 238).

This is one side of the dialectic. On the other side we have no option but to be religious. 'What else can we honestly do than be—religious people, repenting in dust and ashes, wrestling with fear and trembling that we might be blessed and, if we have to take a position, taking that of adoration' (R2: 252). We have no option but to cultivate religion, to reform and revolutionize it. But: 'the more consistently we are involved in religion the deeper the shadow of death which lies over us' (R2: 255). Why? Because it is religion which faces us with the reality of sin, death, and the knowledge that we do not know God, of our radical otherness with respect to the Creator (R2: 250). It is the worst enemy we have—apart from God. Precisely for this reason we have to stay with it, to remain in solidarity with the church, fully aware of the antithesis between church and gospel (R2: 333). The attempt to do without the church is 'pseudo radicalism'. We do not escape from sin by removing ourselves from religion (R2: 241). The rather general account of 'Need', 'Guilt', and 'Hope' of the first commentary are replaced by an account of the tribulation, guilt, and hope of the *church* in the exegesis of chapters 9–11 (R2: 371). The church is not set over against the world; it is the world conscious of its need, the place where the sickness of the world comes to a head and therefore hope for all is included in hope for the church (R2: 407). Properly understood, there are no Christians. 'There is only the opportunity for all alike at once accessible and inaccessible— to become Christians.'

At the same time, doubtless through the influence of Kierkegaard, Barth consciously contradicts what he said in the first commentary about the individual. Human beings do not stand before God via the detour of 'the whole' but 'in their own need and hope'. The individual is not 'part' of anything, but herself 'the whole'. Each individual is met by the eternal distinctness (*Ungleich*) of God (R2: 441/2). At the same time, we note the corrective: 'We announce the right of the individual, the eternal worth of each person (Kierkegaard!) in that we announce that their soul is lost before God and in God taken up (*aufgehoben*) and redeemed' (R2: 116). The neighbour is 'the uplifted finger which by its "otherness" reminds us of the Wholly Other' (R2: 441, 444). The individual of the second commentary is 'identical with the new man . . . characterised by individuality without arbitrariness and community without division into hier-archies' (Plonz 1995: 187).

THE GREAT DISTURBANCE

The letter to the Romans is 'theory of a praxis'. Nowhere are we concerned with abstract thought (R2: 427). Ethics follows from our knowledge of Christ. 'The primary ethical deed is the knowledge of God whose concrete intuitability (*Anschaulichkeit*) is given in the death of Christ and his parable: the concrete Other' (Plonz 1995: 189). Ethics is not 'criticism from high places', but mutual admonition (*Ermahnung*) by those who share solidarity in sin. This mutual admonition is devoid of human justification, but rests on grace, on forgiveness. 'The mature and well balanced man, standing firmly with both feet on the earth, who has never been lamed and broken and half-blinded by the scandal of his life, is as such the existentially godless man. His vigour is the vigour of the lusts of his mortal body' (R2: 235). Grace is the secret of ethics. Grace is 'divine impatience, discontent, dissatisfaction'. It is the enemy of every ethic, even of the essential 'interim ethic'. It is the axe laid to the root of the good conscience which the well-to-do citizen so enjoys in the civil service, in his vocation, or in politics. 'There is no more underhand means of defence than when concerned moral people . . . treat ethics as an account of innerworldly purpose, rather than as the critical negation of all purpose and seek to ground it on goods and ideals rather than on the forgiveness of sins' (R2: 430). Grace is the theory which as such is practice, the indicative which has the force of the categorical imperative, knowledge of the will of God, the knowledge that we are known of God, the power of the resurrection (R2: 207).

Barth distinguishes between primary and secondary ethical action. 'Primary ethical action' is repentance which follows from giving the glory to God, from worship. It is 'offering our bodies as a living sacrifice'. 'Secondary ethical action'—the way we behave to our neighbour and in community—follows from this (R2: 431).

We may understand ethics in terms of negative and positive possibilities. The positive possibility is *agapē* rather than *erōs*. Negative possibilities are those actions in which we find parables of the kingdom in weakness rather than strength, folly rather than wisdom. Christianity 'is always there where there are no apparent solutions, but not there where people have come to terms with things. It has a certain partisan preference for the oppressed, for those falling short, for the immature, for the sullen, those ready for revolution—and to this extent the Socialists in large measure win approval' (R2: 463). The characteristic marks of Christianity are always deprivation and hope rather than possession and self-sufficiency (R2: 36). The twofold possibility is 'either (positive) a demonstration for life in the hope of the resurrection, and as such includes a protest against the many sided evidences of the world's addiction to death. Or (negatively), the dialectical reverse side, a demonstration against all idolatry and for the "exalting" of the lowly' (Plonz 1995: 189). Christianity is purely and simply the protest against all the high places which human beings build for themselves, 'and as such it is the absolute Ethic, and as such proclaims the coming world' (R2: 467).

God's Revolution

In the second edition, according to F. W. Marquardt, Barth carries out 'a sensational anti-revolutionary turn' (Marquardt 1985: 142). This much-quoted remark is less often taken together with the detailed qualifications which follow: 'talk of the "revolution" of God is turned into talk of "God's revolution"' (ibid. 149).[7] So far from this abandoning us to the status quo, what it actually sets up is the principle of permanent revolution.

In the second commentary, as in the first, Barth insists that the attitude of the letter is 'unmistakeably revolutionary' (R2: 484). However, where in the first commentary the target was principally legitimism and principled religious reform, here the target is revolution. Barth's change was made in response to 'a certain stratum of readers of his first commentary who read out of that a "principle of revolution" and expected more of the same from him' (R2: 476). In a heavily ironical rhetorical move, well aware of the reactionary use made of Romans over the centuries, Barth observes that: 'It is highly unlikely that anyone will become a reactionary on the grounds of having read Romans!' (R2: 478). Barth makes plain beyond a peradventure that there is no defence of legitimism in chapter 13. 'There is here no word of approval of the existing order.' But Romans does not endorse the revolution going on in Russia, a 'Titanism of revolt and upheaval and renovation'. The problem is that 'Revolutionary Titanism is far more dangerous and godless than the reactionary kind because in its origin it is so much closer to the truth' (R2: 478). As in the first commentary, Barth insists that evil is never the answer to evil. The true revolution is forgiveness of sins and resurrection of the dead, but the revolutionary chooses hatred and insubordination instead. This choice is worse than the legitimist option for satisfaction, security, and usurpation because 'by it God is far better understood, but so much the worse abused' (R2: 481). What then? An endorsement of the status quo, a 'thorough depoliticization of the concept of revolution' (Jüngel 1986: 102)? To put it this way suggests a turn away from political action and involvement to 'the conversion of the individual' so beloved by right-wing

---

[7] Cf. Marquardt 1985: 158: 'Barth is thinking of a revolution sui generis, an apocalyptic revolution of God happening of its own accord, which can no longer be accomplished in the anti-revolutionary demonstration of revolutionaries but which can only be witnessed to.'

Christians. But Barth intends no such thing. 'No revolution is the best prepara-tion for the true revolution,' he writes 'but even no revolution is no safe recipe' (R2: 483). We need a 'devastating undermining of the existing order' which comes by depriving State, Church, Society, Positive Right, Family, Organized Re-search—but also, of course, revolutionary action—of their pathos. These things 'live off the credulity of those who have been nurtured upon vigorous sermons-delivered-on-the-field-of battle, and solemn humbug of all sorts'. If you stir up revolution against them their pathos is provided with fresh fodder. Depriving them of their pathos starves them out (R2: 483). This is the negative, critical, attacking moment which must be supplemented by the truly revolutionary action of love, 'the great positive possibility'.

> Not a single act but the bringing together of all positive (protesting!) ethical possibilities . . . We define love as the 'Great Positive Possibility', because in it the revolutionary aspect of all ethics comes to light, because it is actually concerned with the denial and breaking up of the status quo (*das Bestehende*) . . . insofar as we love one another we cannot wish to uphold the present order as such, because in love we do the new thing which brings the old crashing down.   (R2: 493)

Love is the denial and demolition of the existing order which no revolt can bring about, the destruction of everything which is—'like God' (R2: 496). It is possible, he claims, in 'the eternal moment, the Now—when the past and future stand still' (R2: 497). 'The "Moment" of the movement of men by God is beyond men, it cannot be enclosed in a system or a method or a "way"' (R2: 110).[8] The Now of revelation is the opportunity for the occurrence of love. This is not only an account of an 'impossible possibility' but a way of insisting on permanent revolution. 'Love enters the realm of evil, in order to leave it again at once. Love builds no tabernacles, for it seeks to create nothing that abides, nothing that "exists" in time. Love does what it does only in the knowledge of the eternal "Moment". Love is therefore the essentially revolutionary action' (R2: 498).

Where, then, does this leave political action? 'A political career . . . becomes possible only when it is seen to be essentially a game; that is to say, when we are unable to speak of absolute political right, when the note of "absoluteness" has vanished from both thesis and antithesis' (R2: 489). What is stated here is some-thing like the 'eschatological proviso' which liberation theology has insisted on as a way of saying that human projects are not identical with God's kingdom. But we also have to ask where Barth's exegesis leaves God, and the answer is that 'from now on the word "God" can no longer be thought without thinking of his revolution' (Marquardt 1985: 159).

---

[8] Jüngel argues that Barth drew on what he had learned from his brother Heinrich to affirm this possibility, exegeting Paul's words that we must act, 'knowing the time'. Plato had solved a famous difficulty about the move from rest to motion with his notion of the *exaiphnes*, the 'moment' (Jüngel 1986: 67/8). Given that Barth had also been reading Kierkegaard, it must also be possible that the language of 'the Moment' is derived from him, or from Plato via Kierkegaard's mediation.

REVOLUTIONARY THEOLOGY

At the end of the commentary Barth turned to the task of theology, in what is clearly a response to Overbeck, from whom he takes the description of the 'fatal prattle of systematic theology' (R2: 333). Of course our language cannot break through to the Absolute, but nevertheless, alongside and indeed, tragicomically, *in* all orderly, regular, bourgeois possibilities of reflection, there exists the revolutionary possibility of theology, which is an out-and-out onslaught on kitsch! (R2: 529). Yes, theology is a totally unpractical and non-religious undertaking, but only because it is concerned with the most practical of all human desires. It represents an unheard-of attack on the human being who seeks security because it is aware that every human venture can be no more than a demonstration or parable. It attacks the nerve-centre of the self-confidence of those who find their security in 'science' (a claim which obviously angered Harnack). Its witness to the gospel constitutes this revolutionary *attack*. Only as it makes this attack does it deserve its place in the academy. Theology is, in essence, an abnormal, irregular, dangerous revolutionary attack on the things the secure human being takes for granted. Why? Because this is what follows from taking its object seriously. 'To be scientific means fidelity to the object. Fidelity to the object in theology is unconditional respect before the uniqueness of the theme . . . humanity in its ultimate distress and hope, humanity before God' (R2: 531). 'Theology today can be based on nothing but daring', is what Barth had taken from Overbeck. This venture or dare (*Wagnis*) becomes a whole manifesto: it is theology which is responsible for setting a question-mark at the outermost edge of the university and of all civilization, and this is why its place within the *universitas litterarum* is vital. Given that, it is a scandal, and one he sought to redress in both commentaries, 'how utterly harmless and unexceptionable most commentaries on the Epistle to the Romans and most books about Paul are' (R2: 13). The Epistle must be read as an advance into the absolute. 'It is theology, a conversation about God, undertaken with penetrating understanding of the One in all. Abnormal, irregular, revolutionary, the Epistle to the Romans is the catastrophe of all catastrophes, the predicament in all other predicaments' (R2: 530). The thirteen volumes of the *Church Dogmatics* were an attempt to try and register this abnormality and to make clear precisely how Christianity was a revolutionary force. The understanding of how theology relates to exegesis which we find in its pages was first forged in struggling with Paul's text. Though the world has moved on, and the context is different, and despite a mountain of commentary on Barth's work, in respect of the understanding of theology which emerged in the course of his struggle both commentaries still—wait.

Works Cited

Barth, Karl (1985), *Der Römerbrief,* 1st edn. 1919, ed. H. Schmidt. Zurich: Theologischer Verlag.

——(1933), *The Epistle to the Romans,* trans. E. Hoskyns. Oxford: Oxford University Press.

——(1978), *Der Römerbrief,* 2nd edn. Zurich: Theologischer Verlag.

Beintker, M. (2005), 'Johann Tobias Beck und die neuere Evangelische Theologie', *Zeitschrift für Theologie und Kirche,* 102/2 (June), 226–45.

——(1985), 'Der Römerbrief von 1919', in G. Sauter (ed), *Verkündigung und Forschung: Beihefte zu Evangelische Theologie,* 2nd edn., 2–28. Munich: Chr. Kaiser Verlag.

Jüngel, E. (1986), *Karl Barth: A Theological Legacy,* trans. G Paul. Philadelphia: Westminster.

Marquardt, F. W. (1985), *Theologie und Sozialismus—Das Beispiel Karl Barths,* 2nd edn. Mainz: Grünewald Verlag.

Plonz, S. (1995), *Die herrenlosen Gewalten: Eine Relektüre Karl Barths in befreiungstheologischer Perspektive.* Mainz: Grünewald.

Winzeler, P. (1982), *Widerstehende Theologie.* Stuttgart: Alektor Verlag.

Further Reading

Burnett, R. (2004), *Karl Barth's Theological Exegesis: The Hermeneutical Principles of the Romerbrief Period.* Grand Rapids, Mich.: Eerdmans.

Webster, J. (2005), *Barth's Earlier Theology.* New York: T. & T. Clark.

CHAPTER 41

AUGUSTINE AND PELAGIUS ON THE EPISTLE TO THE ROMANS

MARK EDWARDS

PERHAPS no scriptural passage has divided the church so bitterly, or so often, as the ninth chapter of the Epistle to the Romans. Predestinarian readings take two forms, one of which maintains that God predestines us to salvation or reprobation in the light of faith or works foreseen, the other that this predestining is itself the unconditioned cause of the good that he foresees. Both can claim the authority of Augustine, the foremost theologian of the first millennium. His adversary Pelagius found a different stratagem—not unknown in modern times—which enabled him to deny that Paul endorsed any species of predestination. To explain how each arrived at his conclusions, we must first sketch the theology of salvation that each set out to reconcile with the difficult text of this epistle.

THE COMBATANTS

Augustine, born in Africa in 354, was a heretic in his youth, then a hesitant Platonist, before he embraced the catholic faith in 386. If we believe the *Confessions*, he was a seeker, not yet a servant of the gospel, when he came upon Paul's account of the divided soul in the seventh chapter of Romans. From this he learned that Plato had been wrong to maintain that knowledge suffices for virtue, since our members are inhabited by an evil soul, so intractable to reason as to make it impossible to perform good works without divine succour. Some years later, a troubled meditation in Milan was interrupted by the cry 'take up and read', and when Augustine turned at hazard to Romans 13:13 he was cut to the heart by the admonition: 'not in rioting and drunkenness, not in chambering and wantonness, not in strife and envying, but put ye on the Lord Jesus and make not provision for the flesh.' As the meaning of this text lies on the surface, the interpretation of it does not exercise Augustine in later writings; on the other hand, it is Romans 7 and 8 that detain him longest in an otherwise cursory *Exposition of Certain Tenets from the Letter to the Romans*, which he wrote around 394.[1] His principal interlocutors were the Manichees, his former instructors, who held that we are bound for eternal darkness or eternal light by virtue of our possessing more of one than of the other in our composition at birth. One goal of his *Exposition*, then, is to show that, since an all-powerful and benevolent God cannot be the author of sin, the cause of this, and hence of the reprobation justly attached to it, must lie in the free will of the sinner. This principle, that damnation cannot be just unless it is voluntary, he upheld throughout his life; yet he also came to hold—at least as early as 397, when he commended a new exegesis of Romans 9 to Simplicianus of Milan—that the absolute sovereignty of God would be infringed if it were in our power to decide whether he would save us. In subsequent works he contends not only that God's aid is required to accomplish whatever good we will, but that the will to good itself is inert unless it is quickened by the Holy Spirit. Some passages, even in his mature works, seem to allow the will some part in accepting or resisting the divine initiative (e.g. *On the Spirit and the Letter* 60); others imply, however, that the sovereignty of God would be abridged if we were free to resist his will. It is only by divine foreordination that we can persevere, for sin is never wholly exorcized from the fallen body this side of death. Adam, who could have avoided sin, lacked the gift of perseverance; the saints receive that gift to make them worthy of the gift of sinlessness in the life to come (*On Punishment and Grace* 26–32).

These arguments matured in a long dispute with Pelagius, a British monk who learned of Augustine's views when he came to Italy. He protested that the lax Christians of this region, once convinced that no act of will could save them, would happily conclude that no act of will could mend their vices. Against this sophistry he urged that, while it is God who endows us with the *posse*, or power of attaining perfection, we are the ones who supply the *velle*, or will to exert that power. The state of being perfect—the *esse*—is thus the joint outcome of divine grace and

---

[1] Text of this and the *Inchoate Exposition*, ed. J. Divjak, *Corpus Scriptorum Ecclesiasticorum Latinorum* 64 (Vienna, 1971).

creaturely endeavour (Augustine, *On the Grace of Christ* 5). Admitting that perfection was rare, he maintained that some had achieved it, and that those who had the pattern of Christ before them should aspire not merely to live without sin but to mortify the appetites by celibacy and other forms of abstention. While he did not believe,[2] with his friend Celestius, that Adam had been created mortal and injured only himself by his transgression, he appears to have held that his offspring suffered not by inheritance but by imitation. As each falls by his own indiscretion, so each is saved by his own resolution, with no hope of vicarious absolution, though with some assistance from the Holy Spirit.

The commentary on Romans now attributed to Pelagius was transmitted under the name of Augustine's mentor Jerome;[3] it is, however, clearly a later work than the *Exposition*, as it skirmishes at times with the later teachings of Augustine. In the following comparison, then, the *Exposition* takes precedence, to be followed by any reflections which betoken a subsequent change of thought, before we turn to Pelagius. Their comments will be most conveniently paired in stages, each corresponding to a natural division of the letter. In chapters 1 and 2 Paul contends that Greek and Jew alike have broken faith with the God who spoke to them by different revelations. In chapters 3 and 4 he shows that neither can be reconciled by works, but only by the faith of Abraham, the uncircumcised progenitor of Israel. Chapters 5 and 6 contrast the universal consequences of Adam's sin with the universal efficacy of Christ's death: much turns on the exegesis of Romans 5:12, *in quo omnes peccaverunt*, which the author whom we know as Ambrosiaster had understood to mean that Adam was the one 'in whom' all have sinned.[4] Chapters 7 and 8 contain a sorrowful affidavit, in the first person, to the inescapability of sin, followed by a celebration of freedom in the Spirit; it was widely agreed that the superficial reading, which takes Paul for the speaker in chapter 7, does not sit well with the character of the apostle. In chapters 9–11 Paul asserts that neither the willing nor the merit of any people, the Jews included, could determine the choice of God; no commentator before Augustine, however, had been willing to infer that faith itself is a gift awarded at God's pleasure. As neither man challenged the cardinal tenets or principles of the other in his exegesis of chapters 12–16, they need not be considered in the present survey.

---

[2] For his answers at the synod of Diospolis (415) see R. Rees, *Life and Letters of Pelagius* (Woodbridge, 2000), 131–5.

[3] T. de Bruyn, *Pelagius' Commentary on Romans* (Oxford, 1993) finds citations of the commentary in Pelagian literature as early as 413, and in Augustine's *On the Merits of Sinners* (412), though he also finds evidence of subsequent revision in 412 or 413.

[4] *Sancti Ambrosii Opera* 2.2 (Benedictine edn., Paris, 1845), 92. See B. Leeming, 'Augustine, Ambrosiaster and the *massa perditionis*', *Gregorianum*, 11 (1930), 58–91.

CHAPTERS 1 AND 2

In his *Exposition* Augustine nowhere ascribes a single purpose to the letter. He does, however, argue that the invective against the gentiles is the justification of Paul's apostolate, since it would be unjust to condemn them for their delinquencies without offering them the chance to share in the blessings of the righteous (p. 4.10–13 Divjak). He also contends that the Jew is already included with the gentile in the denunciation of those who chide their neighbours without passing judgement on themselves (Rom. 2:1 at 5.15–20 Divjak). Pelagius states that the purpose of the epistle is to pacify the dispute which had arisen between the Jews who claimed the privilege of election before the coming of the gospel and the gentiles who retorted that if God's bounty to the Jews was greater, so they committed a greater sin in flouting the law and repudiating Christ (p. 57 Bruyn). Paul concludes his preface and introduces his argument at 1:7 with the admonition that Jew and the Greek alike are saved by the righteousness of faith (p. 61). He next upbraids the gentiles for their want of faith, which leads them to abandon the author of nature, with the consequence that they trespass the natural order and become subject to impiety, which, according to Pelagius, takes the threefold form of secession from God, the dishonouring of one's kin, and a malicious disposition towards one's neighbours (pp. 63–4). The dictum at Romans 2:11 that only those who obey the law will be justified is a reproach to Jew and gentile alike, for to say with Paul that gentiles may be a 'law unto themselves' is to say that they too possess a law which makes them amenable to judgement (p. 72). The sinner is inexcusable because he has been given the capacity for righteousness if he would but exert his will (p. 73).

But in what sense did the Jew fail? Romans 2:21–3 is occasionally translated in modern versions as a battery of questions which invite an affirmative answer: 'you who say *do not steal, do not commit adultery, shun idolatry,* do not you commit theft, adultery and sacrilege?' In fact, however, the Greek, if it is a question, has to be rendered: 'you who say *do not steal,* do you steal?' To this a Jew could readily answer, 'no': if abstinence from adultery, theft, and sacrilege were the test of a blameless life, it could not plausibly be maintained that all have sinned. If, on the other hand, the question-marks have no authority and the original was conceived as a series of statements—'you, who say do not steal, are a thief', and so on—the argument can proceed without the cooperation of the interlocutor, and Paul's words can be invested with a deeper sense that enables him to charge the Jews with crimes of which they would never accuse themselves (pp. 74–5). Finding no interrogative punctuation in the Latin text, Pelagius applies the accusation to the inner man: adultery is the yielding of the soul to another power than its creator, sacrilege any crime against God, and theft the occlusion of Christ by stiff-necked adherence to a carnal understanding of the scriptures. The Jew not only violates his own law in his public conduct, but defies the spirit while he observes the letter, failing to recognize (for example) that the second circumcision performed by Joshua prefigured the circumcision of the heart that Christ effected by his ministry (p. 76). Pelagius echoes the Sermon on the Mount when he interprets Paul's definition of the true Jew at Romans 2:29 as a charter for the transference of the external mandates to the inner man (p. 76).

CHAPTERS 3 AND 4

From chapter 3 Augustine chooses only verse 20 for detailed exposition: '*For no flesh is justified in his sight in the law, since through the law is knowledge of sin.*' His gloss, reproduced in his subsequent exposition of Galatians, is an adumbration of four 'steps' in the perfection of human rectitude. Before the law we pursue the desires of our sullied hearts, under law we strive with the passions but succumb, under grace we begin to prevail, and in the peace which the saint attains after death the regenerate body is free of all temptation (6.17–9.4). Commenting on Romans 4:2–4, Augustine warns that if we aspire to conquer sin by merit rather than grace, we incur a debt while disowning the means of payment (9.10–25). As it was faith, not works, that justified Abraham so it is faith that justifies the impious, not in the sense that it absolves him from the necessity of working, but in the sense that it empowers him to perform the works that none can perform alone (10.4).

Pelagius is the one commentator of ancient times who reads the answer to the apostle's question 'what advantage has the Jew?' at Romans 3:1 as a vaunting speech put into the mouth of the Jew himself (p. 80). On this view, it is not Paul but his interlocutor who imagines that, because God cannot lie, his promises to the Jews remain unshaken when the whole people is forsworn. If that were so (Pelagius continues, now in the person of the apostle), there would be no reprobation of sinners and the doctrine that Paul repudiates at 3:8—'let us do evil that good may come'— would be the gospel (p. 81). The assertion in 3:21 that righteousness has now been made apparent without the law means not the law is overthrown but that Christ set forth a pattern of obedience which the law could not display (p. 82). The conclusion at 3:28 that one is justified without the works of the law is an exhortation to perform the works of grace (p. 83). Justification by faith without works is promised at 4:5 to those who have entered the covenant from without, not to sinners within the covenant (p.85); from the benediction on Abraham we learn not that naked faith is righteousness but that righteousness is the circumcision that God demands of us (p. 86). Faith enables where the law condemns, and it is by faith that we escape the constraints of fallen nature, seeking perfection after the example of the saints (p. 88).

CHAPTERS 5 AND 6

Augustine comments only on the second half of chapter 5 in his exposition, and only to find a series of variations on the principle that the law condemns but cannot cure our sins. According to his text of Romans 5:14, death falls on those who have *not* sinned after Adam's likeness; since he understands sinning after Adam's likeness to signify the infringement of a positive command, he implies that the sin which is not after Adam's likeness is unconscious disobedience to the law (11.14–15). Paul's dictum, that the law came in that trespasses might abound, suffices to demonstrate that Jews who hope to be sanctified by the law do not know for what purpose it was given (13.7). The proclamation at 6:6 that the 'old man' has been crucified interprets, and is interpreted by, the curse on the hanged man at Deuteronomy 21:23, which touches Christ in so far as he takes the delinquencies of the old man on himself (14.3–16). To be under grace in this life, as Augustine explains in his comment on 6:14, is not to be perfect, but to disenthrall the inner man from the weaknesses and transgressions of the flesh (14.21–2).

A verse neglected in the *Exposition*, Romans 5:12, became the cornerstone of his later writings against the Pelagians. His reading of the author whom we know as Ambrosiaster had persuaded him that that clause which the Greeks took to mean 'because all sinned' should be construed instead with reference to Adam, as the one 'in whom all sinned' (*Against Two Letters of the Pelagians* 4.7). He deduced that the whole posterity of Adam was in his loins at the time of the first transgression, and consequently liable to the same punishment, except in the miraculous case of Jesus Christ, who had not been fathered as Adam fathered Seth. Appeals to the Greek and the practice of other interpreters left him unmoved, as it now appeared to him that no other theory could account for the universality of sin.

Pelagius begins his exegesis of chapter 5 by resolving the whole of the letter so far into a single proposition: 'He urges them to be at peace, since none is saved by his own merit, but all are saved in the same way by God's grace' (p. 89). This grace, we learn, includes the pledge of immeasurable glory for those who weather the modest sufferings of the present life, neither shirking Christ's injunctions nor disdaining the promise of the Holy Spirit at 5:5 (p. 90). As we live by the imitation of the second Adam, so it was 'by example or by pattern' that we incurred the death that was merited by the first Adam (p. 92). In his comment on 15:15 Pelagius pauses to canvass the theory that we inherit Adam's moral infirmity by transmission. Against this latter view he records three arguments, all put into the mouth of another, though none is rebutted (p. 94). The objector, who bears a strong likeness to Rufinus the Syrian,[5] an author of the fourth century, urges first that if those who do

---

[5] E. Teselle, 'Rufinus the Syrian, Celestius, Pelagius: Explorations in the Prehistory of the Pelagian Controversy', *Augustinian Studies*, 3 (1972), 61–95.

not sin on their own account are condemned with Adam, those who do not believe on their own account should be saved by Christ. Next, if the purpose of baptism is to wash away Adam's legacy, the child whose parents are both baptized will be born without pollution. Finally, if we inherit the flesh from our parents but receive the soul from God, it is the flesh alone that should be required to expiate the vices of its ancestors. Pelagius seems tacitly to endorse these positions, interpreting the statement at 5:12 that all have sinned as a hyperbole and denying that death has any just dominion over those who have not sinned, as Adam did, by flouting a positive commandment (p. 93).

Christ forgives sins freely, and it is baptism, rather than merit, that brings righteousness (p. 94). This righteousness, however, is the following of Christ that supervenes upon forgiveness (p. 95). To be buried with Christ in baptism, in accordance with the apostle's exhortation in chapter 6, is to yield our vices one by one to death as he surrendered the whole of his body to crucifixion (pp. 96–7). The mortal should live as though it were immortal, every member should become a weapon of rectitude, and this voluntary deliverance of the body will suffice to refute the Manichaean tenet that evil is mixed indelibly in its constitution (p. 99). Cooperative grace is nonetheless required to teach the believer what it is to be free in the service of God (p. 100).

CHAPTERS 7 AND 8

Chapter 7 begins with a parable, which many find equivocal: are we freed from the conjugal tyranny of the law by the death of the law or by our own (pp. 100–2)? Augustine finds the comparison of the law to a jealous husband not quite congruent with its object. In wedlock the woman is subject to the man, and there is no third; in the predicament of the sinner under law, by contrast, the soul is the bride of her overmastering passions, while the law sits over both to enforce the dominion of those passions, thereby rendering the soul more conscious of her own subjection. It is not by the extinction of sinful passion, but by the death of the soul herself to sin, that the power of the law is annihilated. The simile is of universal application, for he who exclaims at 7:8–9 that sin was dead in him before he heard the law and has now revived is speaking only of what was apparent to him. The law not only exposes his transgressions but multiplies them, since the consciousness of breaking a law makes evil more alluring. At the same time, it remains true that the law is good and that its principal office is not to make us sin but to make sin visible: it is those who live under the Spirit, not under law, who obey its mandates without any difficulty, because they themselves are conformed to the law—that is, to Christ the Word. The same Christ, vouchsafing his own blood as a ransom to the devil, takes upon himself the image of the sinner who complains at 7:14 that he is 'sold under sin'. The incontinent man's confession at 7:15 that his sin becomes more apparent to him even while he knows not what he does reveals the paradoxical character of his disobedience; only as he pursues his lament at 7:19 does Augustine decide that the speaker is a man 'under law, before grace', and therefore not the apostle in his current state. The final ejaculation, in which the law of God in the mind is opposed to the law of sin in the flesh, is made in the person of the man under grace, who, having embraced the mercy of Christ, no longer feels the rebellion of his members as his own sin.

Augustine holds, with Pelagius, that the law is made weak by the turpitude of the flesh. Christ, he continues, assumed this flesh to mortify it and thus put away this obstacle to obedience. The wisdom of the flesh is said at 8:7 to be at odds with God because it is not subject to his law; this means, however, not that the flesh does not obey but that it obeys through fear of losing worldly goods. Until fear is expelled by the Spirit, the body's attempts to escape the burdens of mortality will be mortal to the soul. The spirit that holds the graceless man in bondage is not his own—for the human spirit was created good and is capable of conversion—but that of the devil to whom all those who are dead in spirit have been made subject. The creature which Paul declares to be subject to vanity in expectation of God's design (Rom. 8:20) is not, in Augustine's view, the vegetable or the animal creation, for only the Manichees endow such beings with sentience. Nor can it be the angelic race, which is now sure not to fall; it is that element in humanity which, though made by God, remains unreconciled to him. The elect are those predestined to salvation, not because he has arbitrarily decreed it, but because he foresees their faith.

In subsequent works, including the minute examination of chapter 7 which he addressed to Simplicanus of Milan, Augustine still opines that the speaker is a man who is under law but has yet to receive the infusion of grace that accompanies faith. At *Retractations* 23.1 he reports that subsequent study convinced him that the speaker is Paul himself. This change of opinion strengthened Augustine's hand against the Pelagians, for if Paul were not the speaker in chapter 7 there would be no evidence that he was conscious of any moral defect and hence no proof from scripture of the ineradicability of sin.

Pelagius holds that the law is the subject throughout Paul's simile in the first seven verses. The husband who is likened to the law is dead when he lacks the power to punish. That power is taken from him by the atrophy of sin; it is not the human subject but the law that dies when sin dies, leaving the soul free to contract an enduring union with Christ. If Paul speaks openly of the mortification of sin but fails to complete the analogy by announcing the death of the law, that is because he must speak with caution to the Jews (p. 101). The law is not deadly to us because it engenders sin but because of its severity in the chastisement of the sin that infests the unregenerate soul (pp. 101–2). Paul in verse 7 adopts the person of one who first received the commandments when he was already in the habit of breaking them, a violator of natural law whose intellect is so darkened that he literally does not perceive covetousness to be a sin (p. 102). Such a man can say at 7:7 that he was alive before the law in so far as he thought himself alive. When he receives its ordinances, but persists in flouting them, his sin is all the more culpable. This is not to say that the law is a cause of sin: the Marcionites who impugn the law fail to see that in this passage the law is nothing but the minister of the death that the speaker has merited by his perversity (p. 103). Once he consents to the law, his understanding of natural morality is restored; his conscience, however, is now at odds with his ingrained disposition to sin which Paul locates in the outer man, or body (pp. 104–5). That the speaker is not Paul, in his present state at least, is apparent from 7:24, where he throws himself for the first time on the grace of Jesus Christ (p. 105).

Paul's reference to a law of the spirit at 8:2 is sufficient proof that the law works for the ends of grace (p. 105). It is weakened, as 8:3 indicates, by the flesh. It was therefore the task of Christ to assume the likeness of flesh—a likeness which, as in Adam's begetting of Seth in his likeness at Genesis 5:3, comprehends the reality—in order that he might conquer temptation and prove that it is the will, not the flesh itself, that contradicts the will of God (pp. 106–7). We may say that the sin of the devil has been condemned by the sin of the Jews (p. 106); we must not say, with the Manichees, that the flesh and God are naturally at war (p. 107). The fruit of Christ's work is not received vicariously but by imitation; in his comments on 8:11 and the subsequent verses, however, Pelagius makes it clear that when the works of the Spirit supersede the works of the law it is because the Holy Spirit comes to dwell in the believer (p. 108). The presence of the Spirit is attested in prayer, as Paul avers at 8:16; the glory that Paul foresees at 8:18 is the meed of forgiveness, though the believer has still to expiate his past sins by a physical death (p. 109). Paul declares at 8:19 that the whole creation awaits the fulfilment: whether this signifies the deliverance of the lower world from corruption, the satisfaction of longing in the angels, or the redemption of Adam and Eve (p 110), it is not achieved without the cooperation of those who are saved. God's predestination is explicitly said at 8:29 to be based on his foreknowledge; those whom he foreknew he is said to have called, and by a call we commonly mean a summons which invites but does not compel obedience (pp. 112–13). Christ himself was 'given up' so that his example would not impair our freedom (p. 113); the assurance that nothing separates the saint from God at 8:39 is understood to mean not so much that we cannot fall as that we cannot be vanquished by external powers (p. 114).

CHAPTERS 9–11

The younger Augustine grants that if Paul were to deny that our election is contingent on any motion of ours, his reasoning would deprive us of free-will. At the same time, it appears to him that the logic of chapter 9 tells no less strongly against election on the basis of works foreseen than against election on the basis of works accomplished. According to his reading of chapter 9, it is not the works that God foresees but the assent of the human will to his initiative. It is only after the will inclines to God that it is empowered by the Spirit of love to perform good works; the inclination cannot occur unless the will is prompted, and it remains true that the works which are then performed are the consequence, not the cause, of love. Since it is the call that arouses the faculty of volition, it cannot be said that anyone could will his own salvation. Consent to God's overtures, though free in us, is foreknown to him, and, as Paul declares at 8:30, he calls us only when it is foreseen. Predestination is thus the fruit of prescience. God's hardening of Pharaoh's heart, conversely, is no caprice but his anathema on a soul convicted already by its own obduracy. As Paul writes this to abase the pride of Israel, so in chapter 12 he reminds the gentiles that their calling is a work of grace, and not for their sake only, as God's design was to lead the Jews to penitence through emulation.

Treating chapter 9 again in his letter to Simplicianus, Augustine renounces the theory that election depends upon the foreseen assent of the one elected. That some do not assent is proved by the dictum, 'many are called but few are chosen'. It cannot be that the reprobate are those who resist a call that they might have answered, for an omnipotent God would be able, if he chose, to render the summons irresistible. As it is God who creates the will to believe, so it is God who hardens the will against his own proclamation. Intransigence being the natural condition of the fallen soul, this hardening is nothing but a surrender of the will to its own devices; Pharaoh suffers it not because he is more obstinate than others but because God made him a vessel of his wrath. It would, as Paul says, be presumptuous for the fallen creature to plead against its creator, as it is presumptuous in a debtor to complain that his debt has not been remitted, or to construe the remission of it as an index of his own merits. To anticipate the objection that his theory, like that of the Manichees, imputes indelible vice to half the creation, Augustine reasons that when God creates a vessel of wrath, his wrath is directed not to the vessel itself, but to the sin.

Pelagius characterizes chapter 9 as the beginning of a process against the Jews, which is pursued with evident sorrow, and tempered at 9:7 by the hint that, if 'not all' Jews are children of Abraham in the sight of God, there are some who remain secure in their inheritance because they have faith in Christ (pp. 115–16). God's foreknowledge of merits was the cause of his subordinating Ishmael to Isaac and Jacob to Esau; the ground of merit is said to be faith, which in some variants is not even qualified by the word 'subsequent' (p. 116). Paul's statement that the dis-possession of Esau was the consequence not of his works but of God's calling (Rom. 9:12) is construed to mean that Esau was condemned because God foresaw his impenitence, not that his impenitence was predestined (p. 117). The citation from Moses at 9:15—'I will have mercy on whom I will have mercy'—reveals elliptically that God is moved to compassion by his foreknowledge of our deserts (p. 117). The comment in the next verse, that nothing depends on our willing or running but all on God, seems to Pelagius to contradict Paul's judgment on his own race at 2 Timothy 4:7, and is therefore ascribed to a hostile interjector (p. 118). Pelagius allows that Paul is speaking in his own person when he alludes to the hardening of Pharaoh's heart, but offers two palliative interpretations: either God made a spectacle of one whom he already knew to be incorrigibly vicious, or he hardened his heart by forbearance, in the knowledge that he would spurn the opportunity of repentance (pp. 118–19). What follows, from 9:19 to 9:29, is best understood, in Pelagius' view, as an interjection by one who falsely believes that God has the right to use his creatures without regard to our notion of justice. If the apostle speaks for himself at 9.20—'Who are you to answer God?'—he means not that God acts capriciously, but that *even if he did* the creature would have no right to upbraid him (p. 119). If verses 24–9 are spoken on Paul's account, they merely demonstrate that God did not show partiality to Israel; if they belong to the interlocutor, his argument is that God predestinates those whom he chooses to save (p. 120). Whether verse 30 is read as the coping-stone of a Pauline argument or the foundation of his reply to another man's sophistry, it is certainly the apostle who concludes the matter by showing that the elect are those who believe and the reprobate those who decline God's call (pp. 130–1).

Paul's judgment on his countrymen at 10:3—that, in pursuing a righteousness of their own, they fell short of God—is understood to signify not that it was impossible for the law to make them righteous but that they failed to obey it perfectly, and therefore failed to enjoy its fruits, which (as Pelagius declares in his comment on 10:6) were not reserved for the present life (p. 122). We may be surprised to hear, in his annotation to 10:5, that Moses himself knew of a righteousness by 'belief alone', distinct from that of works; yet here as elsewhere, it is evident that it is not the faith that suffices for salvation but the works that faith engenders (p. 122). Belief levels Jew and gentile, and the object of belief is the sacrificial love of God, which was foreshadowed in the prophetic conceit of his stretching out his hands to a stiff-necked people (pp. 123–4). The Jews have faltered, not so much because they relied on works as because they failed to supplement works by faith; election is gratuitous, but it would not be election if there were no criterion of merit (p. 125, on Rom. 11:5). As the Jews have been allowed to transgress in order to bring in the gentiles and thus provoke a renewal of ardour in those who were chosen first, it is clear that mercy and severity are attributes of the same God. Thus those who assign these properties to different gods are confuted (p. 128), and the end of chapter 11, where Paul testifies that all things originate from a single deity, gives the lie to the Arian tenet that the Word through whom all things were created is himself a creature (p. 131).

CONCLUSION

Pelagius and Augustine agree that their task is to ascertain what Paul meant at the time of writing. Neither makes use of allegory or undertakes to harmonize this text with other scriptures. Pelagius is more inclined to argue that Paul's consciousness of his audience, and the particular circumstances of composition, require him at times to say less than he believes. Statements at odds with his own thought which cannot be explained in accordance with this principle of economy are ascribed to a hypothetical interlocutor. This device (called *prosopopoeia* in antiquity[6]) is invoked only once in Augustine's *Exposition*, and even this rhetorical sanction against the plain reading is subsequently withdrawn when he takes a new view of chapter 7. One might suspect that his shifts in interpretation were the result of his having married successive prejudices to his reading; his account of the matter was that meditation and study of better commentators quickened his understanding. It is hard to contradict him, as the predestinarian reading has been endorsed by not a few of the most eminent theologians through the centuries. On the other hand, we should note that the texts which seemed most characteristic of him to admirers for a century after his death were not those that favoured absolute predestination, but those that implied that God calls whom he will, that those who are called have the power to gainsay him, and that the few who embrace him (meritless as they are) receive the grace to persevere.

[6] Cf. Origen, *Commentary on Romans* 6.9.46.

CHAPTER 42

LUTHER ON GALATIANS

PETER MATHESON

THE reception of Scripture has played a key role, often a highly controversial one, in virtually all reform movements in the church. At times it provided a blueprint for institutional change. At others, as in the case of the Lutheran reformation, the primary contribution was a hermeneutical one, although sweeping structural changes rapidly followed. Christian piety, too, individual and corporate, was radically refigured.

BIBLICAL HUMANISM

As the sixteenth century got under way, a European-wide resurgence of interest in the Pauline letters became evident, read less as proof-texts than as communications with a specific genesis and a particular audience. John Colet in England, Jacques Lefèvre in France, Gasparo Contarini in Italy, and Desiderius Erasmus illustrate the trend. Biblical humanism, with its linguistic and historical concerns, combined with a revival of Augustinian theology to encourage the liveliest interest in justification by faith and related issues. Much of this biblical humanism burgeoned outside the universities, at courts, in monasteries, around the new printing-presses in the towns. Lay interest was as prominent as that of reforming clerics, with a focus on daily life, work, and relationships. The initial appeal of Luther's writings in Germany was to personal spirituality and the nurturing of this by a new reading of Scripture. Luther was strongly influenced by his monastic superior, Johann von Staupitz, but from an early point struck out on his own path (Steinmetz 1980).

SCRIPTURE AND TRADITION

The process by which Scripture alone, *Scriptura sola*, elbowed out all other criteria was a remarkable one. The authority of church councils or hierarchies, and on occasion princely courts, was rudely challenged, while immemorial church traditions, feasts, festivals, and social conventions were toppled. The wild animal of Scripture ran free (Matheson 2006). There was a widespread conviction that the key to God's sovereign revelation to humanity had been found, enabling the believer to recognize, and then cross, the threshold from human perceptions to the inner sanctum of the divine. The Word of God was now clear to all (Ebeling 1968).

UNDERSTANDING LUTHER

Today, the comprehension of this process poses acute problems. We approach the interpretation of Scripture and of Paul, including the letter to the Galatians, from a post-Enlightenment perspective. We weigh up our judgements within a rich plurality of options. The imaginative leap required to grasp the elemental optimism of the Reformers about the clarity of Scripture is formidable; drawing analogies to contemporary biblical fundamentalism is misleading.

We are conditioned to assume that Scripture was being 'used' to promote a particular ideology; however, thousands of smudgy pamphlets from the early Reformation testify to the opposite conviction: Scripture's authentic message and God's own promise to his people had been re rediscovered! As Argula von Grumbach, a woman Reformer writing in 1523 put it, neither philosophy nor law nor tradition counted any more. 'I can detect no divine theology in (them)' (Matheson 1995: 90). True theology was to be found in Scripture alone.

Scripture was not seen as a book, an artefact contained within two covers, still less a collection of books (Althaus 1966: 72–104). It was quintessentially verbal, the person-to-person communication of a God who speaks, a *deus redens*. In the Lutheran Reformation the liberating Word, the Word that ran free, was inseparably bound to the letter of Scripture, which had to be authentically recovered by good humanist grammar and philology. The inner clarity of theological discernment, however, was essential to complement the outward clarity of the words (Lohse 1999: 187–95). The Word was the Johannine one, the living Word, was Christ himself, to which the Church itself was subject. To Luther's mind, Paul's thunder-bolt in the first chapter of Galatians demolished the wicked and blasphemous claim of the canonists and commentators that the Church stood in judgement over the Gospel (Pelikan 1963: 57).

LET THE LANGUAGE SPEAK

If it be true that all language is agonistic, every statement a refutation of countless others, then the tone, the style, the flair, as well as the content of Luther's remarkable commentaries will repay the closest attention. Ebeling's classic descrip-tion of Luther's achievement as a 'language-event', or *Sprachereignis*, has never been bettered (Ebeling 1970: 29 f.). The language and images of the Reformers have, as far as possible, to be read on their own terms, not adjusted to our understandings of them (Gregory 1999: 8–14). One pervasive image, taken from contemporary linen chests, is symptomatic: the lid which had obscured the contents of God's revelation has been finally removed.

One's first and last impression of Luther's commentary to the Galatians is its lyricism. Like an orchestral symphony, it takes up a number of key themes and proceeds dynamically to develop, expand, vary, and repeat them in a myriad of different ways, descriptively, logically, and rhetorically, in Latin and in German. The English translation by Jaroslav Pelikan, based on the 1531 printed edition, excellent as it is, cannot convey how Luther commuted between Latin and German in his original lectures, often within a sentence. The German earths or points up an affirmation: 'Don't say: I am perfect, *I've arrived!*', 'Noli dicere: perfectus sum, bin hin vber' (Freitag 1911: 321); or it smuggles in a punchy proverbial saying: 'Many a scoundrel is concealed under a [doctoral] hat' (Freitag 1911: 403). The Rabelaisian flow of language partly explains what Luther himself recognized as the extraordi-nary expansiveness of the commentary (Pelikan 1964: 145, 147).

For Luther the 'discovery' of Paul, and of his 'delicious language' (Pelikan 1963: 155), was a source of endless joy, of open-mouthed wonder. Paul illumined the whole of Scripture, and Galatians was the highway to Paul. Galatians was his bride, his Katie von Bora (Tappert 1967: 20). The doctrine of faith it taught, the freedom from human moralities and traditions, from sin, guilt, terror, remorse, and death, and above all the deadly menace of the Law, was the fount of all good things:

worship, religion, knowledge, social harmony (Pelikan 1963: 3). His entire theology flowed from this doctrine (Pelikan 1964: 145). The reader is whirled along by his unwearying, passionate energy, the text pulsing along like a piece of Bach's music, the genial simplicity of the overall conception providing an assured sense of direction from beginning to end.

CULTURAL AND POLITICAL BACKGROUND

These lectures, Luther's second stab at a commentary on Galatians, were delivered in Wittenberg from 2 July to 12 December in 1531, when he was in his fifties. He writes with the confidence and panache of a mature scholar, one who has seen the 'Lutheran' cause win a degree of acceptance. The Augsburg Diet of 1530 had not removed his heretical stigmata or indeed the Imperial ban, but since the Diet Luther could have been excused for believing that he presided over a success story. In one sense he could relax. Melanchthon's Augsburg Confession had won Lutheranism political legitimacy of a sort. His student audience, too, was far removed from the heady enthusiasms and unpredictability of the early 1520s.

On the other hand, however, the fronts had hardened, not only against 'Rome' and the 'papists', but against the 'enthusiasts'. The Peasants' War of 1524–5, the greatest social conflagration in Europe before the French Revolution, had shaken German society to the core, and Luther put much of the blame for the latter on the 'enthusiasts' or Anabaptists. The Turkish armies, moreover, were actively threatening Christendom from the east. The flip-side to his lyricism, therefore, is the apocalyptic horizon against which the whole commentary was written. The Church was engaged in a quite desperate battle: and not against mere flesh and blood. For the papists and the 'fanatics', who crop up on virtually every page of the commentary, were but shadowy reflections of the cosmic struggle between God and the devil which had dogged the history of Israel and the Church from the beginning.

THE ACADEMIC LUTHER

Luther's commentary, then, shares Paul's lyricism and apocalypticism. There are, however, quite obvious differences. Paul was writing a letter, Luther was a professor, with an academic remit. He inherited the high-medieval assumption that universities were the natural locus for theology. Predictably, therefore, his commentary is studded with succinct summaries, precise analyses, definitions of key terms such as grace, peace, righteousness, freedom, long-suffering. He drew the attention of his student hearers to figures of speech such as synecdoche, or catachresis: 'in peace was my greatest bitterness' (Pelikan 1964: 43). He relished the careful distinctions of the well-trained dialectician, noting, for example, the legitimate place of active righteousness in worldly affairs as opposed to its futility in matters of salvation. He referred extensively, sometimes critically, to other scholars, especially the early Fathers, and offered more than a thousand quotations from other biblical books.

He insisted, too, as a good humanist, that we pay the closest attention to Paul's use of words, weigh them carefully, and read them in context: hope, for example, can mean both that which is hoped for and the feeling of hope (Pelikan 1964: 20). While a differentiation of faith and hope was by no means easy, the former referred more to intellect, knowledge, and dialectic, the latter to will, exhortation, rhetoric (ibid. 22). Luther had the professional's suspicion of autodidacts and scoffed at artisan preachers, deploring the shallowness of their religious experience and their paucity of learning, their pandering to the mob, the *vulgus imperitum* (Pelikan 1963: 46; Freitag 1911: 103). Even the eminent humanist Zwingli came under this condemnation (Pelikan 1959: 125)!

Yet Luther's lectures shared the existential and pastoral concerns of Paul. Virtually every page appealed to personal experience—his own or that of others—or mentioned the confusion of the poor, common folk, who do not know what or whom to believe, and the comfort which Paul's statements would offer them (ibid. 52). He personalized issues by presenting them as conversations between the individual and Christ, Satan, or a hypostasized 'Law'. He focused on the challenges which would face the future ministers of the Word: the temptation to vainglory, their need for confidence in their God-given calling. For only a pure ministry could safeguard the holiness of the Church.

Like Paul, too, Luther's faith statements moved back continually to his own immediate experience and forward to an engagement with the present and with God's future. For all their concern with linguistic and exegetical exactitude, Luther's lectures were conceived as a holistic theology, closer to what we might term systematic or pastoral theology today than to critical exegesis.

Luther's commentary repeatedly cuts through the brushwood of lesser concerns to highlight the liberation which was the central thrust of the Christian message. One of his students summarized: 'Luther's main concern was to transmit the article of justification: because it is so difficult we will remain students of it all our lives. If it takes root in our hearts we will not fall into the errors of the enthusiasts, whose work we see to our great dismay. Therefore we must exercise our faith, so that we do not become surrounded by these evil men who sneak up on all sides' (Brecht 1990: 455). Again and again, as if repetition could compensate for the inadequacy of his previous words, Luther reverts triumphantly to the doctrine of justification, and to warning against the unholy waves of desecration that were raging against God's grace, the one rock we can trust (Pelikan 1964: 145).

THE CENTRALITY OF CHRIST

True Christian theology, Luther insisted, began and ended not with God in majesty but with the Christ born of the Virgin and stretched out on the Cross. Here was our mediator and High Priest. Philosophical speculations about the nature of God were not only futile but precipitated terrifying encounters with the incomprehensibility, wisdom, and majesty of God. The believer must grasp that 'there is no other God than this Man Jesus Christ' (Pelikan 1963: 29) and 'run directly to the manger and the mother's womb, embrace this Infant and Virgin's Child in your arms' (ibid. 30). This alone would enable one to shake off all errors and alarms, for this human Christ was, as Paul taught, the true God, who conquered death, and trampled the devil underfoot. We are to begin and end, then, with Christ, the skilled artisan who conjures joy out of sadness, comfort out of terror, righteousness out of sin, life out of death (Pelikan 1964: 74). This was the path to holiness. Paul taught us that by Christ's grace we were all saints of God, whether prince or magistrate, minister or parent, master or servant, adult or child. Sainthood simply meant claiming Christ as our wisdom, righteousness, sanctification, and redemption, and proceeding to live out our lives in their varied callings in accordance with the Word of God (ibid. 82). All believers in Christ were saints.

DUALITIES WITHOUT DUALISM

Binary oppositions—law and grace, letter and spirit, flesh and conscience, works and faith—have long been recognized as a hallmark of Luther's thought (Ebeling 1970). We need to learn, Luther says, to be good dialecticians and make the right distinctions, to say to the Law: 'Law, you want to ascend into the realm of conscience and rule there ... You want to plunge me into despair, in order that I may perish. You are exceeding your jurisdiction' (Pelikan 1963: 11).

Luther read both Scripture and the text of personal and political life in conflictual terms. One reading informed (and at times deformed) the other. He pointed to Paul, at the beginning of his letter, in Galatians 1: 4, alerting us to the evil of this present age and to the struggle of the kingdoms of this world to extinguish the Gospel of Christ. This evil was unbelievably subtle; the overt fleshly sins were not the problem, but ignorance, hatred, pride, or deceit. The right discernment of these was a life-and-death matter (ibid. 41). The entire history of Israel and the Church demonstrated that Satan commended self-righteousness and appeared under the guise of godliness; and so 'Christ is a laughing stock among His own Christians'

(Pelikan 1964: 147). The devil was truly a clever trickster in this 'game'. He didn't come labelled 'the devil', but masqueraded as goodness incarnate, indeed as Christ himself: he was 'the white devil' (Pelikan 1964: 49). There could be no compromise in such key doctrinal matters as justification, unlike ethical issues, where forgiveness and tolerance should prevail (ibid. 111). 'Paul is concerned to instruct, comfort and sustain us diligently in a perfect knowledge of this most excellent and Christian righteousness', and those who profess an active righteousness, whether Jews or Turks or papists or sectarians, must be resisted because, 'if the doctrine of justification is lost, the whole of Christian doctrine is lost' (Pelikan 1963: 9). Such people are hirelings, not Christians, and peddle a deadly poison; we must resist their rational speculations, their legal demands and ceremonial fussiness, the asceticism to which they made themselves such 'precious martyrs' (ibid. 23, 49).

FREEDOM

Unsurprisingly, given its prominence for Paul, Christian freedom was a constant theme throughout the commentary. Commenting on Galatians 5:1, 'for freedom Christ has set us free', Luther rhapsodized: Christian freedom is immeasurable and ineffable, 'greater than heaven and earth and all creation', a joyous freedom of conscience, of freedom from the wrath to come, from the Law, from sin, death, hell, greater than 'the serpent himself with his head'. Yet, paradoxically, it took agonizing, study, meditation, discipline, and prayer to train one's spirit to embrace it, to exchange for ever the terrors of sin, and the guilt feelings incited by the devil, for 'the freedom of Christ, the forgiveness of sins, righteousness, life, and the eternal mercy of God' (Pelikan 1964: 4 f.). When the devil terrorized our conscience, therefore, we should remember Paul's call to freedom. If Christ appeared to us as a wrathful Judge, 'we should know for certain that this is not really Christ but the devil' (ibid. 11).

Paradoxically, again, this spiritual and theological freedom meant that in moral matters we were to be slaves, there for others. It must not be confounded with the political freedom of the rabble, a demonic freedom to say and do as one pleased (Pelikan 1963: 12; 1964: 4, 49). We must abide by our God-given calling. Some so-called evangelicals had debased the freedom of the Spirit into the licence and lust of the flesh, oppressed the poor, indulged in fraudulent business practices. They were the people of Gomorrah (Pelikan 1964: 50).

Our freedom was not one of the flesh. Indeed, as Paul stressed in Galatians 6:14, the lot of Christians in the world was suffering and rejection. 'Here Paul shows what true Christian boasting is, namely, to boast, rejoice, and be proud in suffering, shame, weakness . . .' The world hated, persecuted, condemned, and killed true Christians with a righteous zeal because they endangered both the spiritual and the earthly realm (ibid. 133). The stumbling-block of the cross could never be taken away (ibid. 44 f.). Persecution was a sign of the true Church.

Life of the Christian

This led into an extended treatment of the Christian life. Faith in God and love toward one's neighbour were what made one a complete Christian, inwardly and outwardly, 'regardless of whether the neighbor is a servant, a master, a king, a pope, a man, a woman, one who wears purple, one who wears rags . . .' (ibid. 30 f.). Holiness was to be worked out in daily life. Those who most loudly claimed to be holy were the most idolatrous. Paul was really asking in Galatians 5:14 why we vexed ourselves so anxiously with laws about foods, seasons, and sacrifices. For the love of one's neighbour was what was critical: putting up with impoliteness, ingratitude, and contempt, being patient with a cranky wife (!). And if one wanted to know how to love one's neighbour one should recall how one loved and looked after oneself (ibid. 56 f.). Our neighbour was no stone or log, devil or wolf, but a living creature like ourselves (ibid. 58). 'Christians should not be harsh and morose; they should be gentle, humane, affable, courteous, people with whom others enjoy associating . . .' (ibid. 94).

We would always remain simultaneously sinners and saints. The lack of realism about the sexual drive, for example, had led to endless hypocrisy (ibid. 67). Apparent victories over sexual desire led to the much worse sin of pride, regarding ourselves as holier than those who were married (ibid. 71). There were, anyway, infinitely worse sins than sexual ones: anger, idolatry, party spirit (ibid. 68, 89). We should not be too hard on ourselves, or lose heart when we faced the battle of the flesh (ibid. 72, 83). All God's saints had been through this battle; the despair we experienced could itself be redemptive (ibid. 73).

God's Righteousness

The gravity of our sins, though, which were 'infinite and invincible', could not be overstated. We should arm ourselves with the doctrine of faith for the onset of temptation in life and for the final struggle at death. 'Then you must be able to say with confident assurance: "Christ, the Son of God, was given not for righteousness and for saints but for unrighteousness and for sinners." ' (Pelikan 1963: 35). The personal, *pro me*, dimension was critical: 'That is, believe that Christ was given not only for the sins of others but also for yours' (ibid. 38).

The self-righteous could not avoid that presumption of confidence which excluded faith in Christ, and so ended up worse than the tax-collectors and harlots (Pelikan 1964: 14). For the more we tried to keep the Law the more we transgressed it. Paul had brutally pointed out (another thunderbolt) that those who put their trust in their own goodness were severed from Christ. By seeking to be justified by the Law, they made God a liar, and Christ redundant. 'These declarations and threats [of Paul] against the righteousness of the Law and against self-righteousness are terrifying...You must give up either Christ or the righteousness of the Law' (ibid. 17).

The 'synagogue' of the papists not only failed to listen to Paul, but exploited the terror of ordinary people, denouncing and excommunicating them, and exercising a wicked tyranny over the conscience (ibid. 110). This tyranny reflected the cosmic tyranny of the Law, sin, and death, through which the devil had always subjugated the human race (Pelikan 1963: 14). Fleshly vices were peccadilloes by comparison. The need to preserve the unity, love, and harmony of the Church could never excuse the tolerance of such abuses. Any love which was observed at the expense of the doctrine of faith was accursed (ibid. 38 ff.). Here, Luther said, I remain a tough nut: 'Ich wil hier der stoltz tropff, hart kropff sein' (Freitag 1911: 181).

He rejected utterly the view of the 'sophists', that when Paul spoke of faith working through love in Galatians 5:6 he meant that divinely infused faith must be formed by love. This was poor grammar. Paul was not saying that we are justified by love—far from it. Nor did he say anywhere that faith in itself was formless or ineffective. This was 'what happens to lazy readers and to those who superimpose their own ideas on the reading of Sacred Scripture' (Pelikan 1963: 29). They should pay careful attention to the words, and to their context, and focus on the intention of the particular passage. Paul was not talking about justification at all, but about the Christian life.

Context

How was Luther's understanding of Galatians affected by the context in which he wrote? First, there was the autobiographical factor. Luther refers frequently to his previous life in the monastery, and in particular to his experience of ascetic and penitential disciplines. The more he tried them, 'the more uncertain, weak and troubled' his conscience became (Pelikan 1964: 13, 73). This paralleled Paul's life before his conversion, and his dismay at the Galatians' reversion to obedience to the Law. Luther was also deeply influenced by humanism, not only in his close attention to language and grammar and the frequent reference to Hebrew and Greek terms, but in his sharp awareness of historical context (Junghans 1985). Luther took care to trace the occasion and necessity of Paul's letter: 'that right after he had gone away false teachers among the Galatians had destroyed what he had built up so painstakingly', these teachers being men of great prestige and authority, adherents of Judaism (Pelikan 1963: 14).

Luther was the child, thirdly, of his apocalyptic age. These false teachers were actually the devil's apostles. 'In fact, St Paul complains in this and in all his other epistles that even in his day Satan was displaying his skill at this business through his apostles' (ibid. 14 f.).

Luther believed that in his own day exactly the same was happening (ibid. 395, 414). He found direct parallels in the 'legalism' of the Anabaptists, which was a falling away from the original Reformation gospel. The Germans were as fickle as the Galatians had ever been (ibid. 47). His commentary repeatedly linked papists and Anabaptists, both of whom were demons, to Paul's false apostles (ibid. 148 f.). 'These wolves are joined at the tail, even though they have different heads': probably a reference, as Pelikan notes, to Judges 15:4 (Pelikan 1964: 149).

Paul's opponents, like Luther's, are 'bewitched', immune to all argument, and themselves bewitchers of others (Pelikan 1963: 194). The 'fanatics' or Anabaptists preyed on those already touched by the doctrine of faith, though they themselves were too fearful to work in papist territories—in reality, a baseless accusation (ibid. 221). Meanwhile the papists spread the calumny that the doctrine the Lutherans preached was subversive of all commonwealth, all harmony and order in society.

There could be no compromise with such legalists, any more than there was for Paul. All priests and monks, even the best of them, trusted in works and asceticism; their papal doctrine rendered Christ useless to us (Pelikan 1964: 18). 'With Paul, therefore, we boldly and confidently pronounce a curse upon any doctrine that does not agree with ours' (Pelikan 1963: 59). Paul's repudiation of the necessity of circumcision as a terrible fall from grace 'gives us marvelous comfort against the ragings of the papists, who persecute and condemn us as heretics because we teach this doctrine' (ibid. 19). One notes the two-way traffic in his arguments. The context in which Paul wrote led him to see his own situation as particularly intractable, while the conflicts with the Anabaptists and his Catholic opponents sharpened his own comprehension of Paul's radical criticism of the Galatians.

RHETORIC

An adequate comparison of Paul's rhetoric with that of Luther would far outrun the scope of this chapter, but it is important at least to raise the issue, for in the reception of Scripture sensitivity to its range of language and images is crucial.

Both Paul and Luther deployed dialectic and rhetoric with the greatest skill, and undoubtedly Luther felt at home in Paul's language, his 'wonderful words of comfort', his exalted and indignant discourse, as well as in the substance of his thought (Pelikan 1963: 32, 36). He appears to have had an intuitive feel for characteristically Pauline expressions, such as 'the world has been crucified to me' (Pelikan 1964: 135); note, too, his deep appreciation of Paul's 'rhetorical exclamation', or epiphonema, that through God we are no longer slaves but sons (Pelikan 1963: 389).

Luther shared Paul's flair for the memorable phrase and his delight in figures of speech (Matheson 1998: 111–31). Paul's language was on innumerable occasions described as a 'thunderbolt'. Both writers thought naturally in metaphorical terms. Luther declared: 'This flame, this raging fire in his [Paul's] heart, cannot be hidden' (Pelikan 1963: 21). Grace is rain. The 'old man' is an ass (ibid. 6 ff.). Hope is a captain battling against despair (ibid. 22). Preachers are royal emissaries (ibid. 16). Someone falling from grace is a man lost overboard (ibid. 18). The examples are endless. Luther delighted in the paradox and the vivid, if not extreme, statement, again not at all unlike Paul. 'For if you do not ignore the Law . . . you cannot be saved' (ibid. 6). 'Here Paul is a heretic', he crowed, when Paul argued that those who were circumcised could not keep the Law, because it was impossible without the Holy Spirit (Pelikan 1964: 131). Rome was worse than Sodom and Gomorrah, yet remained holy, because she retained the marks of the true Church: baptism, the Gospel, the holy name of God (Pelikan 1963: 24). Luther's lyrical tones echoed Paul's adulation of the fruits of the Spirit in Galatians 5:22. 'Joy is the voice of the Bridegroom and the bride. God is repelled by sorrow of spirit; He hates sorrowful teaching and sorrowful thoughts and words, and He takes pleasure in happiness' (Pelikan 1964: 93).

The rhetoric generally remained the handmaid of Luther's core concerns, unlike the coarse writings against the Pope and the Jews ten years later. The polemic was necessary, he argued, to underline the urgency of the crisis, the chasm between the options, the awesome consequences of a fall from grace. Yet even in this commentary the exaggeration shades all too often into distortion, and for this reader at least the categorical, comprehensive condemnation of all Anabaptists, all papists, all Jews and Turks becomes tedious, distracting, and counter-productive.

LUTHER'S UNDERSTANDING OF PAUL

Luther's admiration for Paul knew no bounds (Althaus 1966: 224–73). He was truly an emissary of Christ. Paul 'has nothing in his mouth but Christ' (Pelikan 1963: 32). 'For they are not listening to Paul; but in Paul they are listening to Christ himself and to

God the Father . . . ' (ibid. 16). Luther remarked repeatedly on Paul's fervour, his skilful language, his maternal gentleness in reproof (ibid. 4; Pelikan1964: 109 ff.). Yet although Paul was aware of the weakness of the flesh, and always understanding and encouraging, on the substance of the matter he was wonderfully resolute. Paul had to use such 'passionate words' in his advocacy of freedom in Galatians 5 and his anathemas against false teachers because the choice was between 'eternal freedom or slavery' (Pelikan 1964: 8). His very harsh judgement that circumcision made Christ null and void shows that 'Paul is profoundly moved and in great zeal and fervor of the Spirit he speaks sheer thunderbolts against the Law and against circumcision' (ibid. 9). Paul's boasting about his apostolic authority was necessary to safeguard the Gospel.

Luther may well rank with Augustine as one of the greatest interpreters of Paul. He owed much, of course, to his superior, Johann von Staupitz, and the Augustinian Order which formed his early years. He was anything but a solitary genius in sensing the appositeness of Paul's writings to the church and society of his time and in calling for a return of theology to Augustine and the Fathers. Yet it was no accident that his grasp of the 'edginess' of Paul coincided with his unique role in launching the Reformation. He grasped Paul's apocalyptic outlook and his radical critique of human sinfulness as few have done, before or after. After Luther, the interpretation of Paul could never be the same again.

Recent attempts, for example, to tone down Paul's critique of the Law, by limiting its scope to the validity for ritual prescriptions for gentile converts, have not found wide acceptance. In a recent article, Brendan Byrne, while suggesting that the true dichotomy may be between sin and grace, not Law and Gospel, has remarked on Luther's 'unparalleled interpretive perceptiveness' (Byrne 2000: 302).

However, difficult questions remain. Since the late 1970s a succession of outstanding scholars, such as N. T. Wright and James Dunn, have followed E. P. Sanders and Krister Stendahl in doubting whether Luther really understood Judaism and Paul's relationship to it. Many would question whether justification by faith was the hub of Paul's Gospel in the way Luther understood it, and some even suggest that his emphasis on faith alone has opened the door to modern individualism and anthropocentrism (Morgan 2003: 251). The debate continues.

Thus, the way in which his Galatians commentary circles around the *Anfechtungen*, the agonizing struggles of the individual believer, and the glorious assurance that faith in Christ remedies them, may be magnificent but ultimately reductive. These personal anxieties about salvation generated by guilt and sin and death do not appear to have the same centrality for Paul as for Luther. Moreover, the parallel he drew between Paul's situation when he wrote to the Galatians and his own, that is, of a desertion of the 'original' Lutheran Gospel by those of a legalist bent, may have led him to read Paul with his own agendas in mind, and to assume that his own opponents were but carbon copies of Paul's.

Finally, there is the vexed question of authority. As far as the 'papists' were concerned, Luther's assumption that Paul's 'Gospel' could be identified with 'his', and that those who opposed him came under Paul's condemnation as having fallen from grace, begged the question. Likewise, an Anabaptist or Spiritualist might reasonably argue that Paul's claim to an immediate apostolic authority from God supported their case rather than Luther's. The Wittenberger's admittedly subordinate argument, that he and his followers had a legitimate calling because it was based on the authority of a prince or magistrate unlike the 'pernicious and demonic spirits' (Pelikan 1963: 18 ff.), also carries little conviction today. The demonization of the 'papists' or the 'fanatics' in this commentary reflect the weakness of such arguments. The frequency of references to the devil, who takes centre-stage again and again, is truly extraordinary. It finds no parallel in Paul's letter. Satan or the devil is not mentioned at all in Galatians, or only indirectly, as this evil age or as the 'elements of this world' (Gal. 4:4, 9).

None of this, however, need be seen to detract from Luther's extraordinary achievement. His theological insight enabled him to develop an integrative principle around which the whole of Scripture could be interpreted as liberating. If this involved erecting a canon within the canon, it is hard to see how this could be avoided. Luther was no exception here. For Savonarola, the Dominican preacher to the poor, the prophetic books of the Old Testament set the tone for his reading of the entire Bible. For Erasmus, the Gospels illuminated everything else. For Luther, it was Paul. As an ardent young monk his spirituality had been formed by the Psalms, but it was the light which Romans threw on the Psalms which recast his understanding of righteousness. As the gift of Christ, it was transformed into a 'passive' righteousness.

This 'reading' of Scripture in turn presupposed a specific 'reading' of Christ, a theology of the Cross. The text was not to be spiritualized, allegorically or otherwise. Nor was it to be read literally. It was to be earthed in the Incarnation. *Sola Scriptura* meant *solus Christus*. Galatians was read as proclaiming the good news of the Christ who is God's self-giving to the godless and the undeserving.

WORKS CITED

ALTHAUS, P. (1966), *The Theology of Martin Luther*, trans. R. C. Schultz. Philadelphia: Fortress.

BRECHT, M. (1990), *Martin Luther: Shaping and Defining the Reformation, 1521–1532*, trans. J. L. Schaaf. Minneapolis: Fortress.

BRENDAN BYRNE, S. J. (2000), 'The Problem of Nomos and the Relationship with Judaism in Romans', *Catholic Biblical Quarterly*, 62/2: 294–309.

EBELING, G. (1968), *The Word of God and Tradition: Historical Studies Interpreting the Division of Christianity*, trans. S. H. Hooke. Philadelphia: Fortress.

——(1970), *Luther: An Introduction to his Thought*, trans. R. A. Wilson. London: Collins.

FREITAG, A. (ed.) (1911), *D. Martin Luthers Werke*, vol. 40. Weimar.

GREGORY, B. S. (1999), *Salvation at Stake: Christian Martyrdom in Early Modern Europe.* Cambridge, Mass.: Harvard University Press.

JUNGHANS, H. (1985), *Der junge Luther und die Humanisten.* Göttingen: Vandenhoeck & Ruprecht.

LOHSE, B. (1999), *Martin Luther's Theology: Its Historical and Systematic Development*, trans. R. A. Harrisville. Edinburgh: T. & T. Clark.

MATHESON, P. (1995), *Argula von Grumbach: A Woman's Voice in the Reformation.* Edinburgh: T. & T. Clark.

——(1998), *The Rhetoric of the Reformation.* Edinburgh: T. & T. Clark.

——(2006), 'The Reformation', in J. F. A. Sawyer (ed.), *The Bible and Culture*, 69–84. Oxford: Blackwell.

MORGAN, R. (2003), 'Paul's Enduring legacy', in J. D. G. Dunn, *The Cambridge Companion to Paul*, 242–56. Cambridge: Cambridge University Press.

PELIKAN, J. (1959), *Luther's Works: Introduction to the Exegetical Writings.* St Louis: Concordia.

——(ed.) (1963), *Luther's Works*, vol. 26. St Louis: Concordia.

——(ed.) (1964), *Luther's Works*, vol. 27. St Louis: Concordia.

STEINMETZ, D. C. (1980), *Luther and Staupitz: An Essay in the Intellectual Origins of the Protestant Reformation.* Durham, NC: Duke University Press.

TAPPERT, T. G. (ed.) (1967), *Luther's Table Talk.* In *Luther's Works*, vol. 54. Philadelphia: Fortress.

FURTHER READING

DUNN, JAMES D. G. (1993), *The Epistle to the Galatians.* London: A. & C. Black.

EDWARDS, MARK U. (1994), *Printing, Propaganda, and Martin Luther.* Berkeley, Los Angeles, and London: University of California Press.

WITHERINGTON, BEN (1998), *Grace in Galatia: A Commentary on Paul's Letter to the Galatians.* Grand Rapids, Mich.: Eerdmans.

WRIGHT, N. T. (1991), *Climax of the Covenant: Christ and the Law in Pauline Thought.* Edinburgh: T. & T. Clark.

....

CHAPTER 43

JOANNA SOUTHCOTT: ENACTING THE WOMAN CLOTHED WITH THE SUN

....

GORDON ALLAN

CRIME AND BANDITRY
DISTRESS AND PERPLEXITY
WILL INCREASE
TILL THE BISHOPS OPEN
JOANNA SOUTHCOTT'S BOX

This headline was seen regularly in the first half of the twentieth century over large parts of the British Isles. Its aim was to appeal to twenty-four bishops of the Church of England (the number is significant, as according to Rev. 4:4 around the throne of God are twenty-four elders who were identified with the twenty-four Anglican bishops) to open a wooden box containing manuscripts stored under lock and key since 1804. The group which was responsible for placing these advertisements was a religious society whose members believed that Joanna Southcott (1750–1814), the author of the manuscripts contained in the box, was the 'woman clothed with the sun' spoken of in Revelation 12:1 ('And there appeared a great wonder in heaven; a woman clothed with the sun, and the moon under her feet, and upon her head a crown of twelve stars'). The allusion to Luke 21:25 ('And there shall be signs in the sun, and in the moon, and in the stars; and upon the earth *distress* of nations, with *perplexity*; the sea and the waves roaring') might suggest that they were yet another sect proclaiming doom on the present generation, but the sentiments of the advertisement are only part of the story of a religious subculture of modern England whose effects were widespread and the full account of which remains to be given.

Members of this religious group, the Panacea Society, carried placards announcing this message, placed billboards in Piccadilly Circus in London's West End, and advertised on the sides of London buses. The group was small, composed mainly of women, and was only one of several who looked to Joanna Southcott as the 'woman clothed with the sun'. There were a number of other eighteenth-century claimants to be the embodiments of the Woman clothed with the sun, though Southcott was foremost among them. Mother Ann Lee, claiming to be Revelation's Woman, led a little group of Shakers from Manchester, England, to upstate New York in 1774. After 1780 Sarah Flaxmer and Mrs Eyre appeared in London, filled with the Sun-Woman, and in Ayrshire, Mrs Buchan embodied both St John's Woman and the Holy Spirit herself, readying her followers for the Second Coming (Burdon 1997: 99–100; Harrison 1979: 28–38). Also of relevance, half-a-century after Southcott, is the 'Girlingite' group, a little-known nineteenth-century charismatic and millenarian community of celibates led by Mary Ann Girling, a former Methodist who claimed to be a mystic and the female incarnation of Christ. This group has some affinities with Southcottianism in both its beliefs and practice. The distinctive attitude to gender roles and prophecy made the Girlingites something of a cause célbre, and its rise and fall suggest comparisons with Southcottian groups, all of which were dominated by the belief in the imminence of God's eschatological kingdom. The Girlingite community is believed to have been inspired and shaped in part by the American Shaker movement and Primitive Methodist worship and preaching of the 1830s, as well as Spiritualist and other beliefs and practices of the 1860s and 1870s.

Joanna Southcott's dramatic ministry was far better known, and when Southcott announced that she had been visited by the Holy Spirit in 1814 thousands of followers in London and throughout England prepared themselves to welcome Shiloh, her child, who was identified with the male child of Revelation 12:5. This is a reference to the obscure verse in Genesis 49:10, where the Authorised Version reads 'until Shiloh come', interpreted as a future messianic figure in Jewish interpretations of this verse. In the orthodox Christian biblical interpretation this messianic reference in Genesis 49:10 is said to be fulfilled in Christ. The Geneva Bible note comments: 'which is Christ the Messiah, the giver of prosperity who shall call the Gentiles to salvation.' What is distinctive about Southcott's interpretation (and indeed that of Richard Brothers, a contemporary prophet who claimed to be

Shiloh) is that the fulfilment of this prophecy is not specifically linked with Jesus Christ but with another messianic deliverer.

The Panacea Society was just one of a number of groups, scattered as far afield as Australia and Michigan, with a common origin in early nineteenth-century prophecy, and specifically the career of Joanna Southcott. The prediction of imminent doom was only one of the beliefs, which later included reinstatement of aspects of the Mosaic Law for Christians (though this was not advocated by Southcott herself), and competing beliefs among the different groups about which had the right to be the inheritors of Joanna Southcott's legacy. Her most distinctive belief, that she would give birth to a messianic child, led to the leaders of the various groups claiming to be the embodiment of the child. Taking their cue from Joanna Southcott herself, their reading of scripture not only included prophecy about the future but also attempts to relate biblical passages to individuals and the communal life of the different groups. Previous works on Southcott have not engaged in any detailed discussion of the techniques she used to establish her position. She draws on the authority which scripture held for her readers, and by skilful manipulation of the text, derives her own authority from it, thus 'proving' her claim to be a prophetic biblical figure. She adds support to her case by correcting the false evaluation of Eve's integrity and role in the Garden of Eden story and hence of women in general. This is part of a larger theological framework which includes a higher view of man's perfectibility and the ultimate restoration of all.

The Woman Clothed with the Sun

Southcott's origins were humble. She was born near Ottery St Mary, in rural Devon in the south-west of England, in 1750, the daughter of a tenant farmer. Her education was minimal, as was the norm for a country girl of that time. She was of a religious bent from her youth, steeping herself in the Bible and attending the local Church of England services. However, in 1792 she claimed to have heard the voice of the Spirit of Truth, warning that the coming of Christ was near at hand. She also prophesied about the weather, and local events and personalities, and when these predictions appeared to be fulfilled her reputation as a seer was established. Her role was not to be that of a local soothsayer, but as a prophet in the Old Testament sense—warning of God's coming judgements, and indicating how people might prepare for them and be protected through them.

Having moved to Exeter, and despite some initial interest from a local Anglican clergyman, Joseph Pomeroy, she began to attend Methodist meetings, but this initiative too led to disappointment. With money she had saved, in 1801 she published her first work (a pamphlet of forty-eight pages) *The Strange Effects of Faith*. This was to be the first of sixty-five publications to be completed before her death in 1814. From that very first pamphlet till the very end of her life, she claimed to be the 'woman clothed with the sun' of Revelation 12:1. She says in her first book: 'I am ordered to put in print, the woman in the 12th chap. of Revelation is myself, the 19th and last (chapters)' (Southcott, Book 1: 42). In her exposition of Revelation 12:1 she engaged in a form of allegorical exegesis, interpreting the sun as the light of truth, which the Woman dispenses, the moon as a symbol of Satan, while the world is under his power and in the darkness of night (Southcott, Book 16: 65; Book 4: 161). On the other hand, the Woman herself is literally understood, whereas all the other features are interpreted figuratively.

It was largely the move to print which led to her national profile and increased her following, for Southcott herself travelled little, nor did she preach in public except during a trip to the north of England from November 1803 to April 1804 (Brown 2002: 135–40). With the publication of her prophecies, and the move to London, she attracted several wealthy followers who financed her prophetic ministry (Juster 2003: 239–59). Tens of thousands of readers were reported to have bought her books of communications from the Spirit and, as a result were seeking to be 'sealed' for protection from the coming eschatological tribulation. The start of her prophetic ministry coincided with the war between England and France and her death took place only months before Wellington's defeat of Napoleon at the Battle of Waterloo in 1815. Thus, the social and economic situation was such that the times were particularly susceptible to the rise and acceptance of those who claimed a prophetic ministry (Burdon 1997). Many (including S. T. Coleridge in his 'Religious Musings') had seen the outbreak of the French Revolution in 1794 as a harbinger of the fulfilment of the apocalyptic promise of doom and hope. Southcott was not alone in reading the 'signs of the times' in this way (nor was she alone in claiming a prophetic charisma). Figures like Richard Brothers and, rather differently, William Blake also claimed a prophetic role. Southcott makes frequent reference to political events. The Irish rebellion of 1798 (which she claimed to have foretold in 1795), the possibility of invasion by the French (she was adamant that no invasion of England could be successful), the naval mutiny at the Nore in May, 1797 (which she also claimed to have foretold), and the French Revolution were all the cause of consternation among the public. Southcott's reassurances that the French would never be successful in any attempt to invade were undoubtedly popular, though her other predictions of famine and suffering prior to the return of Christ were not. The fact that Southcott engaged with these events in print, and identified them as evidence that the 'time of the end' had come, were undoubtedly fundamental factors in gaining her renown. In less turbulent times her claims to be the Woman clothed with the sun might well have passed unnoticed by the majority of the public.

INTERPRETING THE BIBLE

A hermeneutical tension pervades Southcott's writings. On the one hand she claimed authority to offer the true interpretation of the Bible, thus grounding what she said on what she found there rather than claiming to offer new revelation. Everything that she taught had to be measured against scripture: 'Now if any man will prove that I have spoken what I cannot bring scripture-proof for, I will give it up. Let men examine my writings, and point out any one passage or page they blame, and if I cannot find scripture-proof for it, then I will resign to man' (Southcott, Book 5: 232). On the other hand, the definitive meaning she offered led to what was in effect a new revelation—a revelation that was necessary in order to identify the Woman aright. Does this mean that her writings are themselves scripture, or on a par with the Bible? She claims to be 'opening up' the Bible rather than bringing a new revelation, but the dividing-line between the two is tenuous. Her sealed prophecies in her box apart, she regarded her words as having immediate relevance to a nation under siege. Drawing on words from Daniel 12:9, she claimed that the appropriate time for the proper understanding of the Bible has come. What is more, her vocation as the Woman is to 'break the seals' and reveal the truth: 'let them know, the spirit is the Spirit of Jesus, that is not come to seal up the sayings of the book, but to reveal them' (Southcott, Book 5: 232). In addition, the new dimension which was brought about by her own actualization of Revelation 12 inevitably set in train a new understanding of the divine purposes, as we shall see.

While Southcott claims that the Bible hangs together and its teachings formed a coherent whole, she makes herself the decisive interpreter, as until her time no one was able to grasp its true import: 'The word of God is as a book that is sealed, so that neither the learned nor the unlearned can read (that is to say, understand) it: for it was sealed up in the bosom of the Father, till he thought proper to break the seals, and reveal it to a Woman, as it is written in the Revelation' (Southcott, Book 1: p. iii). She positions herself as a prophet revealing the true meaning of the divine scriptures. Her role is to unseal those parts of scripture which God had chosen to keep secret till her time.

Joel 2 is a key text in her theology: 'And it shall come to pass afterward, *that* I will pour out my spirit upon all flesh; and your sons and your daughters shall prophesy, your old men shall dream dreams, your young men shall see visions: And also upon the servants and upon the handmaids in those days will I pour out my spirit... before the great and the terrible day of the LORD come.' This verse is quoted in Acts 2:17 in relation to the tongues of fire on the day of Pentecost, but Southcott applies it to her day and to her prophecy, thereby giving authority not only to her own prophecies but also in support of an expectation that there would arise other contemporary prophets, male and female.

In adopting her role as definitive interpreter of what is written in scripture, Southcott reflects key aspects of early Christian hermeneutics. In 1 Corinthians 10, for instance, Paul tells his correspondents that what has been written in former times only now achieves proper understanding; for Paul and his readers, like Southcott, believed that 'these things happened to them to serve as an example, and they were written down to instruct us, on whom the ends of the ages have come' (1 Cor. 10:11; cf. 1 Pet. 1:11–12).

Key to her biblical interpretation is the positive way in which she treats Eve in Genesis 3. On the basis of a careful reading of the text, Southcott argued that although Eve was beguiled by the serpent and persuaded Adam to eat the forbidden fruit, when called to account by God Eve rightly put the blame on the serpent (Gen. 3:12–15). By contrast, Adam blamed Eve. In referring to Eve as 'the woman whom *Thou* [God] gavest me', Adam effectively blamed God for creating Eve in the first place. According to Southcott, in the light of the blame heaped upon Eve down the centuries for leading Adam astray, God purposed to correct the misunderstanding of woman's place in the Creation by providing for a second Eve to redress the wrong done to woman by the church's traditional interpretation. There is a long tradition of interpretation which saw Mary as the second Eve who would rectify the first Eve's fall from grace. That kind of interpretation is here applied not to the past but to the present, and to the eschatological fulfilment which Southcott believed was taking place in her ministry.

Similarly, in her interpretation of Revelation Southcott believed that the time had come for its apocalyptic promises to be fulfilled. She rightly discerned that in the midst of the inevitability of judgement and future hope there is the possibility for escape for those who would repent. Southcott's reading of Revelation went further, however. She took the prophecy of Jonah as an example. When Jonah prophesied the imminent destruction of Nineveh and the people repented, the punishment was not carried out. Alluding to 1 Corinthians 13:8 ('charity never faileth'), she argued that God was 'slow to anger, and loath to punish; and repenteth of the evil' (Southcott, Book 3: 132). While human beings cannot ultimately frustrate the divine purpose, God is always open to his creatures' repentance. Indeed, even Satan might be forgiven, despite the clear indication in Revelation 20 that there is no possibility of forgiveness: 'so shall Satan be let loose *at the end* of the 1000 years, and go over the Earth again: then if he reforms, he may find *some* MERCY!' (Southcott, Book 12: 98). Southcott's teaching is not just a message of doom. Indeed, her theology concerns a loving God who wills that all will be saved (1 Tim. 2:3–4: 'This is right and is acceptable in the sight of God our Saviour, who desires everyone to be saved and to come to the knowledge of the truth'; cf. Rom. 11:32). Though Southcott does not quote any scripture to support her contention that Satan may find mercy, it is, however, a necessary consequence of her belief in the infinite mercy of God and the conditional nature of the divine promise. In Southcott's theological system there is the belief that humans are not inherently evil. While humans are capable of great evils, the temptation to commit sin is primarily the result of external influence. It is the influence of the devil on man that is the cause of sin, and when Satan's power is removed (during the thousand-year kingdom) it will be demonstrated that man is capable of obeying God (Southcott, Book 44: 41). Southcott was opposed to Calvinism, therefore, because it denied that God willed that all men should be saved. She argued that it was impossible for humanity to be eternally alienated from God, as God wills that all should be saved and that in Christ, *all* shall be made alive (1 Cor. 15:22: 'for as all die in Adam, so all will be made alive in Christ'; Southcott, Book 30: 258).

THE WOMAN, THE BRIDE, AND THE BRIDES, OF CHRIST

Southcott's identification of herself with the 'woman clothed with the sun' and the Bride of Christ in her first book appeared to be claiming this role uniquely in the divine economy. But she opens the denomination of bride to all who join with her. She says:

> So now then come, as she hath done;
> Believe my Bible true,
> Then now as brides you all shall be;
> The Bridegroom all shall know.

When it comes to the Woman clothed with the sun, there is no sharing of identity. She, as the Woman, is unique. Southcott did not see it as incompatible that she could be both the fallible Devon farmer's daughter and the interpreter of, and the one who fulfilled, scripture. She believed that when the apostle John saw his vision on Patmos of the portent in heaven, the Woman clothed with the sun, it was her that he was seeing. John saw her in the guise of symbols, but the symbol of the Woman only achieved its objective reality in Southcott herself.

Key to her understanding of the importance of the Woman's role was the fact that, in spite of the death and resurrection of Christ, evil still existed. The promise had been made in Eden that the seed of the woman (Christ) would bruise the head of the serpent: 'And I will put enmity between thee and the woman, and between thy seed and her seed; it shall bruise thy head, and thou shalt bruise his heel' (Gen. 3:15). Southcott believed that the bruising of the heel of the seed of the woman had been fulfilled in the death of Christ. She often quotes the verses from Isaiah, that Christ was 'wounded for our transgressions, he was bruised for our iniquities: . . . and the LORD hath laid on him the iniquity of us all' (Isa. 53:5, 6), in support of her argument. This is orthodox theology. However, she appeals to the gospel records of how Jesus came to be crucified in order to justify her role as the petitioner to God to bring the full implementation of the promise. Jesus was killed because evil men petitioned Pilate for the death of Christ (Luke 23:20–3; Acts 2:23). Therefore, she argues, the fulfilment of the promise to crush the serpent's head must also come through a petition—but this time through righteous men petitioning God to fulfil the promise made in Genesis 3 to bruise the serpent's head. Southcott saw her role as being to lead her contemporaries in petitioning God to bring about the end of Satan's power and to establish the messianic, peaceable kingdom on earth:

> So saints and sinners need not fear,
> If from their hearts they wish it [God's kingdom] here;
> And with their hearts their hands do join,
> They in the end shall all be mine;
> For they will so bruise Satan's head;
> And what against them can be said,
> If they wish every sin to cease,
> That they with me might dwell in peace;
> Then I will give this wish to men;
> As by their wish I died for them.

> (Southcott, Book 17: 44)

This is a good example of Southcott's use of 'types and shadows'. Scripture does not expand on how the prophecy made by God in the garden is to be fulfilled. By using her interpretation of the mechanism of the fulfilment of the bruising of the heel of the woman's seed (which would be familiar to her readers), she then uses this as a type or shadow for the fulfilment of the bruising of the serpent's head—petitioning is the mechanism. Human beings, therefore, have a role to play in the eschatological events in persuading God to bring about the eschatological kingdom. As the Woman clothed with the sun who is in travail and pain (Rev. 12:2), Southcott was to form a vanguard who would tread Satan under their feet. Her role was to gather these petitioners by publishing multiple works, encouraging the 'true' understanding of scripture and emphasizing the urgency of the work to be done in increasing the number of petitioners. But this would expose both herself and her followers to ridicule and insult; the fury of the devil is aimed at herself and her 'children'. Nor is the Woman herself a saviour: Southcott's theology is clear that only a divine person can take away sin (Southcott: Book 18: 3–5). Having given an account of the many women that God used in the Bible story to carry out his acts, Southcott adds: 'But no Saviour can arise in a woman, for her to be a Christ' (Southcott, Book 12: 106), thereby avoiding the charge of blasphemy. However, her argument that Christ's work was not yet fulfilled led to accusations of her teaching 'an insufficient Christ' (Southcott, Book 62: 3). Effectively, her account claimed that the implementation of God's peaceable kingdom would be delayed if men did not recognize the wrong done to women.

At this point in her career the man-child was interpreted as meaning her followers, who will have a position in Christ's peaceable kingdom ruling a perfect earth with Christ. Meanwhile, because of the devil's wrath, the petitioners for Satan's downfall need protection (Rev. 7:2–3). Followers had to sign the Woman's petition, and in return received a seal, comprising a piece of paper signed by Southcott. This would provide temporal protection from the great destruction that was to come on the earth, and contained the words:

> The Sealed of the Lord
> elect precious.
> Man's redemption to inherit the
> Tree of Life
> To be made Heirs of God
> And Joint heirs with
> Jesus Christ

To this the follower's name was usually appended, along with the date. These papers were stamped with Joanna Southcott's personal seal. Each follower was supposed to keep this seal in their possession, to give them protection from the time of great tribulation which was to come on the earth (Rev. 7:14–15). Several scriptural phrases are alluded to here: the sealed of the Lord (2 Cor. 1:22; Eph. 1:13; Rev. 7); elect precious (1 Pet. 2:6); man's redemption (Col. 1:4); inheriting the Tree of Life (Rev. 22:14); heirs of God and joint heirs with Jesus Christ (Rom. 8:17). This sealing was a type or shadow of the great sealing of all humankind in the ultimate universal redemption.

As with many millenarian prophets and groups, the Book of Revelation was key to Southcott's theology. She interpreted it as a chronological prediction, which began to be fulfilled when she received the spirit of prophecy in 1792 (Southcott, Book 1: p. iii). There were eschatological mysteries whose meaning was not understood until the last days, but which (thanks to her) were now made clear (Dan. 12:4, 9; Southcott: Book 20: 51). She understood the apocalyptic imagery to symbolize events to be fulfilled on earth, culminating in the thousand-year reign of Christ on earth (the millennium), similar to the way in which Daniel understood the beasts in his vision to be symbols of a succession of historical epochs. At the end of the thousand years there will be a rebellion led by Satan and his angels, which will result in Satan's power being destroyed forever. The exact sequence of events is not clearly expounded, but a period of severe tribulation will precede the establishment of Christ's peaceable kingdom on earth, and those who join with the 'Woman' in petitioning God for Satan's downfall and are sealed will be protected during these troubles.

Southcott's differs from other interpretations of the millennium as regards its purpose, which in her view is to 'try man without the devil'—to show with whom the fault lies for man's wickedness (Southcott, Book 53: 590–3; Book 44: 41). She concludes that the devil is responsible for man's fall—Eve was correct in her identification. This also was in contrast to the view of many of her religious contemporaries, who believed that man was irretrievably wicked by nature.

Southcott offered detailed explanation of biblical passages. She took a more optimistic view than many in highlighting those texts (e.g. Dan. 2:44; 7:13, 14, 22, 27; Isa. 2:2; 11:9; several sections in Isa. 52–4; and especially Micah 4:1–5) which stress the establishment of Christ's peaceable kingdom on earth. These become the basis of her belief in the ultimate restoration of mankind. In the same texts she finds evidence of times of tribulation prior to the establishment of the eschatological era of peace and happiness. But all her methods of interpretation, whether chronological prediction or the decoding of the symbols (Kovacs and Rowland 2004: 7–11), are used to emphasize the importance and immediacy of her mission to warn the reader of the urgency of the times. These then set the scene for her actualization of scripture, in enacting 'the woman clothed with the sun'.

An event in early 1814 changed her understanding of her vocation to be 'the woman clothed with the sun'. She received a communication from the Spirit of Truth telling her that she was to give birth to a *real* child:

This year, in the sixty-fifth year of thy age, thou shalt have a SON, by the power of the MOST HIGH, which if they [i.e. the Jews] receive as their Prophet, Priest, and King, then I will restore them to their own land, and cast out the heathen for their sakes, as I cast out them when they cast out me, by rejecting me as their Saviour, Prince, and King, for which I said I was born, but not at that time to establish my kingdom. (Southcott, Book 61: 4)

This communication, and other divine messages, brought about a reinterpretation of what had been written before. Her interpretation of the meaning of the reference to the birth changed from being figurative to literal. The remaining months of her life were spent preparing for the birth of the child. Her followers donated baby clothes and a cot. Southcott continued to write, further clarifying the role of the man-child, and devoted her final book (Southcott, Book 65: *Prophecies announcing the birth of the Prince of Peace*) to a detailed analysis of passages from her works prior to 1814, showing how they could now be understood with the identification of the man-child, which must have been their true meaning all along. There has been speculation that she had an underlying psychological reason for introducing this change in interpretation, since her following was waning as the return of Christ had not happened, and she needed something spectacular to regain their enthusiasm; but there is no real historical support for this claim.

THE CONSUMMATION AND ITS AFTERMATH

Southcott began to show the signs of pregnancy, and was pronounced pregnant by several doctors of good reputation, but two days after Christmas Day 1814 she died. An autopsy showed no signs of a child, nor any clear cause of death. Her followers were distraught, trying to make sense of what had transpired before their eyes. Although Southcott herself had been kept in a secret location, the whole event was public and regular updates on the pregnancy appeared in the newspapers, accompanied by less-than-flattering cartoons. The resulting non-appearance of any child brought further derision on her followers.

As with other prophetic groups, when prophecies appear to fail (see e.g. Zygmunt, in Stone 2000: 87–103) explanations are developed and exegetical technique honed to deal with what is often termed the 'cognitive dissonance'; in other words, the stress caused by holding two contradictory beliefs or facts simultaneously. Thus it was with the Millerites after the great disappointment in 1844, and the Bible Students in 1914 (both groups expecting cataclysmic events associated with the return of Christ; on the Millerites see further Chapter 34 above). In the case of both of the last-mentioned groups the adherents reinterpreted their expectations as being fulfilled in a 'spiritual' sense rather than literally. Southcott's committed followers too were spurred on to re-examine the writings to see if they could make sense of what had happened. Several new interpretations were now derived from the writings. First, there was the explanation of the events of her pregnancy and the supposed birth from the Bible itself. Thus, the child was born, but as in Revelation 12:5 ('And she gave birth to a son, a male child, who is to rule all the nations with a rod of iron. But her child was snatched away and taken to God and to his throne was caught up to God and to His throne'), he was taken away to return at some time in the near future. Secondly, Southcott's pregnancy was itself to be interpreted figuratively. The pregnancy was itself a 'type', and the 'substance' would take place at a later time. During Southcott's lifetime she spoke of a time when she would enter a 'trance' which would bring on the return of Christ. There is an unpublished communication, dated 15 September 1814, given when her 'pregnancy' was well advanced, in which she is reputed to have claimed that what she was going through (she had been seized with violent sickness) could not be the fulfilment of the prophecy but only a type. Those followers who accepted this communication as authentic came to the conclusion that the expected trance was her death, and that Southcott must return to give birth to Shiloh. Thirdly, the pregnancy was a type, but the child was to be a living person, one of her followers.

Southcott's actualizing of the apocalyptic image of Revelation 12 is, at least in general terms, not peculiar to herself. As Hans Frei points out, the heart of pre-modern biblical hermeneutic is the insertion of the reading subject into the text of scripture, so that the latter informs and guides belief and conduct. Something more radical and exclusive is going on in Southcott's interpretation, however. Mirroring the ways in which early Christian interpreters saw the biblical stories about the departed Elijah and his return (2 Kgs 2:11; cf. Mal. 4:3) fulfilled in the career of John the Baptist (Matt. 11:14 and 17:11–13), Southcott came to believe that she herself was the one whom John had seen in his vision, and that she, and none other, was the woman who was to give birth to the eschatological man-child, who would rule the earth with a rod of iron (Rev. 12:5). Southcott's own life, therefore, meant that this biblical figure was no longer available as an inspiration or a text to be interpreted figuratively, for in her life she had fulfilled it. Nonetheless, the passage left open the possibility of a succession to Southcott, for the messianic child still had to appear and the claims made by those who succeeded her and claimed to embody her messianic child pervade the history of the Southcottian movement.

What we find are hermeneutical moves which mirror (probably unconsciously) similar processes which were at work in early Christianity. On the one hand, there were those who looked back to Southcott as the authoritative prophet and her prophecies as still awaiting fulfilment. On the other, there were various individuals who claimed to be the incarnation of Southcott's child and thereby to bring her movement to its fulfilment. For example, Zion Ward (1781–1837) claimed not to be a prophet, but the physical embodiment of Southcott's conviction. That meant that his words, both spoken and written, were the result of the indwelling divine, as he had been transformed into a new divine being, Shiloh. He interpreted Southcott's writings and related them to himself. This daring interpretation he offered to the scattered Southcottian communities as the fulfilment of every 'type and shadow', a mode of interpretation familiar to the Southcottian groups. A hundred years later the Panacea Society believed that its founder, Mabel Barltrop, was the incarnation of Southcott's divine child. It was her followers who devoted so much time and effort to get the bishops of the Church of England to open Joanna Southcott's box. This contrast between the conviction that the promises have already, or are already being, fulfilled, and the belief that this fulfilment still remains in the future is at the heart of the intellectual history of Christianity. Southcott and her followers, in their contrasting understandings of the past and the present, recapitulate a pattern in Christian religion which, however deviant it might seem in the light of the orthodox edifice of their day, has many reminiscences of what we find in the pages of the New Testament.

CONCLUSION

Southcott's theology identified her uniquely as 'the woman clothed with the sun'. This chapter has shown how she performed her role as the interpreter of scripture, unsealing those parts that were obscure (or sealed), and as the petitioner to God to fulfil the promise made in Eden to bring an end to evil. She spread her message through her many books, with a view to gathering others who would join with her, as her children, in her petition for the overthrow of Satan. The major change in the interpretation of the identity of her child in the last year of her life, however, led to a literal rather than figurative actualization of the biblical promise, and when the child was not born as expected, others claimed this role. Her interpretation of the Bible combined what she claimed to be definitive interpretations of obscure biblical texts with the fulfilment of a key passage in the way she lived out an apocalyptic prophecy which she believed had always been directed to her. Like the New Testament writers who believed that Elijah had returned in the person of John the Baptist, so Southcott and her followers saw her physical condition as an acting out of the biblical text in preparation for the fulfilment of scripture and the eschatological consummation.

Although more than one alleged Box has been opened, the original Box remains intact in the custody of a few remaining believers, as it has done since 1804, its provenance clearly established. Although less vocal than in previous times, those believers continue to believe that until the bishops open the Box, crime, banditry, distress, and perplexity must inevitably increase.

WORKS CITED

Joanna Southcott's sixty-five books (published 1801–14) are available on-line at www.joannasouthcott.com. Although each book has its own title, it is customary to refer them by number, as throughout this chapter.

BROWN, F. (2002), *Joanna Southcott: The Woman Clothed with the Sun.* Cambridge: Lutterworth.
BURDON, C. (1997), *The Apocalypse in England: Revelation Unravelling 1700–1834.* London: Macmillan.
HARRISON, J. F. C. (1979), *The Second Coming: Popular Millenarianism 1780–1850.* London: Routledge & Kegan Paul.
JUSTER, S. (2003), *Doomsayers: Anglo-American Prophecy in the Age of Revolution.* Philadelphia: University of Pennsylvania Press.
KOVACS, J. and ROWLAND, C. (2004), *Revelation: The Apocalypse of Jesus Christ.* Oxford: Blackwell Bible Commentaries.
STONE, JON R. (ed) (2000), *Expecting Armageddon: Essential Readings in Failed Prophecy.* New York and London: Routledge.

FURTHER READING

ALLAN, G. (2006), 'Southcottian Sects from 1792 to the Present Day', in K. C. Newport and C. Gribben (eds.), *Expecting the End: Millennialism in Social and Historical Context.* Waco, Tex.: Baylor University Press.

DERRETT, J. D. M. (1994), *Prophecy in the Cotswolds 1803–1947*. Shipston-on-Stour: Blockley Antiquarian Society.

GARRETT, C. (1973), *Respectable Folly: Millenarians in the French Revolution in France and England*. Baltimore: Johns Hopkins University Press.

HOPKINS, J. K. (1982), *A Woman to Deliver Her People*. Austin, Tex.: University of Texas Press.

McCALMAN, I. (1988), *Radical Underworld: Prophets, Revolutionaries and Pornographers in London 1795–1840*. Cambridge: Cambridge University Press.

MEE, J. (1992), *Dangerous Enthusiasm: William Blake and the Culture of Radicalism in the 1790s*. Oxford: Clarendon Press.

PALEY, M. D. (1973), 'William Blake, the Prince of the Hebrews, and the Woman Clothed With the Sun', in Morton Paley and Michael Phillips (eds.), *William Blake: Essays in Honour of Sir Geoffrey Keynes*. Oxford: Clarendon Press.

....

CHAPTER 44

BIBLE READING
AND/AFTER
THEORY

....

VALENTINE CUNNINGHAM

In or about September 1969 the nature of modern Bible study changed—I parody Virginia Woolf in the matter of 'human nature' changing 'in or about December 1910' (Woolf 1966: 320)—when the French Catholic Association for the Study of the Bible got the already *renommé* structuralist Roland Barthes to analyse Acts 10–11 (the conversion of Cornelius) for its Chantilly Congress ('The Structural Analysis of narrative: Apropos of Acts 10-11': Barthes 1971*a*; 1985; 1988). This introduction of those curious Catholic Biblicists to the new ways of handling texts that were burgeoning in the *nouvelle vague* of French (post)structuralism, or, as we would now say, of the Linguistic or Theoretical Turn in literary studies, was quickly followed by the two even more momentous evenings in February 1971 at the Faculté de Théologie of the University of Geneva when the *nouveau* critic Jean Starobinski offered 'A Literary Analysis of Mark 5.1–20' (the Gerasene demoniac) (Starobinski 1971; 1972; 1973; 1974) and Roland Barthes, now a neo-Biblicist mage, pulled out of his analytical hat his 'Textual Analysis' of Genesis 32:23–33, 'The Struggle With the Angel', soon to be widely recognized as innovatively absorbing structuralist approaches into post-structuralist ones and highlighting a major way forward for biblical (and literary) studies (Barthes 1972*a*; 1974; 1977; 1985; 1988).

These tentative Biblicist dips into the Barthesian well of Theory dramatically opened the portal for the revolution in recent times in Biblicist hermeneutic practice, the great recent shaking of Biblicism to its established historicizing core, the door through which would rush the literary Theory and theories then muscling their way into the secular literary-critical world—the mixed postmodern bag, or coat of many postmodern colours, sheltering structuralists, Derridean deconstructionists, neo-Freudians, Konstanz School reader-responders (after Wolfgang Iser 1974 and 1980, and Hans Robert Jauss 1982), interpretive communitarians (after the egregious Stanley Fish 1980), and power-spotting Foucauldianized new-historicist/ new-wave feminist/Queer-theorist/post-colonialist body-baggers. All of them committed in their various shades and hues to the pre-eminent textuality of text. And to text conceived, complexly, even contradictorily, as all at once a merely textual, and intertextual, place, a formalist enclosure (differential, not referential; aporetic as to extra-textual meanings) where merely language games are played, *jeux des signifiants*, a site of *jouissant* reader encounters, inciting a hermeneutics of pleasure, but also as a ragged, rebarbative weave, fractured, cryptic, opaque, not least because it's a wily, devious, deviant set of ideologically slanted encodings, demanding decoding by duly suspicious interpreters in a hermeneutics of aroused suspicion. Of reading against the grain. Because no text, even the most formalistically pleasurable one, is to be trusted to say just what it might at first seem to mean, given all of textuality's founding and foundering in the Theory-defined problematics of (always ideological) authorizers, writers, readers, and institutions of reading, and above all of language and text as such. Reading has to be what Roland Barthes called *ungluing* the text (Barthes 1971*b*; 1976), *hulling* it, tearing off its protective husk (*décortiquer* in French) (Barthes 1978; 1981: 284–90)—particularly necessary given the inevitably strong ideological slanting of the Bible and its readers. 'Cracking the binding' is what Bible reading needs, as Timothy K. Beal puts it, thinking of religion, and so the book of religion, etymologically, as a *binding* 'to a web of principles, doctrines, certainities'—the 'binding authority' of the 'mono-lithic and univocal Author/Father' and his 'politics of religious, national, and sexual identity', which need undoing, 'deconstructing', inspecting close up for the inevitable 'tiny cracks and fissures' in the binding (Beal 1997: 1–2).

All a set of hermeneutic dispositions and determinations strutting their stuff in their Theory base camps in English, Literature, and Cultural Studies Departments: enticing siren voices appealing from down the corridor, so to say, to the erstwhile sober, dull even, Biblical and Religious Studies departments. Responding to which, self-exiles from well-worn historicist approaches have flocked in numbers in recent times. Marjorie Garber has astutely described 'Shakespeare' as 'the transferential love-object of literary studies' (Garber 1987: p. xiv). Literary Theory has become the transferential love object of Biblical Studies. Typically the arch-Derridean/Foucauldian Biblicist Stephen D. Moore moons about achingly on the fringes of the North American Modern Languages Association (MLA) convention of 1994, wishing he were really one of the critically smart traders on the Theory front-line, a real member of *that* guild (Moore 2001: 8). Putting yourself confessionally in the hermeneutic story—interpretation as autobiography, telling me when, where, and how you're reading as a womanist, a gay man, a blind Californian (see John M. Hull 2002: 154–77), or whatever, the awful me-generation spin on reader-response theory's insistence on recognizing the implicit and explicit reading situation—is what secular literary critics have been doing for ages, and so Biblicists do it a lot now. Characteristically, Stephen Moore sort of complains about Biblicists imitating their secular guides in this, but then joins relishingly in himself—with 'Me and My Bladder', and so forth. (Moore 1995: 19–50; Krondorfer 2009: 146–62).

'What makes you think you can do that kind of work here?', a male Biblicist's spiteful query punctuates Danna Nolan Fewell's animated feminist-deconstructionist (and, not incidentally, autobiographicized) scramble around Old Testament killing and raping stories: 'Why aren't you in an English Department somewhere?' (Fewell 1997: 134, 143). But she is, in effect, already in the English Department. 'Get thee to a nunnery, go, go', Hamlet urged Ophelia, viciously, knowing *nunnery* meant also *brothel*. Biblicists have become regular buyers of sexy ideas at the Theory-mongers' brothel. But this has not been, and is not by any means, a one-way traffic, a simple textual commerce. Simultaneously with the Biblicists learning from Theory how to modernize and postmodernize the Bible, the Theorists (steeped in the Biblicizings of their Jewish and variously Christian childhoods and adolescences) were adding biblical texts to their repertoire of (especially modernist) illustrative and exemplary texts—it was what Barthes himself was doing—and were finding in ancient Judeo-Christian biblical interpretative practices models and reinforcements for postmodernist assumption, in midrash especially. As part of which interactive Biblicizing movement, Theory-advised literary people—postmodernizers of the canon, textualizers, intertexualizers, (post)structuralizing readers of old and, of course, especially, modernist and postmodernist texts—were putting biblical texts forward as central to secular literary study, as main additions to the syllabus, the canon of studiable literature. Everybody, then—Biblicists, Theorists, EngLit people—a Bible-reader, passing the biblical parcel around, busily unhulling it, with shared postmodernist tools, shared postmodernist assumptions, just as they would any other textual, intertextualized, literary, fictional object.

The Genesis text, says Protestant Barthes in his Wrestling Jacob talk, and typically, demands being recognized as an example of textuality because it 'is called Scripture [*Écriture*], Writing'. This writing works exactly like 'a literary text', if a shade less amply than Balzac's 'Sarrasine' that he's just been analysing into its component codes (Barthes, *S/Z*, 1970). Its intertextuality is, he declares, exactly as predicated by Julia Kristeva in her *Sèmeiotekè* (Kristeva 1969)—she the post-Christian whose later most influential work, as semiotician-turned-feminist psychoanalyst, on the large meanings of abjection, in her *Pouvoirs de l'horreur* (1980; 1982), would turn on her analysis of pollution and the sacred in Dostoevsky, Proust, Artaud, and Céline as inflected through her readings of the biblical matter from

Leviticus to Jesus. *Pouvoirs de l'horreur* is actively incited by Christian convert René Girard's engagement with biblical victims from Job to Jesus (Girard 1978; 1987*a*), foundation of his protracted modelling of human and social behaviour as post-biblical scapegoating (Girard 1982; 1986; 1985; 1987*b*), and by Roman Catholic structural anthropologist Mary Douglas's *Purity and Danger: An Analysis of Conceptions of Pollution and Taboo* (1966), her potent inspection of the 'symbolic system' of filth, taboo, and the sacred with her reading of Leviticus as basic. (Douglas's sense of Leviticus as a socially and symbolically structured piece of literature along the lines of the archaic stories Lévi-Strauss and his disciples analysed would fruit in her remarkable trio of structuralist-anthropolized engagements with Old Testament 'literature': Douglas 1993; 1999; 2004.) Kristeva rightly thought that the recent 'idea of reading the Bible as we might Marx or Lautréamont', 'unravelling its contents as if it were one text among many', was 'born out of structuralism and semiology' ('Reading the Bible', in Kristeva 1993; 1995). She thought this inevitable because the Bible, as represented by John 6, was self-consciously a semiological operation, focused in Jesus the sign and sign-maker ('From Signs to the Subject', in Kristeva 1993; 1995).

Which is indeed Barthes's line. Acts 10 might posit a 'final signified'—'the integration of the Uncircumcized into the Church'—but such anagogical meaning, which of course characterizes Biblical text, is only present as it is encoded as text. (Derrida has, he says, convincingly shown in the *Grammatology* how there is in writings only writing and rewriting, writing as and about writing.) Just so, Barthes will not allow Genesis 32 to be 'reduced' to any non-textual 'truth'—historical, economic, folkloric, kerygmatic. He notes the variations on the Roman Jakobson sender–message–receiver model of communication (here the sender, 'God', is also the receiver) and the presence of folkloric elements from Propp's famous *Morphology of the Folk-Tale* (villain–hero combat, branding of the hero, and so on), but he's moving energetically on from those structuralisms to post-structural interests—the play of woven differences; the problematic dual beginnings of the narrative; the fraught crossings and recrossings of the River Jabbok as an emblematically difficult interpretative border; the consequent friction (*frottement*) and grinding (*grincement*) of legibility. What Derrida would call *aporia: embarras*, in Barthes's word, *blockage*, embarrassment for sense-makers. The text is *embrouillé*, a tangle of textual threads (who *he*, who *him*, in verses 25–30?). The *détournement* (deviousness, avertedness, roundaboutness) of the text is vividly manifest in the wrestling match. In a regular mythical combat a long contest is finally won with a tricky low blow—a *coup de Jarnac*, named for the cheating thrust to the knee by the Comte de Jarnac in his 1547 duel, name of the battlefield where French Protestants thought the Catholics had won an unfair victory in 1569, reminiscent for wrestling fan Barthes of the winning ways of the bad boy, the bastard, *salaud*, or *salope*, bitch, of the French ring (see Barthes 1957; 1972*b*; and Cunningham 1997). But here the low blow that's given (by God the cheating *salop*) is not a decider; narrative logics and expectations are inverted; Jacob the weaker defeats the stronger antagonist, though at the cost of being lamed. Jacob gets his requested blessing, a new name, but it's a kind of curse, its mark a laming. Embarrassing paradoxes these—all sharply illustrative of the paradoxes of language, narrative, text—disruptions, discontinuities—which it is the duty of true (post-structuralist) reading to observe: the self-deconstructions of the text.

So Genesis 32 stands for the embarrassingly aporetic text; its wrestling hero an emblem of the discomfited, cheated reader/interpreter: Barthesian models straight-away seized on in the Theory world. Jewish Harold Bloom, one-time Yale decon-structionist, reads Jacob as ancestor and type of Jewish Sigmund Freud, the prime slayer of Moses, and of the Freudian struggle for meaning; he's the oldest manifes-tation of Bloom's Freudianized model of poetic emergence and survival as a struggle of the young poet against the influence of strong poetic fathers, the oldest of whom is the author of the J, the Jahwistic, biblical texts, which contain, of course, the genetic hermeneutic story of Wrestling Jacob (Bloom 1982; 1991; 1995). For Jewish Geoffrey Hartman, another of the Yale deconstructionists, Jacob's struggle is the exemplum of all of our necessarily hampered interpretative wres-tlings with the aporias of text. It's an allegory of the rabbinical midrashic practices of Hebrew Bible interpretation—layering Bible texts with interpretative rereadings, inviting future rereadings, open-ended, lavishly free, breezily fictional even—which Hartman and his Jewish colleague Sanford Budick have successfully revived as a model, precedent, and legitimation of textual appropriation—celebrated in Hart-man's midrashic reading of Jacob and Barthes's reading of Jacob in 'The Struggle for the Text', provocative opening piece of their propagandizing *Midrash and Literature* (Hartman 1986).

Key contributor to *Midrash and Literature* is, of course, Derrida himself, guru of Yale deconstruction, with his 1984 lecture 'Shibboleth'—a piece of 'Contemporary Midrash' (Derrida 1986a). It's a characteristic Derrida discussion, of poems by the Jewish Paul Celan, modern midrashic but rooted and framed by a midrashic reading of Judges 12, story of the Ephraimites killed at yet another biblical river-crossing because they can't pronounce the word *shibboleth*. This 'unpronounceable word' is taken as emblem of all the unpronounceable words, right down to the Tetragrammaton itself, which for deconstruction are the basis of the literary. Celan's poem 'In Eins' links 'Schibboleth' with the Spanish Republican's cry of 'No pasarán', 'They shall not pass', and Derrida riffs, as he does often, on barred rights of meaning-passage at all the aporetic borders, rivers, doorways, thresholds which so concern him (his protracted lexicon of nostrils, eyeballs, *pharmakon* (poison/medicine), *hymen*, *tympan*, *voile*, *toile*, *tissus*, *écrans*, *parapluie*, *parergon* (all the para- words he can think of), preface, *supplement*, his coinage *différance* (differing/deferring) itself, and so forth). Celan's poem 'Einem, Der Vor Der Tür Stand', 'To One, Who Stood Before the Door', makes Derrida think, as he often does, of the section of Kafka's *The Trial* known as 'Vor dem Gesetz', 'Before the

Law', in which a countryman seeks admittance to The Law and is debarred forever by a Doorkeeper. This is read as an allegory of all the textual threshold frustrations Derrida celebrates (Derrida 1992*a*). The debarring Torah, fundamental biblical text, stands for all texts. All readers are 'essentiellement devant la loi' (Derrida 1986). We all stand before Sinai (Derrida 1997: 65).

The Bible keeps on providing the model for deconstruction like this; repeatedly it's offered as the emblematically self-deconstructing text. Babel, for instance: the place of God's gift of languages, which are however mutually incomprehensible. Derrida is repeatedly drawn to that mock-biblical passage in *Finnegans Wake*, archetypal postmodernist fictional text, where Joyce seemingly joins the enigmas of Babel with Jacob's struggle for meaning: 'And shall not Babel be with Lebab? And he war' (Joyce 1939: 258; Derrida 1980: 257; 1984: 145–59). In his 'Des Tours de Babel' essay, Derrida takes Joyce's modernist struggle, Jacob-style, with the Christian God and the Christian Church for his own name and writing identity ('he war'), as a summary of the aporetic internal warfare within the babelic text of *Finnegans Wake*, but also within its progenitor the Bible, the greatest progenitor text ever, at whose core is the exemplarily unspeakable name of the JHWH of Babel— 'divided, bifid, ambivalent, polysemic: God deconstructing' (Derrida 2002: 108). Like the aporetic gift of tongues at Babel, the Law is given at Sinai, a writing on tablets, only to be immediately smashed in pieces. The Law's interdictions—'Thou shalt not kill', and so on—aporetically presuppose the very possibilities they forbid. So the Mosaic is always a mosaic.

The Law is displayed prominently on orthodox arms, foreheads, doorposts, but locked up in those little leather boxes called phylacteries: for Derrida emblems of the text of the postcard, the letter which 'can always not arrive at its destination' in *La Carte postale*, Derrida's great text of foiled epistolarity (Derrida 1980: 472). Derrida likes knowing that 'phylactery' is etymologically related to prophylaxis, *présérvatif*, condom, instrument of the condomized, the reserved, concealed text (ibid. 91, 472). *La Carte postale* is haunted by the Book of Esther, explicated as the story of a holocaust of Jews prevented by Esther's substitution, her *détournant*, of a letter; and whose text, says its translator André Chouraqui—Algerian Jewish, like Derrida, whose translation Derrida often references—should be read in synagogues 'comme on lit un lettre' (ibid. 79–81): the letter of Haman's law, blunted and reversed by Esther's new legal letter. Letters of the Law: open and shut, like the veiled–unveiled face of Moses after Sinai.

The 'situation of the Jew becomes exemplary of the situation of the poet, the man of speech and writing', declared Derrida early on in his 1964 essay 'Edmond Jabès and the Question of the Book' (it appeared influentially in *L'Écriture et la différence*, 1967; trans. *Writing and Difference*, 1978), his ready response to Jabès's inspiring modernistic, book-celebratory, neo-midrashic *Le Livre des questions* (1963). Writing and text as all at once poetically autonomous and also needing 'commentary', midrash, for their being and understanding, begin, Derrida says, after Jabès, at Sinai, with the breaking of the Tables: the text given, legislative, and also broken, at once imperiously readable and unreadable. 'In the beginning is hermeneutics'—the necessary interpretative attention to broken hermetic words, the 'stifled' voice and 'dissimulated' face of Jahwe. Here at Sinai begin, then, the 'two interpretations of interpretation' (Derrida 1981: 67), which Derrida would spell out in his 1966 Johns Hopkins lecture 'Structure, Sign and Play in the Discourse of the Human Sciences'—at the conference, organized in part by René Girard, intended to bring structuralism to the United States, when they got Derrida and post-structuralism instead (Derrida 1978: 278–93). The two interpretations of interpretation: the one seeking presence truth, origin, foundation, transcendental signifieds, historicist, metaphysical, ontotheological; the other Nietzschean, Freudian, Heideggerean, doing without presence and 'privileged signifieds', enjoying an endless play of signifiers; inseparable as a set of Saussurean binaries (which didn't stop eager US deconstructionists instantly separating them and proclaiming Derrida as the high priest of non-presence, anti-theologocentrism, and so on).

The pair are held together in 'an obscure economy': the economy of Sinai. Which Derrida perceives as the textual, hermeneutic economy of the New Testament as well. His New Testament is a Jewish-Christian midrash on the Old which keeps up the old aporias. Romans 7 especially is a dramatic intertext, 'a kind of movement or trembling between the Old and New Testament'. It's a pre-vision of Kafka's 'Before the Law', and text of the intense Pauline aporetic in which he 'speaks according to the Law, of the Law, against the Law' (Derrida 1992*a*: n. 17, p. 203). Paul is 'the one who says that "apart from the law sin lies dead"; "I was once alive apart from the law, but when the commandment came sin revived and I died"' (ibid. 217, 219).

Of course the strong Theorists are nourished mainly on the Hebrew Bible, even, narrowly, on Harold Bloom's 'Book of J'. Typically, Michel Serres builds his momentous theory of narratological parasitism on readings of Joseph's intepretations of Potiphar's dreams and the positioning of the Genesis story of Tamar, and his meditations on imaginative genetics are of course rooted in biblical Genesis (Serres 1980; 1982). And Hélène Cixous, Derrida's close friend and collaborator, like him an Algerian Jew steeped in the Bible and its aestheticizings, finds an analogy for her 'ladder of writing' in Jacob's Ladder, the one he dreamed at Bethel, subject of 'the first dream of my own life', genetic for her as a writer—as are all the canonical Hebrew stories which light up, she says, the unconscious and provoke paintings and sculpture (Cixous 1993: 66–9; compare her essay on paintings of Bathsheba: Cixous 1998: 1–19). But the New Testament is no less dramatically generative of the Old Testament's hermeneutic dilemmas, at least for Cixous and Derrida. *Memoirs of the Blind*, Derrida's 1990 catalogue for an exhibition of Christian art's dealing with blindness narratives (Derrida 1993), is mightily attracted by Saul's conversionist recovery from blindness, his living through the lifting of the Mosaic veil, which as St Paul he celebrates in 2 Corinthians 3, and by the Pauline move, celebrated in so many paintings, beyond the aporias and shibboleths rampant among the blind OT patriarchs, Samson, Isaac, Jacob. *Veils*, the remarkable late text co-authored with Cixous (Cixous 2001) has Derrida wriggling against God's gift of the separating veil of the temple, and declaring himself fatigued by a lifetime of dwelling on the aporetic figures of his favourite textiles, his 'Penelopean' career of weaving so much aporetic veiling–unveiling metaphoricity. He presents his beloved *tallith*, the Orthodox Jew's prayer-covering he inherited from his father, as a gift from God that's visible, to be seen, and so, he says, a version of the miraculous Pauline seeing, a lifting of the Mosaic veil, a pre-Paulinism of the Old Testament. It prefigures the tearing of the temple veil in the Gospel. But this is a fantasy; the tearing of the temple veil is 'unbelievable'. Like little Samuel, little Derrida once said 'here I am'. Jesus' 'I am the truth and the life' can be thought of as the fulfilment of those old 'I am' declarations, the answer to Levinas's interrogation of Numbers 15 in his (posthumous) *Nouvelles lectures talmudiques* (1996), 'to elaborate the question "Who is oneself?"' But Jesus is actually the one who also said 'I have come, they saw me not, I am coming'—like Derrida's circumcision namesake the prophet Elijah, always coming and never arriving. Jesus, the colour of whose tallith we don't know. Whose prophet is Paul, the unveiling one who is still the aporetic legalist of Romans, still the veiling unveiler of the epistle to the Corinthians, decidedly aporetic about veils (good for women, bad for men), 'terrible' because of the 'monstrous progeny' of this (in)decision in 'history and culture' and for leaving the reader, judge, hermeneute forever stuck at the border of certainty ('Judge for yourselves:/is it appropriate for a woman to pray to Elohim unveiled?/Does not nature herself teach us'). St Paul the Christian legalist burdening the reader with the old perpetual law, afforced by 'Nature', of aporetic judgement and reading.

And this is the profound whole-Bible doublemindedness that keeps deconstruction in place. Confirmed most dramatically, perhaps, in Cixous's wonderful *Portrait of Jacques Derrida as a Young Jewish Saint*, her Jewish-insider's J-text, celebrating Derrida in a commentary on his 'Circonfession' (1991). Beginning with a rhapsody on the letter J, she brings out the incessant Jewish-biblical hermeneutic interests of that extraordinary confession—Derrida's preoccupation with his (forced) circumcision, with Esther (one of his ghosting mother's names), with his namesake Elijah ('Circonfession' even comes with a photo of the chair the eschatological prophet will sit in when the Messiah arrives, hanging expectantly in a synagogue—Derrida 1991: 209), with the orchard (*verger*) in the rue d'Aurelle-de-Paladines in Derrida's birthplace of El-Biar, Algiers, in which some sort of sexual Fall took place (*verger: verge*, penis), an address containing the anagram PaRDes: a 'written paradise, the Paradise before vowels' (i.e. in pseudo Hebrew), with its 'four consonants, PRDS' denoting the four modes of rabbinical reading of the Talmud, so that 'the Pardes' is a 'garden of reading'. A paradise garden (*pardes* in Hebrew story, both orchard and paradise) of aporetic Bible reading (a PaRDes *intact*, untouched, in Derrida's French, but not intact because some trangressive touching, buggery even, has happened there (Cixous 2004: 97 ff.). All Old Covenant stuff, but profoundly infected by Christianity: Derrida's 'Circonfession' deliberately calqued on and blurred into passages from Augustine's *Confessions* (Elie Derrida: Esther; Augustine: Monica, and so on); not Catholic (they do oral confession, Jews don't), but imbricated in the writings of both Testaments, whose differential borders Derrida's readings and reading theory patrol. Hence Derrida, contradictorily, *Saint Juif, Jewish Saint*. And 'Circonfession', one more aporetic blur, at once a *circumcision* and a *confession*. 'Is Deconstruction Really a Jewish Science?' asks John D. Caputo, in perhaps the best book on Derrida's religion, *The Prayers and Tears of Jacques Derrida: Religion without Religion* (Caputo 1997: 279). And the answer is, of course, Yes—if Derrida's betweenness, his eventual inter-testamentality, is acknowledged; as it is by Caputo.

The theoreticians' move on the whole Judeo-Christian book was, of course, an inspirational licence for the 'EngLit' critical machine, led by Robert Alter, Jewish expert in modernist fiction, and Frank Kermode, literary-theorizing ex-Anglican choirboy: Alter in the seventies lectures and articles that culminated in *The Art of Biblical Narrative* (1981)—its first chapter was tried out in December 1976 in the, Jewish, *Commentary* magazine, where he influentially called for 'serious literary analysis of the Hebrew Bible'—and Kermode in *The Genesis of Secrecy: On the Interpretation of Narrative* (1979), his postmodernist reading of Mark which began life as his 1977–8 Charles Eliot Norton lectures at Harvard (Alter 1981; Kermode 1979). And the revolutionary achievement of Alter and Kermode was to assure a repositioning of the Bible as canonical for modern literary studies and also as a set of texts demanding to be read by Biblicists as well as by literary scholars and critics on lines laid down by more or less (post)modern theory. In her editor's 'Introduction: On Biblical Criticism' to the 1990 collection of Theory-affirmative Bible essays by a combined group of literary critics and Biblicists, *The Book and the Text: the Bible and Literary Theory*, Regina Schwartz claims Alter's 1976 alert as foundational to the new interest—and she would be one of the three editors of the nine-person Bible and Culture Collective's swaggeringly Theorizing volume *The Postmodern Bible* (Bible and Culture Collective 1995), which polemicizes forcefully for 'transforming', 'postmodern' Bible readings, which would soon be followed by the reformed Bible and Culture Collective's *Postmodern Bible Reader* (Jobling 2001), anthology of by-now classic essays, including Barthes on Acts, Kristeva on abomination, Michel Serres on Jacob and Tamar, Derrida on the Akedah.) '[S]omething new and exciting is happening', Kermode said of Alter's book in the *New York Times Book Review*, over-modestly handing leadership of the new field to Alter, but the exciting makeover of the Bible as necessarily readable on post-structuralist lines was his doing too.

Mark is 'a sample of what we take literature to be' (Kermode 1979: 138), and of modernist literature at that, the stuff of necessary post-structuralist analysis. Mark's 'latent' senses are like those of Henry Green's 1939 novel *Party Going* (ibid. 5). Its *neaniskos* in the *sindon* (the 'Boy in the Shirt') is parallelled with the Man in the Macintosh who pops up in the graveyard scene of Joyce's *Ulysses* (ibid. 49 ff.). Mark's abrupt first ending in '*gar*' is compared to the final cliff-hanging '*Yes*' of *Ulysses* and '*the*' of *Finnegans Wake*. Mark is famously secretive, but this makes it like classic novels, *Madame Bovary* for instance (ibid. 115). Its withholdings are to be construed as (post)modernistically gappy. Parables are like the Freudian dream-text, the textuality beloved of postmodernist interpreters, notoriously difficult for interpreters (ibid. 24). Mark is midrashic on Old Testament texts (for instance, Pilate's hand-washing is a midrash on Deut. 21: ibid. 97–8), which underlines its fictionality, for midrash is narrative fiction—interpreter fiction which fills earlier textual gaps. The Bible is a long novel: the Old Testament is like the opening pages of a novel, a detective story for instance, whose meanings only become clearer later, in the midrashic New Testament. Midrash creates novel-effects within the big novel. As in John's midrash on Matthew's midrash on Mark's story of Judas at the Last Supper: 'So, after receiving the morsel, he immediately went out. And it was night'—narrative closure of the most sophisticated kind: 'We feel close to the novel' (ibid. 92–3). The Bible texts project themselves, like all this, into the hands of future interpreters, but *inexhaustibly, interminably* (ibid. 35, 36)—an illustration is the story of Salomé and the beheading of John the Baptist, rewritten by 'great artists: Flaubert, Mallarmé, Wilde Yeats, Richard Strauss' (ibid. 130). The 'fulfil-ments' (*pleroma*) of scripture are not final meanings, but the opening out of narrative possibilities in the *jouissance* of endless textual play. All the Bible 'facts' are *figura* (Kermode draws on the influential 1953 *Mimesis* of Erich Auerbach). Jesus' legs are broken and side pierced on the cross in John 19 in an intertextual replay of Psalm 34, Zechariah 12, and Numbers 9. The Gospels' chronicle is 'part of a literary plot' (ibid. 102 ff.). There's no history here, only story, a rhetoric of historicity, what Barthes would call the code of history (ibid. 117). Kermode glosses Jean Starobinski's 'Literary Analysis' of the Gerasene demoniac story to the effect that third-person narratives like Mark's best produce 'the illusion of pure refer-ence'. It's all text, intertext, fiction, to be construed on standard post-structuralist lines. As, more or less, is Alter's Hebrew Bible.

Alter's Bible must be read as historicized prose fiction, or like a Shakespeare History Play, as a fictionalizing of history (Alter 1981: 37). The David Story is a Bildungsroman (ibid. 37). The Bible's multiplied doublings and repetitions are so artfully patterned as to suggest a most cunning authorial hand: too deft to sustain the traditional idea of composite editorializings. There are none of the Biblicist tradition's sloppy intercalations (Alter opens with a bravura explanation of the structural importance of the Tamar story of Genesis 38). Everywhere Alter finds parallels with modernist/postmodernist fiction: Esau selling his birthright reminds him of Nabokov (ibid. 46); the reticences in the David story are Jamesian and Proustian (ibid. 117); modernist enigma is everywhere (ibid.); these stories are as impressionistic, fragmentary, elliptical as Conrad's or Ford Madox Ford's (ibid.

126). *Play* is invoked a lot, even 'flaunted play'—Alter is thinking of post-structuralist favourites Rabelais, *Tristram Shandy*, and *Ulysses* (ibid. 156). (And Alter's attention to patterns of biblical plot and character, verbal play, multivalence and polysemy would continue potently in his books on Bible poetry and Bible literature more generally (Alter 1985 and 1992), and in his great series of translations, *Genesis, The David Story, The Five Books of Moses*, and *The Book of Psalms* (Alter 1996; 1999; 2004; 2007), in whose extended commentaries narratology and poetics meet text-destabilizing dissemination.) Of course there is, as *The Art of Biblical Narrative* has it, a biblical horizon of 'perfect knowledge', but it's only glimpsable momentarily; the Bible text is poised between findable, absolute, fixed, intended meanings— 'theological, psychological, moral, or whatever'—and 'contemporary agnosticism about all literary meanings', inviting 'virtuoso exercises of interpretation, aimed . . . at undermining the very notion that the text might have any stable meanings' (Alter 1981: 158, 178, 179). Alter doesn't acknowledge it, but his Hebrew Bible is stationed precisely between the hermeneutic extremes of Derrida's two interpretations of interpreting.

And all the directions Kermode and Alter were pointing in soon became standard lines of interpretative thought among freshly Bible-conscious members of Literature Departments, busily feeding their theoretized critical fires with biblical cases: in the Sussex University English Department's *Ways of Reading Bible* (Wadsworth 1981), including post-structuralist theorist and novelist Gabriel Josipovici on the Bible's thematic resistance to interpretation; in novelist and University College, London, teacher of English Dan Jacobson's critical turn to the whole Bible (his Bible fictionalizings already established in *The Rape of Tamar*, 1970) as a fiction about Israel, God, sacrifice, and land in *The Story of the Stories: The Chosen People and their God* (1982); in big, old, critical beast Northrop Frye's *The Great Code: The Bible and Literature* (1982)—all (Derridean) writing, verbal play, polysemy, and mythicity built by Lévi-Straussian bricolage; in the theory-eclectic, demythologizing, de-canonizing, feminizing, narratological, midrashic literaturizing Alter–Kermode *Literary Guide to the Bible* (Alter 1987); in Gabriel Josipovici's *The Book of God: A Response to the Bible* (1988), incorporating his pieces from Wadsworth 1981 and Alter–Kermode 1987, in an effusively post-Alterian engagement with the Bible's scrappy, fragmentary textuality, as an ur-modernist (Eliotic, Joycean) montage, midrashic, its meanings and forms endlessly polymorphic and unfixable from the foundational grammatical ambiguity of Genesis 1:1 on ('we do not have to choose' between the two endings of Mark 16, and so forth: Josipovici 1988: 231).

Here was a signing of Bible as canonical for secular literary study that was usefully afforced by the Eng(Lit) guild's massive renewed attention to the strong rereadings and redoings of the Bible—fictional and poetic midrash—in and around the secular canon: studies like Regina Schwartz's of *Paradise Lost* (1988); Jonathan Lamb on eighteenth-century appropriations of Job (1995); Stephen

Prickett on the Romantics (1995); Harold Fisch on the *Biblical Presence* in Shakespeare, Milton, and Blake (1999); Piero Boitani on Thomas Mann, Faulkner, and Joseph Roth in *The Bible and its Rewritings* (1999)—*Ri-Scritture*, 'Re-Scriptures', in its revelatory Italian title; Steven Marx on Shakespeare (2000); Terence Wright on D. H. Lawrence (2000) and on literary readers of Genesis (2007); not to mention the ongoing series of Blackwell Commentaries on Biblical books *Through the Centuries*, which specializes in reporting the various texts' refractions in literature, music, and art; and, of course, the magisterial *Blackwell Companion to the Bible in English Literature* (Lemon *et al.* 2009), inspecting the huge range of English literary Biblicizings from Caedmon to Joyce. And these powerfully revealing studies have been wonderfully supported by the flood of anthologies garnering Bible rewritings from across the world and the ages,[1] by the numerous collections of contemporary writers' responses to the Bible,[2] as well as the torrent of contemporary novels on biblical themes by the likes of Dan Jacobson, E. L. Doctorow, Michel Tournier, Torgny Lindgren, Joseph Heller, Julian Barnes, Timothy Findlay, Jeanette Winterson, Moelwyn Merchant, José Saramago, Howard Jacobson, Norman Mailer, Jim Crace.[3] (And among the novels we have to include Jack Miles's startling but powerful *God: A Biography* (1995), a sort of meta-novel, a novel with commentary, tracking the 'life' of God as it runs from the first page of the standard Judeo-Christian text to the last.) Contemporary literary interest in the Bible and interest in literature's interest in the Bible could not be higher. It's a great bandwagon of writers, critics, and theorizers that the Biblicists have proved arrestingly eager to join.

Not all, of course; you don't have to be an outright fundamentalist/literalist to have concerns about the literary-theorizers' assumption of biblical unreadability

[1] *Chapters into Verse: Poetry in English Inspired by the Bible*, ed Robert Aitwan and Laurance Wieder (2 vols., 1993); their one-volume selection (2000); Laurance Wieder, *The Poets' Book of Psalms: The Complete Psalter as Rendered by Twenty-Five Poets from the Sixteenth to the Twentieth Centuries* (1995; 1999); *Divine Inspiration: The Life of Jesus in World Poetry*, ed. Robert Aitwan, George Dardass, and Peggy Rosenthal (1998); *The Bible and Literature: A Reader*, ed. David Jasper and Stephen Prickett (1999)—which includes critical as well as fictional and poetical voices.

[2] *Congregation: Contemporary Writers Read the Jewish Bible* (1987) and *Communion: Contemporary Writers Reveal the Bible in Their Lives* (1996), ed. David Rosenberg (translator of the Harold Bloom/Rosenberg *Book of J*); *Incarnation: Contemporary Writers on the New Testament* (1990), ed. Alfred Corn; *Out of the Garden: Women Writers on the Bible*, ed. Christine Büchmann and Celina Spiegel (1994); the Canongate, Edinburgh, box-set of twelve pocket-book-size books of the Bible in the Authorised Version, each introduced by a name writer, e.g. David Grossman on Exodus, Doris Lessing on Ecclesiastes, A. S. Byatt on the Canticles, Nick Cave on Mark, Will Self on Revelation, which was a publishing sensation of 1998.

[3] Dan Jacobson, *The Rape of Tamar* (1970), E. L. Doctorow, *The Book of Daniel* (1971/2), Michel Tournier, *Gaspard, Melchior and Balthazar* (1980), Torgny Lindgren, *Bathsheba* (1984), Joseph Heller, *God Knows* (1984), Julian Barnes, *A History of the World in 101/2 Chapters* (1989), Jeanette Winterson, *Boating for Beginners* (1985), Moelwyn Merchant, *Jeshua* (1984), José Saramago, *The Gospel According to Jesus Christ* (1991/1993), Howard Jacobson, *The Very Model of a Man* (1992), Norman Mailer, *The Gospel According to the Son* (1997), Jim Crace, *Quarantine* (1997).

and fictionalism, about their waiving of interest in the claimed sacredness of this 'Sacred' text, their steady hostility to presence and logocentrism, let alone theologocentrism. John Barton's hostility to Derridean indeterminacy and 'all the fun of the ludicity fair' in the post-structuralism-slamming supplements to his *Reading the Old Testament: Method in Biblical Study* is the concernment of a rather liberal historicist (Barton 1996: 220–36). But not for nothing has the Bible proved such a receptive source-book for secular theorists. Its pages, and not least its midrashic history, lie wide open for post-structuralist deconstructors (see e.g. Cunningham 1994), and—it being so patently patriarchal and androcentric and so greatly intimate with Christian white-man colonialist history—wide open to feminists, postcolonialists, and other politicized receptionists. No surprise, therefore, that the Bible and Culture Collectives have had Bible hermeneutic pretty much their own way. Or that the theorized voices of *Semeia: An Experimental Journal for Biblical Criticism* (founded in 1974 to promote the new biblical structuralism; quickly turning post-structuralist) and the Sheffield Academic Press's *Journal for the Study of the Old Testament* supplement series (dominantly textualizing, fictionalist, politicizing, feminist, queer, post-colonialist) are now the norm rather than not. Stephen Moore's polemical *Literary Criticism and the Gospels: The Theoretical Challenge*, with its insistence that 'theological content' other than 'form' is an 'illusory mystique (Moore 1989: 66), its support for Kermode on the 'gaping aporias' of Mark (ibid. 110), for the bottomlessness of interpretation (ibid. 126 ff.), and for Dominic Crossan's centreless, infinitely playful, polyvalent *Finnegans Wake*-like parables (ibid. 143–4; see esp. Crossan 1979), was kicking at an opened door. Revealingly, John Barton presides over *The Cambridge Companion to Biblical Interpretation* (1998), in which guides to postmodern approaches far outweigh every other.

And there is indeed a lot to be said for the claim of André LaCoque and Paul Ricouer that their combined effort of reading the Hebrew Bible in a post-historical-critical way filtered through post-structuralist assumptions about polyvalence, gappiness, multidimensionality, midrash upon midrash, and reader-centrality is indeed *Thinking Biblically* (LaCoque and Ricoeur 1998), and for A. K. M. Adam's notion that reading the Bible the *Postmodern Way* of his farrago of essays on a thoroughly theorized Bible is *Faithful Interpretation* (Adam 2006). Certainly, the new theorized approaches coming out of the marriage of the EngLit and the Bible/Religion Departments have freshened up our sense of the Bible and of its reception no end, with lots and lots of textually and contextually, historically, ideologically, and theologically illuminating readings—interpretatively enticing and, often, actually exciting, as well as duly shaking. I think, to select just a few, of Ricoeur's essays on creation, lamentation, and translation in *Thinking Biblically* (Ricoeur emerging at last from his long theoretical sparring with biblical hermeneutics—for example, in the pieces in his *Essays on Biblical Interpretation* (1981)—to really grip some texts); of Alter on the structural role of the Sodom narrative (Schwartz 1990: 146–60); Herbert Marks on 'Prophetic Stammering' (Schwartz 1990: 60–80);

Christopher Morris's deconstructive take on spirit, apostle, and way (*hodos*) in Acts (Morris 2005: 111–32); Paul Fiddes in Derridean mode on 'the self-unveiling of the God who remains hidden' in a parallel reading of John's Gospel and *The Tempest* (Fiddes 2000: 28–51); post-structuralist feminist tough guy Mieke Bal's decodings of Old Testament narratives of women, love, and violence and their reception (Bal 1987 and 1988)—she's the best of the large phalanx of (post)modern feminist Biblicists, for some of whom see Elizabeth Schüzzler Fiorenza (1992), Letty M. Russell (1985), Ann Loades's chapter on 'Feminist Interpretation' (in Barton 1998: 81–94), and *Bodies in Question: Gender, Religion, Text* (Sherwood and Bird 2005). Also patently powerful are the numerous angry post-Foucauldian, post-Edward Said-esque inspections of the politics of Bible interpretation in terms of race and class (see e.g. Sugirtharajah 2002; Thatcher 2008; Clines 1996), particularly the engagement with the mythicity of ancient Israel and the Biblicized politics of modern Israel (e.g. Whitelam 1996; Davies 1992; 1994; 1997: 104–22). Strong too are the very impressive feminist-deconstructionist Yvonne Sherwood reading Hosea's prostitute-marriage 'Theoretically' (Sherwood 1996) and her book on western culture's way with Jonah—ace literary reception work (Sherwood 2000); and the many lovely Derrida-inspired pieces in *Derrida and Religion: Other Testaments*, edited by Sherwood and Kevin Hart (Sherwood 2004*a*), and in the Sherwood-edited collection *Derrida's Bible (Reading a Page of Scripture With a Little Help from Derrida)* (2004*b*). Not least important here are Sherwood's own potent decon-struction of Genesis 23:2, 'And Sarah Died' (ibid. 261–92), built on the multi-valences of Hebrew *waw*, with the aid of Derrida on *and*, his obituary of Sarah Kofman and *Donner la mort* (Derrida 2001: 165–88; 1999); the literary critic John Mullan on parataxis in the Fall narrative of Genesis 3 and Don DeLillo's fiction; and Frank Yamada on shibboleths of identity in Judges 12 (Sherwood 2004*b*: 119–34), and Mark Brummitt on secrets, secretaries, and scrolls in Jeremiah 36 (ibid. 39–48), and Robert Seesengood reading the Pastoral Epistles as Derridean postcards from God (ibid. 49–60). In his own contribution to Sherwood's volume (ibid. 301–3) John Barton repents of his earlier satire on postmodernizing Biblicists, praising Sherwood's gathering for the illluminations of their slantwise address, their shoot-ing from what historicists think of as the textual margin. They're indeed *ludic* but (as every Theorist's advocacy of the play of signifiers believes of that game) seriously engaged with their texts. These particular Derrideans are not guilty (as critics of post-structuralist reading have often suggested of it) of *Beliebigkeit*—Barton's most useful word for the critical folly, and crime, of hermeneutic freeplay, of Saying Absolutely Anything You Like.

Sadly, though, a lot of theorized Biblicists are as *beliebig* as could be, and infected by the critical daftnesses, follies, and crimes, the sentimental political correctnesses, the neurotic and wishful sightings of oneself in the textual mirror, the canting repetitions about contentless, dehistoricized, utterly abysmal linguistics and textu-ality (founded in misreadings of Saussure and early Derrida, and flying in the face of Derrida's protests) which have all flourished down the literary corridor. And so Jesus emerges startlingly from Dominic Crossan's keen convert-structuralist embrace as existent only 'in, with, and by language', his parables as merely arbitrary signifiers (Crossan 1979). And Dan O. Via, keen purchaser of the awful worst of US (not *echt*-Derridean) deconstruction, offers early Christianity and Matthew's Gospel as mere strands in a 'constitutive linguistic network' (Via 1994: 348–66). In the same Sheffield *JTOS* supplement volume Tina Pippin peers into the abyss of Revelation and finds it representative of what she thinks of as utterly bottomless biblical nothingnessness, endless *différance*, erasure, fissure, rupture, ruptured hymen, (Lacanian) lack, chaos, abysmality—oblivious to the case that the deconstructive lexicon she so blissfully pours out from her theorized critical vials does not denote nothingness but, rather, meaning trembling at the border of presence and absence (Pippin 1994: 250–67). And Stephen Moore (one of the editors of the original Bible and Culture Collective's *Postmodern Bible*), more pun-full than even *Finnegans Wake* and the Joyce-admiring Derrida, mounts a gratuitously more-Derridean-than-Derrida dismantling of scriptural meaning in his *Mark and Luke in Poststructural Perspective* (1992). He jumps excitedly from Derrida on the poet Francis Ponge and the *éponge* of writing (Derrida 1992) to the crucifixion's vinegary sponge in order that Pilate become 'Ponge' Pilate, with Jesus as the 'S[p]ON[ge]' (geddit?) of God, *sponging* off God, who *mops up* Jesus at the stake. Moore's rent veil of the temple is God's torn *hymen*. Loss of the boy's *sindon* marks (and, ho ho, this is indeed *Mark's* story) scripture as *stripture*. The empty tomb of Luke (*Look!* *Lacan: Lack*) stages a word-full void, a silent signifier of absence, so that this Speech Act of the Apostle (*sic*) 'writes the epitaph of the full, simple present', its abandoned cloth the 'sign of an already absent signified' (US deconstructionists never mastered the Sausserean idea that signifiers are inseparable from signifieds, and neither has Moore). So the Gospels are just an endless writing, with no 'Last Supplement', as Paul's attempted supplementation of the Last Supper narrative indicates—or so Moore thinks (Moore 1992: 17, 39ff., 90ff.). And so on and on. Unbelievable *Beliebigkeit*.

   With disciples like these, who needs critics? Especially disciples of Foucault's anti-power classic *Surveillir et punir: naissance de la prison* (1975)/ *Discipline and Punish: The Birth of the Prison* (1977). Biblicists like post-structuralist feminist Elizabeth Castelli (another of the editors of *The Postmodern Bible*), attacking Paul's calls to imitate him and Christ as an egregious discourse of difference-suppressing power: *degrading, debasing, all but destroying* 'alternative knowledges' in the creation of 'the authoritative text' (Castelli 1991). (Compare her line of thought on Paul's allegorizing of the Hagar story in Galatians (Castelli 1994: 228–50) as a doing of violence to a story of violence done to a woman, which illustrates, she thinks, the way allegory, and characteristically biblical allegory, is all hermeneutic bluster covering up real arbitrariness, ruin, emptinesss. A weird take on allegory indeed.) For his part, Stephen Moore just gets truly ludicrous (as well as, presumably, blasphemous) as he assembles *Derrida and Foucault at the Foot of the Cross* in his *Poststructuralism and the New Testament*, for a 'Foucauldian redescription of "the power of the cross" as it has been construed by Paul and certain of his ecclesiastical and critical successors' (Moore 1994: 117). Moore's *God's Gym: Divine Male Bodies of the Bible* (1996)—in which sadomasochistic biblical power-games according to Foucault join glad hands with Foucauldianized Queer Body Studies—has the crucifixion as God's anatomy lesson, in which God does autopsy on his son for his own pleasure and the pleasure of others (*autopses*: eyewitness); surveying and punishing his son in a flogging and execution staged, like the foul French executioners *Discipline and Punish* opens with, for his own orgasmic 'satisfaction' (Moore 1996: 12). The much-flogged Paul, one more biblical sadomasochist, fetishizes 'subjection'. He desires penetration by God's Spirit (God's phallus, the '(rigid) extension of his power': Moore has been reading Howard Eilberg-Schwartz's *God's Phallus: And Other Problems for Men and Monotheism* (1994) with satisfaction). Paul organizes the 'chain-gang' of God's buggerees—who groan orgasmically, as Romans has it, with 'sighs too deep for words' (ibid. 29–30). In these reckonings God is a gay 'she-male' or 'bottom' (he shows his back invitingly to Moses)—just like the very mixed-up Scott Haldeman, a 'professor of worship', apparently, who celebrates the religious joys of his own abjection as a buggeree: it's Christ-like, it's like being filled with god's phallus, and it 'playfully' undoes God's 'sexist' husband-role as in Hosea (Haldeman 2003; in Krondorfer 2009: 381–92; referring to Eilberg-Schwartz 1994 and Ken Stone 2001). God's androgyny comes about, in *God's Gym*, because, like Moore, he's a bodybuilder (all that 'colossal daily intake of animal protein' in the temple's cuisine of sacrifice), with wonderful shoulders and chiselled back muscles, which he uses to divert attention from the bodybuilder's plight of 'bitch-tits' (much 'testosterone . . . oestrogen reaction . . . bona fide breasts') and shrunken testicles. The Bible keeps quiet about those because they are so embarrassingly small (cue again from Eilberg-Schwartz in the matter of Yahweh's lack of a phallus and his buttock display to Moses inviting Israelite males into 'a potentially homoerotic relationship with God: 1994: 105 ff.). God's 'bad temper', his proverbial wrath, is explicable as an extreme bodybuilder's 'anabolic steroid rage' (Moore 1996: 86 ff.).

'Pauline soteriology as pulp fiction?', Moore wonders (ibid. 15). Only on the reckoning of such pulp and pulping critiques as Moore's. Postmodern reading does, of course, find a lot to deplore—the so-called anti-Semitism of the New Testament's midrashic supervention of the Old, and Christian Bible readers' acceptance of it (atoningly popular with the p.c.-overwhelmed likes of Janice Capel Anderson: 1994); the Bible's perceived coercive anti-otherness, its racism, colonialism, masculinism (all exemplarily set out in Laura Donaldson's deploring, in the spirit of Foucault's assault on the invention of madness and the madhouse in his *Birth of the Clinic* (Foucault 1973) of Jesus' curing the 'demon-possessed' Syro-Phoenician woman in Matthew: Donaldson 2005); Jesus's 'use of the expression "blind" as a term of abuse', according to (sympathetic) 'blind disciple' John M. Hull (Hull 2002: 158); the 'divine child-abuse' of the crucifixion (Joanne Brown and Rebecca Parker, in Brown 1989). Brown and Parker's 'divine child abuse' has become standard among postmodern Bible readers (they're quoted in the 'Feminist Readings of the Cross' section of *The Postmodern Bible*, and requoted with relish in *God's Gym*). They're angered by a traditional 'abusive theology that glorifies suffering' (Brown 1989: 26–7). So, plainly, is Moore. But what's greatly troubling about him is the great enjoyment with which, like his sadomasochistic master Foucault, he conducts his deplorings—if that's what they are—of God's sadomas-ochistic treatment of his loyal Jewish and Christian followers (he penetrates the rabbinical scholar with the Torah scroll, which is the phallus of a God who is turned on by the 'French kissing' of the 'Oral Torah', while the onlooking Bridegroom of Revelation, another 'she-male', 'all cleft', enjoys 'spiritual cunnilingus' from the faithful: Moore 2001: 28–35, 40–5, 222). The relish of these wild sexual shenanigans runs disconcertingly through the whole school of the new 'masculinist' Biblicists, led by Moore, Foucault's keenest Biblicist lieutenant, overseen by Foucault's club of secular ancient-world sexologists such as David Halperin, John J. Winkler, and Froma Zeitlin (Halperin 1990; Winkler 1990), who greatly underpin, for example, the essays in *New Testament Masculinities*, edited (naturally) by Stephen Moore and Janice Capel Anderson (Moore 2003).

Utterly representative of those upset masculinists is Chris Frilingos's blood-thirsty 'Sexing' of 'the Lamb' of Revelation. Read against *Daphnis and Chloe* and Roman gladiatorial sports, the Lamb is said to be penetrated by a dominant effeminizing gaze, before turning powerful masculinized pentrating gazer himself. At first a pierced, bleeding, effeminized body, he arms himself with a phallic sickle (Rev. 14), presiding over the fiery punishment of the wicked, like the president of a Roman arena, armed with the 'invasive force of the divine gaze of judgement'. So much arbitrary switching of the overwhelming Foucauldian gaze, so much penetrating and being penetrated—even the Whore of Bablyon gets penetrated in an overexcited reading of Revelation 18:6 (Frilingos 2003: 297–317). Which is perverse, queer reading in the old as well as the new senses of those words. Finding all that sexual abuse in the text is, of course, textual abuse, abusive reading—*abusio*, Latin equivalent of Greek *katachresis*, the rhetoric of exaggeration and distortion. Enjoying the sexual dominating and being dominated, the giving and receiving of gory sexual pain, which you yourself have imagined into the text, is simply reading as, and for, self-abuse. And textual *abusio*—of which there's far too much about in Biblicist reading as in its inspiring secularist counterpart—should be laughed out of court (see Cunningham 2002).

WORKS CITED

ADAM, A. K. M. (2006). *Faithful Interpretation: Reading the Bible in a Postmodern World*. Minneapolis: Fortune Press

AITWAN, ROBERT. (1993), ed., with Laurance Wieder, *Chapters into Verse: Poetry in English Inspired by the Bible*, 2 vols. Oxford: Oxford University Press.

——(1998), ed., with George Dardass and Peggy Rosenthal, *Divine Inspiration: The Life of Jesus in World Poetry*. New York and Oxford: Oxford University Press.

——(2001), ed., with Laurance Wieder, *Chapters into Verse: Poetry in English Inspired by the Bible*, 1 vol. Oxford: Oxford University Press.

ALTER, ROBERT (1975), 'A Literary Approach to the Bible', *Commentary*, December.

——(1981), *The Art of Biblical Narrative*. London and Sydney: George Allen & Unwin.

——(1985), *The Art of Biblical Poetry*. New York: Basic Books.

——(1987), *The Literary Guide to the Bible*, ed., with Frank Kermode. London: Collins.

——(1990), 'Sodom as Nexus: The Web of Design in Biblical Narrative', in Schwartz 1990.

——(1992), *The World of Biblical Literature*. New York: Basic Books.

——(1996), *Genesis: Translation and Commentary*. New York and London: W. W. Norton.

——(1999), *The David Story: A Translation with Commentary of 1 & 2 Samuel*. New York and London: W. W. Norton.

——(2004), *The Five Books of Moses: A Translation with Commentary*. New York and London: W. W. Norton.

——(2007), *The Book of Psalms: A Translation with Commentary*. New York and London: W. W. Norton.

AUERBACH, ERICH (1953), *Mimesis: The Representation of Reality in Western Literature*, trans. Willard Trask. Princeton: Princeton University Press.

BAL, MIEKE (1987), *Lethal Love: Feminist Literary Readings of Biblical Love Stories*. Bloomington and Indianapolis: Indiana University Press.

——(1988), *Murder and Difference: Gender, Genre and Scholarship on Sisera's Death*, trans. Matthew Gumpert. Bloomington and Indianapolis: Indiana University Press.

BARNES, JULIAN (1989), *A History of the World in 10 1/2 Chapters*. London: Jonathan Cape.

BARTHES, ROLAND (1957), 'Le Monde où l'on catche', in *Mythologies*, 11–21. Paris: Seuil.

——(1970), *S/Z*. Paris: Seuil.

——(1971a), 'L'Analyse structurale du récit: apropos Actes X–XI', in *Exégése et herméneutique: colloque de la Société des exégètes de France, Chantilly, 1969*. Paris: Seuil.

——(1971b), *Sade, Fourier, Loyola*. Paris: Seuil.

——(1972a), 'La Lutte avec l'ange: analyse textuelle de Genèse 32, 22–32', in *Analyse structurale et exégèse biblique*. Geneva: Labor et Fides.

——(1972b), 'The World of Wrestling', in *Mythologies*, trans. Annette Lavers. London: Jonathan Cape.

——(1974), 'The Struggle With the Angel: Textual Analysis of Genesis 32, 22–32', in *Structural Analysis and Biblical Exegesis*, trans. Alfred M Johnson Jr. Pittsburgh: Pickwick Press.

——(1976), *Sade/Fourier/Loyola*, trans. Richard Miller. New York: Hill & Wang.

——(1977), *Image–Music–Text: Essays*, selected and trans. Stephen Heath. London: Fontana.

——(1978), 'Propos sur la violence', *Réforme*, 2 September.

——(1981), 'Propos sur la violence', in *Le Grain de la voix: entretiens 1962–1980*. Paris: Seuil.

——(1985), *L'Aventure sémiologique*. Paris: Seuil.

——(1988), *The Semiotic Challenge*, trans. Richard Howard. New York and Oxford: Farrar, Straus and Giroux & Basil Blackwell.

BARTON, JOHN (1996), *Reading the Old Testament: Method in Bible Study*, 2nd edn. London: Darton Longman Todd.

——(ed.) (1998), *The Cambridge Companion to Biblical Interpretation*. Cambridge: Cambridge University Press.

BEAL, TIMOTHY K. (1997), 'Opening: Cracking the Binding', in *Reading Bibles, Writing Bodies: Identity and the Book*, ed. T. K. Beal and D. M. Gunn. London and New York: Routledge.

Bible and Culture Collective (1995), *The Postmodern Bible*. New Haven and London: Yale University Press.

BLOOM, HAROLD (1982), 'Wrestling Sigmund: Three Paradigms for Poetic Originality', in *The Breaking of the Vessels*, 47 ff. Chicago and London: Chicago University Press.

——(1991), *The Book of J*, trans. David Rosenberg, commentary Harold Bloom. London: Faber & Faber.

——(1995), *The Western Canon: The Books and School of the Ages*. London: Macmillan.

BOITANI, PIERO (1999), *The Bible and its Rewritings*, trans. Anita Weston. Oxford: Oxford University Press.

BROWN, JOANNE CARLSON (1989), with Rebecca Parker, 'For God So Loved the World?', in *Christianity, Patriarchy, and Abuse: A Feminist Critique*, ed. Joanne Carlson Brown and Carole R. Bohn, 1–30. New York: Pilgrim Books.

BÜCHMANN, CHRISTINE (1994, 1995), ed., with Celina Spiegel, *Out of the Garden: Women Writers on the Bible*. New York, Toronto, and London: Ballantine Books & Pandora.

CAPUTO, JOHN D. (1997), *The Prayers and Tears of Jaques Derrida: Religion Without Religion*. Bloomington & Indianapolis: Indiana University Press.

CASTELLI, ELIZABETH A. (1991), *Imitating Paul: A Discourse of Power*. Louisville, Ky.: Westminster/John Knox Press.

——(1994), 'Allegories of Hagar: Reading Galatians 4.21–31 with Postmodernist Feminist Eyes', in *The New Literary Criticism and the New Testament*, ed. Elizabeth S. Malbon and Edgar V. McKnight, *Journal for the Study of the Old Testament*, Supplement Series 109. Sheffield: Sheffield Academic Press.

CIXOUS, HÉLÈNE (1993), *Three Steps on the Ladder of Writing*, trans. Sarah Cornell and Susan Sellers. New York: Columbia University Press.

——(1998), 'Bathsheba or the Interior Bible', in *Stigmata: Escaping Texts*. London and New York: Routledge.

——(2001), *Veils*, with Jacques Derrida, trans. Geoffrey Bennington. Stanford, Calif.: Stanford University Press.

——(2004), *Portrait of Jaques Derrida as a Young Jewish Saint*, trans. Beverley Bie Brahic. New York: Columbia University Press.

CLINES, DAVID J. A. (1996), *Interested Parties: The Ideology of Writers and Readers of the Hebrew Bible. Journal for the Study of the Old Testament*, Supplement Series 205, *Gender, Culture, Theory* No 1. Sheffield: Sheffield Academic Press.

CORN, ALFRED (ed.) (1990), *Incarnation: Contemporary Writers on the New Testament*. New York: Viking Penguin.

CRACE, JIM (1997), *Quarantine*. London: Viking.

CROSSAN, JOHN DOMINIC (1979), *Raid on the Articulate: Comic Eschatology in Jesus and Borges*. New York: Harper & Row.

CUNNINGHAM, VALENTINE (1994), *In the Reading Gaol: Texts, Postmodernity and History*. Oxford: Blackwell.

——(1997), 'Roland Barthes (1915–1980): Introduction', in Graham Ward (ed.), *The Postmodern God: A Theological Reader*, 74–83. Malden and Oxford: Blackwell.

——(2002), *Reading After Theory*. Oxford: Blackwell.

DAVIES, PHILIP R. (1992), *In Search of Ancient Israel. Journal for the Study of the Old Testament*, Supplement Series 148. Sheffield: Sheffield Academic Press.

——(1994), '"House of David" Built on Sand: The Sin of the Biblical Maximisers', *Biblical Archaeology Review*, 20: 54–5.

——(1997), 'Whose History? Whose Israel? Whose Bible? Biblical Histories Ancient and Modern', in *Can A History of Israel Be Written?* ed. Lester L. Grabbe, *Journal for the Study of the Old Testament*, Supplement Series 245, *European Seminar in Historical Methodology* No 1. Sheffield: Sheffield University Press.

DERRIDA, JACQUES (1967), *L'Écriture et la différence*. Paris: Seuil.

——(1978), *Writing and Difference*, trans., introduced and annotated by Alan Bass. London and Henley: Routledge & Kegan Paul.

——(1980), *La Carte postale: de Socrate à Freud et au-delà*. Paris: Flammarion.

——(1984), 'Two Words for Joyce', in *Post-structuralist Joyce: Essays from the French*, ed. Derek Attridge and Daniel Ferrer, 145–59. Cambridge: Cambridge University Press.

——(1986*a*), 'Shibboleth', trans. Joshua Wilner, in *Midrash and Literature*, ed. Geoffrey H. Hartman and Sanford Budick, 307–47. New Haven and London: Yale University Press.

——(1986*b*), 'La Loi du genre', in *Parages*, 249–87. Paris: Galilée.

——(1991), 'Circonfession', in *Jacques Derrida*, by Geoffrey Bennington and Jacques Derrida. Paris: Seuil.

——(1992*a*), 'Before the Law', in *Acts of Literature*, ed. Derek Attridge, 181–220. New York and London: Routledge.

——(1992*b*), 'From Signsponge', revised version of the English translation of the original bilingual edition *Signéponge/Signsponge*, in *Acts of Literature*, ed. Derek Attridge, 344–69. New York and London: Routledge.

——(1993), *Memoirs of the Blind*, trans. Pascale-Anne Brault and Michael Naas. Chicago and London: Chicago University Press.

——(1999), *Adieu to Emmanuel Levinas*, trans. Pascale-Anne Brault and Michael Naas. Stanford, Calif.: Stanford University Press.

——(1999), *Donner la mort*. Paris: Galilée.

——(2001), 'Sarah Kofman (1934–94)', in *The Work of Mourning*, ed. and trans. Pascale-Anne Brault and Michael Naas. Chicago and London: University of Chicago Press.

——(2002), 'Des Tours de Babel', in *Acts of Religion*, ed. Gil Anidjar, 102–34. New York and London: Routledge.

DOCTOROW, E. L. (1971/2), *The Book of Daniel*. New York and London: Random House and Macmillan.

DONALDSON, LAURA E. (2005), 'Gospel Hauntings: The Postcolonial Demons of New Testament Criticism', in *The Bible and Postcolonialism*, ed. R. S. Sugirtharajah, 97–113. London and New York: T. & T. Clark International.

DOUGLAS, MARY (1966), *Purity and Danger: An Analysis of Concepts of Pollution and Taboo*. London: Routledge & Kegan Paul.

——(1993), *In the Wilderness: The Doctrine of Defilement in the Book of Numbers*. Oxford: Oxford University Press.

——(1999), *Leviticus as Literature*. Oxford: Oxford University Press.

——(2004), *Jacob's Tears: The Priestly Work of Reconciliation*. Oxford: Oxford University Press.

EILBERG-SCHWARTZ, HOWARD (1994), *God's Phallus: And Other Problems for Men and Monotheism*. Boston: Beacon Press.

FEWELL, DANNA NOLAN (1997), 'Imagination, Method, and Murder: Un/Framing the Face of Post-Exilic Israel', in *Reading Bibles, Reading Bodies: Identity and the Book*, ed. Timothy K. Beal and David M. Gunn. London and New York: Routledge.

FIDDES, PAUL (2000), 'Story and Possibility: Reflections on the Last Scenes of the Fourth Gospel and Shakespeare's *The Tempest*', in *Revelation and Story: Narrative Theology and the Centrality of Story*, ed. Gerhard Sauter and John Barton. Aldershot: Ashgate.

FIORENZA, ELISABETH SCHÜZZLER (ed.) (1992), *But She Said: Feminist Practices of Biblical Interpretation*. Boston: Beacon Press.

FISCH, HAROLD (1999), *The Biblical Presence in Shakespeare, Milton, and Blake: A Comparative Study*. Oxford: Clarendon Press.

FISH, STANLEY (1980), *Is There a Text in This Class? The Authority of Interpretive Communities*. Cambridge, Mass. and London: Harvard University Press.

FOUCAULT, MICHEL (1975), *Surveiller et punir: naissance de la prison*. Paris: Gallimard.

——(1973) *The Birth of the Clinic: An Archaeology of Medical Perception* (= *Naissance de la clinique*, 1963), trans. Alan Sheridan. New York: Vintage.

——(1977), *Discipline and Punish: The Birth of the Prison*, trans. Alan Sheridan. London: Allen Lane.

FRILINGOS, CHRIS. (2003), 'Sexing the Lamb', in *New Testament Masculinities*, ed. Stephen D. Moore and Janice Capel Anderson, 297–317. *Semeia* Studies No. 45. Leiden and Boston: Brill.

FRYE, NORTHROP (1982), *The Great Code: The Bible and Literature*. London, Melbourne, and Henley: Routledge & Kegan Paul.

GARBER, MARJORIE (1987), *Shakespeare's Ghost Writers: Literature as Uncanny Causality*. New York and London: Methuen.

GIRARD, RENÉ (1978), *Des choses cachées depuis la fondation du monde*. Paris: Grasset et Fasquette.

——(1982), *Le Bouc émissaire*. Paris: Grasset et Fasquette.

——(1985), *La Route antique des hommes pervers*. Paris: Grasset et Fasquette.

——(1986), *The Scapegoat*, trans. Yvonne Freccero. London: Athlone Press.

——(1987a), *Things Hidden From the Foundation of the World*, trans. Stephen Bann and Michael Metteer. London: Athlone Press.

——(1987b), *Job the Victim of His People*, trans. Yvonne Freccero. London: Athlone Press.

HALDEMAN, SCOTT (2003), 'Receptivity and Revelation: A Spirituality of Gay Male Sex', in *Body and Soul: Rethinking Sexuality and Justice-Love*, ed. Marvin Ellison and Sylvia Thorson-Smith, 218–31. Cleveland, Ohio: Pilgrim Press. Reprinted in Krondorfer 2008: 381–92.

HALPERIN, DAVID M. (1990), with John J. Winkler and Froma I. Zeitlin, *Before Sexuality: The Construction of Erotic Experience in the Ancient Greek World*. Princeton: Princeton University Press.

HARTMAN, GEOFFREY H. (1986), 'The Struggle for the Text', in *Midrash and Literature*, ed. Geoffrey H. Hartman and Sanford Budick, 1–18. New Haven and London: Yale Universtity Press.

HELLER, JOSEPH (1984), *God Knows*. London: Jonathan Cape.

HULL, JOHN M. (2002), 'Open Letter from a Blind Disciple to a Sighted Saviour', in *Borders, Boundaries and the Bible*, ed. Martin O'Kane, *Journal for the Study of the Old Testament*, Supplement Series 313. Sheffield: Sheffield Academic Press.

ISER, WOLFGANG (1974), *The Implied Reader: Patterns of Communication from Bunyan to Beckett*. Baltimore and London: Johns Hopkins University Press.

——(1980), *The Act of Reading: A Theory of Aesthetic Response*. Baltimore and London: Johns Hopkins University Press.

JABÈS, EDMOND (1963), *Le Livre des questions*. Paris: Gallimard.

JACOBSON, DAN (1970), *The Rape of Tamar*. London: Weidenfeld & Nicolson.

——(1982), *The Story of the Stories: The Chosen People and Their God*. London: Secker & Warburg.

JACOBSON, HOWARD (1992), *The Very Model of a Man*. London: Viking.

JASPER, DAVID (1999), ed., with Stephen Prickett, *The Bible and Literature: A Reader*. Oxford: Blackwell.

JAUSS, HANS ROBERT (1982), *Towards an Aesthetic of Reception*, trans. Timothy Bahti, introduction by Paul de Man. Brighton: Harvester.

JOBLING, DAVID (2001), ed., with Tina Pippin and Ronald Schleifer, *The Postmodern Bible Reader*. Oxford: Blackwell.

JOSIPOVICI, GABRIEL (1988), *The Book of God: A Response to the Bible*. New Haven and London: Yale University Press.

JOYCE, JAMES (1939), *Finnegans Wake*. London: Faber & Faber.

KERMODE, FRANK (1979), *The Genesis of Secrecy: On the Interpretation of Narrative*. Cambridge, Mass. and London: Harvard University Press.

KRISTEVA, JULIA (1969), *Semeiotike: recherches pour une sémanalyse*. Paris: Seuil.

——(1980), *Pouvoirs de l'horreur*. Paris: Seuil.

——(1982), *Powers of Horror: An Essay on Abjection*, trans. Leon S. Roudiez. New York: Columbia University Press.

——(1993), *Les Nouvelles Maladies de l'âme*. Paris: Librairie Arthème Fayard.

——(1995), *New Maladies of the Soul*, trans. Ross Mitchell Guberman. New York: Columbia University Press.

KRONDORFER, BJÖRN (ed.) (2009), *Men and Masculinities in Christianity and Judaism: A Critical Reader*. London: SCM Press.

LACOQUE, ANDRÉ (1998), with Paul Ricoeur, *Thinking Biblically: Exegetical and Hermenutical Studies*, trans. David Pellauer. Chicago: University of Chicago Press.

LAMB, JONATHAN (1995), *The Rhetoric of Suffering: Reading the Bible in the Eighteenth Century*. Oxford: Clarendon Press.

LEMON, REBECCA (2009), ed., with Emma Mason, Jonathan Roberts, and Christopher Rowland, *The Blackwell Companion to the Bible in English Literature*. Malden, Oxford, and Chichester: Wiley-Blackwell.

LEVINAS, EMMANUEL (1996), *Nouvelles lectures talmudiques*. Paris: Minuit.

LINDGREN, TORGNY (1988), *Bathsheba*, trans. Tom Geddes. London: Collins Harvill.

LOADES, ANN (1998), 'Feminist Interpretation', in Barton 1998.

MAILER, NORMAN (1997), *Gospel According to the Son*. London: Little, Brown.

MARKS, HERBERT (1990), 'On Prophetic Stammering', in Schwartz 1990.

MARX, STEVEN (2000), *Shakespeare and the Bible*. Oxford: Oxford University Press.

MERCHANT, MOELWYN (1984), *Jeshua*. Swansea: Christopher Davies.

MILES, JACK (1995), *God: A Biography*. London and Sydney: Simon & Schuster.

MOORE, STEPHEN D. (1989), *Literary Criticism and the Gospels: The Theoretical Challenge*. New Haven and London: Yale University Press.

——(1992), *Mark and Luke in Poststructuralist Perspective: Jesus Begins to Write*. New Haven and London: Yale University Press.

——(1994), *Poststructuralism and the New Testament: Derrida and Foucault at the Foot of the Cross*. Minneapolis: Fortress Press.

——(1995), 'True Confessions and Weird Obsessions: Autobiographical Interventions in Literary and Biblical Studies', in *Taking It Personally: Autobiographical Biblical Criticism*, ed. Janice Capel Anderson and Jeffrey L. Staley, *Semeia*, 721: 19–50. Shortened version in Krondorfer 2009.

——(1996), *God's Gym: Divine Male Bodies of the Bible*. New York and London: Routledge.

——(2001), *God's Beauty Parlour and Other Queer Spaces In and Around the Bible*. Stanford, Calif.: Stanford University Press.

——(2003), ed., with Janice Capel Anderson, *New Testament Masculinities*. *Semeia* Studies No. 45. Leiden and Boston: Brill.

MORRIS, CHRISTOPHER D. (2005), 'Deconstruction and Theology', in *The Figure of the Road: Deconstructive Studies in Humanities Disciplines*. New York: Peter Lang.

PIPPIN, TINA (1994), 'Peering into the Abyss: A Postmodern Reading of the Biblical Bottomless Pit', in *The New Literary Criticism and the New Testament*, ed. Elizabeth Struthers Malbon and Edgar V. McKnight. *Journal for the Study of the Old Testament*, Supplement Series 109. Sheffield: Sheffield Academic Press.

PRICKETT, STEPHEN (1995), *Origins of Narrative: The Romantic Appropriation of the Bible*. Cambridge: Cambridge University Press.

RICOEUR, PAUL (1981), *Essays on Biblical Interpretation*, ed. Lewis S. Mudge. London: SPCK.

ROSENBERG, DAVID (1987), *Congregation: Contemporary Writers Read the Jewish Bible*. San Diego: Harcourt Brace Jovanovich.

——(1996), *Communion: Contemporary Writers Reveal the Bible in their Lives*. New York: Anchor Books.

RUSSELL, LETTY M. (ed.) (1985), *Feminist Interpretation of the Bible*. Oxford and New York: Basil Blackwell.

SARAMAGO, JOSÉ (1993), *The Gospel According to Jesus Christ*, trans. Giovanni Pontiero. London: Harvill.

SCHWARTZ, REGINA M. (1988), *Remembering and Repeating: Biblical Creation in Paradise Lost*. Cambridge: Cambridge Univesity Press.

——(ed.) (1990), *The Book and the Text: The Bible and Literary Theory*. Cambridge, Mass. and Oxford: Basil Blackwell.

SERRES, MICHEL (1980), *Le Parasite*. Paris: B Grasset. (= *The Parasite*, trans. Lawrence R. Scher. Baltimore and London: Johns Hopkins University Press.)

——(1982), *Genèse*. Paris: Grasset et Fasquelle. (= *Genesis*, trans. Geneviève James and James Nielson. Ann Arbor, Mich.: University of Michigan Press.)

SHERWOOD, YVONNE (1996), *The Prostitute and the Prophet: Hosea's Marriage in Literary Theoretical Perspective*. *Journal for the Study of the Old Testament*, Supplement Series 212, *Gender, Culture, Theory*, No 2. Sheffield: Sheffield University Press.

SHERWOOD, YVONNE (2000), *A Biblical Text and its Afterlives: The Survival of Jonah in Western Culture*. Cambridge: Cambridge University Press.

——(2004a), ed., with Kevin Hart, *Derrida and Religion: Other Testaments*. New York and London: Routledge.

——(ed.) (2004b), *Derrida's Bible (Reading a Page of Scripture with a Little Help from Derrida)*. New York and Basingstoke: Palgrave Macmillan.

——(2005), with Darlene Bird, *Bodies in Question: Gender, Religion, Text*. Aldershot: Ashgate.

STAROBINSKI, JEAN (1971), 'An Essay in Literary Analysis—Mark 5, 1–20', *Ecumenical Review*, 23/4: 377–97.

——(1972), 'Le Démoniaque gérasène: analyse littéraire de Marc 5, 1–20', in *Analyse structurale et exégèse biblique*. Geneva: Labor et Fides.

——(1973), 'The Struggle with Legion: A Literary Analysis of Mark 5, 1–20', trans. Dan O. Via, *New Literary History*, 6/2: 331–56.

——(1974), 'The Gerasene Demoniac: A Literary Analysis of Mark 5, 1–20', in *Structural Analysis and Biblical Exegesis*, trans. Alfred M. Johnson Jr. Pittsburgh: Pickwick Press.

STONE, KEN (2001), 'Lovers and Raisin Cakes: Food, Sex and Driving Insecurity in Hosea', in *Queer Commentary and the Hebrew Bible*, ed. Ken Stone, 116–39. London and New York: Sheffield Academic Press.

SUGIRTHARAJAH, R. S. (2002), *Postcolonial Criticism and Biblical Interpretation*. Oxford: Oxford University Press.

THATCHER, ADRIAN (2008), *The Savage Text: The Use and Abuse of the Bible*. Malden, Oxford, and Chichester: Wiley-Blackwell.

TOURNIER, MICHEL (1980), *Gaspard, Melchior & Balthazar*. Paris: Gallimard.

VIA, DAN O. (1994), 'Matthew's Dark Light and the Human Condition', in *The New Literary Criticism and the New Testament*, ed. Elizabeth Struthers Malbon and Edgar V. McKnight, *Journal for the Study of the Old Testament*, Supplement Series 109. Sheffield: Sheffield Academic Press.

WADSWORTH, MICHAEL (1981), *Ways of Reading the Bible*. Sussex and New Jersey: Harvester Press and Barnes & Noble.

WARD, GRAHAM (ed.) (1997), *The Postmodern God: A Theological Reader*. Oxford: Blackwell.

WHITELAM, KEITH W. (1996), *The Invention of Ancient Israel: The Silencing of Palestinian History*. London and New York: Routledge.

WIEDER, LAURANCE (1995 and 1999), *The Poets' Book of Psalms: The Complete Psalter as Rendered by Twenty-Five Poets from the Sixteenth to the Twentieth Centuries*. New York: HarperCollins and Oxford University Press.

WINKLER, JOHN J. (1990), *The Constraints of Desire: The Anthropology of Sex and Gender in Ancient Greece*. New York and London: Routledge.

WINTERSON, JEANETTE (1985), *Boating for Beginners*. London: Methuen.

WOOLF, VIRGINIA (1966), 'Mr Bennett and Mrs Brown', lecture, 18 May 1924, in *Collected Essays*, 1. 319–37. London: Hogarth Press.

WRIGHT, TERENCE R. (2000), *D. H. Lawrence and the Bible*. Cambridge: Cambridge University Press.

——(2007), *The Genesis of Fiction: Modern Novelists as Biblical Interpreters*. Aldershot: Ashgate.

FURTHER READING

STANLEY HAUERWAS and L. GREGORY JONES (eds.) (1989), *Why Narrative? Readings in Narrative Theology*. Grand Rapids, Mich.: William B. Eerdmans.

STEPHEN PRICKETT (ed.) (1991), *Reading the Text: Biblical Criticism and Literary Theory*. Oxford and Cambridge, Mass.: Blackwell.

GRAHAM WARD (ed.) (1997), *The Postmodern God: A Theological Reader*. Malden and Oxford: Blackwell.

SUBJECT INDEX*

* OT and NT refer to the Old and New Testament respectively.

Israel (kingdom) (*cont.*)
  restoration of 64, 69, 71, 81
  social structure 210
Israel (modern state of) 485
Israelites 89, 92, 93, 196, 236, 267, 346, 417, 436–37
  and Rastafarianism 246
  in the wilderness 144, 455
  see also Exodus
'Israelitism', as distinct from Judaism 269
Italy 239
Ithna'asharite (Twelver) Shi'ites 248
ius ad bellum 262, 263
ius in bello 260, 262

Jabbok, River 652
Jabès, Edmond, *Le Livre des questions* 654–5
Jabesh-Gilead 92
Jabin, king of Canaan 89
Jacob (Israel) 11, 12, 14, 15, 16, 18, 20, 21–2, 96, 210,
    319, 345, 346, 388, 393, 618
  Barthes' reading of 652–3
  blindness of 656
  Derrida and 654
  descendants of 21
  dream of ladder 189, 655
  Serres on 657
Jacobson, Dan 660
  The Rape of Tamar 659
  *The Story of the Stories: The Chosen People and
    their God* 659
Jacobson, Howard 660
Jael 89, 90, 100
Jainism 545, 553
Jairus 588
Jakobson, Roman 652
Jallianwalla Bagh massacre, Amritsar 554
Jamaica 245, 246
James, apostle 197, 288, 549, 588
James, Epistle of 286, 532
James, Henry 658
James I, King 98
Japan 239, 242, 323–39, 480
  ecclesial history 337
  militarism 331–2, 337
  nationalism 325, 326
Japhet (son of Noah) 166
Jarnac, Comte de 652
Jauss, Hans-Robert 650
Jeduthun 38
Jehovah's Witnesses 344
Jena, University of 274
Jenkins, Philip 424
Jennens, Charles 294, 296–301, 301, 302, 303, 305

Jenyns, Leonard 402
Jephthah 89, 90–1
  daughter of 320
Jeremiah 52, 67, 80, 328, 662
Jeremiah (prophet) 52, 53, 68, 70, 71–2, 81, 85,
    286, 287, 492
  Uchimura on 328, 329–31, 335, 336
Jerome, St 87, 150, 154, 157, 214–15, 224
  and Augustine 611
  on Ezekiel 70–1, 228–9
  on Isaiah 56–8
  letter to Paulinus 231
  translation of Job 30
Jerusalem 53, 54–5, 59, 61, 115, 152, 552
  apostles in 153
  Christ's entry into 289, 585
  church in 147, 330
  Dante and 285
  destruction of 78, 82, 85, 87
  destruction of temple 54, 68, 86, 297
  Dome of the Rock 376
  Mount Zion, Chamber of the Holocaust 495
  personification as woman 55–6
  prophecies on 80
  temple of 376
  Visitors' Guide 500
  Yad Vashem 499–500
Jesse, Tree of 189–91, 192, 194
Jesuits 324
Jesus Christ
  alleged marriage of 369–75
  ancestors of 188–91
  anti-Semitic dissociation from
      Jewishness 268–78
  'Aryan' origin, attempts to prove 268, 270–3
  Ascension 183, 197, 198
  attitude to violence 253–5, 264–6
  Augustine on 614
  Baptism 183, 188, 190
  biographies of 270–1
  Blake's reading of 464–5
  as *Christus Patiens* 187–8, 197
  as *Christus Victor* 188, 197
  coming of 57–8, 84
  death 108, 123, 138, 611, 641–2
  depicted as child 191–2, 196, 197
  as descendant of David 40, 57
  divinity of 296
  Dylan and 356, 363–4
  Elizabeth Cady Stanton on 320–1
  as emissary and Son of God 107, 111–14
  entry into Jerusalem 289
  exempt from Adam's sin 614

CITATIONS INDEX